Lecture Notes in Computer Science 3334

Commenced Publication in 1973
Founding and Former Series Editors:
Gerhard Goos, Juris Hartmanis, and Jan van Leeuwen

Zhaoneng Chen   Hsinchun Chen
Qihao Miao   Yuxi Fu   Edward Fox
Ee-peng Lim (Eds.)

Digital Libraries: International Collaboration and Cross-Fertilization

7th International Conference on
Asian Digital Libraries, ICADL 2004
Shanghai, China, December 13-17, 2004
Proceedings

 Springer

Volume Editors

Zhaoneng Chen
Yuxi Fu
Shanghai Jiao Tong University
Shanghai, P.R. China
E-mail: znchen@lib.sjtu.edu.cn, yxfu@cs.sjtu.edu.cn

Hsinchun Chen
University of Arizona
Tucson, AZ 85721, USA
E-mail: hchen@eller.arizona.edu

Qihao Miao
Shanghai Library
Shanghai, P.R. China
E-mail: qhmaio@libnet.sh.cn

Edward Fox
Virginia Tech
Blacksburg, VA, USA
E-mail: fox@vt.edu

Ee-peng Lim
Nanyang Technological University
Singapore
E-mail: aseplim@ntu.edu.sg

Library of Congress Control Number: 2004116559

CR Subject Classification (1998): H.3, H.2, H.4.3, H.5, J.7, D.2, J.1, I.7

ISSN 0302-9743
ISBN 3-540-24030-6 Springer Berlin Heidelberg New York

Springer is a part of Springer Science+Business Media

springeronline.com

© Springer-Verlag Berlin Heidelberg 2004
Printed in Germany

Typesetting: Camera-ready by author, data conversion by Scientific Publishing Services, Chennai, India
Printed on acid-free paper   SPIN: 11365358   06/3142   5 4 3 2 1 0

Preface

The International Conference on Asian Digital Libraries (ICADL) is an annual international forum that provides opportunities for librarians, researchers and experts to exchange their research results, innovative ideas, service experiences and state-of-the-art developments in the field of digital libraries. Building on the success of the first six ICADL conferences, the 7th ICADL conference hosted by the Shanghai Jiao Tong University and the Shanghai Library in Shanghai, China aimed to further strengthen the academic collaboration and strategic alliance in the Asia- Pacific Region in the development of digital libraries.

The theme of ICADL 2004 was: Digital library: International Collaboration and Cross-fertilization, with its focus on technology, services, management and localization.

The conference began with an opening ceremony and the conference program featured 9 keynote speeches and 5 invited speeches by local and international experts. During the 3-day program, 40 research paper presentations were given in 3 parallel sessions. The conference also included 6 tutorials and an exhibition. The conference received 359 submissions, comprising 248 full papers and 111 short papers. Each paper was carefully reviewed by the Program Committee members. Finally, 44 full papers, 15 short papers and 37 poster papers were selected.

On behalf of the Organizing and Program Committees of ICADL 2004, we would like to express our appreciation to all authors and attendees for participating in the conference. We also thank the sponsors, Program Committee members, supporting organizations and helpers for making the conference a success. Without their efforts, the conference would not have been possible.

Finally, we hoped everyone who attended enjoyed the conference program and also their stay in Shanghai. We firmly look forward to the impact of ICADL 2004 in the promotion of digital libraries in Asia and beyond.

December 2004

Zhaoneng Chen
Hsinchun
Qihao Miao
Yuxi Fu
Edward Fox
Ee-peng Lim

Conference Organization

The 7th International Conference on Asian Digital Libraries (ICADL 2004) was organized by the Shanghai Jiao Tong University (SJTU) and the Shanghai Library.

Steering Committee

Advisor

Junqi Yan (Vice-Mayor, Shanghai Municipal Government, P.R. China)

Chairman

Shenwu Xie (Professor, President of SJTU, P.R. China)

Co-chair

Hsinchun Chen (Professor, University of Arizona, USA)
Zhaoneng Chen (Professor, Director of the SJTU Library, P.R. China)
Jianzhong Wu (Director of Shanghai Library, P.R. China)
Ee-peng Lim (Professor, Nanyang Technological University, Singapore)

Program Committee

Program Co-chairs

Zhaoneng Chen (SJTU library, P.R. China)
Qihao Miao (Shanghai Library, P.R. China)
Yuxi Fu (SJTU, P.R. China)
Hsinchun Chen (University of Arizona, USA)
Edward Fox (Virginia Tech., USA)
Ee-peng Lim (Nanyang Technological University (NTU), Singapore)

Program Committee Members

Pacific Asia

Jun Adachi (NII, Japan)
N. Balakrishnan (Indian Institute of Science, Bangalore, India)
Abdus Sattar Chaudhry (NTU, Singapore)
Hsueh-hua Chen (Taiwan Univ., Taiwan)
Ling Chen (Management Center of CALIS)
Hsiang-hoo Steve Ching (Teng Chia University, Taiwan)
Key-Sun Choi (KAIST, Korea)
Colin Storey (Chinese Univ. of Hong Kong Library, Hong Kong, China)
Longji Dai (Peking University Library, China)
Qianni Deng (Shanghai Jiao Tong University, China)
Schubert Foo (NTU, Singapore)
Dawu Gu (Shanghai Jiao Tong University, China)
Maruf Hasan (Thailand)
Ching-chun Hsieh (DAP, Taiwan)
San-Yih Hwang (SYSU, Taiwan)
Soon J. Hyun (Information Communication University, Korea)
Hsiang Jieh (Chi-nan Univ., Taiwan)
Yahiko Kambayashi (Kyoto Univ., Japan)
Noriko Kando (NII, Japan)
Ji-Hoon Kang (Chungnam National Univ., Korea)
Wai Lam (CUHK, Hong Kong, China)
Shirley Leung (Hong Kong Baptist University Library, Hong Kong, China)
Jianzhong Li (Harbin Institute of Technology, China)
Min-lu Li (Shanghai Jiao Tong University, China)
Xiaoming Li (Peking University, China)
Dion Goh Hoe Lian (NTU, Singapore)
Wei Liu (Shanghai Library, China)
Fanyuan Ma (Shanghai Jiao Tong University, China)
Tengku Mohd Tengku Sembok (University Kebangsaan Malaysia, Malaysia)
Sung Hyun Myaeng (Chungnam National Univ., Korea)
Liddy Nevile (Univ. of Melbourne, Australia)
Wah Tung Poon (Education and Manpower Bureau, Hong Kong, China)
Zengfu Qin (Fudan University Library, China)
T. B. Rajashekar (Indian Institute of Science, India)
S. Sadagopan (Indian Institute of Information Technology, India)
Ruimin Shen (Shanghai Jiao Tong University, China)
Shigeo Sugimoto (ULIS, Japan)
Yin-Leng Theng (NTU, Singapore)
Shalini Urs (Mysore University, Mysore, India)
Dake Wang (Shen Zhen Library, China)
Ian Witten (Waikato University, New Zealand)
Raymond Wong (Univ. of Macau, Macau, China)

Vilas Wuwongse (AIT, Thailand)
Chunxiao Xing (Tsinghua Univ., China)
Yixin Xu (Fudan Univ., China)
Fangyu Xue (Tsinghua University Library, China)
Jinwei Yan (Wu Han University Library, China)
Christopher C. Yang (CUHK, Hong Kong, China)
Zongying Yang (Shanghai Jiao Tong University Library, China)
Jaffee Yee (GPO Box 701, Bangkok, Thailand)
Jerome Yen (Chinese University, Hong Kong, China)
Masatoshi Yoshikawa (NAIST, Japan)
Halimah Badioze Zaman (Universiti Kebangsaan Malaysia, Malaysia)
Dato' Zawiyah Baba (National Library of Malaysia, Malaysia)
Xiaolin Zhang (Library of the Chinese Academy of Sciences, China)
Qiang Zhu (Shen Zhen University City Library and CALIS, China)

USA

Robert Allen (Univ. of Maryland, USA)
Christine Borgman (UCLA, USA)
Ching-chih Chen (Simmons College, USA)
Su-Shing Chen (Florida Univ., USA)
James Cheng (Harvard-Yenching Library, USA)
Jonathon Furner (UCLA, USA)
Richard K. Furuta (Texas A&M, USA)
Carl Lagoze (Cornell University, USA)
Gary Marchionini (Univ. of North Carolina, USA)
Jian Qin (Syracuse Univ., USA)
Edie Rasmussen (Univ. of Pittsburg, USA)
Howard Wactlar (CMU, USA)
Stuart Weibel (OCLC, USA)
Marcia Lei Zeng (Kent State University, USA)
Foster Zhang (Stanford Univ., USA)

Europe

Thomas Baker (Fraunhofer-Gesellschaft, Germany)
Jose Borbinha (National Library of Portugal, Portugal)
Donatella Castelli (Italian National Research Council, Italy)
Gobinda Chowdhury (University of Strathclyde, UK)
Norbert Fuhr (University of Dortmund, Germany)
Traugott Koch   (Technical Knowledge Center of Denmark (DTV), Denmark /
   NetLab, Lund University Libraries, Sweden)
Marc Nanard   (Laboratoire d'Informatique de Robotique et de Microélectronique
   de Montpellier, France)
Erich Neuhold (Darmstadt Univ. of Technology/Fraunhofer-Gesellschaft, Germany)
Carol Peters (Italian National Research Council, Italy)
Andreas Rauber (Vienna University of Technology, Austria)

Ingeborg Solvberg (Norwegian University of Science and Technology, Norway)
Harold Thimbleby (University College, London, UK)
Keith Van Rijsbergen   (University of Glasgow, UK)

Organizing Committee

Chairman: Weiping Shen (SJTU, P.R. China)

Co-chairs

Haoming Lin (SJTU Library, P.R. China)
Ee-ping Lim (NTU, Singapore)
Long Xiao (Peking University, P.R. China)
Qihao Miao (Shanghai Library, P.R. China)
Xiaoming Li (State Education Commission, P.R. China)
Yi Yang (Qingshua University, P.R. China)

Secretary General

 Haoming Lin

Deputy Secretary General

Fanyuan Ma, Guojing Yuan, Xuyan Chen

Editing Committee

Zongying Yang	Qiaoying Zheng	Haoming Lin
Wei Pan	Guojing Yuan	Jing Guo
Youhua Chen	Ruxing Xu	

Table of Contents

Keynote and Invited Papers

Biomedical Informatics and Security Informatics Research in Digital Library
   Hsinchun Chen.. 1

ChinaGrid: Making Grid Computing a Reality
   Hai Jin... 13

Content Management and Resources Integration: A Practice in Shanghai Digital
Library
   Qiang Xu.. 25

Digital Libraries: Developing Countries, Universal Access, and Information
for All
   Ian H. Witten.. 35

Digital Libraries for Education: A Progress Report on the National Science
Foundation's (NSF) National Science, Technology, Engineering,
and Mathematics Education Digital Library (NSDL) Program
   Lee L. Zia... 45

Digital Libraries for Education: Case Studies
   Edward A. Fox.. 51

Digital Preservation and Workflow Process
   Su-Shing Chen... 61

Global Memory Net: New Collaboration, New Activities and New Potentials
   Ching-chih Chen.. 73

Gold at the End of the Digital Library Rainbow: Forecasting the Consequences
of Truly Effective Digital Libraries
   Michael A. Keller... 84

Information Retrieval Challenges for Digital Libraries
   Edie Rasmussen... 95

Knowledge Service and Digital Library: A Roadmap for the Future
   Xiaoxing Zhang.. 104

Ontological Service Layer for Digital Libraries: A Requirement and
Architectural Analysis
Xiaolin Zhang.. 115

The Distributed Collaborative Virtual Reference System and Its Scheduler
Mechanism for Chinese University Libraries
Min Huang, Haoming Lin , Yi Jin.. 124

The Role of Context for Information Mediation in Digital Libraries
Erich Neuhold, Claudia Niederée, Avaré Stewart, Ingo Frommholz,
Bhaskar Mehta... 133

Papers

Collaboration and Localization

A Policy-Based System for Institutional Web Archiving
Wasuke Hiiragi, Tetsuo Sakaguchi, Shigeo Sugimoto, Koichi Tabata.......... 144

Building a Distributed Heterogeneous CALIS-ETD Digital Library
Yang Zhao, Airong Jiang... 155

Building Digitized Collection: Theory and Practice
Chunrong Luo , Zhinong Zhou, Ying Zhang.. 165

Cataloging and Preservation Toolkit of a Chinese Mathematics Ancient Books
Digital Library
Li Dong, Chunxiao Xing, Lizhu Zhou, Bei Zhang, Airong Jiang................... 174

Exploiting Extended Service-Oriented Architecture for Federated Digital
Libraries
Hao Ding, Ingeborg Sølvberg.. 184

OAI Protocol for Chinese Culture Resources Metadata Harvesting
Qiaoying Zheng, Wei Zhu, Zongying Yang... 195

Preserving Digital Media: Towards a Preservation Solution Evaluation Metric
Carl Rauch, Andreas Rauber.. 203

Technical Issues of Sharing and Integration of OPAC and E-Learning Resources
Qinghua Zheng, Jing Shao, Haifeng Dang, Huixian Bai................................ 213

Technical Issues on the China-US Million Book Digital Library Project
Jihai Zhao, Chen Huang 220

The Construction and Research on Academy Culture Database
Zhangfei Zheng, Zhijian Fan, Xiangbo Tu 227

The Institutional Repository: The Chinese University of Hong Kong 'SIR'
Model
Colin Storey, Rita Wong, Kevin Leung, Ernest Yik 236

The Semantic Architecture for Chinese Cultural Celebrities' Manuscript Library
Wei Liu 245

WebGIS-RBDL – A Rare Book Digital Library Supporting Spatio-Temporary
Retrieval
Ming Zhang, Dongqing Yang, Zhihong Deng, Sai Wu, Feng Li,
Shiwei Tang 255

Approaches to Interoperability Amongst Australian Digital Information
Providers
Philip Hider 266

Knowledge Organization and Representation

An Experimental Study of Boosting Model Classifiers for Chinese Text
Categorization
Yibing Geng, Guomin Zhu, Junrui Qiu, Jilian Fan, Jingchang Zhang 270

CatRelate: A New Hierarchical Document Category Integration Algorithm by
Learning Category Relationships
Shanfeng Zhu, Christopher C. Yang, Wai Lam 280

Constrains in Building Domain-Specific Topic Maps for the Discipline
"Gender Studies in Informatics (GSI)"
M. Suriya, R. Nagarajan, R. Sathish Babu, V. Kumaresan 290

Managing Digital Repositories Through an Ontology-Based Design
Jian Qin, Foster Zhang 300

Metadata Extraction from Bibliographies Using Bigram HMM
Ping Yin, Ming Zhang, ZhiHong Deng, Dongqing Yang 310

Metadata Quality Evaluation: Experience from the Open Language Archives
Community
Baden Hughes 320

New Feature Selection and Weighting Methods Based on Category Information
Gongshen Liu, Jianhua Li, Xiang Li, Qiang Li.............................. 330

Metadata Quality Study for the National Science Digital Library (NSDL)
Metadata Repository
Marcia Lei Zeng, Bhagirathi Subrahmanyam, Gregory M. Shreve.............. 339

Providing Parallel Metadata for Digital Libraries with Linguistically
Heterogeneous Documents
Gregory M. Shreve, Marcia L. Zeng.............................. 341

Multi-media Processing and Knowledge Discovery in Digital Library

A Kind of Index for Content-Based Music Information Retrieval and Theme
Mining
Jianzhong Li, Chaokun Wang, Shengfei Shi.............................. 345

An Implementation of Web Image Search Engines
Zhiguo Gong, Leong Hou U, Chan Wa Cheang.............................. 355

A Relevance Feedback Model for Fractal Summarization
Fu Lee Wang, Christopher C. Yang.............................. 368

A Query Analytic Model for Image Retrieval
Hsiao-Tieh Pu.............................. 378

Character Region Identification from Cover Images Using DTT
Lixu Gu.............................. 388

Multilingual Story Link Detection Based on Event Term Weighting on Times
and Multilingual Spaces
Kyung-Soon Lee, Kyo Kageura.............................. 398

PaSE: Locating Online Copy of Scientific Documents Effectively
Byung-Won On, Dongwon Lee.............................. 408

Temporal Versioning of XML Documents
Vilas Wuwongse, Masatoshi Yoshikawa, Toshiyuki Amagasa.............................. 419

Text-Based P2P Content Search Using a Hierarchical Architecture
Junjie Jiang, Weinong Wang.............................. 429

A Document Image Preprocessing System for Keyword Spotting
C.B. Jeong, S.H. Kim 440

A Gaussian-Fuzzy Content Feature Recognition System for Digital Media Asset
Objects
Sanxing Cao, Rui Lu 444

A Novel Watermarking Scheme Based on Video Content
Guomin Wu, Yueting Zhuang, Fei Wu, Yunhe Pan 449

Subjective Relevance: Implications on Digital Libraries for Experts
and Novices
Shu-Shing Lee, Yin-Leng Theng, Dion Hoe-Lian Goh,
Schubert Shou-Boon Foo 453

Visual Information Retrieval Based on Shape Similarity
Jong-Seung Park 458

Information Retrieval Techniques

A Query Rewriting System for Enhancing the Queriability of Form-Based
Interface
Xiaochun Yang, Bin Wang, Guoren Wang, Ge Yu 462

Digital Library Retrieval Model Using Subject Classification Table and User
Profile
Seon-Mi Woo, Chun-Sik Yoo 473

Hot-Spot Passage Retrieval in Question Answering
Jian Huang, Xuanjing Huang, Lide Wu 483

Query Formulation with a Search Assistant
Lin Fu, Dion Hoe-Lian Goh, Schubert Shou-Boon Foo, Yohan Supangat... 491

Semantic Query Expansion Based on a Question Category Concept List
Hae-Jung Kim, Bo-Yeong Kang, Seong-Bae Park, Sang-Jo Lee 501

Multilingual Collection Retrieving Via Ontology Alignment
Liang Zhang, Guowen Wu, Yanfei Xu, Wei Li, Yang Zhong 510

Using Content-Based and Link-Based Analysis in Building Vertical Search
Engines
Michael Chau, Hsinchun Chen 515

wHunter: A Focused Web Crawler – A Tool for Digital Library
Yun Huang, YunMing Ye.. 519

Personalized Issues in Digital Library

Extending Your Neighborhood-Relationship-Based Recommendations Using
Your Personal Web Context
*Avaré Stewart, Claudia Niederée, Bhaskar Mehta, Matthias Hemmje,
Erich Neuhold*.. 523

Interest-Based User Grouping Model for Collaborative Filtering in Digital
Libraries
Seonho Kim, Edward A. Fox.. 533

Leveraging Enterprise Technology for the Library Portal at the National
University of Singapore
Lee Shong Lin Cecelia, Yulin Yang.. 543

Supporting Field Study with Personalized Project Spaces in a Geographical
Digital Library
*Ee-Peng Lim, Aixin Sun, Zehua Liu, John Hedberg, Chew-Hung Chang,
Tiong-Sa Teh, Dion Hoe-Lian Goh, Yin-Leng Theng*.................................. 553

Academic Digital Library Portal – A Personalized, Customized, Integrated
Electronic Service in Shanghai Jiaotong University Library
Wei Pan, Youhua Chen, Qiaoying Zheng, Peifu Xia, Ruxing Xu.................. 563

Service and Management

A Digital Library of a Service-Orientated Architecture in SJTU– A Case Study
Zongying Yang, Qiaoying Zheng, Guojing Yuan.. 568

A Research to Increase Users' Satisfaction and Loyalty Based on the Customer
Satisfaction Index: A Case Study on the National Taichung Institute of
Technology's Library
Tung-Shou Chen, Rong-Chang Chen, Tsui-Yun Chang.............................. 574

Cross-Cultural Usability of Digital Libraries
Anita Komlodi, Nadia Caidi, Kristin Wheeler.. 584

Design Lessons on Access Features in PAPER
*Yin-Leng Theng, Dion Hoe-Lian Goh, Ming Yin, Eng-Kai Suen,
Ee-Peng Lim*... 594

Information and Communication Technologies, Libraries and the Role of Library Professionals in the 21st Century: With Special Reference to Bangladesh
Md. Anisur Rahman, Md. Hanif Uddin, Ragina Akhter............................. 608

Integrating Electronic Pathfinders in Digital Libraries: A Model for China
Hanrong Wang, William J. Hubbard.......................... 618

Copyrighting Digital Libraries from Database Designer Perspective
Hideyasu Sasaki, Yasushi Kiyoki.................................. 626

Design and Development of Internet Resource Navigation Database on Key Disciplines in CALIS Project
Xiya Zhang, Huijun Zhang, Xiaobo Xiao........................ 630

Live Digital Reference Service: Its Present and Future
Paul W.T. Poon.. 636

Posters

Digital Library Technology

3D Object Retrieval by Bipartite Matching
Xiang Pan, Yin Zhang, Xiuzi Ye, Sanyuan Zhang...................... 640

A Hybrid Neural Network for Web Page Classification
Yukun Cao, Yunfeng Li, ZhuZheng Yu.......................... 641

A Metasearch Engine with Automatic Resource Binding Ability
Guowen Wu, Liang Zhang, Yin Kang, Jun Yin, Xiangdong Zhou, Peiyi Zhang, Lin Zhao.. 642

Certificate-Based Authentication and Authorization Architecture in Digital Library
Lin Chen, Xiaoqin Huang, Jinyuan You...................... 643

Culture Grid and Its Key Technologies
Zhendong Niu, Mingkai Dong, Jie Zhang.................... 644

Face Region Detection on Skin Chrominance from Color Images by Facial Features
Jin Ok Kim, Jin Soo Kim, Chin Hyun Chung...................... 646

Image Assisted Remote Visualization of Volume Data
    Xubo Yang... 647

Improving Multimedia Delivery Performance for Digital Library Applications
    Yunpeng Wang, Xiulin Hu, Hui Guo... 648

Multi-document Summarization Based on Link Analysis and Text Classification
    Jiangqin Wu, Yizi Wu, Jian Liu, Yueting Zhuang... 649

Query Between Heterogeneous Ontology-Based Information Sources Using
Association Matrix
    Jianjiang Lu, Baowen Xu, Wenxian Zhang, Dazhou Kang......................... 650

Research and Development of Digital Library Platform
    Jing Peng, Dake Wang... 651

Understanding the Semantics in Reference Linkages: An Ontological Approach
for Scientific Digital Libraries
    Peixiang Zhao, Ming Zhang, Dongqing Yang, Shiwei Tang....................... 652

Usage of Hybrid Model Based on Concepts Correlations in Adaption to
Changes of User's Interest
    Lizhe Song, Zhendong Niu, Hantao Song, Zhengtao Yu, Xuelin Shi........... 653

WEBDL: A Specific Digital Library for Web Data
    Zhiqiang Zhang, Chunxiao Xing, Lizhu Zhou... 654

Collaboration and Localization

A Practice in the Integration of e-Resources at SJTU Library
    Yongge Bai, Guojing Yuan, Haoming Lin, Jia Peng.................................... 656

An Essay on the Integrated Management of Digital Resources
    Judy L. Cheng, Fred Y. Ye... 658

Analysis, Design and Realization of Metadata Managing System for
Multimedia Resources
    Xu Wu, Ziwei Ma.. 659

Australian Digital Theses Program: Expansion, Partnership and the Future
    Andrew Wells, Tony Cargnelutti.. 660

Building Indian Language Digital Library Collections: Some Experiences
with Greenstone Software
    B.S. Shivaram, T.B. Rajashekar.. 661

Descriptive Metadata Structure and Extended Rules: A Case Study on Ancient
Atlases Metadata Standard
Yunyun Shen, Boyue Yao, Xiangyun Feng.. 662

Featured Collection Digitization and Cooperation: Case Study of Chinese
Mathematics Digital Library
Xiaohui Zheng, Bianai Cheng, Lisheng Feng, Airong Jiang........................ 663

Service and Management

A Stduy on Framework and Methods of Online Information Literacy Instruction
Chunhong Zhang, Zhenbo Lu, Wu Li.. 664

Assessing Users, Uses, and Usage of a Collaborated Digital Library
Natalie Lee-San Pang, Pang-Leang Hiew.. 666

Deepening and Developing the Conception and Service of the Library
JiaZhen Pan.. 667

Design an Ideal Digital Reference Service (DRS) Model for Academic
Libraries
*Jing Guo, Wei Pan, Qiaoying Zheng, Min Huang, Zongying Yang,
Ying Ye*... 668

Discussion of Service Innovation Under the Mode of a Digital Library
Xiaoping He, Liang Wang, Xi Zhang.. 670

Information Services in Digital Library, Fudan's Experience
Yixin Xu, Jun Ying, Xinli Si, Meiqi Mo, Zhiping Xia.................................... 671

Knowledge Management in Library Information Services
Meng Zhan, Ying Liu, Gaokang Yao.. 672

Marketing Academic Digital Library
Jingbo Zhang.. 675

Marketing Information Services in the Digital Age: Viewpoints from
Academic Libraries in North America and the Asia-Pacific Rim
Michael R. Leach, Chihfeng P. Lin.. 676

Models for Sustainability: Three Case Studies
Naicheng Chang.. 677

Research on Academic Personal Portal in Digital Library
Youhua Chen, Wei Pan, Peifu Xia.. 678

Surfing the Hong Kong Baptist University e-Campus in 80 Days: A Pilot
Pocket PC Project with Hewlett-Packard
  Teresa M. L. Kong, Rebekah S. H. Wong.. 680

The Impact of Copyright Upon Digital Libraries
  Min Chou, Oliver G. Zhou.. 681

Online Supervised Learning for Digital Library
  Ning Liu, Benyu Zhang, Jun Yan, Wensi Xi, Shuicheng Yan, Zheng Chen,
  Fengshan Bai, Wei-Ying Ma... 683

Implementation of a Personalized Portal for Academic Library
  Chenggan Quan, Shuang Wang, Lin Mai... 684

The System Design of Military Equipment Digital Library
  Lu Gao, Hongmin Yu, Hongfeng Wang, Sumei Zhang...................................... 685

Author Index... 687

Biomedical Informatics and Security Informatics Research in Digital Library

Hsinchun Chen

Department of Management Information Systems,
The University of Arizona, Tucson, AZ 85721, USA
hchen@bpa.arizona.edu

Abstract. The Internet is changing the way we live and do business. It offers a tremendous opportunity for libraries, governments, and businesses to better deliver its contents and services and interact with its many constituents. After ten years of active research, there appears to be a need towards advancing the science of "informatics" in digital library, especially in several non-traditional but critical application areas. In this paper, we introduce two promising informatics research areas for digital library researchers, namely, Biomedical Informatics and Security Informatics. We discuss some common research elements between these two areas and present several case studies that aim to highlight the relevance and importance of such research in digital library.

1 Digital Library: A Multi-disciplinary Research Framework

The location and provision of information services has dramatically changed over the last ten years. There is no need to leave the home or office to locate and access information now readily available on-line via digital gateways furnished by a wide variety of information providers, (e.g., libraries, electronic publishers, businesses, organizations, individuals). Information access is no longer restricted to what is physically available in the nearest library. It is electronically accessible from a wide variety of globally distributed information repositories.

Information is no longer simply text and pictures. It is electronically available in a wide variety of formats, many of which are large, complex (i.e., video and audio) and often integrated (i.e., multimedia). This increased variety of information allows one to take virtual tours of museums, historical sites and natural wonders, attend virtual concerts and theater performances, watch a variety of movies, and read, view or listen to books, articles, lectures and music, access medical literature and images, all through digital libraries.

Digital libraries represent a unique multi-disciplinary research framework, in which social and policy impact matters as much as system and technical advancement. It is hard to evaluate a new technology in the absence of real users and large collections. Two critical research areas in Biomedical Informatics and Security Informatics are demanding the attention of digital library researchers. Biomedical Informatics needs to consider advanced databases, information systems, standards, and policies for the public health and biomedical professionals. Security Informatics also needs to address both the technical database and information systems issues and

Z. Chen et al. (Eds.): ICADL 2004, LNCS 3334, pp. 01–12, 2004.
© Springer-Verlag Berlin Heidelberg 2004

other related standard, privacy, and policy matters. Both research areas have strong potential in making significant technological advancement and social impacts. They could also benefit from the multi-disciplinary research approach frequently adopted in the digital library community.

2   Biomedical Informatics

Biomedical Informatics refers to the computer and information systems applications in health care and biomedicine. Critical areas under investigation in this important and growing field include databases, information systems, standards, ethics, and privacy consideration, among others. Many medical computing applications have been under active research including: patient record systems, public health systems, biomedical imaging systems, medical digital libraries, clinical decision support systems, and telemedicine.

In Biomedical Informatics, any attempt to solve the problem of information access and usage for discipline specific users - such as those in the field of medicine - requires an understanding of the characteristics of the profession and the attendant information needs. The occurrence of physicians requiring additional information to answer clinical questions is estimated to be 3.2 questions for every 10 patients seen [3], while in inpatient settings the ratio is higher – 1.4 questions per patient [11]. These statistics are staggering in light of recent studies which indicate that the amount of information available to physicians is increasing while the amount of time outside of daily practice to read has remained constant [7].

In addition, researchers in the field of biomedicine generally want information from primary information resources such as journal articles, while clinicians want information from tertiary information resources such as textbooks or reference sources that will help them answer clinical questions [4]. Unfortunately, most physicians and other medical researchers are not able to make full use of these systems because as medical students they are often not adequately trained to use electronic information systems, thus making the task of retrieving timely and relevant sources of information even more onerous and time consuming. In light of the diverse user needs and the overwhelming amount of new biomedical data and information, research in advancing "intelligent" information access, knowledge discovery, and knowledge management is critically needed in biomedicine.

3   Security Informatics

The tragic events of September 11 and the following anthrax contamination of letters caused drastic effects on many aspects of society. Terrorism has become the most significant threat to the national security because of its potential to bring massive damage to our infrastructure, economy, and people. In response to this challenge federal authorities are actively implementing comprehensive strategies and measures in order to achieve the three objectives identified in the "National Strategy for Homeland Security" report [10]: preventing future terrorist attacks; reducing the nation's vulnerability; and minimizing the damage and recovering from attacks that occur. State and local law enforcement agencies, likewise, become more vigilant about criminal activities, which can harm public safety and threaten national security.

Academics in the field of natural sciences, computational sciences, social sciences, engineering, medicine, and many others have also been called upon to help enhance the government's abilities to fight terrorism and other crimes. Science and technology have been identified in the "National Strategy for Homeland Security" report as the keys to win the new counter-terrorism war [10]. Especially, it is believed that information technology will play an indispensable role in making our nation safer by supporting intelligence and knowledge discovery through collecting, processing, analyzing, and utilizing terrorism- and crime-related data [8]. Based on the knowledge discovered, the federal, state, and local authorities can make timely decisions to select effective strategies and tactics as well as allocate appropriate amount of resources to detect, prevent, and respond to future attacks.

In recent years, Security Informatics has begun to emerge as a new discipline for technical, social, and policy researchers in addressing the challenges facing national and homeland security issues around the world. We believe this new discipline could significantly benefit from the multi-disciplinary and community-building nature of the digital library research.

4 Case Studies in Biomedical Informatics and Security Informatics

In the following sections, we present several case studies that aim to address biomedical informatics and security informatics research in a digital library framework. For each case study we summarize research questions, approaches adopted, and potential impacts on users. We hope these case studies can also help digital library researchers broaden their perspective and extend their reach into other non-traditional, but critical application areas.

4.1 HelpfulMed: Medical Knowledge Portal

While the problems of information overload and retrieval are prevalent across the many disciplines represented on the Internet, the ability to accurately search for, access, and process information is particularly pressing in the field of medicine. The availability on the Internet of vast distributed repositories of quality medical information, each with its own unique interface, has placed information access at the center of research.

The goal of this case study is to describe an approach to building a web portal that provides high quality information support in the medical domain with several system-generated knowledge structures. To this end, we present a knowledge portal designed specifically for medical information retrieval called *HelpfulMed*. In developing this system we combined existing AI Lab techniques, including spidering, noun phrase indexing [15], automatic thesaurus (concept space) generation [5], data visualization, and a meta search tool designed to search the invisible web of databases. These techniques have been significantly modified and enhanced for medical information retrieval.

A single search interface ties together the web search, related medical terms, and database search functionalities through the use of an integrated system that allows users to interact with the various technologies offered. This type of "one-stop shopping" system brings together distributed resources the user might need in one place, thus decreasing the time the user would spend moving from one information system to the next, learning the individual idiosyncrasies of each system in an attempt to capture all of the information relevant to their information needs [1].

HelpfulMed provides access to a variety of databases currently publicly available over the Internet. These include citation databases such as MEDLINE and CANCERLIT, online reference works such as the Merck Manual of Diagnosis and Treatment, and Physicians Data Query (PDQ) which provides peer-reviewed summaries on cancer treatment, screening and detection, prevention, genetics and supportive care. Access is also provided to evidence-based medical databases (EBM) such as the American College of Physicians Journal Club (ACP), National Guidelines Clearinghouse (NGC) and the York Database of Abstracts of Reviews of Effectiveness (DARE). Medical librarians at the Arizona Health Sciences Library selected these databases as being those with the most comprehensive and accurate information.

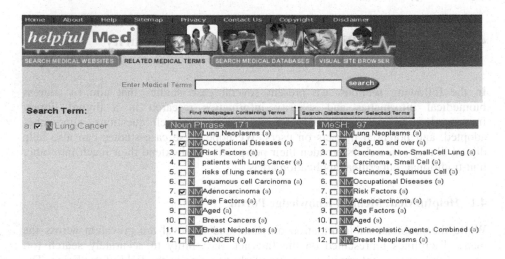

Fig. 1. Concept Space results show terms related to "lung cancer"

A search in the "Related Medical Terms" section (Figure 1) provides the user with a list of additional terms that might more accurately describe the information need. If the user inputs "lung cancer" at this point, the system will return a list of related noun phrases (N) drawn from the concept space, and MeSH terms (M), plus a list of authors (A). Thus, the user can decide if s/he wants to search phrases extracted from the text, related medical subjects headings, authors, or any combination of the three.

The Visual Site Browser, also called MEDMap, is a graphical system designed to facilitate the information browsing behavior of users in the domain of medical-related research. The input data to MEDMap consists of 10 million medical abstracts obtained from MEDLINE. By applying indexing, noun phrasing and self-organizing map techniques, MEDMap generates a subject hierarchy that contains 132,700 categories and 4,586 maps. The MEDMap also combines a text-based alphabetic display and a graphical approach to represent the subject categories generated. Using the Visual Site Browser, the user is able to "drill down" through the levels of a map, browsing for topics of interest until a collection of documents is eventually reached. In the case shown in Figure 2, the user chose to browse the phrase "Liver Neoplasms", which is circled. The user continued refining the search until a relevant document was found.

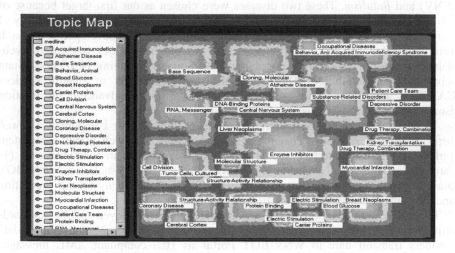

Fig. 2. First layer of MEDMap with "Liver Neoplasms" circled

Previous research into the development of a concept space for cancer information using the CANCERLIT collection resulted in CancerSpace, an automatically created thesaurus of cancer-related terms with 1.3 million unique terms and 52 million relationships [5]. We conducted a study to assess the usefulness of suggested terms from different thesauri: our automatically generated system, the MeSH concept space and Internet Grateful Med, which at the time of the study was the most often cited online tool based on the UMLS Metathesaurus. Cancer researchers affiliated with the University of Arizona Cancer Center participated in our experiment as subjects.

Recall and precision figures for these systems and statistical tests indicate that there were no significant differences among the three systems when used individually. It was also discovered that the three systems rarely returned the same relevant terms. However, when systems were combined, the recall rates went up, while precision rates remained relatively static. Based on this result, a combination of automatic concept space and MeSH terms is provided to the user in our HelpfulMed system.

4.2 WNV-BOT Portal: Disease Informatics

Information technologies and infectious disease informatics are playing an increasingly important role in preventing, detecting, and managing infectious disease outbreaks. This case study presents a collaborative infectious disease informatics project called the WNV-BOT Portal system. This Portal system provides integrated, web-enabled access to a variety of distributed data sources related to West Nile Virus and Botulism. It also makes available a preliminary set of data analysis and visualization tools tailored for these two diseases. This system has helped to demonstrate the technological feasibility of developing a cross jurisdiction and cross species infectious disease information infrastructure and identifying related technical and policy-related challenges with its national implementation [16].

Our research focuses on two prominent infectious diseases: *West Nile Virus* (WNV) and *Botulism*. These two diseases were chosen as our first target because of their significant public health and national security implications and the availability of related datasets in both New York and California states. We developed a research prototype called the *WNV-BOT Portal* system, which provides integrated, web-enabled access to a variety of distributed data sources including New York State Department of Health (NYSDH), the California Department of Health Services (CADHS), and some other sources. It also provides advanced information visualization capabilities as well as predictive modeling support.

Architecturally, WNV-BOT Portal consists of three major components: a *web portal*, a *data store*, and a *communication backbone*. The web portal component implements the user interface and provides the following main functionalities: (1) searching and querying available WNV/BOT datasets, (2) visualizing WNV/BOT datasets using spatial-temporal visualization, (3) accessing analysis and prediction functions, and (4) accessing the alerting mechanism.

To enable data interoperability, we use Health Level Seven (HL7) standards (http://www.hl7.org/) as the main storage format. In our approach, contributing data providers transmit data to WNV-BOT Portal as HL7-compliant XML messages (through a secure network connection if necessary). After receiving these XML messages, WNV-BOT Portal will store them directly in its data store. To alleviate potential computational performance problems associated with this HL7 XML-based approach, we are identifying a core set of data fields based on which search will be done frequently and extracting these fields from all XML messages to be stored in a separate database table to enable fast retrieval.

An important function of the data store layer is data ingest and access control. The data ingest control module is responsible for checking the integrity and authenticity of data feeds from the underlying information sources. The access control module is responsible for granting and restricting user access to sensitive data.

The communication backbone component enables data exchanges between WNV-BOT Portal and the underlying WNV/BOT sources based upon the CDC's Electronic Disease Surveillance System (NEDSS) and HL7 standards. It uses a collection of source-specific "connectors" to communicate with underlying sources. We use the connector linking NYSDOH's HIN system and WNV-BOT Portal to illustrate a typical design of such connectors. The data from HIN to the portal system is transmitted in a "push" manner. HIN sends secure Public Health Information Network Messaging System (PHIN MS) messages to the portal at pre-specified time intervals. The connector at the portal side runs a data receiver daemon listening for incoming messages. After a message is received, the connector will check for data integrity syntactically and invoke the data normalization subroutine. Then the connector will store the verified message in the portal's internal data store through its data ingest control module. Other data sources (e.g., those from USGS) may have "pull"-type connectors which will periodically download information from the source web sites and examine and store data in the portal's internal data store. In general, the communication backbone component provides data receiving and sending functionalities, source-specific data normalization, as well as data encryption capabilities.

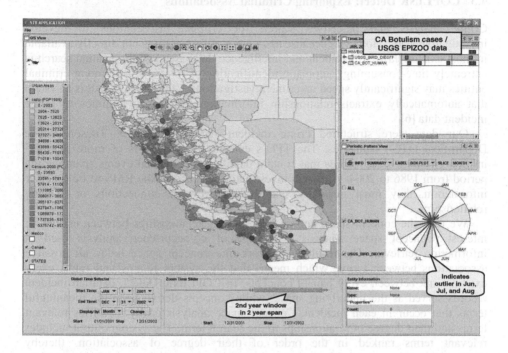

Fig. 3. Using STV to visualize botulism data

WNV-BOT Portal makes available the Spatial Temporal Pattern Visualizer (STV) to facilitate exploration of infectious disease case data and to summarize query results. STV has three integrated and synchronized views: periodic, timeline, and GIS. Figure 3 illustrates how these three views can be used to explore infectious disease dataset: The top left panel shows the GIS view. The user can select multiple datasets to be shown on the map in a layered manner using the checkboxes. The top right panel corresponds to the timeline view displaying the occurrences of various cases using a Gantt chart-like display. The user can also access case details easily using the tree display located left to the timeline display. Below the timeline view is the periodic view through which the user can identify periodic temporal patterns (e.g., which months have an unusually high number of cases). The bottom portion of the interface allows the user to specify subsets of data to be displayed and analyzed.

Our project has supported exploration of and experimentation with technological infrastructures needed for the full-fledged implementation of a national infectious disease information infrastructure and helped foster information sharing and collaboration among related government agencies at state and federal levels. In addition, we have obtained important insights and hands-on experience with various important policy-related challenges faced by developing a national infrastructure. For example, a nontrivial part of our project activity has been centered around developing data sharing agreements between project partners from different states.

4.3 COPLINK Detect: Exploring Criminal Associations

Crime analysts and detectives search for criminal associations to develop investigative leads. However, because association information is not directly available in most existing law enforcement and intelligence databases and the manual search is extremely time-consuming, automatic identification of relationships among criminal entities may significantly speed up crime investigations. COPLINK Detect is a system that automatically extracts relationship information from large volumes of crime incident data [6].

Our data were structured crime incident records stored in Tucson Police Department (TPD) databases. The TPD's current RMS consists of more than 1.5 million crime incident records that contain details from criminal events spanning the period from 1986 to 2004. Although investigators can access the RMS to tie together information, they must manually search the RMS for connections or existing relationships.

We used the concept space approach to identity relationships between entities of interest. Concept space analysis is a type of co-occurrence analysis used in information retrieval. The resulting network-like concept space holds all possible associations between terms, which means that the system retains and ranks every existing link between every pair of concepts. In COPLINK Detect, detailed incident records served as the underlying space, while concepts derive from the meaningful terms that occur in each incident. Concept space analysis easily identifies relevant terms and their degree of relationships to the search term. The system output includes relevant terms ranked in the order of their degree of association, thereby distinguishing the most relevant terms from inconsequential terms. From a crime investigation standpoint, concept space analysis can help investigators link known entities to other related entities that might contain useful information for further investigation—such as people and vehicles related to a given suspect.

Information related to a suspect can direct an investigation to expend in the right direction, but revealing relationships among data in one particular incident might fail to capture those relationships from the entire database. In effect, investigators need to review all incident reports related to a suspect, which can be a tedious work. The COPLINK Detect system introduces concept space as an alternative method that captures the relationships between four types of entities (person, organization, location, and vehicle) in the entire database. COPLINK Detect also offers an easy-to-use user interface and allows search for relationships among the four types of entities. Figure 4 presents the COPLINK Detect interface showing sample search results of vehicles, relations, and crime case details [2].

We conducted user studies to evaluate the performance and usefulness of COPLINK Detect. Twelve crime analysts and detectives participated in the longitudinal field study during a four-week period. The major areas were identified where COPLINK Detect provided improved support for crime investigation. Participants indicated that COPLINK Detect served as a powerful tool for acquiring criminal association information. The cited its value in helping determine the presence of absence of links between people, places, vehicles, and other entity types in investigating a crime.

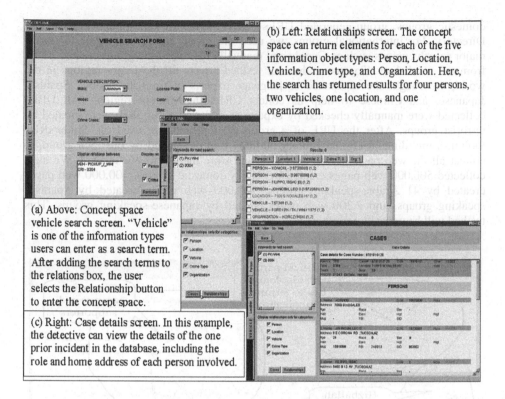

(b) Left: Relationships screen. The concept space can return elements for each of the five information object types: Person, Location, Vehicle, Crime type, and Organization. Here, the search has returned results for four persons, two vehicles, one location, and one organization.

(a) Above: Concept space vehicle search screen. "Vehicle" is one of the information types users can enter as a search term. After adding the search terms to the relations box, the user selects the Relationship button to enter the concept space.

(c) Right: Case details screen. In this example, the detective can view the details of the one prior incident in the database, including the role and home address of each person involved.

Fig. 4. COPLINK Detect interface showing sample research results

In general, users reported that they found COPLINK Detect interface easy to use. Officers noted that the graphical user interface and use of color to distinguish different entity types provided a more intuitive tool than the text-based RMS system. In a direct comparison of 15 searches using COPLINK Detect required an average of 30 minutes less per search than did RMS [2].

4.4 "Dark Web" Portal: Terrorism Research

Because the Internet has become a global platform for anyone to disseminate and communicate information, terrorists also take advantage of the freedom of the cyberspace and construct their own web sites to propagate terrorism beliefs, share ideas of attacks, and recruit new members. Web sites of terrorist organizations may also connect to one another through hyperlinks, forming a "dark web". We are building an intelligent web portal called Dark Web Portal to help terrorism researchers collect, access, analyze, and understand dark web information. This project consists of three major components: Dark Web testbed building, Dark Web link analysis, and Dark Web Portal building.

Relying on reliable governmental sources such as Anti-Defamation League (ADL), FBI, and United States Committee For A Free Lebanon (USCFAFL), we identified 224 US domestic terrorist groups and 440 international terrorist groups. For US domestic groups, group-generated URLs can be found in FBI reports and Google Directory. For international groups, we used the group names as queries to search major search engines such as Google and manually identified the group-created URLs from the result lists. To ensure that our testbed covers all the major regions in the world, we sought the assistance of language experts in English, Arabic, Spanish, Japanese, and Chinese to help us collect URLs in different regions. All URLs collected were manually checked by experts to make sure that they were created by terrorist groups. After the URL of a group is identified, we used the SpidersRUs toolkit, a multilingual Digital Library building tool developed by our own group, to collect all the web pages under that URL and store them into our testbed. We have collected 500,000 web pages created by 94 US domestic groups, 400,000 web pages created by 41 Arabic-speaking groups, 100,000 web pages created by Spanish-speaking groups, and 2,200 web pages created by Japanese-speaking groups. This testbed will be updated periodically.

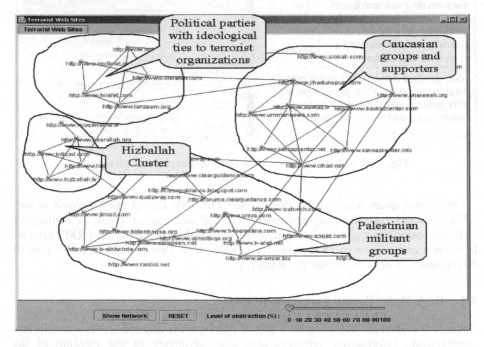

Fig. 5. The "Dark Web": web sites constructed by 46 terrorist organizations or affiliated groups

Terrorist groups are not atomized individuals but actors linked to each other through complex networks of direct or mediated exchanges. Identifying how relationships between groups are formed and dissolved in the terrorist group network would enable us to decipher the social milieu and communication channels among terrorist groups across different jurisdictions. Previous studies have shown that the link structure of the web represents a considerable amount of latent human annotation. Thus, by analyzing and visualizing hyperlink structures between terrorist-generated web sites in our testbed, we could discover the structure and organization of terrorist group networks, capture network dynamics, and predict trends of terrorist attacks.

To test our ideas, we conducted an experiment in which we analyzed and visualized the hyperlink structure between around 100,000 Web pages from 46 web sites in our current testbed. These 46 web sites were created by 4 major Arabic-speaking terrorist groups, namely Al-Gama'a al-Islamiyya (Islamic Group, IG), Hizballa (Party of God), Al-Jihad (Egyptian Islamic Jihad), and Palestinian Islamic Jihad (PIJ) and their supporters. Hyperlinks between each pair of the 46 web sites were extracted from the web pages and a closeness value was calculated for each pair of the 46 web sites. In Figure 5, each note represents a web site created by one of the 46 groups. A link exists between two notes means there are hyperlinks between the web pages of the two web sites. We presented this network to the domain experts and confirmed that the structure of the diagram matches the knowledge of the experts on how the groups relate to each other in real world. The 4 clusters represent a logical mapping of the existing relations between the 46 groups. An example of this kind of mapping is the Palestinian terrorist group's cluster where many of the Palestinian terrorist groups' web sites, as well as their leaders' web sites are clustered together. Examples include Al-Aqsa Martyrs Brigade (www.kataebaqsa.org), HAMAS (www.ezzedeen.net), and Palestinian Islamic Jihad (PIJ, www.abrarway.com). Among others are Palestinian groups fighting the Israeli occupiers.

We believe the Dark Web project allows us to examine the open source terrorist information scientifically and systematically. In addition to aiding intelligence gathering, a more important outcome of the project is to allow us to better understand the social and political context underlying the terrorism phenomena.

5 Conclusions

Digital library represents a multi-disciplinary research community that encompasses both technological advances and social and policy considerations. With the overwhelming growth and opportunities in Biomedical Informatics and Security Informatics, we encourage digital library researchers and practitioners to examine these new emerging applications carefully and to help develop the science of "informatics" for digital library research.

References

1. Chen, H., Lally, A. M., Chau,M.: HelpfulMed: Intelligent Searching for Medical Information over the Internet. Journal of the American Society for Information Science and Technology 54(7) (2003) 683-694
2. Chen, H., Schroeder, J., Hauck, R. V., Ridgeway, L., Atabakhsh, H., Gupta, H., Boarman, C., Rasmussen, K., Clements, A. W.: COPLINK Connect: Information and Knowledge Management for Law Enforcement. Decision Support Systems, Special Issue on Digital Government 34(3) (2003) 271-286
3. Ely, J.W., Osheroff, J.A., Ebell, M.H., Bergus, G.R., Levy, B.T., Chambliss, M.L. Evans, E.R..: Analysis of questions asked by family doctors regarding patient care. British Medical Journal 319(7206) (1999) 358-361

4. Hersh, W.R., Detmer, W.M. Frisse, M.E.: Information Retrieval Systems. Edward H. Shortliffe and Leslie E. Perreault (Eds.), Medical Informatics: Computer Applications in Health Care and Biomedicine 2nd ed. New York: Springer (2000) 539-572. .
5. Houston, A. L., Chen, H., Schatz, B. R., Hubbard, S. M., Sewell, R. R., Ng T. D.: Exploring the Use of Concept Space to Improve Medical Information Retrieval. Decision Support Systems, 30 (2000) 171-186
6. Hauck, R. V., Atabakhsh, H., Ongvasith, P., Gupta, H., Chen, H.: Using Coplink to Analyze Criminal-Justice Data. IEEE Computer 35(3) (2002) 30-37
7. Hunt, R. H. & Newman, R. G.: Medical Knowledge Overload: A disturbing trend for physicians. Health Care Management Review 22(1) (1997) 70-75.
8. Mena, J.: Investigative Data Mining for Security and Criminal Detection. Amsterdam, Holland: Butterworth Heinemann (2003)
9. National Research Council: Making the nation safer: the role of science and technology in countering terrorism. Washington, DC: Committee on Science and Technology for Countering Terrorism, The National Academies Press (2002)
10. Office of Homeland Security: National Strategy of Homeland Security. Washington D.C.: Office of Homeland Security (2002)
11. Osheroff, J. A., Forsythe, D. E., Buchanan, B. G., Bankowitz, R. A., Blumenfeld B. H., & Miller, R. A: Physicians information needs: analysis of questions posed during clinical teaching. Annals of Internal Medicine 114(7) (1991) 576-81
12. Reid, E., Qin, J., Chung, W., Xu, J., Zhou, Y., Schumaker, R., Sageman, M., Chen, H.: Terrorism Knowledge Portal: A Knowledge Discovery Approach to Addressing the Threat of Terrorism. Intelligence and Security Informatics, Proceedings of the Second Symposium on Intelligence and Security Informatics, ISI 2004, Lecture Notes in Computer Science (LNCS 3073), Springer-Verlag (2004)
13. Schatz, B. R., Chen, H.: Building large-scale digital libraries. IEEE COMPUTER 29(5) (1996) 22-27
14. Schatz B. R., Chen, H.: Digital libraries: technological advancements and social impacts. IEEE COMPUTER 31(2) (1999) 45-50
15. Tolle, K., Chen, H.: Comparing Noun Phrasing Techniques for Use with Medical Digital Library Tools. Journal of the American Society for Information Science, Special Issue on Digital Libraries 51(4) (2000) 352-370
16. Zeng, D., Chen, H., Tseng, C., Larson, C., Eidson, M., Gotham, I, Lynch, C., Ascher, M.: West Nile Virus and Botulism Portal: A Case Study in Infectious Disease Informatics. Intelligence and Security Informatics, Proceedings of the Second Symposium on Intelligence and Security Informatics, ISI 2004, Tucson, Arizona, Lecture Notes in Computer Science (LNCS 3073), Springer-Verlag (2004)

ChinaGrid: Making Grid Computing a Reality*

Hai Jin

Cluster and Grid Computing Lab,
Huazhong University of Science and Technology, 430074, Wuhan, China
hjin@hust.edu.cn

Abstract. Grid computing presents a new trend to distributed computing and Internet applications, which can construct a virtual single image of heterogeneous resources, provide uniform application interface and integrate widespread computational resources into super, ubiquitous and transparent aggregation. ChinaGrid project, founded by Ministry of Education of China, is an attempt to achieve above goals by exploring the various resources on existing and well developed internet infrastructure, CERNET (*China Education and Research Network*). In this paper, I will introduce the general picture of ChinaGrid project, its vision and mission. The design of ChinaGrid support platform, called CGSP, is also discussed briefly. To illustrate the reality of ChinaGrid project, five different grid computing applications and its application supporting platform are discussed in detail. The purpose of this paper is to introduce this great grid project to the world completely for the first time.

1 Introduction

Grid computing presents a new trend to distributed computing and Internet applications, which can construct a virtual single image of heterogeneous resources, provide uniform application interface and integrate widespread computational resources into super, ubiquitous and transparent aggregation. According to [10, 11], grid computing is a "resource sharing and coordinated problem solving in dynamic, multi-institutional virtual organizations". The purpose of grid computing is to eliminate the resource islands in the application level, and to make computing and services ubiquitous.

The prerequisites for grid computing lie in three aspects: network infrastructure; wide area distribution of computational resources; and continuous increasing requirement for resource sharing. Nearly all the existing grid computing projects are based on existing network infrastructure, such as UK e-Science Programme [20], Information Power Grid (IPG) [12], and TeraGrid [18]. In TeraGrid, the five key grid computing sites are interconnected via 30 or 40 Tb/s fast network connections. The ChinaGrid project, which will be discussed in detail in this paper, is also based on a long running network infrastructure *China Education and Research Network* (CERNET) [1].

---

* This paper is supported by ChinaGrid project of Ministry of Education of China and National 863 Hi-Tech R&D Research Program under grant 2004AA104280.

Z. Chen et al. (Eds.): ICADL 2004, LNCS 3334, pp. 13–24, 2004.
© Springer-Verlag Berlin Heidelberg 2004

There are five major grid computing projects in China [21], they are: China education and research grid, called ChinaGrid [2]; China National Grid [8]; China Spatial Information Grid; China Science Grid; and Shanghai City Information Grid. In this paper, I will talk about the detail of ChinaGrid project and the applications running on top of ChinaGrid.

The following of this paper is organized as follows: in section 2, the history, vision and mission of ChinaGrid project is introduced. In section 3, the supporting grid computing platform for ChinaGrid project, called CGSP, is presented briefly. In section 4, five ongoing ChinaGrid computing application platforms and pilot applications running on top of these application platforms are discussed in detail. Section 5 ends this paper with conclusions.

2 ChinaGrid Project: Vision and Mission

In 2002, China *Ministry of Education* (MoE) launched the largest grid computing project in China, called **ChinaGrid** project, aiming to provide the nationwide grid computing platform and services for research and education purpose among 100 key universities in China. The vision for ChinaGrid project is to deploy the largest, most advanced and most practical grid computing project in China or even around the world.

The underlying infrastructure for ChinaGrid project is the CERNET, which began to run from 1994, covering 800 more universities, colleges and institutes in China. Currently, it is second largest nationwide networks in China. The bandwidth of CERNET backbone is 2.5Gbps, connected by 7 cities, called local network center. The bandwidth of CERNET local backbone is 155Mbps.

The ChinaGrid project is a long term project with three different stages. The first stage period is from 2002 to 2005, covering 12 top universities in China. They are: Huazhong University of Science and Technology (HUST), Tsinghua University (THU), Peking University (PKU), Beihang University (BUAA), South China University of Technology (SCUT), Shanghai Jiao Tong University (SJTU), Southeast University (SEU), Xi'an Jiaotong University (XJTU), National University of Defense Technology (NUDT), Northeastern University (NEU), Shandong University (SDU), and Sun Yat-Sen University (ZSU). The site view of ChinaGrid project is shown in Fig.1.

The focus for the first stage of ChinaGrid project is on platform and applications on computation grid (e-science). These applications are varied in all scientific disciplines, from life science to computational physics. The second stage of ChinaGrid project will be from 2005 to 2007, covering 20 to 30 key universities in China. The focus will extend from computational grid applications to information service grid (e-info), including applications for distance learning grid, digital Olympic grid, etc. The third stage will from 2007 to 2010, extending the coverage of ChinaGrid project to all the 100 key universities. The focus of third stage grid application will be even more diverse, include instrument sharing (e-instrument).

3   Design Philosophy of ChinaGrid Support Platform (CGSP)

The underlying common grid computing platform for ChinaGrid project is called *ChinaGrid Supporting Platform* (CGSP), supporting all above three different stages grid applications, they are e-science, e-info, and e-instrument. CGSP integrates all kinds of resources in education and research environments, makes the heterogeneous and dynamic nature of resource transparent to the users, and provides high performance, high reliable, secure, convenient and transparent grid service for the scientific computing and engineering research. CGSP provides both ChinaGrid service portal, and a set of development environment for deploying various grid applications.

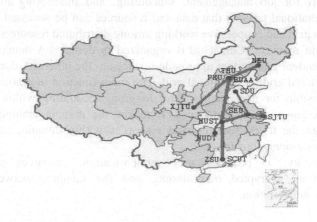

Fig. 1. Site Distribution for the Initial ChinaGrid Project

The detail software building blocks for CGSP are shown in Fig. 2. The current version, CGSP 1.0, is based on the core of Globus Toolkit 3.9.1, and is WSRF [19] and OGSA [13] compatible. According to the roadmap of CGSP development, CGSP 1.0 is to be released in October 2004. There are five 5 building blocks in CGSP 1.0. They are:

1. Grid portal: grid portal is the entrance for the end user to use grid services. By using grid portal, users can submit their jobs, monitor the running of jobs, manage and transfer data, inquiry the grid resource information. Grid portal also provides other facilities such as user management and accounting of grid resource usage.

2. Grid development toolkits: they provide toolkit to pack the resource to grid services, the deployment and management toolkit for grid, and programming model to deploy complex grid application in grid environment.

3. Information service: it is responsible for the management of various resources within grid environment, provides a global resource view and grid information services, and updates grid resource information in real time manner. The main

purpose is to provide real time information of various grid resources for end users and other modules in grid environment.

4. Grid management: it provides basic support for various jobs in grid environment. It consists four parts:

- Service container: it provides a grid service installation, deployment, running, and monitoring environment on each node in grid environment. It also provides necessary support to monitor the real time resources status of each grid node.
- Data manager: it is responsible for the management of various storage resources and data files in grid environment. It provides a global file view, so that users can access various data files transparent.
- Job manager: based on information services and data management, it provides support for job management, scheduling, and monitoring for end users' computational task, so that data and resources can be accessed transparently within grid and cooperative working among distributed resources.
- Domain manager: ChinaGrid is organized in domain. A domain refers to a independent grid system to provide services to the others. A domain can be a specialized grid, or a regional grid. The main function of domain manager is responsible for user management, logging, accounting within domain and interacting with other domains. It makes the domain administrator easily manage the users, services, and resources within domain, and interactive policies among domains.

5. Grid security: it provides user authentication, resources and services authorization, encrypted transmission, and the mapping between users to resources authorization.

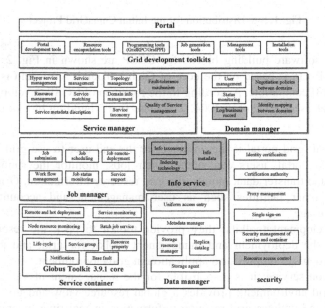

Fig. 2. The Software Building Block of CGSP System

4 Grid Computing Application Platforms

Besides the development of CGSP, another major task for ChinaGrid project is the deployment of grid computing application platform and some pilot grid applications, this makes ChinaGrid very unique to other existing grid projects. In the first stage of ChinaGrid project, five ongoing main grid computing application platforms are under development. They are: bioinformatics grid [3], image grid [6], computational fluid dynamics grid [4], course online grid [5], and massive data processing grid [7]. The first three grids are actually computational oriented. The course online grid is very unique grid, which is the first step to information service grid. The last one, massive data processing grid, is the data grid in nature [9]. Next, I will discuss these grid application platforms in detail.

4.1 Bioinformatics Grid

Bioinformatics merges biology, computer science and information technology into one discipline. The ultimate goal of the field is to enable the discovery of new biological insights. It mainly focuses on grasping biological meaning of plentiful biological data. Bioinformatics uses database, data processing method and software to get results through mass computation. Each bioinformatics research institute holds their own computing facilities, software resources and storage devices. They setup their own research platform independently. Although most of these resources are connected with the Internet, they are only used by their owners, and the utilization rate is low. At the same time, many researchers in Chinese universities have no such research resources to use.

The bioinformatics grid integrates heterogeneous large-scale computing and storage facilities within ChinaGrid to provide bioinformatics supercomputing services for bioinformatics researchers through the Web interface, which is very user-friendly. There are two steps and only two steps are required for users to use bioinformatics grid through this portal. First, input the computing requests according to the submission form from web page. Second, get the computing results from bioinformatics grid. Where the requests are submitted, how the computing requests is allocated, and the monitoring and management for computing tasks are all completed by the bioinformatics grid itself.

When bioinformatics grid server receives the computational requests from the client, it locates a suitable node in the grid to perform the mathematical computation according to the users' requirement and task allocation rule, or integrates a virtual supercomputer to perform the larger computational requests from users.

There are three key modules in bioinformatics grid. They are:

1.   Management of Heterogeneous Resources

In bioinformatics grid, resource management consists of both resource abstraction and resource organization. In order to integrate the diverse resources in a uniform and seamless way, all hardware and software resources are packaged into certain services. A set of attributes is abstracted to describe the services (such as OS information, computation power, software category, software name). Objectives of OMR (Organization and Management of Resources) are:

- Integrated heterogeneous computer;
- Make bioinformatics computing tools grid-enable;
- Basic communication mechanisms;

  These mechanisms must permit the efficient implementation of a wide range of communication methods, including message passing, remote procedure call, and multicast.

- Process creation

  This component is used to initiate computation on a computing grid node once it has been located and allocated. This task includes setting up executables, creating an execution environment, starting an executable, passing arguments, integrating the new process into the rest of the computation, and managing termination and process shutdown.

2.   Monitoring

The bioinformatics grid provides uniform protocol and interface specification for grid resources monitoring. Monitoring is used to identify system bottleneck. The system can be adjusted and optimized by using the information gathered by monitoring. Objectives of Grid Resources Monitoring (GRM) in bioinformatics grid are:

- Maintaining the latest copy of crucial data in the root node;
- Task scheduling;
- Monitoring bioinformatics grid;
- Keeping log of operations, errors and statistics.

3.   Integration of Heterogeneous Bioinformatics Computing Tools

At present, many bioinformatics computing tools have been designed for different application purposes. All of these tools are installed into the grid hardware environment and are used through the Web interface easily and widely. In bioinformatics grid, objectives of Integration of heterogeneous Bioinformatics Computing Tools (IBCT) are:

- Classification and installation of shared bioinformatics computing and research tools;
- Integration of bioinformatics database;
- Pipeline running control of computing flow;
- Graphic user interface;
- Billing system.

4.2 Image Grid

The image grid is a grid image-processing platform based on ChinaGrid infrastructure, which is an integrated environment hiding inner heterogeneous resources and dynamic information. It not only realizes cooperative characteristic, but also affords a secure and transparent image-processing environment with correlative services [23].

The remarkable characteristics of the image-processing platform are: application development, runtime environment, and remote visualization.

The image processing grid application development and runtime environment is based on web service and grid service technology, in which image processing toolkits or software are deployed as web services or grid services components. These services are usually deployed redundantly for all kinds of reasons such as fault-tolerance, availability, and performance. The concept of virtual services, which are the abstract of several physical services, is introduced to implement common functions and interfaces. Therefore during the development of image processing grid application, users just care about the virtual services of image applications, which then convert into different physical services running on ChinaGrid through service-scheduling system.

Various image-processing functions are afforded and extended in the image grid environment with much higher performance and QoS. Currently, the following applications are integrated into image grid as pilot applications: reconstruction of digital virtual human body, image processing of remote sensing, and medical image diagnoses.

The Virtual Human Project (VHP) is the creation of complete, anatomically detailed, three-dimensional representations of the normal male and female human bodies. The long-term goal of VHP is to describe perfectly the conformations and functions of gene, protein, cell and organ so as to achieve the whole accurate simulation of body information in the end.

The basic realization of digital virtual human is to identify and classify inner viscera, rebuild the edge profile data of outer body and three-dimensional profile data of inner viscera, then construct high-precision digital human grid, and use these data to get the visualization for a human body. In addition to the massive amount of body slices (a suit of raw data requires 20GB storage space), the dada amount will increase greatly for mesh construction. Only a computer resource grid can afford its processing. Before we analyze and dispose these data, some optimized resource scheduling algorithm must be bring forward, such as high-precise algorithm for contour extraction and high-precise parallel algorithm for reconstructing three-dimensional grids of digital virtual human.

Remote sensing can be defined as the collection of data about an object from a distance. Geographers use the technique of remote sensing to monitor or measure phenomena found in the Earth's lithosphere, biosphere, hydrosphere, and atmosphere. Remote sensing imagery has many applications in mapping land-use and cover, agriculture, soils mapping, forestry, city planning, archaeological investigations, military observation, and geomorphological surveying, among other uses.

Medical imaging processes are dedicated to the storage, retrieval, distribution and presentation of images, which are handled from various modalities, such as ultrasonography, radiography, magnetic resonance imaging, positron emission tomography, and computed tomography. It consists of a central server which stores a database containing the images. Doctor and his patients can get more reliable and precise medical images (such as X-ray slice, CT and MR) with more quick, exact and simple mode, so as to increase the rate of inchoate morbid detection and diagnoses and the living opportunity.

4.3 Computational Fluid Dynamics Grid

Computational Fluid Dynamics (CFD) grid provides the infrastructure to access different CFD applications across different physical domains and security firewalls. By defining a standard CFD workflow and general interfaces for exchanging mesh data, the platform facilitates interoperating between CFD applications. An application development packages (ADP) is developed and an application development specifications (ADS) is defined shipping with the platform to make migrating CFD applications feasible. The major function of ADP is to schedule jobs, recover from fault and discover service effectively.

The CFD platform includes two levels: high level for Service Oriented Application (SOA) and low level for parallel computing. The physical architecture of the CFD platform is shown in Fig.3.

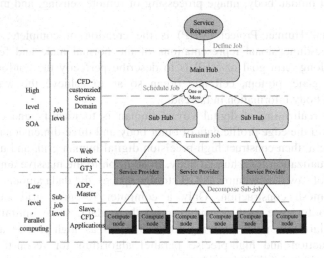

Fig. 3. Physical Architecture of CFD Grid Platform

In the high level, all services are registered in the Main hub or Sub hubs. The function of the Main hub is to provide job definition. Service requestor visits the Main hub for the service interface definition and finds the invocation entrance. Main hub is also responsible for the task scheduling and resources allocation. It collects all the service information from Sub hubs and then find the best resource solution for a given service requestor. The Sub hubs also have those functions which Main hub has, but within a smaller area. Sub hubs delivery the sub tasks (jobs) to the specific service provider, and then collect the results. All the services are provided as web service. By this way (hierarchy architecture and general service interface), the SOA has a good scalability.

In the low level for parallel computing layer, all kinds of parallel environments could be employed. In this system, MPICH2 is used as the low layer parallel environment. The service provider decomposes tasks that distributed by Sub hubs and sends them to computing nodes via MPI mechanism. This feature enable us utilize the distributed computing nodes as a whole to provide scalable and stable services.

4.4 Course Online Grid

Course Online Grid (*realcourse* in short) is a video stream service supported by a collection of physical servers distributed all over China [22]. Since its birth in April of 2003, *realcourse* has been in non-stop operation for more than one and half year, in spite of some of the servers up-and-down, in-and-out from time to time. As of this writing, *realcourse* is composed of 20 servers spanned over 10 major cities distributed on CERNET with 1500 hours quality course videos, which was grown up from initially 4 servers within Peking University campus. As a result we normally observe 20-100 on line users at any time. In turn, these user activities help us to bring the service to a level of robustness.

The 1500 hours of videos are from different universities within ChinaGrid. They are uploaded to different servers with a permanent backup copy created in a server other than original one, and flow from server to server on demand. If one server is down for some reason, its duty is automatically taken up by some other server(s). And once it is up again, a maintenance session will occur automatically to bring it up to a consistent state, in case some transactions occurred during its down time (for example, some more videos were uploaded to the system).

Realcourse is a successful application of distributed computing technologies in a geographically wide area. Different from some traditional distributed fault-tolerant services, *realcourse* emphasizes on giving clients access to the service - with reasonable response times - for as much of the time as possible, even if some results do not conform to sequential consistency. *Realcourse* owns some distinguished characters:

Realcourse aims at non-critical application of video on demand and file storage in which temporal inconsistency is acceptable only if consistency of whole system will finally reached. By eliminating the "update" operation, *realcourse* greatly reduce the consistency requirement. The length of exchanged message among servers is kept constantly small, no heavy communication traffic is observed with the growth of server numbers.

The servers in *realcourse* are not equal to each other. Only two servers are chosen to keep two permanent physical copies of files. No effort is made to keep track of those temporal copies of files but the existence of these copies greatly improve the performance of downloading operation in a way of wide area network cache. In the new version of consistency-check procedure a pervasive search is started to find those "lost" copies in case that both two permanent copies of file are corrupted.

The loop topology of all servers makes it possible for each server to run a consistency-check procedure independently without any overhead. Actually, a more sophisticated consistency-check procedure is in development at the time of this publish. Knowledge from area of "autonomous computing" does much help.

By exploiting the reliable communication provided by Asynchronous Messaging Middleware, *realcourse* hides the failures of network, which is not rare by our observation in a wide area network from servers. The consistency of servers is eventually kept in a "delayed" fashion.

4.5 Massive Data Processing (MDP) Grid

MDPGrid includes three data intensive grid applications: High energy Physics Computing, *Alpha Magnetic Spectrometer* (AMS) Experiment, and University Digital Museums.

High energy physics computing based on MDPGrid, is a solution for the processing and analyzing of the massive data, which are generated by CERN's ATLAS experiment, Sino-Italy cooperated cosmic rays experiment at YangBaJing, Tibet, and BEPC/BES project, at Shandong University.

AMS experiment project is the large-scale physics experiment on *International Space Station* (ISS), with the main purpose to look for the universe composed of antimatter, search for the source of darkmatter, and measure the source of cosmic ray. Space Detector Type Two (AMS-02) will send the space shuttle in 2005 onto ISS to carry on the experiment for three to five years. The data collected by AMS-02 will be finally stored, indexed and analyzed in *Science Operation Centers* (SOC). The Data Processing Center in Southeast University will be able to directly receive the data sent by NASA and carry on data analysis independently. Currently, SOC in SEU has put up a grid platform SEUGrid for the Monte-Carlo simulation computing of AMS-02 MC.

University Digital Museum Grid is to integrate the enormous dispersed resources of various digital museums, to share the resources effectively and eliminate the information island, to filter and classify the collection information, and to provide appropriate information service to users according to their knowledge levels and motivation through unified grid portal. For the time being, the university digital museums involved include the Digital Museum of Aeronautics and Astronautics (BUAA) [15], the Archaeological Digital Museum (SDU) [14], the Geoscience Digital Museum (NJU) [16], and the Mineralogical Digital Museum (KUST) [17]. The services and resources in each university digital museum compose one site. The collection provider service gives access to digital museum's collections as raw data.

5 Conclusion

Although ChinaGrid has just begun for two years, it has gained much attention from all aspects. Just within one year, the coverage of ChinaGrid project has already been to 20 universities in China. Besides, some provinces and cities are trying to deploy their regional grids. CGSP, which is the potential grid computing middleware candidate to use, makes these regional grids as the extension of ChinaGrid system. All these together with above grid computing application platforms and pilot applications make ChinaGrid very unique from other existing grid computing projects. We are very confident that ChinaGrid will be the largest, the most advanced, and the most practical grid in the near future.

Acknowledgement

Special thanks to following people providing materials for this paper of each ChinaGrid application platform: Professor Weiming Zheng from Tsinghua University, Professor Xiaoming Li from Beijing University, Dr. Xiaowu Chen from Beihang University, Professor Minglu Li from Shanghai Jiao Tong University, and Prof. Qin Zhang from Huazhong University of Science and Technology. I also would like to take this opportunity to thank all the experts in ChinaGrid project for their devoting time to this project, and making grid computing a reality in China.

References

1. China Education and Research Network, http://www.edu.cn/
2. ChinaGrid, http://www.chinagrid.edu.cn
3. ChinaGrid Bioinformatics Grid, http://166.111.68.168/bioinfo/tools/index.jsp
4. ChinaGrid Computational Fluid Dynamics (CFD) Grid, http://grid.sjtu.edu.cn:7080/grid/
5. ChinaGrid Course Online Grid, http://realcourse.grids.cn
6. ChinaGrid Image Processing Grid, http://grid.hust.edu.cn/ImageGrid/
7. ChinaGrid Mass Data Processing Grid, http://athena.vrlab.buaa.edu.cn/gcc/
8. China National Grid, http://www.863.org.cn/863_105/applygide/applygide2/information2_app/200206270024.html
9. Data Grid Project WP1, "Definition of Architecture, Technical Plan and Evaluation Criteria for Scheduling, Resource Management, Security and Job Description", *Datagrid document DataGrid-01-D1.2-0112-0-3*, 14/09/2001.
10. I. Foster and C. Kesselman, "Globus: A Metacomputing Infrastructure Toolkit", *International Journal of Supercomputer Applications*, Vol.11, No.2, pp.115-128, 1997.
11. I. Foster, C. Kesselman, and S. Tuecke, "The Anatomy of the Grid: Enabling Scalable Virtual Organizations", *International Journal of High Performance Computing Applications*, 15 (3), 200-222, 2001.
12. W. E. Johnston, D. Gannon, and B. Nitzberg, "Grids as Production Computing Environments: The Engineering Aspects of NASA's Information Power Grid", *Proceedings of 8th IEEE Symposium on High Performance Distributed Computing*, 1999.
13. Open Grid Services Architecture, http://www.ggf.org/Public_Comment_Docs/Documents/draft-ggf-ogsa-specv1.pdf.
14. The Archaeological Digital Museum, http://museum.sdu.edu.cn/index/index.asp
15. The Digital Museum of Aeronautics and Astronautics, http://digitalmuseum.buaa.edu.cn/
16. The Geoscience Digital Museum, http://202.119.49.29/museum/default.htm

17. The Mineralogical Digital Museum, http://www.kmust.edu.cn/dm/index.htm
18. The TeraGrid Project, http://www.teragrid.org/
19. The Web Services Resource Framework, http://www.globus.org/wsrf/.
20. UK e-Science Programme, http://www.rcuk.ac.uk/escience/
21. G. Yang, H. Jin, M. Li, N. Xiao, W. Li, Z. Wu, Y. Wu, and F. Tang, "Grid Computing in China", *Journal of Grid Computing*, accepted.
22. J. Zhang and X. Li, "The Model, Architecture and Mechanism Behind *Realcourse*", Technical Report, Beijing University, 2004.
23. R. Zheng, H. Jin, Q. Zhang, Y. Li, and J. Chen, "IPGE: Image Processing Grid Environment Using Components and Workflow Techniques", *Grid and Cooperative Computing – Lecture Notes in Computer Sciences*, Vol.3251, 2004.

Content Management and Resources Integration: A Practice in Shanghai Digital Library

Qiang Xu

Shanghai Library, No.1555, Huai Hai Zhong Lu, Shanghai 200031, China
qxu@libnet.sh.cn

Abstract. The purpose of this paper is to show the resources integration procedure of Shanghai Digital Library, which hope to manage the content of digital collections, electronic resources and free web-based resources. According to the goals of SHDL, it will integrate the resources to gives our end-users a single point of access to a wide variety of digital collections, indexing and abstracting databases, full-text databases, and other e-resources. At the same time it offers the librarians easy administration tools for managing the resources and collections to support the one-stop services. Therefore, this paper presents the framework and design concepts of the Shanghai Digital Library, focusing on resource navigation and cross-databases searching. SHDL will offer the practical model as soon as possible and support the further resources in the future.

1 Introduction

As a large, comprehensive research and public library, Shanghai Library has a collection of 48.5 million items; including 55826 current serials and newspapers, 1.7 million rare books, genealogies, manuscripts, and patent documents, technical standard documents, science & technology reports, maps, audio & video materials, over 150+ online databases and 11500 titles of electronic resources, etc. Shanghai Library is becoming an organizer in a consortium named as Shanghai Municipal Central Library (SMCL). It has 32 branches distribute in the whole Shanghai region composing of district/country libraries, academic libraries and special libraries.

2 Overview of the Shanghai Digital Library (SHDL)

The Shanghai Library is the first public library in China that began the construction of a digital library environment. When the new building of the library was opened to the public in December 1996, the library began to consider digitizing many items in its treasured collections and regularly acquiring electronic resources. The Shanghai Digital Library (SHDL) was launched in 1997 and by 1999, 7 digitization projects were completed, and began to provide services to the public in 2000.

Shanghai Digital Library already has 7 digital collections, the detail is as follow.

Z. Chen et al. (Eds.): ICADL 2004, LNCS 3334, pp. 25–34, 2004.

(1) Shanghai pictures—over 20000 old pictures and issued 9000 pictures to reappear one hundred years of Shanghai developing period.

(2) Shanghai Local Documents—has 114 titles and 227 volumes such as annuals and Shanghai local documents.

(3) Chinese opera collection—16 kinds of traditional operas, 90 actors and actresses, 311 arias and about 3,000 minutes, Many arias are over half a century old.

(4) Chinese Rare Books—about 1.3 million pages, 313 CD-ROMs, 3,223 titles, are available for the intranet of library and 19 titles for internet.

(5) Min Guo books (1911-1949)—about 18 titles, are a part of library special collections.

(6) Chinese Periodicals & Newspapers—support by the National Index to Chinese Periodicals & Newspapers that first published in the 1950s, it has 5 million titles as an index and abstract database.

(7) Popular Science Video Clips—142 episodes of popular science serials and 700 minutes of programs.

Shanghai Library also have many electronic resources currently available for the users to retrieve indexes, abstracts, full text articles and dissertations, but many electronic resources often access via different interface, usually Interfaces and functionalities differ considerably and they change without due notification to the library. Under these circumstances the training of end-users is almost an impossible task for the library staffs. Although SHDL integrated some digital collections and electronic resources, it's not enough. These digital collections and electronic resources are difficult to find for end-users. Therefore, this paper presents the framework and design concepts of the Shanghai Digital Library, focusing on extending and enhancing the functions of content management and resources integration so as to replace the existing SHDL service with an updated portal aimed at general users and needs.

3 Goals

Content is what we published. It can be text, graphics, audio and video. As the library, there are books, newspapers, serials, tapes, digital collections and electronic resources store on the different mediums. The library users want to retrieve information they need in any formats, anytime, anywhere. According to these certain resources, we should focus on the content management to make it easily reuse, search and share effectively. We should not only deal with the mediums but also manage the content.

SHDL is different from traditional library, it should cover all the numerous digital collections and electronic resources, and serve by uniform interface, uniform operating mode. A highly prioritized area for us was the development of a system that integrated all our digital services, transferring from the distributed application to the digital library aggregation service. We aimed to offer the library a complete system. SHDL integrate the resources to gives our end-users a single point of access to a wide variety of digital collections, indexing and abstracting databases, full-text databases, open archives, and other e-resources. At the same time it offers the library staff easy administration tools for managing the resources and collections to support the library one-stop services.

4 SHDL Application Requirements

In Shanghai Library, there are many digital collections, indexes, abstracts, e-journals and e-books. These resources can be divided into three types:

Catalogues and digital collections: we have bibliographic databases (public access catalogue) that currently contain over 1.9 million bib records and over 6.9 million holdings, indexing and abstracting databases over 7 million titles and digital collections that library can basically manipulate resources construction, data structure, storage mode (RDBMS or File System) and update period.

E-resources on the mirror site: these electronic resources are locally loaded on servers in our library such as TsingHua TongFang China Academic Journals Full Text Database, VIP Journals of Chinese Science & Technology, China Law Database, etc. For these licensed databases library only maintain the servers and update the data but don't know well the data structure and storage or retrieval method.

Remote access resources: including major foreign electronic resources, some native databases and free internet-based resources. Library can access these resources via internet or ISP, but mostly provide patrons to access them in the library's local network by IP filter or authorized users. The publishers and providers control the resources and retrieval method.

Shanghai Library has already provide users a variety of functions such as PAC, digital collections searching, document delivering, but each kind of resources are basically separate and did not get effective integration. Along with the resources gradually expanding, accessing to hundreds of research databases and other information resources, in fact, if our users make it to the library's web site at all, chances are they are confronted with library terminology they don't understand and a long list of databases they have to decipher and choose among. Libraries are losing potential users. Librarians license valuable and costly full-text databases that we know contain the information researchers are seeking, but the result is that it can be difficult to know where to start. So we urgently proceed to integrate related resources, and make it easier to discover useful information.

4.1 The Users

To better enable Shanghai Library to serve the information needs for their readers and users. SHDL will construct user-oriented system and face to the four types users: readers and users, librarians (acquisition and cataloguing librarians), general staffs, system administrators. SHDL will organize library resources so they can be used to meet the basic needs of the average users or the casual information users. For the librarians—the expert users, they will navigate and describe the resources to provide easy access for the users to complex resources, and the general staffs should get the access information and utilization rate of the resources so as to feed back to the librarians who make the decision to the resources construction.

4.2 The Function of SHDL

- Cross-databases searching and federated searching for the resources.
- Navigation for the various types of resources.
- User single-sign-on.
- Integration with linking services.

- Resources registration, Resources auditing, Resources registration and usage statistics, users' administration and keyword admin.
- System administration, uniform users management, uniform authority control.

4.3 The System Framework of SHDL

SHDL is to provide a digital service environment with application integration, uniform resources registration profile, similar as the "Infobus" concept from the Stanford Digital Library Project. We need put the resources or collections into the resources registration module and acquire the resource collections description metadata and make them available on resources level in one single user interface, with cross-searching, merged search results and also providing orderly access and guidance to the digital resources, and integrating them into library service programs.

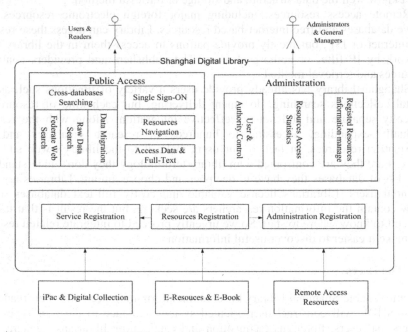

Fig. 1. The System Framework of SHDL

4.3.1 Resources Registration

If we will process resources registration, we should define how to describe these resources. Due to have been widely used for the resources composing of the heterogeneous collections, we refer to the Dublin Core Collection Description Application Profile (DC CD AP) to identify the location of the collections and the services that provide access. According to the DC CD AP, the term "collection" can be applied to any aggregation of physical or digital items. Those items may be of any type, so examples might include aggregations of natural objects, created objects, "born-digital" items, digital surrogates of physical items, and the catalogues of such collections (as aggregations of metadata records). We regard these digital and e-resources as the "collections" and define their elements so that the librarians can add and modify resources identifier, title, alternative title, description, physical characteristics, collector, language, type, rights, subject, and browse them based on resources registration module.

4.3.2 Resources Navigation

For the certain sources, the variety types of resources can display from classified tree that the librarians' team predefined. The classified navigation tree will be defined by different aspect such as different subject, language, resources types and browsing alphabetically. It can set up sub classification and each node of the tree can be repeatable. This navigation tree should give the novices or common users a clear interface to discover the resources independently and they can directly access the resources that they are interested in.

4.3.3 Cross-Databases Searching

The cross-databases searching has basic and advanced search. In the basic search users can do word and phrase searches combined with Boolean operators and truncation, and search electronic resources and digital collections available in full text. If the users need search the information in the specific field such as economy, law or health, Cross-databases searching merge the classified tree that make the users predefine the databases range or select the checkbox to designate group of databases and then search the information by appointment. The search fields contain the titles, creators, subject/keywords, abstracts, issue date, language, full text and sources. The search results are presented as a list with basic information that the records can serve as active links, allowing the users to navigate in the native system and to download records to view. One of the major advantages of cross-databases searching is that results can be obtained from multiple databases without having to repeat a search.

4.3.4 Single Sign-ON

Single sign-on (SSO) is mechanism whereby a single action of user authentication and authorization can permit a user to access all computers and systems where he has access permission, without the need to enter multiple passwords. An authentic "account" (username and password) provides access to the licensed resources (the majority of e-journals, databases or e-books that use identity authentication). Access may be available from any location in library, at home, or elsewhere. SSO provides users with a more efficient, effective and seamless approach to accessing online resources. This means that once the user has logged on an electronic resource using your Athens username and password, you should not have to login to any other Athens authenticated resources unless he logged off or closed down the browser.

4.3.5 Resources Administration

SHDL supply the resources administration consists of four parts: resource collections administration, resources registration statistics and usage statistics, users' admin and keyword admin. Collections administration will make the librarians of staffs create, modify, delete, copy, input and output the description of the resource collections according to the definition with a set of elements refers to the DC CD AP. Statistics report is essential for the general managers of the library, so they can be clearly understood various resources circumstance, resources total amount, resources gathering the quantity, take upping the space quantity, usage and access statistics etc. Users' and keyword admin allow the system administrator assign the users' authority in order to manage the resource collections and give the keyword to describe the resources so as to make the users easily find the resources.

5 SHDL Integration Procedure

The process of integrating resources was accomplished in four steps:

1. Resources analysis and definition.
2. Resources registration.
3. Resources integration for cross-databases searching.
4. Resources navigation and cross-searching integration.

These are further described as follows.

5.1 Resources Analysis and Definition

Resource Description concerns the definition of data elements describing a collection. For the purpose of Resource Discovery, we should analysis the resources components and describe a set of metadata elements and set boundaries for resource/collection types to be covered.

The Resource collections can be applied to any aggregation of physical or digital items. Collections are exemplified in the following list:

- Library catalogues.
- Digital collections such as Shanghai picture, Popular Science Video Clips and so on.
- Digital archives—Chinese Rare Books, Chinese opera.
- Electronic resources, e-journals, e-books, indexes and abstracts.
- Web-based resources and subject directories on the internet.

These collections will be defined resource description metadata elements and mechanism for collecting resource descriptions.

5.2 Resources Registration

If we want to integrate the resources for the one-stop access, we should clearly navigator the resources and supply the cross-searching or Meta searching, so we describe the resources or collections and define the navigator tree and classification of the collections. Our goal is to provide access to the collections through subject, title, language, resource type and other classification.

For the purpose of resources registration requirement, we define the resource description metadata elements refer to the DC CD AP in the following list:

Resource Description is a way of exposing the collection so users can find and use the contents. Librarians or staffs register the resources by the module of resources registration in order to make the users find the resources and collections.

Element	Definition	Defined by
Identifier	A globally unique formal identifier for the collection	dc:identifier
Title	The name of the collection	dc:title
Alternative Title	Any form of the name used as a substitute or alternative to the formal name of the collection	dcterms:alternative
Description	A summary of the content of the collection	dcterms:abstract
Format	The physical or digital characteristics of the collection	dc:format
Size	The size of the collection	dcterms:extent
Language	A language of the content of the items in the collection	dc: Language
Type	The type of the collection	dc:type
Rights	A statement of any rights held in/over the collection	dc:rights
Access Rights	A statement of any access restrictions placed on the collection, including allowed users, charges, etc	dcterms:accessRights
Accrual Periodicity	The frequency with which items are added to a collection	cld:accrualPeriodicity
Audience	A class of entity for whom the collection is intended or useful	dcterms:audience
Subject	A subject or topic associated with the items in the collection	dc:subject
Spatial Coverage	The spatial coverage of the content of the items in the collection	dcterms:spatial
Accumulation Date Range	The range of dates over which the collection was accumulated	dcterms:created
Collector	An entity who gathers (or gathered) the items in a collection together	dc:creator
Owner	An entity who has legal possession of the collection	marcrel:own
Is Available Via	A service that provides access to the collection	gen:isAvailableVia
Sub-collection	A second collection contained within the current collection	dcterms:hasPart
Super-collection	A second collection that contains the current collection	dcterms:isPartOf
Associated collection	A second collection that is associated with the current collection	dc:relation

5.3 Resources Integration for Cross-Databases Searching

Cross searching or metasearch engines utilize a variety of methods to search and retrieve records from the resources and databases. The protocols include Z39.50,

APIs, HTTP, XML gateways, SQL and other adapters. Most of these protocols have no provision for providing information, either the set of records returned of the individual records returned. Through the Cross-databases searching, users can search the resources name, type, description and select one of subjects or topics by which to limit a search or link directly to that collection. The Cross searching also identifies collections by format (e.g. indexes, abstracts, full text, images or audio) and collections themselves have a mouse followed point view design that represents the description information beside them. With the various collections, one-stop searching will be integrated by three ways:

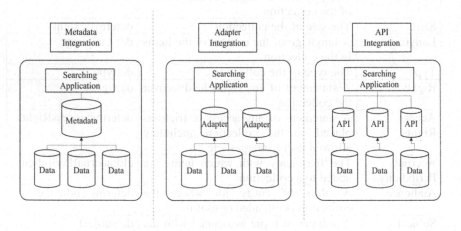

Fig. 2. Resource Integration Framework

(1) Metadata Integration: We extract the metadata from digital collections or databases and concentrate to a new index databases for the searching. It can be available for active-indexes, Open-URL or content-sensitive reference linking to the full-text or content.

(2) Adapter Integration: If the database targets will be established by RDBMS, we could construct adapters to access them, which supporting SQL and search deep to the databases.

(3) Several content vendors have created proprietary APIs that allow a search to be submitted as a URL via HTTP and the response returned in HTML format or XML format.

Cross-databases searching provide search services by forwarding users' queries to separate database search engines and combining the results of all searches and displaying the merged set in the search summary database list with the number of relevant results found in each database and each search status. If users will refine the search, they could click the checkbox before the database name. When they finish the search, clicking the databases summary result list, selected records list will appear. Cross searching also provide the "my favorite resource list", "single sign-on" and "my account" information, which users could change the session preferences and view the personalized lists.

5.4 Resources Navigation and Cross-Searching Integration

For the benefits for our patrons, cross-searching is not enough. With the increasing of the resources and collections, we should supply the navigation tools to manage the confusing list of resources, locate appropriate resources and enable cross-searching of a focused set of databases. We create the navigation tree to refine the resources type, language, format or the other attributes, provide the discovery tool to find the appropriate databases, and make it easier to change databases attributes and classification, so then merging the resources navigation and cross-searching together.

Fig. 3. Resource Navigation and Cross-Searching Integration

5 Future

SHDL has developed a useful framework for challenges of various types of resources and providing guidance and tools for the patrons' service. While the architecture of SHDL has been completed, it will continue to expand the response to an ever-changing information need. Depending on the framework of SHDL, we intend to enhance the resources navigation more features such as "my search history", "my alert" for "my library" personality service and combine with the virtual reference desk and document supply system to provide the high quality service for the patrons. Digital collections can be more created and organized through some topics, which are successfully integrated into library collections, relying on the SHDL architecture and performance. Although cross-searching has some problems, which been mentioned, speed and performance, results repeatable, different ranking algorithms, maintenance of databases, little standard of metadata and application profile, libraries are the important role to find the solution with their knowledge and skills. SHDL will offer the practical model as soon as possible and support the further protocol and resources in the future.

References

1. Coleman, A., Brackc, P., Karthik, S.: Integration of Non-OAI Resources for Federated Searching in DLIST, an Eprints Repository. D-Lib Magazine. Jul/Aug 2004. http://www.dlib.org/dlib/july04/coleman/07coleman.html
2. Ma, Yuanliang., Liu, Wei.: Digital Resources and Metadata Application in the Shanghai Library. http://www.libnet.sh.cn/sztsg/fulltext/reports/2001/DigitalResources.htm
3. Luther, J.: Trumping Google? Metasearching's Promise. Library Journal Magazine. Oct 2003. http://www.libraryjournal.com/article/CA322627?display=searchResults&stt=001 &text=trumping
4. Susan, S.S.: Building the Collections of the California Digital Library. http://www.library.ucsb.edu/istl/98-winter/article2.html
5. Paepcke, A., Baldonado, M., Chang, C.-C.K., Cousins, S., Garcia-Molina, H.: Building the InfoBus:A Review of Technical Choices in the Stanford Digital Library Project. http://www-diglib.stanford.edu/
6. Brogan, M.L.: A Survey of Digital Library Aggregation Services. http://www.diglib.org/pubs/brogan/
7. Dublin Core Collection Description Working Group.: Dublin Core Collection Description Application Profile. http://www.ukoln.ac.uk/metadata/dcmi/collection-application-profile/2004-08-20/
8. The Open Group.: Introduction to Single Sign-On. http://www.opengroup.org/security/sso_intro.htm
9. NISO.: Resource Description. http://www.niso.org/committees/MSpapers/Resource_Description.pdf
10. Getting Around Metasearch: A Guide to New Terms, Features, and Searching Options. http://www.lib.duke.edu/fsb/MetaSearch%20Guide.doc
11. Randall, S., Goldner, M.: Resource Set and Single Record Metadata. http://www.niso.org/committees/MSpapers/MSResultSet.pdf
12. Jordan, M.: Metadata and Interoperability for Digital Collections. http://www.slais.ubc.ca/jdavis/559g/lecture_notes_july07.htm

Digital Libraries: Developing Countries, Universal Access, and Information for All

Ian H. Witten

Department of Computer Science,
University of Waikato, New Zealand
ihw@cs.waikato.ac.nz

Abstract. Digital libraries are large, organized collections of information objects. Well-designed digital library software has the potential to enable non-specialist people to conceive, assemble, build, and disseminate new information collections. This has great social import because, by democratizing information dissemination, it provides a counterbalance to disturbing commercialization initiatives in the information and entertainment industries. This talk reviews trends in today's information environment, introduces digital library technology, and explores applications of digital libraries—including their use for disseminating humanitarian information in developing countries. We illustrate how currently available technology empowers users to build and publish information collections. Making digital libraries open to all, as conventional public libraries are, presents interesting challenges of universal access.

1 Introduction

Digital libraries are large, organized collections of information objects. Whereas standard library automation systems provide a computerized version of the catalog—a gateway into the treasure-house of information stored in the library—digital libraries incorporate the treasure itself, namely the information objects that constitute the library's collection. Whereas standard libraries are, of necessity, ponderous and substantial institutions, with large buildings and significant funding requirements, even large digital libraries can be lightweight. Whereas standard libraries, whose mandate includes preservation as well as access, are "conservative" by definition, with institutional infrastructure to match, digital libraries are nimble: they emphasize access and evolve rapidly.

What will the future hold for digital libraries? The dizzying rate of change in the core technologies clouds even the brightest crystal ball. Perhaps the most striking feature of the digital library field, at least from an academic point of view, is the inherent tension between two extremes: the very fast pace of technological change and the very long-term view that libraries must take. We must reconcile our aspiration to surf the leading edge of technology with the literally static ideal of archiving material "for ever and a day." Any future we create must run on everyone's computer today—for libraries are universally accessible, and should remain so—and it must also preserve the treasures of the past, including past digital libraries.

Z. Chen et al. (Eds.): ICADL 2004, LNCS 3334, pp. 35–44, 2004.

This paper is particularly concerned with the future for developing countries. It sometimes happens that technological advances in developing countries leapfrog those in developed ones. This occurs because established infrastructure, a strong and necessarily conservative force, is absent. Alternative sources such as solar energy are widely used in place of traditional power generation and distribution, while many developing countries have experienced far higher levels of mobile phone growth than developed ones. Digital libraries provide another example, compensating for the failure of traditional distribution mechanisms to address local requirements and deliver information where it is needed. Indeed, developing countries already have a competitive edge, for the labor-intensive process of optical character recognition (OCR) is often outsourced from the Western world to countries such as India, the Philippines, and Romania. More intellectually demanding tasks such as metadata assignment and collection building will not be far behind.

In the next section we examine the social need for digital libraries by briefly sketching some trends in commercial publishing and contrasting them with a growing international perspective of information as a public good. Then we review a project that is applying digital library technology to the distribution of humanitarian information in the developing world, a context that is both innovative and socially motivated. Next we discuss issues of universal access and illustrate them with reference to the Greenstone digital library software [9]. We include a brief demonstration of a system that is intended to allow anyone to build and disseminate information collections, and illustrates some human interface challenges that arise when providing necessarily complex functionality to a non-computer-oriented user base. We close with the hope that future digital libraries will find a new role to play in helping to reduce the social inequity that haunts today's world, both within our own countries and between nations.

2   Books, Libraries, and the Socially Disadvantaged

Today, the long-standing three-way tension between the commercial interests of publishers, the needs of society and information users, and the social mandate of public libraries, is being pulled and stretched as never before.

2.1   Books

What future has the book in the digital world? The question is a complex one that is being widely aired (see [3] for a particularly thoughtful and comprehensive discussion). Authors and publishers ask how many copies of a work will be sold if networked digital libraries enable worldwide access to an electronic copy of it. To counter the perceived threat, the entertainment industry is promoting "digital rights management" (DRM) schemes that permit a degree of control over what users can do that goes far beyond the traditional legal bounds of copyright. Indeed, they seem to be concerned solely with content owners rights and not at all with user's rights. Anti-circumvention rules are sanctioned by the Digital Millennium Copyright Act (DMCA) in the US (similar legislation is being enacted elsewhere).

Can DRM be applied to books? The motion picture industry can compel manufacturers to incorporate encryption into their products because it holds key patents on DVD players. Commercial book publishers are promoting e-book readers that, if widely adopted, would allow the same kind of control to be exerted over reading material. Basic rights that we take for granted (and are legally enshrined in the concept of copyright) are in jeopardy. DRM allows them to be controlled, monitored, and withdrawn instantly, and DMCA legislation makes it illegal for users to seek redress by taking matters into their own hands. Fortunately, perhaps, standardization and compatibility issues are delaying consumer adoption of e-books.

In scholarly publishing, digital rights management is more advanced. Academic libraries license access to content in electronic form, often in tandem with purchase of print versions too. They have been able to negotiate reasonable conditions with publishers. However, the extent of libraries' power in the consumer book market is moot. One can envisage a scenario where publishers establish a system of commercial, pay-per-view, libraries for e-books and refuse public libraries access to books in a form that can be circulated.

These new directions present our society with puzzling challenges, and it would be rash to predict what society's response will be. But one thing is certain: they will surely increase the degree of disenfranchisement of those who do not have access to the technology.

2.2 Public Information

In parallel with publishers' moves to reposition books as technological artifacts with refined and flexible control over how they can be used, an opposing trend has emerged: the ready availability of free information on the Internet. Of course, the world-wide web is an unreliable source of enlightenment, and undiscriminating use is dangerous—and widespread. But search engines and other portals have enormously increased our ability to locate information that is at least ostensibly relevant to any given question.

Teachers complain bitterly that students view the Web as a replacement for the library, harvesting information indiscriminately to provide answers to assignments that are at best shallow and at worst incoherent and incorrect. Nevertheless, the Web abounds with accessible, high-quality information. Many social groups, non-profit societies and charities make it their business to create sites and collect and organize information there. Widespread use is strongly encouraged, and arrangements could surely be made for re-distribution of the material, particularly as a not-for-profit service, with appropriate acknowledgement.

A key problem with information distribution via the Web is that it disenfranchises developing countries. Although the Web does not extend into the homes of the socially disadvantaged in developed countries either, programs are working to provide access. But network access varies enormously across the world, and it is still true that, as Arunachalam wrote in 1998, the Internet "is failing the developing world" [2]. Prompted by this inequity, the importance of public information is today being highlighted by prominent international bodies. For example, UNESCO's "Information for all" programme was established in 2001 to foster debate on the political, ethical and societal challenges of the emerging global knowledge society and to carry out projects promoting equitable access to information. Information literacy is described as "a new frontier" by the Director of UNESCO's Information Society Division [6].

The International Telecommunications Union's World Summit on the Information Society (Geneva in 2003 and Tunis in 2005) is promoting a global discussion of the fundamental changes that are being brought about by the transformation from an industrial to an information society, and confront the disparities of access to information between the industrialized countries and the developing world.

2.3 Libraries and Their Role

What is the librarian to make of all this? The mandate of public libraries is to facilitate the open distribution of knowledge. Librarians strive to enable the free flow of information. Their traditions are liberal, founded on the belief that libraries should serve democracy. A recent promotional video from the American Librarian's Association exults that "the library is democracy's place of worship" [1].

Clearly, the impending redefinition of the book as a digital artifact that is licensed rather than sold, tied to a particular replay device, with restrictions that are mechanically enforced, goes right to the heart of libraries. The changing nature of the book may make it hard, or even impossible, for libraries to fulfill their mandate by providing quality information to readers. And the emergence of a vast storehouse of information on the Internet poses a different kind of conundrum. Librarians, the traditional gatekeepers of knowledge, are in danger of being bypassed, their skills ignored, their advice unsought. Search engines send users straight to the information they require—or so users may think—without any need for an intermediary to classify, catalogue, cross-reference, advise on sources.

The ready availability of information on the Internet, and its widespread use, really presents librarians with an opportunity, not a threat. Savvy users realize they need help, which librarians can provide. A good example is Infomine, a cooperative project of the University of California and California State University [4]. Infomine contains descriptions and links to a wealth of scholarly and educational Internet resources, each of which has been selected and described by a professional academic librarian who is a specialist in the subject and in resource description generally. Participating librarians see this as an important expenditure of effort for their users, a natural evolution of their traditional task of collecting and organizing information in print.

New trends in information access present librarians in developed countries with difficult and conflicting challenges. Meanwhile, however, the situation in the developing world is dire. Here, traditional publishing and distribution mechanisms have failed tragically. For example, according to the 1999 UN Human Development Report [7], whereas a US medical library subscribes to about 5,000 journals, the Nairobi University Medical School Library, long regarded as a flagship center in East Africa, last year received just 20 journals (compared with 300 a decade before). In Brazzaville, Congo, the university has only 40 medical books and a dozen journals, all from before 1993, and the library in a large district hospital consisted of a single bookshelf filled mostly with novels.

2.4 Open-Source Software

Open source software is a powerful ally for librarians who wish to extend liberal traditions of information access. Open source projects make source code freely available for others to view, modify, and adapt; and the very nature of the licensing

Fig. 1. A selection of recent humanitarian digital library collections on CD-ROM

agreement prevents the software from being appropriated by proprietary vendors. But the open-source movement is more than just a vehicle for librarians to use: its link with library traditions goes much deeper. Public libraries and open source software both enshrine the same philosophy: to promote learning and understanding through the dissemination of knowledge. Both enjoy a sense of community, on the one hand the kind of inter-institutional cooperation exemplified by inter-library loan and on the other teams of designers and programmers that frequently cross national boundaries.

3 Disseminating Humanitarian Information with DLs

Digital libraries provide perhaps the first really compelling *raison d'être* for computing technology in the developing world. Priorities in these countries include health, agriculture, nutrition, hygiene, sanitation, and safe drinking water. Computers *per se* are not a priority, but simple, reliable access to practical information relevant to these basic needs certainly is. Witten *et al.* [8] mention ten information collections in which Greenstone is being used to deliver humanitarian and related information in developing countries. For example, the *Humanity Development Library* is a compendium of practical information aimed at helping reduce poverty, increasing human potential, and giving a useful education. Rather than recapitulating parts of the above-cited paper, we describe four new ones (Fig. 1).

The *Researching Education Development* library is a project of the Department for International Development (DFID), a British government department whose central focus is a commitment to a target of halving the proportion of people living in extreme poverty by 2015. Associated targets include ensuring universal primary education, gender equality in schooling, and skills development. It has created a CD-ROM library containing many education research papers and other documents. Each one represents a study or piece of commissioned research on some aspect of education and training in developing countries.

The *Energy for Sustainable Development* library, initiated jointly by the United Nations Development Programme (UNDP), the United Nations Department of Economic and Social Affairs (UNDESA), and the World Energy Council (WEC), contains a collection of 350 documents (26,000 pages). It includes titles that all these organizations have published on the subjects of energy for sustainable development—technical guidelines, journals and newsletters, case studies, manuals, reports, and other training material. The documents are in English, Spanish and French, and one document has Arabic, Russian and Chinese translations as well.

The *UNAIDS Library* contains publications that form a unique resource for those working in planning and practice. It is produced by the Joint United Nations Programme on HIV/ AIDS, whose mission is to lead, strengthen and support a response to the AIDS epidemic that will prevent the spread of HIV, provide care and support for those infected by the disease, reduce the vulnerability of individuals and communities to HIV/AIDS, and alleviate the socioeconomic and human impact of the epidemic.

The *Health Library for Disasters*, a collaboration between the emergency and disaster programs of the World Health Organization (WHO) and the Pan American Health Organization (PAHO), with the participation of many other organizations, contains over 300 technical and scientific documents on disaster reduction and public health issues related to emergencies and humanitarian assistance. A follow-up to the Spanish-language *Biblioteca Virtual de Desastres* discussed in [8], it includes technical guidelines, field guidelines, case studies, emergency kits, manuals, disaster reports, and training materials.

4 Universal Access

Universal access to digital libraries presents huge challenges to software engineers. The Greenstone digital library software [9] allows us to glimpse some of the issues. We summarize some technical details in the next subsection, before turning to more interesting questions of access for readers, collection builders, and international users.

4.1 Platforms and Distribution

Most digital libraries are accessed over the web. However, in many environments in developing countries, web access is insufficient and the system must run locally. And if people are to build and control their own libraries, a centralized solution is inadequate: the software must run on their own computers. Thus digital library systems intended for broad access should run on a wide variety of computer systems, particularly low-end ones.

The Greenstone server runs on any Windows, Unix, or MacOS/X system. All versions of Windows are supported, from 3.1 up. Supporting primitive platforms poses substantial challenges of a rather mundane nature: for example, Microsoft compilers no longer support Windows 3.1 and it is necessary to acquire obsolete versions (e.g. at software auctions).

In an international cooperative effort established in August 2000 with UNESCO and the Belgium-based Human Info NGO, Greenstone is being distributed widely in developing countries with the aim of empowering users, particularly in universities, libraries, and other public service institutions, to build their own digital libraries. UNESCO recognizes that digital libraries are radically reforming how information is acquired and disseminated in its partner communities and institutions in the fields of education, science and culture around the world, particularly in developing countries, and hopes that this software will encourage the effective deployment of digital libraries to share information and place it in the public domain.

4.2   Access for Readers

Greenstone collections can be published as standalone libraries on removable media such as CD-ROM, or presented on the Web. Any Greenstone collection can be converted into a self-contained Windows CD-ROM that includes the Greenstone server software itself (in a version that runs right down to Windows 3.1) and an integrated installation package. The installation procedure has been thoroughly honed to ensure that only the most basic of computer skills are needed to install and run a collection under Windows.

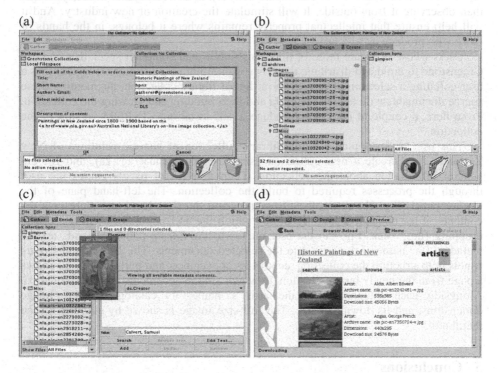

Fig. 2. Building a collection with the Greenstone Librarian Interface

The Unicode character set is used throughout Greenstone, and documents in any language and character encoding can be imported. Collections in Arabic, Chinese, Cyrillic, English, French, Spanish, German, Hindi, and Maori are publicly available (see nzdl.org). The Greenstone web site (greenstone.org) links to sites that contain further examples.

It makes little sense to have a collection whose content is in Chinese or Hindi, but whose supporting text—instructions, navigation buttons, labels, images, help text, and so on—are in English. Consequently, the entire Greenstone interface has been translated into a range of languages, and the interface language can be changed by the user as they browse from the *Preferences* page. Currently, interfaces are available in over 30 languages.

4.3 Access for Librarians: Building New Collections

Effective human development blossoms from empowerment rather than gifting. As the Chinese proverb says, "Give a man a fish and he will eat for a day; teach him to fish and he will eat for the rest of his days." Disseminating information originating in the developed world is no doubt useful for developing countries. But a more effective strategy for sustained long-term human development is to disseminate the capability of creating information collections, rather than the collections themselves. This will allow developing countries to participate actively in our information society, rather than observing it from outside. It will stimulate the creation of new industry. And it will help ensure that intellectual property remains where it belongs, in the hands of those who produce it.

Users whose skills are those of librarians rather than computer specialists can use Greenstone to build and distribute their own digital library collections. Fig. 2 shows a user collating a selection of images for a digital library collection, augmenting these source documents with textual metadata and then building and viewing the collection. From here, a couple of clicks can produce a self-installing CD-ROM version of the collection.

This user is developing a digital library collection of historic paintings of New Zealand. They create a new collection using the file menu (Fig. 2a), and fill out general information about the collection. Then a series of panels guides the user through the processes required to build the collection. The left-hand pane of the *Gather* panel (Fig. 2b) shows the file system and the right-hand one represents the contents of the collection, initially empty, which the user populates by dragging and dropping files. Then (Fig. 2c) the user moves to the *Enrich* panel and adds textual metadata (the name of the artists) to the selected documents. The *Design* and *Create* panels help structure the collection, control its appearance, and build it. Fig. 2d shows a page from the newly built collection, in which source documents are listed by artist. Alongside each thumbnail are the artist's name, its catalog number, image dimensions, and its download size. The full-size image is shown by clicking on the thumbnail.

5 Conclusions

By allowing people to easily create and disseminate large information collections, digital libraries extend the applications of modern technology in socially responsible directions, and counter a possible threat towards the commercialization of information in line with practices developed by the entertainment industry. As far as the developing world is concerned, digital libraries may prove to be a "killer app" for computer technology—that is, an application that makes a sustained market for a promising but under-utilized technology. The World-Wide Web is often described as the Internet's killer app. But the Internet does not really extend to developing countries, and the developing world is missing out on the prodigious amount of basic, everyday human information that the Web provides, and its enormous influence on promoting and internationalizing business opportunities. There is little incentive to make copies of the entire Web available locally because of its vast size, rapid change, and questionable information value per gigabyte. However, it is easy to provide focused information collections on both the Web and, in exactly the same form, on removable media such as CD-ROM, DVD, or bulk disk storage devices—indeed, the Greenstone software described above allows one to create a complete, runnable, self-installing CD-ROM image from a Web collection in just a few mouse clicks.

Public libraries are founded on the principle of universal access, and digital libraries should be too. Universal access means running on low-end devices, but one does not want to provide a lowest-common-denominator solution that sacrifices high-end capability where it is available. Universal access means that interfaces should be available in the world's languages, but one does not want the burden of translation to stifle the development of new functionality and features. Universal access means educating users: UNESCO is mounting training courses on building collections with Greenstone in Almaty, Bangalore, Senegal, and Suva, and discussions are underway for Latin America; the Tulane Institute has run courses that use Greenstone collections as a resource in many locations in Africa (e.g. Burkina Faso, Cameroon, Cote d'Ivoire, Democratic Republic of Congo, Ghana, Rwanda, Senegal, Sierra Leone, Togo) and Latin America (e.g. Argentina, Bolivia, Colombia, Ecuador, Guatemala).

Universal access also means that non-textual material should enjoy first-class status in a digital library—perhaps first-class status in "the literature." This has important cultural ramifications. It should be possible to create digital library collections intended for people in oral cultures, who may be illiterate or semi-literate. Or people who, though literate in their own language, cannot speak or read the language of the documents. Opening digital libraries to the illiterate is a radical and potentially revolutionary benefit of new interface technology.

Digital libraries give software engineers a golden opportunity to help reverse the negative impact of information technology on developing countries and reduce the various "digital divides" that cleave our world [5]—the "social divide" between the information rich and the information poor in our own nations, the "democratic divide" between those who do and do not use the panoply of digital resources to engage, mobilize and participate in public life, as well as the "global divide" that reflects the huge disparity in access to information between people in industrialized and developing societies.

Acknowledgements

I gratefully acknowledge all members of the New Zealand Digital Library project for their enthusiasm, ideas and commitment, particularly David Bainbridge and John Thompson who worked on the Greenstone Librarian interface. I have benefited enormously from cooperation with John Rose of UNESCO, and Michel Loots of Human Info NGO.

References

1. ALA (2002) "Rediscover America @ your library." Video produced by the American Library Association, Chicago, IL. www.ala.org/@yourlibrary/rediscoveramerica.
2. Arunachalam, S. (1998) "How the Internet is failing the developing world." Presented at *Science Communication in the Next Millennium*, Egypt; June.

3. Lynch, C. (2001) "The battle to define the future of the book in the digital world." *First Monday* 6(5)..
4. Mason, J., Mitchell, S., Mooney, M., Reasoner, L. and Rodriguez, C. (2000) "INFOMINE: Promising directions in virtual library development." *First Monday* 5(6).
5. Norris, P. (2001) *Digital divide? Civic engagement, information poverty and the Internet worldwide*. Cambridge University Press, New York
6. Quéau, P. (2001) "Information literacy: a new frontier." *UNISIST Newsletter* 29(2): 3-4.
7. UNDP (1999) *Human development report 1999*. UNDP/Oxford University Press.
8. Witten, I.H., Loots, M., Trujillo, M.F. and Bainbridge, D. (2002) "The promise of digital libraries in developing countries." *The Electronic Library*, Vol. 20, No. 1, pp. 7–13.
9. Witten, I.H. & Bainbridge, D. (2003) *How to build a digital library*. Morgan Kaufmann.

Digital Libraries for Education: A Progress Report on the National Science Foundation's (NSF) National Science, Technology, Engineering, and Mathematics Education Digital Library (NSDL) Program

Lee L. Zia*

Lead Program Director, NSDL Program, Division of Undergraduate Education,
National Science Foundation, Arlington, VA 22203

Background

The decade since the introduction of the World Wide Web has witnessed dramatic advances in the underlying communication capabilities of the Internet. These include greater numbers of access points; increased bandwidth of existing and new networks; growth in the deployment of new transmission technologies (e.g. various versions of DSL, cable modems, and in remote areas, satellite providers); and the emergence of wireless technologies, from Wi-Fi to WiMax (see www.wimaxforum.org). Indeed, the ability for the latter technologies to "untether" the user from the Internet is quickly permitting new and in some cases unforeseen uses of the Internet, posing interesting questions and challenges to our assumptions about user behavior and information needs.

Simultaneously, advances in computational power have lowered the financial barriers to entry for individuals using the Internet (e.g. fixed and mobile computers, and a variety of low-cost devices that are blurring the lines between cell phones and personal digital assistants). Increases in computational power have also led to increases in multimedia capabilities that offer greater levels of interactivity for the user's experience via modeling, animations, simulations, and voice and other audio applications.

Finally, if only measured by the sheer number of Web sites added daily and the increasingly international dimensions of that growth, the Web itself continues to evolve. New Web-based technologies are also changing the nature of the Web and the way in which users and, more specifically, learners can interact. One particular capability that has emerged is for individuals to express themselves, contribute their commentary, provide expertise, and otherwise participate in potentially wide and wide-ranging conversations. Through instant messaging and other variants of peer-to-peer communication, and blogging and other self-publishing models, content, commentary, and community are commingling at an unprecedented scale.

---

* All views expressed in this article are solely those of the author and do not represent an official NSF policy statement.

Z. Chen et al. (Eds.): ICADL 2004, LNCS 3334, pp. 45–50, 2004.
© Springer-Verlag Berlin Heidelberg 2004

Taken together these various communication and computational developments continue to strengthen the potential that information technology has to transform education by enlarging the concept of access – both spatially ("anyplace") and temporally ("anytime") – to this fundamental societal good. And, at a deeper level, the "why, where, and when" of the classroom and learning is changing, as well as the associated underlying cost structures.

A Role for Digital Libraries

Although the advances described above have resulted in a so-called "democratization of access" to Internet and Web resources, proponents also recognize the enormous challenges brought on by this state of affairs. For example, individuals clamor for help in the process of "sense-making" in the face of the voluminous data that is available. This is particularly important in educational settings. In the same vein, there is an opportunity to better connect learners with resources that are appropriate to their educational needs, but this relies on the willingness of the end user to reveal enough personal information so that a reasonable profile may be passed to a discovery system. This issue poses new challenges in the area of user identification, authentication, and maintenance of privacy. However, one need only look at the degree of technical development shown in this area by commercial and other retail businesses to appreciate how much personalization and/or customization of Web interfaces and experiences remain a prime interest of the industry.

Against this background research and development (R&D) agendas in digital libraries have been implemented throughout the world primarily through the funding initiatives of various governments. Indeed it has long been seen that digital libraries offer opportunities to provide critical infrastructure in the form of content and services that can enable transformations in learning. In some cases the motivations for these R&D agendas has emphasized cultural heritage and preservation needs, and in other cases they have focused more on basic digital library research questions, and in still others they have focused specifically on applications to education.

To investigate the basic research and development challenges associated with digital libraries, the National Science Foundation (NSF) – along with the National Aeronautics and Space Administration (NASA) and the Department of Defense Advanced Research Projects Agency (ARPA) – initiated the Digital Libraries Initiative (DLI) in 1994. Subsequently, the Digital Libraries Initiative – Phase 2 (DLI-2) began in 1998 with several additional federal agency partners supporting digital library research (see http://www.dli2.nsf.gov). This included a pilot program *Special Emphasis: Planning Testbeds and Applications for Undergraduate Education* program. After two years of pilot projects, NSF formally launched the National Science, Technology, Engineering, and Mathematics Education Digital Library (NSDL) program in fiscal year (FY) 2000. The program structure was based on ideas explored and developed through a series of workshops and planning meetings [1-6]. Subsequent papers considered evaluation and dissemination issues [7] and the organization and architecture of a digital library [8].

NSDL Vision and Current State of Development

The NSDL program (http://www.ehr.nsf.gov/ehr/due/programs/nsdl/) resides formally in the NSF Division of Undergraduate Education, however its ultimate user base is comprehensive. Indeed, through this program NSF seeks to stimulate and sustain continual improvements in the quality of science, technology, engineering, and mathematics (STEM) education at all levels. The resulting digital library targets a broad audience – pre-K to 12, undergraduate, graduate, and life-long learners – in formal and informal settings, and individual and collaborative modes. NSDL will be a virtual facility, and as a "national treasure" (and hopefully part of an "international treasure") it will enable seamless access to a rich array of interactive learning resources and learning environments, and services not bound by place or time (see [9]).

December 2002 saw the initial release of an "operational" NSDL at http://www.nsdl.org/. In that initial release the library featured a small set of collections addressing a variety of STEM content. Since then NSDL has continued to grow through the efforts of the many NSDL supported projects in Collections, Services, and Targeted Research, and a core integration project that provides the technical and organizational "glue" to bind distributed users with distributed collections and services. To visualize current collections within NSDL, (see http://nsdl.org/collections/ataglance/browseBySubject.html).

Since that time the program has also seen the emergence of an information architecture framework for the library resulting from the joint efforts of many principal investigators of the NSDL supported projects. Complete information on technical and organizational progress including links to the community workspaces may be found at the NSDL Communications Portal, see http://comm.nsdl.org. All workspaces are open to the public and interested organizations and individuals are encouraged to learn more about NSDL and join in its development.

Recent Grant Cycle

The NSDL program held its fifth formal funding cycle during fiscal year 2004 with a proposal deadline in mid-April 2004. In FY 2004 the NSDL program supported projects in the Services and Targeted Research tracks, but replaced the Collections track with a Pathways track. Within the Services track, two particular types of projects were strongly encouraged: (1) selection services and (2) usage development workshops.

- Pathways projects assume a stewardship role for the educational content and/or the services needed by a broad community of learners.
- Selection services projects focus on increasing the amount of high-quality STEM educational content known to NSDL.
- Usage development workshops promote the use of NSDL and its resources by various communities of learners.

These three elements reflect an appropriate expansion in emphasis for NSDL from its initial (and necessary) collecting of educational resources, materials, and other digital learning objects, towards enabling learners to "connect" or otherwise find pathways to resources that are appropriate to their needs. Simultaneously, these projects develop both the capacities of individual users and the capacity of the larger community of learners. In addition, the workshops are expected to enable the study of user information-seeking behavior and user interaction with specific NSDL content.

As of this writing, not all new grants for FY 2004 projects have been officially awarded. The Appendix lists the anticipated new projects displaying the title, the grantee institution, the name of the Principal Investigator (PI), and the official NSF award number. Full abstracts are anticipated to be available from the Awards Section at the NSDL Program site http://www.ehr.nsf.gov/ehr/due/programs/nsdl/ by mid-October. Projects with shared titles are formal collaborations and are grouped together. Several NSF sister directorates to EHR, the Directorate for Biological Sciences (BIO), the Directorate for Geosciences (GEO), the Directorate for Mathematical and Physical Sciences (MPS), and the Directorate for Social, Behavioral, and Economic Sciences (SBE) are providing significant co-funding on approximately 15 projects in the combined multi-year NSDL portfolio of awards. These jointly funded projects illustrate the NSDL program's facilitation of the integration of research and education that is an important strategic objective of NSF. For information about projects from the previous funding cycles, see [10-13].

Future Directions

The NSDL program expects to have another funding cycle in fiscal year 2005 with an anticipated deadline for proposals in mid-April, 2005. Optional letters of intent would be due in mid-March, 2005. Support for **Pathways, Services, and Targeted Research** will be available again. The new solicitation is expected to be available online in early January 2005, see http://www.ehr.nsf.gov/ehr/due/programs/nsdl/.

As the NSDL continues to mature development is proceeding on several fronts that the expected new awards complement along with many of the established collections and services efforts. Several "recommending" systems are anticipated to be underway along with emerging public annotation capabilities. NSDL-wide user authentication and registration work is proceeding and private annotation is possible for certain user audiences that have registered with specific sites. Many challenges remain of course including user interface provision that reflects differing user experiences and expertise; services that promote the stability of content metadata that has been aligned with national, regional, and local standards even as the underlying standards evolve; dealing with multiple metadata frameworks; and digital preservation and archiving issues.

Numerous opportunities also exist particularly from a high-level international perspective. First is the ability that digital libraries provide to leverage and otherwise share excellent STEM educational content. Second is the similar sharing of effective and proven approaches and strategies for learning and teaching, including assessment practices. Third is the sharing of human expertise, with experts communicating with novice learners, for example through the askNSDL service, see http://nsdl.org/asknsdl/. To be sure enabling such sharing in a language independent manner poses an interesting research agenda. But there are important long-term social and cultural advantages (if not also political) to such an effort, specifically the breaking down of barriers through education.

References

1. *Information Technology: Its Impact on Undergraduate Education in Science, Mathematics, Engineering, and Technology* (NSF 98-82), April 18-20, 1996. http://www.nsf.gov/pubsys/ods/getpub.cfm?nsf9882.
2. *Developing a Digital National Library for Undergraduate Science, Mathematics, Engineering, and Technology Education*, NRC workshop, August 7-8, 1997. http://www.nap.edu/catalog/5952.html.
3. *Report of the SMETE Library Workshop* (NSF 99-112), July 21-23, 1998. http://www.dlib.org/smete/public/report.html.
4. *Serving the Needs of Pre-College Science and Mathematics Education: Impact of a Digital National Library on Teacher Education and Practice*, NRC workshop, September 24-25, 1998. http://www.nap.edu/books/NI000781/html/.
5. *Digital Libraries and Education Working Meeting*, January 4-6, 1999. http://www.dli2.nsf.gov/dljanmtg.pdf.
6. *Portal to the Future: A Digital Library for Earth System Education*, workshop report, August 8-11, 1999. http://www.dlese.org/documents/reports/panelreports/reports.html
7. Mogk, David W. and Zia, Lee L. "Addressing Opportunities and Challenges in Evaluation and Dissemination through Creation of a National Library for Undergraduate Science Education." Invited Symposium in Proceedings of the 31st Annual Meeting of the Geoscience Information Society, October 28-31, 1996, Denver, CO (1996). Available at http://gdl.ou.edu/rp1.html.
8. Wattenberg, Frank. *A National Digital Library for Science, Mathematics, Engineering, and Technology Education*, D-Lib Magazine, October 1998. http://www.dlib.org/dlib/october98/wattenberg/10wattenberg.html.
9. Zia, Lee L. *Growing a National Learning Environments and Resources Network for Science, Mathematics, Engineering, and Technology Education: Current Issues and Opportunities for the NSDL Program*. http://www.dlib.org/dlib/march01/zia/03zia.html.
10. Zia, Lee L. *The NSF National Science, Mathematics, Engineering, and Technology Education Digital Library (NSDL) Program: A Progress Report*. http://www.dlib.org/dlib/october00/zia/10zia.html.
11. Zia, Lee L. *The NSF National Science, Technology, Engineering, and Mathematics Education Digital Library (NSDL) Program: New Projects and a Progress Report*. Available at http://www.dlib.org/dlib/november01/zia/11zia.html.
12. Zia, Lee L. *The NSF National Science, Mathematics, Engineering, and Technology Education Digital Library (NSDL) Program: New Projects in Fiscal Year 2002*. http://www.dlib.org/dlib/november02/zia/11zia.html.
13. Zia, Lee L. *The NSF National Science, Technology, Engineering, and Mathematics Education Digital Library (NSDL) Program: New Projects in Fiscal Year 2003*. Available at http://www.dlib.org/dlib/march04/zia/03zia.html.

Appendix (Anticipated NSDL Awards for FY 2004)

Teachers' Domain Pathways to Science: Rich-Media Sources for K-12 Teachers. Institution: WGBH Educational Foundation. PI: Theodore Sicker. DUE-0434813.

The Computational Science Education Reference Desk. Institution: Shodor Education Foundation Inc. PI: Robert Panoff. DUE-0435187.

The Math Gateway. Institution: Mathematical Association of America. PI: Lawrence Moore. DUE-0435198.

AMSER: Applied Math and Science Education Repository. Institution: University of Wisconsin-Madison. PI: Rachael Bower. DUE-0435310.

Collaborative Project: Nuclear Pathways - A Model for Composite Digital Collections. Institutions: Washington and Lee University and Kennesaw State University. PIs: Frank Settle and Laurence Peterson. DUE-0434253 and DUE-0434278 (respectively).

The Science Knowledge and Education Network Building a User Base around Scientific Publications: Editing Online Content and Annotating Scientific Materials. Institution: Cornell University - State. PI: Steven Kelling. DUE-0435016.

Collaborative Project: Assessing the User-base and Expanding the Usability/Reach of the Analytical Sciences Digital Library through Developmental Workshops. Institutions: University of Kansas Center for Research Inc. and University of Illinois at Urbana-Champaign. PIs: Cynthia Larive and Alexander Scheeline. DUE-0435327 and DUE-0435422 (respectively).

IntegraL (Integrating Libraries): Expanding the NSDL's Reach to Traditional Libraries through Resource Integration. Institution: Foundation @ NJIT, New Jersey Institute of Technology. PI: Michael Bieber. DUE-0434581.

Annals of Research on Engineering Education (AREE). Institution: National Academy of Sciences. PI: Norman Fortenberry. DUE-0434960.

General Recommendation Engine (GRE) for NSDL. Institution: Foundation @ NJIT, New Jersey Institute of Technology. PI: Il Im. DUE-0434998.

Online Psychology Laboratory. Institution: American Psychological Assoc. PI: Maureen McCarthy. DUE-0435058.

PRISMS- Phenomena and Representations for the Instruction of Science in Middle Schools. Institution: Maine Mathematics and Science Alliance. PI: Page Keeley. DUE-0435217.

CoMPASS-DL: Design and use of a concept map interface for helping middle school students navigate digital libraries. Institution: University of Wisconsin-Madison. PI: Sadhana Puntambekar. DUE-0434624.

Collaborative Project: Superimposed Tools for Active Arrangement and Elaboration of Educational Resources. Institutions: Villanova University and Oregon Health and Science University. PIs: Lillian Cassel and Lois Delcambre. DUE-0435059 and DUE-0435496 (respectively).

Computer-Assisted Content Standard Assignment & Alignment. Institution: Syracuse University. PI: Anne Diekema. DUE-0435339.

Faculty Participation in the NSDL - Lowering the Barriers. Institution: University of Wisconsin-Madison. PI: Alan Wolf. DUE-0435398.

Creating Interactive Educational Activity Templates for Digital Libraries. Institution: McLean Media. PI: Lois McLean. DUE-0435464.

Collaborative Research: DLConnect: Connecting Underserved Teachers and Students with NSDL Learning Resources and Tools. Institutions: Eastern Michigan University and Utah State University. PIs: Ellen Hoffman and Mimi Recker. DUE-0435098 and DUE-0434892 (respectively).

Collaborative Project: Personal Collections: Enhancing the Utility of the NSDL. Institution: New Media Studios and Eduworks Corporation. PIs: Martin Landsfeld and Robert Robson. DUE-0434922 and DUE-0435084 (respectively).

Digital Libraries for Education: Case Studies

Edward A. Fox

Virginia Tech Dept. of Computer Science, 660 McBryde Hall,
Blacksburg, VA 24061 USA
fox@vt.edu
http://fox.cs.vt.edu

Abstract. Digital libraries may have extraordinary impact on education, especially in Asia where vast communities could benefit from improved teaching and learning. We highlight opportunities and challenges, drawing upon three case studies. Thus, we explore how CITIDEL, a discipline-specific Digital Library for Education (DLE), oriented toward computing, has evolved, and constitutes a part of the US National Science Digital Library (NSDL), which includes over 160 projects. By way of contrast, we describe the grass-roots and low-cost global movement toward electronic theses and dissertations led by NDLTD. Summarizing lessons learned from these case studies, we suggest ways forward so that DLEs in Asia may engage the diverse stakeholders whose serious involvement can ensure sustainable success.

1 Introduction

Education can be a powerful force for the advancement of civilization. Starting with our earliest years, we may all engage in lifelong learning, if given a proper environment, replete with suitable resources. Commonly, we consider educational resources as being made available at five levels: personal, local, regional, national, and international. Yet while the WWW does provide support at the global level, to ensure quality it is wise to have national programs, often with goals like those discussed in Section 2. Thus, each nation can have a Digital Library (DL [4, 22, 42]) for Education (DLE) [33]. In USA this function is met in part by the National Science Digital Library [45, 54, 68]. Understanding NSDL, however, can be aided by studying it in conjunction with one or more of its constituent projects. Thus, based on discussion in Section 3 of the Computing and Information Technology Interactive Digital Educational Library [9, 34, 57, 67], we explore more about NSDL in Section 4.

Success at a national scale with DLEs, however, also depends upon change at the local level, coordinated across institutions. Hence, in Section 5 we consider the Networked Digital Library of Theses and Dissertations [11, 17, 35], which operates at all five levels mentioned above. Thus, in China, operating at the national level, CALIS is already mirroring the NDLTD Union Catalog [7], but at present it only includes a relatively small number of full-text works from students in China. With relatively minor expense (and money savings in many cases), all nations can enter easily into the DLE arena by instituting policies encouraging universities to manage the Electronic Theses and Dissertations (ETDs) already being produced by the next

Z. Chen et al. (Eds.): ICADL 2004, LNCS 3334, pp. 51–60, 2004.
© Springer-Verlag Berlin Heidelberg 2004

generation of scholars. Building upon such efforts, we can broaden work on DLEs, as suggested in Section 6 (where we present our conclusions).

2   Goals of Digital Libraries for Education

Based on analysis of DLE-type activities in Europe, UK, and USA, it was noted that they may transform the way we learn, providing supporting resources and services, operating as decentralized but integrated/virtual learning environments that are adaptable to new technologies [33]. Advanced frameworks and methodologies may spread the benefits of instructional and course development into learning module repositories which promote learning object reuse – ensuring increased quality and comprehensiveness. Communities may organize around such universally available DLEs, which can become central to our cyberinfrastructure, supported by fast networks and powerful data grids. Concept-based organization of learning materials and courses can build upon suitable ontologies and benefit from concept maps [46]. These will be part of the global learning environment of the future, facilitating group work, and targeting enhanced performance on student-centered, personalized, interactive, dynamic, and lifelong activities. Students may increase their excitement about science and scholarship, through materials that are easy to discover, retrieve, and render. Driven by educational and science needs, DLEs will facilitate innovation, but be stable, reliable, and permanent [33].

With this clear vision in mind, we consider progress on CITIDEL, discussed in the next section, as one part of NSDL, a research program aimed toward a US DLE (see Section 4).

3   Case Study: CITIDEL (Computing Education)

The Computing and Information Technology Interactive Digital Educational Library was launched in 2001 through support from the US National Science Foundation as one of the NSDL collection projects. It builds upon prior work on the Computer Science Teaching Center [36], Curricular Resources in Interactive Multimedia [19, 20], and CS Virtual History Museum [40], as well as CiteSeer [6, 24] and other systems. Included are almost a million metadata records, from ACM DL, IEEE-CS DL, DBLP, NDLTD, PlanetMath, and many other sources. Part of the work in CITIDEL has been to collect as many as possible of the high-quality key records available. Since our focus is education, we worked closely with the ACM Special Interest Group on Computer Science Education (SIGCSE), including full-text of their collection [60], as well as of the ACM Journal of Educational Resources in Computing (JERIC) [8]. Thus we balanced including broad digital libraries from professional societies (ACM [1] and IEEE-CS [31]), large collections obtained by web crawling (CiteSeer), and curated bibliographies covering key conferences and journals (DBLP). Using the Open Archives Initiative Protocol for Metadata

Harvesting [39], we were able to gather the subset of records for electronic theses and dissertations (ETDs) relating to computing [67]. Several students engaged in term projects or independent studies at Virginia Tech prepared small collections, each with about 100 items, on topics they found of particular interest, such as genetic programming or artificial intelligence. We hope that this practice can spread, so that many universities around the globe identify and catalog useful resources, helping students prepare the modern equivalent of an annotated bibliography, which subsequently can assist others involved in learning and research.

Another goal of NSDL collection efforts has been to provide improved support for targeted communities, such as through portals. Thus, CITIDEL can aid distance education and teaching [41]. In the latter regard, the VIADUCT portion of CITIDEL [10] helps with the creation of lesson plans built around learning resources, extending earlier NSDL-funded work on the Instructional Architect [59] and on Walden's Paths [23]. With enhanced usability, such systems can become easier to use [57]. With visualization support, users can more quickly learn about the collection as well as manage large result sets [34]. Further, to provide enhanced browsing support, four different category systems relevant to computing have been mapped by hand so that an automatic process has categorized works, previously indexed in only one scheme, into all applicable schemes [37].

Assessment of CITIDEL is ongoing, to guide further enhancements. Our main emphasis has been on using logs. We perceived that the Digital Library field should have specially designed logging support, going beyond conventional support for web logs. We proposed [25] and refined [26] a suggested standard for DL logging, covering all important behaviors and activities. Our ongoing work on DL logging has been referred to the technical and evaluation committees that are part of NSDL – which is discussed in more detail in the next section.

4 Case Study: NSDL (US Initiative in Science Education)

NSDL evolved out of the earliest discussions on digital libraries [12]. Though funding was needed in the early 1990s for basic research [28] and applied research [43] on digital libraries, it is clear that education has been one of the most important applications to be studied and developed [29, 64, 66]. In conjunction with several years of workshop discussions [3], the US National Research Council helped move forward the NSF plans for a prototype DLE program [51]. Planning for NSDL also was informed by work on several pilot efforts [32, 50, 63].

The first call for NSDL proposals was distributed in 2000 and a first set of projects funded [68]. Early governance ideas were captured in a definitive vision document [45]. Further work on governance and on establishing a volunteer structure for policies and coordination was assigned to the Policy Committee [52], which helps run an all-project annual conference. Funding continues from NSF, through a succession of annual calls and panel reviews [55]. NSDL is supported by a Core Integration (CI) team based at UCAR in Boulder, CO, USA, that also manages core services [38].

However, the majority of the funding for NSDL has been assigned to over 160 projects; more will be supported later in 2004. Details are available through the NSDL homepage [54]. Beyond the CI work, projects have been categorized as "collections" (e.g., CITIDEL), "services" (e.g., GetSmart that provides tools for concept maps [46], and the digital-library-in-a-box toolkit [15]), and "targeted research" (recall the earlier mentioned aids for teachers [23, 59]). In 2004, a new set of "pathways" projects will "provide stewardship for the content and services needed by major communities of learners" [54]. Also, looking toward the future, an important NSDL standing committee focuses on the problem of sustainability [53], which we discuss further in Section 6.

5 Case Study: NDLTD (International Initiative for Theses)

Complementary to the heavily financed approach illustrated by NSDL is the development of a specialized global DLE, largely as a grass-roots / member-driven phenomenon – NDLTD [11, 18]. About $200,000 of funds from the US Department of Education in 1996-1998 supported work on a National Digital Library of Theses and Dissertations [16]. However, except for some support for related research [13, 14], there has been minimal additional US federal support for what quickly evolved into a global effort, the Networked Digital Library of Theses and Dissertations (www.ndltd.org). UNESCO has helped spread the ETD movement since 1999 [58], especially in Latin America, Africa, and Eastern Europe, and funded preparation of a Guide in English, French, and Spanish [49]. NDLTD, a non-profit organization with international board of directors, coordinates activities. An annual international conference (in Sydney in 2005) ensures effective communication. Corporate support has been provided by many sponsors, especially including OCLC [56], VTLS [62], and Adobe [2].

Related research has focused on usability [35], interoperability standards and methods [5], a union catalog [7, 61], the evolving new genre of ETDs [21], library issues [47], and enhanced services [27, 44, 67]. Much of the progress towards a global DLE occurs on the campuses of over 200 members, and of the many others affiliated through involvement in consortial activities (e.g., national efforts in Australia, Brazil, Germany, and India – as well as state efforts such as that managed by OhioLink). In effect, the move toward managing local collections of ETDs, and facilitating their submission and processing, as well as sharing through mechanisms connected with the Open Archives Initiative [39], has been one of the most successful aspects of what sometimes is referred to as the institutional repository movement, most recently considered in connection with the DSpace system [48] (which is being studied by an NDLTD sub-committee in partnership with the DSpace Federation).

Using DLs, universities can replace cumbersome handling of paper theses and dissertations by requiring students to submit electronic works (that they in any case prepare, in order to turn in paper copies that are hardly ever read). With automated workflow, and suitable handling of intellectual property rights issues, universities thus can manage a key part of their intellectual output – saving shelf space (and costs of binding and shipping), and at the same time increasing visibility in the global research community (since ETDs are downloaded by hundreds or thousands of interested scholars). Thus, Virginia Tech alone has a collection of over 5000 full-text ETDs, and there were over 15 million requests for PDF files against this collection over the period 1997-2003 (see http://scholar.lib.vt.edu/theses/data/somefacts.html#logs).

In China, members of NDLTD include Shanghai Jiao Tong University and Xiamen University Library. There has been collaboration between NDLTD and CALIS, leading to a mirror site in China [7], affording free access to over 100,000 metadata records for ETDs. Further collaboration is encouraged, so that ETD activities in the world's most populous nation can be coordinated with Asian and global efforts in this arena.

6 Conclusion

Digital libraries have evolved since their inception in the early 1990s. Education continues as one of their key applications. Large domain-specific projects, such as CITIDEL, which is focused on computing, are parts of even larger national programs, such as NSDL. However, much lower cost and clearly sustainable global educational digital library efforts, such as for electronic theses and dissertations, offer a complementary approach. Countries in Asia are encouraged to officially engage in the movement toward institutional repositories, by joining NDLTD, and by collaborating as well in efforts targeting different genre. In particular, it would be of great interest to have connections between the US National Science Digital Library (NSDL) and possible similar activities in Asia.

We believe, however, that careful attention must be given to three key issues if sustainable success is to result. First, in keeping with the principles that led to the proliferation of the WWW, simplicity must rule. Too much concern with elaborate systems must yield to componentized construction of networked infrastructure that employs lightweight protocols [15]. Too much concern for detailed metadata must yield to descriptive information provided by authors/editors or by programs (trained on large collections of previously cataloged publications) [65]. Second, the entire enterprise must become user-centered [30]. Students must be able to find what they need for classes and reports. Teachers must be supported in preparing lesson plans, reading lists, assignments, laboratory exercises, and exams. DL software must be made to effectively and efficiently support real educational tasks and activities. Third, sustainability and scalability must be built-in from the beginning. Sharing of high quality educational resources among teachers must be rewarded professionally and socially. The motivation of practical benefit must be highlighted when collections and systems are developed. Training regarding re-use and re-packaging must be ubiquitous among educators, while students must be guided to broaden from their focus on WWW search engines to also draw upon high quality DLs. Barriers to sharing across institutional, regional, and national boundaries must be removed as cooperation is facilitated and encouraged.

Clearly, as can be seen by considering the case studies discussed above, each country can advance toward a locally appropriate model and infrastructure for a national Digital Library for Education (DLE). Thus, it appears that the notion of DLE, as encouraged by UNESCO [33], may be of particular importance in the future of global digital library development.

Acknowledgements

The work discussed in this paper was funded in part by the US National Science Foundation through grants DUE-0333531, DUE-0121741, DUE-0136690, DUE-0121679, IIS-0080748, IIS-0086227, IIS-0002935, and IIS-9986089. Additional support has been provided by Adobe, IBM, Microsoft, OCLC, Solinet, Sun, SURA, UNESCO, US Dept. of Education (FIPSE Program P116B61190), and VTLS. Special thanks go to the many faculty, students, staff, and other collaborators whose efforts have led to the abovementioned accomplishments.

References

[1] ACM. "ACM Digital Library", 2000. *http://www.acm.org/dl/*.

[2] Adobe. Adobe ETD Initiative (homepage), 2004. *http://www.adobe.com/education/digitalcampus/etd/main.html*.

[3] Arms, W. "Report of the NSF Science, Mathematics, Engineering, and Technology Education Library Workshop, July 21-23, 1998", National Science Foundation, Division of Undergraduate Education. NSF 99-112, 1999. *http://www.dlib.org/smete/public/report.html*.

[4] Arms, W. Y. *Digital Libraries*. Cambridge, MA, MIT Press, 2000.

[5] Atkins, A., Fox, E. A., France, R. K., and Suleman, H. "ETD-ms: An Interoperability Metadata Standard for Electronic Theses and Dissertations". Blacksburg, VA: NDLTD, 2001. *http://www.ndltd.org/standards/metadata/current.html*.

[6] Bollacker, K., Lawrence, S., and Giles, C. L. "CiteSeer: An autonomous Web agent for automatic retrieval and identication of interesting publications", in *Proceedings of the Second International Conference on Autonomous Agents*, K. P. Sycara and M. Wooldridge, Eds. New York: ACM Press, 1998, pp. 116-123.

[7] CALIS. NDLTD Union Catalog Mirror Site in China, 2004. *http://ndltd.calis.edu.cn*.

[8] Cassel, L. and Fox, E. A. "ACM Journal of Education Resources in Computing". New York: ACM, 2000. *http://purl.org/net/JERIC/*.

[9] CITIDEL. "CITIDEL: Computing and Information Technology Interactive Digital Educational Library", E. A. Fox, D. Knox, L. Cassel, J. A. N. Lee, M. Pérez-Quiñones, J. Impagliazzo, and C. L. Giles, Eds. Blacksburg, VA: Virginia Tech, 2002. *http://www.citidel.org*.

[10] CITIDEL. Virginia Instructional Architect for Digital Undergraduate Computing Teaching (VIADUCT), 2004. *http://www.citidel.org/?op=viaduct_front*.

[11] Fox, E. "NDLTD: Networked Digital Library of Theses and Dissertations", 1997. *http://www.ndltd.org*.

[12] Fox, E. A. "Sourcebook on Digital Libraries: Report for the National Science Foundation". Blacksburg, VA: Dept. of Computer Science, Virginia Tech, 1993. *http://fox.cs.vt.edu/pub/DigitalLibrary/*.

[13] Fox, E. A. Networked University Digital Library (including Digital Library in a Box), 2000. *http://www.nudl.org*.

[14] Fox, E. A. "NSF SGER IIS-9986089: Core Research for the Networked University Digital Library (NUDL)". Blacksburg, VA, 2000.

[15] Fox, E. A. *Case Studies in the US National Science Digital Library: DL-in-a-Box, CITIDEL, and OCKHAM*. Presented at 6th International Conference on Asian Digital Libraries (ICADL 2003), Kuala Lumpur, Malaysia, Dec, 2003.

[16] Fox, E. A., Eaton, J., McMillan, G., Kipp, N., Weiss, L., Arce, E., and Guyer, S. *National Digital Library of Theses and Dissertations: A Scalable and Sustainable Approach to Unlock University Resources*. D-Lib Magazine, vol. 2(8), Sept., 1996. *http://www.dlib.org/dlib/september96/theses/09fox.html*.

[17] Fox, E. A., Eaton, J. L., McMillan, G., Kipp, N., Mather, P., McGonigle, T., Schweiker, W., and DeVane, B. *Networked Digital Library of Theses and Dissertations: An International Effort Unlocking University Resources*. D-Lib Magazine, vol. 3(8), Sept., 1997. *http://www.dlib.org/dlib/september97/theses/09fox.html*.

[18] Fox, E. A., Feizbadi, S., Moxley, J. M., and Weisser, C. R. *Electronic Theses and Dissertations: A Sourcebook for Educators, Students, and Librarians*. New York, Marcel Dekker, 2004.

[19] Fox, E. A., Heller, R. S., Long, A., and Watkins, D. "CRIM: Curricular Resources in Interactive Multimedia", in *Proceedings ACM Multimedia '99*. Orlando: ACM, 1999.

[20] Fox, E. A., Heller, R. S., and Watkins, D. "CRIM: Curricular Resources in Interactive Multimedia", 2000. *http://ei.cs.vt.edu/~crim*.

[21] Fox, E. A., McMillan, G., and Eaton, J. *The Evolving Genre of Electronic Theses and Dissertations*. Presented at Digital Documents Track of HICSS-32, 32nd Annual Hawaii Int. Conf. on Systems Sciences (HICSS), Maui, HI, Jan. 5-8, 1999. *http://scholar.lib.vt.edu/theses/presentations/Hawaii/ETDgenreALL.pdf*.

[22] Fox, E. A. and Urs, S. "Digital Libraries", in *Annual Review of Information Science and Technology*, vol. 36, Ch. 12, B. Cronin, Ed., 2002, pp. 503-589.

[23] Furuta, R. Walden's Paths, 2004. *http://csdl.cs.tamu.edu/walden/*.

[24] Giles, C. L., Bollacker, K., and Lawrence, S. "CiteSeer: An Automatic Citation Indexing System", in *Proc. Third ACM Conf. Digital Libraries, DL'98 (Pittsburgh)*, I. Witten, R. Akscyn, and F. M. Shipman III, Eds. ACM Press: ACM, 1998, pp. 89-98. *http://www.neci.nj.nec.com/homepages/lawrence/papers/cs-dl98/*.

[25] Gonçalves, M. A., Luo, M., Shen, R., Farooq, M., and Fox, E. A. *An XML Log Standard and Tool for Digital Library Logging Analysis*. Presented at Sixth European Conference on Research and Advanced Technology for Digital Libraries, Rome, Italy, 2002.

[26] Gonçalves, M. A., Panchanathan, G., Ravindranathan, U., Krowne, A., Fox, E., Jagodzinski, F., and Cassel, L. *Standards, mark-up, and metadata: The XML log standard for digital libraries: analysis, evolution, and deployment*. Presented at 3rd ACM/IEEE-CS joint conference on digital libraries, IEEE Computer Society, 2003.

[27] Gonçalves, M. A., Zhou, Y., and Fox, E., A. *Providing Extended Services and Resources to the NDLTD Community*. Presented at ETD'2002, Provo, Utah, May 30 - June 1, 2002.

[28] Griffin, S. "Digital Libraries Initiative". Arlington, VA: NSF, 1999. *http://www.dli2.nsf.gov/dlione/*.

[29] Gupta, A., Ludäscher, B., and Moore, R. W. "Ontology Services for Curriculum Development in NSDL", in *Proceedings of the second ACM/IEEE-CS joint conference on digital libraries, JCDL'2002*, G. Marchionini, Ed. Portland, OR: ACM, 2002, pp. 219 - 220. *http://doi.acm.org/10.1145/544220.544266*.

[30] Heath, L., Hix, D., Nowell, L., Wake, W., Averboch, G., and Fox, E. A. *Envision: A User-Centered Database from the Computer Science Literature*. Communications of the ACM, vol. 38(4), pp. 52-53, 1995.

[31] IEEE-CS. IEEE Computer Society Digital Library, 2004. *http://www.computer.org/publications/dlib/*.

[32] iLumina_Project. "iLumina: A Digital Library of Reusable Science and Math Resources for Undergraduate Education (home page)", 2001. *http://www.ilumina-project.org*.

[33] Kalinichenko, L. *Digital Libraries in Education: Analytical Survey*. Moscow, UNESCO Institute for Information Technologies in Education, 2003.

[34] Kampanya, N., Shen, R., Kim, S., North, C., and Fox, E. A. "Citiviz: A Visual User Interface to the CITIDEL System", in *Proc. European Conference on Digital Libraries (ECDL) 2004, September 12-17, University of Bath, UK*, 2004.

[35] Kengeri, R., Seals, C. D., Harley, H. D., Reddy, H. P., and Fox, E. A. *Usability study of digital libraries: ACM, IEEE-CS, NCSTRL, NDLTD*. International Journal on Digital Libraries, vol. 2(2/3), pp. 157-169, 1999. *http://link.springer.de/link/service/journals/00799/bibs/9002002/90020157.htm*.

[36] Knox, D., Grissom, S., Fox, E. A., Heller, R., and Watkins, D. "CSTC: Computer Science Teaching Center", 2000. *http://www.cstc.org*.

[37] Krowne, A. and Fox, E. A. "An Architecture for Multischeming in Digital Libraries", in *Proceedings 6th International Conference on Asian Digital Libraries, ICADL 2003, Digital Libraries: Technology and Management of Indigenous Knowledge for Global Access;Kuala Lumpur, Malaysia, Dec.; Springer, Lecture Notes in Computer Science 2911*, T. Mohd, T. Sembok, H. B. Zaman, H. Chen, S. R. Urs, and S. H. Myaeng, Eds., 2003, pp. 563-577.

[38] Lagoze, C., Hoehn, W., Millman, D., Arms, W., Gan, S., Hillmann, D., Ingram, C., Krafft, D., Marisa, R., Phipps, J., Saylor, J., Terrizzi, C., Allan, J., Guzman-Lara, S., and Kalt, T. "Core Services in the Architecture of the National Digital Library for Science Education (NSDL)", in *Proceedings of the second ACM/IEEE-CS joint conference on digital libraries, JCDL'2002*, G. Marchionini, Ed. Portland, OR: ACM, 2002, pp. 201-209. *http://doi.acm.org/10.1145/544220.544264*.

[39] Lagoze, C., Van de Sompel, H., Nelson, M., and Warner, S. "The Open Archives Initiative Protocol for Metadata Harvesting - Version 2.0, Open Archives Initiative", 2002. *http://www.openarchives.org/OAI/2.0/openarchivesprotocol.htm*.

[40] Lee, J. A. N. Computer History Museum, 1996. *http://virtualmuseum.dlib.vt.edu/*.

[41] Lee, J. A. N., Impagliazzo, J., Cassel, L. N., Fox, E. A., Giles, C. L., Knox, D., and Pérez-Quiñones, M. A. "Enhancing distance learning using quality digital libraries and CITIDEL", in *Quality Education @ a Distance*, 2003, pp. 61-71.

[42] Lesk, M. *Practical Digital Libraries: Books, Bytes and Bucks*. San Francisco, Morgan Kaufmann Publishers, 1997.

[43] Lesk, M. *Perspectives on DLI-2 - Growing the Field*. D-Lib Magazine, vol. 5(7/8), 1999. *http://www.dlib.org/dlib/july99/07lesk.html*.

[44] Luo, M. and Fox, E. A. "ETD search services", in *Proceedings of ETD 2004: Distributing knowledge worldwide through better scholarly communication, June 3-5, Lexington, KY*, 2004.

[45] Manduca, C. A., McMartin, F. P., and Mogk, D. W. "Pathways to Progress: Vision and Plans for Developing the NSDL", NSDL March 20 2001. *http://doclib.comm.nsdlib.org/ PathwaysToProgress.pdf (retrieved on 11/16/2002)*.

[46] Marshall, B., Zhang, Y., Chen, H., Lally, A., Shen, R., Fox, E. A., and Cassel, L. N. "Convergence of Knowledge Management and E-Learning: the GetSmart Experience." in *Proc. JCDL'2003, Third ACM / IEEE-CS Joint Conference on Digital Libraries, May 27-31, Houston*, 2003.

[47] McMillan, G. *What to Expect from ETDs: Library Issues and Responsibilities*. Presented at Digital Library Symposium, Cleveland, OH, Sept. 22, 1999. *http://scholar.lib.vt.edu/ staff/guilmac/presentations/CWRUGMc2.pdf*.

[48] MIT. "DSpace: Durable Digital Depository". Cambridge, MA: MIT, 2003. *http://dspace. org*.

[49] Moxley, J. M., Masiello, D., and Fox, E. The Guide for Electronic Theses and Dissertations, 2002. *www.etdguide.org*.

[50] Muramatsu, B. and Agogino, A. *NEEDS - The National Engineering Education Delivery System: A Digital Library for Engineering Education*. D-Lib Magazine, vol. 5(4), 1999. *http://www.dlib.org/dlib/april99/muramatsu/04muramatsu.html*.

[51] NRC. "Developing a Digital National Library for Undergraduate Science, Mathematics, Engineering, and Technology Education: Report of a Workshop", National Research Council, Washington, August 7-8, 1997 1997. *http://books.nap.edu/catalog/5952.html*.

[52] NSDL. NSDL Policy Committee Workspace, 2004. *http://policy.comm.nsdl.org/*.

[53] NSDL. NSDL Sustainability Standing Committee Home Page, 2004. *http://sustain. comm.nsdl.org/*.

[54] NSF. "National Science, Technology, Engineering, and Mathematics Education Digital Library (NSDL)". Arlington, VA: National Science Foundation, 2004. *http://www.ehr. nsf.gov/EHR/DUE/programs/nsdl/*.

[55] NSF. *National Science, Technology, Engineering, and Mathematics Education Digital Library (NSDL): nsf04542*. Arlington, Virginia, National Science Foundation, 2004. *http://www.nsf.gov/pubsys/ods/getpub.cfm?nsf04542*.

[56] OCLC. XTCat NDLTD Union Catalog, 2004. *http://alcme.oclc.org/ndltd/index.html*.

[57] Perugini, S., McDevitt, K., Richardson, R., Perez-Quinones, M., Shen, R., Ramakrishnan, N., Williams, C., and Fox, E. A. "Enhancing Usability in CITIDEL: Multimodal, Multilingual, and Interactive Visualization Interfaces", in *Proceedings Fourth ACM/IEEE-CS Joint Conference on Digital Libraries (JCDL2004), Tucson, AZ, June 7-11*, 2004, pp. 315-324.

[58] Plathe, A. "Workshop on an international project of electronic dissemination of theses and dissertations". Paris: UNESCO, 1999. *http://www.unesco.org/webworld/etd*.

[59] Rucker, M. Instructional Architect, 2004. *http://ia.usu.edu/*.

[60] SIGCSE. SIGCSE Education Links, 2004. *http://sigcse.org/topics/*.

[61] Suleman, H. and Fox, E. A. *Towards Universal Accessibility of ETDs: Building the NDLTD Union Archive*. Presented at ETD'2002, Provo, Utah, May 30 - June 1, 2002, 2002. *http://rocky.dlib.vt.edu/~hussein/etd_2002/etd_2002_paper_final.pdf*.

[62] VTLS. Networked Digital Library of Theses and Dissertations Union Catalog, 2004. *http://hercules.vtls.com/cgi-bin/ndltd/chameleon*.

[63] Wattenberg, F. *A National Digital Library for Science, Mathematics, Engineering, and Technology Education*. D-Lib Magazine, vol. 4(9), 1998. *http://www.dlib.org/ dlib/october98/wattenberg/10wattenberg.html*.

[64] Wattenberg, F. *Stretching the Zero Sum Paradigm with a National Digital Library for Science Education*. Information Impacts, 1999. *http://www.cisp.org/imp/june_99/ wattenberg/06_99wattenberg.htm*.

[65] Weinstein, P. C. and Birmingham, W. P. *Creating Ontological Metadata for Digital Library Content and Services.* International Journal on Digital Libraries, vol. 2(1), pp. 19-36, 1998.

[66] www.smete.org. "www.smete.org (home page): Information Portal: A Digital Library for Science, Mathematics, Engineering, and Technology Education". Berkeley, CA: NEEDS, 2000. *http://www.smete.org.*

[67] Zhang, B., Gonçalves, M. A., and Fox, E. A. "An OAI-Based Filtering Service for CITIDEL from NDLTD", in *Proceedings 6th International Conference on Asian Digital Libraries, ICADL 2003, Digital Libraries: Technology and Management of Indigenous Knowledge for Global Access; Kuala Lumpur, Malaysia, Dec.; Springer, Lecture Notes in Computer Science 2911*, T. Mohd, T. Sembok, H. B. Zaman, H. Chen, S. R. Urs, and S. H. Myaeng, Eds., 2003, pp. 590-601.

[68] Zia, L. L. *The NSF National Science, Mathematics, Engineering, and Technology Education Digital Library (NSDL) Program.* CACM, vol. 44(5), pp. 83, 2001. *http://doi.acm.org/10.1145/374308.375359.*

Digital Preservation and Workflow Process

Su-Shing Chen

Department of Computer and Information Science and Engineering,
University of Florida, Gainesville, Florida 32611, USA
suchen@cise.ufl.edu

Abstract. The digital societies of E-government, E-learning, and E-business have grown by leaps and bounds worldwide during the last several years. While we have invested significant time and effort to create and maintain those workflow processes, we do not have the ability to make digital objects generated by the processes all available across generations of information technology, making it accessible with future technology and enabling people to determine whether it is authentic and reliable. This is a very serious problem for which no complete solutions have been devised yet. This paper discusses three important factors - archival stability, organizational process, and technology continuity – for digital preservation to succeed, and describes a general framework of digital libraries (or the life cycle of information) to address this important problem so that we may find reasonable ways to preserve digital objects that can be analyzed and evaluated in quantitative measures and incremental manners.

1 Introduction

Although digital societies have emerged and digital communities have formed of E-government, E-learning, and E-business, we are still facing a fundamental paradox in digital preservation: On the one hand, we want to maintain digital information intact as it was created, but on the other we want it to be accessible in a dynamic context of use [2]. Why the rapid progress being made in information technology today to create, capture, process and communicate information in the digital form threatens the accessibility in the near future? This is because of two reasons: First digital information has mushroomed, and secondly hardware and software products are being upgraded and replaced roughly every eighteen months. Companies in the information technology sector have reported that the majority of products and services they offer did not exist five years ago. For cost-effectiveness, we have to change hardware and software products from generation to generation. The digital library community, which is a part of digital societies, needs to pay attention to digital preservation.

The digital environment has fundamentally changed the concept of preservation. Traditionally preservation means keeping things unchanged. For example, we can still read the Rosetta Stone of Ptolemy V in hieroglyphic, demotic, and Greek today. However if we could succeed in holding on to digital information without any change, the information would become increasingly harder, if not impossible, to access. Even

Z. Chen et al. (Eds.): ICADL 2004, LNCS 3334, pp. 61–72, 2004.
© Springer-Verlag Berlin Heidelberg 2004

if a physical medium could hold digital information intact, the formats in which information is recorded digitally do change and the hardware and software to retrieve the information from the medium often become obsolete. In summary, we can not predict the future of information technology, and thus can not plan our digital preservation well in the present.

In [4], we have emphasized how important it is to preserve digital objects as the essential information memory for our society, and introduced the life cycle of information for addressing the requirements and strategies of preserving digital objects. By establishing the long-term requirements and strategies, we can stabilize the development of digital objects and archives/libraries. In this paper, we argue that *archival stability* must be coupled with *organizational process*, and *technology continuity* in digital preservation, and propose a new approach beyond traditional digital preservation that these factors are interrelated and must be considered together. We introduce the new technical concept of "dynamic" objects which are digital objects associated with workflow processes, and the idea of process repositories (to preserve workflow processes) in addition to the traditional object libraries/archives. Therefore librarians/archivists cannot achieve *archival stability* without the coupling with *organizational workflow processes* and *technology implementations*. Likewise organizations and technology companies must seek librarians/archivists to participate in their planning.

2 A New Framework for Digital Preservation

Digital societies are concerned with the participants - human citizens, software agents, and robots (e.g., ATM and vending machines), information (knowledge bases, databases, and repositories of records), and workflow processes (E-government, E-business, E-learning and etc.). It has become evident that objects must be "dynamic", that is they are not only traditional objects but also associated with appropriate workflow processes. Thus not only objects must be preserved, so are their workflow processes. The traditional archival requirements alone may not work well, because workflow processes are dynamic and subject to change due to administrative and legislative changes.

We believe that this new framework will need the research, design, and implementation of IT technologies – secure networking, distributed computing, information fusion, dynamic records, process repositories, and intelligent record archives. These technologies are necessary for the economic vibrant and civil digital societies. In this paper, we can only introduce briefly some concepts and argue for their importance. The technologies will be developed in subsequent work. The framework consists of five components:

(1) A digital society has a governance model with the organizational structure that consists of a role hierarchy of participants carrying out various collaborative workflow processes (e.g., accessing and processing information and other activities). The maintaining and updating of role hierarchy databases assures the democracy of the society [26].

(2) An object/process management server that manages workflow processes and provides core workflow services and supporting services (e.g., ontology services synchronize semantics from heterogeneous dynamic objects into a consistent dynamic object for relevant processes. It has a user interface that visualizes the logic of the workflow and dependencies of dynamic objects and their fusion. It associates each dynamic object with the associated workflow process.

(3) An archive server of societal databases that provides reliable access for participants to all dynamic objects based on the processes and the role hierarchy. Here we are concerned about the preservation of a digital society's memory. In a digital society, digital objects proliferate and propagate. How to assure that digital objects are appraised, authenticated, and preserved in a societal memory for the long-term? We must develop a digital preservation management model for a digital society, by examining archival stability, organizational process, and technical continuity of the society.

(4) Information (objects) fusion and workflow process integration have broad impacts on digital societies of E-government, E-learning and E-business. Practical case studies must be made to study the dynamics and to understand the advantages and disadvantages to societies. Case studies should not be carried out by librarians/archivists alone. A multidisciplinary team of social scientists is needed to study the social impacts, process models, and object keeping.

(5) The development of consistent hardware, software and applications sustaining the technology continuity is the responsibility of the IT industry. The IT industry must realize that technology continuity means good business. Although disruptive technologies are the driving force of IT advancement, the technology continuity makes good business sense by keeping customers in the long-term. The industry norm should not be chaotic new products and services that win competition in the IT industry. Recently governments around the world have introduced funding opportunities to the IT industry that will influence this outcome (e.g., [18-20]). The industry has also developed future visions that potentially include digital preservation (e.g., [17]).

A general digital society can be modeled as workflow systems on the Internet. This digital society model supports the five components of the new framework. Such model consists of three major parts: user interfaces, workflow dynamics and societal databases. Users interface through the use of portals and clients to the web-based system. The workflow dynamics is supported by a collection of services, including the core workflow processes and affiliated digital library services: ontology, administration, evaluation, discussion and visualization. In our proposed framework, the core workflow processes access the workflow template depositories and the subject role hierarchy databases, which represent the organizational structure of workflow participants. Workflow information sources are in the societal databases, whose objects are indexed for multiple contexts and services to generate dynamic objects.

One of the most important issues of digital preservation is to know what to preserve and how to preserve? The new framework places emphasis first on the *organizational process* to preservation and clarifies the overall picture of digital preservation. The responsibility of the holding organizations - government offices, companies, hospitals, and institutions - will affect the ultimate outcome. In addition to *organizational process*, the information science community (e.g., librarians and archivists) must provide *archival stability*, and the computer industry must develop *technical continuity* for *archival stability* in synchrony. For this purpose, we will formulate the digital preservation problem within a life cycle of information. The life cycle of information spans acquisition, preservation, collection, indexing, accessing, and utilization in a dynamic manner [3]. If preservation is missed, then the life cycle is broken and will be disrupted. *Thus organizations should design their preservation of digital libraries/ archives seamlessly in the life cycle of information so that technology can provide the necessary continuity.*

3 Organizational Process

Different organizations have very different requirements and implementations of their archives/libraries, which depend much on the nature of organizations. For example, hospitals will maintain their patient records, school systems their student records, and companies their financial records. In general, there is no standard on whether organizations should preserve, how they preserve and what they preserve? In the more focused context of digital societies, organizations' process in relevance to digital preservation must be evident for their sustainability. This section examines various issues of this kind of processes. One must factor this process as an archival variable into the future organizational management equation. Digital preservation will assume a variety of storage and preservation functions. Traditionally, the preserved objects have been in the forms of books, monographs, reports, maps, photographs, analog sound tracks and films, which are readable, listenable and viewable directly by humans with the aid of magnification, scanning, playing and projection devices. The preservation of physical and analog media has to ensure long-term stability and accessibility. The preservation of digital objects takes on a somewhat different direction, because the technology advances so rapidly that hardware and software products are being upgraded and replaced constantly. Companies in the information technology sector report that the majority of their products and services they offer did not exist 5 years ago. Simultaneously, the explosive growth of information in digital forms has posed a severe challenge for organizations and their information providers because the digital information can be easily lost or corrupted. The pace of technology evolution is further causing severe pressure on the ability of existing data structures or formats to represent information for the organizations in the future. The supporting information necessary to preserve the digital information is available or only available at the time when the original digital information is produced. Usually after the information is produced, the running software may be updated and its version may be changed. Organizations must start to preserve in long-term, otherwise their information will be lost forever.

There are several functions of organizations in preservation. Except some national archives and research groups, these functions are generally ignored by the IT people. We emphasize three of them here. The organizations must monitor community needs, interact with consumers and producers to track changes in their service requirements and available product technologies. Such requirements might include data formats, media choices, software packages, computing platforms, and mechanisms for communicating with the digital libraries/archives. This first function may be accomplished via surveys, a periodic formal review process, community workshops where feedback is solicited, or by individual interactions. It provides reports, requirements alerts and emerging standards for developing future preservation strategies and standards. It sends preservation requirements to the digital library/archive developers and managers. The second function is the responsibility of tracking emerging digital technologies, information standards and computing platforms (i.e., hardware and software) to identify technologies which could cause obsolescence in the archiving computing environment and could prevent access to some of the archives' current holdings. This function may contain a prototyping capability for better evaluation of emerging technologies and receive prototype requests from the digital archive developers. This function is also responsible for developing and recommending strategies and standards to enable the digital archives to better anticipate future changes in the community service requirements or technology trends that would require migration of some current holdings or new acquisitions. The third function approves standards and migration goals from the digital library/archive managers. The standards include format standards, metadata standards and documentation standards. It applies these standards to preservation requirements. The migration goals received by this function involve transformations of the preservation package, including transformations of the content to avoid loss of access due to technology obsolescence. The response to the migration goals may involve the development of new preservation designs, prototype software, test plans, community review plans and implementation plans.

Facing the ever-increasing cost of preservation, digital libraries/archives need sound policies and strategies to preserve the essential information in the long-term. To develop policies and strategies digital libraries/archives need a generally accepted framework or a life cycle of information. A life cycle of information is not only for preservation and access, but rather for the full business model of digital libraries/archives. In the following we discuss the important aspect of the organizational structure – workflow process in general. The specific life cycle of information will be discussed in the next section.

A workflow process is the computerized representation of a business process. It specifies the various activities of a business process that have to be executed in some order, the flow of data between activities and the multiple collaborating agents that execute activities to carry out a common objective. A workflow management system is a software system for defining, instantiating and executing workflows and is currently the leading technology for supporting business processes (e.g., financial markets, banks, retailing stores, transportation and others).

Existing workflow solutions focus on the capability of representing project information and information exchange between applications. However, the ever-changing nature of organizations requires solutions equipped with facilities that are able to treat information (e.g., records) as a dynamic entity. The information changes either because of the normal progress of the business from preplanned activities, or because of events, which occur due to uncertainty. In both cases, they are the results of the life cycle of information!

We believe that the design of a flexible and expressive workflow system can and should be tackled through an interoperable and dynamic information process model. This architecture allows participants and information objects flow in a flexible workflow process architecture, where data and service providers will interact through the Internet in the workflow system. For such system architecture, there is an open harvesting protocol of metadata of data providers by service providers proposed by the Open Archives Initiative (OAI) [23-25]. By exposing a sufficient amount of metadata, data providers openly advertise their content for retrieval and usage by other data providers and service providers. This open architecture must certainly be protected by security mechanisms. In this paper, we will not discuss this issue. In [26], we have focused on this access control issue in the framework of life cycle of information.

The database system is further interfaced to the workflow system through certain service protocols (depending on the functionality of organizations). The workflow engine executes and manages workflow processes with the underlying information model. Applications (e.g., digital society services) reside in the domain-specific middleware layer which is also not discussed in this paper.

Now some discussions on the workflow process repository. The flexibility of workflow architecture is accomplished by the construction of basic workflow building blocks as directed graphs, and indexing of basic workflow processes into a repository from which several processes can be composed into more complex processes, as graph rewriting. During workflow enactment, a workflow can be modified due to on-line constraints and subsequently ingested into the repository as a new entry for future use. The idea of treating workflows as an archival component greatly improves the preservation principle in the long-term. Apparently the design of a workflow system for preservation needs much further research. Our effort has been to investigate the applicability of formal models such as graph-rewriting, Petri-net, and extended transaction for the flexible and dynamic configuration of workflows. More detailed results will be reported elsewhere. Such an interoperable and dynamic information model consists of networked application services with distributed users, objects, workflow processes, and their repositories. This kind of application services can be implemented based on the dynamic object model which originates from our research (described in the next section). This section has discussed the overall system architecture only, while the details at the object level must be considered in the next section.

4   Archival Stability of Objects

The object-oriented methodology has emerged to be a standard representation scheme of information technology, preservation and thus archival science [12]. The information encapsulation principle provides a representation of digital objects. It wraps the information content by its accompanying procedures, which are applied whenever necessary. Processes in the life cycle of information may be expressed as complex objects of objects [3]. In each organizational infrastructure, we will use the object-oriented framework of the life cycle of information. The life cycle consists of acquisition, preservation, collection, indexing, accessing, and utilization (including various workflow processes discussed in the previous section), where preservation is an important component of the life cycle.

The information encapsulation principle provides a general representation scheme of various multimedia data content of the life cycle. The multimedia data content is wrapped by its representation information and accompanying software programs, which are applied whenever necessary. The representation information maps the bit streams of data content into understandable information of certain format, structure, and type. Thus data content, representation information, and software programs become modular and reusable. Digital objects are convertible and transformable, and operable under processes of the life cycle of information. Since digital objects are encapsulated, they are active, dynamic, and extensible. They are active, because software agents may be embedded in objects so that activities may be initiated by objects. They are dynamic under any process that is associated with accompanying software programs of objects. They are extensible in the sense of multimedia content and networked sources. Any object can be augmented by other objects of multimedia content and from networked sources. It is highly plausible that a digital object pulls several networked records into itself. The multimedia digital content is composed of one or more bit sequences. The purpose of the representation information is to convert the bit sequences into more meaningful information. It does this by describing the format, or data structure concepts, which are to be applied to the bit sequences and that in turn result in more meaningful values such as characters, numbers, pixels, arrays, tables, etc. For simplicity, we will call such active, dynamic and extensible objects by a single adjective: "dynamic". Thus in this paper, "dynamic" has the characteristics of active, dynamic and extensible. In our subsequent work, we will provide more details on the development of dynamic objects (DO's) in this convention.

How can we develop a preservation strategy for these objects? The data types, their aggregations, and mapping rules which map from the underlying data types to the higher level concepts are referred to as the structure information component of the representation information. These structures are commonly identified by name or by relative position within the associated bit sequences. The representation information provided by the structure information component is usually insufficient to understand the digital content. The additional required information is referred to as the semantic information. Semantic information may be quite complex. It may include special meanings associated with all the elements of the structural information, processes that may be performed on each data type, and their inter-relationships. Moreover representation information may contain further associative references to other representation information.

In order to preserve a digital object, its representation information, both structural and semantic, must also be preserved. This is commonly accomplished when the representation information is expressed in text descriptions that use widely supported standards such as ASCII characters for digital versions. If text descriptions are ambiguous, we should use standardized, formal description languages (e.g., XML markup languages) containing well-defined constructs with which to describe data structures. These markup languages will augment text descriptions to fully convey the semantics of the representation information.

Software programs associated with digital objects commonly are representation rendering software and access software. Representation rendering software is able to display the representation information in human-readable forms, such as the PDF display software to render the record human-readable. Access software presents some or all of the information content of a digital object in forms understandable to humans or systems. It may also provide some types of access service, such as displaying, manipulating, processing, to another object (e.g., scientific visualization systems supporting time series or multidimensional array). Again its future existence and migration depend highly on the *technology continuity*, which is a very difficult prediction to make. Since representation rendering software and access software are provided at the desktop, their preservation is not necessary at each object level, but only at the environmental level.

It is tempting to use Internet-based access software to incorporate some of the representation information as a cost-effective means. Many web-based services actually do use web access software as the full representation information, and the WWW consortium is doing an excellent job for this effort. Access software source code becomes at least the partial representation information of those digital objects. First such information may be mixed with various other processing and display algorithms, and may be incomplete since the code assumes an underlying operating environment. Secondly, if executables of access software are used, without the source code, such archives have great risks for loss of representation information. It is more difficult to maintain an operating environment for software than to migrate over time. If the organizational computing environment supports the software, it is not difficult to access the preserved package. The environment consists of the underlying hardware and operating system, various utilities that effectively augment the operating system, and storage and display devices and their drivers. A change to any of these will cause the software no longer function properly. This is why preservation of software is complex and complicated. To push one more level, representation information may need to include dictionary and grammar of any natural language (e.g., English) used in expressing the digital content. Over long time periods the meaning of natural language expressions can evolve significantly in both general and specific disciplines.

An important step of preservation is the *bundling* of necessary preservation information to a digital object so that we can still access and retrieve the content whatever the hardware, software, and media migration may advance. A preservation package is a conceptual container of these two types of information, content information and preservation information [13]. The content information and preservation information are encapsulated and identifiable by the package information. The resulting package is accessible by the descriptive information of the preservation package. The content information is the original target information of preservation. It consists of the digital content and its associated representation information and software programs. The preservation information applies to the content information and is needed to preserve the content information, to ensure it is clearly identified, and to understand the environment in which it was created.

The preservation information is divided into four types of preserving information called provenance, context, reference, and fixity. Briefly, they are described in the following four categories:

1. Provenance describes the history and source of the content information: who has had custody of it since its origination, and its history (including processing history). This gives future users some assurance as to the likely reliability of the content. Provenance can be viewed as a special type of context information.

2. Context describes how the content information relates to other information outside the information package. For example, it would describe why the content information was produced, and it may include a description of how it relates to another content information object that is available.

3. Reference provides one or more identifiers, or systems of identifiers, by which the content information may be uniquely identified. Examples include an ISBN number for a book, or a set of attributes that distinguish one instance of content information from another. Further examples include taxonomic systems, reference systems and registration systems.

4. Fixity provides a wrapper, or protective shield, that protects the content information from undocumented alteration. It provides the data integrity checks or validation/verification keys used to ensure that the particular content has not been altered in an undocumented manner.

The packaging information is that information which binds, identifies, and relates the content information and preservation information either actually or logically. The descriptive information of the package is the information, which is used to discover which package has the content information of interest. It may be a full set of attributes or metadata that are searchable in a catalog service. In OAIS [1], the total archival information over an indefinite period of time is called preservation description information (PDI). The packaging information does not necessarily need to be preserved since it does not contribute to the content information or the PDI. The preservation should also avoid holding PDI or content information only in the naming conventions of directory or file name structures. These structures are most likely to be used as packaging information. Packaging information is not preserved by migration. Any information saved in file names or directory structures may be lost when the packaging information is altered.

The life cycle of information is also represented in an object-oriented framework [3]. The life cycle consists of at least the following processes of information: acquisition, preservation, collection, indexing, accessing, and utilization. In particular, utilization may further include many other workflow processes in organizations. In any organization, information is received from external transactional sources, generated by its own workflow processes, or accessed from information resources (e.g., libraries and archives). The life cycle starts, only after an object is acquired (ingested or initiated) by an organization. An object acquired will be preserved for long-term use. All preserved objects are stored into appropriate collections, each of which is properly indexed for future accessing and utilization. The life cycle captures a spiral (rather than a linear) cycle, because acquisition follows utilization in a repetitive and iterative pattern. Information generated by utilization is often ingested into the life cycle!

There are also secondary processes. It is impossible to have a complete listing of secondary processes. These secondary processes may be embedded in various stages of the life cycle. In this paper, workflow processes are assumed in general forms and not described in details. Workflow processes may include secondary processes. To illustrate, we discuss a few secondary processes. Conversion and transformation of formats and structures of digital objects permits the interchange among them. They are used in preservation for example. Communication and transmission sends digital objects from computer hardware and storage systems through communications networks. They are needed perhaps in every process of the life cycle. Brokerage and integration mediates query results from networked sources into unified objects for users. They are essential to the accessing process. Delivery and presentation brings information in useful manners to users in access and utilization.

Since digital objects are associated with processes in the life cycle of information, it is natural to develop the definition of dynamic objects as those with associated processes. Let us envision the following scenario: On the Internet, dynamic objects automatically transmit in the network from one stage to the next stage according to some associated processes, supporting dynamic horizontal and vertical information flows of the life cycle. For each stage of the process, dynamic objects will do the following: build their metadata, join a group of objects of the same purpose, and offer-of-access-of-metadata to processes and members of the organization through some automatic indexing and clustering algorithms. To accomplish this scenario, some sophisticated techniques must be employed. For examples, knowledge discovery and data mining must be used. Knowledge discovery has been used to extract useful knowledge from large volumes of data and it is one of the many potential objectives of information fusion. Data mining is defined as the nontrivial extraction of implicit, previously unknown, and potentially useful information from data and can be used as a means of accomplishing the objectives of knowledge discovery. Dynamic objects can be constructed by simultaneously indexing objects with their workflow processes and dynamically organize and search the resource space by constructing links among the objects based on the metadata that describes their contents, types, context, and workflow processes. The offer-of-access-of-metadata is specified by the user profiles, and the semantics of the type of dynamic objects. The links will be used to generate a virtual graph, with a flexible set of multiple hierarchies to provide searching and browsing facilities in the organized concept space. We may also build an ontology space by using the graph constructed. The ontology space is an explicit specification of a conceptualization of objects. The use of ontology provides an effective way to describe objects and their relationships to other objects.

5 Conclusions

We have proposed a potential solution to the digital preservation problem in digital libraries/archives. The interplay of organizational process, archival stability, and technology continuity is evident in our discussion that more innovative research should be conducted in this direction. Our solution has also developed a new model of digital libraries that is dynamic and associated with workflow processes.

References

1. CCSDS and ISO TC20/SC13, "Reference Model for an Open Archival Information System", July 2001, http://www.ccsds.org/documents/pdf/CCSDS-650.0-R-2.pdf.
2. S. Chen, The paradox of digital preservation, IEEE Computer, March 2001.
3. S. Chen, Digital Libraries: The Life Cycle of Information, BE Publisher, 1998.
4. S. Chen, Digital preservation and the life cycle of information, Advances in Computers, M. Zelkowitz (ed.), volume 57, Academic Press/Elsevier Science, 2003.
5. S. Chen, C. Choo, and R. Y. Chow, Internet security: A novel role/object-based access control for information domains, under revision by Journal of Organizational Computing and Electronic Commerce, http://phoenix.lite.cise.ufl.edu:8080/dllsl/papers.html
6. C. M. Dollar, Archival Theory and Information Technologies: The Impact of Information Technologies on Archival Principles and Methods, Macerata: University of Macerata Press, 1992.
7. L. Duranti, Diplomatics: New uses for an old science (Part V), Archivaria, 32 1991, pp. 6–24.
8. J. Garrett and D. Waters, Preserving digital information, Report of the Task Force on Archiving of Digital Information, May 1996, <http://www.rlg.org/ArchTF/>.
9. M. Hedstrom, Descriptive practices for electronic records: Deciding what is essential and imaging what is possible, Archivaria, 36, 1993, pp. 53–63.
10. InterPARES, http://www.InterPARES.org/.
11. J. Rothenberg, Ensuring the longevity of digital documents, Scientific American, 272, 1995, pp. 42–47.
12. J. Rumbaugh, M. Blaha, W. Premerlani, F. Eddy, and W. Lorensen, Object-Oriented Modeling and Design, Prentice Hall, 1991.
13. T. Shepard, UPF User Requirements, http://info.wgbh.org/upf/.
14. Victorian Electronic Records Strategy Final Report, Public Record Office Victoria 1999, http://www.prov.vic.gov.au/vers/
15. National Digital Information Infrastructure and Preservation Program, http://www.digitalpreservation.gov/.
16. OCLC, http://www.oclc.org/services/preservation/default.htm.
17. IBM Vision of Autonomic Computing (IEEE Computer January 2003), www.ibm.com/research/ autonomic/.
18. NARA ERA, http://www.archives.gov/electronic_records_archives/research/research.html.
19. Australian Standards and Framework: Records Management and Metatagging of Web Pages, http://www.lester.boisestate.edu/metatags/Australian_Standards_and_Framework1.htm.
20. Sue McKemmish Describing Records in Context in the Continuum: the Australian Recordkeeping Metadata Schema, http://www.sims.monash.edu/research/rcrg/publications/archiv01.htm.

21. H. Kim and S. Chen, Ontology Search and Text Mining of MEDLINE Database, Conference on "Data Mining in Biomedicine", February 16-18, 2004, University of Florida, Gainesville, FL; Book published by Kluwer.

22. S. Shi, O. Rodriguez, S. Chen and Y. Shang, Open learning objects as an intelligent way of organizing educational material, International Journal on E-Learning, Vol. 3 No. 2, 2004, pp. 51–63.

23. H. Kim, C. Choo, and S. Chen, An Integrated Digital Library Server with OAI and Self-Organizing Capabilities. In *Proceedings of the 7th European Conference on Research and Advanced Technology for Digital Libraries (ECDL 2003)*, Trondheim, Norway, August (2003)

24. C. Lagoze and H. Van de Sompel, The Open Archives Initiative: Building a low-barrier interoperability framework. In Proceedings of the First ACM/IEEE Joint Conference on Digital Libraries, Roanoke, VA, 2001. Pages 54–62.

25. C. Lagoze, H. Van de Sompel, M. Nelson and S. Warner, The Open Archives Initiative Protocol for Metadata Harvesting. Open Archives Initiative, 2001. http://www.openarchives.org/OAI/openarchivesprotocol.htm.

26. S. Chen, C. Choo, and Y. Chow, Internet Security: A Novel Role/Object-Based Access Control for Digital Libraries, Journal of Organizational Computing and Electronic Commerce, Lawrence Erlbaum Publisher, under revision.

27. InterPARES Project, http://www.interpares.org/rws/login.cfm?accessdenied=%2Frws%2Findex%2Ecfm.

Global Memory Net: New Collaboration, New Activities and New Potentials

Ching-chih Chen

Professor, Graduate School of Library and Information Science,
Simmons College, Boston, MA 02115, USA
chen@simmons.edu

In technological terms, it has been a long time since my *PROJECT EMPEROR-I* -- a multimedia interactive videodisc project on the First Emperor of China's famous terracotta warriors and horses in 1984. At that time, *PROJECT EMPEROR-I* demonstrated that multimedia technology could change the way we seek, demand, and use information. Two decade later, fueled by enormous progress in science and technology, we have come a very long way from the use of interactive multimedia technology in the workstation environment to the global networked environment. We have moved from the use of hardcopy and analog resources to digital content, which users can search, retrieve and use instantly to meet their needs over the global network with no national boundaries. We have also moved from the offering of multimedia content of one specific subject topic to the digital content of all media formats on all related subject topics to the world instantly. We are truly living in a new period of unprecedented opportunities and challenges [1]! So, in this digital era, we have witnessed the exciting convergence of content, technology, and global collaboration in the development of digital libraries [2] with great potential for providing universal information access.

Thus, today's information seekers, regardless whether they are general public, school children, or those from research and higher education communities seek information for education, research, entertainment, or enrichment in very different ways from before. From the information resources point of views, the old model of "owning" a collection has given way to "sharing," and the new emphases have shifted from possessing large "physical libraries" to "virtual libraries" digitally distributed all over the world.

In the last two decades, I have experienced much of these transformations up-close and personal through my own R&D activities – from the creation of interactive videodisc and multimedia CD in the 80s and 90s to leading a current international digital library project, *Global Memory Net*, supported by the International Digital Library Program of the US National Science Foundation [2, 3].

Global Memory Net and Recent Development

From PROJECT EMPEROR-I to Chinese Memory Net to Global Memory Net

In the early 80s, the by-product of *PROJECT EMPEROR-I's* is a set of interactive videodisc, called *The First Emperor of China*, content of which later was converted to

Z. Chen et al. (Eds.): ICADL 2004, LNCS 3334, pp. 73–83, 2004.

a popular multimedia CD product of the same title in 1991 and published by the Voyager Company. The core image collection of this product together with the extensive descriptive annotations (later known as metadata) of these resources has become the core collection of *Chinese Memory Net (CMNet)* which I proposed to NSF's International Digital Library Program (NSF/IDLP) in 1999, and funded from 2000.

The NSF's supported *CMNet* since 2000 is intended to develop a model for international collaboration with various R&D activities in digital libraries. It hopes to accomplish "more" with "less," avoid duplication efforts, and capitalize R&D results from other major funded digital library R&D projects. *CMNet*'s Chinese partners are Peking University, Shanghai Jiaotong University and Tsinghua University. Although we did not achieve one of the original goals in bringing the digital contents available in our partner institutions together, in the short four years, it has made progress in developing collaborative infrastructure for digital library development. Both *CMNet* and my *NIT 2001 conference* in Beijing played important role in fueling the development of digital libraries in China [4].

While building the digital library community and infrastructure, *CMNet* also started the labor-intensive R&D activity in content and metadata building. This activity has paid off because these invaluable image resources and metadata have formed attractive basis for a number of exciting and productive technology-oriented collaborative works with computer scientists, such as a few listed in the following with more complete reference provided in [5, 6]:

- Open Archive Initiative (OAI) research,
- Intelligent agent and text-based image retrieval [7, 8],
- Semantic sensitive content-based image retrieval [9],
- Digital video using the Informedia technologies [10], and
- Machine learning for annotation [11].

Once it is possible to develop a multimedia digital library in one subject disciplinary or for one geographical area, it is upward scalable to include more subject topics and bigger geographical areas. This was the case with the expansion of the scope of *CMNet* to *GMNet since 2002*. *GMNet* developed out of the *CMNet* project which concentrates on images and video related to China's ancient culture. In the last two years, more collaboration with several major institutions in different countries has become a reality and thus *CMNet* is changed to *Global Memory Net*. It is being expanded to cover the 'memory' of other parts of the globe [3].

As shown in Figure 1, the tentative *GMNet* homepage, *GMNet* literally has space holder for all countries in the world although this tentative homepage has listed tentatively only a few continents and countries under each at this moment.

The Scope of Global Memory Net

The name of *Global Memory Net* clearly articulates both the potential coverage and scope of this project [1, 2, 3]:

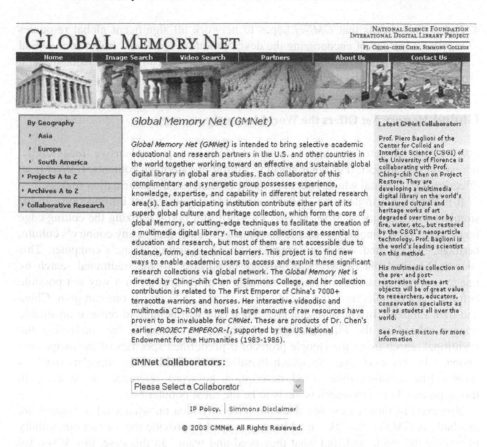

Fig. 1. Home Page of the Global Memory Net

1. **Global** – It means global coverage.
2. **Memory** – "Memory" refers to all types of treasures, thus *GMNet* has the structure to cover all kinds of invaluable memories related to culture, heritage, history, art, music, science, technology, medicine, etc. However, at this initial stage, and with initial entry of the extensive visual memory related the First Emperor of China's terracotta warriors and horses, *GMNet* is focused on the world significant cultural, historical, and heritage materials. Once this focus is well underway, *GMNet* will expand to cover other kinds of "memories."
3. **Memory** – "Memory" refers to all types of treasures, thus *GMNet* has the structure to cover all kinds of invaluable memories related to culture, heritage, history, art, music, science, technology, medicine, etc. However, at this initial stage, and with initial entry of the extensive visual memory related the First Emperor of China's terracotta warriors and horses, *GMNet* is focused on the world significant cultural, historical, and heritage materials. Once this focus is well underway, *GMNet* will expand to cover other kinds of "memories."

4. **Net** – This means that *GMNet* hopes to network all significant global resources together. Instead of encouraging the development of small and fragmented digital libraries, it hopes to be a networked portal to offer needed resources instantly with the simple click of the mouse.

Global *Memory Net* Offers the World Instantly

For the First Emperor of China's content, *GMNet* is a comprehensive image digital library on that subject. For other world's cultural and heritage contents, *GMNet* is an effective digital portal which offers the world instantly to the information seekers.

It is impossible to describe all the features of in such a short introduction. In the simplest way, consider *GMNet* an easy to use digital portal utilizing the cutting edge image retrieval technology to enable one to take a visual tour of any country's culture, heritage, history, and world contributions, all while sitting at one's computer. This soon to be available *GMNet* will provide, in addition to the traditional search by image retrieval capabilities with considerable textual supports in a way not possible before. For example, from the page like that shown in Figure 1, one can go to China and then Emperor Image Base quickly. Then one will be able to retrieve invaluable images related to the First Emperor of China, for example, by conducting the traditional search using the Google protocol if predefined specifics of the images are known. In this case, one can search literally every field of the metadata, such as creator, title, location, time period, description, keyword, reference source, etc. In this approach, keyword search is likely to be the most popular one.

However, in most cases, one does not have any idea on what kind of images are available in *GMNet*. Just like in a library, we need to provide the user an opportunity to browse the stack, and find what they need and want. In this case, in *GMNet*, we powered our images' random retrieval with the cutting edge content-based image retrieval technique, SIMPLIcity, developed at the Stanford University under NSF's DL-I phase, and then at the Penn State University under NSF/ITR [Ref. 9 provides more references]. This allows users to browse, retrieve, enjoy, and learn in just seconds through multiple thousands of digital images accurately and effectively.

For example, when the icons of the images of the Emperor collection are displayed randomly in Figure 2, one spots the image related to "Han silk" of interest. In this case, one can ask the system to provide "SIMILAR" images by clicking "Similar" without typing any word, *GMNet* will display in seconds all the images in the collection similar to the one selected. This opens up all possibilities for all related maps which are totally unknown to the user (see Figure 3).

Once these massive numbers of images are displayed, one would be able to enlarge a chosen image by clicking on "larger", and multiple levels of zooming will be possible and dynamic digital water mark will be instantly generated to offer the "ownership" information of the image as shown in Figure 4. One will be able to find more textual descriptive information as well as reference sources and in some cases, full-text original source on a chosen image instantly by clicking "Info" Fig. 5).

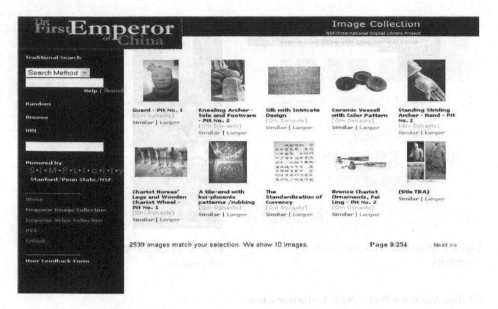

Fig. 2. Random images for user's browsing and selection

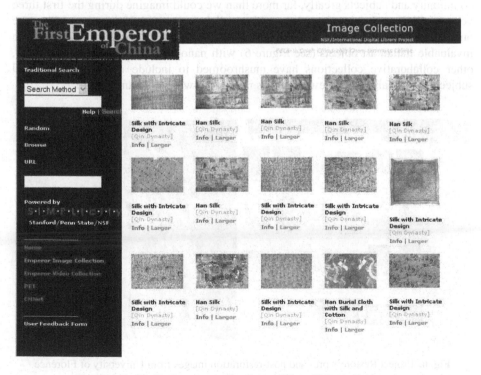

Fig. 3. Similar images on the chosen "Han silk" are displayed

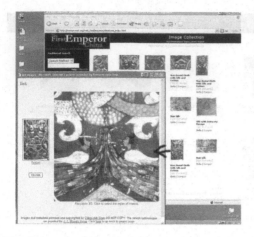

Fig. 4. Chosen image enlarged with digital watermark

Fig. 5. Metadata information is on the left column

Global Memory Net – New Collaboration

The move to *Global Memory Net* has enabled us to expand our collaborative community and subjects greatly, far more than we could imagine during the first three years of *CMNet*. Starting from our exciting collaboration with University of Florence on Project Restore [12] with the exciting pre- and post- restoration images of the invaluable Italian art objects (see Figure 6) with nano-particle chemistry technology, other collaborative collections have mushroomed to include many countries and subjects. We shall name a few examples in the following table and Figure 7:

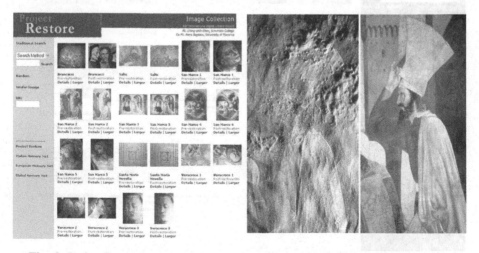

Fig. 6. Project Restore's pre- and post-restoration images from University of Florence

China - Chinese painting, many historical unique collections, architecture, etc.

- Cambodian - Ancient temples, etc.
- India - Architecture, palaces, temples, goddess, etc.
- Vietnam - Historical development of the former Saigon
- Italy - Historical artifacts
- Europe - Cathedrals, Castles, etc.
- World - Global musical instrument, national libraries, etc.

Fig. 7. Some sample image collections

In addition to these, the collaboration with the Asian Division of the Library of Congress is an exciting development. Currently we have included the unique Naxi manuscripts' images of the Library of Congress in *GMNet* (see Figure 8). In addition, we are also exploring the collaboration with Unesco's *Memory of the World* Programme. We have identified over 1000 digital collections in the world, and it is possible for us to retrieve all web sites of digital collections of similar color and design of an organization instantly, such as those of the Unesco's *Memory of the World* Programme as shown in Figure 9. Once the website is selected, information on the site can be located instantly, and the user can be linked to the

Fig. 8. Images of the unique NAXI manuscripts' can be retrieved instantly

Fig. 9. Images of Unesco's *Memory of the World* sites can be retrieved and linked instantly (in yellow)

site instantly. Currently, Unesco has 91 digital collections from 45 countries of this nature, thus, our digital portal has certainly boosted the accessibility and value of these collections instantly.

Global Memory Net – New R&D Activities

As mentioned earlier, although *GMNet* has concentrated thus far on digital image cultural and heritage collections thus far, we have already collaborated with Carnegie Mellon University in exploring the sophisticated digital video retrieval capabilities using the world renown Informedia Technologies [2,3,10], see Figure 10. The Chinese University of Hong Kong has extended the Informedia Technology capability to handle Chinese language, and we are exploring the possibility of using that.

Fig. 10. Screens from Informedia's Emperor Application

Fig. 10. Screens from Informedia's Emperor Apllication

In addition to digital videos, our research will also incorporate sound and music. One of the perfect starting points will be with the world's musical instruments. Another possible area would be with the language learning and writing.

One final mention of an exciting new activities would have to be our newly funded NSF/IDLP [NSF/IIS-Special Projects (IIS)] 2-year project from 2004-2006, entitled *"International Collaboration to Advance User-oriented Technologies for Managing and Distributing Images in Digital Libraries"* with James Z. Wang of Penn State University and Jianbo Shi of University of Pennsylvania as my co-PIs. This project will develop user-oriented image management of distribution technologies for digital libraries. An interdisciplinary team of computer and information scientists from US, China, and Taiwan will investigate efficient ways to search digital collections of images using an integrated approach. The team will use real-world digital library datasets to develop user-oriented technologies suitable for practical deployment. Notably, the research will utilize an existing collection consisting of a large quantity of images associated with The First Emperor of China's terracotta warriors and horses of all types of resolution and with enormous cultural significance as well as the existing rich descriptive information. In addition to Ontology-based image retrieval, machine learning based content-based image retrieval including, we will explore the difficult object-based partial image searches. We also hope to extend the intellectual property (IP) protection techniques.

Conclusion

During 1998-2002, I was privileged to serve on the US President's Information Technology Advisory Committee's (PITAC). Our PITAC's Digital Library Panel's Report, *Digital Libraries: Universal Access to Human Knowledge,* has a vision for digital libraries:

"All citizens anywhere anytime can use any Internet-connected digital device to search all of human knowledge. … In this vision, no class-room, group, or person is ever isolated from the world's greatest knowledge resources." [13]

This is a vision easily said than done! There are many obstacles on the road, thus we are a long way from approaching this "elusive" vision.

From "sharing" and "accessing" points of view, we must first have much more "quality" digital contents, we must collaborate internationally in content building because no one can have everything, then we must have the technology to cope with these contents, and the infrastructure to deliver, access and retrieve them [2,3]. This is what *Global Memory Net* is inspired to do specifically in content building and method development areas. The new collaboration and new R&D activities have expanded our research horizon, and have offered us great opportunities for digital library community building, for making digital collections alive and accessible, and for contemplating much more practical R&D agenda in areas of metadata standards, interoperability, scalability, retrievability of difficult multimedia contents, and usability of these resources for knowledge creation.

Acknowledgments

Chinese Memory Net and *Global Memory Net* is supported by the US NSF/IDLP under grant no. IIS-9905833.   PROJECT EMPEROR-I was supported by the

Humanities in Libraries Program of the US National Endowment for the Humanities. Examples given on the use of SIMPLIcity is a collaboration with James Z. Wang of the Penn State University whose work is supported by the NSF/ITR program under grant no. IIS-0219271.

References

1. Chen, Ching-chih, "Global Memory Net Offers Users the World Instantly," Library Times International, 21 (1): 1-4 (July 2004)
2. Chen, Ching-chih, "The promise of international digital library collaboration for innovative use of invaluable resources," in Human Information Behaviour & Competences for Digital Libraries (Keynote in Proceedings of the Libraries in the Digital Age, May 25-29, 2004, Dubrovnik and Mljet, Croatia. pp. 7-15.
3. Chen, Ching-chih, "Global Memory Net offers the world instantly: Potentials for universal access to invaluable contents," in Proceedings of CCDL: Digital Library – Advance the Efficiency of Knowledge Utility, Beijing, September 5-8, 2004. Beijing: National Library of China, 2004.
4. Chen, Ching-chih, ed. Global Digital Library Development in the New Millennium: Fertile Ground for Distributed Cross-Disciplinary Collaboration. Beijing: Tsinghua University Press, May 2001.
5. Chen, Ching-chih, "Global Memory Net: Potential and challenges for archiving and sharing cultural and heritage resources," Proceedings of the ICDL (International Conference on Digital Libraries) 2004, Delhi, India, February 25-27, 2004. Delhi, India: TERI, 2004. pp. 3-10.
6. Chen, Ching-chih, "Past forward - Digital media for cultural heritage: The case of the Global Memory Net," Invited lecture given at the 10th Annual Lecture of Informatics, sponsored by Informatics, Bangalore, India, February 29, 2004.
7. Soo, V. W., C. Y. Lee, C. C. Lin, S. L. Chen, and Ching-chih Chen, "Automated semantic annotation and retrieval based on sharable ontology and case-based learning techniques," full-length paper accepted for present at the ACM/IEEE Joint Conference of Digital Libraries, Houston, TX, May 29, 2003. Published in Proceedings of the ACM/IEEE JCDL Conference, 2003. 12 pages.
8. Soo, V. W., C. Y. Lee, C. C. Yeh, and Ching-chih Chen, "Using sharable ontology to retrieve historical images," ACM/IEEE JCDL Proceedings, Portland, OR, July 15-18, 2002. pp. 197-198.
9. Wang, James Z., Jia Li and Ching-chih Chen, "Interdisciplinary research to advance digital imagery indexing and retrieval technologies for Asian art and cultural heritage," Proc. ACM Multimedia, Workshop on Multimedia Information Retrieval, Juan Les Pins, France, December 2002. 6 pp.
10. Wactlar, Howard D. and Ching-chih Chen, "Enhanced perspectives for historical and cultural documentaries using Informedia technologies," Proceedings of the ACM/IEEE Joint Conference of Digital Libraries, Portland, OR, July 15-18, 2002. pp. 338 – 339.
11. Wang, James Z., Kurt Grieb, and Ching-chih Chen, "Machine annotation and retrieval for Digital Imagery of Historical Materials," Submitted to Journal of Digital Libraries: Special Issue on Multimedia Contents.

12. Baglioni, Piero, Rodorico Giorgi, and Ching-chih Chen, "Nanoparticle technology saves cultural relics: Potential for a multimedia digital library," in Online Proceedings of DELOS/NSF Workshop on Multimedia Contents in Digital Libraries, Crete, Greece, June 2-3, 2003.

13. US. President's Information Technology Advisory Committee (PITAC). Digital Library Panel. Digital Libraries: Universal Access to Human Knowledge. February 2001. www.hpcc.gov/pubs/pitac/pitac-dk-9feb01.pdf

Gold at the End of the Digital Library Rainbow: Forecasting the Consequences of Truly Effective Digital Libraries

Michael A. Keller

Green Library, Stanford University, Stanford, CA 94305
makeller@stanford.edu

Abstract. This paper contemplates a truly effective digital library from the user's point of view. It will contain vast amounts of information, comparable to, but different from, the public web; it will help the user make real sense of that information by organizing, evaluating, and testing the reliability or authenticity of needed information; it will help the user manage, adapt, and reuse the information gathered. We will have to understand the digital library as both consumer of information and as publisher and partner with the scholarly author. Digital preservation is and will be a paramount concern.

Creating digital libraries is not easy or inexpensive. The literature on the subject is vast and growing, and a considerable part of that literature is concerned with architecture, design, methods of digitizing and building digital collections, meta-data for digital objects, intellectual property issues and digital rights management, and other "technical" or "professional" matters. We must not lose sight of the true goal of academic digital libraries and that is to make research and teaching better, faster, more penetrating, more intuitive, more powerful. This exhortation concerns itself with that goal and only in passing with the "technical" and "professional" matters. The metaphor of gold at the end of the rainbow is a Western literary allusion, for many of us one that is associated with Irish culture, no doubt in part because there is enough rain and sun mixed in Irish days to make rainbows more common than perhaps they are elsewhere. The problem with the metaphor is that rainbows are not constructed and operated by men, but by nature. And one who chases the rainbow to find its end is chasing an illusory goal, for it is very difficult to pin down the end of a rainbow. For many, the end of the rainbow keeps moving, resetting itself. That part of the metaphor, at least, is apropos of building digital libraries!

As this conference and many others like it attest, we, as information professionals, are challenged deeply by the practices, assumptions, and implications of an increasingly digital and global information space. In my own library, we are struggling to change the whole organizational structure in light of digital collection and service issues. Over the course of 2004, we have been working to structure our support of digital information. Bear in mind, we have been aggressively pursuing digital technologies, collections and services for perhaps two decades, but we find that the many currents and streams have become such a torrent that the very foundations of library

Z. Chen et al. (Eds.): ICADL 2004, LNCS 3334, pp. 84–94, 2004.

services require examination. It is probable we will create a Digital Services Bureau within the Stanford Libraries, separate from, but of lesser stature than, the Collections and Services and Technical Services division.

In fact, some of my staff have suggested humorously that we should rename Technical Services as the Analog Services division, in recognition that much of their work continues to revolve around the physical artifact. That may be premature, but it may be instructive. The core of what we do continues to depend on the two pillars of Collections and Services: the traditional Technical Services function shares with the Digital Services function a supporting role in making collections available to our readers and providing them with the services necessary to assure access, discovery, interpretation, and continuity to those collections. On the one hand, I have estimated that creating the Digital Services Bureau would shift the organizational position of perhaps 25 individuals. On the other hand, the changes implied by this reorganization will directly influence the working environment for the other 350 or so staff.

I will address here some issues pertaining to "a truly effective digital library" (per the title of this presentation), but the first thing to say is that a truly effective digital library will not be entirely digital: it will complement, supplement, enrich, and inform collections that remain, for whatever reason, in analog form, whether that form is cuneiform tablet, parchment manuscript, silk scroll, printed book, silver-halide image, annotated typescript, or magnetic tape. The original of a text, to the extent it can be preserved, needs to be preserved and kept accessible for scholarly use. After we digitize it, of course.

For some years, I have been referring to the "both/and" dilemma: we must maintain our collection development and services for printed books and serials, while also growing (both by acquisition and creation) our digital collections and services, despite the relatively static budgets universities have provided. The "both/and" dilemma is shifting: we will be buying more digital material and less analog material. But the dilemma will, if anything, become more pointed in these coming years of the early digital age: we must not only spend on digital services and materials, we must continue to acquire what exists only as analog material. Concurrently we must digitize collections and preserve digital materials. At the same time, we must also retain access to the hardcopy, as a safeguard and as an alternate form of access. The stacks in libraries are not going away anytime soon. My provost wishes to believe the digital age will decimate the space needs of the campus libraries; it is my duty to contradict those wishes.

Three Key Aspects of the Digital Library

Let us look briefly at a truly effective digital library from the user's point of view. In the first place, it will provide truly vast amounts of information. The public web now contains an unaccountably large volume of information – Google indexes over four billion pages, and worries rightly that it doesn't access nearly enough content. The digital library I envision contains a similar or larger scale of information not presently on the Web at all.

In the second place, the effective digital library – very much unlike the public web, despite the Googles of the world – helps the user make real sense of that vast amount of information. It not only helps retrieve, but organize, evaluate, and test the reliability or authenticity of needed information.

In the third place, the effective digital library will help the user manage, adapt, and reuse the information gathered. In fact, we will have to understand the digital library as both consumer of information and as publisher, or at least as a form of partner with the scholarly author.

The remainder of this talk will expand these three aspects. First, though, we as information professionals must ponder something the user probably assumes or ignores: preservation. We know that digital collections, while inherently reproducible, are also inherently unstable and at risk of catastrophic loss. I will not dwell here on the fundamental mandate for us to preserve the digital collections we assemble, but I wish you to bear in mind this mandate critically influences nearly everything we do.

Building Digital Collections

Unlike conventional collections, digital collections may be accumulated in four ways:

- **by Purchase** - we may buy digital sets much as we do books or serials. Doing so, creates the need to house the materials on our servers or other technology. It also provides us with control, but the corollary is that we hold the responsibility not only for preservation, but also for format migration, an issue that will come to occupy much of our attention in years to come.

- **by Licensing** – The popular rubric is "access, not ownership." This is an important and attractive – indeed inevitable – method of providing information to our readers/users. The downside, of course, is that we in the library pay, but have no say or control in the long-term access to the licensed content. If a publisher (here using that term to mean the provider of licensed content, whatever it calls itself) decides to increase its prices arbitrarily, if it removes content, if it goes out of business, the library has little option, and its prior investment is for naught. On the other hand, issues such as format migration, archiving, and hosting remain with the publisher, thus limiting the managerial complexity to the library. It may be a pact with the devil.

- **by scanning** or other digitization means - There are many mass book digitization schemes afoot today – I am deeply in discussion with several parties about this effort – each of which is hampered by financial, technological and intellectual property (copyright) issues. We hope that key libraries will be able to undertake mass digitization projects so as to make millions of books available to the world in digital form. Whether this is something practical within the next few years, as opposed to a decade or more hence, has yet to be determined, but I am confident that there will be successful mass digitization efforts to the benefit of the world's readers sooner or later. And the impact of such an expansion of access to the world's literatures is almost incalculable and tremendously exciting. But under any scenario, there will be a tremendous volume of material held by collections that will not be covered by such mass schemes: there is a great deal of locally unique material. I think there is at least as much promise in digitizing local, rare, manuscript, media, and other special collections as there is in converting general collections. And the quantities are enormous.

- **by Exchange** – Collaboration among libraries in collection access can acquire a tremendous life of its own in the digital age, dependent on, of course, and limited by copyright and related issues. If your institution has digitized a half-million works, and my institution has digitized some similar volume in a different range of subject areas, we may strike a barter agreement, either by exchanging data (and thereby beginning to address digital preservation concerns) or by exchanging the right for our users to access the other's collection. The Digital Library Federation, of which I am pleased to be an active member, is currently planning a Distributed Online Digital Library, or DODL, the premise of which is to make the digital holdings of each participating library available to the others' user community. I suggest you track our progress with this cooperative model. Needless to say, there are many other collaborative models in discussion at present, some of which are reported upon in this conference.

We know from many sources, not least of which is the "E-Journal User Study" that Stanford conducted with support of the Andrew W. Mellon Foundation a few years ago, that scholars are extremely interested in depth and breadth of the serial literatures.[1] We know from usage logs of the HighWire Press client publications that, while the number of clicks on a given article taper off very rapidly after publication, the number of clicks does not go to zero. Rather, there is what statisticians call a very long tail to the usage curve. One of the primary desiderata for e-journal users is online access to the backset, to old issues of journals, in some cases back the full history of the journal. And, of course, they want the same flexibility of searching, linking, viewing options they have come to rely on for the current issues of the same journals. The demand is there, I assure you.

We are spending a great deal already on digital resources, though in ways I find almost reprehensible, as I have argued elsewhere.[1] As reported in the most recent *Charleston Report* (v 9, no. 1), a recent report by ARL (the Association of Research Libraries) notes that expenditures on electronic resources between FY95 and FY02 for the typical university research library grew nearly 400% to almost $1.4 million. During the same period the overall library materials expenditures grew 61%. Electronic journals accounted for 92% of the e-resource expenditures in FY02 and 26% of the library's overall serials expenditures, up from 5% in FY95. Expenditures on electronic books or other one-time purchases account for less than 4% of current monographic expenditures.[2]

---

[1] See: http://ejust.stanford.edu

At Stanford, we are also dedicating increasing proportion of our internal effort to digitizing materials – at the rate currently of hundreds of thousands of documents and thousands of books a year. Although this is not the place to go into detail, I have been very deeply involved in trying to increase the rate of digitization efforts and funding for such efforts, by several orders of magnitude. I believe we are on the threshold of a revolution in conversion of analog content to digital form. Frankly, the problem space – which began as mainly technical – focuses even more on intellectual property issues than on funding. I think you will see some exciting headlines in this area in the next months or at most years.

Making Sense of Digital Collections

We know quite a bit about how users find research material, online and otherwise, and we can say that the digital age introduces literally unimagined possibilities for discovery and analysis. Clearly, we do not know enough about how users behave and which tools of the future they will embrace. Here are just a few of the potentially profound issues having to do with making one's way through the literatures:

- Searching vs. browsing
- Searching across genres, across collections, across institutions, across artificial boundaries – even across the digital-analog frontier
- Searching tools: Google et al. work where they work, and fail dismally otherwise.
- Controlled vs. uncontrolled lexicons
- Taxonomic vs. text searching
- Organizing search results, including visualization tools
- Saving, as well as refreshing, search results – both links and content
- Annotating search results persistently
- Using technology to make value judgments, e.g., to favor trusted sources and suppress dubious material in transparent and controllable ways
- Text analysis
- Image analysis
- Linking of references within the literatures, especially Toll-Free Linking
- Social evaluation of literature – knowing how many others have read or cited a work and even knowing who those readers are (notwithstanding issues of privacy)
- Alert services and other customized means of selective dissemination of information.

We cannot delve into all of these issues at this time, but the messages I would leave you with are that:

- Digital discovery is very much in its infancy.
- Despite some seminal work, at Yahoo, at Google, and even within the library-supported areas of abstracting and indexing and other subscription-driven resources, librarians have not assumed a leadership role to date in developing discovery methods or interpreting user needs and behaviors for developers.

• Librarians can and should have a vital role in helping to develop, test, and promulgate emerging modes of digital discovery. Not to do so would be a real loss to the academy, to the profession, and to the world at large.

Let me focus on searching for a moment, as much of what is listed above bears on what we understand generally as searching. If I wish to search a query exhaustively at Stanford, depending on the discipline, I may need to conduct dozens of separate queries, using dozens of user interfaces, dozens of search rules or conventions. And each search result will come up in a different form, in a separate page, with different caveats as to coverage, currency, depth, etc. Some of the separate search results will be more relevant than others, of course, but some will be filled with spurious hits or duplicates or dead links or links to sources I am not allowed to view. And, of course, no matter how diligent I am using the considerable wealth of sources available to me at Stanford, the probability is low that my efforts will be truly exhaustive.

Despite our efforts as librarians and information professionals to provide controlled and competent tools to our users, the net result is fundamentally uncontrolled and uncontrollable, just like the public web. As some of my colleagues enjoy saying, "Get used to it." The price of vastly increasing access to information in an "information age" is reduction of control.

Please do not misunderstand me: I do not advocate a chaotic information space; in fact, I strongly support our utmost diligence in assisting our readers/users to navigate, understand, and exploit information in relatively controlled ways. But I also think we need to be clear that the library traditions of highly controlled information spaces is a dying anachronism.

The key idea, I believe, is not to try to control the information space, as we used to, but rather to try to provide the user with an armamentarium of tools and techniques to forge a path of meaning through the sector of the information space they wish to explore. Specifically, we need to provide better searching capabilities to our readers. For starters, the tools we offer on our home pages, the OPAC catalog searches and the like, need to become a great deal more powerful. Federated searching, a fancy way of saying searching multiple databases at once, really must become the rule, rather than the exception, such that we don't force the user to predict where the material of interest is hidden or what form of ownership it takes. It is a simple and fundamental point, and one that we can influence, in developing services and encouraging our system and service vendors to improve. There will be much behind-the-scenes development of search standards, proxy management, and like technical support for federated searching. I do not think its importance can be overemphasized.

There will also be a great deal of organizational cooperation to make federated searching more effective. Let me mention the DODL in the context of cross-institutional discovery, retrieval, and sharing. Even though the DODL is not yet underway (early technical meetings are ongoing), the very fact that a dozen institutions are committed to trying to develop some means of crossing boundaries is an encouraging sign. I look forward to the day – perhaps not too far in the distance – when a researcher at Stanford can find and retrieve a digital text from, say, Virginia, without even realizing that it was not local.

Taxonomic indexing, as an adjunct to uncontrolled term searching, is a challenging, but very valuable method of organizing a literature. The easiest way to explain it is to show an example, and the HighWire Press topic map serves well.[2] By clicking on "TopicMap" at the lower center of the HighWire home page, we see graphically the relatedness among topics, clusters of meaningful likeness, and a means of understanding relations among sub disciplines. This topic map – shared among the 361 journals supported by HighWire – was built by one person, an ex-cataloger, and accommodates some 1.4 million articles. Note also there are over 54,000 topics in this relational set – a relatively literal "web of science." Populating these topics has required a great deal of coordination with the publishers, but it is in essence an automated process, and one we think very powerful and promising.

Next, sorting and making sense of the search result are vital areas. At Stanford, for example, we are in the middle of a year-long joint development with a software producer called Groxis to provide another visual aid in organizing search results. Their product is called Grokker.[3]

Compare a Grokker set map, a visualization of a search result, against the now-traditional set of search results: it is virtually impossible to get a sense of the hundreds or thousands of hits from the latter, all one can do is scroll through a page at a time. As a means of finding a known site or a common fact, this is a fine technique – I am sure we have all been pleasantly surprised to find the one page we need at the top of the Google search result list. But as a means of understanding an information space or a range of sources, it is completely inadequate.

Let me mention in passing that Grokker allows a form of federated searching and enables handling several sorts of data to coexist and be managed together by the user.

We can understand the taxonomic or topic map as a form of browsing, as opposed to searching. We know that browsing – more or less in its traditional definition independent of Web "browsers"- is a valued and productive form of library discovery. For a century and more, we have been putting like together with like in the hope that this collocation assists the reader. That is still an important aspect of the digital age. For example, a recent article in the *New York Times* [3] talks to this point: "the Internet cannot replace many of the built-in benefits of the library, like browsing the stacks for related information that could add spark and depth to an essay or a report." That article goes on to discuss tools being developed at Berkeley and at IBM to assist "cross-linking" descriptive elements of collections, in the case of Berkeley's Flamenco system, and to explore use of a "collection layer" in organizing folders and files and links, in the IBM example. I think we will see a great deal of important growth in ways to simulate the human capacity for association, fuzzy logic and sets, and partial or sloppy matching of ideas, as opposed to matching of terms, which is much of what we have available now.

A critical element in facilitating research is citation linking. This is something HighWire Press has emphasized in its e-journal services since 1995, and our research verifies that users value this extremely highly. Good scholarship requires checking

---

[2] http://highwire.Stanford.edu
[3] Grokker can be downloaded at http://www.groxis.com

and rechecking, including examination of worked cited by other scholars. Given the explosive growth of all the literatures in recent decades, resulting in the literal impossibility for scholars to cover all the relevant literatures, making it easy to get to referenced citations is absolutely critical to scholarly productivity. Thus, with HighWire, not only can the reader get from a reference in one article to the full text of that article in another journal with a single click, her or she may do so without charge, actually free to the reader, and whether or not the scholar otherwise has access rights to the journal in which the cited article appears. This is genuinely profound, and I am extremely proud that HighWire led this development. Of course, this requires both technology and a rethinking of stakeholder interests, but it is certainly the only way to go. There are rumors currently that JSTOR is about to re-code its whole system and corpus of literature so citation linking can be accomplished, and I fervently hope the rumors are true. I have long felt that the lack of such linking has compromised the utility or even viability of the otherwise exemplary JSTOR model.

Another form of assessing one's potential interest in a particular source is learning how many others (and perhaps who) have made use of it. This is actually a very popular and common technique: vide the New York Times Best Seller List, amazon.com reader reviews and rankings, Oprah Winfrey's Book Club list, and simple word of mouth. In fact, this is the dominant mode of evaluating literature in the general public: "Everybody's reading it"; "This summer's must-read novel"; even, "Soon to be a major motion picture." These are absolutely rational determinants (even if they are easily manipulated by marketers) for deciding what to pick up from the airport bookshop. And while this does not sound dignified enough for the scholarly realm, analogous methods could be used in our world. If I knew that the futurist Paul Saffo and the business guru Tom Peters both have studied a certain new book on information practices, you can be fairly sure I would make it my business to check it out. If I knew that Stanford electrical engineer Stephen Boyd personally subscribes to a certain journal, I would certainly advise my friend's daughter, a promising young engineer, to start reading it. If I were an ambitious graduate student in bio-informatics casting about for promising research areas, I would be very interested in what Stanford's Doug Brutlag has been reading lately, whether or not he cites it in recent research results. We all need to know what is hot, whether deservedly or not.

Thus, social aspects of the literatures are important. We as research librarians have all but ignored this – our colleagues in public libraries buying multiple copies of best sellers are far ahead of us in this respect. We do have some tools, however, such as the concept of knowledge communities. At Stanford, we have worked with publishers and scholars to develop several Knowledge Environments, which support in various ways the idea of virtual knowledge communities.[4] I believe there is much more we could do in this area, ranging from statistical reporting on demand ("this item has been downloaded 34 times this quarter") to supporting peer-to-peer communications based on the literatures. Amazon.com does this extremely well, and it would be tragic for us as librarians to ignore these models of success.

---

[4] See, for instance: http://stke.sciencemag.org

Another form of discovery that works well – both for Amazon and for HighWire Press – is individual email with readers, based on sign ups for alerting services, whether periodical – e.g., advance Tables of Contents– or topical, e.g., abstracts of newly published articles that may be of interest to me, based on preferences I established. Within a few years, major research institutions will be adding access to multiple millions of digital objects a year – databases, articles, books, images, models, syllabi, drafts, presentations, etc. If we don't have means in place to notify users of material they may need , but not know about in advance, no amount of search capability can enable them to keep up with this onslaught. There is a huge opportunity for us, and one that our traditional efforts in this area cannot begin to address.

Integrating Digital Material

Perhaps for the best of reasons, librarians have really not started to think very much about the results of research except in the context of published results. Let's take a look for a moment at what we may call the traditional scholarly cycle:

- Scholar performs research (including examination of literature via the library)
- Scholar writes paper
- Scholar submits paper to journal (or book to editor)
- Editor manages peer review, editing, format, etc.
- Publisher publishes paper or book
- Libraries subscribe to journal or buy book
- Libraries make materials accessible, discoverable, etc. – perhaps by subscribing to discover services – so that cycle can begin again

There are other, somewhat similar, cycles for student papers, conference proceedings, and other essential elements in academia.

As we have seen over the past few years, this cycle is under attack, in large part because certain publishers – and I emphasize certain publishers, particularly European for-profit publishers, but not the scholarly society publishers – have extracted obscene profits with outrageous subscription price increases. Certain others, including scholars and bureaucrats, have countered by promoting alternate publication models, taking some slight advantage of the fact that online editions eliminate printing and mailing costs. As many of you may be aware I strongly support the publication models of responsible publishers, mainly not-for-profit scholarly societies, such as those that use the Stanford HighWire Press service for online editions. I also advocate and show by example resistance to the "big deals" and escalating pricing of those certain other publishers, in other words, to encourage libraries not to remain hapless and passive victims of commercial predation.

But what I wish to emphasize here is another kind of activism, namely, the active role libraries can and should have in the future of the scholarly cycle. Here is one scenario among many to illustrate the role of a more active and effective digital library:

- Scholar searches online digital information acquired or created by library, using discovery tools, such as federated or taxonomic searching, provided by library.
- Scholar organizes search results using visualization tools provided by library.
- Scholar organizes and stores digital information in library-provided online work-space. Library-supported tool allows local, remote, and original materials to be handled in common, secure, flexible environment.
- Scholar uses digital tools provided by library to extract, model, reformat, and embed earlier digital information in work, which becomes the "research paper."
- Scholar posts draft "paper" to library-supported institutional repository, along with supporting data and literature, and makes them available to specific colleagues.
- Scholar revises "paper" and releases final version to the repository and the public.
- A virtual electronic journal, after a review process, links to the library repository as the published edition of record, and the library provides various kinds of access to the paper and its supporting documents.

Note that the scholar in this scenario may or may not physically visit the library. The scholar may or may not have discussed what material is of interest with library curators. The key materials may be primary source documents, digital representations of primary source documents, private notes, or the research literatures. They may be texts, hypertexts, databases, visual materials, models, simulations, or some other carrier of information. Indeed, the scholar may not fully realize.

Conclusion

Our traditional measures of library services and, indeed, library empires – e.g., the infamous ARL annual statistics – are absolutely silent on effectiveness. At best, most of us conduct an occasional "satisfaction" survey. Such surveys are important and reveal some interesting insights, but the brutal truth is we librarians have never yet begun to measure results. That may persist into the digital age.

I come back to the user or reader as the measure of a truly effective digital library. We could stipulate as an easy approximation that a truly effective digital library is one in which the user gets what he or she needs or wants. It should be clear to you that I do not think this begins to address the challenge. Perhaps the right measure is something like this:

The truly effective digital library is one which anticipates, addresses, and tests, the way scholars seek, understand, handle, store, annotate, synthesize, manipulate, and publish information such that it is integral, whether or not visible, to the entire scholarly enterprise and supports the productivity of scholars' research, thinking and expression.

In sum, the truly effective digital library, freed in part from the shackles of physicality, is the information infrastructure of the academy, not a support service, but rather the backbone of intellectual effort, whether applied to teaching, learning, or research. I don't know whether libraries are capable of this transcendent mission, and I know I can at best dimly understand its implications, but I am fairly sure that is what constitutes a truly effective digital library.

94   M.A. Keller

References

1. Keller, M. Casting Forward: collection development after mass digitization. Fiesole Collection Development Retreat, March 18th 2004
   http://digital.casalini.it/retreat/2004_docs/KellerMichael.pdf
2. E-Journals Take Lion's Share of E-Resource Budgets. *ARL Bimonthly Report* 235, August 2004 http://www.arl.org/newsltr/235/snapshot.html.
3. Eisenberg, A. Making a Web Search Feel Like a Stroll in the Library. *New York Times*, August 19, 2004.

Information Retrieval Challenges
for Digital Libraries

Edie Rasmussen

School of Library, Archival and Information Studies,
University of British Columbia,
Vancouver, BC, Canada V6T 1Z3
edie.rasmussen@ubc.ca

Abstract. Information retrieval is an important component of digital libraries, and there is a high degree of synergy between the two research communities. Much of the current research in information retrieval is potentially relevant to digital libraries, and digital libraries present a challenging environment in which to incorporate new information retrieval methods.

1 Introduction

There is a strong relationship between the information retrieval (IR) research community and the digital library (DL) research community; for example, the Joint Conference on Digital Libraries is co-sponsored by the ACM Special Interest Group in Information Retrieval, and the programs of digital library conferences such as this one include many papers on information retrieval as it relates to digital libraries. Given this synergy, it would appear that digital library developers have the opportunity to incorporate the best results of information retrieval research, combining it with the knowledge on access developed over years of library automation. However, in their study of the information retrieval functions offered by 20 digital libraries, Chowdhury and Chowdhury, found that "Boolean, proximity and truncation search facilities are commonly available" and that "most digital libraries do not allow users to enter natural language search expressions" [4]. Their results suggest that retrieval in the digital library owes more to the models underlying the current generation of OPACs (online public access catalogues) in use in libraries than to the state of the art in information retrieval.

What has the information retrieval research community to offer to digital library developers, and what challenges does the digital library environment present for information retrieval researchers? A study of IR research suggests some of the factors that have hindered and helped adoption in the past. Much of the current research in IR is very relevant to digital libraries, but there are additional areas in which research is needed.

Z. Chen et al. (Eds.): ICADL 2004, LNCS 3334, pp. 95–103, 2004.
© Springer-Verlag Berlin Heidelberg 2004

2 Early Information Retrieval Research

At the system level, the goals of the ideal information retrieval system (IRS) are straightforward: to provide, in response to a query, all the useful documents (measured as recall), only the useful documents (measured as precision), to prioritize the documents by their value to the searcher, and to perform the retrieval function in a timeframe which is virtually imperceptible to the user. At the user level, the system should interact with the searcher in a meaningful way to help achieve these goals, and produce results which can be interpreted by the searcher in the context of the information need (for example, through visualization, summarization, organization, and question-answering).

Computer-based information retrieval research, as a field of endeavour concerned with the performance of information retrieval systems, took, at least initially, a "black box" view of IR, and resulted in some significant successes at the system level. These successes were achieved largely by minimizing or ignoring the goals of system design at the user level. As a simplifying assumption, a number of other important aspects of the information retrieval process were eliminated from consideration, as summarized in Table 1. For instance, for perhaps the first 30 years of endeavour, the assumption was made that information was equivalent to textual documents, excluding the information value and retrieval issues associated with images, video and sound. After some early attempts to deal with the semantics of documents, it was found more convenient---and, in terms of the results achieved, acceptable---to reduce textual documents to the so-called "bag of words", in which documents were treated, for the purpose of retrieval, as if they contained words which were independent of context and semantics. The problem of document representation or indexing was reduced to a statistical process, in which term importance was derived from frequency of occurrence and distribution across documents, and matching and ranking documents against a query was derived from term co-occurrence in document and query. Information retrieval was treated as a static process, with no query development or change, and feedback was incorporated largely as an automatic process. To accomplish IR system evaluation, success in meeting the goals of recall and precision was measured on an aggregate rather than an individual basis, and very little failure analysis for individual queries or types of queries was performed.

Table 1. Characteristics of early IR Research

- Assumes information = textual documents
- Reduces documents to "bag of words"
- Assumes indexing is a statistical process
- Emphasizes "processor" (matching) component
- Treats IR as a static process
- Considers feedback to be an automatic process
- Measures success on an aggregate, rather than individual, basis
- Ignores failures

Given the complexity of the information retrieval process, and despite this remarkably simplified view of it, significant progress was made toward solving a difficult problem. Systems based on this classic approach to IR provide very reasonable results, showing that these automated, non-semantic approaches carry us a surprisingly long way. Moreover, the very rigidity of the model made it possible to establish an evaluation paradigm, which in turn led to rigorous testing and system comparisons, a major factor in refining information retrieval system performance.

Major contributions from this era of system-centred information retrieval include the pre-eminence of a range of statistical models for describing text, which were quickly shown to be better than the early Boolean models. These include the vector space model, probabilistic model, and more recently, language models [2,9]. Output ranked in order of predicted relevance has emerged as the preferred mode of presentation of results, and relevance feedback, though much less commonly implemented, has been shown to provide significant improvements in original results. An evaluation paradigm was developed based on the so-called "Cranfield model", using a test collection of some reasonable size, standard queries, known relevance judgments and standard performance measures. Although unrealistic, these controlled conditions in laboratory experiments have led to continuing improvements in system performance. A close knit research community with a culture of shared retrieval tools, including search engines such as SMART, InQuery, Okapi and Lemur, has also promoted information retrieval research and development.

After steady progress over the first 30 years of information retrieval research, there was some evidence of a plateau. Performance improvements, though significant, were increasingly difficult to achieve. Moreover, the results which had been achieved in the laboratory tended to remain there. There were almost no implementations at the operational level, since the major database vendors continued to rely on traditional Boolean models, while in libraries, OPACs lagged one or two generations behind the database vendors in terms of search techniques. Analyses of this disconnect with the commercial world suggested at least two major problems: first, that researchers had failed to communicate their work effectively to the industrial sector, and second, that they had not convincingly proven the scalability of their methods, since test collections tended to be small, with the largest around 50,000 documents, and containing abstracts rather than full text---far smaller than the commercial databases then available [6,10]. Skepticism about scalability applied not only to the problem of achieving a rapid response rate on systems serving hundreds of users, but perhaps more importantly, to the performance levels which could be achieved with databases several orders of magnitude larger than those on which the retrieval techniques had been demonstrated.

3   An Information Retrieval Revolution

This low point in information retrieval research was followed by what amounted to an IR revolution during the 1990's. The information retrieval techniques which had been developed in laboratory-like conditions were validated through large-scale experimentation, through implementation on the World Wide Web, and through limited adoption by some library OPACs. The new visibility of information retrieval attracted researchers in the academic and commercial sectors. At the same time, the funding and publicity surrounding digital libraries suggested another new environment for information retrieval research.

A significant factor in establishing the credibility of modern information retrieval techniques was the annual TREC (Text REtrieval Conference)[1] series, in which participants from academia, government, and industry met to discuss system performance on a structured set of IR tasks. By providing the infrastructure to conduct systematic laboratory experiments on a large scale, with large volumes (gigabytes) of text, large number of queries, and relevance judgments on pooled retrieved documents, TREC was able to demonstrate scalability, and the use of a common testbed also resulted in significant performance improvements [11,14]. The results for the basic retrospective retrieval task (called ad hoc retrieval in TREC) were validated, and as performance improvements leveled off, this task was "retired" in 2000 as other retrieval tasks were added to the research agenda. As a forum for discussion and debate, TREC also resulted in community building and the technology transfer which had been notably missing in the 1980s.

With infrastructure and a community of researchers addressing the same set of tasks, the scope of TREC was broadened as new tasks or 'tracks' were added. At various times, these included cross-language retrieval, spoken document retrieval, question-answering, high precision retrieval, document summarization and categorization, novelty, and interactive retrieval, among others [14].

As TREC was providing validation and community, a new IR environment emerged with the World Wide Web, presenting a new set of challenges. The characteristics of the Web as an information retrieval environment were quite different from the homogenous document collections of the past. This highly distributed, redundant collection of materials embodies multiple formats, languages and cultures and adds new information in the form of hyperlinks. It is highly dynamic, growing and changing frequently. The characteristics of its users are also different: with users at all skill and knowledge levels, with a wide range of information needs, and an expectation of instant gratification, the Web has created a new group of active searchers, whose searching patterns have been extensively studied [12].

Web search engines moved quickly to incorporate and validate many experimental IR techniques. Early search engines built on readily available algorithms and implementation techniques published in journal articles and monographs. A second generation of search engines found ways to take advantage of the additional information and structure of Web pages, adding new techniques using the information in hyperlinks, networked pages, and anchor text. The Web proved to be an excellent large scale testbed to demonstrate the viability of information retrieval techniques, and as a wholly new environment with freely

---

[1] http://trec.nist.gov/

available, unregulated content, it lacked the inherent risks and costs of conversion which had impeded adoption of new techniques in the commercial sector. The Web provides a venue for experimental systems and prototypes in which researchers can not only describe, but also demonstrate new IR techniques for summarization, question-answering, and multimedia IR, spurring further research. And in the process, it has created a new generation of searchers, who view retrieval not as a formal, structured experience, perhaps to be delegated to experts, but as a casual, daily occurrence which they are comfortable undertaking.

4 Information Retrieval for Digital Libraries

Digital libraries present still another new environment for information retrieval, presenting new and different challenges and an expanded research agenda. Some of these challenges arise from the nature of the content in digital libraries, others from the nature of the tasks performed in them, and others from the characteristics of the users of digital libraries.

Like the Web, digital libraries incorporate mixed data types. The data may be structured, semi structured, or unstructured; and incorporate text, images, video, and audio information. Information retrieval from this mix of structure and formats is relatively unstudied, since research has usually been based on an assumption of a homogenous collection, and metadata, where available, has been treated as unstructured text. How do we incorporate evidence from these multiple sources to create an ordered list?

Since digital libraries are by definition often distributed or federated systems, another level of complexity is added by the need to make retrieval from multiple sites and multiple collections transparent to the user. Given multiple sites, we need to give priority for search to sites with the highest probability of success. Searching on multiple sites leads to a data fusion problem as the system must integrate and rank information from different datasets, with different data and metadata.

Global in nature, digital libraries may include documents in many different languages, and users may wish to query them in still others. Most information retrieval techniques are based on the statistics of the occurrence of words and word stems, and were originally developed for English. Research on multi-lingual and cross-lingual IR has been conducted on several languages, especially French, Spanish Russian, and the CJK (Chinese, Japanese and Korean) languages, and recently on Arabic. But there are many other languages to explore, and further research is needed to develop successful algorithms for them [8]. A lack of testbeds and parallel corpora hampers research in the less common languages.

Research in the retrieval of documents in non-textual formats such as image, video, speech, sound, and music has grown considerably in the last ten years. Work on content-based information retrieval (CBIR), in which information is extracted automatically from an image or sound file, has resulted in new search functions. However this work has focused on low-level document features which can easily be identified---in the case of images, usually colour, texture, and shape---and there is a difference between the kinds of queries users would like to pose, based on conceptual or emotive aspects of the document, and the kinds of queries which systems are able to answer. To provide this kind of conceptual information, some systems rely on text associated with the image, for example text surrounding the image location, or the anchor text. The challenge for digital libraries is to develop better ways to incorporate all available information regarding non-textural documents, as well as to add value to them through the use of appropriate metadata.

Recent trends include the use of relevance feedback to add information to image documents, and the use of free text captioning, often by users of the collection. One current study in which Web users are invited to provide information about images by participating in a game ("The ESP Game"[2]) demonstrates a creative, Tom Sawyer approach to user-based indexing [13]. By asking paired players to agree on a match in the context of an entertaining game, the system builds in inter-indexer consistency while harnessing the power of Web users. Attempts to obtain formal metadata from users in the past have met with limited success; it will be interesting to see what quantity and quality of metadata can be obtained from this game-playing approach.

Current research in information retrieval has moved beyond comprehensive retrospective research, which was the basic task of laboratory IR. The Web, and potentially many digital libraries, offer so much redundancy, and search has become so casual, that many searchers are looking for "the answer" at best, or at least a few good references. Researchers have turned to the development of "question-answering" systems, which produce a text passage containing the answer to a specific question. For example, the START natural language question-answering system[3] developed at MIT's Infolab, when asked "What is the temperature in Shanghai in December?", produces a table which shows an average high of 51 degrees, an average low of 37 degrees, and record high and low of 73 and 18 degrees. This comes much closer to meeting an information need than a list of documents which may, somewhere, contain the information needed.

The digital library environment offers opportunities for designing for new types of interactivity in IR systems. At the interface level, support can be provided to the user in formulating an appropriate query, through tools for manual and/or automatic query expansion. Relevance feedback, in which the search is modified based on relevance judgments from the user on the initial results presented, has been shown to enhance retrieval performance, yet it has rarely been used in operational systems. Current research explores different types of search, recognizing that there are different types of information need. Algorithms for high precision search attempt to produce a few targeted, high quality results. Other techniques attempt to identify what is new or novel, and produce only documents which add new information. These tasks have been addressed in TREC experiments. However, in practice, current operational IR systems rarely allow users to specify their needs to fit the circumstances of their search.

---

[2] http://www.espgame.org/
[3] http://www.ai.mit.edu/projects/infolab/

The design of the user interface also offers opportunities for supporting the post-retrieval function. Automatic categorization or clustering of documents can enhance the presentation of search results, allowing for easier interpretation. Visualization of results can aid in browsing as well as interpretation. And automatic summarization can facilitate document selection. Users have become accustomed, in the Web environment, to seeing brief summaries or snapshots of a document's contents, generated on the fly using a variety of summarization techniques. These techniques can be used to add value to retrieval from the digital library.

A major challenge for information retrieval researchers is to find ways to evaluate information retrieval systems with real users interacting with the system, rather than a formalized laboratory evaluation. Browsing, which is a major retrieval activity in the traditional library, continues to be understudied in the digital environment. Research which has studied and built models of information seeking behaviour, such as the work of Bates [1] has not often been used to support the design of information systems. One example of a system design based on user searching behaviour is the Daffodil system, in which Fuhr et al. provide an interface to support user activities identified in Bates' model of users' search behaviour [5].

As Borgman has noted, definitions of the digital library have evolved to represent the viewpoints of the communities developing them [3]. In the research community, the emphasis is on digital libraries as collections of content, while in the library community, functions and services are emphasized. The opportunity to interact with the digital library in support of the retrieval process could add significantly to the value of the digital library. A suite of tools for the user, in the form of a searcher's toolkit, could perform functions such as building personalized collections, tracking documents, providing support for reading of retrieved materials, providing and creating citation trails, and automatically creating bibliographies in a variety of formats.

The third component in this challenging mix is the users of digital libraries. Librarians have always prided themselves on knowing their users, but in the digital world this is increasingly difficult. With global access to digital libraries, it is difficult to predict how a particular collection may be used; a collection of Japanese poetry intended for scholars may be used by schoolchildren in the US studying Japanese, or a collection of botanical engravings for historians of horticulture may be used by wallpaper designers. Marchionini et al., in a study of users of the Library of Congress National Digital Library, developed a taxonomy of users showing nine categories, including students, teachers, scholars, rummagers and searchers. Each group had a unique profile in terms of its motivation, domain knowledge, system knowledge, focus, and time allocation for searching [7]. Providing retrieval functionality across a wide spectrum of user types is a daunting challenge.

5 IR, DLs, and the Future

Research in information retrieval has led to significant improvements in the basic task of retrospective retrieval of text, and has begun to focus on identifying and addressing additional tasks. In recent years, a much greater range of retrieval goals, document types and content have been examined, spurred in part by the need to adapt to the Web environment. Finding ways to build on and incorporate this work is a challenge for digital libraries. However, research in information retrieval has focused primarily on unstructured text, and has not taken advantage of available structure or metadata; nor has it recognized the wide range of users and their information needs and behaviours, and designing for the flexibility and interactivity needed by digital libraries represents a further challenge for information retrieval research.

References

1. Bates, M.J. Where Should the Person Stop and the Information Search Interface Start? Information Processing & Management 26 (1990) 575-591
2. Baeza-Yates, R., Ribeiro-Neto, B. Modern Information Retrieval. Addison-Wesley 1999
3. Borgman, C.L. What are Digital Libraries? Competing Visions. Information Processing and Management 35 (1999): 2778-243.
4. Chowdhury, G.G., Chowdhury, S. An Overview of the Information Retrieval Features of Twenty Digital Libraries. Program 34(4) (2000) 341-373
5. Fuhr, N., Klas, C.-P., Schaefer, A., Mutschke, P. Daffodil: An Integrated Desktop for Supporting High-Level Search Activities in Federated Digital Libraries. In: Agosti, M., Thanos, C. (eds.), ECDL 2002, LNCS 2458, 597-612.
6. Ledwith, R. On the Difficulties of Applying the Results of Information Retrieval Research to Aid on the Searching of Large Scientific Databases. Information Processing and Management 28 (1992) 451-455
7. Marchionini, G., Plaisant, C., Komlodi, A.   The People in Digital Libraries: Multifaceted Approaches to Assessing Needs and Impact. In: Bishop, A.P., Van House, N.A., Buttenfield, B.P. (eds): Digital Library Use: Social Practice in Design and Evaluation. Cambridge, MA: MIT Press (2003) 119-160
8. Oard, D.W. Serving Users in Many Languages: Cross-Language Information Retrieval for Digital Libraries. D-Lib Magazine (December 1997) http://www.dlib.org/dlib/december97/oard/12oard.html
9. Ponte, J., Croft, B. A Language Modeling Approach to Information Retrieval. Proceedings of the 21st Annual ACM SIGIR Conference on Research and Development in Information Retrieval. New York: ACM (1998) 275-281
10. Smit, P.H., Kochen, M. Information Impediments to Innovation of On-line Database Vendors. Information Processing and Management 24 (1988) 229-241
11. Sparck Jones, K. Further Reflections on TREC. Information Processing and Management 36 (2000) 37-85
12. Spink, A., Jansen, B.J. Web Search: Public Searching of the Web. Kluwer Academic 2004

13. Von Ahn, L., Dabbish, L. Labeling Images with a Computer Game. CHI 2004, April 24-29, Vienna, Austria. http://www-2.cs.cmu.edu/~biglou/ESP.pdf
14. Voorhees, E. Overview of TREC 2003. Proceedings of the Twelfth Text REtrieval Conference (TREC 2003), Gaithersburg, Maryland, November 18-21, 2003. http://trec.nist.gov/pubs/trec12/papers/OVERVIEW.12.pdf

Knowledge Service and Digital Library: A Roadmap for the Future

Xiaoxing Zhang

National Library of China, Beijing 100081, China
zhang@nlc.gov.cn

Abstract. In the age of explosive growth of information, the objective of the digital library (DL) is to systematically and effectively organize, process and manage massive information resources, and to acquire meta-knowledge by integrating and displaying the knowledge accumulated in the process of reading, understanding, disseminating and utilizing information resources in order to provide readers with a systematic, complete, fast and accurate knowledge service. In this paper we analyze the problems in the existing DL information systems, and put forward a knowledge service model (KSM) to support the requirements of knowledge services. The proposed KSM consists of three layers: an information layer, a knowledge layer, and a knowledge service layer. We also describe service modes of KSM and finally discuss KSM applications in DL. The KSM is not a description of what we can accomplish tomorrow, rather it is a vision of what we should be aiming for.

1 Introduction

With the development of information technology, DL emerges as the times demand and becomes one of the key indicators of the level of a country's information infrastructure. However, if DL is merely an information repository like the World Wide Web, it will put users into a state of "information overload" and will prove unsatisfactory for satisfying the user's demand for knowledge [1, 10]. Among the various services provided by a traditional library, the main one is the interaction between librarian and user or the direct interaction between user and various resources. If a library fails to analyze and summarize the experience and knowledge acquired during this interaction, it cannot accumulate experiences and knowledge, nor share these experiences and knowledge with other users. Therefore, the resources remain static, without any discovery or addition of new knowledge.

Solving this problem requires the introduction of a knowledge service mechanism into DL. The knowledge service model (KSM) presented in this article comprises three layers: an information layer, a knowledge layer, and a knowledge service layer. In the base information layer, we use technologies such as ontologies to design knowledge concept systems, extract knowledge from information, construct knowledge bases, and form inherent knowledge. The Knowledge Layer can be divided into two sub-layers: the lower level is knowledge from specific domains or disciplines. Such knowledge is contained in resources and requires users' study, absorbing and

Z. Chen et al. (Eds.): ICADL 2004, LNCS 3334, pp. 104–114, 2004.
© Springer-Verlag Berlin Heidelberg 2004

digestion. The upper level is dynamically developing knowledge: it is accumulated through understanding, thinking, analyzing, inference, concluding, summarizing, organizing, managing, disseminating, and utilizing of resources by experts and users; it is the enrichment, extension, value addition, and evaluation of inherent knowledge. It is knowledge about knowledge, or what we call meta-knowledge. On the basis of this knowledge base, the KSM provides users with intelligent knowledge services such as browsing, searching, and customization. At the same time the KSM also accumulates new experiences and knowledge through interaction with users and thus form meta-knowledge. KSM is an intelligent and dynamic knowledge service model. This is an ideal model, but one for which we should aim.

2 Analysis of Status Quo

The scale and diversity of documents and information within the DL are immense, so existing information service systems are unable to find, organize, access and maintain the information required by users. Therefore a knowledge service mechanism is needed to resolve the said problems.

2.1 The Inadequacy of the Existing Information Service System

In the existing information service system, various information resources are roughly organized and managed, and basic features of the information are indexed, so as to provide the users with information navigation and information retrieval services. Such a system usually provides keyword-based searches, which may assist the users to carry out simple and quick searching. But this system has no classification mechanism and relies on simple pattern matching, so it cannot exploit the semantic relationship between a given query and information within the system.

Therefore, existing information service systems have shortcomings as follows: (1) information is redundant and unordered with bad organization and management, (2) systems do not store knowledge generated by users during accessing services, (3) systems do not understand the semantics and the context of information. Such problems lead to information overload and hamper users finding what they need.

2.2 The Requirements for Knowledge Service

With the arrival of the information age as well as the popularization and deepening of the Internet, people put forward ever higher demands for traditional information services. The existing information services cannot satisfy these demands. A fully satisfactory system has to address the demands of particular groups, further explore information resources, and provide guidance for decision making as well as solutions for specific issues. People expect a knowledge service oriented to content and solutions, a service driven by users' objectives. The information resources provided from the knowledge layer should be demand-oriented, specific, and effective. The content provided should be organized as a knowledge concept system. There should be rich semantic association between knowledge resources according to different concepts and disciplines to form various knowledge bases and to establish a huge expandable "knowledge network" which crosses geographic boundaries. Such a network will satisfy user's demands for larger scale knowledge services on a more specialized and customized level.

The people's demands for knowledge service may be summed up into various types of services: a service based on the user's activity and decision making, a service based on user's interaction and knowledge sharing, a service based on solutions, a service based on specialization and customization, a service based on dynamic resources and systems that are distributed and diversified, a service based on information integration, a service based on self-dependence and innovation, etc. From the user's perspective, a desirable knowledge service resembles consulting an expert: it should promptly provide customized, convenient, comprehensive, intelligent, systematic, and all-round services that can solve the issues at hand. A tall order to be sure.

3 Knowledge Service Model

The objective of the ideal DL is to provide "all citizens anywhere anytime can use any Internet-connected digital device to search all of human knowledge" [13]. To realize this goal, DL should organize, process, and manage massive information resources systematically and effectively; it should effectively gather and represent knowledge accumulated during reading, understanding, disseminating, and utilizing information resources to provide complete, fast and accurate knowledge services to readers that "search without delay, rubbish, or omissions" and "push without delay, rubbish, or omissions". In line with this demand, we put forward a model KSM based on the concept of meta-knowledge and integrated with various service models.

3.1 Knowledge Service in the Digital Library

In DL, knowledge service is not only provided by librarians and the DL system, but more through interaction between readers and between experts and readers, who share knowledge during their interaction. When we access knowledge services, we provide knowledge at the same time. A real effective knowledge service model should play 4 roles: the librarian, the reader, the expert, and the intelligent computer system. The librarian and the expert are the initial providers of inherent knowledge. They convert their experiences and specialist knowledge into knowledge rules, which are a part of the knowledge base. The role of the intelligent computer system is a complicated one. Strictly speaking, it is a service provider, but often it requires knowledge, learning, and training. The user not only creates knowledge, but also benefits from it, i.e. he/she provides his/her experiences and knowledge to others while accessing knowledge services.

The knowledge service of DL should be a cyclic, intelligent, dynamic, and interactive process. It mainly functions to provide a platform of knowledge interaction for various users. By effectively classifying, filtering, and merging the users' interaction logs, it may form an ordered knowledge system, build an effective knowledge base for problem solving and provide them to users through knowledge Q&A, retrieval, recommendation, etc.

Furthermore, the platform of knowledge interaction should be associated with existing knowledge bases. On the one hand, other users and experts can solve user's demands and problems; on the other hand, potentially they can also be solved via a computer system's machine inference. In the development of such a platform, the ideal system will continuously learn, carry out effective research, discovery, analysis, and summarizing of experiences and knowledge formed during interaction, and create new knowledge. Such new knowledge will be the basis of the knowledge services provided by the system. The knowledge in the existing knowledge base and the new knowledge formed in this interaction should be classified, organized, and ordered so that they can be easily managed by the computer system. It establishes the basis of an intelligent knowledge service.

The knowledge service of DL functions in several roles. The first is to provide structured resources; the second is to provide a knowledge interaction platform; the third is to research and accumulate new knowledge from users' activities; the last is to provide systematic, ordered, structured, and customized solutions and knowledge services on the basis of this static and dynamic knowledge.

To sum up, the knowledge service of DL should be implemented by a dynamic model, which integrates organically the user, computer system, and knowledge resources. Therefore, we put forward a three-layer model of KSM, introducing the concept of meta-knowledge. Meta-knowledge is the new knowledge formed through exploring, discovering, analyzing, and summarizing experiences and knowledge created during the users' interaction. Meta-knowledge is the basis of the knowledge services provided by the system.

3.2 Meta Knowledge

Meta-knowledge, first put forward by Driscoll in 1994[12], is a process of critical thinking, reasoning and understanding of knowledge, through which it turns into a kind of skills of problem-solving and decision-making. Meta-knowledge serves not only knowledge management, but more importantly it serves the provision of knowledge services, problem-solving methods, and decision-making processes.

In DL, meta-knowledge refers to knowledge that has been accumulated during the process of browsing, retrieval, disseminating and utilizing knowledge sources. Meta-knowledge is the exploitation, analysis and presentation of the users' wisdom and experience, including analysis, evaluation, and recommendations concerning inherent knowledge resources. Through placing more emphasis on activities and intelligence that are used to accurately represent the inherent knowledge, it provides more instantaneousness and practical results for customers. Such dynamic knowledge is a process of gradual accumulation in which users take an active part and a manifestation of what has been implicit in activities of users. Since much meta-knowledge is not explicit or is difficult to express, the knowledge is obscure and has to be represented and manifested by certain means.

3.3 Knowledge Service Model

Our knowledge service model (KSM) of DL is shown in Fig 1. The model consists of three layers, i.e. information resources, knowledge, and knowledge services.

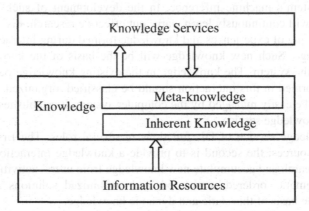

Fig. 1. Knowledge service model

The layered architecture of KSM is easily extensive and scalable. Each layer implements some functions and communicates with other layers. We illustrate the three layers in details as follows.

(1) Information Resources Layer

The layer consists of various types of digital resources, and their basic systems of storage, management, and retrieval. The major form of representation is the knowledge base of fundamental resources object and related fundamental metadata databases.

The digital resources of DL are immense, heterogeneous, and dynamic, and it is semi-structured. For this reason the information layer must integrate heterogeneous information sources in different formats, especially in processing semi-structured data. In addition, masses of dynamic data also need to be processed, which requires expandability to support dynamic expansion.

To fulfill the above requirements, the information resources layer in our design has been encapsulated with heterogeneous data sources of various data formats and interface protocols. Global query dispatch and result synthesis are based on the design to implement integrated information retrieval (IIR).

(2) Knowledge Layer

The knowledge layer consists of two sub-layers:

- Inherent knowledge, the lower layer, is the knowledge extracted from the information resources: This knowledge layer consists of two parts, i.e. rules for knowledge classification and knowledge about resource objects, which is created and managed on the basis of classification. The knowledge base is used not only to facilitate users' browsing, retrieval and utilization, but also to provide precise and highly effective services to users. It which stores inherent knowledge from the information resources layer and is the primary source of the knowledge service. The key point of a knowledge base is the presentation and management of knowledge. We adopt a technology combining ontology and semantic nets to represent the knowledge in the knowledge base, and use knowledge retrieval and navigation technology to implement retrieval and browsing of this knowledge base.

- Meta-knowledge, the upper layer, is the analysis, evaluation, comprehension, inference, and interpretation of inherent knowledge and is the exploitation, including analysis and manifestation of the users wisdom and experience. The meta-knowledge derives from three sources: (1) analysis and inference by algorithmic computer technology of the inherent knowledge in the knowledge base, (2) meta-knowledge established by experts (librarians) through evaluation and analysis of inherent knowledge and using their professional knowledge, and (3) knowledge accumulated as users browse, retrieve, disseminate, and utilize the knowledge. Therefore, the meta-knowledge is continuously and dynamically expanded, which support the intelligence of the knowledge services in DL.

Inherent knowledge is the major source of meta-knowledge, but the two types of knowledge are not independent of each other. As the meta-knowledge is accumulated and expanded, the inherent knowledge will be updated with new meta-knowledge rules. In operation of knowledge service systems, inherent knowledge and meta-knowledge are always in a state of mutual supplementation and expansion.

(3) Knowledge Services Layer

This layer provides various types of intelligent knowledge services on the basis of the knowledge layer and provides platforms for knowledge exploitation and accumulation, thus providing a knowledge interaction platform for users. Besides providing services on the basis of inherent knowledge, more importantly, the knowledge service layer, through exploitation, accumulation, and utilizing meta-knowledge, provides services to users, solves users' problems, and meets users' demands.

In order to help a user obtain the knowledge required, the knowledge service layer will not only retrieve and locate the knowledge, but also actively and dynamically provide intelligent knowledge services through customized technology.

Customized service components will assist the users to clarify and specify queries intelligently through users' interest models. Furthermore, the component will record basic operations when a user uses the system. These logs, which will display the interests of the user in certain information resources, will be used by the interest analyzing machines to conduct training on positive samples and negative samples, to generate and study users' interests automatically, and to consummate user interest models.

In the knowledge service model, people will accumulate more abundant meta-knowledge during knowledge service and interaction. The dynamic change and increase of meta-knowledge will improve the development of knowledge services in both content and form. The critical characteristic of the knowledge services layer can be said to be the dynamic increase and accumulation of meta-knowledge, which enables users to gain knowledge and solve problems during their interaction   with knowledge services.

4 Service Modes of KSM

In order to solve problems in the traditional library, KSM should mix several service models so as to provide the users with a flexible and capable intelligent knowledge service platform.

Knowledge services in a traditional library mainly include reference consultation, retrieval, and mutual communication. The reference consultation includes consultation of the conventional library, catalog search, subject guides on the Internet, database building and so on. Many of these are done manually or semi-automatically. The service is one to one. It is an interaction between the reader and the librarian, and is a service provision process from the librarian and the reader. The following problems exist in these services:

- Service architecture is not open. Service systems are developed and delivered individually and repeatedly, so interoperation and sharing are rare.
- Service modes are too simple. Users are usually confined to a certain scope. Content, form, and quality of the service are seldom evaluated.
- There is little communication between users.
- Passive service: Active and customized services to the user are rare. Content and form of the service are at a low level and lack deep exploration and critical review of the resources.

In order to solve the above problems, the following service modes are mixed in our KSM. Service form and scope are expanded and an active and customized service is offered to the user.

Active Push Service: Through analyzing and learning the interests and preferences of the user automatically, the KSM will build an individual user model and actively deliver knowledge resources from DL to the user, in particular,: news about an area or specialty the user is interested in, specialist opinions and feedbacks and comments from other users. The push service is active: it knows the interests and preferences of the user clearly and pushes dynamic knowledge to the user.

Knowledge Navigation and Association Services: These services classify and organize all types of digital resources in an effective manner and offer a knowledge classification system and a navigation mechanism. In addition, they provide related knowledge corresponding to the basic problems and requirements of the user. They associate and expand various and diverse types of knowledge from different sources so as to make available comprehensive and valuable knowledge to the user.

Customized Service: The KSM provides customized service as required by users. In response to the requirements and feedback from the user, it collects knowledge type, knowledge area, organization, and presentation method, service method, service period, and other information required by the user. Then the system provides the required service according to the individual characteristics, features, and requirements of the user in order to implement a customized service for both content and form. In addition, an overall solution may be provided for a special user.

Knowledge is now the key competitive battleground for knowledge intensive industry and providing satisfactory service to users is the object of the knowledge service architecture. Different lines of work have their own experience of research and practice of service content and form. Service forms vary across users, areas, locations, and time. The knowledge service provided by DL can use more existing mature service modes and constantly develop and innovate to ensure maximum customer satisfaction.

5 The KSM Application in Digital Library

KSM is a dynamic and open architecture of knowledge services for digital libraries. It offers the user both organized and structured resources and a knowledge interaction platform. It provides a systematic, ordered, structured, and individualized problem resolution and knowledge service including evaluation and recommendation of knowledge resources. This section analyzes the application of KSM in DL and an evaluation of its function.

5.1 Some Critical Issues for Knowledge Service

To evaluate application of KSM in DL, we must first clarify critical issues of knowledge service in digital libraries. We should analyze the application of KSM with that as the evaluation standard. We believe the following issues should be addressed for the knowledge service in DL:

(1) Demands of the user: It needs to analyze and acknowledge what the user really needs; what is the appropriate content and manner of service? How to implement self-adaptation and expandability of the knowledge service?

(2) Knowledge extraction and discovery: How to explore and find meta-knowledge from the resources available? How to increase the value of the current knowledge and deduce more knowledge?

(3) Knowledge representation and modeling: How to build the knowledge model and represent knowledge in order for the system to easily understand, process and apply knowledge? How to express and transform knowledge, especially dynamic and implicit knowledge?

(4) Knowledge management: How to organize and manage the large quantity of knowledge and retrieve and use it conveniently? How to organize and manage properly the existing knowledge and experiences of the user in order to build a foundation for the knowledge service?

(5) Knowledge sharing: How to break through obstacles of knowledge sharing? What technical solutions can be used? How to implement a knowledge-sharing platform?

In many cases the technology to accomplish these ambitious goals is not here yet, nor is it quite around the corner, but we won't get there as expeditiously as we might if we don't have a road map of what we want to accomplish.,Those areas which in particular are still not mature and need further improvement include: knowledge representation and ontology technology [3,5]; knowledge discovery technology [11]; knowledge retrieval technology [6,8]; knowledge analysis and evaluation technology [2]; knowledge management technology [4]; E-learning technologies and customized service technology [7, 9].

DL knowledge services must use technology to resolve the above issues to satisfy requirements of practical applications. Next we will discuss the performance of KSM based upon these standards.

5.2 Performance Discussion

Adopting multiple service modes, KSM provides a dynamic and open service for digital libraries.

Through customized services and multiple service modes, the top layer of KSM provides active and customized knowledge retrieval functions in order to meet the users' demands.

The knowledge layer is the key module of the overall KSM. The layer embraces many technologies especially the introduction of meta-knowledge, and the dynamic development of the meta-knowledge expands the knowledge categories of traditional knowledge services. On the basis of inherent knowledge, human activities and wisdom have been taken into account by introducing meta-knowledge. Meta-knowledge embodies the exploitation, analyses, and manifestation of users' wisdom and experience, which include analysis, evaluation, and recommendation of inherent knowledge resources. Meta-knowledge includes the abstract reflection and high level expansion of inherent knowledge. It is ultimately the basis of high level knowledge search.

The information layer is the basic information source for KSM, which provides search results to the upper layers by means of the integrated retrieval of heterogeneous resources.

6 Conclusions and Future Work

In the age of the knowledge economy, knowledge is now widely recognized as the forth production factor.[15] People are in great need of enhanced knowledge services. And it is intelligent services that can help people solve problems. As knowledge portals based on digital resources, such a DL will provide high quality knowledge services to users by maximizing dissemination and sharing to meet users' demands. Therefore, this paper puts forward the concept of a KSM of DL. The KSM consists of three layers, i.e. information resources, knowledge and knowledge services, and is dynamic and interactive. The KSM has two contributions to knowledge services: (1) automatically building a knowledge base from heterogeneous information resources, and (2) it is a dynamic knowledge interaction platform, in which meta-knowledge is formed and accumulated during interaction and participation to provide enriched knowledge services.

In addition, KSM comprises multiple knowledge service modes and adopts knowledge engineering technology from various fields to implement knowledge services in DL.

The objective of DL is to provide users satisfying service. The future DL should support knowledge management to build an ordered knowledge and meta-knowledge base from immense information resources. Such a DL should introduce different service modes to provide intelligent services to users. To accomplish this, the knowledge service modes must be improved and meta-knowledge must be clarified and classified. And even more challengingly, we must introduce evaluation mechanisms to conduct effective evaluation and feedback on various types of services in order to provide high quality knowledge service.

This article has attempted to chart what will be needed in the ideal DL, and what are the pieces that will need to be constructed to achieve this goal.

References

1. William Y. Arms. Digital Libraries. The MIT Press, Cambridge, Massachusetts, London, England. 2000.
2. Sergey Brin and Lawrence Page. The anatomy of a large-scale hypertextual Web search engine. In Proceedings of the Seventh International World Wide Web Conference, p107–117, April 1998.
3. Ying Ding, Schubert Foo, Ontology Research and Development, Journal of Information Science, 28(5), 375-388, 2002.
4. Joseph M. Firestone, Mark W. McElroy, Key Issues in The New Knowledge Management, Knowledge Management Consortium International Press, 2003.
5. T. R. Gruber, A translation approach to portable ontology specifications, Knowledge Acquisition, vol.5, 199-220, 1993.
6. Jim. Hendler, T. Berners-Lee, and E. Miller. Integrating applications on the semantic web. Journal IEE Japan, 122(10):676-680, 2002.
7. D. Hicks, K. Tochtermann, Personal Digital Libraries and Knowledge Management, Proceedings of I-KNOW '01, Springer, Graz (2001), 96-111.
8. Norbert Lossau, Search Engine Technology and Digital Libraries, D-Lib Magazine, 10(6), 2004.
9. Bamshad Mobasher, Robert Cooley and Jaideep Srivastava, Automatic personalization based on Web usage mining, Communications of the ACM, 43(8), 142-151, 2000.
10. Sudha Ram, Jinsoo Park and Dongwon Lee, Digital libraries for the next millennium: challenges and research directions, Information Systems Frontiers, 1(1), 75-94, 1999.
11. Zhongzhi Shi, Knowledge Discovery, Tsinghua University Press, Beijing, 2001.
12. http://www3.sympatico.ca/lgrightmire/META.HTM. (Date: 2004-06-10).

13. David Nagel, et. al. Presidents Information Technology Advisory Committee Digital Libraries Panel. http://www.itrd.gov/pitac/meetings/2000/20000225/pitac-dl/pitac-dl.pdf, 2004-8-18.
14. Gail Hodge, Systems of Knowledge Organization for Digital Libraries: Beyond Traditional Authority Files, 2000.
15. John Davies, Dieter Fensel, Frank Van Harmelen, Towards the Semantic Web: Ontology-Driven Knowledge Management, John Wiley & Sons Ltd, England, 2003

Ontological Service Layer for Digital Libraries: A Requirement and Architectural Analysis

Xiaolin Zhang

Library, Chinese Academy of Sciences, Beijing, China 100080

Abstract. Based on a brief analysis of the emerging challenges and development strategies for digital libraries facing the convergence of the cyber-infrastructure, Semantic Web, and Web Services, the author advocates a new paradigm of digital libraries that encompass knowledge content, context, and communities, using as an example the three-tiered Digital Library Framework of the Chinese Science Digital Library strategic plan. Within this framework, an Ontological Service Layer (OSL) plays the central role as a semantic glue for knowledge-based integration of digital resources, services, and processes. Further analysis is given to the functional requirements of the OSL and a high level architecture of the OSL is presented. An exploration of the structure, faceted ontology components, and possible construction tools of the underline Integrate Ontology System of the OSL is then made to illustrate approaches to implement the OSL.

Keywords: Digital libraries, Ontology, Ontological Services, Requirements, Architecture.

1 Challenges from the Convergence of the Cyberinfrastructure, Semantic Web, and Web Services Technologies

While digital libraries making great strives in providing universal access to vast amount of information resources, the very environment where information is created and used is going through some fundamental changes that inevitably affect the strategies of DL development.

First and foremost, there comes the cyberinfrastructure[1] that drives for a comprehensive, advanced infrastructure based on information and communication technology that serves as a platform for new organizations and methods for conducting scientific and engineering research. We already saw the proliferation of various digital resources, including data grids, computing grid, co-laboratories and collaboratories, digital or digitally representable instruments, virtual communities, digital libraries, and so on. (we will use the phrase 'digital resources' to represent all these throughout this paper). We also witnessed the development of computational science and engineering that makes computational emulation and analysis basic instruments for research, and that is data intensive, collaborative, network-based, and knowledge discovery-driven. Adding to this cyberinfrastructure is the Semantic Web[2] movement (and Networked Knowledge Or-

Z. Chen et al. (Eds.): ICADL 2004, LNCS 3334, pp. 115–123, 2004.
© Springer-Verlag Berlin Heidelberg 2004

ganization Systems[3] in digital libraries) that aims to semantically enrich the representation, description, organization, and utilization of knowledge content and relationships often embedded in the depth of various digital resources. Adding again to the cyberinfrastructure is the Web Services[4] movement that openly and dynamically integrate resources, systems, and processes to develop virtual organizations and processes on time. Open Grid Service Architecture[5], Web Service Composition[6], and many other efforts are rapidly turn this dream of open integration into reality. As matter of fact, Semantic Web and Web Services are combining forces to develop Semantic Web Services[7] that will realize knowledge-based user-driven or problem-driven open integration of resources, systems, and processes.

With the development of cyberinfrastructure, we clearly see the convergence of information resources, communication processes, and information utilization process (i.e., research processes) in the same digital space. Here, the ways and processes to acquire, discover, access, apply, and create knowledge will be diffused into and connected with the various aspects of user knowledge process, and will be built around and interrelated with the cyberinfrastructure-enabled knowledge communities[8]. Stimulated and pushed by further convergence of Cyberinfrastructure, Semantic Web, and Web Services, we can envision an ambient intelligent environment[9] for knowledge application and creation that is user-centered, knowledge-based, problem-driven, dynamic, and openly integratible.

Digital libraries are yet to prepare themselves for the change. They are often built as a digital copy of the print library, resource-centric as relying on massive resource they acquire to prove their usefulness, document-centric as relying on document retrieval and delivery to manifest their contribution, and library-centric as relying on improving their own capacity and capabilities to sustain their viability. They lack the abilities to effectively organize, integrate, and utilize, in a user-centered, knowledge-based, and problem-driven fashion, the full range of digital resources in cyberinfrastructure to support user knowledge application and creation. To tackle this challenge, a paradigm shift is required to build DLs for enhancing user knowledge productivity.

2   A DL Framework Incorporating Content, Context, and Communities

A quantum leap of faith, or a re-examination of the key concepts involved is necessary for us to broaden and enlighten our understanding of DL development[10].

Libraries are knowledge institutions, but there are much richer facets of knowledge than we usually realized[11]. Knowledge is a thing, a flow, and an experience. As a thing, knowledge is manifested as data, documents, or databases. As a flow, knowledge becomes a process during which information is parsed, filtered, transformed, interacted, related, re-organized, and integrated through multiple stages in an applied context. As an experience, knowledge is dynamic, personal, subjective, and purposeful, often requiring interaction and exchange. From this point of view, then a knowledge process, on which information systems are built to serve, will not only deal with content, but also deal with context and communities. Knowledge (and knowledge service) is only meaningful in a context that serves to define a problem and provides the integrating framework. And, it is the community that provides an interactive experience to enable better understanding of the problem and knowledge. With this understanding of knowledge and knowledge process, an effective knowledge system should present an integrated and interrelated organization of digital content, scholarly communications and problem-solving process, and cyberinfrastructure-enabled knowledge communities. This posture makes DLs more capable to take full advantages of the convergence of the Cyberinfrastructure, Semantic Web, and Web Services.

Based on the analysis, the CSDL plans to develop its DL as part of CAS user knowledge creation platform in an e-Science environment, integrating content, context, and communities with an objective to enhance user knowledge productivity. Hence, a framework for CAS Digital Library is produced to guide the next phase development, as showed in Fig. 1.

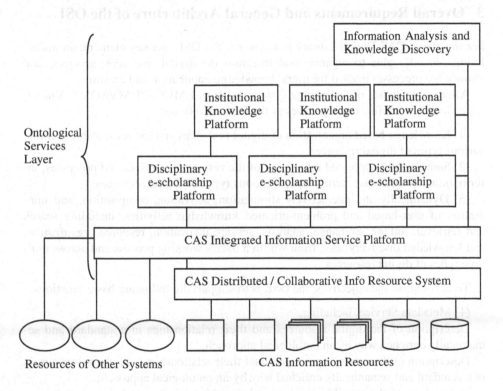

Fig. 1. CAS Digital Library Framework

This Framework consists of three major tiers: an Integrated Information Service Platform (IISP), a series of Disciplinary eScholarship Platforms (DeSPs), and a series of Institutional Knowledge Platforms (IKPs). An information analysis module is added on top to aid in knowledge discovery. An Ontological Service Layer is planed to provide the semantic glue to intelligently integrate digital resources at various tiers and "outside" resources.

The IISP, which is in place now, includes a distributed information resource system and an integrated service platform that will also integrate resources from the former and from other systems for a coherent and integrated information service. DeSPs provide support for the whole range of user scholarly communications activities by integrating information resources (library or otherwise), communications resources, and research resources. IKPs serve individual research institutes, laboratories, or project teams from a community and context point of view, by integrating information resources, communications resources, research resources, institutional resources, and programs/projects resources, with an institutional knowledge repository, a series of knowledge wares such as data mining and community building, and interfaces with e-science, e-learning, and workflow management.

3   Overall Requirements and General Architecture of the OSL

For the above CAS Digital Library Framework, the OSL is a key element, an underlining semantic glue to organize and integrate the digital resources, services, and knowledge processes needed for users' knowledge application and creation.

After some studies of knowledge systems such as UMLS[12], FAO/AOS[13], Knowledge Grid[14], we define the objectives of the OSL as follows:

(1) Knowledge-based organization of digital resources and the relationships among various types of digital resources;

(2) Semantically-supported integration of the resources, services and processes, informational or otherwise, across heterogeneous types of digital resources;

(3) Dynamically and interactively stimulation, activation, composition, and integration of user-based and problem-oriented knowledge activities, including search and retrieval, linking, exchange, analysis, service invocation, resource organization, and knowledge discovery, etc., from within a user's working process and across multiple types of digital resources.

To accomplish the objectives, the OSL is to support the following basic functions:

(1) Metadata Service, including,

Description of the digital resources and their relationships in a standard and semantically enriched way by an ontological approach;

Description of the services, processes, and their relationships with digital resources, in a standard and semantically enriched way by an ontological approach;

Description of the possible mapping relationships between existing metadata or ontologies and the OSL ontologies.

(2) Knowledge Directory Service, including,

Registration of the digital resources and their relationships on a standard open registry mechanism such as UDDI[15];

Registration of the services, processes, and their relationships with digital resources, on a standard open registry;

Provision of an open discovery mechanism for these resources, services, and processes, that can be embedded into the following Presentation Service and any third-party service;

(3) Search and Presentation Services, including,

Ontological search processor that supports third-party search services with semantically augmented capabilities such as expansion, refinement, semantics negotiation, relationship construction, and result organization, etc.

Integrated browsing and visualization of the ontologies used to describe digital resources;

Integrated browsing and visualization of the ontologically organized digital resources;

Dynamical and interactive linking and interfacing of the semantically related services and processes with corresponding digital resources;

Customization of browsing, visualization, and interfacing;

Provision of an open interfacing mechanism that can embed the Presentation Service in any third party service.

(4) Process Management Service, including,

A process invocation mechanism that can activate, by an explicit trigger or an inference from implicit actions or relationships, a resource node to present necessary service process in a transparent way, and the resource node itself can be a service process too;

Process composition engines that can discovery, compose, validate, execute, and evaluate multiple processes across multiple resources or even heterogeneous resources, using Web Service composition technologies[16] with XML-based languages like BPEL4WS[17], and the engines can be triggered again by explicit actions or implicit inference;

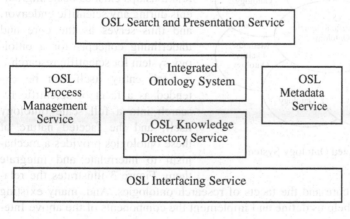

An extension process engine that supports further processing of the resources and their content by third party systems or agents for complicated tasks such as knowledge discovery, collaboration, virtual organization, and service customization;

Fig.2. Ontological Service Layer Architecture

A process re-organization module that will extract semantic descriptions from the composition process about the newly formed composite service processes, register them in the OSL Knowledge

Directory, and attach them to according to the integrated ontology system of the OSL in a semantically meaningful way.

(5) Interfacing Service, including,

An open mechanism that will provide standardized methods to embed the OSL services in a resource, service, or process, for example OpenURL linking[18] or SOAP invocation[19];

An open mechanism that will provide a standardized way to trigger the OSL services from within a resource, service, or process, usually by some kind of intelligent agents;

An open mechanism that will allow the OSL to discover and harvest resources, services, and processes, by crawler or registry services;

An open metadata transformation engine that supports standardized mechanisms to map the ontologically enriched metadata from the OSL to the original or proprietary metadata of a resource, service, or process, or vice versa.

Figure 2 gives a very general presentation of the OSL architecture.

4   The Integrated Ontology System of the OSL

Central to the OSL is a concept of the integrated ontology system that based on a faceted approach[20]. A research **program** is started by a researcher who belongs to an **institution** or a **community**, in a **subject** area, through a series of **scholarly communications processes**, utilizing some research **methods** that may in turn require certain **facilities**, making use of a number of **information resources**, and maybe managed as **workflow**. This set of entities and their semantic relationships exist as basic ingredients during any scientific endeavor, and thus serves as the core and underlining concepts for a ontology system for scientific research.

Each entity itself can be extended as a facet of scientific research into a full scale ontology itself, and the faceted nature of these ontologies provides a mechanism to interrelate and integrate them. Figure 3 illustrates the relationships among the core and the facets of research ontologies. And, many existing R&D programs may help us define and implement the components of the above Integrated Ontology System.

Fig. 3. OSL Integrated Ontology System

To develop subject ontologies, or knowledge organization systems many would like to call, classifications and thesauri can be used as a basis, excellent examples exist like FAO/AOS and UMLS. In these systems, multi-layered semantic types are defined, and so are the complicated semantic relationships that go beyond simple concepts of broader, narrower, related, used for, uses. The openness and interoperability of these knowledge systems can be enhanced by XML-based semantic tools, such as RDF[21], OWL[22], or XTM[23] and SKOS[24].

For institutional ontologies, work in enterprise modeling and ontology[25-26] provides semantic instruments that, on one hand, define the organizational structure, units, members, facilities, responsibility lines, collaboration relations, policies and procedures, and on another hand, define the strategies, capabilities, plans, activities, events, processes, and effects or results. These entities and their relationships can also be defined by XML-based languages for machine-understanding and interoperability.

To model scholarly communications processes, early efforts such as the Scholarly Community Ontology[27] explored basic concepts involved, such as activity, organization, publication, person, research theme, team, etc. Newer experiments go more deeply into the dynamics of the scholarly communications. The ScholOnto[28] project and its ClaiMaker[29] system try to model the interactive relationships such as addresses, analyses, uses/applies, modifies/extends, is an example of, encapsulates, envisages, predicts, confirms, is enabled, proves/refutes, supports/challenges, is consistent/inconsistent with, takes issue with, raises problems with, etc., so that a chain of meaningful communications can be delineated and acted upon. Combined with subject and institutional ontologies, one can trace the knowledge exchange and intellectual interaction across multiple disciplines and organizations.

Tools already exist for modeling processes and workflows, such as high level standards Workflow Reference Model[30], workflow markup languages like Wf-XML[31], web-oriented process choreography languages for modeling workflows and composition of processes[32], like BPSS[33] and BPEL4WS[17].

Development has been active in knowledge-based organization of information resources. Metadata, semantically enriched classification schemes and thesauri, collection description metadata, semantically rich languages for description of management mechanisms such access control, DRM, privacy protection, service organization, personalization policies, and many others, begin to provide a fabric of information objects, resources, systems, and processes, that are semantically understandable, openly accessible, and dynamically integratible[34]. Helped by technologies such as OWL-S[35], we can extend Web Services stack of capabilities into semantically description and understanding of service profiles and processes. From another angle, e-Science communities are pushing for Knowledge Grid[36] and ontology-based services on the grid[37] which will contribute to the development of ontologies for e-Science services utilizing facilities, methodologies, and processes.

Though the above development encourages us in terms of the progress and availability of ontological tools, some key questions remain to hinder the implementation of a real and effective OSL. A better understanding of the underline conceptual model will help us to construct the core ontology for scientific research. Here theoretic considerations like ABC ontology[38] and the modeling of socio-technical systems[39] may reveal a more abstract framework that will more accurately and flexibly capture the essence of the concepts and relationships. Another need is for the easy-to-harness methods to develop large number of ontologies for subject fields, types of institutions, and types of services and processes that we commonly encountered during scientific research. Still another challenge is to semantically describe or connect the huge amount of existing digital resources, services, and processes.

The technological challenges are tremendous. However, the biggest challenge is to the vision and the approach for digital library development that integrates content, context, and communities. It is the author's believe, as I said in an earlier presentation, that strategies to meet the challenges of the convergence of the cyberinfrastructure, semantic web, and web services, lie in building digital libraries into user knowledge process and making digital libraries part of the so-called cyberinfrastructure-based knowledge communities. It is also the author's believe that the viability and sustainability of digital libraries lie in their effort in this direction, not in massing more resources and making better access alone.

References

[1] Atkins, D. E. et al. Revolutionizing Science and Engineering Through Cyberinfrastructure. National Science Foundation Blue-Ribbon Advisory Panel on Cyberinfrastructure, January 2003.
[2] W3C Semantic Web Activity. http://www.w3.org/2002/ws/
[3] Networked Knowledge Organization Systems and Services. http://nkos.slis.kent.edu/
[4] W3C Web Service Activity. http://www.w3.org/2002/ws/
[5] Open Grid Service Infrastructure, Version 1.0, April 5, 2003. http://www.ggf.org/ogsi-wg/drafts/draft-ggf-ogsi-gridservice-29_2003-04-05.pdf
[6] Srivastava, B. Koehler, J. Web Service Composition: Current Solutions and Open Problems. http://www.zurich.ibm.com/pdf/ebizz/icaps-ws.pdf
[7] Semantic Web Services Initiative. http://www.swsi.org/
[8] Atkins, D. E. Research Libraries and Digital Library Research for Cyberinfrastructure-enabled Knowledge Communities. In The Proceedings of Digital Library-Advances the Efficiency of Knowledge Utilization, ed. Furui Zhan, Beijing: Scientific Documentation Press, 2004.9
[9] ISTAG Scenarios for Ambient Intelligence in 2010. ftp://ftp.cordis.lu/ist/docs/istagscenarios2010 .pdf
[10] Zhang, X. Building DLs into User Knowledge Process. In The Proceedings of Digital Library-Advances the Efficiency of Knowledge Utilization, ed. Furui Zhan, Beijing: Scientific Documentation Press, 2004.9
[11] Norris, D., Mason, J. and Lefrere, P. Transforming e-Knowledge. http://www.transformingeknowledge.info/index.html
[12] Unified Medical Language System. http://www.nlm.nih.gov/research/umls/documentation.html
[13] The Agricultural Ontology Services Concept Note: A Tool for Facilitating Access to Knowledge. Draft 5.5. http://www.fao.org/agris/aos/Documents/AOS_Draftproposal.htm.
[14] Cannataro, M. and Talia D. The Knowledge Grid: Designing, Building, and Implementing an Architecture for Distributed Knowledge Discovery. CACM, 46(1), 2003.
[15] Bellwood, T. et al. Universal Description Discovery and Integration. Version 3.0.1. UDDI Spec Technical Committee Specification, Oct. 14, 2003. http://uddi.org/pubs/uddi_v3.htm
[16] Srivastava, B. and Koehler, J. Web Service Composition: Current Problems and Open Solutions. http://www.zurich.ibm.com/pdf/ebizz/icaps-ws.pdf

[17] Andrews, T. et al. Business Process Execution Language for Web Services Version 1.1, 05 May 2003, http://www.ibm.com/developerworks/library/ws-bpel/

[18] NISO. Development of an OpenURL Standard http://library.caltech.edu/openurl/

[19] Gudgin, M. et al. SOAP Version 1.2 Part 1: Messaging Framework, W3C Recommendation, 24 June 2003. http://www.w3.org/TR/soap12-part1/

[20] Spiter, L. A simplified Model for Facet Analysis. Canadian Journal of Information and Library Science, v.23, 1-30, April-July, 1998

[21] Klyne, G. and Carroll, Resource Description Framework (RDF): Concepts and Abstract Syntax. W3C Recommendation 10 February 2004. http://www.w3.org/TR/rdf-concepts/

[22] Patel-Schneider, P., et al. OWL Web Ontology Language: Semantics and Abstract Syntax. W3C Recommendation 10 February 2004. http://www.w3.org/TR/owl-semantics/

[23] Pepper, S. and Moore, G. XML Topic Maps (XTM) 1.0: TopicMaps.Org Specification. http://www.topicmaps.org/xtm/1.0/

[24] Miles, A. J. et al. SKOS-Core 1.0 Guide: An RDF Schema for thesauri and related knowledge organisation systems. http://www.w3.org/2001/sw/Europe/reports/thes/ 1.0/guide/

[25] Enterprise Modelling and Ontology for Interoperability. http://www.cs.rty.lv/caise2004/ W_INTEROP.asp

[26] The Enterprise Ontology. http://www.aisi.ed.ac.uk/project/enterprise/enterprise/ontology.html

[27] Scholarly Community Ontology. http://www.kampa.org/phd/ontology/s_community.html.

[28] ScholOnto: an Ontology-based digital library server for research documents and discourse. International Journal of Digital Library. 2000(3)237-248

[29] Li, G. et al. ClaiMaker: Weaving a Semantic Web of Research Papers. http://kmi.open.ac. uk/publications/papers/kmi-tr-126.pdf

[30] Workflow Management Coalition. The Workflow Reference Model. http://www.wfmc. org/standards/docs/tc003v11.pdf.

[31] XML-Based Workflow and Process Management Standards: XPDL, Wf-XML. http://xml.coverpages.org/wf-xml.html

[32] W.M.P. van der Aalst. Web Services Composition Languages: Old Wine in New Bottles?.http://tmitwww.tm.tue.nl/research/patterns/download/wscl-euromicro.pdf

[33] ebXML Business Process Specification Schema 1.1. April 2001. http://www.ebxml.org/ specs/ebBPSS.pdf

[34] Zhang, X. Metadata Research and Application. Beijing: Beijing Library Press, 2002.

[35] The OWL Service Coalition. OWL-S: Semantic Markup for Web Services, 27 December 2003, http://www.daml.org/services/owl-s/1.0/owl-s.html

[36] Sure, Y. Towards the Knowledge Grid. In Workshop of Grid for Integrated Problem Solving Environment", Bonn, 29. April, 2003. http://www.scai.fraunhofer.de/fileadmin/ download/vortraege/KNOWLE3.PDF

[37] Cannatora, M. Knowledge Discovery and Ontology-based Services on the Grid. http://www.semanticgrid.org/GGF/ggf9/mario/

[38] Lagoze, C. and Hunter, J. The ABC Ontology and Model. Journal of Digital Information, 2(2), 2001. http://jodi.ecs.soton.ac.uk/Articles/v02/i02/Lagoze/

[39] An Ontology for Modelling Socio-Technical Systems. http://www.campus.ncl.ac.uk/ unbs/sbi/emad/ontology2.html (All internet URLs accessed Spt. 19, 2004)

The Distributed Collaborative Virtual Reference System and Its Scheduler Mechanism for Chinese University Libraries*

Min Huang, Haoming Lin, and Yi Jin

Shanghai Jiao Tong University Library, 1954 Huashan Road,
Shanghai 200030, P.R. China
minhuang@sjtu.edu.cn
{hmlin, yjin}@lib.sjtu.edu.cn

Abstract. The resource-oriented digital library, the system-oriented digital library and the service-oriented digital library best illustrate the development phrases of the digital library. The service-oriented digital library should consist of the following components: three kinds of resources, two service platforms, and one portal. The virtual reference system, as one of two service platforms, is playing an important role in the service-oriented digital library. A distributed collaborative virtual reference system and its framework are presented in the paper. And an automatic task scheduler for the synchronous reference and the asynchronous reference is also described in detail.

1 The Service-Oriented Digital Library

With a view of the whole and further application, development of the digital library should go through three periods as the construction of resource, system, and service. Digital libraries then can be accordingly classified as resource-oriented, system-oriented and service-oriented.

As a foundation of the digital library, the resource-oriented digital library is changing the dominating media type from printed format to digital format, so that it can meet the needs of network environment featured with modern communication technologies. In this period, people would pay more attention on digitized resources and digitized methods. The digitized resources are mainly based on the following three digital resources: library's special collections, commercial online e-journals or databases, and useful literature information resources on the Internet[1]. As a symbol that the digital library goes to mature, the system-oriented digital library is trying to change the situation that multiple systems and multiple platforms could not work cooperatively because of lacking the standards and the specifications. In this period, the specifications for resource construction and system construction are more considerable, so the further development of digital libraries will be more open and more

---

* This project is one of the China Academic Library & Information System (CALIS) sub-projects developed during the 10th five-year-plan period.

Z. Chen et al. (Eds.): ICADL 2004, LNCS 3334, pp. 124–132, 2004.

interoperable by adopting the unified specifications. As a symbol that the digital library moves towards perfect, the service-oriented digital library, which is based on the resource-oriented and system-oriented digital library, is trying to improve interaction and communication between the system and its users, so that the friendly, convenient and individualized service platform should be provided.

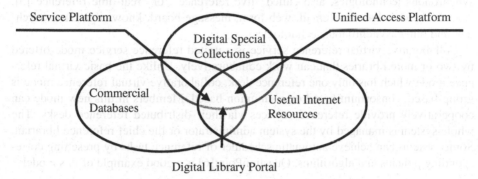

Fig. 1. Framework of the Service-Oriented Digital Library

So an ideal framework of the Service-Oriented Digital Library should compose of three resources, two platforms and one portal, as showed in Figure 1.

It forms an applied and effective digital library firstly by having digital resources (including library's special collections, commercial online e-journals & databases, and useful literature information resource on the Internet) of the Resource-Oriented Digital Library as fundamental elements, secondly by taking uniform information accessing platform and digital library gateway of the System-Oriented Digital Library as a prospective path, and thirdly by developing digital library services of the Service-Oriented Digital Library as an efficient implement.

2   The Service Platform of the Digital Library

The virtual reference system (VRS) plays a key role on the service platform of the digital library[2]. Since Maryland University USA Health Service Library firstly launched 'EARS - The Electronic Access to Reference Service' by using network and information technologies in 1984[3], online reference service has drawn considerable attention in library communities around the world. Especially in recent years, with the further development of information technologies and applications, VRS has been a significant part of the digital library. And it plays a more and more important role in library reference services, due to its flexible access ways, efficient reference modes and web-based management.

As more people rely on the online information resources and less people approach the reference desks at their local libraries for assistance, there is an increasing need of establishing remote communication between patrons and librarians. Many libraries and organizations have responded to this need by providing reference service to their users via the Internet. VRS can combine traditional reference services with digital and network technologies, and it also provides a digital reference platform that allows a patron to get assistance from a librarian without having to physically come to the library. VRS can provide two service modes: the synchronous reference and the asynchronous reference[4]. The former can provide real-time communication between patrons and librarians by using chatting, co-browsing, web-page pushing, and other synchronous technologies, also called "live reference", or "real-time reference"[5]. And the latter is based on email, web-form, message board, knowledge base searching, and other asynchronous technologies.

Collaborative virtual reference service is a united reference service mode offered by two or more libraries that can work collaboratively. Unlike the basic virtual reference mode which has only one reference desk, collaborative virtual reference mode is group-based, consortium-based or even union-based. Members in this new mode can cooperatively provide reference services via their distributed reference desks. The whole system is managed by the system administrator or the chief reference librarian. Some systems can achieve automatic scheduler of reference tasks by presetting corresponding policies and algorithms. QuestionPoint[6] is a good example of this model.

3   The Distributed Collaborative Virtual Reference System

3.1   The System Introduction

China Academic Library & Information System (CALIS) is one of the two communal service systems of the "211 Project"[1] sanctified by the State Department. During the second phase of the project, CALIS has initiated a China Academic Distributed Collaborative Virtual Reference System (CVRS) project in order to provide best possible reference service for patrons and enable reference staff of CVRS members to work collaboratively. Librarians can answer patrons' questions online without the limitation of time and location. Thereby, it resolves the technical problems and makes it possible to realize the 24/7 ideal service mode. This project has started in 2003, and will be accomplished and running in 2005.

3.2   The System Framework

CVRS application system is a two-level distributed framework, including the local virtual reference systems located at CVRS members, and the CALIS central virtual reference system hosted by CVRS center, as shown in Figure 2.

Most system functions are supported by both levels, and each level would also have some unique functions. All the reference systems are distributed.

A distributed reference system is an independent system that has independent system functions and runs independently. It can also establish complete connections

---

[1] Project 211 is supported by the Chinese government and the aim of this project is to improve the level of research capability and higher education for top 100 universities in the 21 century.

among local reference systems, and between the CALIS central reference system and local reference systems. So it is possible to let all the reference systems serve the patrons as a whole.

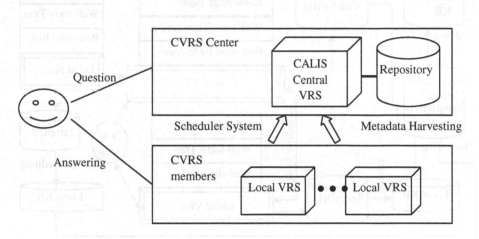

Fig. 2. Two-level distributed framework of the CVRS application system

3.3 The Service Modes

The combination of the central reference system and all distributed local reference systems makes it possible to form one or several reference networks that can provide reference services together by means of assigning duty times among members or working collaboratively.

Figure 3 shows that patrons can enter the CVRS system in two ways:

1. Log on the central reference system, and communicate with the on-line librarians via the real-time reference service provided by the chief virtual reference desk; or fill in a question form, and get the answer from a librarian at the chief virtual reference desk.
2. Log on the local reference system, and communicate with the local on-line librarians; patrons can be transferred to the chief reference desk if there are no local librarians on duty. Patrons can also fill in a question form and send it to the local reference desk.

The records of previous asked questions and answers from the local reference system are saved to the local temporary database first, and then are added to the local knowledge base after being edited by reference librarians to enhance clarity and search ability. The OAI harvest server of the central reference system would harvest the marked records from the local knowledge databases periodically to the central temporary database, and records then can be added to the central knowledge base after being edited. This makes the central knowledge base a primary discovery resource for all patrons and reference librarians.

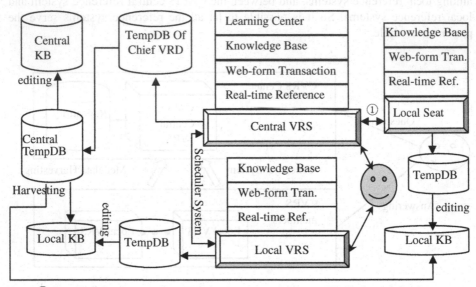

Note: ① for scheduler system; TempDB for temporary database; KB for knowledge base.

Fig. 3. CVRS system service flow chart

3.4 The Scheduler System

In order to realize real collaborative reference, a scheduler system is needed between the central reference system and the local reference systems. The scheduler system can route every question to the librarian/library best able to answer it.

3.4.1 The Scheduler Modes

CVRS has adopted several scheduler modes including:

1. Scheduler by time: Service time of the central system can be assigned to different CVRS members. So the reference service can be switched to the corresponding online reference desk that is on duty. The time unit of this mode is one hour.
2. Scheduler by subject: the system presets profiles of subject specialists, which include their strengths, such as subject strengths, language strengths, etc. Patrons can choose the specialists to answer their questions. The librarians can also transfer the questions to the related specialists if they can't answer them.
3. Scheduler by member: the system presets profiles of CVRS members, including their collections, subjects, reference scope, reference items and so on. CVRS members can look over profile information and transfer questions from each other. The system can also route a question automatically to the member best able to answer it based on the profile information.
4. Scheduler by the status of the reference librarian: when there are more than one librarian online, the system can automatically transfer the new patron to the reference librarian who is not busy or has the shortest waiting list.

5. Any questions that are unable to be answered can be routed to the "On-Call" module, which means to request for answers publicly.

CVRS' scheduler system can route questions for both asynchronous and real-time reference. Scheduler modes used for real-time reference is mainly by time and the status of the reference librarian, it can switch online reference desks by the scheduling strategy. Scheduler modes used for asynchronous reference is mainly by subject, member and "On-Call" module, and these scheduler modes decide the way how questions are to be routed.

3.4.2 Non-real-time Scheduler

Non-real-time scheduler is mainly used for the automatic question routing. This can be achieved in two ways: the questioner can submit the question directly to a reference desk or a librarian/subject specialist that has been chosen to answer the question. If the questioner does not make a choice, the system will analyze attributes of the question first, such as language, related subjects etc. and then compares these attributes with the profiles to find the best candidate most likely to be able to answer the question. A rank list will be generated and the question thus can be routed to the most appropriate candidate on the list. If first candidate is unable to answer, the question can be rerouted to the next likely candidate, and so on. If the automatic matching process cannot find appropriate candidates, the question will be handled manually. Figure 4 shows the process of non-real-time scheduler.

The CVRS member/librarian/subject specialist that receives the routed question may answer directly, and send the question and answer back to the questioner. The question and answer record is saved simultaneity to the temporary database of the chief reference desk and the local reference desk. And at the same time, the question is marked "answered".

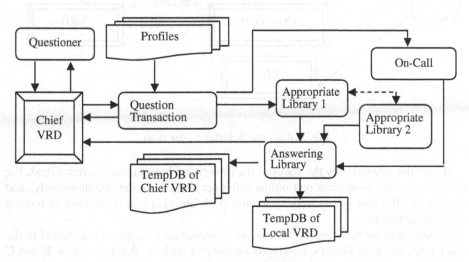

Fig. 4. Non-real-time scheduler flow chart

If the CVRS member can't answer the routed question, it can reroute the question to the next appropriate library, and so on. If finally a question is still unable to be answered, it could be submitted back to the chief reference desk and be handled manually.

The librarian/subject specialist who receives the question will handle it in the same way as described above. The question and answer record will be saved to the temporary database of the chief reference desk and the local reference desk where the librarian/subject specialist works. If the library is not a CVRS member, the answer will be only saved to the temporary database of the chief reference desk.

3.4.3 Real-Time Scheduler

Real-time scheduler is mainly planned by time, and the status of the reference librarian and reference desk.

As for the scheduler by time, the system presets the timetable of duty times. When patrons log on the chief reference desk and ask for real-time reference, the system will automatically transfer patrons to the local reference system that is on duty according to the timetable. The question and answer records will be simultaneously sent to the local temporary database and the temporary database of the central reference desk.

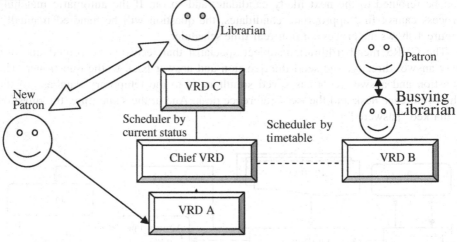

Fig. 5. Real-time Scheduler flow chart

As for the scheduler by the status of the reference librarian and reference desk, the system supports more than one online reference desk/librarian simultaneously, and can transfer the new patron to the reference desk/librarian that is not busy or has the shortest waiting list.

As shown in fig 5, a new patron logs on reference desk A, and is transferred to the chief reference desk because nobody is on duty at desk A. Reference desk B and C are on duty at this time according to the timetable of the chief reference desk. But desk B is busy, so the patron is transferred to the idle reference desk C.

Both real-time scheduler mode and non-real-time scheduler mode are transparent to patrons. If they are available simultaneously, patrons can choose any one of the following reference means: queuing, logging on the local online reference desk, sending question form, and searching knowledge base.

Reference librarians, according to the status of patrons, can directly transfer them to other online reference librarians or other online reference desks. Patrons themselves can also choose to visit other online reference desks.

To realize the automatic question routing, the system needs to collect profiles of CVRS members, reference librarians and subject specialists. Each one should fill in an information table following the archive criterions. The system uses these profiles for automatic routing. A reference desk scheduler server is needed in order to realize real-time reference desk scheduler. A CVRS member must register to the server if it wishes to make its local reference desk a node of the central reference system's collaborative reference network. The central reference system's reference desk scheduler server will dynamically check the status of each reference desk.

4 Conclusion

The construction of CVRS will fall into two phases. The first phase is the developing and running phase of the local system that is supposed to be tested in several universities including Shanghai Jiaotong University by the end of 2004. The second phase is the developing and running phase of the central system that will be accomplished and running by the end of 2005. By then the local and central virtual reference systems of more than 10 universities will work collaboratively to realize the distributed collaborative virtual reference system. By considering the possibility of collaboration with global reference groups, the standard we have defined for our system is compatible with QuIP[7] and DC[8]. We have also studied the draft standard of virtual reference Question/Answer Transaction Protocol[9] that was released by NISO, the US National Information Standards Organization, in March of 2004. We hope being protocol compliant will guarantee the smooth exchange of questions and answers from our system to other systems such as QuestionPoint.

Collaborative virtual reference services can benefit libraries and patrons by sharing expertise and resources, expanding service hours, and providing access to a larger collection of knowledge accumulated from virtual reference service. However, collaboration with other libraries can also raise some challenges, such as ensuring the quality and consistency of responses, reaching consensus in developing procedures and policies, and adopting appropriate technologies. Now many overseas organizations have established virtual reference desks[10]-[15], and in China, more and more libraries have realized the importance of offering VRS and some virtual reference desks have been developed to provide better responses to patrons' information needs[16].

With the growth of virtual reference services and collaborative networks, there is a strong requirement to define the standards that can ensure service quality and interoperability. It is now natural and necessary for libraries to participate collaborative virtual reference that can combine individual virtual references and support better resources sharing rather than just provide local virtual reference. And Service area of the collaborative virtual reference is from among campuses, universities, to regions, consortia and even global. This will be the developing trend in the next few years[5] and it is also a symbol that the digital library moves towards perfect.

References

1. M. Huang, Z.Y. Yang, H.M. Lin: On the Major Models and Development Trends of Online Virtual Reference Service. Journal of Academic Libraries, Volume: 21 No.1 Page 33-36; 2003
2. Gobinda G. Chowdhury: Digital libraries and reference services: present and future. Journal of Documentation, Vol: 58 No: 3 Page: 258 - 283; 2002
3. Wasik, Joann M.: Building and Maintaining Digital Reference Services. http://www.michaellorenzen.com/eric/reference-services.html
4. Catherine Jane, Dawn McMillan: Online in real-time? Deciding whether to offer a real-time virtual reference service. The Electronic Library, Volume: 21 No. 3 Page: 240-246; 2003
5. Lesley M. Moyo: Reference anytime anywhere: towards virtual reference services at Penn State. The Electronic Library, Volume: 20 No. 1 Page: 22-28; 2002
6. Barbara Quint.: QuestionPoint Marks New Era in Virtual Reference. Information Today, Vol. 19, no. 7, pp.50-54; 2002
7. http://www.vrd.org/Tech/QuIP.shtml
8. http://dublincore.org/
9. http://www.loc.gov/standards/netref/qatp-trial.pdf
10. Kaba Abdoulaye, Shaheen Majid: Use of the Internet for reference services in Malaysian academic libraries. Online Information Review, Vol: 24 No: 5 Page: 381-389; 2000
11. Gobinda Chowdhury, Simone Margariti: Digital reference services: a snapshot of the current practices in Scottish libraries. Library Review, Vol: 53 No: 1 Page: 50-60; 2004
12. Rory Patterson: Live virtual reference: more work and more opportunity. Reference Services Review, Volume: 29 No. 3 Page: 204-210; 2001
13. Wayne Daniels, Kathy Scardellato: Past into future: capturing library expertise in a virtual library. Library Hi Tech, Volume: 17 No. 2 Page: 181-188; 1999
14. Catherine Jane, Dawn McMillan: Online in real-time? Deciding whether to offer a real-time virtual reference service. The Electronic Library, Volume: 21 No. 3 Page: 240-246; 2003
15. James A. Stemper, John T. Butler: Developing a model to provide digital reference services. Reference Services Review, Volume: 29 No. 3 Page: 172-189; 2001
16. M. Huang, H.M. Lin, Z.Y. Yang: Building of the Distributive and Collaborative Virtual Reference System. Journal of Shanghai Jiaotong University, Volume: 37 Sup. Page 12-15; 2003

The Role of Context for Information Mediation in Digital Libraries

Erich Neuhold, Claudia Niederée, Avaré Stewart, Ingo Frommholz,
and Bhaskar Mehta

Fraunhofer IPSI, Integrated Publication and Information Systems Institute,
Dolivostrasse 15, 64293 Darmstadt, Germany
{neuhold, niederee, stewart, frommholz, mehta}@ipsi.fhg.de

Abstract. Mediating between available information objects and individual information needs is a central issue within the functionality of a digital library. In the simplest case this is an information request answered by a search engine based on an analysis of information objects within the digital library's information collection. However, neither the information access activity nor the information objects within the collection are isolated entities. They are both equipped with a multifaceted context. The invited talk, which is summarized by this paper, analyzes this context and discusses complementing approaches to make such context explicit and to use it for refining the mediation process within digital libraries.

1 Introduction

"The context of something consists of the ideas, situations, events, or information that relate to it and make it possible to understand it fully" [1]. When information is represented, context is generally left implicit. This strategy enables concise representation and communication under the assumption that relevant parts of the context are shared or given as common background knowledge. If context is represented explicitly (e.g. in knowledge representation [2]), it can be used for reasoning and decision making and enables interpretation in spite of diverging contexts. For an effective use of context, it is important that the "right" aspects of the context are modeled, that the relationship between the context representation and the representation of the "something" in the context is clearly defined, and that there is a systematic way to deal with context changes.

The most common way to represent context for information objects in digital libraries (DLs) are bibliographic meta data. Bibliographical meta data define a *creation context* by embedding an information object into a context which describes mainly its creation and publication processes (e.g. the author and the publication date). There are, however, further context related issues involved in the information mediation process of DLs:

Z. Chen et al. (Eds.): ICADL 2004, LNCS 3334, pp. 133–143, 2004.

1. Within a DL an information object is embedded in a library context that is determined by the collection(s) and information structures it is part of as well as by the library processes it is subject to.
2. When an information object is used and interpreted, this is done in an *interpretation context* that is typically different from the creation context.
3. The collaborative reflection of the information object content by community members leads to new insights and valuations that contribute to *community context*.
4. An information request, or more generally the information access activity, is embedded in a *user context*, i.e. a user's task, interests, skills and other relevant characteristics, as well as results of preceding activities.

This paper systematically examines the types of context that influence the mediation process in DLs, taking the information and knowledge lifecycle of an information object as a starting point (see Section 2). The resulting context typology is used to structure the discussion of approaches that exploit context in the information mediation process in Section 3. Section 4 introduces the additional aspect of context interpretation in heterogeneous environments. The paper concludes with ideas for further work in the area of context exploitation in DLs.

2   A Typology of Context in Digital Libraries

An information object is subject to a number of processes throughout its lifecycle. This section discusses the different types of contexts implied by such a lifecycle and their relevance for the information mediation process in DLs. Furthermore, it reviews basic issues on representing context, a crucial prerequisite for exploiting context.

2.1   The Role of Context in Information Mediation

A DL mediates between the information needs of its user community and the globally available content. This is achieved by contributions in four areas (see [3] and Fig.1): 1) *pre-selecting* content potentially relevant for the members of its user community; 2) *structuring* content according to the predominant domain understanding of its user

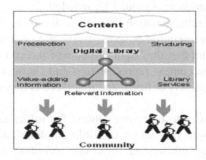

Fig. 1. Digital Library Mediation

community; 3) enriching content objects with value adding metadata; and 4) providing services which support the identification of relevant material and facilitate content access.

These contributions allow a DL to reduce the gap that exists between the wide variety and large amount of globally available content and specific information needs of individuals and small group within its community. However, there still exists a considerable gap since the content and service offer is tailored toward the community as a whole and the individual has specific information needs determined by the current task. This gap can be further reduced by refined information mediation processes.

The mediation process can be refined by achieving an improved understanding of the user's information needs, on the one hand, and of the information objects available, on the other. For this purpose, context information can be taken into account. Context information for an information object (*information context*) provides additional background information about it. Context information for users (*usercontext*) can describe the current situation influencing their information needs (see next section).

If the user's information need is specified by a model of the user context, in addition to the pure information request articulated by the user, the DL can compute matching information objects more accurately also taking into account the modeled information context. Furthermore, selected parts of information context can be presented to the user together with information objects providing additional information for its interpretation and contributing to a better understanding. Thus, context may contribute to the information mediation process on the more pragmatic level of identifying relevant information objects by search and retrieval methods as well as on the perceptual level in contributing to an improved understanding of information objects.

2.2 Context Types Along the Information and Knowledge Lifecycle

An information object is part of an Information and Knowledge Lifecycle (ILKC, see Fig. 2 a) that starts with its (possibly cooperative) creation. Further, important stages within the ILKC are the (electronic) publication of information objects and their policy-driven management and archival in a digital collection. As part of an information collection the information object is enriched with metadata and made available e.g. by a DL and can be accessed by a community. Accessed information objects are interpreted by users. Their interpretation may trigger new insights and, in the area of scientific content, scientific discourse, which may result in the creation of new information objects. Starting from this IKLC, different types of context relevant for the information mediation process can be identified and are structured in a context taxonomy (see Fig. 2b):

User Context: captures the user and his situation in accessing and using information objects.

Community Context: considers the information object as part of community processes like scientific discourse, censorship, content commentary. An information object is perceived, interpreted, reflected or enriched. These process may stimulates other work in the domain or new ways of interpreting the information object.

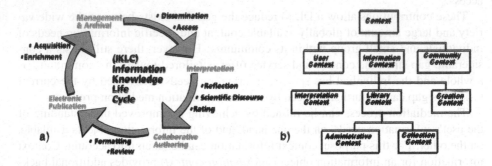

Fig. 2. The Information and Knowledge Lifecycle and related context types

Information Context: includes information about the information object that is directly related to the individual artifact and to its surrounding information structures like an information collection it is part of.

Creation Context: the context an information object is created in. The influence of different context dimensions (cf. section 2.3) like time, political situation, skill of the author, purpose and genre depend on the type of artifact created. If we consider the film "All Quiet on the Western Front" (based on Remarque's novel "Im Westen Nichts Neues" [4]) as an example information object, the creation context is clearly determined by the First World War experience of the author. Creation context also is determined by the reflection of this experience in the time of the creation of the book (1928)[1] . In this example, we can even distinguish a publication context as an important part of the creation context, since Remarque had to revise his book to reduce its anti-war characteristic following the wishes of the publisher.

Library Context: contributes to the interpretation of an information object due to the fact that it becomes part of a DL or another type of a digital collection.

Collection Context: refers to both the information object as part of a collection and information structure of related (possibly explicitly connected) information objects. The aforementioned film could e.g. be part of a collection of anti-war films or it can be linked to other films based on novels by Remarque.

Administrative Context: refers to the information object as subject of administrative library processes like acquisition, preservation, and maintenance. The reasons for acquiring an information object for a specific collection and the reasons of its long-term preservation are e.g. part of this type of context.

---

[1] The chosen example also reflects the idea of the IKLC very well, because the original information object (the novel) triggered the creation of another artifact, the film.

Interpretation Context: the context an information object is interpreted in. The context of the information object creator (creation context) and the context of a person that interprets an information object (interpretation context) are not identical, but only partly overlapping. Differences between these two contexts may be due to cultural differences or a large time span between information object creation and information object consumption. Finally, Interpretation and Community context are related but Community context considers the results of interpretation processes on the community level contributing to new ways of interpreting the information object.

2.3 Context Representation

Each of the context types identified in the previous section consists of a large number of facets that could be represented. The first challenge in context representation is, thus, to identify the relevant facets for the targeted service or as it is put in [5] for information retrieval context: *"The problem is in detecting which of the many contextual elements (that may be applied to the process) actually make a difference to search outcomes."* Determining what facets are relevant depends on the actual approach to be implemented. Therefore, the question of *what* context information is represented is discussed together with the selected context-based approaches in Section 3.

Bibliographic metadata, a popular form of context in DLs, are typically captured by attribute value pairs based on controlled vocabularies for the attributes as well as for parts of the values (e.g. ACM classification schema). Further approaches for *how* to represent context can be found in the area of user and user context modeling for personalization and context aware access support as well as in knowledge representation.

User modeling for personalization services typically focuses on cognitive pattern like user interests and preferences. User model facets are represented by keyword lists, concepts or vector representations that describe user is interests (e.g. [6]). However, there are also more comprehensive modeling approaches, also called user context models [7], that capture further aspects of a user and his current situation like a user's task [8]. Approaches for context aware access are more focused on the physical situation of users like current location, time, present persons or used devices (see e.g. [9]).

In knowledge representation a systematic consideration of context modeling can be found. In [10] twelve dimensions for modeling context are identified including time, location, and topic that can be used as a starting point for modeling context for information mediation. A systematic discussion of different approaches toward context modeling can be found in [11], where a unifying approach is taken based on a metaphor that considers context as a box that is described by a set of parameters and associated values.

A similarly approach is presented in [12] for user context modeling - the Unified User Context Model (UUCM). UUCM describes by an extensible set of facets and structured into four dimensions: cognitive pattern, relationships, task, and environment.

3 Context Exploitation for Information Mediation

The different types of context identified in the previous section can be used to support the information mediation process in different ways. This section discusses representative examples for such approaches to context exploitation. Two advanced approaches are presented in more detail: the systematic use of annotation to capture community and interpretation context, and the Personal Web Context.

3.1 Overview of Approaches

Existing approaches that exploit context for refining the information mediation process differ in the context facets they use and in the way they use the context information. Therefore, for each of the approaches presented in this section the following three aspects are considered: 1) representation: What type of context from the context taxonomy is addressed? What exact context facets are represented by the approach? 2) collection: How is the information for filling the context model collected? 3) exploitation: How is the modeled context used to improve information mediation?

The most obvious way of representing and exploiting context for information mediation in digital libraries is the enrichment of information objects with bibliographic metadata and the use of such metadata in retrieval. Metadata standards for bibliographic metadata like Dublin Core [13] or MARC [14] typically represent parts of the creation context like the author and the publication date. By also capturing classification information (subject, keywords, etc.) a connection between the creation and the interpretation context is made by giving an idea of the intended interpretation of the information object.

An especially interesting case of context information is geo-referencing of information objects as it is done in the Alexandria DL project [15]. Information objects are equipped with references to geographical coordinates that provide context information for their access and interpretation. In some cases the geo-referencing models a type of creation context (e.g. place, where an ancient artifact has been created or found); in other cases the geographical metadata refers to the content of the information objects (e.g. a book about Tuscany) and, thus, rather provides a type of interpretation context.

There are different approaches that take collection context into account in information retrieval and text classification. In [16], for example, links pointing to a documents and the text surrounding such links in the referencing document are considered as relevant information context that contribute to the interpretation of the referenced document. The surrounding text is considered as some type of review of the information object itself and the aggregation of such texts is used as a basis for automatic text classification. Another approach for using collection context can be found in [17]. Links pointing to a document are used to decide if this document is authorative (many other documents refer to it) and documents that point to many authorative documents are considered informative or a "hub" (for a certain topic). A similar approach is used for search engine Google.

One way of refining the information mediation process is personalization based on information filtering. There are two major approaches: content based filtering [18] and collaborative filtering [19]. In both approaches, the overall goal of the information filtering process is to select and deliver "relevant" information objects based on knowledge about the user. In the collaborative case, relevance is computed based on correlations between "like-mined" persons, e.g. those with similar ratings. In the content-based correlations are based on similarity between information objects. The collaborative approach builds a user context as well as a community context. The ratings of user A are used for building a user (context) model for user A. The ratings of different users for an information object B are used to build a community context model of B. The two types of context models are matched with each other to compute recommendations. Content based filtering builds a user context model. This is done when the profiles are constructed by analyzing the content of information objects the user rated in the past.

3.2 Annotations: Creating, Reconstructing and Exploiting Context

Within a DL, annotations can serve several purposes. They aid in realizing features of digital libraries, like creation and interpretation, access, and usage of digital resources. They are helpful in creating, reconstructing and exploiting the different types of contexts.

Annotations (pieces of free text) are a special kind of metadata. Typed links between annotations can form an annotation thread and thus can create a context and new information resources. They are able to capture parts of the *creation context* since they contain the results to be found in the new information resource and provide information about the process of finding the results, the motivations and decisions which finally led to the new content. Annotation can assist in reconstructing the *creation context* which might not be available, e.g. historic documents.

Annotations also support the *interpretation* of documents by providing a framework in which the interpretation of information sources takes place [21]. Using discourse structure relations [21], annotators can provide background information about the authors of other annotations. Such annotations contain information for *Interpretation context*. Regarding the *collection context*, information resources can be linked using annotations, creating new explicit relationships between resources. Annotations can be exploited for information retrieval create new index terms to an information resource, allowing for matching query terms. Additionally, annotation threads based on discourse structure relations can be analyzed, e.g., by using a logic based retrieval function [21,22]. The rich and diverse information contained in annotation threads enables us to discuss advanced context based retrieval frameworks, as it is done in [20].

3.3 Personal Web Context: An Extended View on User Context

As mediator, digital libraries seek to tailor content and services to its users. One fundamental prerequisite for a DL to do so, is the representation of characteristics of its users e.g. the users needs, environment, cognitive patterns etc. Such representations are typically captured by a user model. The most prevalent models of DL users to date limited to representing interests and skills. However, studies have shown that one of the main hindrances to personalization in digital libraries is a limited understanding of users and their information needs [23, 24].

One approach to fulfilling the demand for more comprehensive user models is the Personal Web Context [3]. The PWC approach models the salient interrelationships of individuals in a community context [25]. The provision of valid and expressively annotated Resource Networks is in the core of the PWC approach. Digital libraries may provide such networks extracted from their information collection as value-added service to other or a DL can also implement the PWC approach as part of their own services to support personalized information mediation (see [26] for more details on the PWC).

4   Context Interpretation in Heterogeneous Environments

The two-fold challenge faced for future context based information mediation in DLs is to make increasingly heterogeneous information collections accessible to increasingly heterogeneous communities [23]. Furthermore, the trends toward dynamically federated services replacing integrated systems [27] and toward ubiquitous computing and multi-usage environments, give rise to additional challenges. These challenges are in the areas of extensible and reusable context models, that can be easily combined and exchanged as well as interpreted in different environments. The use of ontologies and ontology based context models and approaches for exchanging context models in heterogeneous environments are important steps in addressing these challenges.

4.1   Ontology and Context

All types of context are captured by some type of metadata. The interpretation of metadata by humans as well as by machines relies on a shared understanding of the concept underlying the metadata schema. Thus, one abstraction level higher, ontologies [28] provide context for context interpretation. This context can be made explicit by referring to formally defined ontologies which define the concepts used in the metadata schema. Ontologies also support combining context information based on different metadata schemata by tracing them back to a shared context (the more basic concepts). The shared understanding and the semantic description achieved by relying on adequately formalized ontologies can be used to develop intelligent services interpret context models that have been created in other independent environments.

One example for an ontology-based (user) context model is the UUCM [12]. In the UUCM, the characteristics and contexts of users are modeled along an extensible set of facets. The facets as well as facet values can be flexibly attached to ontologies or agreed upon vocabularies to enable interpretation in heterogeneous environments.

4.2 Cross-System Context Exchange

Conflictingly, given the current trends toward more heterogeneous populations of DL systems, the mediation on behalf of users usually uses information collected about a user and his current context. The user context however, is traditionally restricted to a single system. The role of context must be reconsidered when tasks require information handling activities that span several systems. Cross-systems context exchange is considered as a way to meet the challenge of interpreting context when the boundary or system interface between the content and the user changes, as in heterogeneous environments.

An example of Cross-System context exchange is the "Context Passport" - which metaphorically accompanies users on travels through the information space [12]. The context passport is a compact representation of the user's current context model. A user, who has an information need, seeks to satisfies this need by a DL system. A user then performs some tasks and the system informs the Context Passport about the user interaction. In an interaction with a second system , the Context Passport provides meaningful interpretation on how the user's context may have evolved as a result of interactions with the previous system.

5 Conclusions and Future Work

In this paper we presented a typology of contexts that are relevant for information mediation within a DL and for the interpretation of information objects. Based on this context typology different approaches for context exploitation in the information mediation process have been discussed. However, there are still some open issues for future work in order to further refine the mediation process based on context information.

- Most contexts evolve and this has to be reflected by the respective context models, else they loose their usefulness for the mediation process;
- The effect of context exploitation might be increased by combining different context types in one approach in a synergetic way.
- For many context types context information is defined manually. The development of further (semi-)automatic methods to collect context information makes context exploitation in information mediation more affordable and enables the implementation of further methods of context exploitation.

References

1. Akman, V., Surav, M.: Steps toward formalizing context. AI Magazine 17 (1996) 55—72
2. D.B., L.: Cyc: Large-scale investment in knowledge infrastructure. Communications of the ACM 38 (1995) 33–38
3. Neuhold, E.J., Niederée, C., Stewart, A.: Personalization in digital libraries: An extended view. In: Proceedings of ICADL 2003. (2003) 1–16
4. Remarque, E.: Im Westen nichts Neues. 1998 edn. Kiepenheuer and Witsch (1929)

5. Toms, E., Dufour, C., Bartlett, J., Fruend, L., Szigeti, S.: Identifying the significant contextual factors of search. ACM SIGIR 2004 Workshop on Information Retrieval in Context (2004) 26–29

6. Konstan, J., Miller, B., Maltz, D., Herlocker, J., Gordon, L., Reidl, J.: Applying collaborative filtering to usenet news. Communications of the ACM 40 (1997) 77–87

7. Goker, A., Myrhaug, H.: User context and personalization. In: Proceedings of the European Conference on Case Based Reasoning (ECCBR 2002) - Workshop on Personalized Case- Based Reasoning, Aberdeen, Scotland, 4-7 September 2002. Volume LNCS 2416 of Lecture Notes in Artificial Intelligence., Springer-Verlag (2002)

8. Souchon, N., Limbourg, Q., Vanderdonckt, J.: Task modeling in multiple contexts of use. In: Proceedings of 9th International Workshop on Design, Specification, and Verification of Interactive Systems DSV-IS'2002. Volume 2545 of Lecture Notes in Computer Science., Springer-Verlag (2002)

9. Schmidt, A., Beigl, M., Gellersen, H.W.: There is more to context than location. Computers and Graphics Journal 23 (1999) 893–902

10. Lenat, D.B. : The dimensions of context space. http/www.cyc.com/publications (1998)

11. Benerecetti, M., Bouquet, P., Ghidini, C.: Contextual reasoning distilled. Journal of Theoretical and Experimental Artificial Intelligence 12 (2000) 279–6305

12. Niederée, C.J., Stewart, A., Mehta, B., Hemmje, M.: A multi-dimensional, unified user model for cross system personalization. In: Proceedings of Advanced Visual Interfaces International Working Conference (AVI 2004) - Workshop on Environments for Personalized Information Access, Gallipoli (Lecce), Italy, May 2004. (2004)

13. Weibel, S.: Metadata: The foundations of resource description. D-Lib Magazine (1995) http://www.dlib.org/dlib/July95.

14. Crawford, W.: MARC for Library Use, 2nd ed. G.K. Hall & Co, Boston (1989)

15. Chen, H., Smith, T. R.and Larsgaard, M.L.H.L.L.: Ta geographic knowledge representation system for multimedia geospatial retrieval and analysis. International Journal on Digital Libraries 1 (1997) 132–152

16. Attardi, G., Gullí, A., Sebastiani, F.: Automatic Web page categorization by link and context analysis. In Hutchison, C., Lanzarone, G., eds.: Proceedings of THAI-99, European Symposium on Telematics, Hypermedia and Artificial Intelligence, Varese, IT (1999) 105–119

17. Kleinberg, J.: Authoritative sources in a hyperlinked environment. Journal of the ACM (JACM) 46 (1999) 604–632

18. Mooney, R., Roy, L.: Content based book recommending using learning for text categorization. In: Proceedings of the Fifth ACM Conference on Digital Libraries, San Antonio, TX, June 2000. (2000) 195–204

19. Bouthors, V., Dedieu, O.: Pharos, a collaborative infrastructure for web knowledge sharing. In Abiteboul, S., Vercoustre, A.M., eds.: Research and Advanced Technology for Digital Libraries, Proceedings of the Third European Conference, ECDL'99, Paris, France, September 1999. Volume LNCS 1696 of Lecture Notes in Computer Science, Springer-Verlag (1999) 215 ff.

20. Agosti, M., Ferro, N., Frommholz, I., Thiel, U.: Annotations in digital libraries and collaboratories -- facets, models and usage. In: Proc. 8th European Conference on Research and Advanced Technology for Digital Libraries (ECDL). (2004)

21. Brocks, H., Stein, A., Thiel, U., Frommholz, I., Dirsch-Weigand, A.: How to incorporate collaborative discourse in cultural digital libraries. In: Proceedings of the ECAI 2002 Work- shop on Semantic Authoring, Annotation & Knowledge Markup (SAAKM02), Lyon, France (2002)

22. Frommholz, I., Thiel, U., Kamps, T.: Annotation based document retrieval with four valued probabilistic datalog. In Roelleke, T., de Vries, A.P., eds.: Proceedings of the 1st SIGIR Workshop on the Integration of Information Retrieval and Databases (WIRD'04). (2004)

23. Callan, J., Smeaton, A.: Personalization and recommender systems in digital libraries. Technical report, DELOS-NSFWorkshop on Personalization and Recommender Systems in Digital Libraries (2003) Further Contributors: Beaulieu M., Borlund P., Brusilovsky P., Chalmers M., Lynch C., Riedl J., Smyth B., Straccia U., Toms E.

24. Hanani, U., Shapira, B., Shoval, P.: Information filtering: Overview of issues, research and systems. User Modeling and User-Adapted Interaction 11 (2001) 203–259

25. McDonald, D.: Recommending collaboration with social networks: A comparative evaluation. In: Proceedings of the ACM Conference on Human Factors in Computing Systems (CHI'03), 2003. Volume 5., ACM Press (2003) 593–600

26. Stewart, A., Niederée, C., Mehta, B., Hemmje, M., Neuhold, E.: Extending your neighborhood - relationship based recommendations for your personal web context. In: Proceedings of Seventeenth International Conference of Asian Digital Libraries. (2004)

27. Frommholz, I., Knezevic, P., Mehta, B., Niederée, C., Risse, T., Thiel, U.: Supporting information access in next generation digital library architectures. In Agosti, M., Schek, H., Trker, C., eds.: Digital Library Architectures: Peer-to-Peer, Grid, and Service-Orientation. Proceedings of the Sixth Thematic Workshop of the EU Network of Excellence DELOS. Lecture Notes in Computer Science (2004) 49–60

28. Gruber, T.: Towards principles for the design of ontologies used for knowledge sharing. In Guarino, N., Poli, R., eds.: Formal Ontology in Conceptual Analysis and Knowledge Representation, Deventer, The Netherlands, Kluwer Academic Publishers (1993)

A Policy-Based System for Institutional Web Archiving

Wasuke Hiiragi, Tetsuo Sakaguchi, Shigeo Sugimoto, and Koichi Tabata

Graduate School of Library, Information and Media Studies, University of Tsukuba
{ragi, saka, sugimoto, tabata}@slis.tsukuba.ac.jp

Abstract. Archiving Web content is an important topic for digital libraries and especially for deposit libraries. Web archiving systems usually collect Web resources using search robot software and/or by human labor. However, these resource gathering methods have disadvantages: for example, it is difficult to collect all historical versions of a resource or to collect hidden or dynamic resources. This paper proposes a Web archiving system which is designed to collect resources in accordance with a resource archiving policy determined by the person or organization which provides the resources on the Web. This paper presents the model of the Web archiving system and a prototype system implemented based on the model.

1 Introduction

Today, there are huge number of Web resources on the Web and the number of the resources are increasing very rapidly. The importance of the Web resources is increasing not only for professional and scholarly activities but also for cultural, social and daily activities. Many organizations such as universities, governments, and companies are providing information resources on the Web which we call institutional Web. They have been making significant efforts to keep them updated. As the Web matures, it has become a crucial task to provide users with legacy resources as well as new resources. Since resource archiving is an important but hard and inconspicuous task, the majority of the organizations do not archive their Web resources well. A goal of this study is to build a system which supports the organizations to collect and archive their Web resources.

There are global and nation-wide Web archiving services, e.g. Internet Archive in cooperation with the Library of Congress, the PANDORA archive in Australia, and WARP by the National Diet Library, Japan. These services collect resources through the global Internet and archive the resources based on their own policies. However, these services have experienced many difficulties caused by the nature of Web resources; for example, Web resources are updated frequently, they are occasionally moved to other locations or suddenly disappear, some resources are created on-the-fly, and intellectual property issues to archive the resources by a third party is not clear. Since these problems are mainly caused by the basic task model of these conventional services in which there is no collaboration between resource providers and archiving agents. In this study, we propose a task model in which resource providers, which are resource creators and site administrators, and archiving agents cooperate for

Z. Chen et al. (Eds.): ICADL 2004, LNCS 3334, pp. 144–154, 2004.

collecting and archiving resources. Cooperation between the providers and archiving agents is hard to realize in the global Web environment, but they can collaborate for archiving their Web resources in an organizational or community network environment.

In this paper, the authors propose a model to collect and archive Web resources and provide the archived resources for users[1]. This paper describes the implementation of a prototype of a Web archiving system based on the model, and discusses the lessons learned from the development of the system.

2 Web Page Archiving Oriented to Organizational Network

2.1 Web Contents and Archiving

An ordinary Web page is an instance composed of one or more objects. Each object is identified by a URI. Most commonly used identification scheme is URL which points a location. There are various kinds of component objects of Web pages including active or dynamic objects, e.g. HTML texts, XML texts, still and motion pictures, animations, programs, and so on. These Web pages are primarily classified into two classes, i.e., static resource and dynamic resource. A static page is directly transferred to Web clients from a Web server without any processing on-the-fly. On the other hand, a dynamic page is produced from a source object on-the-fly. To archive a dynamic resource, there are two ways of collecting a resource; one is to collect the source object and a set of program codes to produce the resource, and the other is to collect the resource in the form that is transferred to a client. In this paper, the former is called *internal form*, and the latter is called *external form*. [Fig. 2.1]

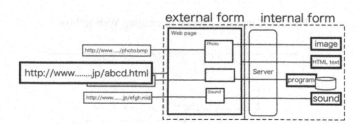

Fig. 2.1. Structure of Web page

2.2 A Brief Survey of Web Archiving Services

There are several Web archiving projects and services which are primarily collecting resources from the global Web or nation-wide Webs. Internet Archive is a project to archive Web pages accessible by a search robot which collects resources on the Internet [2]. A small JavaScript code is added to every resource in order to keep hyperlinks in each resource consistent. The PANDORA Archive by the National Library of Australia selectively collects and archives Web resources. They add metadata to each resource manually [3][4]. WARP by the National Diet Library collects contents in Web sites of national and local governments, universities and public sectors [5][6]. They also collect Web sites hosted by major international and domestic events, e.g. festivals, expositions, and sports games. Resources are collected by software. WARP provides the categorized Web sites and a search function.

There are a few crucial problems in the conventional resource gathering method which uses software robot as described below.

(1)   These Web archives collect the contents via the Internet periodically. As shown in Figure 2.2, if Web pages are revised more than once within a collection interval, some versions will be lost. If the contents are not revised during the interval, the archive collects the same contents two or more times.

(2)   Web pages are sometime moved to another location. Fig.2.3 shows an example of history of migration of a Web page; a Web page is moved to a new location from an original location, and then the page is split into two pages. Fig.2.3 also shows that a location can be re-used by different contents. Although Web archiving systems should be able to keep track of the location changes of the resources, it generally is not easy to find the changes without notifications from resource providers or intelligent tools to keep track of migration of the Web pages.

(3)   There are resources valuable to archive but are not accessible from the archiving agent because of accessibility, i.e. hidden Web.

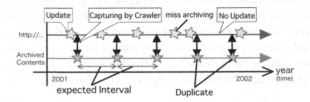

Fig. 2.2. Capturing interval of existing Web archive

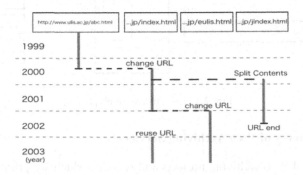

Fig. 2.3. History of URLs of pages

These problems are hard to solve without collaboration between providers of the resources and archiving agents. In conventional Web archiving systems which are mostly oriented to collect resources from the global network environment, it is not realistic to assume collaboration between the providers and the archiving agents. Therefore, in this study, we propose a collaborative archiving model which is primarily oriented to an organization or a community.

2.3 Basic concepts for Institutional Web Archiving

Organizations such as universities and governments have serious demands to archive and preserve their Web resources published by their members. Although there are well-known Web archiving services, technologies for the organizations to archive their Web resources are immature yet. This model assumes that cooperation between resource providers and archiving agents for archiving. The fundamental difference between global Web archiving and organization-oriented Web archiving is the incentive of the organizations to archive their contents. The core concepts of this model are description of archiving policy associated with every resource to be archived and metadata to store Web pages.

The Web archiving system proposed in this paper obtains a Web resource each time it is revised. This revision includes update of the contents of the resource, removal of the resource and relocation of the resource. In order to obtain all revisions of the resource, the archiving system has to be notified each time the resource is revised. The system has an interface for receiving events of revision from Web servers, which we call *update event*. Since the archiving system is triggered by update events to archive resources, archiving decision is controlled by the Web servers that send events to the archiving system. The Web servers which cooperate with the archiving system determine archiving factors which are, for example, events to initiate archiving, a method to archive, access control of archived resources, and so on. These factors are associated with the resources as policy description and stored in the Web servers. The policy description is used by the Web servers and the archiving system.

In this paper, an archived Web page is organized into a set of *Archived Components*, *Archived Resource*, and *Set of Archived Resources*. An *Archived Resource* is composed of one or more *Archived Components*. An *Archiving Resource Set* is a series of resources collected from a single location or a single site which may have changed its location. [Fig. 2.4]

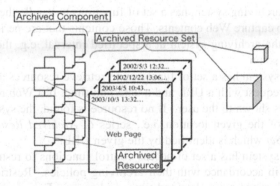

Fig. 2.4. Model of archived Web pages

Archived Component.   An *Archived Component* is a primitive object which is stored into the archive. An archived component is a file stored in a location identified by a URL. It is identified in the system by its URL and date-and-time when it was captured. Components are used to reconstruct an *Archived Resource* on a client, e.g. Web browsers, when the resource is requested.

Archived Resource.   An *Archived Resource* is a composite instance composed of one or more *Archived Components*. It is a snapshot of a Web page at the time the page was captured. An archived resource is identified by the location of the page and the date-and-time of capture.

Archived Resource Set.   An *Archived Resource Set* is an ordered set of *Archived Resources* captured from a single location or a logically single site. *Archived Resources* in *Archived Resource Set* is ordered by date-and-time of capture. Every *Archived Resource Set* has a date-and-time of creation and that of removal. The creation and removal date-and-times are used to identify the period of existence of the *Archived Resource Set*.

Metadata is created for each instance of *Archived Component*, *Archived Resource*, and *Archived Resource Set*. The metadata schema for these components is discussed in section 3.3.

3   Archiving System Model

3.1   Overview

The authors have designed a Web archive system based on the concepts described in the previous section. The Web archive system cooperates with Web servers where resources to be archived are stored. Since this archiving system is designed for an organization or a community, we call it an institutional Web archive which is an intranet-oriented archive. As shown in Fig.3.1, in an institutional Web environment, Web page creators and administrators of the Web servers and administrators of the archiving system collaborates in order to effectively archive their resources. In the proposed model, these people collaborate to determine their archiving policies. In this system, Web servers have a set of functions to send update events to the archiving system. The archiving system has a set of functions to handle the events. It has a set of functions to capture Web contents. Those contents that are periodically updated are collected by the archiving system at a specified interval, e.g. the bulletin board, news articles and so on.

The archiving system has a set of functions to retrieve resources archived. A user gives a retrieval request with a URL and a date-and-time. If a Web resource is found in the archive, it is shown to the user. If no resource is found, the system displays the resource history of the given location, i.e., series of *Archived Resources* in an *Archived Resource Set* which is identified by the given URL.

The archiving system has a set of access control functions to restrict access to archived resources in accordance with their archiving policies. Restrictions are determined by network range, user, date and time, and so on. For example, a university can make an archived dissertation open to off-campus users after three years from its first publication.

The system archives the Web pages when it receives the following events.

Create a new Web page. This event is occurred when a new page is created at a new location. When this event is notified, the system creates a new *Archived Resource* and a new *Archived Resource Set*, and stores the captured files as new *Archived Component*.

Change a Web page. This event is occurred when an existing Web page is updated. When this event is notified, the system adds a new *Archived Resource* to an existing *Archived Resource Set*, and stores the captured files as *Archived Component*.

Remove a Web page. This event is occurred when a Web page is removed. When this event is notified, the system sets the date-and-time of deletion to the corresponding *Archived Resource Set*.

Relocate a Web page. This event is occurred, when a Web page is relocated to a new location. When this event is notified, the system adds a new *Archived Resource* and a new *Archived Resource Set* which is linked to the *Archived Resource Set* of the previous URL. The system stores the captured files as *Archived Component*. The system sets the date-and-time of deletion to the previous *Archived Resource Set*.

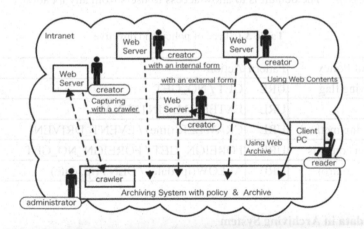

Fig. 3.1. Overview of this system

3.2 Policy Description

The policy descriptions are given by administrators and creators of Web resources and stored in Web servers. A policy description is composed of a pattern and actions. A pattern is a regular expression used to specify a location or a domain of locations of resources to which a policy description applies. When a Web page is created, updated or deleted, its URL is examined using registered patterns. If a pattern matches the URL, its corresponding action is applied to the Web page. The policy types and the actions are shown in Table 3-1.

Archiving flag. The action *GET* means to capture a Web page. *NO_GET* means not to capture the Web page. The default action is *GET*.

Form. This type of action specifies to capture the Web page in *internal form* or *external form*. The action *EXTERNAL* means external form and *INTERNAL* means internal form. The default action is *INTERNAL*.

Capturing method. This type describes a triggering method to automatically collect by search robots. *EVENT_DRIVEN* specifies to capture resources at an update event. *CRAWLER(time)* specifies that a search robot captures periodically by an interval specified in *time*.

Foreign components. In the case a captured Web page has a component stored in the Web server that is not included in a cooperation circle for archiving, the system cannot receive the update events caused by actions on the component. This policy type specifies how to handle those foreign components. *FOREIGN_GET* means capturing by the crawler, and *FOREIGN_NO_GET* means not capturing. The system does not capture the foreign components by default.

Access control. The system controls access to archived Web pages. *ALLOW(ip, date)* means the system allows access to the Web pages from users at the network address *ip* during specified date. *DENY(ip, date)* does not allow access from the network address *ip*. The default is to allow access to users from any location.

Table 3.1. Type of policy and directive

Type of Policy	Pattern	Action
Archiving flag	URL	GET / NO_GET
Form	URL	EXTERNAL / INTERNAL
Capturing method	URL	CRAWLER(time) / EVENT_DRIVEN
Foreign contents	URL	FOREIGN_GET / FOREIGN_NO_GET
Access control	URL	ALLOW(ip, date) / DENY(ip, date)

3.3 Metadata in Archiving System

This system maintains metadata of *Archived Component*, *Archived Resource*, and *Archived Resource Set*. Metadata schema for these data components is shown in the following paragraphs. Every metadata instance of a data component is identified by a pair of URL and date of creation of the data component.

An *Archiving Component* has four metadata elements given in Table3.2. *componentURL* is a location of a component when it was captured. *ComponentDate* is the date-and-time of capture. All components have own Content-Type in the HTTP header, this data is used as a *componentType* value. Conditions to reproduce resources are given by an administrator or a creator in *componentMemo*.

Table 3.2. Metadata of Archived Component

componentURL	URL of the component, i.e., URL of a file capture and stored into the archive.
componentDate	Date-and-time of capture of the component.
componentType	Type of the component which is derived from the HTTP header.
componentMemo	Comments

Table 3.3. Metadata of Archived Resource

resourceURL	URL of the resource which is a composite instance composed of one or more components at the time of capture.
resourceDate	Date-and-time of the resource at the time of capture.
resourceComponent	Identifiers of the archived components which are a part of the resource.

An *Archived Resource* has three metadata elements shown in Table3.3. The metadata of *resourceURL* is the location of the captured resource. *Archived Components* that constitute the resource are described in *resourceComponent*.

Table 3.4. Metadata of Set of Archived Resource

resourceSetURL	URL of the archived resource set.
resourceSetPast	URL of the predecessor of the archived resource set.
resourceSetCreated	Date-and-time of the creation of the archived resource set, i.e., date-and-time of the first capture of the first resource in the set.
resourceSetDeleted	Date-and-time of the last deletion of a resource in the archived resource set.

An *Archived Resource Set* has four metadata elements shown in Table3.4. Resource set is a collection of Archived Resources located at a single location described in *resourceURL*. *ResourceSetURL* is a location of collected Archived Resources. URL of the previous location is recorded in *resourceSetPast* in the case that the captured resource is relocated from an old location to a new location. A period during which the location was used is described in *resourceSetCreated* and *resourceSet-Deleted*, and they are used in order to choose a resource with *resourceSetURL*.

4 Implementation

The system consists of the three parts which are Updating Part, Capturing Part, and Archive Access Part. DSpace is used to build the Updating Part and the Capturing

Part [7][8]. Since DSpace does not have a function for archiving multiple versions of a resource captured from a single location, the metadata schema of DSpace is extended to satisfy the requirements described in section 3.3. [Fig. 4-1]

The Web Archiving Server is synchronized with a Web server by an updating event from the Updating Part in the Web server in the capturing process. The capture process is carried out as follows:

1. A creator updates the contents with the Updating Part on its the Web Server,
2. The Updating Part detects the change by the creator's action and sends an update event and the resource to the Capturing Part, and then
3. The Capturing Part receives them with metadata automatically generated based on the event and policy description, and then, it archives the resource with the metadata.

A user inputs a date-and-time and a URL and gets a Web page from the archive. The system provides the archived Web contents as follows:

1. A user inputs a URL and a date-and-time via the user interface,
2. A system finds an Archived Resource Set based on the URL, and check the date-and-time with metadata of *resourceSetCreated* and *resourceSetDeleted*,
3. If the Web page has not been relocated from the location specified by the user, the system finds an Archived Resource based on the date-and-time in the set, and then
4. Based on metadata of the Archived Resource, the system sends Archived Contents to the User Interface via the Accessing Part. A Web browser assembles these files into a Web page.
5. If the Web page has been relocated, the system finds a preceding or following Archived Resource Set and continues the steps 3 and 4.

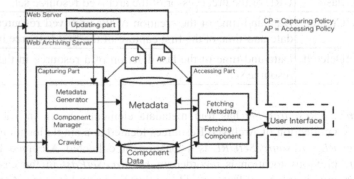

Fig. 4.1. The prototype system

5 Discussion and Conclusion

We designed this system in order to satisfy the following three requirements, which are widely recognized as crucial issues from the experiences in the existing Web archiving services described in section 2.2.

- Capturing all versions of Web resources based on archiving policy,
- Capturing dynamic resources in appropriate forms determined by archiving policy, and
- Tracing a history of a Web page which has been relocated from a location to another.

The primary reason of the difficulty for the existing Web archiving systems to satisfy these requirements is that it is hard for the archiving systems to get information required to satisfy the requirements from resource providers. The model proposed in this paper has solved the problems by cooperative resource archiving between an archiving system and Web servers.

Archiving resources located in restricted locations for external search robots to access is a well-known issue for Web archiving. Collaboration by resource providers and Web archive agents are inevitable in order to solve this issue which is primarily deeply related to intellectual property rights and publishing policies.

Thus, this model requires human efforts to establish cooperation between the archiving system and Web servers and to write policy descriptions. The cost of the human efforts is not negligible but we consider that the cost is affordable for organizations and communities who want to archive their Web resources systematically.

Another advantage of this model is that every resource is archived exactly in the form that it is captured. Consistency of hyperlinks between resources is maintained by the archiving system using metadata attached to the archived resources and no additional script is inserted to the captured resource. Dynamic contents may loose their source resource if *external form* is chosen. However, this information loss depends on the archiving policy.

Not only new resources but also legacy resources are important and useful for Web users, especially for those users who use the Internet like a library. As the existing global and nation-wide Web archiving services have shown, there are several unsolved problems. The model is proposed to solve some of the issues as described above by building an archiving system for an institutional Web environment but not for the global or nation-wide Internet. We need to evaluate the functionality of the model in depth using the prototype. Cooperative archiving network by multiple institutional Web archiving systems is left for our future work to bridge the gap between the institutional Web archiving and the global Web archiving.

Acknowledgements

The authors would like to express our thanks to Profs. Atsuyuki Morishima and Mitsuharu Nagamori for their useful discussions on this study.

References

[1] Wasuke HIIRAGI, Tetsuo SAKAGUCHI, Shigeo SUGIMOTO, Koichi TABATA, "A Web Archiving System for Information Providers" Digital Libraries, No 24, September 2003. in Japanese

[2] Internet Archive. <http://www.archive.org/>. (accessed 2004-9-9)

[3] PANDORA Archive. <http://pandora.nla.gov.au/index.html>. PANDRA. (accessed 2004-9-9)

[4] Warwick Cathro, Colin Webb and Julie Whiting, "Archiving the Web: The PANDORA Archive at the National Library of Australia" <http://www.nla.gov.au/nla/staffpaper/2001/cathro3.html>, National Library of Australia (accessed 2004-9-9)

[5] WARP. <http://warp.ndl.go.jp/>. National Diet Library Japan. (accessed 2004-9-9)

[6] Machiko NAKAI, "Consideration and plan for metadata description of the National Diet Library" Digital Libraries, No 22, March 2002. in Japanese (accessed 2004-9-9)

[7] DSpace Federation. <http://www.dspace.org/>. MIT and Hewlett-Packard. (accessed 2004-9-9)

[8] DSpace Public API. <http://jehu.leosandbox.org/doc/dspace/>. MIT and Hewlett-Packard. (accessed 2004-1-17)

Building a Distributed Heterogeneous CALIS-ETD Digital Library

Yang Zhao and Airong Jiang

Tsinghua University Library, Beijing, China 100084
{zhaoyang, jiangar}@lib.tsinghua.edu.cn

Abstract. CALIS Electronic Thesis and Dissertation Digital Library (CALIS-ETD-DL) is a distributed heterogeneous digital library system funded by CALIS with goals to share the ETD resource among the universities in China and speed up knowledge spreading. It is a prototype system based on the advanced digital library technology and open standards. This paper focuses on the following issues: 1) architecture of CALIS-ETD-DL and its implementation that is centralized metadata repository and distributed digital object; 2) interoperability protocol and standard interface used in CALIS-ETD-DL including international widely used protocol such as OAI, METS, OPENURL, Web Service etc. and self-defined protocol such as ODL-MAP protocol etc; 3) ETD Digital Right Management System for ETD copyright protection; 4) CALIS-ETD metadata specification for describing and administrating ETD resource; 5) ETD persistent identifier and long-term preservation format of ETD. Conclusions are drawn and future works of CALIS-ETD-DL are introduced in the end.

1 Introduction

Theses and Dissertations are a type of the important academic resource for the application and development of knowledge. Generally the print theses and dissertations have a very limited reach and are rarely viable in a massive way. The development of computer and network technology makes it possible to collect, preserve, manage and access ETDs (Electronic Thesis and Dissertations). There are more advantages for the ETD service in the digital library environment than the print TD service in the traditional environment. ETD service makes it possible for anyone worldwide to access ETD and can improve graduate education through more effective sharing. ETD is more expressive than the print thesis and dissertations. Many ETDs include color diagrams and images, interactive forms such as animations, and multimedia resources including audio and video that can enhance the expressive force of ETDs and help users to better understand the content of ETDs. At the same time, ETDs can reduce the need for library storage spaces and improve library services.

There are over 1000 universities in the China. The students in universities create a considerable amount of ETDs every year. To make these ETD resources become more readily and more completely available and speed up technology and knowledge sharing, the China Academic Library & Information System (CALIS) funded the three-year national CALIS-ETD digital library project. The Tsinghua University staff

Z. Chen et al. (Eds.): ICADL 2004, LNCS 3334, pp. 155–164, 2004.

is in charge of implementing the project in 2003-2005. The project will achieve the following objectives:

1) Establishing the CALIS-ETD-DL that is centralized metadata repository and many distributed digital object repositories, share the ETD resource among the universities and provide the wider access to ETDs.

2) Helping the member universities establish the submission and retrieval system that is OAI and METS compatible, design and develop the ETD workflow module, decrease the cost of managing the ETDs.

3) Harvesting the ETD metadata and pre-16 page PDF files by the OAI and METS technologies, establish the central CALIS-ETD merged metadata collection, centrally manage and preserve the pre-16 pages of ETD in PDF format.

4) Enabling ETD metadata and the pre-16 page PDF files to be searchable, link metadata to ETD digital objects by the OpenURL technology or URN resolver.

5) Implementing and designing the standards and specifications related to ETDs.

6) Establishing strategy of long-term preservation of ETDs.

7) Formulating policies to safeguard the copyright and intellectual property rights of ETDs.

Not only is the CALIS-ETD-DL an applied digital library system for ETD services, but also it is a prototype system of digital library that uses the many advanced technologies such as OPENURL, DRM (Digital Right Management), OAI-PMH, METS Harvest, Persistent Identifier name resolution and so on.

There are an international and several national ETD digital library projects that have established or are implementing now. NDLTD is the most influential international ETD cooperation project and has 210 worldwide members now. NDLTD uses the OAI-PMH to harvest the metadata from the members, but it only harvests the static URL of ETD digital object. Users cannot link to ETD digital object through the static URL when ETD is moved to a new location and the URL address has been changed. And there is no specified method for the creation of a globally unique identifier within the NDLTD system. So it is impossible to provide with mechanism for the persistent identification and resolution of ETD digital object. Many universities in British have used or are planning to use Dspace for individual institutional ETD collections, but there is not a nationwide repository of ETDs now. DiTeD(Digital Thesis and Dissertation) project initiated by national library of Portugal uses URN to identify ETD and describe ETD in METS structure for storage in the preservation space. The national library of Portugal centrally manages ETD resources and provides services for users. Malaysia national ETD project uses grid technology to establish ETD digital library within Malaysia Context that can realize to formally manage the distribution of ETD across institutional boundaries.CALIS-ETD-DL has some similar characteristics with other existing ETD digital library systems in the technology implementation process. And they also have many different points because of the local status, characteristics and copyright of Chinese ETD resource. This paper will mainly discuss and introduce some of the key technologies applied in the CALIS-ETD-DL.

The rest of the paper is organized as follows. Section 2 presents the architecture of CALIS-ETD-DL. In Section 3 we discuss the interoperability protocol and standard interface in the CALIS-ETD-DL. Section 4 introduces the DRM system for ETD copyright protection. In section 5 we introduce the ETD metadata specification. Section 6 presents the persistent identifier and long-term preservation format of ETD. Section 7 concludes and discusses the future work.

2 Design of CALIS-ETD-DL Architecture

CALIS-ETD-DL is a distributed digital library system that consists of central CALIS-ETD collection and ETD submission and retrieval systems in the member universities. Figure 1 shows the CALIS-ETD-DL architecture. The lower part in this figure is the function module of ETD submission and retrieval systems in the member universities. The upper part is the function module of central CALIS-ETD collection. They all include four layers consisting of storage layer, application layer, interface layer and safe communication layer.

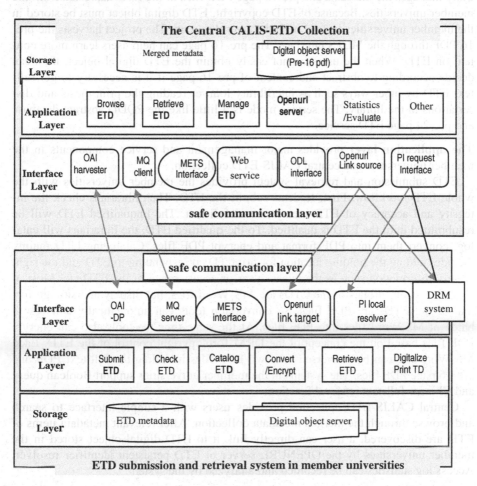

Fig. 1. CALIS-ETD-DL Architecture

The storage layer consists of ETD metadata repositories and digital object servers. ETD metadata repositories in the member universities are responsible for managing and storing all their own ETD metadata stored in RDBMS or Chinese full-text retrieval databases. Metadata Repository provides some methods to store and index text abstracted from full-text PDF files in order to realize ETD full-text retrieval function in the member university system. Digital object servers in the member universities provide the mechanism for storing and organizing all kinds of ETD digital objects that include PDF full-text files, multimedia files related with ETD such as audio or video files, software demo, experimental data etc. Administrators in the member universities can flexibly configure access right of ETD digital object. Access right granted by the students has three levels including within each campus, within the CALIS-ETD-DL member universities and on the Internet.

The ETD merged metadata repository in the central CALIS-ETD collection centrally manages the metadata and pre-16 page PDF files of the ETD harvested from the member universities. Because of ETD copyright, ETD digital object must be stored in the member universities instead of in the central system. The project harvests the pre-16 PDF through the METS interface. The pre-16 page can help users learn more content on ETD. When the users cannot easily obtain the ETD digital object, they can decide according to abstract and content of pre-16 page if it is necessary to get full-text ETD by other ways such as interlibrary loan or reading the print thesis and dissertations in the library. The service mode is a little like the PQDD abstract database and pre-24 page ETD service.

The application layer provides major management and service components in the member universities and central CALIS-ETD collection.

ETD submission and retrieval system provides the member universities with the whole ETD workflow. First, students submit the ETD. Then librarians check the integrity and accuracy of ETD metadata and full-text. The unqualified ETD will be resubmitted until the ETD is qualified. To the qualified ETD, the librarians will catalog, convert them into PDF format and encrypt PDF files. Cataloging ETD mainly includes adding the holding location for print TD corresponding to ETD and the right control information such as the release year or access range of the ETD etc. Most of the submission formats of the ETDs are MS-Word files, but display and storage format of the ETDs are PDF files. So conversion tools can automatically converse a batch of MS-Word files into PDF files. At the same time the tools also can encrypt PDF files based on the concept of the DRM for copyright control of the ETD. Each MS-Word file can be conversed into two PDF files including the full-text PDF and pre-16 page PDF files. The systems in the member universities support Boolean query and Chinese full-text retrieval function.

Central CALIS-ETD collection provides users with a simple interface to search and browse through the merged metadata collection. After relevant metadata items of ETD are discovered, a user can directly link it to ETD digital object stored in the member universities by the OPENURL server or ETD persistent identifier resolver. Access log statistics can be recorded and analyzed by the system.

The Interface Layer can realize interoperability between the member universities and central system or between the central system and other digital libraries. The protocol and interface will be introduced in detail in section 3.

The safe communication layer can ensure the data exchange safety among interactive systems. The safe communication mechanism for CALIS-ETD-DL is established according to three basic principles: simple configuration, no impact on total system performance, safe communication. The SSL protocol is the industry standard and the most effective way to conduct secure communication. It provides a safe channel for message exchange between a client and server. SSL is very easy to use and is transparent to web service. That is to say, the program code for SSL is the same as the no-SSL except the different configuration.

But SSL adds the communication times and the cost of encryption and decryption, SSL will lower total system performance during the large data transmission. So we will use the web service via SSL for the safe communication (for example, personal identification or precious data transfer). We will use the common web service or other methods for the large data transfer. To balance the security and performance, SSL and no-SSL can coexist in the same the system.

3   Interoperability Protocol and Standard Interface

Because of the CALIS-ETD Digital Library is the distributed system, it is necessary to comply with universal protocols and interfaces for both the member universities and central CALIS-ETD system in order to realize the communication and interoperability between them. The central CALIS-ETD system as portal need also conform to some standards and protocols to realize the interoperability with the other digital libraries. The main interfaces and protocols used will be introduced as follows:

OAI Interface: The member universities as the data provider support the OAI-PMH2.0. The datestamp of the record indicates the date of creation, modification or deletion of the record. The repository of the member universities supports datestamp format YYYY-MM-DDThh:mm:ssZ and does not support the sets defined by OAI . The repository supports metadata formats including Dublin Core, ETD-MS by NDLTD, CALIS-ETDMS by the workgroup of the project. The OAI harvester in the Central CALIS-ETD system as the service provider can harvest the metadata of the data providers and provides the web interface for the system administrator to schedule and monitor harvest jobs. The administrator can flexibly configure harvest strategy and can analyze the harvest result according the log files. The member universities can register their basic information of the repository by the web interface provided by the harvester.

METS Interface: The Central CALIS-ETD system centrally manages the pre-16 page PDF files. So both the Central CALIS-ETD system and member universities need to support METS interface in order to successfully harvest the pre-16 page PDF files. METS(Metadata Encoding and Transmission Standard) is developed by the Digital Library Federation. METS provides a standard way to represent resource structure and encode metadata (using XML). The content of the ETD METS package includes the description metadata of ETD, the administration metadata of ETD, binary code of the pre-16 page PDF files. They are organized and encapsulated according to the METS encoding schema. The transfer method of ETD METS digital object package adopts the widespread Message Queue Technology (MQ) based on the message. MQ provides guaranteed message delivery, efficient routing, secure and reliable approach to communication, and priority-based messaging. It can be used to implement solutions to both asynchronous and synchronous scenarios requiring high performance. The METS interface between the Central CALIS-ETD system and member universities system adopts the CALIS digital object transfer protocol designed by the CALIS technical workgroup. The protocol includes 6 verbs (GetMetsItem, GetMetsItems, GetMetsItemByDate, GetObjMetsItem and GetObjMetsItems).

OPENURL Interface: The OPENURL interface between the central CALIS-ETD system and member university systems can realize to link metadata to the ETD digital object, the interlibrary loan system or something else etc. Administrator in the central CALIS-ETD system can flexibly configure the OPENURL link server, developed by CALIS whose functions resemble those of SFX, which can complete the efficient and effective link between OPENURL link sources and link objects. The metadata in the central CALIS-ETD system can be regarded as the link source. The ETD digital object in the repository of the member universities or other systems can be regarded as the link object.

ODL Interface: The central CALIS-ETD collection needs to support CALIS ODL-MAP (Open Digital Library-Metadata Access Protocol) protocol in order to provide the required services using a network of components rather than a monolithic system and realize the functions, such as the federated search, browse service and recent record list service etc, between the central CALIS-ETD collection and the other digital library systems using ODL protocol. ODL components are designed to conform to a set of principles for maximum reusability at the levels of design, implementation, and information sharing. CALIS ODL-MAP protocol includes ODL-Search component, ODL-Browse component, ODL-Recent component, ODL-Recommend component and ODL-Index component. CALIS ODL-MAP protocol defined by the CALIS technical workgroup is based on extensions of OAI protocol and ODL protocol designed by Virginia Polytechnic Institute and State University.

Web Service Interface: The central CALIS-ETD collection, as the service provider of web service, supports web service interface in order to make more users easy to find the services provided by the CALIS-ETD-DL. First, CALIS-ETD-DL defines a service description for the web services and publishes it to service discovery agency through a UDDI registry. Then the service requestor uses a find operation to retrieve the service descriptions from the service discovery agency and acquire what they ask for service descriptions based on WSDL. The service requestor uses the service descriptions to generate SOAP requests and sends the SOAP requests to CALIS-ETD-DL. After the CALIS-ETD-DL receives the SOAP requests, they invoke corresponding web service and return SOAP message to requestor. So one-time web service is over.

4   DRM System for ETD Copyright Protection

There is very strict control and rule for ETD copyright in China. It is prerequisite to get the students' grant before ETDs are used on the network. But some students are afraid of unauthorized distribution of their own research result. They do not agree to their own ETD used on the network. We think the copyright is an important issue to hinder the implement of CALIS-ETD in China. To encourage more students release their ETDs in the network, on the one hand, we will introduce to the students advantages of releasing ETDs in network, gradually change their ideas that such release should in no wise be viewed as in conflict with publishing of related articles or monographs, and encourage them to release their own ETD in network.

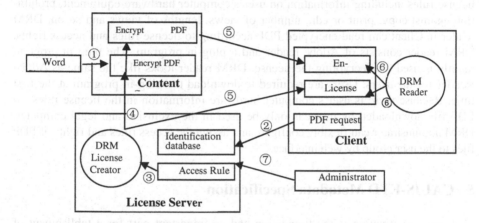

Fig. 2. DRM system architecture in the member universities

On the other hand, we will protect the copyright of ETD by the DRM technology and remove student's worry about their ETD copyright. Access control based on IP address or username/password in general lacks the power to provide more complex protection for ETD digital object and cannot control the unauthorized distribution of digital object. But DRM system provides a higher level of granularity to control and protect content of digital object. An important concept that forms a foundation for DRM is the separation between the content and the rights for access to the content. Rights describe precisely what a user is allowed to do with the content. The DRM systems in the member universities is very simple and do not involve in business model for the commercial distribution of the content, different types of purchase models, use models and so on. The main functions of DRM systems include:

1) To guard PDF files against unauthorized use and make PDF available for authorized users.
2) To flexibly configure the access right of PDF files according to user identification.
3) To provide the open interface and high extensibility to flexibly and easily connect with many kinds of application system.
4) To provide PDF files with high security and powerful encryption mechanism.

Figure 2 shows the DRM system architecture in the member universities and the sequence number in Figure 2 illustrates the implementation order of system. DRM system consists of three components including content server, license server and client. Content server encrypts the PDF files according to some encryption algorithms. It is also responsible for writing the license rules into PDF contents. License server assigns the the license rules for accessing PDF to user according the identification database based on IP address or username/password. When user sends a request, license server can obtain some information from user's computer hardware equipment (for example, MRC address for network card) as the part of license rules. In general, license rules including information on user's computer hardware equipment, prohibition against copy, print or edit, number of views, lengths of views and so on. DRM reader in Client can read encrypted PDF according to license rules and access rights. DRM reader consists of Adobe reader and a plug-in program. The plug-in program mainly is used for decrypting the license. DRM reader looks like the same as Adobe Reader for the users. Users are required to download the plug-in program at the first time. Because there is user's computer hardware information in the license rules, so PDF file downloaded by user can only be used in the exclusive and legal computer. DRM administrator can flexibly configure and assign the access rules and rights of PDF files to the user group by web interface.

5   CALIS-ETD Metadata Specification

Metadata specification is the foundation and an important part for establishment of digital library, and a powerful tool for the organizing, administering and describing of ETD resources in CALIS-ETD-DL。We define two kinds of metadata in CALIS-ETD-DL including descriptive metadata and administrative metadata.

Descriptive Metadata Standard: It usually refers to the metadata that descript the content of the ETDs. ETDMS designed by NDLTD is one of the ETD description metadata adopted widely in the world. We carefully research it and find it is not enough to descript the Chinese ETD resource. On the basis of referring to DC and ETDMS, we designed the CALIS-ETDMS that is an extension of Dublin Core with additional elements or qualifier for the provision of information about the ETD. Extension principle of the elements or qualifiers includes: 1) Semantic of new additional elements and existing elements can not overlap, 2) To follow dumb-down principle, that is to say, qualifiers are supposed only to refine but not extend the semantic scope of elements. CALIS-ETDMS includes 14 elements and 23 qualifiers. Among the 14 elements, the 12 elements come from DC and we add 2 new elements (degree element and location element) according to the Chinese ETD characteristic.

Degree element is special for describing the related information with ETD degree such as degree name/level, discipline and grantor. Location element comes from DC-lib and describes holding location of print thesis and dissertations corresponding with ETD in order that users can find print copy in the library in case they have no access right to use ETD. The description object of ETD metadata is a piece of ETD full-text. We descript the multimedia files related with ETD full-text by the qualifier of relation element. CALIS-ETDMS has good interoperability with the DC and ETDMS. We have established the mapping among the CALIS-ETDMS, DC, ETDMS, USMARC and CNMARC.

Administrative Metadata Standard: The administrative metadata provides information regarding how the files were created and stored, intellectual property rights, metadata regarding the original source objects from which the digital object derive, and information regarding the provenance of the files comprising the digital object. We divide the administrative metadata into four main forms according to METS. They include Technical Metadata(regarding ETD files format, size etc). Rights Metadata(regarding copyright, release year and access range of the ETD etc). Source Metadata(regarding the analog source such as the print thesis and dissertation from which ETD derives etc) and Digitization Process Metadata (regarding digitization process of the print thesis and dissertations etc).

6   Persistent Identifier and Long-Term Preservation Format of ETD

Long-term availability of digital objects is an important and hot issue in the development of digital library. An essential component to achieve long-term availability is the use of Persistent Identifier (PI) that solves the problems of unequivocal resource identification and reliable resolution. In this section we will introduce the name rule of ETD persistent identifier and long-term preservation format of ETD in CALIS-ETD-DL.

CALIS ETD Persistent Identifier: The CALIS-ETD-DL can automatically assign a PI called CALIS-OID to each record of ETD. CALIS-OID is globally unique and persistent names for digital objects of ETD and will remain the same regardless of ETD changes of location or other current state information. URN namespace is used by CALIS-OID for naming ETD. CALIS-OID syntax definition as follows:

urn:CALIS: Library digital code-ETD[.CollectionName]/ObjID.type.format

The Uniform Resource Name "urn" stands for the urn namespace, "CALIS" stands for the officially registered namespace, each university library in China has a unique 6-bit digital code assigned by the ministry of Education, objID is local unique identifier and may be identified by the personal identification number (PIN), type stands for the function of the digital objects and the project define the type list, format stands for the file formats of the digital object. For example, " urn:calis:211030-ETD/S02024.P.PDF" stands for a record of ETD in the tsinghua university, its author's pin is S02024 and P stands for per-16 PDF file. " urn:calis:211030-ETD/S02024.T.PDF" stands for the full-text PDF file of former record.

The resolution service of CALIS-OID that is similar in function to the handle resolution is made of the Central CALIS resolver and the local resolvers in the member universities. The Central resolver is responsible for knowing the locations of CALIS-OID and routing CALIS-OID to local resolver that knows how to resolve it. The local resolver can communicate with the central CALIS resolver and resolve the CALIS-OID to where its actual URL address is.

Long-Term Preservation Format of ETD: ETD as a kind of multiple digital object includes description metadata, administrative metadata, pre-16 PDF file and full-text PDF file. It is important to determine how to express their logical relationship and how to encapsulate such information and establish the logical model of ETD for the long-term preservation. We choose METS scheme as ETD descriptive encoding scheme and long-term preservation format. We define the ETD long-term preservation format that is XML file made of the description metadata, administrative metadata, binary code of pre-16 PDF file and full-text PDF file. Each of the ETD digital object is expressed by an XML file whose name is CALIS-OID (not including "type" and "format"). And this can ensure an XML file corresponding to a record of ETD and facilitate management .The syntax of XML file fits into METS Schema1. 3.

7 Conclusion and Future Works

The CALIS-ETD-DL project includes about 50 member universities now. These members have established their own submission and retrieval systems and provided the metadata and pre-16 pages PDF files for the central merged collection. As this project develops and gains popularity, we believe more and more universities in China will join this project in the near future. We hope to harvest and manage more ETD resources and make them more visible and accessible to the broader users. At the same time, we will continue to expand and improve the functionality of the CALIS-ETD-DL. We will apply more advanced and mature technologies in the CALIS-ETD-DL in order to better satisfy the users' needs.

In the future works, we will research some challenge issues deeply and broadly, for example, description and display of multimedia ETD, personalized active service, long-term preservation of ETDs, access and display of special characters such as mathematical expressions or chemical molecular formula and so on. Finally, we will undertake more research in these directions.

References

1. Networked Digital Library of Thesis and Dissertations [online] Available: http://www.ndltd.org.
2. Jose Borbinha, Jorge Machado etc: DiTeD – Digital Thesis and Dissertations in Portugal [online] Available:http://www.uky.edu/ETD/ETD2004/program.html.
3. Hussein Suleman, Edward A. Fox: A Framework for Building Open Digital Libraries. D-Lib Magazine, vol.7, No.12(2001).

Building Digitized Collection: Theory and Practice

Chunrong Luo[1], Zhinong Zhou[1], and Ying Zhang[2]

[1]Zhongshan University Library, Guanzhou 510275, P.R. China
{puu107, puu105}@zsu.edu.cn
[2]School of Communication, Information and Library Studies, Rutgers, USA
yzhang@scils.rutgers.edu

Abstract. The digitization of library collection is one of the most important tasks for electronic collection development of a library. Digital collection development tends to be more complex than electronic resource licensing and subscription. There are many factors to be considered in the digitization of collection, such as selection policy, organization, access, preservation, funding, and so forth. In this article, the authors discuss some issues associated with collection digitization, including copyright control, intellectual nature, added value, users and their needs, human resource management, technical requirement, funding, and digital content preservation. Several collection digitization principles emerge from the discussion, with respect to standardization and specification, extensibility and integration, security and reliability, preservation and service, collaboration and sharing. as well as evaluation of the digital collection. Finally, the theoretical discussions are further demonstrated by using digital dissertation development at Zhongshan University Libraries, P.R.China, as a pragmatic instance.

Library collection digitization is one of the core missions in developing digital resources of a library. Compared with direct subscription of e-journals, databases and other electronic resources, the digitalization of library collection tends to be more complex, because one has to take different aspects (e.g. copyright, resource, personnel, technology, and fund) in to account simultaneously. In US, UK, and other developed countries, has been a theoretical and pragmatic topic for years regarding how to digitalize library collection. Similarly, China has seen a surge of library collection digitization and a number of related projects in recent years. Among the existing projects, there has been either successes or failures. To ensure the quality of future projects, it is essential to examine some crucial issues in library collection digitization, such as selection criteria for digitization, development principles, evaluation of the digital products and services, and so forth.

1 Selection Collection for Digitization

In general, library collection digitization requires a great amount of human, physical, and financial resources. Any inappropriate selection of resources and inadequate project planning may result in an unfinished digitization project or a forever test-bed. Moreover, the ignorance of intellectual property may end in a troublesome lawsuit. Eventually, the project can never be integrated into library collection and service.

Z. Chen et al. (Eds.): ICADL 2004, LNCS 3334, pp. 165–173, 2004.

Therefore, it is crucial to decide which library collection is appropriate for digitization. One may easily find successful (e.g. American Memory at Library of Congress, USA) and unsuccessful cases from the past 10 years of library collection digitization all over the world. As such, we argue that libraries must take a serious consideration on copyright, staffing, fund, and physical resource, for any collection digitization project. Collection digitization should be implemented on a highly selective and focused ground and should refrain from blindfold and hasty actions following main streams.

To date, a number of academic libraries abroad have proposed collection digitization standards and procedures, such as *Selection Criteria for Preservation Digital Reformatting* (Library of Congress)[1], *University of California Selection Criteria for Digitization* [2], *Columbia University Libraries Selection Criteria for Digital Imaging* [3], and *Selection for Digitization* (Harvard University Libraries)[4]. The Selection for Digitization from Harvard University Libraries, for instance, contains a decision-making matrix, which is represented in a question-answering format. When a question receives "yes" decision, the decision-making can thus moves on. Otherwise, the process has to be paused for reassessment. The criteria and procedure in the Harvard Model involve the following factors: the intellectual and physical nature of the source materials, current and potential users, actual and anticipated nature of use, the format and nature of the proposed digital product, describing, delivering, and retaining the digital product, relationships to other digitization projects, cost and benefits, and so forth. Harvard University Libraries' *Selection for Digitization* can be employed as not only a specification for digital resource selection, but also a tool for making executive digitization plans. Several university libraries (e.g. Indiana University) have applied the Harvard Model in their collection digitization projects with notable outcomes[5].

To learning from overseas' existing experiences in the context of our domestic political, social and cultural state of art, we argue that the following factors, should be taken into a serious consideration in library collection digitization.

(1) Copyright Control and Protection. The following questions need to be addressed regarding this issue: What are the copyright conditions of library collections? Whether they belong to public or private property? Whether or not a given library collection has a clear statement on intellectual property? If yes, whether it is owned by individual, or corporate entities? Whether copyright release can be acquired?

(2) Content and Physical nature of Library Collection. The pertinent key questions include: How significant is a given library collection? Which of the following categories the collection belongs to: rare book; general publication; special collection (library, university, or district); research collection; historical documentation related local or national political, economic, or cultural; monograph, serial, microfiche, microfilms, audio, or video? What is the current physical status in terms of preservation and whether there are any damages on the physical items? What is the relationship between the library collection and the other digital resources? Whether the collection is formal publication? Are there any digital forms available? Whether the library can benefits more from collaborative digitization with a given partner?

(3) Added Value of Library Collection. Some representative key issues are: Whether there are any foreseeable added value given the collection is digitized?

Whether the collection digitization may increase accessibility, service scope and quality?

(4) Users and User Needs. The questions need to be answered are: Who are the current users and who will be the potential users? Whether the collection is in high demand? Is current access to the source materials so difficult that digitization should be done? Does the physical condition of the library collection limit their use? What is the distribution pattern of other relevant resources? Whether or not local needs can be satisfied after digitization?

(5) Technical Factors. Are there any special technical and equipment requirements for digitization, preservation, and transformation? What is the availability of corresponding techniques and standards for a reference purpose? How can metadata schema be developed for resource organization and description.

(6) Fund and Budget. The related issues include: What is the size of the library collection for digitalization? Whether it is historical or non-historical documentations? For non-historical documentations, what is the annual volume-increasing rate? What are the budgets for entire project implementation and service maintenance, including equipment, technical platform, digitization, digital preservation and transformation? Among the total budget, how much can be acquired from an external source and whether or not the internal fund is sufficient? For any large-scale project, it is crucial to seek external funds and/or partners.

2 Implementation Principles

Digitalization project in libraries should follow pre-determined implementation principles[6]. Similarly, the library collection digitization project should follow the following principles.

(1) Standardization and Specification. The implementation of digital collection should be in accordance with uniformed standards, protocols, and specifications, while using compatible software and hardware, As such, a digitized collection can be readily accessed and searched by users without any geographical and physical restriction. Additionally, the digitized collection can be compatible and easily integrated into other digital library systems. Some representative standards and specifications include uniformed data format, network communication protocol, and ISO approved network equipments.

(2) Extensibility and Integration. Library collection digitalization should have an open-ended architecture, flexible technical specification, as well as extensible hardware and software. It should be able to support multi-protocols. Only through the implementation of compatible and extensible digital collection, can the digital resources be integrated seamlessly and smoothly with other library and digital resources and services.

(3) Security and Reliability. It is crucial to protect data and network in any digital process, preservation and transformation. A successful digital collection is highly associated with matured techniques, and reliable equipments for data storage and transformation. Additionally, there are some essential premises for securing digital

collection and service, such as automatic data backup, advanced network management system, flexible virtual sub-net, as well as efficient and effective functions for system monitoring, problem diagnosis, and recovery. Moreover, campaign for intellectual property protection and online monitoring actions against any offences of copyrights are necessary as well.

(4) Interwoven Digital Collection Development and Utilization. Different from the subscription of commercial databases, the implementation of digital library collection, in particular those in large scale, requires longitudinal efforts, ranging from several months, decades to lifelong. Accordingly, it is wise to make the implemented part of a digital collection accessible to users whereas the other part of the collection still under development.

(5) Equivalent Emphasis on Preservation and Service. For any types of digital library collection, there are essentially two ultimate goals, namely, optimized preservation of library resources and maximized utilization of library collection. The two goals should be simultaneously represented in plan, design and implementation stages of digitalization.

(6) Collaboration and Sharing. Considering the complexity of a digital project, which is associated with copyright, personnel, budget and technical factors, it is unrealistic for a single library to develop a large-scale digital collection. Rather, collaborative and resource sharing for the collection digitization at various levels, including national, regional or local level, tends to be a wiser option. Furthermore, collaboration and resource sharing can be implemented at any of the following aspects: technique, equipment, service and staffing. In general, collaboration and resource sharing is more likely to yield to a highly cost-benefit outcome.

3   Evaluation for Digitization Collection

Systematic and holistic evaluation should be regarded as a highlighted activity in any library collection digitization. The majority of the early digitization projects were implemented in the form of test-bed, as a mean of exploring digitization techniques, methods, and tools, as well as accumulating experiences and lessons. Accordingly, evaluation criteria were limited in these aspects. In contrast, current digital collection projects, where techniques and development tools are fairly matured, tend to emphasize practical rather than experimental values[7]. As such, evaluation criteria should be changed accordingly to highlight the following aspects.

(1) Comprehensiveness and Currency. What is the coverage of the digital collection? Whether there are any significant resources not included in the collection? What is the update frequency?

(2) Usability and Accessibility. Is the digital information organized and represented fully and accurately without any bias? Are users provided with flexible and usable search functions? Is the digitized collection easy to search with the assistance of a user-friendly interface? Can the digitized collection be only used by restricted users? How easy can the resources in the digitized collection be accessed, searched, browsed, and downloaded via the Internet?

(3) Integration. The integration related evaluation questions could be whether the digitized collection can be integrated to other library resources and services in an interconnective and interoperatable way.

(4) Sustainability. Can the digital library collection be sustainable overtime? Specifically, can archived resources be well maintained and new resources be continuously added to the collection even after the original funds are used up?

(5) Adaptation. Whether the digital collection is implemented in a way that it can be adapted into national digital library projects? Whether the collection can interoperate and interchange with other systems?

4 Case Study–Zhongshan University Digital Dissertations

Zhongshan University is a prestigious higher education institution in China. The graduate programs, including master and PhD. have been receiving special administrative attention from the university. There are totally 10329 students (excluding medical school students) graduated from the programs from 1981 to 2003. In accordance with new university goal of enhancing academic and educational status, the amount of graduate students admitted has been increasing every year. Whereas there were 3250 new graduate students in 2003, there will be 3800 graduate students in 2004. To date, the total number of enrolled graduate students is 11900 and accounts for one third of total graduate students in Guangdong Province. Zhongshan University has become one of the core bases for graduate education in China. In general, the dissertations are in good quality. During the past five years, there have been more than 20 dissertations received Excellence Awards from China Higher Education Board. The dissertations are unique academic resources in Zhongshan Univ..

Zhongshan University Digital Dissertation (ZSUDD) is regarded as a core project of the libraries. In 1999, the libraries initiated the ZSUDD. Since the past five years, there have been more than 11000 dissertations in the database, among which 10800 are in full-text format. These dissertations have become one of the core digital library collections.

4.1 Project Demonstration

The idea of developing ZSUDD can retrospect to 1996, when the university libraries started paying attention to collecting dissertations discs. Meanwhile, some texts were entered into a test database. However, for some reasons, there had been only a slow progress until March 1999 when we reexamined the digitization project thoroughly in the following several aspects.

(1) Copyright Control and Protection. Dissertations are informal publications. The copyright owners are graduates who finish these dissertations. Without their copyright release, one cannot make full copy of a given dissertation. However, there should not be any violation of copyright given university libraries provide bibliographic data for online searching and full-text digital dissertations for restricted use.

(2) Content Characteristics. Dissertations are unique and core academic resources. According to the existing rules, copies of each thesis or dissertation should be submitted not only to university libraries, university archives, graduate school, and departments, but also to National Library and China Science and Technology Institute. However, for unknown reasons, university is usually the institution with the most comprehensive collection of the dissertations by their students. Therefore, dissertations are somewhat the unique treasury of university libraries.

(3)Preservation and Utilization. Due to some historical reasons, dissertations in Zhongshan University are collected in university libraries, university archives, departments and graduate school. The paper version has low quality in terms of the papers used, print techniques, and bindery effects. Currently, a fair amount of the paper copies are in an ever-decreased preservation status. Some of them cannot be vertically shelved on stacks, and consequently cause some inconvenience and management obstacles. Similarly, the dissertations discs submitted by students from 1995 to 1997 have encountered more or less damage because of inappropriate management. It is crucial to preserve the discs and hard copies.

(4) Added Value. The ZSUDD can be accessed, searched, and downloaded via the Internet so that the utilization of the unique academic resources can be maximized. The user community can be expanded beyond on-campus faculty and students.

(5) Users and Their Needs. Dissertations are academic products by graduate under the supervision of their advisors. They should have large user community (both current and potential) with learning, teaching, and research purposes.

(6) Technical Factors. In general, dissertations can be regarded as text format resources although some of them may have small portion of graphs and figures. As such, there should be no extra needs for special equipments, software, and techniques in digitizing, storage, delivering and management.

(7) Cost and Benefit. Compared with other digitized library resources, the implementation of digital dissertations should be of low cost, due to a limited size. In ZSUTDD, only 4000 early dissertations in paper format need to be scanned. The late-electronic submissions are digital editions. What we need to do is to receive submissions, transform formats, and go through , transform, and a short administrative process before final digital version of dissertations can be generated. Additionally, the preservation and transmission of digital formats are in low cost.

(8) Collaboration. 1999 saw the initiation of CALIS (China Academic Library and Information System) Digital Dissertations Project, a national funded project. As being the South China Center of CALIS, Zhongshan University Libraries become not only one of the active participants in the National project, but also the administrator and sponsor for South China regional digital dissertations collaborative development. As such, the libraries have responsibility and obligation to identify an effective collection digitization model for other regional libraries through the ZSUDD development.

Based on the preceding discussion, we may claim that it is essential and feasible to push the implementation of Zhongshan University Digital Dissertations.

4.2 Implementation

(1) Goal and Objective. The primary goal of ZSUDD is to provide users with a comprehensive and robust special library collection in high quality. Correspondingly, there are essentially two core objectives in the development, namely preserving dissertations in a long run and offering easy search and use functions.

(2) Submission Receiving. A comprehensive submission and resource collection is the prerequisite for developing a successful dissertations database. Previously, students submitted their dissertations to the graduate school and university archives. The university libraries then received copies from the graduate school or university archives. As such, the collection was difficult to become comprehensive. After several runs of negotiation with the graduate school, a policy was made asking each graduate student to submit the electronic copy of his/her dissertation to the university libraries and paper copy to the graduate school before they can receive their diplomas. The policy became valid in the year of 2001. Since then, the dissertations submission rate amount to 100% each year. Additionally, the graduate school provides us a graduated student list since 1981. The list is very useful for us to develop the retrospective collection. Eventually, the database receives on-time update and comprehensive maintenance.

(3) Platform Development. When the project was initiated in 1999, the database platform was developed internally by library staff. In 2000, during the system upgrade, the libraries decided to ask professional software developers to design a powerful platform based on our requirements and needs. To shorten the cycle from receiving submission to being available online, the new platform has been implemented as an integrated system with multiple functions, including submission, digitization, search, and so forth. The current system has essentially three sub-systems, namely submission, search, and administration. Moreover, the system can be integrated seamlessly into CALIS Digital Dissertation Administration system. The followings demonstrate some basic functions supported by the platform.

(a) Submission. There are essentially two types of online submission forms. One is for theses, while another is for dissertation. Both forms have multiple options (e.g. manual input and pull-down menus) for assigning values to different fields.

(b) Review. By using the administrative sub-system, each ZSUDD staff can monitor and edit his/her part of new submissions pre-determined in individualized department channels. The review results are sent automatically to corresponding students' email accounts. There are essentially several types of submission status, including: dissertation received, with an incomplete forms; finished forms, without dissertation submission; dissertation submitted, with errors; error submission, and final acceptance. For the final acceptance status, the students are instructed to go to http://library.zsu.edu.cn/paper/search.htm and search for results for receiving diploma. Figure-1 and Figure-2 are two sample status reports to students.

(c) File Transformation. For the dissertations finally accepted, standardized transformation is processed for generating PDF format of full text and the first 16 to 24 pages (depending on the size of dissertation). The digitized dissertation can be accessed and retrieved immediately after they are added to the database.

Dear student,

Greetings. You have successfully finished the online form. Please send your final electronic version of thesis/dissertation to *lunwen@aimc.asiainfo.com* or *puul17@zsu.edu.cn* as an email attachment or hand in person to the 3rd floor in the new library building (South Campus)

Contact: Ms. Liang, Phone: 84111666

Thank you very much for your support.

Fig. 1. Sample Report (Finished form without thesis/dissertation submission)

Dear student,

Greetings. Your online submission of thesis/dissertation has been final accepted. Please go to *http://library.zsu.edu.cn/paper/search.htm* and search for your record and come in person to the 3rd floor in the new library building (South Campus) for receiving your certificate.

Please contact us at *lunwen@aimc.asiainfo.com* or *puul17@zsu.edu.cn* or call us at 84111666, if you have any questions and concerns.

Contact: Ms. Liang, Phone: 84111666

Thank you very much for your support.

Fig. 2. Sample Report (Final acceptance)

(4) Search/Browse Functions. The ZSUDD provides both search and browse functions. Users can either browse by disciplines and subjects or search by different fields. Whereas the basic function allows search within various fields, such as: author, title, keyword, advisor name, and abstract as well as graduation year, the advanced function adds the Boolean logic combination and diploma, discipline, subject, and graduation year limitation.

(5) Preservation. To preserve digitized dissertation is a long run goal, as well as a prerequisite for the improvement of library service. Currently, the database is maintained at the library server.

(6) Copyright Protection. For the sake of copyright protection, users can only access bibliographic information and the first 16 to 24 pages (depending on the size of dissertation) in PDF format. The full text can be only accessed by the author (student) or his/her student fellows who have the same advisor as the author and present the authorized signature from the advisor.

(7) Staffing. Due to the limited human resources in the libraries, the dissertation project is implemented mainly by part-time. However, in order to ensure the quality of the database, one department head has been assigned responsibility of supervising the project. Additionally, a few student assistants are hired for data entry. During the peak months (June and July every year), it usually takes about one or two days to make a dissertation searchable online under staff's collaborative work. During the non-peak months, the staff process retrospective work.

(8) Fund. There are no specific funds for the project. The limited allowances from the CALIS Digital Dissertation Project and "211 project".

4.3 Future Plan

Having experienced the past several years' exploration and practice, the ZUSDD development becomes a routine workflow in the libraries. The digitalized collection has been integrated into other library resources and services. Our near future plan for further improvement include:

(1) To complete the first stage implementation by December of 2004, that is to finish the digitization of more that 11,000 dissertations dated back to the year of 1981. Currently, we have finished 10,800 volumes of retrospective digital dissertations. Additionally, we have found that there are approximately 900 dissertations not in the library collection, among which about 90% volumes are held in the university archive. We plan to hire more student assistants to do the retrospective data entry during the summer break, 2004. It is anticipated that about 96% of the proposed work (i.e. more that 11,000 dissertations) will be digitalized by November 11th, 2004—80 Anniversary of Zhongshan University.

(2) To upgrade system platform in particular to add statistical administration function.

(3) To strength cooperation with other university libraries in China and to participate actively in the CALIS Digital Dissertation project. Meanwhile, we plan to seek more partners, such as domestic and overseas database vendors, so that the database can reach more users.

(4) To prepare for the second stage project. There are several dozens of earlier dissertation finished during the period 1920 to1930. Among the old collection, some are in worsen physical conditions. We plan to digitize these valuable academic resources for a long-term preservation and utilization.

References

1. Library of Congress. Selection Criteria for Preservation Digital Reformatting. http://lcweb.loc.gov/preserv/prd/presdig/presselection.html
2. University of California. University of California Selection Criteria for Digitization. http://www.library.ucsb.edu/ucpag/digselec.html
3. Columbia University. Columbia University Libraries Selection Criteria for Digital Imaging. http://www.columbia.edu/cu/libraries/digital/criteria.html
4. Harvard University. Selection for digitization. http://preserve.harvard.edu/ resources/digitization/selection.html
5. Brancolini, Kristine R. Selecting Research Collection for Digitization: Applying the Harvard Model. Library Trends, 48(4), 783-798
6. Luo Chunrong. On the Principle and Strategy of Academic Digital Library Construction. Journal of Academic libraries, 21(3), 16-20
7. Institute of Museum and Library Services (IMLS).A Framework of Guidance for Building Good Digital Collections. http://www.imls.gov/pubs/index.htm
8. http://library.zsu.edu.cn/paper/search.htm

Cataloging and Preservation Toolkit of a Chinese Mathematics Ancient Books Digital Library

Li Dong[1], Chunxiao Xing[2], Lizhu Zhou[2], Bei Zhang[1], and Airong Jiang[1]

[1] System Division of Tsinghua University Library
{dongli, beizhang, jiangar}@lib.tsinghua.edu.cn
[2] Computer Science and Technology Department of Tsinghua University
{xingcx, dcszlz}@mail.tsinghua.edu.cn

Abstract. This toolkit is designed for the Chinese Mathematics Digital Library (CMDL) System of Tsinghua University. The aim of CMDL is to preserve digitalized Chinese Mathematics ancient books available and provide mathematics research and education service to the public. This toolkit fulfills the cataloging and preservation functions of CMDL. METS encoded documents are used as the final storage format of metadata, including descriptive metadata, structural metadata and administrative metadata. The final XML documents with original digital resources can be packaged into an electronic book record extended from OEB, and submitted to a management system based on Fedora Open Source System. This software is a pure-Java application for platform-portable consideration, and JAXB is used to process XML for its convenient and powerful performance at XML processing.

1 Introduction

In recent years, long-term preservation of digital resources began to gain focus from libraries widely over the world, some related projects have been or being carried out. In Summer 2001, Cornell University Library, State and University Library Goettingen, Tsinghua University Library and Orsay Library agreed to take part in the research and development related to archiving, preserving, and providing access to digital mathematics material, this cooperative project EMANI (Electronic Mathematics Archives Network Initiative)[1] was initiated by Springer-Verlag and was formally started in Feb. 2002. After that, Tsinghua University Library associated with the CS department, Mathematical Sciences department and EE department of Tsinghua University, got the support of the University Research Foundation, began to set up a Chinese Mathematics Digital Library System for long-term preservation of Ancient Books.

The main purpose of the CMDL system is to provide a platform of preservation, management and service of digitalized Chinese Mathematics Ancient Books, preservation is an important feature compared to former systems such as THADL(Tsinghua University Architecture Digital Library)[2]. Some related projects have been or being carried out for digital resources preservation and management in recent years, such as MOA2(Making of American 2)[3] in UCB, the Library of Congress Audio-Visual

Z. Chen et al. (Eds.): ICADL 2004, LNCS 3334, pp. 174–183, 2004.
© Springer-Verlag Berlin Heidelberg 2004

Prototyping Project[4], the Fedora(Flexible Extensible Digital Object and Repository Architecture) project[5]. Many achievements have been done from these projects: the practice of MOA2 came out with an encoding format for descriptive, administrative, and structural metadata for textual and image-based works, the encoding format is defined in XML DTD (Document Type Definition), which is usually referred as MOA2 DTD later; METS (Metadata Encoding and Transmission Standard)[6], a Digital Library Federation initiative, attempts to build upon the work of MOA2 and provide an XML document format for encoding metadata necessary for both management of digital library objects within a repository and exchange of such objects between repositories; Fedora has become a general-purpose and an open-source digital object repository system that can be used in whole or part to support a variety of use cases including: institutional repositories, digital libraries, content management, digital asset management, scholarly publishing, and digital preservation[5]. Enough have been done for preservation of simple-structured images and texts with standard ASCII characters, while few have been researched on complex-structured digital objects and texts with nonstandard ASCII characters, such as those digitalized resources from Chinese mathematics ancient books. In this paper, we will introduce some general information of CMDL system, and as an important part of CMDL, we will mainly discuss our experience of design and implementing a Cataloging and Preservation Toolkit, which is developed to record and organize the digital resources with metadata properly.

2   General Information About CMDL

The main process of creating and submitting the digitalized resources is described as Figure 1.

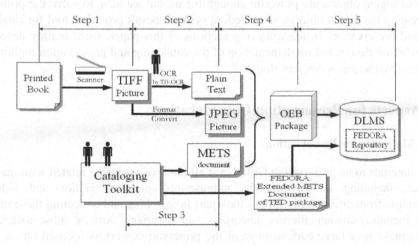

Fig. 1. CMDL workflow

In Step 1, we use scanners to scan the ancient books in different resolutions. We decide whether the page should be color, grayscale or black-and-white, and what resolution to use. These decisions are made on a case-by-case basis, weighing the quality, file size, and staff time[7]. Typically an original copy for preservation is scanned in 600 dpi and saved in tiff file format with different colors as needed; an copy for OCR(Optical Character Recognition) is scanned in 300 dpi with 256 gray levels, saved in tiff file format; other copies for browsing can be converted to lower resolutions as needed and saved in JPEG file format.

In Step 2, scanned images are processed by TH-OCR(Tsinghua – Optical Character Recognition) software provided by Tsinghua UNIS WINTONE Info Technology Ltd.[8], which is a famous company in Chinese OCR technology field. After that, we can get plain text files corresponding with the images.

In Step 3, librarians can use the Cataloging and Preservation Tool to input metadata information of the digital resources and save them into standard METS documents.

In Step 4, those standard METS documents with original digital resources created in Step 3 are submitted to an Electronic Book Maker, after the E-Book Maker's process, we get an electronic book package extended from OEB (Open eBook), which can be viewed with a special E-Book Viewer developed by the CS Department of Tsinghua University.

In Step 5, a Fedora-Extension METS document with the E-Book package files is exported from the standard METS document, and submitted to a digital objects management system based on the Fedora System. After that, those digital objects with metadata and related resources can be accessed through the management system.

It's lucky for us to find that Fedora is an open-source project and provides flexible interfaces for us to do extensions on it, it's full-featured to act as a foundation upon which interoperable web-based digital libraries can be built. The management functions of digital objects are powerful enough for us, but we have to solve the problem of creating the digital objects, since Fedora system doesn't provide a tool for cataloging and preservation. In the following sections of this paper, we'll mainly describe our work on design and implementation of the cataloging and preservation toolkit for Chinese Mathematics Ancient Books.

3 Aspects for Preservation Consideration

3.1 Materials for Preservation

The materials to be preserved in CMDL are all kinds of resources related with mathematics, including books, journals, manuscripts, pictures, audios and videos. Specialists from different disciplines took part in searching and collecting those materials, including mathematicians, historians and librarians. Among those materials, books make up a large part, so most of the preservation work is focused on ancient books, written from Han Dynasty to Qing Dynasty.

3.2 Metadata for Preservation

For preservation purpose, not only the digitalized resources themselves should be saved, the metadata of the digitalized resources should also be saved and packaged with them properly, so that those resources can keep original status after transmission and refreshment. In CMDL, we use 3 types of metadata for preservation, descriptive metadata, structural metadata and administrative metadata.

1. **Descriptive Metadata:** Descriptive metadata is for digital object description to find or identify the resource. In CMDL we use a special DC-extension standard for description metadata of Chinese Mathematics Ancient Books, there are 11 top-level elements extended from Dublin Core (DC)'s 15 elements[9], other 4 elements are mapped from the source and rights metadata in administrative metadata set. For every top-level element, some sub-elements are defined for detailed description of ancient books. For example, as the relationships between ancient books are rather particular, we use 6 types of relation sub-elements to represent them: Serials, Subdirectories, PartOf, IsVersionOf, HasVersion, and Reference. An XML Schema definition of the descriptive metadata can be found at our technique website[10].
2. **Structural Metadata:** For simple-structured digital objects, such as separate images, it's easy to catalog and load them into some management systems as Fedora, but for those images constructing a book, we must find a way to represent the relationships inside a book. Structural metadata is designed to solve this problem. In CMDL, we use the <structMap> section of a METS[6] object to record the structural metadata, each <div> represents a node of the book structure.
3. **Administrative Metadata:** Administrative metadata is data that supports the unique identification, maintenance, and archiving of digital objects, as well as related functions of the organization managing the repository. There are 4 parts of administrative metadata: technical metadata, rights metadata, source metadata and digital provenance metadata. In CMDL, we studied the administrative metadata standards recommended by METS Official Web Site[6] and define some simplified metadata definitions for them at our technique website[10].

3.3 Metadata and Characters Encoding

Maintaining a library of digital objects of necessity requires maintaining metadata about those objects. We use METS[6] to incorporate metadata of digital objects in CMDL. The METS schema is a standard for encoding descriptive, administrative, and structural metadata regarding objects within a digital library, expressed using the XML schema language of the World Wide Web Consortium.

Unicode is chosen for internal document representation and storage. Considering data exchange between different systems from different countries, Unicode is the best choice of character encoding method compared with some other local standards for Chinese characters, such as GB2312, GBK, GB18030, because it's global interoperable and supported widely by most popular software platforms. Since the basic docu-

document storage format of CMDL is XML, whose legal accepted character set is specified by ISO/IEC 10646:2000(Unicode)[11], using Unicode in CMDL is a wise choice for software implementation and data maintenance, as a result, UTF-8 and UTF-16 are used for character encodings.

4 Functions of the Toolkit

This cataloging and preservation toolkits provide main functions as following:

4.1 Metadata Cataloging

You can use this toolkit to input and edit metadata, including descriptive metadata and administrative metadata following CMDL metadata standards mentioned in section 3.1. Although the top-level elements of the descriptive metadata are extended from Dublin Core, the whole metadata structure is rather complex. Most of the top-level elements have sub-elements, some elements are repeatable, while some ones are with qualifiers, all those features should be included in the cataloging procedure.

4.2 Cataloging the Structure

To describe and record a resource's inner structure, this toolkit provides the function of cataloging a resource's inner structure. You can use this toolkit to create a complete structure of the resource, from the whole book node, chapter node, and section node to page node. The node can extend to any level with free types, which are not limited by pre-defined structure types; and each node can be added, edited, or deleted freely on the structure tree, as the cataloger needs. For cataloger's convenience, the toolkit provides auto-construction of page nodes, so that the cataloger need not create so many page nodes as they construct the resource's structure, thus to save much time of cataloging the structure.

4.3 Resource Linking

To organize the metadata and digital resources with correct structure, this toolkit provides linking functions for metadata (such as structural metadata) with resource files. Cataloger can finish the linking steps as constructing the resource structure, while creating each node; he can assign the linked resource files to the node. As the structure construction, page node resource linking can be done automatically without cataloger's operation.

4.4 Previewing the Resource Images

To associate cataloging and resource linking, this tool provides an image viewer for resource images. In general consideration, the viewer supports image files in JPEG format.

4.5 Importing Metadata

Sometimes we have some existing metadata records stored in other formats (such as standard DC XML), or have some template input metadata files, to reduce the cataloger's work, we provide metadata importing function in this toolkit. For most administrative metadata items, such as those for digital provenance metadata, technical metadata and rights metadata, which are almost the same for a batch of digital resources, we can import those metadata from a template file instead of input them one by one, reducing the time of inputting data by hand.

4.6 Packaging and Creating METS Objects

After cataloging and resource linking, we can use this toolkit to package all types of metadata with linking information to create METS objects. The result objects are verified and ensure validation; documents are saved in standard METS format.

4.7 Exporting Metadata

The result documents of CMDL are saved in standard METS format conforming to the schema defined on the Library of Congress official site. Since we use Fedora

Table 1. Metadata Elements Mapping from CMDL to Fedora

Elements in th_mathdmd, th_mathsrcmd, th_mathrightsmd	Elements in oai_dc
<thmdm:Identifier>	<dc:identifier>
<thmdm:TitleMain>, <thmdm:TitleAlternative>	<dc:title>
<thmdm:CreatorMain>, <thmdm:CreatorCountry>, <thmdm:CreatorTime>, <thmdm:CreatorType>	<dc:creator>
<thmdm:ContributorMain>, <thmdm:ContributorCountry>, <thmdm:ContributorTime>, <thmdm:ContributorType>	<dc:contributor>
<thmdm:SubjectMain>, <thmdm:Keyword>, <thmdm:Classification>	<dc:subject>
<thmdm:Abstract>, <thmdm:TOC>, <thmdm:Note>	<dc:description>
<thmdm:Type>	<dc:type>
<thmdm:Format>	<dc:format>
<thmdm:Language>	<dc:language>
<thmdm:Spacial>, <thmdm:Temporal>	<dc:coverage>
<thmdm:RelationName>, <thmdm:RelationLocator>	<dc:relation>
<thmdm:DatePublishedAD>, <thmdm:DatePublishedImperial>	<dc:date>
<thmdm:PublishingPlace>, <thmdm:PublisherMain>	<dc:publisher>
<thmdm:HoldingAddress>, <thmdm:HoldingClassification>	<dc:rights>
<thmdm:Binding>, <thmdm:Number>, <thmdm:Size>, <thmdm:Page>, <thmdm:Edition>	<dc:source>

System as the digital objects management system for CMDL, this format of document can't be used directly, it is converted to the format conforming to Fedora-Extension METS XML schema before submitting to Fedora system. This conversion is accomplished through metadata exporting function. On exporting to Fedora-Extension documents, main operation is handling some mappings between the two document formats. Of those mapping items, descriptive metadata is an important part, here is an example mapping table for descriptive metadata, one is conformed to the 'th_mathdmd', 'th_mathsrcmd' and 'th_mathrightsmd' schema[10] for CMDL, the other is conformed to 'oai_dc' schema[12] for Fedora.

5 Implementation

5.1 Implementation Technologies

XML is used as the final format of metadata storage, not to store metadata into RDBMS, because XML documents can carry data independent with different system, and play an increasingly important role in the exchange of a wide variety of data on the Web and elsewhere.

We use pure Java solution to develop this toolkit, so that this application can be ported to other platforms easily as needed and it is more convenient and powerful than other languages for XML processing. There are many kinds of Java-based XML processing APIs and toolkits, such as JDOM, DOM4J, JAXP, JAXB, we choose JAXB as XML processing framework in our programs.

5.2 User Interface Design

As the metadata for CMDL is much more complex than simple applications, for example, the structure representation, sub-elements and repeating elements, if those metadata are not properly arranged on the screen, the cataloger would often get into trouble for so many kinds and numbers of metadata elements. In this application, we use Java Swing Components to build up the UI. To represent the resource structure, JTree component is used, each node on the tree represent a node of the book content, as you choose one node of the tree in the left panel, the metadata information of this node will appear in the right panel at the same time. To arrange the sub-elements and repeating elements in a panel properly, we use JTable component, so that the UI looks orderly for catalogers. For some elements with qualifiers, dropping Lists are provided to aid cataloger to choose values from a value set, so that to ensure value validation. If the cataloger likes, she can view a brief display of the whole metadata content by selecting the preview button. Figure 2 is an example picture of the toolkit UI.

6 Main Process of Creating a METS Object

We can use this toolkit to catalog and package the metadata into a METS object as following steps:

1. Create a new project package. This step initializes the framework of a METS document.
2. Create the file groups representing digital resource files. To cataloger's convenience, we can only choose the file directory containing the resource files, no matter what kind of resource files existing, this toolkit can check the resource files automatically, and create different file groups according to the sub-directories in the base directory. As a part result, this step accomplishes the <fileSec> part creation of a METS document, which links the FILEID attribute to physical files.
3. Construct the structures of the digital resources, and link resources with structures. We can use the structure constructing toolbars in the left panel of the toolkit to add the content node of a book, which is represented in a tree view. When creating each node, only the node type and starting page number are required, the program can compute out the page numbers of each node and linking relations of resource files automatically. This step fulfills the <structMap> part creation of a METS document, which links each structure node to FILEID.
4. Input metadata, including descriptive metadata and administrative metadata. This step create the <dmdSec> and <amdSec> of a METS document.
5. Verify and create a package in METS format.

Figure 2 is an example of cataloging a Chinese Mathematics ancient book "Zhou1 Bi4 Suan4 Jing1".

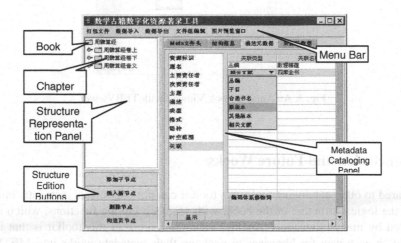

Fig. 2. An example of an Ancient Book being cataloged

7 Results and Example

After cataloging and saving metadata with resources in standard METS format, the original digital resources' preservation has been completed, which contains full information of the resources. Those documents with resources are submitted to a

E-Book Maker which we call TEBMaker(Tsinghua Electronic Book Maker), the TEBMaker organizes the input documents with resources into a package file extended from OEB format, with a suffix file name 'teb'. The '.teb' file can be opened by a software called 'TEBViewer', by which we can explore the structure of a digital book, the images view and text view of the book, Figure 3 is an example of viewing 'Zhou1 Bi4 Suan4 Jing1' with 'TEBViewer'. To provide access service for mathematics research and education, those preserved digital resources should be submitted to the digital objects management system based on Fedora System. The digital objects being submitted to the management system are those packaged into 'teb' format, not the original images and texts, so the input documents for Fedora should be converted to a Fedora-Extension format describing the 'teb' objects, this conversion can be accomplished by using the 'Metadata Exporting' function of the toolkit.

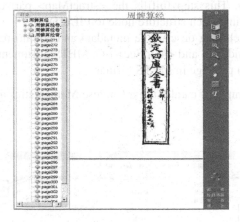

Fig. 3. An Ancient Book Viewed with TEBViewer

8 Conclusion and Future Works

Compared to other cataloging tools, this toolkit can not only create metadata, but also create the logical structure of the book, with resource linking functions, which is not provided by many other tools. Another valuable feature of this toolkit is that it can provide an easy way for librarians to package their metadata works into METS encoded XML documents. In reality, it's very difficult for librarians to understand and master writing a METS encoded XML document by hand, even for a technique engineer, writing such kind of document by hand is a time-consuming work. According to our experience, it may cost an engineer about 3~6 hours to write out such a document with existing metadata, with no warrant of content correctness, while using this toolkit, a librarian can finish the catalogue process in at most one hour, including metadata creation, with ensured correct result.

This cataloging and preservation toolkit for CMDL is being tested by catalogers and will soon be applied into real use. After this, we're going to extend the program to some other subjects, such as Mechanics, Hydraulics. These applications have different metadata schemas to those in CMDL, we are trying to find a solution for fast-extending applications in other fields. In an ideal model, we shall research and develop a software kit like the OCLC SiteSearch Record Builder, which is an end-user application to allow you to create, modify, and maintain searchable databases for local collections of digital objects and data[13]. You can modify the template file of the metadata for your data without modifying the program code in Record Builder, which is flexible for different applications with different metadata, but there are still some limitations with Record Builder: the storage format of XML format is an internal XML format not conforming to W3C XML standard; it's difficult to implement multiple complex metadata input areas on user interface; structural metadata is difficult to implement and can't extended to free level, etc. It's still a lot of work for us to do to implement a toolkit flexible enough to handle these problems.

References

1. Electronic Mathematical Archiving Network Initiative (EMANI), http://www.emani.org/
2. Chunxiao Xing, Lizhu Zhou: A study and development of THADL digital library. Proceedings of the Sixth International Conference for You Computer Scientist: in Computer Science and Technology in New Century. Hang Zhou, P.R., China, Oct 23-25 2001, International Academic Publishers, 2001, 605-609.
3. The Making of America, http://sunsite.berkeley.edu/MOA2/
4. Digital Audio-Visual Preservation Prototyping Project, http://lcweb.loc.gov/rr/mopic/avprot/
5. The Fedora Project: An Open-Source Digital Repository Management System, http://www.fedora.info
6. Metadata Encoding and Transmission Standard (METS), http://www.loc.gov/standards/mets/
7. Karen Caron: Military medical history is being saved in a digital archive. Computers in Libraries. Jun 2003. Vol. 23, Iss. 6, 20-22.
8. Tsinghua UNIS WINTONE Info Technology Ltd., http://www.wintone.com.cn/
9. Dublin Core Metadata Element Set, Version 1.1: Reference Description, http://www.dublincore.org/documents/dces/
10. XML Schema for Tsinghua University Mathematics Digital Library Preservation Metadata, http://dlib.lib.tsinghua.edu.cn/cmdl/th_mathdmd.xsd, th_mathtechmd.xsd, th_mathrightsmd.xsd, th_mathsrcmd.xsd, th_mathdigiprovmd.xsd
11. 11.Extensible Markup Language(XML) 1.0 Third Edition, http://www.w3.org/TR/2004/REC-xml-20040204/
12. 12.Dublin Core XML Schema for Open Archives Initiative, http://www.openarchives.org/OAI/2.0/oai_dc.xsd
13. 13.OCLC SiteSearch Record Builder, http://sitesearch.oclc.org/helpzone/rb/rb_01-00-00i.html

Exploiting Extended Service-Oriented Architecture for Federated Digital Libraries

Hao Ding and Ingeborg Sølvberg

Information Management Group, Norwegian University of Science and Technology,
Sem Sælands vei 7-9, NO-7491, Trondheim, Norway
{hao.ding, ingebog.solvberg}@idi.ntnu.no

Abstract. In order to support various requirements from the user's perspective, digital library (DL) systems may need to apply a large variety of services, such as query services for a specific DL, mapping services for mapping and integrating heterogeneous metadata records, or query modification and expansion services for retrieving additional relevant documents. This paper focuses on exploiting an extended Service-Oriented Architecture - Peer-based SOA (PSOA) for DL development with the goal of alleviating the weaknesses in the basic SOA infrastructure, especially in the aspects of scalability and interoperability. We also present our work in how to combine the Semantic Web and Web Services together to support interoperability over heterogeneous library services. A query service example is also presented.

1 Introduction

Exposing online resources as web services to the users is becoming prevalent recently. The promise of web services is to enable a distributed environment in which any number of applications, or application components, can interoperate seamlessly among and between organizations in a platform-neutral, language-neutral fashion [1] [2] [3]. In library community, introducing web services into digital library (DL) systems has appeared in some creative initiatives, such as digital preservation [4], metadata harvesting [5], and schema mapping [6] etc. However, few approaches have considered the composition of fine-grained services into coarse-grained services such that more complicated requirements can be met, and not to mention how to construct a stable environment for such applications.

In this paper, we talks about the exploitation of the Service-Oriented Architecture (SOA) into DL systems construction. The main advantages of our approach over the others is that we extend the basic SOA infrastructure into a Peer-to-Peer (P2P) based SOA model (PSOA) with the goal of achieving a more stable infrastructure which can dynamically composing and interoperating from fine-grained services to coarse-grained ones in a large and heterogeneous DLs environment. P2P technology provides an approach that does not rely on centralized registries as that in the basic SOA. Each peer can serve as both the server and client, that is, a peer can be a service pro-

Z. Chen et al. (Eds.): ICADL 2004, LNCS 3334, pp. 184–194, 2004.

vider, requestor, or both. Powered by the P2P-based registry capability, the system will be more stable even if certain core servers, such as registry servers, are degraded.

We believe that more and more research projects will come to the web services technologies that make specific applications straightforward to implement them. It is now the time to look at a bigger picture of how to move forward from simple models to a large scale model of arbitrary complexity.

The remainder of the paper is structured as follows. The next section describes the motivations of exploiting extended SOA for DLs. We present in Section 3 the basic SOA architecture and describe in Section 4 our approaches in extending SOA for DL systems, and the system architecture is described in the section as well. Section 4 describes a walking-through example as well as the implementation details. Section 5 concludes with a discussion of problem issues and future work.

2 Motivations

Our motivations originate from the following questions: Why we need web services and SOA? What weaknesses lie in SOA? And how to improve such an infrastructure?

Since almost anything can be a service, such as security, transaction and clustering, etc., coming up with an exhaustive list is difficult. However, we mention a few straightforward examples especially in DL systems:

- *Query Services for a Specific DL*: It is very often that you (users) prefer to access a service portal which can provide more flexible searching interface, for example, searching for documents published between 1970 and 1990 (*from* 1970 *to* 1990). In such a situation, you may feel frustrated unless a fuzzy searching for the publishing date is available.
- *Mapping Services*: for handling heterogeneity of schemas, classification or languages. Taking metadata schemas for example, there are various metadata formats, such as Dublin Core [7], EAD [8], LOM [9], MARC [10], and ONIX [11]. In large-scale and complex applications (eg., federated digital libraries), the functionality of metadata translation may be embedded. To the small libraries or libraries with specialized needs, however, it may not be accessible [12]. Fortunately, recent research [13] is approaching for this problem by adopting the web services in order to increase the accessibility to clients whose data management problems cannot be solved by expensive turnkey systems.
- *Query Transformation Services*: for retrieving additional relevant documents, e.g. query expansion, relevance feedback. Query transformation is slightly different from the metadata schema mapping. The former need use certain predefined semantic relations between classification categories or controlled vocabularies, etc for term translation and expansion. There are many such components available, but corresponding accessible web services are still in shortage.

In a matter of fact, there are numerous mature components, algorithms and open collections available and it will be a waste of resources and time to re-implement them from scratch. Currently, interest has been highly activated in a number of initiatives. Reference [12] describes a prototype for a web service that translates between pairs of metadata schemas. Hunter et.al. [4] developed a web-services-based system which enables organizations to semi-automatically preserve their digital collections. Another interesting work can be found in [5] which developed web services to support searching for their metadata collections by third parties.

3   The Basic Service-Oriented Architecture (SOA)

Most of the library services are somehow isolated although the compositions or integrations on these services will provide more benefits to the service consumers. SOA represents a way to achieve a vision of seamlessly composing and interoperating between services. It is particularly applicable when multiple applications running on varied technologies and platforms need to communicate with each other [2]. Conceptually, SOA is comprised of three roles, namely, *Provider*, *Registry* (broker), and *Requestor*. A general service-oriented architecture which can be deployed in federated DLs is illustrated in Figure 1.

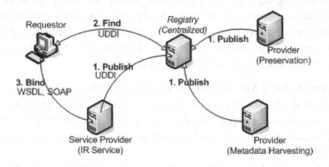

Fig. 1. The General Service-oriented Architecture

The interactions between these roles involve: library services providers define service descriptions for services and publish them to registry (a centralized node generally); a requestor then uses a registry to find service descriptions for services they are interested in using; with the service description available, the requestor sends a service request to a specific provider (i.e. for the metadata harvesting service). Such centralized registry-based mechanisms are effective since they guarantee discovery of providers that have registered. However, on the opposite side, they also suffer from the traditional problems of centralized systems, namely they are performance bottlenecks and single point of failure [14]. Additionally, the possible storage of vast numbers of service descriptions (advertisements) on centralized registries hinders the timely update, but the capabilities of providers may change now and then.

Moreover, some libraries may on one hand provide services to the consumers, and need as well some special services, such as harvesting appropriate records in order to enrich collections. For example, consider that some service consumers can access L_1 for query services. Meanwhile, L_1 itself may need to harvest favorite records from L_2

by using the metadata harvesting services provided from L_2. After this phase, L_1 can also request preservation services provided by L_3 in order to index the new collections. Obviously, we need to extend the basic SOA architecture so as to fulfill such requirements.

4 Extending SOA for DL Services

We enrich the basic SOA with the Peer-to-Peer (P2P) network features and generate the a P2P-based SOA model (PSOA) with the goal of dynamically composing and interoperating over varied library services and alleviating the constraints from single point of failure and associated performance bottlenecks. P2P computing fits well in a dynamic environment. In PSOA, each library system (peer) contains its own indexing of the existing requesters and providers so there is no danger of a bottleneck effect. Here, we use 'requesters' to differentiate the library system which may 'request' for other library services from the ordinary users who can access library services. Such architecture does not need a centralized registry server since any peer will respond to the queries it receives. If the query matches the service it exposes, then it replies, otherwise, it forwards the query to the peers in the indexed list. Finally, if a connection is set up, peers contact each other directly, so there are no delays with the communication of new information. This mechanism is illustrated in Figure 2.

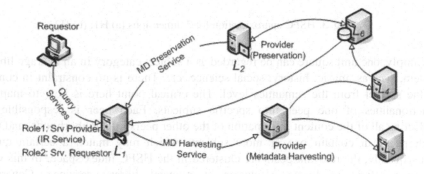

Fig. 2. Peer based Services Discovery and Coordination

Other problems emerge from this approach. Since each peer in the network has to provide certain resources needed to guarantee query propagations and response routing, which in turn means that most of the time the peer acts as a relayer who has to forward queries which may be of no interest to the peer itself. This results in inefficiencies and large overhead especially as the number of the peers becomes huge and connectivity increases. The output of the Gnutella system shows such results. Furthermore, there is no guarantee that a request will definitely find the providers of critical information even if they are available, since it depends on the network bandwidth, routing path and TTL value (Time To Live), etc.

In [15] [16], we designed a feasible prototype and discovery algorithms which can efficiently find appropriate peers. We based our prototype in JXTA framework because currently it is used by a number of other projects in the DL and peer-to-peer areas. In such a large scale environment, the critical issue is how to generate, index, store and re-locate peers capabilities information. We adopt the Distributed Hash Table (DHT) approach for locating library systems in the overall architecture. Moreover, instead of simply mapping peers' identifiers to indices, the Hilbert Space Filling Curve (HSFC) [17] method is used to indicate relevant peers. A HSFC is a one dimensional curve which visits every point within a two dimensional space. Each point in the dimension space can be regarded as a peer. The HSFC can be regarded as the limit of a sequence of curves which are traced through the space. For example, in Figure 3, curve H1 has four vertices at the center of each quarter of the unit square. Curve H2 has 16 vertices each at the center of a sixteenth of the unit square.

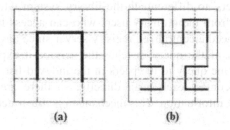

(a)   (b)

Fig. 3. HSFC approximation for 2 dimensions (a) H1; (b) H2

Simply, one unit square can be regarded as a subject category in an average library system, such as, music, history, social science, etc. There is no constraint in content of the subject from the semantics level. The critical point here is how to map the functionalities of one peer into specific subjects. Each peer is responsible for collecting all of the content information of the other peers in neighborhoods, and then each peer can contain one or more subjects which may match a certain query. Consequently, the relevant peers are clustered in the HSFC index space. In this way, we can efficiently locate a cluster of relevant library services. Generally, the query processing procedure can be carried out in two steps: 1). finding the relevant clusters of the HSFC based index space according to specific query; 2). querying the selected peers in the overlay network for metadata information.

In implementing a basic SOA platform, both applications and infrastructure must support SOA principles. Enabling an application for SOA involves the creation of service interfaces to existing or new functions, either directly or through the use of adaptors. Enabling the infrastructure, at the most basic level, involves provision of the capabilities to route and deliver service requests to the correct service provider. However, it is also vital that the infrastructure supports the substitution of one service implementation by another with no effect to the clients of that service. This requires not only that the service interfaces be specified according to SOA principles, but also that the infrastructure allows client code to invoke services in a manner independent of the service location and the communication protocol involved.

5   Semantics in PSOA

In the basic SOA, one weakness in adopting web services is its lack of semantic information. The web services technologies, SOAP, WSDL, UDDI, rely exclusively on XML for interoperation, but the structural XML guarantees only syntactic interoperability. Expressing message content in XML allows web services to parse each other's message but does not allow semantic 'understanding' of the message content [18]. For example, consider a DL system which advertises a scientific publication information retrieval (IR) service (such as CiteSeer[1]) and a requestor looking for 'book' searching service. Relying on keyword matching alone, a UDDI style registry will not be able to match the request to the existing 'publication' IR advertisement, since keyword matching is not powerful enough to identify the relation between 'publication' and 'book'.

However, the efforts in the Semantic Web hold great promise of making the Web a machine understandable infrastructure. We adopt OWL-S (OWL-based Web Service Ontology) [19] in PSOA in order to increase the inferential power in matchmaking web services. OWL-S adds a formal representation of content to web services specifications and reasoning about interaction and capabilities. OWL-S allows *concepts* and *relationships* rather than keywords to be expressed. Since the adoption of ontologies on the Semantic Web makes relations between concepts explicit, it would be able to perform a semantic match and recognize the relation between the request and the advertisement [20]. For example, an ontology may indicate that 'a book is a publication'. It can be modeled as a rule in the matchmaking component, which uses a reasoner to recognize 'book searching service' is a kind of 'publication searching service'. In this way, the DL which exposes publication searching service is selected for answering the requests.

The embedding of OWL-S into a specific DL (peer) is illustrated in Figure 4.

In PSOA, the **Web Service Invocation** component is responsible for receiving web service requests from outside. It translates the message into OWL-S based service description or forwards the OWL-S description directly to **Ontology Parser**. Ontology parser is responsible for importing ontologies harvested from outside resources automatically or manually, and transforming them into Lisp-like rules. **OWL-S Process Engine** is the kernel component in the framework because it processes web services in OWL-S specifications, together with the ontologies gathered from ontology parser, and outputs the decisions to the interface. To make the decisions, it also refers to the concrete rules generated from the OWL-S Grounding and Service Model components. The former specifies the details of how an agent can access a service, while the latter describes what to do when the encapsulated service is carried out [19]. The 'decisions' generated by the process engine are passed to the *Interface* and wrapped

---

[1] http://citeseer.ist.psu.edu/

into a concrete message and then sent off to the shared matchmaking component. As an average user, one can access the local library services exposed. Besides, one can also access transparently other library services which are harvested by local library according to user's profile. In this way, library is powered to fulfill more complicated requirements.

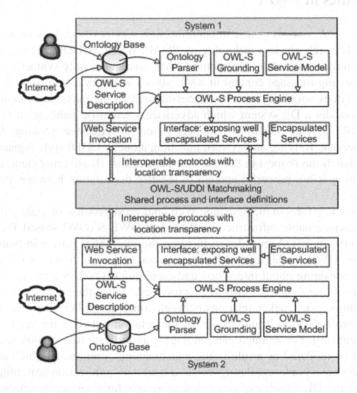

Fig. 4. Service Description of Other Accessible Services Indexed by Local Peer

6 An Example: Query Services from User's Perspective

In order to make the changes in the architecture as transparent as possible to the user, PSOA provides a list of the services references if such functionality is activated. As an example, a query service for searching IEEE conference and journal papers (INEX collection) is shown in Figure 5. There are multiple ways to invoke the query service. It is presumed that SOAP [21] protocol is supported by all of the services. Based on the service description and the SOAP protocol, new client interfaces can be easily built according to users' preferences.

One straightforward way to access the service is by an embedded URL. For example: http://129.241.102.88:8000/soap/jsp/inexSrch/search.jsp. Moreover, by activating other services (c.f. left and bottom figures in Figure 5), users can also access the other available services which are indexed and accessible by the local peer. Such functionality brings users more possibilities to extend/complement the limited capabilities of a monotonic query service provided by local library. For example, in Figure 5, Carol wants to search the articles in IEEE Intelligent Systems Journal from 2001 to 2003. Accordingly, she has to input '2001', '2002', '2003' into the 'year' segment respectively. However, there are also many other query services which support the fuzzy search on 'date', such as the ACM digital library portal. Obviously, it is laborious if we fail to find appropriate services for our routine work.

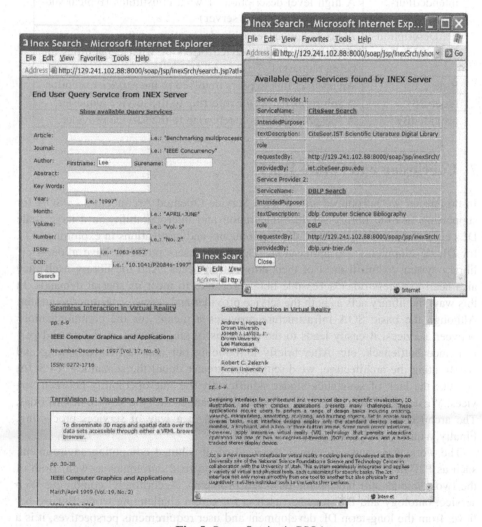

Fig. 5. Query Service in PSOA

By activating the link on the query interface, we can obtain extra services exposed by other providers. The figure on the right of Figure 5 illustrates the available services along with their descriptions. User can simply click into the favorite links to access the practical services. The comments of all items in the service descriptions are introduced in Table 1.

Table 1. Service Description Properties

Property	Comments
serviceName	The name of the service
intendedPur-pose	A high-level description of what constitutes (typical successful execution of a server)
textDescription	A brief, human readable description of the service, summarizing what the service offers or what capabilities are being requested.
Role	An abstract link to peers involved in the service execution.
requestBy	A sub-property of role referring to the service requester.
providedBy	A sub-property of role referring to the service provider.

7 Conclusion and Future Work

In this paper, we introduced an extended Service-Oriented Architecture - PSOA for supporting flexible library services integration and interoperability in a large scale DLs environment. We described the requirements and motivations in exploiting SOA for DL developments and applications. Generally, users prefer to have a 'one-stop' library system to fulfill most of their information needs. And the library itself may also need to access other accessible library services to meet its special demands. In this way, the library acts as both the service provider and service consumer/requestor. Although the basic SOA infrastructure provides a means for the communications between services, it easily leads to the problems of single point of failure and performance bottleneck, etc. After briefly introducing our approach in designing and constructing the architecture, we discussed in greater detail the semantics in PSOA, because the lack of semantics hinder significantly the interoperability between services. We adopted OWL-S in order to embed semantics into the service descriptions. The architecture of a library node was described in a way of services processing. Finally, a query service example was presented.

The work presented here shows the need of distributed computing environment, such as P2P network, and the importance of widespread ontologies as well. Both of the two domains still have some unsolved problems. Accordingly, combining Web service, ontology and P2P together itself is for sure a challenging work. But we believe, from the long-term DL development and user requirements perspectives, it is a necessary and important research work to bring these efforts together. And our approach acted as a stepping stone.

Acknowledgement

Thanks Lars Edvardsen and Trond Aalberg for letting us use their INEX system. Thanks for the discussion with Peep Küngas and Øyvind Vestavik. This work is partially supported by the Norwegian Research Foundation in the framework of Information and Communication Technology (IKT-2010) program.

References

1. Booth, D., Haas, H., et.al, F.M.: Web services architecture. W3CWorking Group Note, Web Services Architecture. http://www.w3.org/TR/ws-arch/ (2004)
2. Papazoglou, M.P.: Service -oriented computing: Concepts, characteristics and directions. In: Fourth International Conference on Web Information Systems Engineering (WISE'03). (2003)
3. Chappell, D.A., Jewell, T.: Java Web Services. O'Reilly, USA (2002)
4. Hunter, J., Choudhury, S.: A semi-automated digital preservation system based on semantic web services. In: Joint Conferece on Digitial Libraries, Tucson, Arizona, USA. (2004) 269-278
5. Anan, H., Tang, J., Maly, K., Nelson, M., Zubair, M., Yang, Z.: Challenges in building federation services over harvested metadata. In: International Conference on Asian Digital Libraries (ICADL), Kuala Lumpur, Malaysia (2003) 602 -614
6. Nottelmann, H., Fuhr, N.: Combining daml+oil, xslt, and probabilistic logics for uncertain schema mappings in mind. In: European Conference on Digital Libraries (ECDL), Trondheim, NORWAY (2003) 194-206
7. Dublin core medata initiative. http://www.dublincore.org (2003)
8. Encoded archival description: Official ead. Version 2002 web site. http://www.loc.gov/ead/ (2002, Last visit: September 15, 2004)
9. Draft standard for learning object metadata. http://ltsc.ieee.org/wg12/ (2002, Last visit: September 15, 2004)
10. Marc standards. (n.d.). library of congress network development and marc standards office. http://lcweb.loc.gov/marc/ (Last visit: September 15, 2004)
11. Editeur: Onix international. (n.d.). release 1.2. http://www.editeur.org/onix_les1.2/onix_les.html (Last visit: September 15, 2004)
12. Godby, C.J., Smith, D., Childress, E.: Two paths to interoperable metadata. In: Dublin-Core Conference, DC-2003: Supporting Communities of Discourse and Practice Metadata Research & Applications, Seattle,Washington (USA). (2003)
13. 13.Metadata switch: schema transformation services. a project of oclc research. http://www.oclc.org/research/projects/mswitch/1 schematrans.shtm (2002, Last visit: September 15, 2004)
14. Sycara, K., Paolucci, M., Lewis, M.: Information discovery and fusion: Semantics on the battle_eld. In: Proceedings of the Sixth International Conference of Information Fusion, Volume 1. (2003) 538 -544
15. Ding, H., Solvberg, I.: Towards the schema heterogeneity in distributed digital libraries. In: 6th International Conference on Enterprise Information System (ICEIS). Volume 5, Porto, Portugal (2004)
16. Ding, H., Solvberg, I.: A schema integration framework over super-peer based network. In: 2004 IEEE International Conference on Services Computing (SCC 2004), Special Session, Wuhan, China (2004)
17. Sagan, H.: Space-Filling Curves. Springer-Verlag Telos (1994)

18. Paolucci, M., Sycara;, K.: Autonomous semantic web services. Internet Computing, IEEE (2003) 34-42
19. Members., D.S.C.: Owl-s 1.0 release. http://www.daml.org/services/owl-s/1.0/ (2003, Last visit: September 15, 2004)
20. Sycara;, K.: Dynamic discovery, invocation and composition of semantic web services. Hellenic Conference on Arti_cial Intelligence (SETN) (2004) 3-12
21. Gudgin, M., Hadley, M., et.al, N.M.: Soap version 1.2, w3c recommendation. http://www.w3.org/TR/soap12-part1/ (2003, Last visit. September 15, 2004)

OAI Protocol for Chinese Culture Resources Metadata Harvesting

Qiaoying Zheng, Wei Zhu, and Zongying Yang

Shanghai Jiao Tong University Library,
1954 Hua Shan Road Shanghai, 200030, P.R. China
zheng@mail.lib.sjtu.edu.cn,
{wzhu, zyyang}@lib.sjtu.edu.cn

Abstract. This paper presents a part of the research result, according to the research of the International Digital Library Project (IDLP)— CMNet (Chinese Memory Net – US-Sino Collaborative Research Toward A Global Digital Library in Chinese Studies) founded by the America[1]. The Open Archives Initiative (OAI) Protocol for Metadata Harvesting presents one promising method by which metadata regarding Chinese Culture resources can be shared and made more interoperable with metadata from other sources. In this international cooperative project, Shanghai Jiaotong University mainly undertakes the research of key theories, methods and technologies for the Chinese folk music DL and the major content of the research are digitalization processing methods for the Chinese folk music, metadata standards and criteria, metadata interoperability for the Chinese folk music and so on. This paper introduces the OAI-based metadata interoperation framework for Chinese cultures resources, OAI-based system framework for CMNet, OAI protocol for metadata harvesting, administration and value-added services of metadata harvesting for Chinese Folk Music DL (CFMDL) and so on.

1 Introduction

Nowadays digitized information resources on the Internet are increasing at a tremendous speed. Facing such widely distributed, large quantity of information which has so many types of carriers, how to organize and manage it effectively, provide high quality, diversified, and unified global information services that surpass traditional libraries in level and efficiency, is the problem to be solved urgently, and is also the content of the research of digital libraries (DLs). The rise and evolution of DLs marks the Internet gradually walking out of the category of technical development, striding toward the multi-subject, creative fields of human activities including science exchange, art creation, culture propagation, economy growth, and knowledge management. We can say anyone that grasps this direction of development will have the

---

[1] This research was supported by National Natural Science Foundation of China. No 60221120145.

initiative in the competition of science and economy of the century. Therefore, every country of the world highly values the research and practice of DLs, makes it an important task of present, and carries out various plans and projects in succession.

2   CMNet Project Background

Chinese civilization has a centuries-old history and accumulated abundant culture resources. How to carry forward our plentiful information resources, to digitize them and provide users with DL services conveniently is the main aspect of current DL technical research both domestic and abroad.

In 1998 the research of US DLI project phase 1 was finished and more large-scale project of DLI2 was initiated immediately. Library of Congress (LOC), National Library of Medicine (NLM), National Endowment for the Humanities (NEH), and Federal Bureau of Investigation (FBI) were added to the list of sponsors that cooperated with National Archives & Records Administration (NARA), Smithsonian Institute, and Institute of Museum and Library Services (IMLS). Tens of universities and research institutes participated in this project, which launched more extensive, indepth research and practice against DL technologies. The noticeable point of US DLI project phase 2 is to push the International Digital Library Project (IDLP) founded for global digital libraries. American scientist of Chinese origin, member of President's Information Technology Advisory Committee (PITAC), Professor Ching-chih Chen headed the list to apply for the research project of CMNet (Chinese Memory Net – US-Sino Collaborative Research Toward A Global Digital Library in Chinese Studies) which was supported by the National Science Foundation (NSF) in1999. Ching-chih Chen invited Tsinghua University, Peking University, Shanghai Jiaotong University, and Cornell University, UC Berkeley, University of Pittsburgh of US to cooperate internationally to share the fundamental research of Chinese culture on the Internet by means of digital library.

In order to promote the DL research and construction of our country, Tsinghua University, Peking University, and Shanghai Jiaotong University applied jointly for the major project, "Theories, Methods and Technical Research of the Globalization of the Chinese Culture Digital Library". This project will study the worldwide Chinese culture information aiming at Chinese culture, which will overcome the limitation of location, media type and language to achieve free exchange visits and resource sharing. Key issues include the digitalization techniques of typical resources of Chinese culture; standards of metadata description and organization, architecture and interoperation techniques of DLs on the Internet; collection, sharing, and administration of distributed mass-capacity of information; services and technologies needed to globalize Chinese culture DL, human machine interface, and searching techniques.

Through the research of international cooperative project, we can learn and master foreign advanced experience. Secondly international cooperation will push the spreading of Chinese culture because one of the uses of DL is to provide the sharing and all-purpose services of global information resources. Thus we should study basic problems of the translation and transformation between Chinese and other languages since currently our DL researches and practices are mainly digitization and services of local resources, less studying the key theories, technologies and methods of providing global services.

In this international cooperative project, Shanghai Jiaotong University mainly undertakes the research of key theories, methods and technologies for the Chinese folk music DL and the major content of the research are digitalization processing methods for the Chinese folk music, metadata standards and criteria, system interoperability, and visiting methods toward distributed, heterogeneous resources, all of which are crucial issues in DL technologies.

3   OAI-Based Metadata Interoperation Framework for CMNet Project

3.1   Metadata Standard of Chinese Folk Music DL

Chinese folk music includes various types of musical works in every historical period of Chinese nations. The data collection of Chinese folk music database metadata gives priority to Chinese ancient music, also considers modern music, including musical works (composition), musical characters (e.g., composers, executants), musical instruments, etc.

Music metadata is composed of three data modules: descriptive metadata, administrative metadata, and structural metadata.

Descriptive metadata: Describes the content and form of musical resources, which is the basic metadata to show resources to users.

Administrative metadata: Administers the metadata of musical resources described above, providing information about details to construct and store electronic documents of resources, the relationship with maternal resources and history of technical processing.

Structural metadata: Determines the relationship between electronic document format and musical resources.

Descriptive metadata has 15 elements and 22 qualifiers.

Through reviewing and analyzing current metadata format (MARC – Machine Readable Catalogue, DC – Dublin Core, SMDL – Standard Music Description Language) applying to describe music resources, according to CMNet project's requirement analysis, we decided to resume using the 15 basic elements and part of qualifiers, making whole' element set compatible with "Chinese Metadata Standard Framework".

3.2   Brief Introduction of the OAI Protocol

OAI is a protocol for searching and publishing digitized information resources applied to interchangeable platform, which was mainly designed to solve the interoperation of different resources to achieve effectively extracting, publishing, and utilizing digitized information resources on the Internet. OAI is composed of service provid-ers and data providers. Service providers harvest the metadata regularly or randomly from data providers through OAI requests and provide value-added services on the acquired metadata. Data providers publish the metadata to service providers through OAI responses and they must provide at least DC format metadata, or provide other format of metadata according to the requests of service providers. OAI protocol allows many-to-many interchangeable way, i.e. one data provider can publish metadata to several service providers simultaneously while one service provider can also obtain metadata from several data providers. The OAI component has multiple properties: it can be a data provider as well as a service provider. As OAI is an application protocol based on HTTP, commands set triggers corresponding server programs at the back end by means of the variable names and its contents used by HTTP to transmit between front end and back end, which sends back the results after processing them according to variable contents and it must conform to the XML format set by the XML Schema of OAI protocol.

Table 1. Metadata Standard of Chinese Folk Music

Element	Qualifier	DC Mapping
1. Title/name	Alternative	dc:title
2. Creator	Role	dc:creator
3. Subject and keywords		dc:subject
4. Description	Abstract	dc:description
	MusicInstrument	
	Score	
	Genre	
	Work	
	Phrase	
	Range	
	Voice	
	Key	
5. Publisher		dc:publisher
6. Contributor	Role	dc:contributor
7. Date	Created	dc:date
	Issued	
8. Type		dc:type
9. Format	Extent	dc:format
	Medium	
	Technique	
	Scheme = IMT	
10. Identifier	Scheme = URI	dc:identifier
11. Source		dc:source
12. Language		dc:language
13. Relation	HasPart	dc:relation
14. Coverage	Temporal	dc:coverage
	Spatial	
15. Rights management		dc:rights

3.3 OAI-Based CMNet System Framework

Data providers that own information repository are responsible for creating and publishing metadata, meanwhile organize the numerical objects in the information repository to produce structural metadata and make end-users or service providers can use and browse the information repository. Data providers can organize metadata in accordance with the standards defined by themselves, while they must reflect and publish the metadata format conformed to OAI protocol (DC standard).

Service providers send requests to data providers that publish the metadata to extract metadata, process and organize them, as well as build value-added services that are based on the metadata collected from data providers. Service providers can harvest part of the metadata needed according to requirement definition.

A registration sever provides the registration interfaces for data providers and service providers, and the server also administers and organizes the data providers and service providers. A service provider can look for data providers through the registration sever, and the users can look up suitable service providers through the registration interfaces provided by the registration sever.

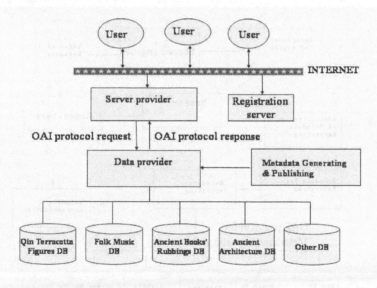

Fig. 1. CMNet System Framework based on OAI Protocol

3.4 Metadata Harvesting, Administration and Value-Added Services

The major technical mechanism of OAI protocol is to obtain metadata from data providers. It uses HTTP to deliver requests, decides what data to obtain from data providers, and transmits records using XML that resolves the data into metadata that can be distinguished by computers. Metadata harvesting is achieved by service providers' functional modules through which service providers harvest metadata regularly from data providers and construct data repository of metadata. Meanwhile, these metadata will be used for establishing value-added services, e.g. metadata reorganization according to classification system, metadata publishing, etc.

3.4.1 OAI Protocol for Metadata Harvesting

The OAI Protocol defines the following requests and responses:

(1)Identify: to retrieve basic information about a data provider.

(2)List Metadata Format: to retrieve the metadata formats available from a data provider. OAI protocol also permits other metadata formats in addition to OAI_DC (Dublin Core) format defined by the protocol.

(3) List Sets: after sending the ListSets request to a data provider, the set structure of metadata will be returned.

(4) List Identifiers: to retrieve the related item number of the data provider.

(5)List Records: a data provider return the metadata required by the service provider according to certain subject, category or time scope.

(6) Get Record: to retrieve the record contents according to designated item number and metadata format.

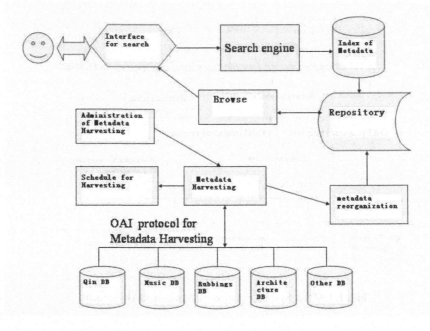

Fig. 2. Metadata Harvesting Administrator

3.4.2 Metadata Harvesting, Administration and Value-Added Services

(1)   Information Management of Data Providers: users can add information about data providers that require metadata harvesting at any time. Through registration service, the system will list the information of registered data providers for users to choose, and also allows users to add information of unregistered

data providers. The main information of data providers is repositoryName, baseURL, protocolVersion, and Metadata format, etc.

(2)   Administration of Metadata Harvesting: users can set up the system in advance to periodically harvest the metadata record for selected data providers, update local metadata repository, in the meantime set conditions for metadata harvesting, including: set, date, identifier, and metadata types. The frequency of metadata harvesting and updating can be modified and set at any time through administration module. If the processes of metadata harvesting cannot be completed successfully during set time due to network problem or data provider's server breakdown, users can restart or cancel these unfinished processes.

(3)   Administration and Reorganization of Metadata: in local metadata repository, store and update the metadata periodically harvested, reorganize and classify them in accordance with the requirement of value-added services, so that users can search and browse.

(4)   Query Module: the system provides users with search interfaces, search routes, and search methods for users to search information resources of metadata repository, while full-text browsing directly links to the targeted databases through data providers' URI. Search routes include simple searching and advanced searching in which users utilize music name, composer, executants, composition, sentence, times, and location, all of which are searching required information resources. The system also provides Boole logical search, truncate search, vague search, and knowledge-based search. Moreover the searching scope is restricted through the conditions of metadata generating time, metadata categories, and document types.

(5)   Data Browsing Function: to provide several types of data browsing and ordering, mainly including: displaying simple information of the data, displaying detailed information of the data, browsing according to alphabetical order of the digital resources, and browsing according to the categories of the digital resources. Users can align the data by times, music name, or composer during browsing.

4 Conclusions

OAI protocol has good features of opening, applicability, and interoperability, which can seamlessly connect to databases under different platform with flexibility. Although OAI is a simple protocol which is easy for designing programs, some issues that OAI protocol has not refer to will still occur in practical system design. How to obtain digital objects, how to design the interface to data service port, etc., are all the parts that OAI protocol has not stipulated for, but they must be considered and handled in real systems. While the OAI-based interoperable system for the Chinese culture digital library is in developing, we hope we can accumulate more experience in the system development process to exchange with everybody.

References

1. Wang Shuan, Wang Meng, Zhang Ming: The Design and Implementation of a Metadata Interoperable Architecture Supporting OAI-PMH, Computer Engineering and Applications, 2003, No.20
2. Shen Yi: Open Archives Initiative Protocol for Metadata Harvesting and Its Application, New Technology of Library And Information Service, 2004.2
3. Wang Aihua, Zhang Ming, Yang Dongqing, etc.: OAI-based Metadata Interoperation Framework in Digital Library, Computer Engineering and Applications, 2002, No. 1
4. Xiaoming Liu, Kurt Maly, Mohammad Zubair,: Arc – An OAI Service Provider for Digital Library Federation
5. The University of Illinois Open Archives Initiative Metadata Harvesting Project—UIUC OAI Harvester Architecture: http://oai,grainger.uiuc.edu/papers, 2003.5.16
6. The Open Archives Initiative Protocol for Metadata Harvesting, http://www. openarchives.org/OAI/2.0/openarchivesprotocol.htm: 2003.5.24
7. Chen Zhaozhen: OAI-based Joint Catalog Construction Plan for the National Digital Collection

Preserving Digital Media: Towards a Preservation Solution Evaluation Metric

Carl Rauch and Andreas Rauber

Department of Software Technology and Interactive Systems, Vienna University of
Technology, Favoritenstr. 9 - 11 / 188, A-1040 Wien, Austria
{Rauch, Rauber}@ifs.tuwien.ac.at
http://www.ifs.tuwien.ac.at/ifs/

Abstract. With an increasing amount of information being digitized or directly
created and subsequently existing only electronically, and coupled with an ever
increasing variety of file formats and integrated document functionalities, long-
term preservation solutions become crucial. While different approaches, such as
Emulation, Migration, or Computer Museums were developed, neither of them
excels in all circumstances, and the selection of the most appropriate strategy
poses a non-trivial task. In this paper, an adapted version of Utility Analysis is
presented, which can be used for choosing an optimal preservation solution for
each individual situation. This analysis method comes from infrastructure
projects and is here used to combine the wide range of requirements which are
to be considered in order to choose a suitable preservation strategy. The
evaluation metric will be presented and demonstrated with the help of two
practical examples.

1 Introduction

Present day rapid expansion of digital data and the trend towards digitally saved files
and documents leads to an increasing demand for robust and trustworthy digital
archives. Research in the preservation area has been focussed on storage media. CD-
Rs with a reported lifetime of over a hundred years [14], or systems that automatically
migrate data to the most adequate storage media are available in the market.

In the last couple of years a second issue became urgent - the preservation of objects
in digital libraries, existing in a range of formats. Due to rapid file format changes, it is
nowadays very unlikely that it will be possible to reopen a digital object 10 years after
its creation without loosing parts of the original creation. Typical examples are changes
in the format or problems with interpreting certain character encodings. In some cases
the result of reopening the file might be just an uninterpretable bit stream. A number of
projects and working groups elaborated two major strategies to preserve digital objects
over a longer period, namely Emulation and Migration, which can be subdivided into a
wide array of possible realizations. Additionally, some alternative solutions have been
found, ranging from computer museums to machines with an independent energy
supply and very stable components [8].

These various solutions have been tested, rated and implemented, but until now,
none of them is clearly better than all others for all scenarios. Unfortunately the

Z. Chen et al. (Eds.): ICADL 2004, LNCS 3334, pp. 203–212, 2004.
© Springer-Verlag Berlin Heidelberg 2004

decision which solution to choose for which scenario is not only influenced by the size and composition of a collection, but also by many other attributes, such as user satisfaction or costs, which leads to complex decision processes.

In the research area of infrastructure projects, complex decisions have long played a major role. Bridges, dams, and highways have to be built the best way possible while obeying many different constraints. Therefore *Utility Analysis* [16] was developed as a tool to integrate and evaluate different aspects, to give an overview over them, and to accumulate them into a single decision value. As presented in this paper, the tool can be applied with some modifications to preservation solutions as well, which we will demonstrate in theory and in practice. We will use the preservation of an audio collection of the Austrian Phonogrammarchiv and the preservation of an journal's digital library in MS Word 2002 format as practical examples to evaluate various migration strategies. Emulation or Migration of files into an Emulation environment was not considered since no sufficiently specified solutions were available.

The remainder of this paper is organized as follows: Following some related work in Section 2 and a short description of the Utility Analysis in Section 3, the individual steps of the Analysis are presented in detail. In Section 4, the first step is to define the project objectives and to construct an objective tree. After the target definition, Section 5 describes the choice and enlistment of alternatives, which will be evaluated in Section 6. The measurement results are then transformed into comparable numbers. Finally the objectives defined at the beginning are weighted according to their importance, aggregated with the comparable numbers and added to a final ranking of the alternatives, as described in Section 7.

2 Related Work

The basis of this paper comes from two different research areas, the long-term preservation of digital media and the economic evaluation of alternatives.

During the last couple of years, a lot of research has been done to define, improve, and evaluate single preservation strategies. A good overview over the state of art was prepared by the National Library of Australia [15] and published by the UNESCO as a handbook accompanying the UNESCO charter on the preservation of the digital heritage. It not only describes specific preservation strategies, but also management and legal issues. The research on technical preservation issues is focussed on Migration and Emulation. Scientific results on Migration, which is at the current time the most common preservation strategy, were published for example by the Council of Library and Information Resources (CLIR) [10], where different kinds of risks for a migration project are presented.

Work on the second important preservation strategy 'Emulation' was done by Jeff Rothenberg together with CLIR [13] envisioning a framework of an ideal preservation surrounding. In order to make Emulation useable in practice, several projects developed it further. One of them is the CAMILEON project [7] trying to implement first solutions and to compare Emulation to Migration. Other important projects in the preservation field are the CEDARS project [2], the PADI project [12], or the 'digitale duurzaamheid' project [5].

Another aspect is the description of digital objects with metadata. Research in this area has focussed on a description that facilitates the reopening of files in the future or the search and cataloguing functionalities [4]. In this paper metadata will be necessary for verifying changes which happen as a result of the preservation process. Important criteria for this purpose have sometimes been mentioned in literature, but always as a side argument or as a short introduction or preparation for other theories. The objective tree built from such criteria constitutes a core issue of the presented approach as shown in this paper.

The second research area which contributes to our solutions here is the area of economic evaluation. Utility Analysis is often used for ranking alternatives for complex infrastructure projects. A good introduction to Utility Analysis was published by Hanusch [6]. It describes several predecessors of the concept and the different analytical steps which have to be followed to receive a final ranking. A software to support the decision process was implemented by the Institute of Public Finance and Infrastructure Policy at the Technical University of Vienna [9].

In economic research, the Utility Analysis is often mentioned together with two other decision instruments. The first is 'Cost-Effectiveness Analysis', which focuses strongly on the representation of costs. Reasons for not choosing this alternative are that the status-quo alternative is not evaluated, that the weighting metric is not as well developed as in the Utility Analysis, and that no clear ranking of alternatives can be done. In the second model, the 'Cost-Utility Analysis', all attributes are only measured with monetary units. On the one hand this simplifies the comparison process, but on the other hand it reduces the explanatory power of the attributes and the decision's transparency. Without the existence of life-cycle cost models for digitally preserved files, it requires a lot of effort and a high level of uncertainty to define such costs. Considering these disadvantages Utility Analysis is probably the best choice for a preservation setting.

3 Introduction to the Utility Analysis

Utility Analysis has its origins in the evaluation and ranking of infrastructure projects and public projects. The first scientific research in this area started around 1970, the version presented here was introduced by Arnim Bechmann [1] in 1978. In English language literature this concept is also referred to as 'cost-effectiveness', 'value-benefit', 'multicriteria' or 'benefit-value' analysis [16]. Still, 'Utility Analysis' seems to be the best translation. In order to be applicable for preservation issues, the Utility Analysis has to be slightly altered, but equals in most parts the original process. It consists of eight steps which are described and discussed in this paper.

The letters 'A' and 'U' in the listing specify whether a step has to be done mechanically by an Administrator or a software system that moderates the process, or by a User who is responsible for the decisions:

1. U: Definition of the project's objectives by generating a decision tree
2. A (for already defined), U(for new objectives): Assignment of effects on the objectives
3. U: Definition of alternative solutions
4. U: Measurement of the alternative's outcome
5. A, U (for new objectives): Transformation of the measured values
6. U: Weighting of the objectives
7. A: Aggregation of partial and total values
8. A, U: Ranking of the alternatives

To demonstrate the usability of the Utility Analysis, examples from two areas are taken: The first describes the preservation of an editor's electronic book collection, which is stored in MS Word 2002. The second one describes an implementation at the Austrian Phonogrammarchiv, where the preservation of audio files was evaluated. The numbers used in the following chapters are taken from the first example.

4 Definition of the Project Objectives

The first step of the Utility Analysis is to define the project as a whole and its goals, i.e. the file characteristics to be preserved. This is made by constructing a so-called objective tree, where many different goals, high-level and detailed ones, are collected and put in relation to each other in order to gain a certain structure.

For defining the objective tree, a synthesis of a top-down and a bottom-up approach is probably the best solution. Here high-level aims (which are suggested in the generic objective tree in Table 1) are combined with basis requirements (which are usually collected in a brainstorming process).

In the generic objective tree, the main objective - preserving digital objects without major modifications and with reasonable cost - is detailed into the three subgoals to preserve the objects characteristics, to optimize the preservation process to meet surrounding goals and to keep costs at a reasonable level.

These objectives are further divided into a wide variety of subgoals. It is tried to avoid overlap of different subgoals although duplicity is not really a problem in Utility Analysis. As can be seen in Table 1, these second level goals are again further split into third level goals, only listed as an incomplete excerpt in the table due to possible differences between implementations at this and at deeper levels. Although costs are basically a process characteristic, it seems beneficial to list them as a top-level entry since they form an orthogonal decision dimension. The final hierarchy's depth depends on the criteria's complexity and on the user's possibility of finding exactly measurable subgoals.

Combining this generic objective tree with the bottom-up approach, users take a look at the actual files in their collection, listing all relevant document characteristics to be preserved (such as page numbering, colour, links, resolution of images, presence of macros, interactivity, storage size, etc.) and sort them into the previously defined top-down structure. The resulting objective tree may be rather extensive and complex for heterogeneous preservation settings, with some parts being common to many preservation initiatives, whereas others will be very specific for a given collection.

When implementing an objective tree, it proved helpful to start with a brainstorming process to identify targets. After a certain time, the use of the generic objective tree will help to focus the thinking on the wide array of possible criteria.

In the first setting of e-journal documents 63 criteria were found, in the second practical example, where criteria for preserving audio files are collected, 136 different objectives in five levels of the hierarchy were identified. The creation of an objective tree proofed even useful for settings with a clear and already determined strategy, where new requirements were found by applying the structured approach of identifying potential requirements.

Table 1. Generic objective tree: Hierarchical order of goals

Top level	Level 2	Level 3 (selected)
File Characteristics	Appearance	Page (margins, breaks, . . .)
		Paragraph (formatting, . . .)
		Character (font style, colour, . . .)
		Sound (bit rate, . . .)
		Video (frame rate, . . .)
	Structure	Caption, tag description, . . .
	Behaviour	Reaction on user inputs, search, links, . . .
Process Characteristics	Authenticity	Traceability of changes, . . .
	Stability	Supplier independency, . . .
	Scalability	Data or format range increase, . . .
	Usability	Process complexity, functionality, . .
Costs	Technical	Hardware, Software, per file, . . .
	Personnel	Maintenance, . . .

In order to demonstrate the Utility Analysis' usability, four characteristics selected as examples are described in detail. Three of them concern the appearance of a file, namely 'Numbering of chapters', 'Page margins' and 'Page break'. The fourth one, 'Running additional SW costs' stands for all software costs that are dedicated only to the preservation solution.

In a next step, the objectives identified in the objective tree are made measurable. It does not matter, whether the targets are in the second, third, or fourth level of the tree, but whether they are leaves or internal nodes. Theoretically, all kinds of measurements could be used, such as ordinal, cardinal or proportional scales. Usually, cardinal measures are preferred, such as EURO per year for the running additional SW costs or the deviation from the original page margins in millimetre. In cases where no numerical measurement is possible, subjective measures can be applied: the user chooses a value according to her or his impression of a criterion's fulfilment. Examples are the evaluation of paragraph formatting or the numbering of chapters. The worst measure level is always be the 'not acceptable' possibility. If this is chosen, the result in the objective's field is so bad that the evaluated approach cannot be seen as useable.

5   Listing Alternative Strategies

After the definition of the objective tree and the measures for the single criteria, which helps to obtain a clearer picture of the project's perspective, the next step is to search for different approaches that could be used to preserve the collection. Alternatives have to be significantly different from one another and verbally described with their names and a short overview of the preservation process. This is done to assure that the alternatives are understood by the project team. In addition to possible alternatives, the status-quo should be considered and added, plus the case where no planning process is made, the zero-planning case. Due to the fast technical evolution and due to very different user environments, this alternatives' enlistment alters significantly in each implementation of the analysis.

For the practical example of preserving a Word 2002 collection, the following four alternatives are evaluated; constraints arc, to use no additional hardware, thus reducing the solution on the personal computer of the editor:

1. Migration from the MS Word 2000 format to MS Word 2003
2. Migration to the XML-based, public OpenOffice.org 1.0.3 Writer format
3. Migration to PDF with Adobe Acrobat Distiller 2017.801
4. Not making any changes, keeping the MS Word 2002 files

Emulation or Migration of files into an Emulation environment are not considered as an alternative, because for the present scenario no software and no specifications were available or published. Other possibilities worth considering might include conversion to level-1, level-2 Postscript files, with the possibility of Migration to PDF later-on based on the PS-file, Migration to pure ASCII-text, and others, as well as the separate handling of different tools for the respective steps.

For the implementation for the audio collection, alternatives affecting the compression rate and the sample rate but also concerning the metadata were combined, additional to the alternative of not changing the actual strategy and to the 'no changes' alternative.

6 Measuring and Transforming the Strategies' Performance

In this step, the real test work has to be done. Every alternative has to be tested with a couple of representative files and evaluated according to the criteria of the objective tree. Some test beds are available or under construction, some well described files in different formats and types can be downloaded from the Internet, such as [5] or [11]. Alternatively, representative files from the collection to be preserved are used, although care has to be taken that these are really representative with respect to the variety of document characteristics, e.g. to include equations, embedded images of various types used in the collection, etc. The different preservation alternatives, which were defined in Chapter 5, are then executed with these files. The average outcome per alternative is stored such as in Table 2, for the subjective choice a range from zero to five is chosen.

Table 2. Performance of the four different preservation alternatives

Objective \ Strategy	MS Word	OpenOffice	PDF	No Changes
Numbering of chapters	5	5	5	5
Page margins	0	+3	0	0
Page break	5	N.A.	5	5
Running additional SW costs	100	0	0	0
...	...	...	...	...

In the first evaluation line of this table all alternatives get the highest score, because all of them fulfil the requirement: the pages were correctly numbered. Some first differences appear at the page margins, which changed for 3 millimetres in the Open Office environment. This leads to the effect that also the paragraph structure alters in such a significant way that the outcome of the OpenOffice alternative cannot be accepted as a preservation solution for this scenario any more.

Research on assessing the risk of migration was made by the Council on Library and Information Resources [10]. The costs are zero in all cases except for the first one, where it is estimated that a newer version of MS Word is published every two years with average costs of around 200 EURO.

All objectives which are here used as an example concern appearance oriented aspects and costs, so the 'no changes' alternative ranks very high. In the practical implementations it was nevertheless never chosen because of its 'Not Acceptable' result concerning long-term stability.

When a file does not exhibit a certain characteristic (say, an animation or sound embedding) making an evaluation not possible, the criteria of all alternatives are assigned the same values. Because of the equality of all possible solutions, this would not influence the final choice for this particular document.

After the measurement of the various criteria, the result is a table with 'the number of leaves' times 'the number of alternatives' values, which are measured in different categories, such as EURO, minutes, or subjective estimations. The next step is to transform these values into comparable numbers.

To this end, all previously obtained subjective results are transformed to a uniform scale, e.g. from zero to five, as in our example. It is useful to work with the same range as it is used for the subjective evaluation of characteristics, because then the results can be directly taken as uniform numbers. The only difference is to change the lowest (knock-out) values from zero to the term 'not acceptable'.

Table 3. Transformation of measured values to a 5 to 0 (N.A.) scale

Objective	Val. 5	Val. 3	Val. 4	Val. 2	Val. 1	N.A.
Numbering of chapters	5	3	4	2	1	N.A.
Page margins [mm]	0	2	1	3	4	> 4
Page break	5	3	4	2	1	N.A.
Running additional SW costs	0	]20;40]	]0;20]	]40;80]	]80;150]	> 150
...	...	...	...	...	...	...

Table 4. The comparable values

Objective \ Strategy	MS Word	OpenOffice	PDF	No Changes
Numbering of chapters	5	5	5	5
Page margins	5	2	5	5
Page break	5	N.A.	5	5
Running additional SW costs	1	5	5	5
...	...	...	...	...

The transformation is more difficult with cardinal scales. In this paper, the approach of defining intervals is chosen. Table 3 shows the transformation function for the previously defined values. These values may differ significantly from other users' needs. Especially the costs cannot be generally categorized, because of their direct dependence on the collection's size. The values which are presented in Table 3 were elaborated together with the user and define her expectations regarding the characteristics of the single objectives.

While in principle the definition of the transformation functions could take place immediately after defining the measurement scales, it is recommended to do it only after the performance measurements of the various strategies have been made. This is in order to first get an overview of the scope of the values, such as e.g. the displacement of page margins in the example listed in Table 2. After applying the transformation functions we obtain the results as listed in Table 4. These values form the input to the final rating.

7 Weighting the Objectives and Final Ranking

The output of the previous step is a large table with the size of 'number of alternatives' times 'number of characteristics'. In this step the numbers are aggregated to a single value per alternative while allowing for different weighting of the various objectives. The first part is to choose the importance of the four top-level criteria 'File characteristics', 'Costs', 'Usability', and 'Process performance' by distributing the weight of 100 percent among them. Another 100 percent are distributed on every single level of each branch. The next step thus is to choose the relative importance of 'Appearance', 'Structure', and 'Behaviour'. The process goes on like this until all leaves and nodes have a specific weight. Finally, the weights of the single leaves are obtained by multiplying their own value times the importance of their parent nodes. For example, the weight of the criterion 'Numbering of chapters' is multiplied with the weight of 'Pages', 'Structure' and the weight of 'File characteristic'. Such, the weights for all characteristics' leaves are calculated, summing up to 100% for each individual branch. Although, again, these weights could be set immediately after defining the objective tree, it is advisable to set them after evaluating the performance of the various preservation strategies.

Weights should be adapted by the user for every single implementation of Utility Analysis. The values presented in Table 5 are chosen subjectively and only reflect the requirements of our specific preservation scenario. They are best set interactively in a brain- storming session evaluating the outcome of different decisions and their effect in the usability of the collection in the future. With some simple mathematics the final ranking is obtained. The first part is to multiply the objective values of Table 4 with the objectives' weights, resulting in so called part-values. By adding all part-values of the same alternative, the total-value of it is obtained. Before ranking the results and determining the best solution, a sensitivity analysis is usually performed. It controls, how close different alternatives are to each other, which characteristics were decisive, and if they are affected with a certain risk and uncertainty. Finally, the ranking of the alternatives is made, not only based on the numerical results of the Utility Analysis, but also on side effects, which were not considered in the calculation. Such effects are good relationships with a supplier, expertise in a certain alternative or individual assessment, that one solution might become the market leader within a couple of years. Nevertheless, the numerical evaluation of different alternatives provides a powerful tool to weight their strengths and weaknesses and to make them comparable. Table 6 presents the result of the practical example, which advises to vote 'MS Word Migration'. This solution may be completely different from other, even similar, scenarios, because of subjectively chosen weights and values and because of the focus on these four specific alternatives.

Table 5. Weights of the different objectives and of the leaves-

Top level	Level 2	Level 3 (selected)	Percent	Weights
File Characteristics			0.4	
	Appearance		0.3	
		Numbering of chapters	0.1	0.012
		Page margins	0.1	0.012
		Page break	0.1	0.012
		. . .		
	Structure		0.2	
		Paragraph formatting	0.3	0.024
	. . .			
Process performance			0.4	
	. . .			
Costs			0.2	
	Technical		0.4	
		Running additional SW costs	0.4	0.032
	. . .			

Table 6. Total-Values and final ranking of the alternatives

Rank	Solution	Total-Value
1	MS Word Migration	4,175275
4	OpenOffice Writer	Not Acceptable
2	PDF	3,895975
4	No Changes	Not Acceptable

8 Conclusion

One major problem in the preservation research area is the choice of the right strategy for a certain data collection. The Utility-Analysis is a good approach to cope with that complex situation. Because of its stringent process, while at the same time allowing subjective weighting and even evaluation of solutions which fail to fulfil knock-out criteria to a sufficient degree, it helps to reduce the complexity and increases the objectivity of the decisions taken. It allows the analysis of a range of scenarios, providing a high-level overview due to the hierarchical structure and aggregation of extensive lists of preservation requirements into higher-level objectives.

Acknowledgements

Part of this work was supported by the European Union in the 6. Framework Program, IST, through the DELOS NoE on Digital Libraries, contract 507618.

References

1. Bechmann. Nutzwertanalyse, Bewertungstheorie und Planung. In: Beiträge zur Wirtschaftspolitik, Band 29. Bern, Stuttgart. 1978.
2. CURL Exemplars in Digital Archives. University of Leeds. Website. http://www.leeds.ac.uk/cedars/.
3. Consultative Committee for Space Data Systems. Reference Model for OAIS. CCSDS 650.0-B-1 Blue Book. ISO 14721:2003. Washington, DC. 2002.
4. Dublin Core Metadata Initiative. Website. http://dublincore.org/.
5. Digitale Duurzaamheid. ICTU. Den Haag. http://www.digitaleduurzaamheid.nl.
6. H. Hanusch, P. Biene, M. Schlumberger. Nutzen-Kosten-Analyse. Verlag Franz Vahlen München, Germany. 1987.
7. M. Hedstrom, C. Lampe. Emulation vs. Migration. Do Users Care? RLG DigiNews Dec. 2001. Vol. 5, Nr. 6. http://www.rlg.org/preserv/diginews/.
8. D. A. Kranch. Beyond Migration: Preserving Electronic Documents with Digital Tablets. Information Technologies Libraries 17(3):138-148. 1998.
9. G. Krames, J. Bröthaler. NWA-Applet - Nutzwertanalyse im Internet. Institute for Public Finance and Infrastructure Policy. Vienna Technical University. http://www.ifip.tuwien.ac.at/forschung.htm. [04/04/2004].
10. G.W. Lawrence, W.R. Kehoe, O.Y. Rieger, W.H. Walters, A.R. Kenney. Risk Management of Digital Information. CLIR. Washington, DC. 2000.
11. V. Ogle, R. Wilensky. Testbed Development for the Berkeley Digital Library Project D-LIB Magazine, Vol 7. 1996.
12. Preserving Access to Digital Information. National Library of Australia. Website. http://www.nla.gov.au/padi/. [03/03/2004].
13. J. Rothenberg. Avoiding Technological Quicksand: Finding a viable technical foundation for digital preservation. CLIR. Washington, DC. 1999.
14. D. Dinston, F. Ameli, N. Zaino. Lifetime of KODAK Writable CD and Photo CD Media. Digital & Applied Imaging. http://www.cd-info.com/CDIC/Technology/CD-R/Media/Kodak.html. [03/03/2004].
15. UNESCO Information Society Division. Guidelines for the preservation of digital heritage. National Library of Australia. 2003.
16. P. Weirich, B. Skyrms, E.W. Adams, K. Binmore, J. Butterfield, P. Diaconis, W.L. Harper. Decision Space: Multidimensional Utility Analysis. Cambridge University Press. 2001.
17. P. Wheatley. Migration-A CAMILEON discussion paper. Ariadne Issue 29. http://www.ariadne.ac.uk/. [03/03/2004].

Technical Issues of Sharing and Integration of OPAC and E-Learning Resources

Qinghua Zheng[1], Jing Shao[2], Haifeng Dang[1], and Huixian Bai[1]

[1] Department of Computer Science and Technology, Xi'an Jiaotong University,
Xi'an, 710049, P.R. China
[2] Xi'an Jiaotong University Library, Xi'an, 710049, P.R. China
jshao@mail.lib.xjtu.edu.cn

Abstract. Based on the analysis of the characteristics of both OPAC and e-learning resources respectively, some key issues of sharing and integration, such as data exchange format, searching interface, and supporting platform, were discussed, and a total model for integration of the two resources was proposed. Moreover, a prototype of sharing search system named Fsearch was developed, with which users can search for both OPAC system and e-learning system simultaneously. The result shows that Fsearch system can effectively improve the efficiency of acquiring knowledge for users and bring forward a preferable application prospect.

1 Introduction

OPAC means Online Public Access Catalog system, which mainly shows bibliographies and holdings of various print and electronic literature including books, periodicals and journals, scientific dissertations, and standards. E-learning resources are the basic materials or documents of e-learning, which include multimedia courseware, electronic teaching materials, examination database, question and answer database, and other related network courses. The distance learners can learn these materials via e-learning web site.Currently, OPAC and e-learning resources are independent each other because of the following facts:

- OPAC resource is stored in library system and maintained by library system administrators, but the e-learning resources are saved in e-learning database and maintained by network education college or e-learning center.
- The inherent relation or hyperlink between OPAC and e-learning resources has been not constructed.
- The two kinds of resources above are quite different in data format, coding method, technical standard, storage mode, and supporting platform.

In fact, Both OPAC and e-learning resources are indispensable study materials for learners. For example, when they want to study "computer network" curriculum over internet, not only they need to learn the teaching materials such as powerpoint, word document or the network courseware stored in e-learning materials database, but also do they need to search for some reference books from OPAC. When learners want to

Z. Chen et al. (Eds.): ICADL 2004, LNCS 3334, pp. 213–219, 2004.

obtain, extend and reinforce relational knowledge during on-line learning, or when learners need to find and consult interrelated holding information such as appointed reference books, dissertations, and periodical papers, learners have to search for his/her interesting material in the two resources respectively, which will certainly cause much inconvenience for learners. Therefore, how to integrate these two kinds of heterogeneous and distributed resources efficiently so that learners can retrieval any kind of learning material conveniently via one website and one uniform query is a very vital and challengeable problem.

Motivated by the above requirement, we consider that if e-learning resources can be related tightly with OPAC resources, not only can the educational quality and the ability of learners' acquiring knowledge be improved more effectively, but also can library's resources be utilized more sufficiently. Thus, it is absolutely necessary to study the technical issues of sharing and integration of OPAC and e-learning resources. Here, we propose one feasible solution to this problem to provide learners with the uniform search engine which is designed as one common website and query mode, users just input a query expression on it one time, and the merged results, which are joined by the result of OPAC and that of e-learning resources, will be returned.

In this paper, we analyze some key issues of Sharing and Integration of OPAC and e-learning resources, such as system function, data exchange format, searching interface, resources storage mode, and supporting platform, and then propose a viable solution of integrating the two resources. Now we have successfully developed a prototype of sharing search system with which users can search both OPAC system and e-learning system simultaneously, which has been tested on the heterogeneous and distributed XJTU Library's OPAC and E-learning resources. The result shows that the proposed solution can effectively improve the efficiency of acquiring knowledge for users.

2   Issues of Sharing and Integration of OPAC and E-Learning Resources

In this section, we will take Xi'an Jiaotong University (XJTU) library and network education as an example to describe the issues of sharing and integration of OPAC and E-learning resources.

2.1   Different Application and Function

XJTU's Integrated Library System (ILS) is INNOPAC system developed by Innovative Interfaces Inc., which consists of OPAC subsystem oriented to users and the modules of acquisition, cataloging and circulation system management. OPAC system is used for searching bibliographies and holdings of various print and electronic literature including books, periodicals and journals, scientific dissertations and other media included in library collection, while other subsystems are used for library management such as order, check-in, processing data, cataloging and circulation.

XJTU's Network Educational Resource Management System (ERMS for simple) is composed of e-learning resources, system management, and e-learning database. E-learning resources management includes cataloging and upload; system management consists of access rights management, security management, and learning log management; e-learning database is for saving various e-learning resources composed of multimedia courseware, teaching materials, examination database, question and answer database, teachers and learners' information database, study log file and other related materials. ERMS is based on Linux OS and Oracle 9i database, which is different from the platform of OPAC system. Distance learners can search, browse, and learn network educational materials of ERMS through WWW browser.

2.2 Different Data Format and Standard

The metadata of OPAC is MARC record. MARC is very mature standard. There are application software and data processing specification adapted to MARC. Various literature bibliography and holding information, such as title, author/publisher, ISBN/ISSN, call number, and location, can be described by MARC.

In China, both USMARC and CNMARC records are mainly used for cataloging in libraries. Foreign language literature is cataloged in USMARC and Chinese literature in CNMARC. The two MARC records are conformed with ISBD (International Standard Bibliographic Description) formula and ISO2709 format. The two MARCs' structures are entirely same. According to formula of ISO2709, a MARC record is composed of four parts such as its Leader, Directory, Data, and delimited field except that the other three part of CNMARC are same as that of USMARC. A fully ISO2709 structure of MARC record is illustrated in Figure 1.

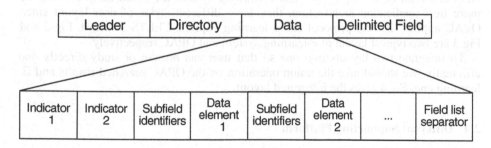

Fig. 1. A fully ISO2709 structure of MARC record

Each record has a 24 bytes leader, containing data concerning record structure and some items of data element defined by ISO2709. Directory, which is used to locate data in Data Area, is generated by system automatically. Data Area contains two parts. One is content structure including display field and data element, the other is value structure that indicates external standard used in content structure or descriptive cataloguing for data element.

LTSC (Learning Technology Standards Committee) is a standardization organization founded by IEEE Standards Committee, which specializes educational software, e-learning resource, management, and maintenance specification of educational information system. LOM(Learning Object Metadata) , issued by LTSC, is currently most important data model of e-learning resources[2]. In China, Long-distance Education Technology Committee proposed a local but more complete and practical E-learning standardization system after referring to IEEE LOM standard. That is CELTS (Chinese E-learning Technology Standardization). CELTS-3 defines Learning Object Metadata Specification, which is derived from the Chinese translation version of IEEE LOM. CELTS-3 defines nine categories of digital or non-digital learning objects. These learning objects are General, Lifecycle, Metametadata, Technical, Education, Rights, Relation, Annotation, and Classification. Each may include more than one items or subclasses or both, and each subclass contains at least two items. Furthermore, core or optional data elements can be determined according to the element's generality. E-learning resources are a subset of learning object. Their data elements are defined by Chinese and English name, interpretation, data type, range of value, value and sequence[3].

CELTS-41 is Technical Specification for Educational Resource Construction. It is a guidance specification of e-learning resources development[4]. This specification mainly includes nine types of resources such as material media, test questions, examination paper, courseware, case course, materials, network courseware, and FAQ. In term of different types of resources, a series of interrelated resource attribute label standard are made. CELTS-41 supplements extended data elements of each type. Xi'an Jiaotong University's e-learning resources keep to CELTS-3 and CELTS-41 specification.

2.3 Different Retrieval Interface

Although both of OPAC system and e-learning system are based on Web three or more tiers application architecture, they have different styles of user layout since OPAC applies Z39.50 protocol and e-learning exploits CELTS standard, Fig.2 and Fig.3 are two typical layout of e-learning system and OPAC respectively.

To integrate two layouts into one so that user can browse or study directly and efficiently, we should take the union operation on the OPAC searched results and E-learning one. Fig.4 gives the integrated layout.

2.4 Different Supporting Platform

Advanced integrated library systems are mostly based on UNIX operating system and large database management system, such as INNOPAC. It runs on professional servers, such as IBM, SUN or HP. INNOPAC is a autonomous ILS, but it provides application programming interface (API) to access its database through Z39.50 gateway. E-learning systems are mostly based on Windows or Linux operating system and general commerce database system, such as oracle DBMS, SQL DBMS. In general, E-learning systems are based on J2EE component technology and J2EE/JSP three layers application architecture. Therefore, it is a challengeable technical question that how we design and develop a middleware through which learners can access OPAC system and E-learning system simultaneously.

Fig. 2. E-learning   **Fig. 3.** OPAC

Fig. 4. Fsearch

3   A Scheme of Federal Searching on OPAC and E-Learning Resources

On the basis of analysis of the issues of integration and sharing of OPAC and E-learning above, we proposed a technical scheme to realize federal search for the two Resources. Fig.5 gives the implementation model of the scheme.

The key part of this model is the middleware named Fsearch system, which is based on J2EE component technology and Jsp/Java programming language. Fsearch system is composed of 4 modules as follows:

– Query Construction Module: accept user's search expression such as keywords, key title or subjects and convert the search expression into two different queries corresponding to OPAC system and E-learning system. One is accordant with Z39.50 protocol as RPN(Reverse Polish Notation) expression, The other is designed as SQL expression.

– OPAC Search Agent: accept a query accorded with Z39.50 protocol from Query Construction Module and submit it to Z39.50 gateway. Get the results with

ISO2709 format from OPAC and convert them into a common presentation with XML.
- E-learning Search Agent: accept a query with SQL expression from Query Construction Module and submit it to E-learning Database Search Engine. Get the results with SQL ResultSets format and convert them into a common presentation with XML.
- Result Join Module: In order to provide users with a final and unified search result set, this module should do the join of the two kinds of the results from both OPAC Search Agent and E-learning Search Agent module. The main operations of JOIN include describing every record with a uniform attribute set, eliminating duplicate records, ranking records retrieved, and canceling unnecessary fields in result record. Finally, the ranked and refined result will be returned to web users.

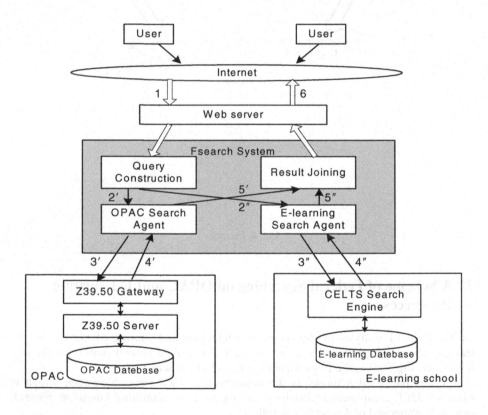

Fig. 5. Fsearch System Model

In Fig.5, those digits and arrow symbols indicate operating processes order and data flow direction respectively. Such digits as 2'and 2'', 3'and 3'', 4'and 4'', or 5'and 5'' express simultaneous operation.

Now we have already developed a prototype named Fsearch system according to this model, which is based on XJTU INNOPAC system located in XJTU library and XJTU E-learning system in Network Education School respectively.

4 Conclusion

For the requirement of integration of e-learning resource and OPAC database, so as to provide users with one website resource retrieval service, this paper proposes a novel and practical scheme of how to realize federal search for the two heterogeneous and distributed resources. And we have successfully developed a prototype of Fsearch system with which users can realize federal search for OPAC system and E-learning System simultaneously. Fsearch system has been tested through XJTU Library's OPAC and network educational resource system. The result of its application shows that the proposed solution can effectively improve the efficiency of acquiring knowledge for users and bring forward a preferable application prospect. Furthermore, the significance of sharing and integration of the two resources is accomplishment of one stop search, and an attempt of solving cross-find various sources retrieval technology, which has definite practical significance.

References

1. Pan, Y., Jin, P.: MARC: From Bibliographic Data to Generic Information: An Outlook to the Future Information Service. http://www.datatrans.com.cn/DTMARC/art01.htm
2. WG12: Learning Object Metadata : http://ltsc.ieee.org/wg12/
3. CELTS-3.1 CD1.6. Specification for Learning Object Metadata:Information Model(2002)
4. CELTS-41.1 CD1.0. Technical Specification for Educational Resource Construction: Information Model(2002).
5. Moore, J. ,Cvetkovic, S., Hung, K., Kraner, M.: The Z39.50 information retrieval standard. Comput. Control. Eng. J. 11(2000) 143-151

Technical Issues on the China-US Million Book Digital Library Project

Jihai Zhao and Chen Huang

Zhejiang University Libraries, Hangzhou, 310027 China
{Jhzhao, chuang}@lib.zju.edu.cn

Abstract. The China-US Million Book Digital Library Project (MBP) is a cooperated project of universities and institutes in China and USA, with funding from the Ministry of Education of China (MOE) and National Science Foundation of USA (NSF). The objective of MBP is to create a free-to-read, searchable collection of one million books, available to everyone over the Internet. This task will be accomplished by scanning the books and indexing their full text. Based on the plan and experience in MBP, six technical issues are presented in this paper, such as content selection, copyright clearance, data production, metadata creation, digital preservation and access, and quality control. The current status of the project and the future plan are discussed.

1 Introduction

It is estimated that about 100 million volumes of books and other materials have been accumulated since the beginning of recorded history in the world, among which about 55 million titles were indexed in OCLC's WorldCat up to April 2004[1]. The task of preservation of and access to the huge printed resources is a big challenge. With new digital technology, this task may be within the reach of a concerted effort by the cooperation among libraries, museums, and other groups in all countries.

The China-US Million Book Digital Library Project (MBP) is a cooperated project of universities and institutes in China and USA, with funding from the Ministry of Education of China (MOE) and National Science Foundation of USA (NSF). MBP is the first part of the Universal Library Project put forward by Dr. Raj Reddy, Herbert A. Simon Professor of Computer Science, Carnegie Mellon University(CMU)[2]. The objective of this project is to create a free-to-read, searchable collection of one million books, with a half in the Chinese language and the other half in the English language, available to everyone over the Internet. This task will be accomplished by scanning the books and indexing their full text.

The State Development and Reform Commission, Ministry of Education and Ministry of Finance of China decided to support MBP as a part of the Public Service System in the Project 211 in the Tenth Five-year Plan (2001-2005). MBP in China is led by Zhejiang University and Chinese Academy of Sciences as the Principal Investigators, and is jointly implemented by Peking University, Tsinghua University, Fudan University, Nanjing University, Shanghai Jiaotong University, Xi'an Jiaotong University, Wuhan University, Huazhong University of Science and Technology, Zhongshan University, Jilin University, Sichun University and Beijing Normal University. RMB 80 million yuan will be funded to support the organization,

Z. Chen et al. (Eds.): ICADL 2004, LNCS 3334, pp. 220–226, 2004.

scanning and processing of one million books by the Chinese government and the above 14 partners, and American partners will provide scanning equipment, storage servers and other related hardware and software. MOE has allocated the first funding of 40 million yuan to this project.

In this paper, six technical issues are presented based on MBP plan and experiences in the past year, such as content selection, copyright clearance, data production, metadata creation, digital preservation and access and quality control, which are important factors in the project implementation. The current status of the project and the future plan are discussed.

2 Technical Issues

2.1 Content Selection

Based on the MBP plan, 500 thousand volumes of Chinese Language books and 500 thousand volumes of English Language books will be selected for digitization. For Chinese Language books, the content will include 100 thousand ancient books published before the year 1911, 300 thousands academic books and journals published since 1911 in the public domain or of receiving permissions for digitization and Internet access, 100 thousands dissertations and theses in the partners, and other valuable traditional cultural resources.

The selection of English books is mostly carried out in USA, and it focuses on non-copyrighted materials and copyrighted ones of receiving permissions for digitization and Internet access. Non-copyrighted materials include all the publications before 1922 and part of the ones published after 1922, as many publishers and authors did not exercise the copyright renewal option based on US 1909 copyright law.

Government documents are in the public domain and are included in this project. The inclusion of these documents will allow for more recent materials to enter MBP legally and to become available to a broader audience and in a more accessible manner. Many recently released government documents are currently available in digital form. The creation of these back files will enhance those resources.

2.2 Copyright Clearance

All the books and other materials available at MBP are either out of copyright or permission to scan has been granted.

According to the China Copyright Law, the copyright is granted to authors for their lifetime plus 50 years. Suppose that the average lifetime of authors is 75 years and the average publication age is 40, then, we can estimate that the copyrighted materials are those published within 85 years. In other words, most books published in China after 1920s are copyrighted.

The US 1909 Copyright Law granted copyright for 28 years. Rights holders could then renew the copyright for another 28 years. Based on the current US Copyright Law, copyright in a work created on or after January 1, 1978, subsists from its creation and endures for a term consisting of the life of the author and 70 years after the author's death.

The project should obtain the permission from the right holders if copyrighted materials are selected for digitizing and Web access. Books often go out of print in two or three years but remain in copyright for a long period, which might not produce profits to the right holders. Certain publishers, including the National Academy Press, have had the experience that when they digitized their books, sales increased because attention was focused on the material and the users were not yet ready to read the books online. Therefore, the right holders may grant non-exclusive permission of digitization to the project[3].

MBP will make a good faith effort to clear copyright on appropriate materials by the following three approaches: (1) if the copyright of a book belongs to a publisher, MBP will send the publisher a letter asking for permission. Replies will be recorded in the administrative metadata; (2) if the publisher has returned the rights to the author, the author will be contacted, and subsequent copyright holders will be contacted as needed; and (3) as the individual authors or right holders are difficult to find and contact, it is recommended that the project would ask collective administration organizations to manage the copyright issues. The copyright clearance approaches are necessary though they are complicated, time consuming and may be costly.

2.3 Data Production

The scanning approach of MBP is to digitize the documents at the archival quality of 600 dots per inch (dpi) as a binary image (1 bit per pixel) for B/W pages. The resulting images are stored as Tagged Image File Format (TIFF). The resolution of the images is high enough so as to permit printing as legible as the original pages, say nothing of reading on the screen.

Typical TIFF data are provided for most tags. A specification for the TIFF header is produced to include scanner technical information, filename, and other data, but to be in no way a burden on the production service as the data are supplied by software default settings[4].

Images are named in sequential order, with corresponding 8.3 filenames, e.g., 00000001.tif as the first image in volume sequence and 00000341.tif as 341st image in volume sequence. Volumes provided to the project are assigned unique identifiers that conform to 8.3 format. The images are in directories named with the corresponding identifier. Images and directories are written to DVD discs according to agreed upon specifications.

Minolta PS-7000 overhead scanners, which are provided to the Chinese scanning centers by CMU are used in the project. The image processing software for curvature correction, de-skewing, de-speckling and cropping allows for thick books to be scanned either flat or in an angled cradle that reduces wear on the spine.

The English OCR program Abby Fine Reader and the Chinese program TH-OCR 2000 are tested in the project. The OCR output is not corrected manually, as the primary function of OCR is to allow searching inside the text. Therefore, the output of the OCR text will not be used for direct displaying, and only be used for creating a searchable index.

2.4 Metadata Creation

For Chinese books, a new MBP defined metadata standard (Edocument Metadata, Version 2.0) has been released by Zhejiang University Libraries with the help of Peking University Library, Shanghai Jiaotong University Library and other institutes, which combines DC with MARC. DC is used to describe digital objects produced from the project, while MARC is used to describe documentation objects or the original books. In this way, the available MARC records will be utilized, the digital library metadata standards will be followed, and the digital books will be fully described in MBP. The software named "MetaCreator" has been developed by Zhejiang University Libraries and applied in 14 scanning center.

For English books in MBP, we will use Digital Library Federation standards and metadata best practices.

Bibliographic metadata are derived from existing library catalog records. CMU libraries developed Metadata capture software that uses the standard Z39.50 protocol to search and retrieve relevant metadata from catalog records fields. Thus, author, title, and publication data do not have to be re-keyed[5].

Entering metadata information manually is time-consuming. One of the current research projects is software development for "automatic discovery of document structure". This will permit users to create hyperlinks which are not present in the original printed version of the book and navigate through the chapters.

Administrative metadata are maintained internally as file descriptions in the project databases and externally as part of the copyright permission database, which support the maintenance and archiving of the digital objects and ensure their long-term availability.

2.5 Digital Preservation and Access

MBP will produce approximately 300 million pages or 600 billion characters of information when it is completed. The database will house both an image file and a text file at about 50-60 megabytes per book. Creating and managing such a vast information base poses many technological challenges and provides a fertile test bed for innovative research in many areas. Mirroring the database in several places in China and USA will not only provide fast access, as the network speeds at the various nodes would be different, but also ensure security and long-term preservation. The Internet Archive is a project partner, providing a permanent archive for the Million Book Collection, quality control tools, and assistance with acquiring books. Research in distributed caching and active networks would be needed to ensure that the look and feel of the database is the same from any location.

The images of the MBP digital books are used for viewing, while the texts produced by OCR are used for searching. In order to speed up the viewing of the images, we have tested and applied the DjVu as the publishing format to replace HTML with TIFF images in Zhejiang University Libraries. DjVu technology is a highly sophisticated imaging language based on six advanced technological breakthroughs developed at AT&T Labs. Conventional image-viewing software decompresses images in their entirety before displaying them. This is impractical for high-resolution document images like the MBP digital books because the large file sizes involved typically exceed the memory capacity of most computers. DjVu technology, on the other hand, keeps the image in memory in a compact form and decodes only the area displayed on the screen in real time as the user views the image. As a result, the initial view of the page loads very quickly, and the visual quality progressively improves as more bits arrive[6]. DjVu technology can achieve file size reduction ratios as great as 500:1 while preserving excellent image quality.

2.6 Quality Control

The process of digitizing a book involves finding the book in the public domain or receiving the permission of scanning, locating a library that owns the book, printing the call number, pulling the book, checking out it, transporting it to the scanning site, scanning the pages, creating metadata, and returning the book to the original library. This process is expensive. Maintaining high quality the first time the book is scanned is essential. The standards established for quality control in MBP are those currently endorsed by the Digital Library Federation. The project must maintain a 98% accuracy rate for the quality of images and the inclusion of all pages. Nevertheless, a process must be developed to allow for users to report missing pages and for those missing pages to be scanned and dropped back into the existing scanned text.

3   Current Status

The first funding at RMB 40 million yuan (US$4.84 million) from the MOE was allocated to MBP in Sept. 2003, for support of the staffing and operation of the 14 scanning centers and 2 technical centers in China, which means the initiation of the project in the country. The Chinese partners have established 12 scanning centers in their libraries or in cooperated companies, with a total floor space at above 1400 square meters and 105 workers fully engaged in data production. CMU has provided the Chinese partners with 9 Minolta Overhead PS-7000 scanners, 40 AVA3+ scanners and 6 servers, and another 26 Minolta PS-7000 scanners, 20 Terabyte storage, DVD writers and DVD-R discs will be delivered to the Chinese partners in autumn 2004. By August 31,2004, 68940 volumes of Chinese books and materials had been scanned, and another 40 thousand Chinese books and materials had been selected for scanning in the coming months. Over 30 thousand volumes of English books and government documents were pulled from the stacks in CMU libraries in summer 2004, and the first container with more than 25 thousand books were shipped from USA to China for scanning in August 2004.

Two technical centers have been established in Zhejiang University (South Technical Center) and in Chinese Academy of Sciences (North Technical Center) to provide technical support for the scanning centers in southern and northern areas respectively. In Zhejiang University Libraries, a Digital Library Technology R&D Laboratory was established for the project in March 2004. In the lab, the technicians from the computer school and the libraries of the university, who are the main R&D personnel of the South Technical Center of the project, will jointly develop and test the technologies used in MBP. Our technicians have developed a system to digitize Chinese books, which is integrated with commercial OCR software (TH-OCR 2000) and has been applied in the scanning centers.

Carnegie Mellon School of Computer Science has developed a system to support free-to-read access to the digitized books on the web. The system provides tools to add books to the collection and generate PURLs and usage reports. Future developments will enable the Million Book Collection to be indexed by popular Internet search engines like Google and harvested via the OAI protocol.

4 Future Plan

In the libraries of the Chinese project partners, non-copyrighted books and other materials will be selected for digitization. More English books will be selected in the academic libraries of the American partners. CMU Libraries and the National Agricultural Library (NAL) are discussing the possibility for selecting and scanning the non-copyrighted books and government documents in NAL for MBP.

In order to speed up the book digitization of the project, more scanners will be equipped in the 14 Chinese scanning centers, and a new scanning center will be established in Shenzhen to specifically scan the books shipped from US. We hope that when the scanning centers in China are put into full operation, the data production output will reach 30 thousand digital books or about 9 million pages a month.

Copyright clearance will be further implemented, focusing on obtaining the permission of scanning and Web access to modern academic books and dissertations from the right holders. MBP is not developing a for-profit system. All of the content will be available free-to-read on the Internet. Participating publishers will get copies of the digitized books and metadata, and they can themselves provide or enable others to provide value-added services to access the digital books. Permission granted to MBP is non-exclusive.

The computer experts in both the Chinese and American MBP partners are doing essential research on multi-linguistics, multimedia and multi-modal digital library to provide knowledge service. The project will produce an extensive and rich test bed for use in further textual language processing research. It is hoped that at least 10 000 books among the million will be available in two or more languages, especially both in Chinese and English, providing a key testing area for problems in machine translation. In the last stage of the project, books in multiple languages will be reviewed to ensure that this test bed feature is accomplished.

5 Conclusion

Digital technology can make the works of man permanently accessible to the billions of people all over the world. It is impossible to digitize all the books accumulated in the history, but as a first step we are undertaking to digitize 1 million books or less than 1% of all books in all languages ever published, which is possible with the cooperation of the partners.

As MBP is a collaborative project with different academic libraries, computer schools, librarians and IT specialists in different nations, we have discovered that although the partners share a common vision and objective, there are also many differences that need to be communicated and addressed along the way. Differences in approaches, expectations, understanding and philosophy must be negotiated among the disciplines, and between the nations. With the development of MBP, the common understanding on how to deal with the challenges in the project has being established among the partners. As more partners are joining the project, we believe that the objective will be realized, and MBP will promote the digital library development in China and around the world, so as to improve the information infrastructures in education and research.

References

1. OCLC: WorldCat Gold Records. http://www.oclc.org/worldcat/goldrecords.htm
2. Reddy, R., St. Clair G.: The Million Book Digital Library Project. http://www.rr.cs.cmu.edu/mbdl.htm
3. George C. A.: Exploring the Feasibility of Seeking Copyright Permissions. January 31 2002. http://zeeb.library.cmu.edu/Libraries/FeasibilityStudyFinalReport.pdf
4. Michalek, G. V.: Million Book Universal Library Project: Manual for Metadata Capture, Digitization, Post Processing, and OCR. May 7 2003. http://www.library.cmu.edu/Libraries/MillionBookManual.pdf
5. Carnegie Mellon University Libraries: Report to the Digital Library Federation, January 15, 2002. http://zeeb.library.cmu.edu/Libraries/DLF_CMrept2.html
6. Haffner P, Bottou L, Howard P, LeCun Y.: DjVu : Analyzing and Compressing Scanned Documents for Internet Distribution. Proceedings of the International Conference on Document Analysis and Recognition. (1999) 625–628

The Construction and Research on Academy Culture Database

Zhangfei Zheng, Zhijian Fan, and Xiangbo Tu

Hunan University Library, 410082 Changsha, China
{zfzheng, fanzj, lib-calis }@hnu.cn

Abstract. Academies are culture educational institutions, where ancient Chinese scholars carry out various activities concerning books which include book storing, reading, teaching, lecturing, carving to accumulate, create, and impart culture. Relying on our cultural background of the academy of classical learning, we utilize the extant original academic literatures and consult national and international scholars' research on Chinese traditional culture of the academic of classic learning to construct Academy Culture Database, characterized by the distinctively Chinese traditional culture. This database is also built on the basis of modern information technique and complied with the international universal format of the database. We aim at revealing the essence of Chinese traditional culture to the world through the modern information processing technique and digital measures, as well as providing a convenient public research platform for home and abroad experts of academy culture studies, education history studies, Confucian studies and of culture history studies.

1 Introduction

Academies are culture educational institutions, where ancient Chinese scholars carry out various activities concerning books which include book storing, reading, teaching, lecturing, revising, writing, and carving to accumulate, create, and impart culture. Academy has had a history of over 1000 years, covered all the provinces of China except Tibet and outnumbered 7000 during the period from the Tang Dynasty to the Qing Dynasty. Academies have made great contribution to the development of Chinese education, learning, culture, publish and book storing, to the cultivation of the folk-custom, and to the forming of the national concept and ethic value. It can be traced back to the Ming Dynasty that academy culture was introduced to Korea, Japan, Southeast Asia and even to Italy and America, which has contributed to the transmission of Chinese culture and the development of indigenous culture. Under the influence of Chinese culture revitalization since 1980's, academy research has received great attention from all fields including education, history, philosophy, culture and etc.

Z. Chen et al. (Eds.): ICADL 2004, LNCS 3334, pp. 227–235, 2004.

2   The Significance of Constructing Academy Culture Database

2.1   The Construction of Academy Culture Database is a Need for the Preservation and Utilization of the Precious Cultural Legacy of China's Ancient Academies

The academy is a special educational form in the history of education, which started from the Tang Dynasty, flourished in the Song Dynasty and changed till the end of Qing Dynasty. It has a history of over 1000 years, and covers all China. Most converted private schools and schools of modern times (the period from the mid-19th century to the May 4th Movement of 1919) were developed from academies, The academy is main channel that links up China's ancient and China's modern education, and it has a peculiar significance in the history of Chinese education development.

The advanced stage of Chinese feudalistic education produced the academy educational system, which promoted the development of common education, proposed the educational principle, that is, "taking the responsibility of cultivating talented people to benefit mankind", and contributed to development of local education, the transmission of academy cultural, the forming of folk-custom and the cultivation of ethnic value. All these made by the academy could not be achieved by the official education. The academy has fundamentally changed the traditional education and symbolized the great reform in China's traditional education.

The Chinese academy is the place where ancient Chinese scholars accumulated and transmitted culture, for instance, Confucian school of idealist philosophy of Song Dynasty, the psychics of Ming Dynasty and the Han study Qing Dynasty once all carried out academic research and personnel cultivation in academies. The academy has a peculiar status and value in the history of Chinese education and even in the cultural history, so it needs to be efficiently preserved and carefully studied. However, our survey of a large proportion of academies throughout the country finds academy relics are continuously being damaged and lost due to the vicissitude of history, and it becomes even worse. Considering that relics cannot be reproduced, educational researchers should take the salvage of academy relics as their due and urgent task. It is an unprecedented all mankind-beneficial act to construct a comprehensive database of original historical materials and research data for China's academy culture.

2.2   The Construction of Academy Culture Database is Necessary to the Development of Modern Educational Cause with Distinctive Chinese Characteristics

The ancient academy education can be taken as a reference for modern education in many aspects, such as educational object, personnel training model, pedagogy, management form, cultivation of both body and mind, researching spirit, and etc. The Academy Culture Database, constructed by conducting well-planned survey and collecting relevant cultural relics and literatures which benefit a profound study of ancient academy education, to summarize its experience and discover its rule of development, has played an important role in reforming educational system and had a great significance in the development and prosperity of modern educational undertaking with distinctive Chinese characteristics.

As a typical representative of China's ancient culture and humanistic spirit, the academy is a rich resource of humane education. The construction of Academy Culture Database can fortify a position of quality-oriented characteristic education, promoting national cultural quality, inspiring patriotic enthusiasm and cultivating virtuous sentiments.

2.3 The Construction of Academy Culture Database is Complementary to the Resources of China's Education of Higher Learning

At present, China does not have a comprehensive subject database reflecting the past and present of academy culture as well as the research achievements of academy culture of academies in both china and all over the world. Hunan University Library bases itself on Yuelu Academy and relies on the historical literatures and modern research achievement of the Yuelu Academy to construct China Academy Culture Database, which fills in the blanks in special academy culture database of China, does good to take the advantage of the Yuelu Academy's culture resources, and combines Chinese academy culture with the teaching and researching of institutions of higher learning. Academy Culture Database will become an important culture education resource of China.

2.4 The Construction of Academy Culture Database is a Need for Developing International Cultural Exchange

From the Ming Dynasty, academy culture was introduced to Korea, Japan and Southeast Asia, which resulted in its further development. Especially in recent years, with the participation of "western studies", academies bridge the cultural exchange between the east and the west. Academy Culture Database is constructed as a comprehensive aggregation of literatures on China's academy culture and made to further radiate in both home and abroad in order to propel international culture exchange at great speed.

3 The Overall Planning of Database Construction

3.1 The Project Construction Background

Yuelu Academy is a typical example of China's academy of classic learning, an epitome of the development of cultural and educational work from the ancient China to the modern China, the most persuasive historical evidence of the changes of China's educational system, and the "alive specimen" of the history of China's educational development.

Dated back to the Song Dynasty, Yuelu Academy, the representative of academies, is a prominent academy of "the four major academies" in ancient China, Emperor Zhenzong of North Song, learning its remarkable achievements in running the school, awarded it his Majesty's own handwriting "Yuelu Academy" on the horizontal tablet to praise its achievements in education.

The distinguished Confucius scholar Zhangshi held the post of Yuelu Academy and fund "Huxiang school of thought" on the basis of Yuelu Academy. The famous "Zhu Zhang co-lecture " promoted the exchange of Min school and Huxiang school. The Yuelu Academy flourished at the time when it was honored as "a sage's hometown of Hunan". To honor Yuelu Academy's brilliant feats of carrying forward Confucian school of idealist philosophy, Emperor Kangxi and his grandson Qianlong bestowed it with horizontal tablet which read "Learn before you can probe the infiniteness of tian, the universe" and "The doctrines taught here in the south are genuine Confucian doctrine". Yuelu Academy was converted into Hunan Institute of Higher Education until Guangxu 29th in the end of Qing Dynasty (1903). After that, it was consecutively renamed as Hunan Normal School (1912-1917) and Hunan Senior School of Industry (1917-1926). In 1926, it was officially named Hunan University. Yuelu Academy has experienced the changes from the ancient academy of classic learning to modern university and has a history of over 1000 years, so it is called "a-thousand-institution of higher education". It is exactly appraised that "The Kingdom of Chu, unique home of the talents, The Academy of Yuelu, the very cradle of all".

It is known that other ancient famous academies have lost their educational function; but Yuelu Academy, relying on Hunan University' favorable conditions of economy, talented people and education, has always kept up with the development of modem education. Yuelu Academy has Culture Research Institute that recruits postgraduates and conducts studies of historical science, the right to award doctorate of both Chinese ideology historical and of Chinese ancient history, and a sound overseas influence that attracts numerous overseas students. Especially in 2003, Hunan University was funded by the state to construct Chinese Museum of Academy in Yuelu Academy, and consequently it becomes a world-recognized academy research center.

Based on the above cultural background, we construct Academy Culture Database in order to reveal the world the essence of Chinese traditional culture by the means of modern information-processing technique and digital measures.

3.2 Database Planning

Academy Culture Database consists of five columns: A view of Academy, Academy Figures, Academy Literatures, Academy sightseeing and Academy Encyclopedia. Each column has different subject, displayed to readers through navigate content. It covers a wide variety of subjects, including general introductions and reforms of over 8000 academies of China, Korea, America, Italy and Southeast Asia, people of academy, academies' extant collection of first-hand data, research data, and multimedia information of some relevant historic relics picture, architecture art, scenic spots and historic interests. The ultimate goal of constructing the database is to reflect fully and accurately academies' historic vicissitudes, original literatures, scenic spots and historic interest, historic relics and research developments of academies, and become world's most authoritative database of academy culture.

4   Database Construction Design and Function Realization

4.1   Classification of Database System

First named in the Tang Dynasty, academy appeared in the time of Emperor Taizong, the first Emperor of the Tang Dynasty. Academy has experienced over 1000 years history from the Tang Dynasty till the Qing Dynasty's academy conversion of "Reform Movement of 1898". Academy's thousand years of development witnessed the growth of many academic entities that have formed their own distinctive culture with numerous literatures, salient scenic spots, architectures and different groups of people. According to these characteristics, we classify the database as following.

A View of Academies. Academy is one of the main threads of database construction, and so many data are arranged concerning academies. The column is classified according to different nations like China, Korea, Japan and so on, and under each nation, it further divides into provinces, prefectures, cities, areas and etc.

Academy Figures. Academies cannot be developed without people. For over 1000 years, numerous ancient Chinese scholars, literatures and senior official of the imperial courts had come to academies, chanting poetry and drawing pictures. They had left thousands of poetic masterpieces and treasurable calligraphies and paintings. The information are classified in this column by status, such as the super intendant of the academy, teachers and students of the academy, masters of lecturing, other figures, researchers and experts. Academy figure is another main thread of the database construction.

Academy Literatures. This column contains catalogues: original literatures, researching literatures, developments records and so on. Among these, the original literatures of ancient Chinese academies are the richest one, which are classified according to their genres like chapter literatures, book literatures and atlas. Chapter Literatures have records of events inscribed on a tablet, prefaces and postscripts, imperial edicts, teaching sheets, student's written homework, poems, prose-poetries, couplets and so on; book literatures includes academy annals, rules, teaching materials, quotations, poetry anthology, records of fellow disciples, lists of book collection and carve printing books and etc. It should be mentioned that original literatures are the main body of Academy culture Database and its collection and selection are rather difficult, for most part of the historical literatures require maintenance of their original features in storing. While people today collect and select academy studies complying with academy research, academy history study, academy education research, academic entities and academic schools, study of academy book collection, study of academy carve printing books, academy sacrificial rites study, academy architecture culture, academy and local culture, and etc.

Academy Sightseeing. It provides a full-round collection of pictures of academy historic relics, architecture, scenes and sights of cultural interest and multi-media materials concerning academy historic relics, fabulous scenic spots and renowned historical site of scenic beauty.

Academy Encyclopedia. It introduces to readers the academy's general knowledge under categories concerning academy historical narrative, lecturing and exam paper, sacrificial rites, book collection and carving printing books, tuition fee, duty and position, stipulations and management, architecture and equipment, and so on.

Special Treatment Type. Besides the above mentioned five columns, the database resources system supplies readers with the data of the extant well-protected famous academies, brilliant figures, poetic masterpieces throughout the ages and elegant academy random thoughts under the titles of famous academies of the world, brilliant figures, well-known antithetical couplet and sentences, realization of academy, and etc.

4.2 Database Structure Design

In constructing characteristic database, Content is the most important standard of high-quality database. Considering the characteristics of the relevant stored literatures of Yuelu Academy Database, we set up two sub-databases, Index Databases and Full Text Databases, in order to guarantee the full coverage of resources with distinctive features of academy culture. The main function of index database is to serially connect the frame structure of database system, which does not have much importance and worth detailed suggestion. Here much emphasis is laid on Full-text Database structure introduction.

Academy Culture Database consists of three main parts of information: academy general information, general information of academy figures and academy literature information (including text-format information, picture-format information, audiovisual format information). Academy general information includes the following glossaries: literature' title (brief introduction of academy), reform (academy used names), academy address, fund time, founder, academy conditions (protection of academic entities), nation, areas, key word, academy brief-introduction body, academy image picture; relevant document appendix and so on; general information of academy figure contains literature titles (brief introduction of people), surname, native place, birth date, category, figure picture, literature resource, publishing year, page, key word, relevant picture, relevant literature appendix and so on. We have made new tries in the practices of database structure design: to simplify database structure and increase database searching speed, we put the above three kinds of information in one storage and apply some techniques to converge different glossaries, because the above three types of information can all be viewed as literature information and share many glossaries according to our analysis.

4.3 Database Function Realization

Form is another important symbol of high-quality database in constructing characteristic database. No matter how abundant and high-qualitative the database is, it must be presented to users through foreground quick retrieval services and friendly user interface database. Academy Culture Database adopts today's most advanced BIS system for the whole systematic structure, and users can read all the information of the database through browser.

Academy Culture Database applies illustration and text storage supportable TRS Full-text Database server of the UNIX operation system and TRS WEB applied releasing system of JAVA to set up and release database. Database system sets up on HP9000 UNIX server and HP VA7410 network-storage device of SAN frame. The server systematically realizes the thermal function of double servers, and the high function of the server system and storage system ensure the high-speed, stable function of the database system of Academy Culture Database.

The system adopts three-layer frame structure: application, business-logic and database strict classification, to maximally protect data security and easy maintenance, make sure that changes in any part of system, that is, data structure, application and releasing, data processing, will not affect the other part, and to benefit system supply. Database and releasing system separately set up on one or two computers, and firewall's function can be better served (database server only allows WEB application server in order to maximally protect database from Hacker's attack).

We have designed two retrieval strategies: navigator searching and full-text retrieval. Database foreground presents five columns: a view of academies, academy figures, academy literatures, academy sightseeing, and academy encyclopedia. And under each column, there are some subjects. All the literatures are revealed to users under titles of five columns and relevant subjects by navigator. At the same time, with two main threads, academy and academy figures, navigator serves better to present every academy and its people. Users can directly learn database resources system through foreground page that is equipped with full-text retrieval entrance. With high-efficient full-text retrieval function of TRS, through various ways of retrieving full text, G text response time is kept within sub-second and full-text retrieval is conducted by database through automatic word-separation processor to give due consideration to the requirement of complete and accurate Full-text retrieval.

5 Resource Construction and Relevant Problems Consideration

5.1 Database Collection and Construction

Academy Culture Database adopts various ways of collecting data, notably, internet searching and field collection by digital camera. But most resources are original historical literatures of academies such as historical material chronicles and local chorography that can only be acquired through scanning and shooting. Special attention should be paid to the protection of historical relics when scanning and shooting them. Therefore, Unfold and non-touch scanning processors are adopted.

Digital Text Standard Format. The present practice is that various producers adopt their own Text format after taking pictures of the materials by scanning, and supply readers with their own browser, which, in consequence, results in lots of inconvenience for later data exchange and full-text retrieval. Universally-adopted text formats today are mainly: PDF & OEB Format. In constructing Academy Culture Database, we use PDF format, by which users throughout the world can visit us through free universally adopted PDF READER and realize managing and publishing in varied storage.

Original Text Brower and Full-Text Retrieval Treatment. In order to guarantee processing quality and information integrity, we adopt pictorial PDF which is the exactly same with the original materials for users to read, and background automatic OCR text provides readers with more convenient full-text retrieval service. But for those ancient literatures that cannot be OCR we make notes and quotations from them. Therefore, we have not only kept the format and the original features of the original materials and supported the original browsing of the ancient literatures, but also provided full-text retrieval service.

5.2 Database Intelligence Property Rights

Here mentioned intelligence property rights mainly refers to two aspects:

Firstly, that database is constructed to present the public information of text, picture and audio-visual is, in some sense, a publishing behavior so that its copyright should be taken into account. Even if most literatures of Academy Culture Database are original historical literatures whose copyrights are unable to be traced back, there are still other original historical literatures kept intact in some academies that need to establish a relevant acquisition mechanism. But for some modern research literatures whose copyright are protected by the state law, we should contact the author to obtain his or her authorization before we can use them; secondly, database itself concern the problem of intelligence property rights. We have tried to classify two kinds of users: browse users and download user, in order to protect the data technically.

Secondly, database itself also involves the problem of intellectual property rights protection. In constructing database, we apply database management of the processed literatures and design internet users' visiting limitation. To be specific, the internet users' visiting limitation permits users to read only the front 24 pages of the text (the universal-adopted practice, and specific pages can be set up); Text copyright protection processor forbids users to print or copy texts even if users can read them fully. So we have fully played our role in transmitting China's traditional culture and marvelous civilization, and also strengthened effective copyright protection and improved database sustainable utilization and characteristic application.

5.3 Foreground Page Art Design

Foreground page presentation, especially its art design, is very important in constructing database. And this is especially important in the construction of characteristic database that takes traditional culture, folk culture and local culture as its themes. Therefore, page style, page patter and page color must be pertinent to themes. Constructing Academy Culture Database, we design the page with ancient and simple style and succinct color to bring the elegant humanistic atmosphere into its full play. Among them: three brushes in the fore-page, free and unaffected, describes poets and painters' works of image, which implies academy's representatives "poem, book, picture, print"; the inner-page, restraining and elaborative, relic on meticulous brushwork; the copyright page uses the image of winter sweet from a poem, "without the trial of deadly cold, how can winter sweet finally give out sensational fragrance", suggesting the ups and downs in constructing our database and our final remarkable achievements; and the characteristic page "Academy under the Sun" dots famous academies in the picture of history.

6 Conclusion and Prospective

For the sake of learning, Scholars of the Song and Ming Dynasties braved thousands of miles and spent decades of years to visit and learn from "Four Major Academies ". Academy Culture Database built by Hunan University Library, on the basis of modern information processing techniques and new internet technology, has already been successfully connected with the internet. Only with a touch of the mouse, all the data are available on the internet and academy culture information exchange can be made. Academy Culture Database construction has gained a wide attention from the state, people and media throughout the country. Academy Culture Database will provide a convenient public research platform for home and abroad experts of academy culture study, educational history study, Confucian study and of cultural history study, and open a new window for the world to learn brilliant Chinese culture.

References

1. Chen Gujia, Deng Hongbo: Chinese Academy History Data. Zhejiang Education Press, Hangzhou (1998)
2. 2.Deng Hongbo: Chinese Academy Culture Series. Hunan University Press, Changsha (2000)
3. Yang Shenchu: Chinese Academy Culture and Architecture. Hubei Education Press, Wuhan (2002)
4. Ji Xiaofeng: Chinese Academy Glossary. Zhejiang Education Press, Hangzhou (1996)
5. Cheng Hongli: Characteristic CALIS Database Building: Current Status Analysis. Library Journal. 2 (2001) 5–7
6. Li Liangxian, Xu Wenxian: A Study on the Design and Development of a Couplet Database. Journal of Academic Libraries 6 (2003) 60–62
7. Song Guangshu, Zhang Yuefeng, etc: On the Development of the Featured Database of Southwest China Nationalities Studies. Journal of Academic Libraries 4 (2002) 43–46
8. Yao Boyue, Zhang Lijuan, etc: On the Design of Rare Book Metadata Standard and its System Implementation. Journal of Academic Libraries 1 (2003) 17–21

The Institutional Repository: The Chinese University of Hong Kong 'SIR' Model

Colin Storey, Rita Wong, Kevin Leung, and Ernest Yik

The Chinese University of Hong Kong, University Library System
{storey, rita-wong, ckleung, ernestyik}@cuhk.edu.hk
http://www.lib.cuhk.edu.hk

Abstract. To be in line with The Chinese University of Hong Kong's (CUHK) mission of assisting in the preservation, creation, application and dissemination of knowledge, the CUHK online institutional repository, known as the 'SIR' (Scholarly Information Repository), is designed to serve the University community and its constituent four Colleges, the people of the Hong Kong Special Administrative Region (SAR) and China, and academics and researchers in the wider world. This paper reviews the planning and implementation of the CUHK SIR model. Discussions on what materials needed to be included in the SIR database are highlighted – for example, not only preprints, published articles, theses and dissertations, but also University and College publications, audio and video clips, etc. The paper details certain system design parameters - it runs on DSpace, and a simple interface is available for faculty to submit citations of their publications and other documents for digitization and inclusion. Finally, the challenges facing the future growth and use of the SIR are noted – not least in securing both the intellectual property rights and the financial and human resources to sustain and develop a major online initiative of this kind.

1   Introduction

The Chinese University of Hong Kong (CUHK) is one of the eight higher tertiary institutions in the Hong Kong Special Administrative Region (HKSAR). In the past 41 years, the CUHK has proved herself to be one of the most energetic and fast-growing universities in the Far East. High quality research and teaching are emphasized in the University. The search for excellence is a core value shared by everyone in the CUHK community.

The University Library System (ULS) of the CUHK aims to collect scholarly periodicals, to digitize them and make them available on the Internet. In the summer of 2003, the ULS initiated a pilot project on e-prints. Working closely with partners such as research officers, teaching staff and University administrators, the ULS has played a key role in promoting scholarly information sharing and dissemination. Through deep collaboration among different parties in the University, the e-print project has developed into more comprehensive information repository model for the University and benefited not only the local community but also the academic world in general. The CUHK model – the Scholarly Information Repository (SIR) is a

Z. Chen et al. (Eds.): ICADL 2004, LNCS 3334, pp. 236–244, 2004.

noteworthy reference model for an information repository in an academic environment.

1.1 The University

The CUHK was established in 1963 following the amalgamation of three post-secondary colleges. These colleges are New Asia College (founded in 1949), Chung Chi College (found in 1951) and United College (founded in 1956). Each of these institutions always had its own library, with collections in specific subjects built up with the assistance from Colleges' teaching and research staff. The University Library came into existence after the establishment of the CUHK in 1963. Shaw College was founded in 1986 and became the fourth college of the CUHK. The University has articulated her mission "to assist in the preservation, creation, application and dissemination of knowledge by teaching, research and public service in a comprehensive range of disciplines, thereby serving the needs and enhancing the well-being of the citizens of Hong Kong, China as a whole, and the wider world community"[1]. Nowadays, the six libraries of the ULS in CUHK are under a central administration with a collection of 1.8 million items in print, as well as myriad online resources. The ULS serves a community of 14,000 students and 4,000 teaching, research and administrative staff and supports research and teaching activities in the University.

1.2 Research and Publication in CUHK

The CUHK fosters quality research over a broad front in its seven faculties. It offers opportunities for significant advances in human knowledge, and provides scope for academic staff to undertake consultancy and collaborative projects with industry. There are already 11 major research institutes established in the CUHK and in 2003, the CUHK staff secured HK$97 million in the form of competitive grants from the Research Grants Council of the HKSAR and more than 30 patents worldwide[2]. Most of this high quality research is published in international and local peer-reviewed journals.

According to *ISI Essential Science Indicators,* between 1994 to 2004 CUHK academies published a total of 9,898 papers; they were cited 54,338 times.

In addition, the University, Colleges, faculties and departments themselves publish reports or research journals throughout the year. These administrative or research publications are valuable documents for the University. They are the assets and historical records of the University and the treasure of its academic community. These records need to be properly archived and conserved.

The ULS is the ideal hub for preserving and disseminating knowledge. The Library already plays a role in information deposit and promotes information sharing and exchange. A University Archive was established as one of the special collections in the ULS. It collects all University publications including ephemera such as posters and invitation cards. This Archive can be regarded as the very first step initiated by the ULS to conserve University publications for Library users through the collection and preservation of the printed form of University publications.

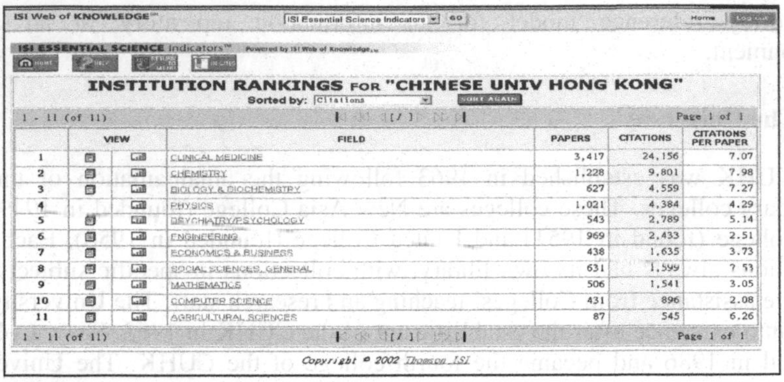
ISI Web of KNOWLEDGE
ISI ESSENTIAL SCIENCE indicators™ Powered by ISI Web of Knowledge

INSTITUTION RANKINGS FOR "CHINESE UNIV HONG KONG"
Sorted by: Citations

1 - 11 (of 11) Page 1 of 1

	VIEW	FIELD	PAPERS	CITATIONS	CITATIONS PER PAPER
1		CLINICAL MEDICINE	3,417	24,156	7.07
2		CHEMISTRY	1,228	9,801	7.98
3		BIOLOGY & BIOCHEMISTRY	627	4,559	7.27
4		PHYSICS	1,021	4,384	4.29
5		PSYCHIATRY/PSYCHOLOGY	543	2,789	5.14
6		ENGINEERING	969	2,433	2.51
7		ECONOMICS & BUSINESS	438	1,635	3.73
8		SOCIAL SCIENCES, GENERAL	631	1,599	2.53
9		MATHEMATICS	506	1,541	3.05
10		COMPUTER SCIENCE	431	896	2.08
11		AGRICULTURAL SCIENCES	87	545	6.26

1 - 11 (of 11) Page 1 of 1

Copyright © 2002 Thomson ISI

Fig. 1. ISI Essential Science Indicators for CUHK

1.3 The RTAO Online Publication Input System

The Research and Technology Administration Office (RTAO) of the CUHK is the primary office responsible for research administration and technology transfer. It is also the central clearinghouse of intellectual property rights of the University. Researchers are required to submit their research reports, conference papers and other publications to RTAO for record.

In 2002, RTAO launched an Online Publication Input System (OPIS) which allows CUHK staff to submit brief records of their research publications such as books, book chapters, conference papers, working papers, patents and etc. to the RTAO. Although an important advance, while the OPIS does allow the staff to submit or search their own publications, they cannot search the publications submitted by others. Annually, RTAO publishes a list of staff research projects and publications for users' reference.

2 CUHK SIR

In the summer of 2004, the ULS launched the CUHK SIR system which is both an extension of the existing e-print pilot project and the University Archive print collection. The system is running on open source DSpace software and allows browsing and searching of all publication records of the University and its staff.

2.1 The Need for an Online Information Repository

There was an increasing demand for a more sophisticated online information retrieval system to search and retrieve staff publications in the University. Users may be interested in knowing the research interests of their colleagues and seek collaboration. The existing OPIS maintained by RTAO is much more like a self-input publication submission system than an information repository. No full-text of any publication is available in OPIS. Some modifications must be done in order to develop the OPIS system into an open and a more sophisticated information retrieval system for staff publications.

Another reason for the development of the CUHK SIR system is the lack of a centralized system for collecting all research publications for other researchers to view. Some faculty members post a list of their publications in their personal webpages while some academic departments or faculties do the same. Therefore, a researcher has to go through a number of websites and consolidate the research publications of other colleagues in different formats.

2.2 System Design

The CUHK SIR system serves as a bridge between users and published information, including pre-prints. The submitters send their publication details to a new interface – the Citation Input System (CIS). Information is then passed on to RTAO's OPIS and also to the CUHK SIR system. Besides the citation and brief bibliographic information of a given publication, the CUHK SIR system also provides linking to the full-text as far as possible. The articles submitted via the CUHK SIR system are linked to Library subscribed databases and e-resources and other free online resources from which the full-text is available.

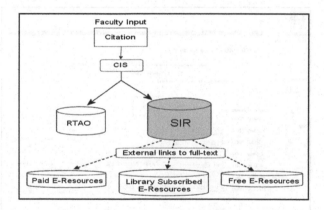

Fig. 2. Workflow of CUHK SIR system

2.3 Coverage

The CUHK SIR system covers as many University publications and staff research publications as is possible. The categories in the CUHK SIR system include University publications, college publications, department and faculty publications, staff working papers, journal articles, newspaper articles, books, book chapters, theses, conference proceedings, technical reports and patents. Both citations and full-texts of publications are available in the CUHK SIR system.

2.4 Features and Benefits

The CUHK SIR system is an online system for the storage, retrieval and, where permitted, downloading of all the research output of the whole University community. It has been designed as a user-friendly self-submission and information retrieval system for University and staff bilingual publications.

Fig. 3. CUHK SIR brief record display

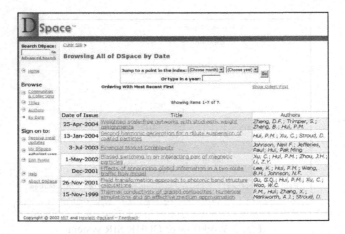

Fig. 4. CUHK SIR Browsing mode

2.4.1 Updating of Contents

The publication details are provided by the submitters directly, or imported from the RTAO's OPIS system through data conversion. The submitters can modify and delete any information supplied by themselves, but are not permitted to modify other people's data.

2.4.2 Name Authority

The OCLC's Library of Congress (LC) Name Authority Service has been integrated into the SIR system. The searching of an Author's name will be matched against the LC's Name Authority File, which consequently improves the hit rate.

2.4.3 Accessibility

The CUHK SIR system provides full-text searching of metadata such as Author, Title, Subject, Keyword and Abstract. It also provides browsing modes according to Subject, Author and Title. The system is opened to the public but as would be expected, only CUHK Library users can be authenticated to access any full-text version available in the Library subscribed databases.

2.4.4 Interoperability

This system is Open Archives Initiative (OAI) compliant and supports cross-search and metadata harvesting between different archives. It is a more flexible option for data exchange with other system.

2.4.5 Benefits

The use of CUHK SIR system has many advantages and applications for its users.

2.4.5.1 For the University

The system is opened to the public which helps to raise the University profile by making its research output available in the wider academic community. The organized and centralized structure of the CUHK SIR system helps to present a uniform image of the University to the users. Moreover, publication details once uploaded by the submitters, will be stored and available until they are removed from the system. It will thereby preserve the valuable research output of the University.

2.4.5.2 For the Faculty Members and Researchers

The system allows users to locate the researchers' publications. It thereby increases visibility of researchers' works by sharing with others. Collaboration among researcher is also thus encouraged. Through the CUHK SIR system, it is easier for users to obtain the latest research trends and access the full-text of research publications. As a result, the easier the publications is located and read, the higher the possibility of being cited by other researchers.

3 Planning and Implementation

A detailed feasibility study and a number of discussions were held with various parties in the University. A careful selection of software was done as there are a number of software systems that specialize in building institutional repositories.

3.1 Selection of Software

The Library based its selection of software on the "OSI Guide to Institutional Repository Software"[3] which provides a detailed introduction and outlines the most important issues in the selection process. Three basic criteria must be met: Open source, OAI compliance and availability. Open source is extremely important as it means that the source codes of the software are open for inspection and modification. The users have the freedom to customize the software to suit their own needs. Besides the repository software, supporting tools such as database systems and the operating system should have the same freedom.

The CUHK system is compliant with the latest OAI[4] metadata harvesting protocols[5]. This means that the Repository will be able to join a global network of interoperable research repositories. Researchers can search across multiple repositories located everywhere at the same time with a single search interface. At the outset, the CUHK policy stated that the system should be available for public use, thereby adhering to the third and last criterion – availability.

3.1.1 EPrints and DSpace

In the software evaluation phase, the Library selected two systems for further studies: Eprints[6] and DSpace[7]. Both systems satisfy the three base criteria stated above and each has unique features. Both are widely adopted by universities and research institutions worldwide.

EPrints is developed by the University of Southampton and was publicly released in November 2000. It is one of the earliest publicly available systems for institutional repositories and has a very large installed base. It is distributed under the GNU General Public License. The implementation platform for EPrints includes Perl, MySQL database system and Apache WWW server on top of a Unix-like operating system such as Linux. All required supporting tools are freely available under an open-source license.

DSpace was designed by MIT Libraries in collaboration with Hewlett-Packard and released in November 2002. DSpace is freely available as open-source software under the BSD distribution license. The BSD license allows anybody to make changes to the system to suit their needs. The implementation platform for DSpace includes the Java SDK, PostgreSQL database system, Lucene search engine and a Java servlet engine on top of an Unix-like operating system such as Linux. All required supporting tools are freely available under an open-source license. Commercial software such as operating systems and database systems can also be used if desired.

3.2 Testing and Evaluation

In order to evaluate EPrints and DSpace, the Library set up both systems for demonstration on a test machine. Comparisons were made in the installation process, supporting tools, architecture and technology and the process of batch uploading 5,000 digital items of both systems. After due comparison DSpace was selected as the platform for the CUHK Repository. One of the features of DSpace is the community and collections model. This model provides flexibility in grouping and organizing the users and the digital items. A community can be sub-units of an institution such as faculties, departments, research centres or laboratories. Each community can adapt the system to meet its own special needs.

Batch uploading is another important issue. The Library will be making use of the batch uploading feature to process some existing collections as well as other new additions suitable for batch processing. DSpace employs a customized XML architecture in batch uploading of digital items into the Repository. The process, although non-trivial, is robust and flexible. The Library was in fact able to convert its batch of sample items into suitable XML format for batch uploading and finished the process without many problems.

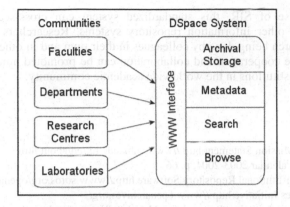

Fig. 5. DSpace system diagram

DSpace provides full-text search capability through Jakarta Lucene[8], an open-source Java search engine. Slight modifications to the Java source codes are required to support searching Chinese characters. DSpace also supports the Handle System from CNRI[9] to provide a persistent identifier for each digital item. This system makes sure that the name of the digital items in the Repository can persist even if there are changes in the location, protocols or other state information.

3.3 Intellectual Property Issues

Copyright is obtained from Colleges, teaching departments and faculty members, so that, whenever possible, full-text is available for research purposes. However, since many of the peer-reviewed journals articles are linked to Library subscribed databases or e-resources, only eligible Library users are entitled to access the full-text. Otherwise, the users have to purchase the published online articles through the publishers.

4 Future Development

The CUHK SIR system is a University project for all the faculties and researchers. The success of SIR relies on the publications submitted by the faculty, teaching departments and Colleges and their willingness to share their work. In order to promote the use of SIR among them, it is important the advantages of the CUHK SIR to the faculties and researchers are highlighted so that they can continue to support the system by providing new data in a consistent and comprehensive way.

To promote deeper collaborations in the academic community, any university should encourage its staff to submit their publications to their institutional repository. A good collection of research publications through a single showcase is proved to be an efficient and effective way to share scholarly information and to promote institutional advancement.

With the use of SIR, this standardized system can cross-search and harvest metadata with other information repository systems. Researchers can know more about the research being done by colleagues in their own and in other universities. As the result, more cooperation and collaboration can be promoted amongst universities and research institutions in the worldwide academic community.

References

1. The CUHK Mission Statement.http://www.cuhk.edu.hk/en/about.htm
2. The CUHK Calendar 2003-2004, p. 66.
3. A Guide to Institutional Repository Software.http://www.soros.org/openaccess/software/
4. Open Archives Initiative.http://www.openarchives.org/
5. Open Archives Initiative Protocol for Metadata Harvesting.http://www.openarchives.org/OAI/openarchivesprotocol.html
6. Eprints.http://software.eprints.org/
7. Dspace.http://www.dspace.org/
8. Jakarta Lucene:http://jakarta.apache.org/lucene/
9. Handle System, Corporation for National Research Initiatives.http://www.handle.net/

The Semantic Architecture for Chinese Cultural Celebrities' Manuscript Library

Wei Liu

Shanghai Library, No.1555, Huai Hai Zhong Lu, Shanghai 200031, China
wliu@libnet.sh.cn

Abstract. Semantic architecture is crucial for a digital library application especially in a distributed system environment. It provides various approaches to overcome semantic interoperability problems and usually consists of metadata solution with open system architecture. The design of the digital library system for the China Cultural Celebrities' Manuscripts Library (CCCML), which is a branch of Shanghai Library, has taken into account a lot of the main aspects from the requirement of semantics, including the metadata profiles, encoding consistence, authority control, ontology functioning, semantic integration, etc. We argue that it is very important to establish an articulated layered semantic architecture for digital libraries in the semantic web environment. And it becomes more and more clear that the semantic services can be settled with the Semantic Web Services technologies, which is supported by and consisted of a wide range of standards and protocols. And a lot of mainstream interoperability architecture, such as OAI, OpenURL etc., can be conformed or implemented by Semantic Web Services. This paper gives some major considerations and overviews on the design of semantic architecture for CCCML, which shows a lot of similarity in typical digital library systems.

1 Introduction

Metadata is usually defined as data about data, and semantics is the meaning of meaning. When computing involving with semantics, metadata is becoming more and more obvious important to be the semantic building blocks of all kinds of information systems such as digital libraries. But metadata itself, without some sort of mechanism, including term selection, profile composition, encoding formalization, ontology annotation, vocabulary mapping, authority controlling and service allocation etc., will not realize its full potential to implement semantics. In this paper, we call such a mechanism the "semantic architecture".

The most significant and difficult requirement for digital libraries (usually considered as distributed information systems on the web to bring together collections and services) is to achieve a high level of "semantic interoperability". We can never expect that digital library applications will be developed with a uniformed data model or conformed to just a few metadata sets, such as Dublin Core, EAD, VRA Core etc. There will be emerging numerous domain specific metadata sets continuously, while

Z. Chen et al. (Eds.): ICADL 2004, LNCS 3334, pp. 245–254, 2004.

at the same time the sharing of metadata standards becomes widely accepted and popular. We have to find some ways to deal with the heterogeneous problem and to integrate the diversity information systems of a digital library into one consolidated view.

An articulate layered semantic architecture will help us to achieve such a goal. With the design and development of the digital library system for Chinese Cultural Celebrities' Manuscript Library (CCCML), we propose and implement a semantic architecture to accomplish a high level of interoperability and to reserve a good scalability, extensibility and integratibility for the system. But in this paper we are not focusing on the technical details of the implementation and arithmetic of the developing, such as schema matching, ontology mapping etc. The remainder of this paper is structured as follows. The next section introduces the semantic requirements of the CCCML digital library system. Section 3 reviews some related works in this area. Section 4 describes a semantic architecture which is the main contribution of the paper, following with the Section 5: the future consideration under the emerging technology of Semantic Web Services.

2   CCCML Application Requirements

Unlike a traditional library, CCCML has a collection with tens of thousands various kinds of documents and physical objects, including manuscripts, letters, diaries, photographs, books with signature and remarks, notebooks, account books, paintings, calligraphies, seal cuttings, badges, diplomas, print materials as well as audio visual materials. A large portion of the collections is expected to be digitized in the near future to provide better preservation and services. Items in the collections are all connected with (made by or related to) "Chinese cultural celebrities" and can be referred or linked to other related applications like OPAC system, union cataloguing system and inventory systems of special libraries and museums across the country.

The CCCML digital library can be roughly considered into three sub-systems: the Digitalization System (DS), the Metadata Management System (MMS) and the Digital Object Repository System (DORS), in which all consist of software modules or components and interconnected with each other (see Fig. 1). We take the MMS as the key system to be designed and accomplished at the first phase before the end of 2004. It provides the base data and information model and shapes the overall architecture of the digital library.

The goal of the CCCML Digital Library System is to provide a digital repository with preservation and retrieval services for the resources of Chinese Cultural Celebrities' collections in the Shanghai library. The application should make the full use of IT infrastructure and digital library architecture which have been developed and maintained since 1999, and integrated into the whole digital resources and services framework within Shanghai Library. It is by no means another stand alone autonomous system for a series of special collections. So it should be designed to be component based and loose coupled, even to share the same software environment and server capabilities with other applications.

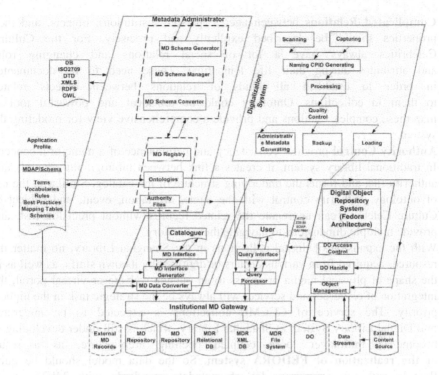

Fig. 1. The system architecture of CCCML

We have encountered several special requirements and difficulties regarding the semantic discovery in construction of CCCML digital library system:

1. **The Variety Types of Resources** in CCCML collections are always with different but overlapping properties need to discover, at the same time all the metadata terms should be "standard" and conforms to Metadata Guidelines of the Shanghai Library, which contains a "core set" of metadata elements derived from DC-Lib application profile, with a set of encoding rules and best practices for metadata manipulating. Metadata Application Profile (MAP) provides a practical approach to fulfill domain specific description needs while remains compatibility with major metadata standards. But the implementation of MAP is still in its early stage with ambiguous in a few aspects like qualification and keeping encoding consistency. And MAP encoded with XML Schema cannot represent semantic restrictions and formalize all constrains required by the system.

2. Each type of resource has its own metadata profile expressed with XML Schema. So the system should **support multi-schema management**, including input, load, open, edit, parse, error detect, and convert between different types of schemas: DTD, XML Schema, RDF Schema etc. The most important function is to generate type and context aware interfaces for metadata instance manipulation (input, edit, convert, output, and storage) according to different types and properties of resources.

3. **Complicated Relations** between agents (person, institution), objects, and their properties should be described explicitly and precisely. For the Cultural Celebrities always have a lot of social relations and changing roles and attributes during their life long time. These need to be documented in order to establish all kinds of relations between objects related to them in collections. Ontology could be an ideal and powerful tool to map these complex relations and provide a comprehensive view for modeling the system.

4. **Authority Control** provides consistency and permanence of a name or a concept. In traditional library system, it creates a link between bibliographic records and authority file, and forms the underlying structure of the catalog. Similar to the use of ontology, authority control with the name, affiliation, event, and subject of Culture Celebrity can aggregate the related records without precision lost, and provide multiple dimensions to navigate the repository.

5. With the expansion of digital collections in the Shanghai Library, no matter the resources acquired from various dealers or digitized by its own staffs, as well as in the shape of physical media or access to an outside website or virtual portal, the integration of resources and services will always be the strategic task in the highest priority. The service of CCCML collections is expected to be integrated into Digital Library System in Shanghai Library, which is still under developing to become a multilayer loose coupled opening architecture, as a result of **the realization of FEDORA system**. So the data model should be quite flexible and can support a lot of metadata standards with METS[1] as a standard schema container. The use of web service exposure layer in FEDORA adopted a lot of communication protocols such us HTTP, SOAP, OAI, Z39.50 etc., will bring the CCCML digital library a wide range of interoperability and adaptability.

3   Related Work

Semantic interoperability is a major challenge in resources and services integration. Semantic heterogeneity comes from the mismatch in meanings with different tags represented by different terms from different vocabularies, when expressed with different schemas conformed to different guidelines. There are various kinds of conflicts that cause semantic inconsistencies with naming, data structure, attributes, granularity, types of values, etc. We think an integrity semantic architecture can help a lot to facilitate the semantic interoperability between systems.

This paper was inspired by FEDORA[2], HARMONY[3] and ARIADNE[4] projects, as well as some researches on enterprise data integration [11][12]. Semantic Web as a

---

[1] See: http://www.loc.gov/standards/mets/
[2] See: http://www.fedora.info/
[3] http://www.ilrt.bris.ac.uk/discovery/harmony/
[4] http://www.ariadne-eu.org/

significant movement about Web technologies, which aims to move from syntactic interoperability to semantic interoperability and relies on machine interpretable semantic descriptions, is also a technical resource for the designing of Semantic Architecture of CCCML digital library.

Chen's paper [1] reviews two results of semantic research from the early digital library projects: feasible scalable semantics and semantic indexes of large collections. They all deal with the retrieval effectiveness of massive information instead of description and architecture aspect of the interoperability solution for heterogeneous repositories. Norm Friesen [3] analyzed the meaning of semantic interoperability and metadata approach to achieve it in detail, but with a somehow pessimistic conclusion—"The goal of increased interoperability ... will clearly not be achieved through further formalization and abstraction". ABC ontology [4][5] from Harmony project proposed by Carl Lagoze, Jane Hunter etc. derived from FRBR[5] can model the complexity of relations between resources and properties. It is a good abstract model for resource integration, but for the lack of application specifications, it does not provide an articulate semantic architecture and can be implemented in different levels with different approaches. Paper [8] by Jérôme Euzenat roughly layered interoperability into five levels: encoding, lexical, syntactic, semantic, and semiotic based on a classification of possible requirements, from which each level can not been achieved without the completion of the previous one. The discussion is based on the purpose of implementation of a totally machine executable semantic representation and transformation on Semantic Web. These researches shed light on the approach of establishing a semantic architecture for CCCML digital library.

4 The Semantic Architecture

4.1 The Purpose

Semantic architecture brings structure to the content of a digital library. The structure can expose some interfaces to outside world accessed by people as well as mediator agents. The design of semantic architecture is to give a practical approach under the consensus of semantic interoperability within and between communities.

We see the main purpose to establish a semantic architecture is to formalize the semantic description of digital resources, for the better serving of resource and service discovery and exposing adequate interfaces for the integration of digital resources, and finally to achieve high level interoperability between digital libraries.

4.2 The Approach

The specification of Metadata Application Profile (MAP) provides the foundation of a semantic architecture for digital libraries. MAP is defined as a kind of metadata schema which consists of data elements drawn from one or more namespaces,

---

[5] FRBR: Functional Requirements for Bibliographic Records. see: http://www.ifla.org/II/s13/-br/frbr.pdf

combined together by implementers, and optimized for a particular local application [17]. It becomes a standard approach with methodologies and procedures to reuse metadata terms from various metadata standards authorities, share the semantics and structures all in once without the burden of setting up one's own metadata registry. One example of MAP is a CEN standard: CWA14855- "Dublin Core Application Profile guidelines", which is a declaration specifying which metadata terms to use and how these terms have been customized or adapted to a particular application. But it stopped in terminology level which can help to share a common data model underlying the applications but not information model which specifies complex relations among resources and properties during its life cycle.

The use of controlled vocabularies (thesauri), authority files and ontologies are practical means of system level to achieve consistency and integrity within and between digital libraries. To get the better flexibility and extensibility, especially in large institutions or enterprises with a number of various kinds of information resources and applications, the metadata registries which collect and maintain data dictionaries, metadata elements, schemas and vocabularies are the sources and repositories of formal semantics. They are the key mechanism to the semantic architecture, especially when the registries can provide web services for software agents by the request of digital library applications.

4.3   The Implementation

The semantic architecture for CCCML consists of schemas in data model level (which consists of the formal definition and restrictions of "core" elements, extended elements, metadata profiles, schema encoding rules) and information model level (which consists of relations between elements, ontologies, procedures and methodologies and Institutional registry for local qualified terms, schemas and namespaces), which serves for consistent description and discovery of semantics of the resources in CCCML. The architecture takes the form of a collection of schemas, tools and documentations which support semantics manipulating needs within the life cycle of the resources. The following paragraphs introduce the semantic architecture of CCCML system in a sequence of workflow:

1. Resource Analysis and Definition
The resources in the CCCML collections are defined from a practical point of view, from which the system can never anticipate what a set of properties of next object will be. We predefined twelve categories of resources with fixed metadata set and encoding schema in a form of Metadata Application Profile. But the system can accept multiple number and any kinds of MAP at the same time in the form of DTD, XML Schema or RDF Schema. The only necessity is the category of a resource should be defined explicitly with a set of properties (metadata elements from multiple namespaces with definitions), guidelines for cataloguing and encoding.

2. Metadata Set Definition (Core and Extended)
Shanghai Library had issued a specification with a "Core" set of metadata elements and encoding guidelines for the interoperation of all its digital library applications. The specification derived elements from DC-Lib application profile and takes a

reference to "the IFLA Guidance on the Structure, Content, and Application of Metadata Records for Digital Resources and Collections"[6]. As a digital library application of Shanghai Library, the CCCML system takes the "Core" as its mandatory set of elements. But this does not mean every element should be in use with the resource of CCCML. The element in the "Core" only becomes mandatory when it is needed.

At the same time each type of resources in CCCML 'borrows' some elements from other metadata standards like MODS, VRA Core etc., and proposes its own elements, as its the domain specific MAP. So a local metadata registry should be established to maintain terms in a local namespace for the proposed elements as well as for those terms from other metadata standards without namespaces.

It is not recommended to invent elements or terms for any resource. But the content owners and users of CCCML want to discover the properties of the resources exhaustively. So we developed a rigorous procedure for approving the proposed terms.

3. Encoding and Mapping Rules

The Schema Suite is a stand alone utility to manipulate (open, load, input, parse, edit, save, delete, convert, output etc.) metadata schemas and generate web interfaces for metadata cataloguing as well as help to generate the query interface. It is designed to support DTD, XML Schema and RDF Schema according to the rules of encoding from time to time. All empty schemas (without instances) can be kept and managed with the tool.

Basically the tool is fed with an original schema of the "Core" set. But it supports aliases for core elements so that it can be user-friendly to the domain expert for inputting and retrieving to the resources. It can support to accept records with ISO2709 format and transform it to any form of a MAP according to a mapping table.

4. Guidelines and Best Practices

For the limitation on the capabilities of different formalization language like XML Schema or RDF Schema, not all of the restrictions and constrains can be expressed and encoded with them. Some of the functions have to accomplish during implementation.

So the metadata element set and its encoding is not enough to carry the semantics of an information model. It must assist with restrictions, constrains, rules, guidelines etc. That's why the semantic architecture has documentation for people readable instead of machine readable. All these documents would better be kept and maintained in a mechanism of registry system so as to provide open access by people or agents. What's more it can be extended to construct web service to provide semantic support services (discussed below).

5. Metadata Registry, Ontologies and Authority Files

Registries are essential to the scalability of a digital library, for it provides a mechanism in the distributed environment to get the semantic architecture reusable, sharable, integrity and consistence. Local registry is a kind of "have-to" facility for institutions and enterprises as the scale of application becomes bigger and bigger and

---

[6] See: http://www.ifla.org/VII/s13/guide/metaguide03.pdf

eventually get out of control. Registry can be considered as data dictionary for local systems. But the metadata registry should synchronize with open registries distributed on the internet. And it's better to open itself to serve as a member of the metadata registry cluster.

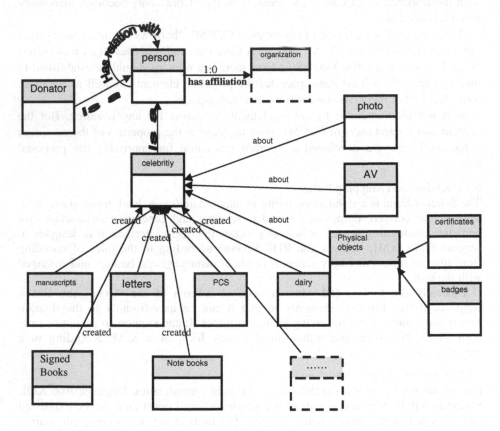

Fig. 2. The ontology of CCCML resources

Ontology brings the semantic integrity of a digital library. The formalization of an information model which consist of metadata profile and relations between objects and properties within a digital library can be considered as a ontology. Fig. 2 illustrated the ontology of CCCML in brief. Some resources and properties in the ontology should be controlled with authority files, such as the "person" in Fig.2, and some subject properties can be controlled with encoding scheme.

5 Future work

There are three kinds of implementation models to accomplish the semantic architecture for consistency and interoperability among applications:

a) Simple model: schema/mapping;
b) Formal model: registry and agent mediator; and
c) Full functional model: metadata services by means of semantic web services which depends on a series of standards and protocols to be settled down.

We just proposed an implementation in level b) mentioned above. The registry function we plan to realize illustrated in Fig. 3. For the second phase of the project, we plan to accomplish FEDORA Architecture to set up digital objects repository. And we expect that the system will eventually support multi-interoperable linkage with protocols such as OpenURL, OAI, and Z39.50.

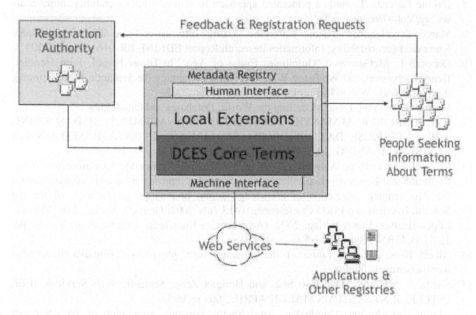

Fig. 3. Single metadata registry overview[7]

References

1. 1.Chen, H.: Semantic Research for Digital Libraries. D-Lib Magazine. Oct 1999. http://www.dlib.org/dlib/october99/chen/10chen.html ()
2. Schreiber Z.: Semantic Information Architecture: Creating Value by Understanding Data published in DMReview.com October 1, 2003 http://www.dmreview.com/articlesub.cfm?articleId=7438 ()
3. Friesen, N,: Semantic Interoperability and Communities of Practice. February 5, 2002 http://www.cancore.ca/documents/semantic.html ()

---

[7] From Harry Wagner's presentation on the "Open Forum for eBusiness and Metadata Technology Standardization" Xi'an, China, May 2004.

4. Hunter, J., Lagoze, C.: Combining RDF and XML Schemas to Enhance Interoperability Between Metadata Application Profiles. http://www.cs.cornell.edu/lagoze/papers/HunterLagozeWWW10.pdf ()

5. Doerr M., Hunter J., Lagoze C.: Towards a Core Ontology for Information Integration. Journal of Digital Information, Volume 4 Issue 1. (Article No. 169, 2003-04-09) http://jodi.ecs.soton.ac.uk/Articles/v04/i01/Doerr/

6. Amit Sheth, Vipul Kashyap , and Tarcisio Lima: Semantic Information Brokering: How Can a Multi-Agent Approach Help? http://cgsb2.nlm.nih.gov/~kashyap/publications/cia.doc

7. Jehad Najjar, Erik Duval, Stefaan Ternier, Filip Neven: TOWARDS INTEROPERABLE LEARNING OBJECT REPOSITORIES: THE ARIADNE EXPERIENCE. Proc. IADIS Int'l Conf. on WWW/Internet 2003, Vol. I, P. 219-226. ISBN 972-98947-1-X

8. Jérôme Euzenat: Towards a principled approach to semantic interoperability. http://ceur-ws.org/Vol-47/euzenat.pdf

9. Marco Schorlemmer, Yannis Kalfoglou: Using Information-Flow Theory to Enable Semantic Interoperability. Informatics Research Report EDI-INF-RR-0161. March 2003

10. Deborah L. McGuinness. "Ontologies Come of Age". In Dieter Fensel, J im Hendler, Henry Lieberman, and Wolfgang Wahlster, editors. Spinning the Semantic Web: Bringing the World Wide Web to Its Full Potential. MIT Press, 2002.

11. Michael Breu, Ying Ding: Modelling the World: Databases and Ontologies.

12. ZVI SCHREIBER: SEMANTIC INFORMATION MANAGEMENT (SIM): SOLVING THE ENTERPRISE DATA PROBLEM BY MANAGING DATA BASED ON ITS BUSINESS MEANING. 2003(V2).

13. Maria Inês Cordeiro, Aida Slavic: Data Models for Knowledge Organization Tools: Evolution and Perspectives. Challenges in knowledge representation and organization for the 21st century: integration of knowledge across boundaries: proceedings of the the Seventh International ISKO Conference, 10-13 July 2002, Granada, Spain). Eds. María J. López-Huertas. Ergon Verlag, 2002. (Advances in Knowledge Organization; Vol 8). pp. 127-134. ISBN 3-89913-247-5

14. Albert Benschop: The future of the semantic web. http://www2.fmg.uva.nl/sociosite/websoc/semantic.html.

15. Sheila A. McIlraith, Tran Cao Son, and Honglei Zeng: Semantic Web Services. IEEE INTELLIGENT SYSTEMS MARCH/APRIL 2001 pp46-53.

16. Abhijit Patil, Swapna Oundhakar, Amit Sheth: Semantic Annotation of Web Services (SAWS). http://lsdis.cs.uga.edu/~abhi/SAWS-TR.htm.

17. Thomas Baker, Makx Dekkers, Rachel Heery, Manjula Patel, and Gauri Salokhe, "What Terms Does Your Metadata Use? Application Profiles as Machine-Understandable Narratives". Journal of Digital Information, Volume 2 Issue 2 (November 2001)

18. (Acknowledgement to my colleague Leon Zhao for his inspired discussion with me occasionally and to Miss Lu Ying for drawing the Fig. 1 for me)

WebGIS-RBDL – A Rare Book Digital Library Supporting Spatio-Temporary Retrieval

Ming Zhang[1], Dongqing Yang[1], Zhihong Deng[1], Sai Wu[1], Feng Li[2], and Shiwei Tang[1]

[1] School of Electronics Engineering and Computer Science,
Peking University, Beijing, 100871, China
{mzhang, ydq, zhdeng, wsai, lifeng, tsw}@db.pku.edu.cn
[2] National Earthquake Infrastructure Service,
China Seismological Bureau, Beijing, 100036, China

Abstract. In order to help researchers of humanities study the cultural ancient resources from temporal and geographical perspectives, we build WebGIS-RBDL at Peking University. In WebGIS-RBDL, metadata records and historical map layers are linked together, and therefore users can get more spatio-temporal information about rare books through folded map layers, including historical maps, modern maps and landform images. In this paper, the architecture of WebGIS-RBDL is introduced. Then, the principles, rules and methods for metadata extracting and correlating in WebGIS-RBDL are discussed. Furthermore, efficient tools to extract spatio-temporal information automatically from rare-book metadata are developed. The WebGIS-RBDL can be extended to include other ancient collections easily. Our efforts show that using GIS in digital libraries is a new and promising method to build more effective user-friendly interfaces in digital libraries.

1 Introduction

Peking University Rare-Book Digital Library (PKU-RBDL) is one of the most important components of Peking University Digital Libraries. It is built on the large special collection of Chinese rare books, rubbings, ancient atlases, Dunhuang Scrolls, and old journals published before 1949 [1].

Emphasized on "Historical and Geographical researchers work in the same field", spatio-temporal information is very important for scholars of humanities to study the cultural resources from both temporal and geographical perspectives. So we utilize Geographic Information System (GIS) to explore spatio-temporal information and develop a user-friendly interface to enhance human-machine interaction [2].

There are several distinguished projects using GIS technology, such as ECAI, Perseus project, and CHGIS [3, 4, 5].

ECAI (Electronic Cultural Atlas Initiative) is an international collaborative project, which uses GIS (Geographic Information Systems) to integrate electronic atlas with various digital resources to facilitate the access and availability of information distributed around the world [3].

Z. Chen et al. (Eds.): ICADL 2004, LNCS 3334, pp. 255–265, 2004.

TimeMap is one of the key components in ECAI [6]. One of its aims is to archive and visualize historical and cultural resources in order to analyze the temporal evolution of those resources. Creating key historical maps as temporal snapshots, TimeMap can cartoon AVI to demonstrate the evolvement of historical maps in its database.

Perseus is a project developed by the Department of the Classics, Tufts University. It is used as an entrance to temporal, geographical, historical and cultural information for historical-geographers, travelers and environment planning officers [4]. Perseus automatically extracts place-names from documents, then creates spatial indices and organizes data to be reflected on the GIS maps.

CHGIS was formally launched in 2001 by Fudan University Historical-Geography Center with the financial support from Luce Foundation [5]. CHGIS tries to create a fundamental geographic information database of China's history to show the continuous changes of China's historical periods. It provides a GIS data platform with timelines and access tools for researchers.

Map plug-ins are needed at client ends for most of these projects. Thus, the means to access map data and metadata in these systems are pretty much limited.

WebGIS-RBDL applies the WebGIS technique, which only requires a web browser for an end user. The client sends a request, and then the server takes charge of building the new map layer and sending the JPEG map back to the user's browser.

With more than 20,000 items in WebGIS-RBDL, the key of WebGIS services lies in how to obtain spatio-temporal metadata automatically and how to correlate them with the WebGIS maps.

Researches on Chinese rare books have very distinct characteristics. Actually, geographical information in literature is mostly conveyed through place-names. We devise a historical gazetteer, dynasty thesauri, and many extracting rules, and then develop efficient tools to extract spatio-temporal information automatically out of rare-book metadata.

Based on the time-slice model and the 11 historical Maps of China developed by our group, we have built linkages between metadata records and historical map layers, such as the migration of boundaries, cities and rivers. Therefore users can get more spatio-temporal information about rare books through the folded map layers, including historical maps, modern maps and landform images.

The remainder of this paper is organized as follows. Section 2 presents the main architecture of the system. Section 3 describes the spatio-temporal information extraction in WebGIS-RBDL. Section 4 shows how we correlate metadata in the WebGIS-RBDL. Section 5 provides a case study for querying WebGIS-RBDL. And the final section gives our conclusions and future work.

2 The Architecture of the WebGIS-RBDL

The WebGIS-RBDL is developed with ArcIMS HTML Viewer from ESRI Corporation [7]. Different from plug-in technique with Java Applet map, HTML Viewer adopts the customized "thin client" model. The maps and data are stored on the server, and the queries are also processed on the server. The maps are delivered to clients in JPEG forms. The WebGIS-RBDL customizes the client ArcIMS HTML Viewer to support spatial, temporal, and attribute queries.

Fig 1 shows the three-tier software architecture of WebGIS-RBDL: the back-end is the Data Service layer; the middle is the Application layer; the front is the Web Browser layer. The Data Service layer supports accesses to data repositories. Data in the repositories can be non-structured images, map layer files, semi-structured XML files or structured metadata. The Application layer consists of the Web information service and the WebGIS service. The Application layer returns processed results to the Web browser according to query requirements from the front Web browser and data from the back-end data repositories. The Web Browser layer provides the WebGIS interface and the OAI-PMH metadata interface.

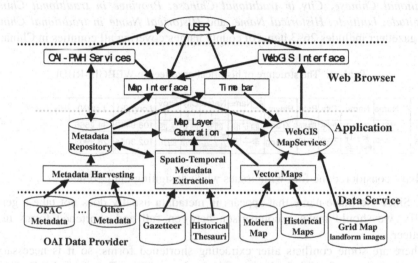

Fig. 1. The software architecture of WebGIS-RBDL

So far, OAI-PMH is the most important and convenient metadata interoperable framework in Digital Libraries. Therefore, The PKU-RBDL OPAC (Open Public Access Catalog) system communicates with WebGIS-RBDL via OAI-PMH [7, 9].

PKU-RBDL OPAC system releases OAI metadata of rare books and notifies the WebGIS-RBDL, and then WebGIS-RBDL harvests the metadata and starts up the Map Layer Generator to get new layers for further map services.

3   Automatic Information Extraction from Inscriptions

3.1   Automatic Spatial Information Extraction

It is very important to get guiding rules for metadata extraction [10]. Researches on Chinese rare books (e.g. rubbings) have very distinct characteristics, one of which is that they abound in historical names and dynastic titles such as "the place of being excavated", "the place of preservation", "spatio-temporal range", etc. We should think about automatic extraction of historical places and ages from metadata.

In ancient times, there were not such concepts as longitude and latitude. Actually, geographical information in literature was mostly conveyed through place-names. However, the relative positions of place names might be changed for many times in a long history. As a result, the identification of historical place-names becomes a real challenge. For example we should deal with ambiguities in place-names: similar place-names, variances of place-names, and so on.

With the help of the historical gazetteer, we scan Chinese texts to look for some frequently used place-names. Table 1 shows the structure of the historical gazetteer, which consists of *ID, Abbreviated Name, Name, City, Province, Pinyin Name* (pronunciation in Chinese), *Abbreviated name in traditional Chinese, Name in traditional Chinese, City in traditional Chinese, Province in traditional Chinese, Longitude, Latitude, Historical Name,* and *Historical Name in traditional Chinese.* Our gazetteer includes 2693 items of county names covering all counties in China.

Table 1. The structure of historical gazetteer in WEBGIS-RBDL

ID	A_Name	Name	City	Prov	Pinyin	A_Name_T	Name_T	City_T	Prov_T	Long.(E)	Lat.(N)	His_Name	His_Name_T
1091	西安	西安市	西安	陕西	Xi'an	西安市	西安	西安	陕西	108.9442	34.2666	长安	長安
1906	李子坪	李子坪彝族乡	石棉	四川	Liziping	李子坪	李子坪彝族乡	石棉	四川	102.3054	28.9903		

We have considered the following issues while designing the gazetteer.

1. Since the place-name that appears in metadata usually does not take a general postfix, we should make a comparison between full and shortened forms in the gazetteer.

There are some conflicts after extracting shortened forms, so it is necessary to reserve full forms for relatively uncommon place-names. For example: Dongxiang autonomous county of Mongolian Nationality in Henan has the same short form as Dongxiang county in Jiangxi.

2. Because the partition of districts in China is very complex, some places share the same name or have more than one name.

- City and county homonyms, different places: Shanghai city vs. county.
- District homonyms, different places: Xinrong district (Shanxi) vs. Xinrong district (Xizang, Tibet); Deqing (Xizang, Tibet) vs. Deqing (Guangxi).
- The duchy district and the duchy county share the same name of the superior city: Chaoyang municipal district, Chaoyang county, Chaoyang city.

In order to get the correct location information, we must use the full form of a place-name and the province the place belongs to. Generally speaking, different places are not allowed to use the same name. In the gazetteer, we have dealt with about 100 groups of analogous place-names. Finally, only three groups of homonyms with different places are left; all of them are related to Tibet (Xizang in Chinese).

3. The metadata for ancient Chinese Literature usually use traditional Chinese but the ArcIMS map displays only simplified Chinese. So the place-name gazetteer must include both simplified and traditional Chinese. In addition, variant names are possibly used at different times, which are different from modern place-names. These problems must be solved by unifying metadata records in the gazetteer [11].

4. Longitude and latitude: they are key attributes of place-names and essential to link metadata with maps.

Now we will consider the rules for place-name extraction. We use some assistant tables for heuristic words to extract place-names. The principal rules and related tables for rubbings metadata are:

- Using postfixes for identification. We have designed a Loc_suf table for location suffixes, in which there are states, counties, cities, districts, towns, etc., especially place-names used in Ming Dynasty: Wei, Suo and so on.
- Assigning high priorities to provinces and considering administrative relations. For example, in "excavated in Luoyang Longmen of Henan", we record "Henan" (the province name) and "Luoyang" to avoid eliciting "Longmen (county)" (in Guangdong province).
- Extracting the annotated modern place-names first: "excavated in Yunzhou Rencheng county of Shandong province, now located in the south of Jining city of Shandong". We extract the place-name "Jining" according to "now located". The tense adverbs, such as "now" and "present", are saved in table Time_Adv.
- Proceeded by prepositions and verbs, such as "from", "In". For example, "from Baocheng Shimen west wall of Shanxi". We get Loc_VerbPrep, the table for prepositions and verbs with location objects: "in", "from", "of", "excavated in", "preserved at" and so on.
- Merging some cities-subordinate to one city: Chongwen district, Chaoyang district, and Xicheng district of Beijing are all considered as (parts of) Beijing.
- Considering important historical place-names as bynames.

According to the rules, we extract the place-names step by step. The procedure for place-name extraction is described as follows:

Input: one string of "time/place sculpted" in the field "spatio-temporal range" for a piece of rare-book metadata.

Output: a place-name.

Step 1. Use the tables Loc_suf, Loc_VebPrep, and Time-Adv to segment the input string to get candidates.

Step 2. Match the candidates with frequently used location names stored in the gazetteer to get initial place-names.

Step 3. Use the rules and the gazetteer to expand the contexts of initial place-names to get exact place-names.

We get most place-names (95%) without ambiguity. Those place-names that cannot be determined will be recorded into another database separately.

3.2   Automatic Temporary Information Retrieval

We apply the A.D. year as the time unit while recording metadata for rare resources, but use the Chinese dynasty while displaying. So when we distill temporal information from metadata, we should settle the corresponding relations between A.D. years and the Chinese dynasties.

Some typical problems with temporal information in metadata of rare resources are:

- The problem to determine the time of dynastic changes.
- Similar dynasty names, such as the Wei of three Kingdoms vs. the Northern Wei, Tang vs. the Tang of the Five Dynasties and so on.
- Duplicated reign titles, such as Donghan Yonghe (beginning from 136 A.D.), Xijin Yonghe (beginning from 345A.D.).
- The ascription of years in dynastic changes, such as the reign title of Southern Ming regime and Qing Dynasty.
- The comparisons of simplified and traditional year names.

Table 2. The dynasty thesaurus

ID	Dynasty	Nation	Start_Year	End_Year	Dynasty_T	Nation_T	Ref
06	西汉	西汉 新	-206	23	西漢	西漢 新	
08	三国	魏 蜀 吴	220	265	三國	魏 蜀 吴	

Table 3. The reign thesaurus

ID	NianHao	Start_ Year	End_ Year	Dynasty	Nation	DiHao	PinYin	NianHao_ T	Dynasty_ T	Nation_ T	DiHao_T
319	天成	926	930	五代	唐	明宗	TianCheng	天成	五代	唐	明宗
400	崇祯	1628	1644	明	明	思宗	CongZhen	崇禎	明		思宗

We created complete thesauri with 400 entries for Chinese historical years, including dynastic thesaurus a shown in Table 2, and thesaurus of reign titles shown in Table 3.

- Dynasty thesaurus: including ID, dynasty name, nation name, the beginning and the end of a dynasty, dynasty name in traditional Chinese, nation name in traditional Chinese, and reference.
- Reign thesaurus: including dynasty, beginning year, final year, year name in traditional Chinese, and corresponding name of the emperor (DiHao).

With the help of the historical thesauri and effective technique of Chinese segmentation, first, we can get the year name, and then extract the exact dynasty information. The procedure for temporal information extraction is stated as follows.

Input: one string of "time/place sculpted" in the field "spatio-temporal range" for a piece of rare-book metadata.

Output: the A.D year and corresponding dynasty information.

Step 1. If there is a year number of A.D calendar
then goto step 4.

Step 2. Get the dynasty name using the Dynasty thesaurus.

Step 3. Get the year number of the dynasty using Reign thesaurus.

Step 4. Get the A.D year and corresponding dynasty information using
Reign thesaurus.

4 Correlating Metadata in WebGIS-RBDL

The major purpose of WebGIS system is to provide spatio-temporal queries on the Web browser-based GIS platform. Since the 1980s, researchers have paid much attention to GIS and made some progress.

4.1 Spatio-Temporal Model

There are three most common spatio-temporal models: the snapshot-transition model, the vector model, and the grid model [12]. The advantage of the snapshot-transition model is that it is very easy to implement, so it can use conventional 2D-GIS techniques. But there are huge data redundancies of unchanged spatio-temporal features. The vector model can denote the spatial and attribute changes but it cannot present gradual changes. The grid model denotes times by adding a time stamp on the grid data, but if the geographical objects or their topological structures change, the history or variance information will be broken up.

WebGIS-RBDL uses the snapshot-transition model [6], which presents the historical data into a series of snaps taken from known dynasties and these snaps will be displayed as time-slices. The temporal queries will be translated to queries on the time-slice collections.

In Chinese history, the evolvement of administrative areas, cities and culture is very distinct in the periods of dynastic changes. It can be regarded as a series of sudden spatio-temporal changes, so we developed 11 representative historical vector maps for main dynasties as time-slices.

One dynastic map is a projection on the temporal section from the beginning year to the final year. The historical gazetteer is generated from the vector of dynastic maps. The rubbing metadata can be connected with historical maps by the field "spatio-temporal range", when using MapObject API from ESRI Co [7].

Since GIS uses layers to organize different types of data, we consider rubbing metadata as point elements and then create many rubbing layers according to the types and times of the metadata.

According to the corresponding place-name and dynasty extracted from metadata elements, we can get the longitude and latitude from the historical gazetteer, and then add the metadata record to the corresponding coordinates of the suitable map layer.

4.2 Map Services

Before specifying the map services, we should know the work flow of WebGIS software. When using ArcIMS to create the basic WebGIS website, first, we integrate data (such as: Shape file, ArcSDE layer, grid images and so on) onto the map layers; then we set up gradual displaying scales, basic representation features and geographical codes; finally, we export one map configuration file written in ArcXML. Using this map configuration file, ArcIMS creates a MapService running on the server. The Spatial Server of ArcIMS parses the users' requests and sends these data back to the client according to the definitions in this map configuration file.

The process of specifying map services is as following:

1. First, create metadata layers of the specific rubbing types, places, and dynasties per users' demands.
2. Create a map configuration file: define the layer attributes displayed on the map service, including the layer type, name, figure, font, color, diaphaneity, attributes, displaying scales, folding sequences, on-off states and so on. In the end, create one map configuration file with suffix .axl.
3. Create a MapService: The ArcIMS Manager imports the map configuration file, and then creates a corresponding MapService. The Spatial Server deals with the query requirements, takes out the layer elements from the MapService, and then gets correlative data from the shapefile and transforms the data into a geometric graph and exports the graph to the client.

   The map configuration file offers information to every layer for MapService. By overwriting the element parameters in ArcXML queries to overlay the information in the MapService, we can control the effects of displaying maps from the client end.

   WebGIS-RBDL integrates layers of the same dynasty into one MapService, and links map layers of modern times as references. The purpose is to reflect:
   - The boundaries of nations and counties, the administrative districts, the changes of city places.
   - The changes of nature physiognomy: rivers, coastal lines etc.
   - The changes of rubbing centers vs. the changes of political and cultural centers.
   - At the same time, the map services are divided into two types:
   - Map services for different dynasties.
   - Map services for different data types (such as different metadata harvested from different digital libraries).
4. Create WebGIS websites: define essential things for Web publishing in ArcIMS Manager, such as website names, service paths, MapService, client Viewer types and displaying models.
5. Update the related MapSevices every time after harvesting metadata and regenerating the layer.

   In order to integrate various query methods for metadata, we have implemented different map interfaces based on HTML Viewer of ArcIMS.

   There is an interoperable interface between WebGIS-RBDL and PKU-RBDL OPAC system. The interface can pass ID List of query results between WebGIS-

RBDL and PKU-RBDL based on OAI-PMH, and display corresponding map elements on the map.

- Dynamically create new layers for new metadata. Customize and pass the requests of map layer updating via ArcXML.
- Call different map services directly: get different dynastic maps on the temporal selection toolbar, or get metadata on OAI-PMH Server.

5   A Case Study for Querying the WebGIS-RBDL

As shown in fig 2, the WebGIS-RBDL has been published in the Internet with URL "http://162.105.203.89/website/rub2/viewer.htm". Users can use web browsers (Internet Explorer or Netscape) to get services we provide without downloading or installing any client-end software.

The WebGIS-RBDL system consists of WebGIS toolbars (including map operating tools, spatial selection and query tools, and attribute query tools, printing tools), the map displaying areas (including indexing maps, scale, orientation marks), the layer displaying area, the temporal selection toolbar, the links for OAI-PMH service and OPAC queries, etc.

Map displaying and List displaying are two primary displaying methods. When the query results are shown up on the map with highlight, the collected metadata will be displayed in a list. The OPAC system offers a high-level metadata method for queries for detailed contents and image links.

The default Web page will display the current map of China (published in 1983 as a standard), which includes layers of provinces, cities, towns, roads, rivers, lakes and mountains in the center frame, and searching/displaying tools for users in the left frame. At the bottom frame lists the temporal selection toolbar, by which users can travel through China history.

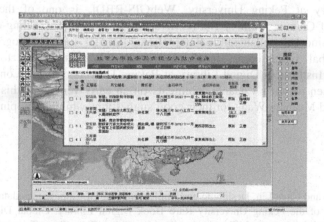

Fig. 2. The spatial query results displayed by the OPAC

The tools we provide can efficiently express users' queries which always have spatial and temporal requirements in the visualization way. First, users can use the searching tools to select the right region in the center map or even type the keywords of the region. Second, users can select the right dynasty via the temporal selection toolbar or input the specific year for precision. The tools translate this information into queries and send them to the system. Once the system receives the request, it will select the right layer for users. Since the layers have been built-in in the background, the result will be returned immediately to the users without delay.

For more complex queries, users can use both tools and logic expressions, which can deal with most requests. And users can also query through the last result.

6 Conclusions and Future Work

In this paper we devise and implement the WebGIS-RBDL system. With the help of the historical gazetteer, dynasty thesauri, and many extracting rules, we extract spatio-temporal information automatically from the metadata of ancient rare books with accuracy of 95%. The system also integrates OAI-PMH-based metadata harvesting service, OPAC Database queries and WebGIS-based spatio-temporal queries through the map-display interfaces. Several experts on rare books have tried out the system and they encouraged us with some valuable advices. In the future, we would provide visual and statistical tools for query results and the dynamic cartoon function for historical rare books as well as map transitions, improve the extracting tools with more linguistic rules and provide WebGIS special services on more collections, such as Silk Road, the Emperor Qing Shihuang, etc.

Acknowledgements

Our work (funded by NSFC grant 60221120144) is a key project of Institute of Digital Library at Peking University. WebGIS-RBDL is one of the important components of Chinese Memory Net (CMNet, inspected by Prof. Ching-chih Chen), which is a Sino-US collaborative International Digital Library Program (IDLP) toward a global digital library in Chinese studies. We would like to thank our colleagues of Institute of Digital Library at Peking University, Prof. Long Xiao and Prof. Ling Chen for their valuable comments on an early version of this paper, Ms. Ying Feng and Ms. Yan Wang for their good suggestions while developing WebGIS-RBDL.

References

1. Long Xiao and Chen Lin. Designing and implementation of Chinese metadata standards: a case study of the Peking University Rare Book Digital Library. Global Digital Library Development in the new Millennium, edited by Ching-Chih Chen. Tsinghua University Press, 2001.

2. Ming Zhang, Long Xiao, Dong-qing Yang, Shi-wei Tang, Exploring Spatio-temporal Information in a Rare Book Digital Library, Proceeding of PNC2002 "Collaboration in the Digital Age". Osaka, Japan. September 2002.
3. http://www.ecai.org/
4. Robert F. Chavez, "Using GIS in an Integrated Digital Library." Proceedings of the 5th Annual ACM Digital Library Conference 250-251. 2000. http://www.perseus.tufts.edu/
5. http://yugong.fudan.edu.cn/chgis/
6. Ian Johnson. The Electronic Cultural Atlas Initiative: Global Access to Cultural Data Using Time Map Methodology. Computer Applications in Archaeology Conference, Ljubljana April 2000. http://www.timemap.net/
7. http://www.esri.com/
8. Carl Lagoze, Herbert Van de Sompel. The Open Archives Initiative: Building a low-barrier interoperability framework. Digital Library Research Group, Cornell University, 2001
9. Aihua Wang, Ming Zhang, Dongqing Yang and Shiwei Tang. The Framework for Metadata Interoperability Based on OAI. Journal of Computer Engineering and Application. PP5-7, Vol 38, No.1, 2002.
10. Peixiang Zhao, Ming Zhang, Dong-qing Yang, Shi-wei Tang. Automatic Metadata Extraction from Digital Documents. Journal of Computer Science, Oct. 2003, PP221-226.
11. Qixiang Tan, The Collection of Historical Chinese Maps, the Map Press of China, 1991.
12. May Yuan. Temporal GIS and spatio-temporal Modeling. In Proceedings of Third International Conference Workshop on Integrating GIS and Environment Modeling, Santa Fe, NM, 1996. Santa Barbara.

Approaches to Interoperability Amongst Australian Digital Information Providers

Philip Hider

School of Information Studies, Charles Sturt University,
Locked Bag 675, Wagga Wagga, NSW 2678, Australia
phider@csu.edu.au

Abstract. The results from a questionnaire survey distributed to Australian institutions hosting digital collections, are presented. It was found that few metadata schemas are being used, although several others are being contemplated; that content standards tend to follow format standards; and that in-house standards are often required to supplement these. A fairly low level of resource and metadata exchange is taking place. Standards were considered important for a variety of reasons, a leading reason being interoperability. However, when it came to practice and new initiatives, there was a range of approaches taken to achieve interoperability. Some institutions concentrate on interoperability across their own systems, others focus on cross-institutional projects. Some institutions stress adherence to metadata standards, others are implementing new technologies that can handle different metadata formats and content.

Survey

A questionnaire survey was emailed in April 2004 to forty Australian institutions with digital collections, and also disseminated through two lists. Nineteen completed questionnaires were received. These represented mostly major libraries, with some museums, archives and other related information services. Most of the digital collections were freely accessible on the Web, and all institutions had digital collections supported by some kind of retrieval system that indexed metadata for query-based searching. There was a broad range of original formats, including born-digital materials, printed text, manuscript, and audio-visual.

Metadata Format Standards. The format standards used for the metadata of the digital collections did not vary as much as might have been expected, with the two leading standards being MARC21 and Dublin Core (DC). The distribution of standards is shown in Table 1. Only one institution did not apply any format standard; several applied more than one.

There were a considerable number of reasons offered as to why the institutions chose their respective metadata formats. The reasons given by the respondents were categorised into types, as listed below in Table 2, with the frequencies indicated.

Six of the institutions are contemplating adopting a new schema. However, given the range of schema under consideration – EAD (3), IEEE LOM (2), METS (2),

Z. Chen et al. (Eds.): ICADL 2004, LNCS 3334, pp. 266–269, 2004.

CIMI, DC, and MODS – this does not indicate an homogenisation; if anything, it indicates the opposite, with further proliferation of standards likely over the next few years.

Table 1. Format Standards Employed

Standard	Fully	Partially	Total
MARC21	10	3	13
Dublin Core	9	4	13
AGLS	3	4	7
EAD	3	2	5
METS	0	1	1

Table 2. Reasons for Format Selection

Reason	f
Most appropriate standard for nature of collection	7
Existing standard for non-digital collections (so facilitates integration)	6
Community's favoured standard	3
Government standard	3
"Interoperability"	3
Supported by system	3
Existing expertise in the standard at the institution	2
Requirement for participation in a cross-institution project	2
"Simplicity"	2
"Extensibility"	1
Facilitates record exchange	1
"International"	1
"Lowest common denominator"	1
Suitable for local context	1
Supplements other standards	1

Seven of the respondents (37%) stated that the retrieval system(s) supporting their digital collections could accommodate other metadata formats not used for their own metadata. However, again, no particular schema stood out as an alternative format, not even Dublin Core.

Metadata Content Standards. With respect to metadata content, five institutions (26%) do not apply any external standards, eight (57%) apply AACR2; five apply the AGLS usage guide produced by the National Archive of Australia [1], three institutions follow guidelines based on EAD; three apply the National Library of Australia's *Guidelines for the Creation of Content for Resource Discovery* [2]; while one institution applies DC and MARC21 usage guides. It would appear that the relationship between content and format standards is generally quite close, with

AACR and MARC historically interdependent, and in the case of the newer format standards, content standards often based on the particular schema selected, rather than vice-versa. All but one of the institutions had developed in-house guidelines, suggesting that many institutions still pay considerable attention to local context; it may also indicate a need for the further development of content standards.

The majority of responding institutions use one or more controlled vocabularies, mostly for subject indexing purposes, with the Library of Congress Subject Headings (LCSH) are assigned by eleven institutions (58%).

Importing and Exporting of Resources. Only six of the institutions (32%) had imported digital objects into their collections from outside, and in only three of these cases were objects accompanied by metadata, indicating a fairly low level of metadata importing amongst Australian digital collections at present. On the other hand, eight (42%) of the institutions had allowed digital objects to be exported from their collection to an external collection. Of these, only two also imported digital resources; whereas four of the importing institutions had not exported. There seems little correspondence, then, between importing and exporting of digital resources.

Federated Searching. Respondents were then asked whether it would be beneficial for their end-users to be able to search on digital collections provided by other institutions at the same time as they search on the digital collections provided by their own institution. Most considered it "extremely beneficial," and all thought it beneficial to some degree. While it might not be a priority, access is thus considered an important feature of interoperability.

Importance of Metadata Standards. Respondents were asked how important it was for their institution to describe its digital resources using established metadata standards. Fifteen believed it to be "very important;" only one thought it "not important." The respondents were then asked to give reasons why they considered such standards important. These have been categorised by the author as listed in Table 3 below.

Table 3. Reasons for Importance of Standards

Reason	f
Interoperability	9
Optimise external access	6
For cooperative ventures	5
Portability	4
Enhance retrieval	3
For federated searching	3
Standardisation	3
Government condition	1
To fully •tilize retrieval technologies	1

The range of reasons ties in with the range of reasons given for choice of format standards. The word "interoperability" was used by many of the respondents, suggesting that standardisation is seen as a key facilitator of interoperability. Three important considerations appear to help standardise the metadata used in Australian digital collections: "interoperability;" economics; and optimisation of access, both internally and externally.

Interoperability Initiatives. Many of the institutions are working towards achieving greater interoperability for its digital collections in concrete ways. These initiatives were categorised as listed in Table 4 below.

Table 4. Interoperability Initiatives

Type of initiative	*f*
Part of cross-institutional federated search projects / portals	6
System development	5
Adherence to metadata standards	4
Part of Open Archives Initiative	3
Development of internal federated search	2
Providing access through external search engines	2
Implementation of Z39.50 client	1
Cross-institutional resource sharing	1
Partnerships with NLA	1

From these responses, we may observe that institutions are working towards interoperability in some quite different ways. Some see interoperability as a means to improve external access to their collections, through cross-institutional portals, external search engines, or the Open Archives Initiative (OAI). Others are looking primarily at integrating internal access, across their own institutions' systems. Some institutions emphasise standardisation, others systems development.

We have noted that when it comes to exchange of resources and their metadata, the survey indicates that Australian digital libraries and other digital information providers have a long way to go, although this might be due not only to low levels of interoperability, but also to a lack of critical mass of resources worth exchanging. There appears to be more emphasis on access, yet even here it is more "work-in-progress" than "work-completed." On the other hand, the *goal* of interoperability is supported by most institutions. The importance of standards and the desirability of federated searching are also widely acknowledged. However, as far as *practice* is concerned, different institutions appear to vary significantly in their approaches to achieving interoperability.

References

1. National Archives of Australia: AGLS Metadata Element Set Part 2. Version 1.3. National Archives of Australia, Canberra (2002)
2. National Library of Australia: Guidelines for the Creation of Content for Resource Discovery http://www.nla.gov.au/guidelines/metaguide.html (14 July 2004)

An Experimental Study of Boosting Model Classifiers for Chinese Text Categorization

Yibing Geng, Guomin Zhu, Junrui Qiu, Jilian Fan, and Jingchang Zhang

Library, Second Military Medical University, 800 Xiangyin Rd.,
200433 Shanghai, P.R. China
{Yibing, Zhugm, Junrui, Fanjl, JCZhang}@smmu.edu.cn
http://www.smmu.edu.cn/library.html

Abstract. Text categorization is a crucial task of increasing importance. Our work focuses on the study of Chinese text categorization on the basis of Boosting model. We chose the People's Daily news from TREC5 as our benchmark datasets. A minor modification to AdaBoost algorithm (Freund and Schapire, 1996, 2000) was applied for this hypothesis. By way of using the F1 measure for its final evaluation, the results of the Boosting model (AdaBoost.MH) is proved to be effective and outperforms most of other algorithms reported for Chinese text categorization.

1 Introduction

With the popularity of the Internet and the development of digital libraries, Chinese information, especially Chinese text processing, has gradually developed into a higher "knowledge" level. Among those developments, text categorization which classifying a large number of texts into different categories automatically according to the content of the text on the basis of a predefined category system will help people better in understanding and management of information. In recent years, the technologies for text categorization, developed with *sense disambiguation* and *feature extraction*, combined together with *information filtering* and text *search engine*, have greatly improved the service quality of text information. But, text categorization, the automated assignment of natural language texts with predefined categories based on their contents, still remains a crucial task of increasing importance.

In this paper, we introduce the study of the automatic classification methods of Chinese texts on the basis of machine learning. The basic conception of these methods is to use a general inductive process (called "the learner") to automatically build a classifier by "learning" from a set of previously classified documents. The extensive experiments using Boosting model were described at length. And comparing with other recently works, such as Simple Vector Distance, Naive Bayesian, and kNN, the results of Boosting algorithm for Chinese text categorization is proved to be effective and outperforms most of other algorithms in this field.

Z. Chen et al. (Eds.): ICADL 2004, LNCS 3334, pp. 270–279, 2004.

2 Description of Text Categorization Problem

The systematic task of text categorization is that: given a classification system, texts are to be assigned with one or several categories. For more precisely, text categorization is a classifier that uses a hypothetic function $f': D \times C \to \{0,1\}$ to estimate the unknown real function $f : D \times C \to \{0,1\}$, where, $C = \{c_1, c_2, \cdots, c_m\}$ are a set of predefined categories, and $D = \{d_1, d_2, \cdots, d_n\}$ are set of texts. The closer the function f' meets f, the better the category system is.

To be success with the function f', a learning method based on machine learning must have some corpora $C_o = \{d_1 \ldots, d_s\}$ for training purpose. We call this the training set $T_r = \{d_1 \ldots, d_k\}$. These are texts having been previously assigned with categories by human experts. This process is also called a supervised learning process.

For its evaluation, we need a test set $T_e = \{d_{k+1} \ldots, d_n\}$, which also are texts previously assigned with categories by human experts. The evaluation of a classifier usually reflected by two different aspects of category assignment.

Precision is the rate of accuracy of all the correct category assignment. It is expressed as:

$$precision = \frac{\text{number of categories correctly assigned}}{\text{number of categories assigned}} \tag{1}$$

Recall is the rate of capability of all the correct category assignment. It is expressed as:

$$recall = \frac{\text{number of categories correctly assigned}}{\text{number of categories should be assigned}} \tag{2}$$

In the evaluation of a given text categorization task, we usually use a one single criteria, which is usually called F1 measurement, The formula for F1 evaluation is as follows:

$$F1 = \frac{precision \times recall \times 2}{precision + recall} \tag{3}$$

3 The Boosting Classifier

There are a lot of methods for text categorization [5], such as Rocchio, Decision Tree, Naïve Bayes, Support Vector Machines (SVM) and Classifier Committees and so on.

For the method of Classifier Committees, it makes a classifier by merging all the simple rough decision to form a smart rule. This is sometimes called a voting process.

The core sense behind this is that for a given task which need experts' knowledge in making a decision, then, with a number of experts getting involved in making independent judgment, we will get better results. While applying this idea to the text categorization, we use different classification devices $\Phi_1, \cdots, \Phi_S$ to identify whether a given text d_j belongs to a category c_i. Hereby, the classification device Φ_k is said to be a weak hypothesis, or a weak learner, because it only makes a decision better than a random guessing.

The Boosting method, in fact, is one kind of the Classifier Committees. It can use any kind of special classification devices as its weak hypothesis such as the Decision Tree and Neural Network etc. The most difference between Classifier Committees and Boosting method is that: for the method of Classifier Committees, on a broad sense, it makes weak hypothesis on a parallel and independent manner over training set, while for the method of Boosting, it makes weak hypothesis on a sequential and recursive manner over training set. That is to say that the weak hypothesis Φ_i depends on the result of its $\Phi_1, \cdots, \Phi_{i-1}$, and it concentrates more on the training text which appears to be abnormality.

3.1   The Boosting Algorithm

The original description of AdaBoost was given by Freund and Schapire [6]. Boosting algorithm is implemented by amalgamating a series of weak hypothesis then producing its final hypothesis to form a highly accurate rule in the task of text categorization.

It's input is $T_r = \{\langle d_1, C_1 \rangle, \cdots; \langle d_g, C_g \rangle\}$ from training collection, where a text d_j has certain category C_j assigned, and $C_j \subseteq C$. The learning process recursively combined S times with a series of weak hypothesis $\Phi_1, \cdots, \Phi_S$. And finally, we get a linear amalgamation $\Phi = \sum_{s=1}^{S} \alpha_s \Phi_s$, where α_s is a tunable parameter for the amalgamating.

This algorithm has three characteristics: (1) With no previous knowledge in hand, the initial probability distribution for Φ_i is a uniform. That is to say if there is N samples in the training set, its distribution of each sample is $1/N$. (2) The boosting algorithm finds a highly accurate classification rule by calling the weak learner recursively in a series of rounds. (3) As boosting progresses, training samples and their corresponding categories that are hard to classify correctly get incrementally higher weights while samples and categories that are easy to predict get lower weights. The intended effect is to force the learning algorithm to concentrate on samples that will be most beneficial to the overall goal of finding a highly accurate classifier.

The systematic description of this algorithm is as follows:

Given training set $T_r = \{\langle d_1', C_1 \rangle, \cdots, \langle d_g', C_g \rangle\} \subset D_o$,

where $C_j \subseteq C = \{c_1, c_2, \cdots, c_m\}$, $j = 1, \cdots, g$.

Initialize $D_1(d_j', c_i) = 1/mg$.

For all $j = 1, \cdots, g$, and $i = 1, \cdots, m$, repeat the following steps in a series of rounds $s = 1, \cdots, S$, we get s weak hypotheses Φ_s:

(1)Pass distributed $D_s(d_j', c_i)$ to weak learner.

(2)Compute weak hypotheses Φ_s.

(3)Choose a parameter α_s;

(4)Update $D_s(d_j', c_i)$ recursively:

$$D_{s+1}(d_j', c_i) = \frac{D_s(d_j', c_i)\exp(-\alpha_s \cdot C_j[c_i] \cdot \Phi_s(d_j', c_i))}{Z_s} \tag{4}$$

where $Z_s = \sum_{i=1}^{m} \sum_{j=1}^{g} D_s(d_j', c_i)\exp(-\alpha_s \cdot C_j[c_i] \cdot \Phi_s(d_j', c_i))$ is a normalization factor.

The final output for the classifier after all would be:

$$\Phi(d, c) = \sum_{s=1}^{S} \alpha_s \Phi_s(d, c) \tag{5}$$

3.2 Algorithm Analysis

The classifier based on Boosting algorithm mentioned above is in fact trying to find sensitive words in the text. For a given text d_k, it computes s rounds to get s sensitive words. Each sensitive word is responsible for its corresponding category c_j. These sensitive words are sometimes called a rough rule or weak hypotheses. And finally, the weak rules are combined into a single classification rule.

Weak Learner Selection. Formally, we denote a possible term in a text by w. Thus,

$$\Phi_s(d_j', c_i) = \begin{cases} c_{0i} & w_{kj} = 0 \\ c_{1i} & w_{kj} = 1 \end{cases} \tag{6}$$

Among them, c_{0i} and c_{1i} are real numbers.

Weighting Calculation. For each round, the weighting calculation has the form of $\Phi_s : D \times C \to IR$, among them D is the training collection, and C is the category set. The value $\Phi_s(d_j, c_i) > 0$ indicates text d_j belongs to C_i, otherwise not belongs to. The Absolute value $\left| \Phi_s(d_j, c_i) \right|$ represents its believe coefficient.

Still in each round, the newly generated weak learner Φ_s must be validated. The value $D_{s+1}(d_j', c_i)$ indicates whether $\Phi_1, \cdots, \Phi_s$ correctly associated d_j' with category C_i. And the value $D_{s+1}(d_j', c_i)$ is also uniformed in updating the weighting distribution $\langle d_j', C_i \rangle$.

For the parameter α_s, if it is positive, which means an error takes place in the categorization, because $C_j[c_i]$ and $\Phi_s(d_j', c_i)$ usually have opposite signs. Therefore, to the factor $\Phi_s(d_j', c_i)$, it will increase the weighting of the training pair $\langle d_j', C_i \rangle$, otherwise it will decrease its weighting.

Weak Rule Combination. For each $T_r = \{\langle d_1, C_1 \rangle, \cdots, \langle d_g, C_g \rangle\}$, we want to get the Φ_{best}^i by selecting Z_s the smallest. In this way, for a given t_k and its corresponding classification C_i, when $\alpha_s = 1$ and $c_{xi} = \dfrac{1}{2}\ln\left(\dfrac{W_1^{xik}}{W_{-1}^{xik}}\right)$, then we get Φ_{best}^i. Where,

$$W_b^{xik} = \sum_{j=1}^g D_t(d_j', c_i) \cdot \left\| w_{kj} = x \right\| \cdot \left\| C_j[c_i] = b \right\|$$

among them $b \in \{1, -1\}$, $x \in \{0, 1\}$, $i \in \{1, \ldots, m\}$, $k \in \{1, \ldots r\}$.

For its abstract value $\left\| \pi \right\|$, if π is true, then return 1, otherwise 0. In its implementation, we use $c_{xi} = \dfrac{1}{2}\ln\left(\dfrac{W_1^{xik} + \varepsilon}{W_{-1}^{xik} + \varepsilon}\right)$ in replacement of $c_{xi} = \dfrac{1}{2}\ln\left(\dfrac{W_1^{xik}}{W_{-1}^{xik}}\right)$, where $(\varepsilon = \dfrac{1}{mg})$.

In doing so, we get its final classifier as:

$$\Phi(d_k, c_j) = \sum_{s=1}^S \alpha_s \Phi_s(d_k, c_j) \tag{7}$$

4 Experiments and Results

Boosting method has been tested empirically by many researchers. For instance, Freund and Schapire [6] tested AdaBoost using C4.5 [9] as its weak learning algorithm. Schapire and Singer [10] also used boosting for text categorization. For their work, base classifiers were used to test on the presence or absence of a word or phrase. Our experiment is trying to use Boosting method for Chinese text categorization.

4.1 Test Corpora

Reuters-21578. The Reuters-21578 text categorization test collection was originally compiled by David Lewis [8]. Texts in this collection were collected from Reuter's Newswire in 1987. We used the modified Apte split [1] which contains 12902 texts, and 9603 for the training set, 3299 for the test set. All its texts belong to 90 categories.

In order to comparable with other recently works, we performed the following pre-processing prior to the experiments: All words were converted to lower case, punctuation marks were removed, and function words from a standard stop-list were removed.

People's Daily News. For the test of Chinese text categorization, we use the People's Daily News from TREC5 as our benchmark datasets. The texts in this corpus are all press news. All the texts are classified in advance by domain experts. And there are 40 categories and a total number of 3208 texts.

For the experimental purpose, we did two experiments. The closed test use all the texts as training set and also use the same data set as test set. The open test divided 3208 texts into 10 subsets randomly. One set was chosen as test set, while the rest of 9 sets as training set.

4.2 Chinese Segmentation

Many works have been done for linguistic preprocessing [2], [3], [4]. For the special characteristics in Chinese text, we apply Maximum Matching method (MM method) as a preprocessor for Chinese text segmentation. A self-defining special-purpose dictionary (having 49248 words) was also supplied.

The Maximum Matching method is a general purposed segmentation method based on word form information. Its purpose is to pick up the longest complex words in the text. That is to say: For every word in the text, we will try to find a phrase in the dictionary. According to its possible maximum length of that word in the dictionary, the MM method tries to find the longest character string of that word.

Its implementation could be simply described as follows:

First, we chose n Chinese characters in the present character bunches on the text as a startup. Try to find a match in the dictionary using binary searching. If this match succeeded, pick up this character string as a segment.

If the character string was not found in the dictionary, the last Chinese character of this string are removed, then dealing with the rest of the string again. By doing so, this algorithm finishes until finds out a segment that it is succeed in cutting a word or the length of bunch of surplus characters is zero.

Then we choose the word next to the matched segment as a new start to search repeatedly until the file is scanned over.

In practice, MM algorithm is inefficient for its matching operations. In dealing with this problem, we build an index for every first word in the dictionary as a plus. In doing so, we search this index first, if it is not among the index, we choose the one that most close to it, and then looking for the longest and totally matching entry within this index. There are two conditions that will stop this searching progress: (1) The character string is smaller than the largest length of matching to match the length at present; (2) The entry in the index is bigger than the character string. Then use it to the next entry of the segmentation.

4.3 Dimensionality Reduction

There are usually a lot of words r that only appears once in the corpus base C_o.

Therefore, the dimensionality is very high over its vector space after indexing of the corpus. This will bring out problems because complicated classification algorithms are unsuitable in dealing with such a large dimensionality. So we must apply some dimensionality reduction technologies to reduce its vector space dimension to $r' \ll r$.

Dimensionality reduction can also reduce the problem of over-fitting. Over-fitting means that the algorithm was absorbed in those randomly characteristics instead of those inevitable characteristics in the training text. Our experiments indicate that, for avoiding the over-fitting problem, the number of train samples may be proportional to the number of categories. That is to say that if we applied dimensionality reduction by using less train samples, the problem of over-fitting could be somewhat overcome.

The concept of dimensionality reduction usually was divided into two categories, the local and the global. The local dimensionality reduction is for a single category. In practice, for each category c_i, we generally choose its corresponding training text $10 \le r' \le 50$. For the global dimensionality reduction, it is meant to all categories, choose the term $r' \ll r$ that represents text d_j.

4.4 Boosting Algorithm Modification

Boosting is a method for generating committee of classifiers that are characterized by state-of-the-art effectiveness and a strong theoretical grounding in computational learning theory. In the method, the S classifiers that make up the committees are not trained in a conceptually parallel and independent way, as in other committee-based methods, but sequentially. In this way, when generating the i-th classifier the learner can take into account how the previously generated classifiers perform on the training documents, and can force the i-th classifier to concentrate on those training documents where the previously generated classifiers performed the worst.

What we used for each classifier is a one-level decision tree. It tests for the presence or absence of a term in a document, depending on whether a positive or negative classification decision is taken. The term on which this decision hinges is generally different for each of the S classifiers and is chosen each time, according to a complex error-minimization policy. The key step of this policy consists in scoring each term by a scoring function, and picking the term with the smallest score.

The scoring function is extremely complex, and computationally onerous. As this computation has to be performed for each of the terms and this has to be iterated S times, boosting is a computationally expensive method.

Therefore, we have made a minor modification to AdaBoost algorithm, based on the construction of a sub-committee of classifiers at its each iteration of the boosting process. Instead of using just the best term, as the standard AdaBoost algorithm does, we select the best K terms, and generate K classifiers, grouping them in a sub-committee. This is almost the same as AdaBoost.MH [10].

This idea comes from the observation that, in the first iteration the scores of the best terms are remarkably different from each other and from the worst ones, while in the last iteration, the differences among scores are very small. In AdaBoost.MH we choose, at each iteration, K top-ranked terms that would be good candidates for selection in the next K iterations. We can thus build a committee composed of S sub-committees at a computational cost comparable to that required by AdaBoost to build a committee of S classifiers. In fact, most of the computation required by the boosting process is devoted to calculating the term scores, and by using only the top-scoring term AdaBoost.MH exploits these hard-won scores only to a small extent.

4.5 Experimental Results

In Table1, it shows our experiments using different algorithms in English text categorization. This experiment uses Reuters-21578 as its corpus. And the Apte split was applied. Compared with most famous category algorithms such as Decision Trees (C4.5) [7], Decision rules (RIPPER), Neural Networks (NNET) and Supporting Vector Machine (SVMLIGH) [11], [12], the Boosting.MH algorithm is found to be the highest for the macro-breakeven point evaluation.

In Table2, for the Chinese text categorization, we still got the conclusion that the Boosting. MH algorithm is much better than the others. In the tests, we use the People's Daily News from TREC5 as its corpus. We did two round of tests in the experiments. One is for a closed test (results expressed in left half column in Table 2), and the other is for an open test (right half column in Table 2).

In a brief analysis of the results from Table2, we got the assumption that the ocular thought of kNN algorithm is to consider the incoming text to be affiliated with its nearest samples. The advantage of this algorithm is that it is easy to gain its base success. But it is easily been influenced by text noises and the selected parameter of K .

Table 1. Comparison of different algorithms used in English text categorization

Algorithms	Systems	Breakeven
Probabilistic	NB	0.795
Decision Trees	C4.5	0.794
Decision rules	RIPPER	0.820
Regression	LLSF	0.849
Batch Linear	ROCCHIO	0.776
Neural Networks	NNET	0.838
Example-based	GIS-W	0.860
SVM	SVMLIGH	0.859
AdaBoost.MH	AdaBoost.MH	0.876

Table 2. Different algorithms used in Chinese text categorization and also its comparison between closed and open test

Algorithm	Closed Test Precision	Closed Test Recall	Closed Test F1 Value	Open Test Precision	Open Test Recall	Open Test F1 Value
AdaBoost.MH	94.68	96.78	95.72	88.03	87.72	87.87
Simple Vector Distance	87.08	87.08	87.08	80.23	80.23	80.23
Baye's	82.39	83.78	83.08	76.17	77.26	76.71
kNN	89.11	91.42	90.25	83.29	85.12	84.20

For the Naive Bayesian categorization method, its basic principle is based on the Bayes' probability theory. Its parameter estimation largely depends on well-trained samples. And this algorithm is highly under the assumption that the features for each category are independent with each other. Therefore, this may give some explanations for its worst accuracy rate for the text categorization task.

Simple Vector Distance uses the concept of category centroid. Coming texts are classified into its nearest centroid. This may unsuitable with a large category system.

To our understanding, the key contribution for the success of AdaBoost.MH algorithm may counts for its T times iteration (we chose T equals to 10). Because the weightings for the error prone samples are increased in its next iteration, it makes the algorithm pay closer attention to these samples next time they encounter. Thus, making the AdaBoost.MH algorithm ultimately improvement of precision and efficiency.

5 Conclusions

We have implemented a text categorization system both for Chinese text and English text based on the Boosting algorithm. Test results show that, Boosting algorithm is suitable for the text categorization for English text as well as for Chinese text. And what's more is that: Compared with other Chinese text categorization algorithms that have published previously, our results are much better.

Of cause, more research works for the next step in the domain of text categorization still remains around the following three respects:

(1) Try to further improve Boosting algorithm by using different weak learners, in order to make the classifier to have higher capability in dealing with incidental texts.

(2) Change the thinking from word frequency based vector space to concepts based vector space. Study the methodology of feature selection under concepts, to see if these will help in text categorization.

(3) Make the dimensionality reduction more efficient over large corpus.

References

1. Apt'e, C., Damerau, F., Weiss, S. M.: Towards language independent automated learning of text categorization models. In Proceedings of the 17th Annual International ACM SIGIR Conference on Research and Development in Information Retrieval, (1994) 23–30
2. Biber D.: Using Register-Diversified Corpora for General Language Studies. Computational Linguistics, 19(2) (1993) 219-241
3. Brown P., Della P. V., DeSouza P., Lai J., Mercer R.: Class-Based n-gram Models of Natural Language. Computational Linguistics, 18(4) (1992) 567-480
4. Church K., Mercer R.: Introduction to the Special Issue on Computational Linguistics Using Large Corpora. Computational Linguistics, 19(1) (1993) 1-24
5. Fabrizio Sebastiani.: Machine Learning in Automated Text Categorization. Journal of the ACM, 34(1) (2002) 1-471
6. Freund Y. and Schapire R. E.: Experiments with a New Boosting Algorithm. In *Machine Learning: Proceedings of the Thirteenth International Conference*, pages 148–156, 1996.
7. Quinlan, J. R.: Bagging, Boosting, and C4.5. In Proceedings of the Thirteenth National Conference on Artificial Intelligence, (1996) 725–730
8. Lewis, D.: Representation and Learning in Information Retrieval. Tech. rep. (1992) 91-93, Computer Science Dept., University of Massachusetts at Amherst. PhD Thesis.
9. Schapire R. E., Singer Y.: Improved Boosting Algorithms Using Confidence-rated Predictions. Machine Learning, 37(3) (1999) 297-336
10. Schapire R. E., Singer Y.: BoosTexter: A Boosting-based System for Text Categorization. *Machine Learning*, 39(2/3) (2000) 135–168
11. Sebastiani F, Sperduti A, Valdambrini N.: An Improved Boosting Algorithm and its Application to Automated Text Categorization. In Proc. of CIKM-00, (2000) 78-85
12. Vladimir N. Vapnik.: The Nature of Statistical Learning Theory. Springer, (1995)

CatRelate: A New Hierarchical Document Category Integration Algorithm by Learning Category Relationships*

Shanfeng Zhu[1], Christopher C. Yang[2], and Wai Lam[2]

[1] Bioinformatics Center, Institute for Chemical Research, Kyoto University, Japan
zhusf@kuicr.kyoto-u.ac.jp
[2] Department of System Engineering and Engineering Management,
The Chinese University of Hong, Hong Kong
{yang, wlam}@se.cuhk.edu.hk

Abstract. We address the problem of integrating documents from a source catalog into a master catalog. Current technologies for solving the problem deem it as a flat category integration problem without considering the useful hierarchy information in the catalog, or deal with it hierarchically but without a rigorous model. In contrast, our method is based on correctly identifying relationships among categories, such as Match, Disjoint, SubConcept, SuperConcept, and Overlap, which come from the relations of sets in Set theory. Compared with traditional Match/NotMatch relationship in literature, our approach is more expressive in defining the relationship. The relationships among categories are first learned in a probabilistic way, and then refined by considering the hierarchy context. Our preliminary experiments show that it can help to correctly identify category relationships, and thus increase the accuracy of document integration.

1 Introduction

With the development of the WWW, the amount of information (such as documents, Web pages) increases dramatically. To organize them effectively, hierarchical categorization, classifying documents into a hierarchical category, is widely adopted, such as Yahoo! Directory, and Google directory. The rapid growth of Internet and E-commerce has spurred people and enterprize's interest on integrating information from different sources that are organized in their specific hierarchies. How to integrate documents organized in one taxonomy (source catalog) into documents that are organized according to another taxonomy (master catalog) efficiently and effectively becomes increasingly important.

---

* The work described in this paper was substantially supported by a grant from the Research grant Council of the Hong Kong Special Administrative Region, China (Project No: CUHK 4179/03E) and CUHK Strategic Grant (No: 4410001).

Z. Chen et al. (Eds.): ICADL 2004, LNCS 3334, pp. 280–289, 2004.

This problem was first proposed and studied by Agrawal and Srikant [1]. They squeezed the hierarchical structures of the catalogs into flat structures, and extended Naive Bayes approach to build more accurate classification models by using the similarity information implicit in the categorization of documents in the source catalog. Cheng and Wei subsequently explored the hierarchical structure of the source and master catalog for the integration without rigorous definition and algorithm [2]. To locate the merging target in the master catalog, the similarity between the source category and master category is examined based on the vector space model. If the similarity score is greater than a predefined threshold, the source category and master category will be conceived as two matching categories, otherwise they would be deemed as not matching. One obvious limitation is that similarity based measurement can hardly identify subtle relationship among categories, for example, one category subsumes another category.

In this paper, we give a formal definition of the problem by modeling the hierarchical structure of the catalog by tree and category by set of documents that could be classified into the category, as well as a new algorithm for the problem. This paper has the following major research contributions:

- Our algorithm discovers five types of relationships among categories in different catalogs: Match, Disjoint, SubConcept, SuperConcept and Overlap.
- Our algorithm also considers the discovered relationships of the neighboring categories in the hierarchy to which is referred as a hierarchy context.

2 Problem Statement

The problem of hierarchy category integration can be regarded as classifying the source documents in one hierarchical structure according to another master hierarchical catalog. If we assume that each category (document), except the uppermost one, belongs to only one parent category, it is natural to model this kind of hierarchical structure by tree. Furthermore, we can model each category as a set of document members, which stand for the concept of the category. In this paper, if there is no ambiguity, we will use category C to stand for both the category node C in the catalog tree and the set of documents that can be classified into this category.

Hierarchical Catalog. A document organization $DO(D, H, E)$ is a hierarchical catalog H on a certain domain D with a set of example documents E. With tree structure and set theory, it can be expressed by a tree T.

- (I). The Universal is all documents in the D (maybe infinite), and each document is an individual member of the Universal.
- (II). There are two sets of nodes in Tree T, $CN(T)$ (category nodes) that are internal nodes of the tree, and $DN(T)$ (document nodes) that are leaf nodes of the tree. Each category in original catalog corresponds to an internal node in the Tree T, and each example document in E corresponds to a leaf node in the Tree T. We also call the category nodes, which only have children of document nodes, as leaf category nodes, and denote the set of leaf category nodes as $LCN(T)$.

- (III). Given two category nodes $A, B \in CN(T)$, if $A = Parent(B)$ then $B \subset A$. Given one category node B and one document node d, if $B = Parent(d)$, then $d \in B$.
- (IV). Mutual exclusive constraint: Given three category nodes $A, B, C \in CN(T)$, if $A = Parent(B) \wedge A = Parent(C)$, then $B \cap C = \phi$.
- (V). Exhaustive constraint: Given category node A and all its children category nodes $A_1, A_2, ..., A_k$, $A = \bigcup_{i=1}^{k} A_i$.

With above definition, we can easily get following characteristics.

Lemma 2.1 *If* $A, B \in CN(T)$ *then* $B \in descendant(A) \longleftrightarrow B \subset A$.

Lemma 2.2 *If* $A, B \in CN(T)$ *then* $(B \subset A) \vee (A \subset B) \vee (A \cap B = \phi) = TRUE$.

Catalog Integration. Given another document organization $DO'(D', H', E')$, which organizes another set of documents E' in Domain D' with respect to hierarchical structure H', we can also construct a Tree T' for DO'. Our problem is how to integrate documents E' into $DO(D, H, E)$. In order to integrate documents in E' to DO, D' should be homogenous, or at least comparable to D. To simplify the problem, we don't modify the structure of the master catalog during integration. With DO and DO', we can obtain two corresponding trees, T and T'. If we choose one category node from each tree, e.g. A from tree T and B from tree T', the relations between these two nodes (categories) can be classified as follows:

- **Match** $\forall d \in (D' \cap D), d \in A \longleftrightarrow d \in B$. We denote it as $Match(A, B)$.
- **Disjoint** $\forall d \in (D' \cap D), (d \in A) \wedge (d \in B) = FALSE$. We denote it as $Disjoint(A, B)$.
- **SubConcept / SuperConcept** Here we assume concept A is subsumed by concept B. Then, $\forall d \in (D' \cap D), d \in A \longrightarrow d \in B$. We denote it as $SubConcept(A, B)$ or $SuperConcept(B, A)$.
- **Overlap** $\exists d \in (D' \cap D), (d \in A) \wedge (d \in B) = TRUE$. We denote it as $Overlap(A, B)$. In this paper, Overlap relationship doesn't include those special cases, such as Match and SubConcept(SuperConcept).

3   CatRelate Algorithm

Exploiting the hierarchical structure of catalog can improve the effectiveness of the integration. For example, suppose we want to integrate the document leaf nodes of Tree T' into Tree T, if one intermediate category node S_a in T' matches one category node M_b in T, then all document leaves, which are children of S_a in T', should be merged into the categories, which are children of M_b in T, without need of considering other category nodes. It could be explained in the following lemmas that can be easily proofed in our models.

Lemma 3.1 *Given* $S_a \in CN(T')$ *and* $M_b \in CN(T)$, *if* $Match(S_a, M_b)$ *then* $\forall d \in (D' \cap D), d \in S_a \longrightarrow d \in M_b$.

Lemma 3.2 *Given* $S_a \in CN(T')$ *and* $M_b \in CN(T)$, *if* $Disjo int(S_a, M_b)$ *then* $\forall d \in (D' \cap D), d \in S_a \longrightarrow d \notin M_b$.

Correctly identifying category relationship is the basis of our integration algorithm. In this paper, we call our algorithm CatRelate.

3.1 Learning Category Relationship

Overview
Since we represent each category by the set of documents that can be classified into this category, the relationship between two categories is analogous to the relationship between two sets, which can be inferred from two probability values $P(A|B)$ and $P(B|A)$. Note that $P(A|B)$ means $P(d \in A | d \in B)$, that is, randomly selecting a document d from category B, the probability of d that can be also classified into category A. If we have the prior knowledge of all the documents that belong to A and B, then $P(A|B) = P(A \cap B)/P(A) = |A \cap B|/|A|$. We denote $P(B|A)$ as p_a and $P(A|B)$ as p_b . In ideal case, if $p_a = p_b = 1$, we know that $Match(A, B)$, and if $p_a = p_b = 0$, then $Disjo int(A, B)$. As there exist classification errors in practice, we determine α_{high} and α_{low} for relationship identification.

- **Match** $Match(A, B)$ iff $p_a \geq \alpha_{high} \wedge p_b \geq \alpha_{high}$
- **Disjoint** $Disjo int(A, B)$ iff $p_a \leq \alpha_{low} \wedge p_b \leq \alpha_{low}$
- **SubConcept / SuperConcept** $SubConcept(A, B)$ iff $p_a \geq \alpha_{high} \wedge p_b \leq \alpha_{high}$
- **Overlap** $Overlap(A, B)$ iff $\alpha_{low} < p_a < \alpha_{high} \wedge 0 < p_b < \alpha_{high}$ or $\alpha_{low} < p_b < \alpha_{high} \wedge 0 < p_a < \alpha_{high}$

Probability Estimator
Here we illustrate the method of estimating the probability with the example of $P(A|B)$, where A is a category in the master catalog M and B is a category in the source catalog S. As proposed in [3], we could select documents from both two domains to smooth the parameters, and reduce the bias caused by sampling documents from only one domain. We denote $N(U_S^B)$ as the number of documents selected in the source catalog S that belong to category B, and $N(U_S^{A,B})$ as the number of documents selected in the source catalog S that can be classified into both A and B, $N(U_M^B)$ as the number of documents selected in master catalog M that are

predicted into category B, and $N(U_M^{A,B})$ as the number of documents selected in master catalog M that can be classified into both A and B. Then,

$$P(A|B)=(N(U_M^{A,B})+N(U_S^{A,B}))/(N(U_M^B)+N(U_S^B))$$

To estimate the values of $P(A|B)$ and $P(B|A)$, we need to train binary classifiers for both category A and category B. For instance, to train a binary classifier for B, all documents that belong to category B in source catalog S are trained as positive instances, and all other documents in S are trained as negative instances.

3.2 Locating Related Master Categories for Each Source Category

With above techniques, we can learn the relationship between any two category nodes, respectively in the master and the source catalog. By exploring the hierarchical structure of catalogs according to top-down and breadth-first strategy, we don't need to compare all category pairs to integrate documents in the source catalog into the master catalog. That is, the nodes in the source catalog will be explored according to breadth-first order from top to bottom. At the same time, for a given category node in the source catalog, we will find its most relevant category nodes in the master catalog from top to bottom. For each category node in the source catalog, its most relevant category nodes in the master catalog and corresponding relationship will be stored into a table LR.

The first node in T' to explore is the root of T'. Assume the node in T' that waits for processing is S_a.

Step 1, Finding the Starting Points in T.
We first scan the table LR to see whether its relevant category nodes has already been found and recorded. If the answer is YES, then proceed to Step 3.

If S_a is the root of T', then the starting point is the root of T. Proceed to Step 2.

If S_p is the parent of S_a in T', then we obtain the relevant category nodes of S_p in master catalog T by scanning table LR, which have several possible cases:

- $Match(S_p, M_q)$ Then the starting points in the master catalog for S_a include all category children of M_q.

- $SubConcept\ (S_p, M_q)$ M_q must be a leaf category node, otherwise the relationship between S_p with some children of M_q will be stored in the table LR instead of $SubConcept\ (S_p, M_q)$. Under this situation, all descendants of S_p are subconcept of M_q. We add these relationships into LR. Proceed to Step 3.

- $\exists M_1,..., M_k \in T, SuperConcept(S_p, M_i)$ where $(1 \le i \le k)$ and $\exists O_1,..., O_m \in T$,
  $Overlap(S_p, O_j)$ where $(1 \le j \le m)$ and $depth(M_i) = depth(O_j) = h$
  $\forall X \in T, SuperConcept(S_p, X) \longrightarrow depth(X) \ge h$ and
  $\forall X \in T, SuperConcept(S_p, X) \longrightarrow depth(X) \ge h$

In this case, the set of starting points for S_a include the overlap nodes $O_1,...,O_m$ and other related nodes $M_1,...,M_k$.

- $Disjoint(S_p,T)$ It means all nodes in T disjoint with S_p, then all the descendants of S_p disjoint with T. We add these relationships into LR, and proceed to step 3.

Step 2, Exploring Process.
In step 1, we obtain the starting point or a set of starting points in T for S_a. Then for each one of these start points, e.g. M_b, we begin to search most relevant category nodes in T for S_a by comparing the M_b with S_a.

- $Match(S_a,M_b)$ Then add it into LR, and proceed to step 3. Here we treat it specially if M_b is a leaf category node. Under this, $\forall S_d$, if $Descendant(S_d,S_a)$, we will add $SubConcept$ (S_d,M_b) into LR.
- $Disjoint(S_a,M_b)$ if there is no more starting points for S_a, then add $Disjoint(S_a,T)$ into LR, and $\forall S_d$, if $Descendant(S_d,S_a)$, we add $Disjoint(S_d,T)$ into LR. Otherwise fetch next starting point for further exploring.
- $Overlap(S_a,M_b)$ Then add it into LR. If there are other starting points, then fetch it for further processing. After processing all of them, proceed to Step 3.
- $SubConcept$ (S_a,M_b) Then empty the starting point set, add all the children of M_b into starting point set, repeat Step 2. Here we treat it specially if M_b is a leaf category node. Under this case, in addition to adding $SubConcept(S_a,M_b)$ into LR, $\forall S_d$, if $Descendant(S_d,S_a)$, we will add $SubConcept(S_d,M_b)$ into LR.
- $SuperConcept(S_a,M_b)$ then add it into LR. If there exist other starting points, then fetch them for further processing. This is because that there may exist several nodes overlap/subconcept with S_a.

Step 3, Fetching the Next Node of Tree T' According to Breadth First Strategy.
Then we repeat Step 1 and Step 2, until we traverse all category nodes of T'.

3.3   Merging the Documents

For each leaf category node S_f in Tree T', we scan the table to get its most relevant category nodes in the master catalog, which have several possible cases.

- $Match$ (S_f,M_f) If M_f is also a leaf category node in T, then the documents in S_f should be merged into category M_f in the master catalog. If M_f is not a leaf category node in T, then the documents in S_f should be classified into leaf categories, which are descendants of M_f in T.
- $SubConcept$ (S_f,M_f) In this case, M_f must be a leaf category in T. Then the documents in S_f should be merged into category M_f in the master catalog.

- *SuperConce* $pt(S_f, M_f)(1 \le i \le k) \wedge$ *Overlap* $(S_f, O_j)(1 \le j \le m)$

We know that these nodes locate in same depth of Tree T. If they are leaf category nodes, the documents in S_f should be classified into these categories. If they are not leaf category nodes, all the leaf category nodes that are descendants of M_i, O_j in T will be fetched for further comparison with S_f. Finally we can obtain a set of leaf category nodes in the master catalog that are related to S_f. Then we can train a classifier over these categories to classify documents in S_f into most suitable categories in the master catalog.

- *Disjo*int(S_f, T) The documents in S_f don't belong to the master catalog.

4 Considering Hierarchy Context

Correctly identifying category relationship is the basis of CatRelate algorithm. In last section, we present a probabilistic estimator to learn the relationship between two categories. If we don't have enough example documents in the categories, or some document instances are misplaced into the category, the relationship we learned may be not correct, and need further refinement. Here we focus on discovering category relationship by considering hierarchy context. We illustrate it using the example of identifying relationship of category A in the source catalog and category B in the master catalog. We need to determine a threshold value $\alpha_{context}$ that is slightly smaller than α_{high}. If A and B don't match each other, but satisfy $p_a > \alpha_{context} \wedge p_b > \alpha_{context}$, we can check the hierarchy context of A and B to see whether they satisfy following rules (as shown in Figure 1). If they satisfy one of following rules, we will relabel the relationship as *Match*.

- *Rule 1: Node A also matches node B if their children match.*

A has three children $A1$, $A2$, $A3$, and B also has three children $B1$, $B2$, $B3$. If we know that $Match(A1, B1)$, $Match(A2, B2)$ and $Match(A3, B3)$, we can easily get $Match(A, B)$. It could be relaxed into $x\%$ of children matching in practice.

- *Rule 2: Node A matches node B if their leaf category descendants match.*

A has six leaf category descendants A11, A12, A21, A22, A31 and A32, and B has six leaf category descendants B11, B12, B13, B21, B22 and B23. If we know that $Match(A11, B11)$ $Match(A12, B12)$ $Match(A21, B13)$ $Match(A22, B21)$, $Match(A31, B22)$ and $Match(A32, B23)$, we can easily get $Match(A, B)$. The condition could also be relaxed into $x\%$ of descendants matching in practice.

- *Rule 3: Node A matches node B if their parents and siblings match.*

M is the parent of A, C and E, and N is the parent of B, D and F. If we know that $Match(M, N)$, $Match(C, D)$ and $Match(E, F)$, we can easily get $Match(A, B)$. It could also be relaxed into $x\%$ of siblings matching in practice.

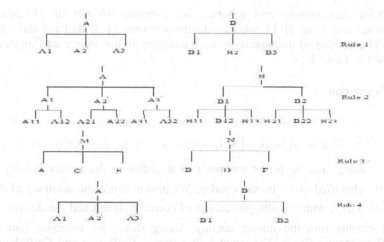

Fig. 1. Example Refining Rules for Match Relationship between *A* and *B*

– *Rule 4: Node A matches node B if the children of node B are all subconcept of node A, and the children of node A are all subconcept of node B.*

A is the parent of *A1,A2* and *A3*, and *B* is the parent of *B1* and *B2*. If we know that *SubConcept(A1,B)*, *SubConcept(A2,B)*, *SubConcept(A3,B)*, *SubConcept(B1,A)* and *SubConcept(B2,A)*, we can easily get *Match(A,B)*.

5 Experiments Results

5.1 Document Corpus and Catalog Structure

We used the same document corpus and catalog structure that were used in [2] by Cheng and Wei*. There are 384 scientific research articles collected from CiteSeer Scientific digital library (http://citeseer.nj.nec.com). These articles belong to nine leaf categories, namely, Data Mining, Robotics, Network Protocol, Wireless, EC, Security, XML, IR and Data Compression. Moreover, two intermediate categories are formed by some leaf categories. Intermediate category AI has two children, namely, Data Mining and Robotics. The category network also has two children, namely, Network Protocol and Wireless. In the experiment, we keep the structure of the document corpus as the structure of the master catalog, and establish a source catalog that differs with the master catalog only in the children categories of AI and Network. For example, in contrast to the master catalog, AI category in the source catalog has two different children categories, namely, AI_1 and AI_2, which are formed by combining documents from both data mining and robotics in the corpus. Half of documents in the original corpus are randomly selected and kept in the master catalog, and the other half are put into the source catalog. For example, AI in the source catalog consists of 31 data mining documents and 14 robotics documents that are, respectively, half of all data mining documents and robotics documents in original corpus. Since we have AI_1 and AI_2 categories as the children of AI

---

* Special thanks to Prof. Cheng and Prof. Wei for providing the dataset.

instead of data mining and robotics, we combine 16 out of 31 data mining documents and 7 out of 14 robotics documents into AI_1, and put the others into AI_2. The number of documents in each category in the source and master catalog is shown in Table 1.

5.2 Evaluation

We propose a criterion A_c to measure the accuracy of discovered category relationship. That is, $A_c = m_c / |S_c|$, where $|S_c|$ is the number of categories in the source catalog, and m_c is the number of categories in the source catalog that are correctly identified in the master catalog. We also evaluate the accuracy of document integration A_d, which is the percentage of correctly integrated documents from the source catalog into the master catalog. Using them, we compare four different algorithms, Naive Bayes, Enhanced Naive Bayes, CatRelate and CatRelate(without hierarchy context).

5.3 Experiment Results

To reduce the bias, we run the experiment 100 times. Each time half of documents in the corpus have been randomly selected and put into the master catalog, and the others are put into the source catalog. We first compare CatRelate with and without considering the hierarchy context on the accuracy of discovering category relationship. The result is given in the Table 1. In the experiment, we set α_{high}=0.8 and α_{low} =0.05 for CatRelate (without hierarchy context) algorithm, and $\alpha_{context}$=0.7 for CatRelate (with hierarchy context) algorithm. The rule 3 of considering hierarchical context discussed in section 4 is used in our experiment. That is, A match B if their parents match and no less than 50% of their siblings match. Without considering the hierarchy context, the average accuracy of category relationship discovering A_c out of all 100 experiments is 60.45%, while it improves to 71.09% by considering the hierarchy context. Among Match category node pairs, three of them (AI, Network and XML) can be correctly identified in most cases, and the other four (EC, IR, Security and Compression) are often wrongly identified. The average size of three often correctly identified Match categories is 36.67, and the average size of four often wrongly identified Match categories is 20.75. For the category without sufficient document instances, considering hierarchal context can greatly improve the accuracy of category relationship discovering. For example, the times of correctly identifying match relationship for category EC out of 100 experiments is improved from 24 to 78 by considering the hierarchical context. Furthermore, we compare all four different algorithms on the accuracy of document integration. We find that in this experiment CatRelate has the best performance with accuracy 89.47%, then followed by CatRelate without considering the hierarchy context (85.35%), Enhanced Naive Bayes (81.71%), and Naive Bayes(79.85%).

5.4 Discussion

First we can see that CatRelate (without considering hierarchy context) method outperforms Enhanced Naïve Bayes method and Naive Bayes method. We think this is because CatRelate (without considering hierarchy context) method can effectively identify related master categories for the source category to integrate documents, without the need of considering all master categories, which may increase the errors of classification. Second, with insufficient example documents, we may not correctly discover category relationships, which will reduce the accuracy of document integration. Third, when some categories do not have enough example documents, we can consider hierarchy context to increase the accuracy of category mapping, and thus increase the accuracy of document integration.

Table 1. The accuracy of category relationship discovery by CatRelate with and without considering the hierarchy context of 100 experiments

Source node (size)	Related Nodes in Master node(size)	Correct relationship found by CatRelate without considering the hierarchy context (times out of 100)	Correct relationship found by CatRelate with considering the hierarchy context (times out of 100)
AI(45)	AI (45)	Match (94)	Match (100)
Network(39)	Network(40)	Match (83)	Match (100)
EC(16)	EC(16)	Match (24)	Match (78)
Security(30)	Security(30)	Match (0)	Match (16)
XML(25)	XML(25)	Match (98)	Match (100)
IR(22)	IR(23)	Match (0)	Match (0)
Compression(14)	Compression(14)	Match (1)	Match (23)
AI_1(23)	Data Mining (31) Robotics (14)	Overlap (100)	Overlap (100)
AI_2(22)	Data Mining (31) Robotics (14)	Overlap (100)	Overlap (100)
Net_1(20)	Network Protocol(9) Wireless(31)	Overlap (86)	Overlap (86)
Net_2(19)	Network Protocol(9) Wireless(31)	Overlap (79)	Overlap (79)

References

1. R. Agrawal, R. Srikant. On Integrating Catalogs. Proceedings of WWW10 Conference, May 1-5, 2001, Hong Kong, pp 603-612
2. T. H. Cheng, C. Wei. Integration of Document-category Hierarchies: A Clustering-based Approach. Web 2003 (The Second Workshop on e-Business), December 13-14, 2003, Seattle, Washington, USA
3. A. Doan, J. Madhavan, R. Dhamankar, P. Domingos, A. Halevy. Learning to match ontologies on the semantic Web. The VLDB Journal (2003) 12: 303-319

Constrains in Building Domain-Specific Topic Maps for the Discipline "Gender Studies in Informatics (GSI)"

M. Suriya[1], R. Nagarajan[2], R. Sathish Babu[2], and V. Kumaresan[2]

[1] Prof. & Head & Librarian, Dept. of Library & Information Science,
Annamalai University, Annamalainagar –608 002, India
au_surya@hotmail.com
[2] Programmer, University Central Library, Annamalai University,
Annamalainagar – 608 002, India

1 Introduction

The 21st century has witnessed an overwhelming research output on GSI but due to publication scattering and want of organized database, the outcome of these publications have not been visible to the policy makers and gender scientists. Further, the traditional document management system put a heavy burden on the user in the process of information access, extraction and interpretation. Besides, the absence of domain-specific semantic index in the discipline GSI results in irrelevant retrieval of records resulting in high recall but low precision. In addition, the existing system makes the process of literature-search difficult and time consuming. The exponential growth of literature, the information overload, and the time wasted in searching and browsing in the field of GSI demanded a semantic information processing system. This situation calls for the development of Knowledge Management System (KMS) in GSI by building dynamic (i) knowledge repositories, (ii) semantic index and (iii) knowledge maps and thereby alleviates the problems encountered by the user in the traditional document management system.

2 Need for Knowledge Management System in GSI

The gender problem received wider attention in the field of informatics across the globe in the recent years. While discussions about these gender issues are useful, there is no effort to consolidate these deliberations in an organized form. Similarly, research on GSI is gaining momentum in the last two decades but there is no knowledge management system (KMS) or subject portals in this area. Therefore an attempt has been made in the direction of constructing a KMS on a sample database in the field of GSI. It further attempts to identify the modalities for organizing knowledge in GSI, despite the fact that there is an absence of supporting tools like the semantic index or subject thesaurus in this field. It further identifies the appropriate tools and techniques to standardize the unstructured and complex data in order to represent the knowledge in an accurate and precise manner without time consumption. Attempts have also been made to capture the intellectual structure of the domain through concept maps/topic maps.

Z. Chen et al. (Eds.): ICADL 2004, LNCS 3334, pp. 290–299, 2004.

3 Focus of the Study

1. The focus of study is to trace the evolution of the research literature on GSI since the conceptual contours and their evolution in the discipline GSI is lacking. A large number of publications from 1983-2003 are analyzed to determine themes and trends in GSI.
2. The study also aims at creating different knowledge maps consisting of different types of objects like keywords, institutions and authors.
3. It further aims at designing efficient information retrieval tools in GSI using co-occurrence analysis.

4 Backgrounds and Previous Work

Creation of knowledge database like CiteSeer Citation index that provides access to over 300,000 articles is a pre-requisite to promote research in GSI. Automatic indexing and categorization of publication have become an integral part of establishing knowledge repositories in the recent years. The propagation of digital libraries has fuelled much work in the area of automatic categorization and meta-data extraction.. Topic maps for repositories and for knowledge organisation have been the trend in the last decade, which is a step forward in the area of KMS. It is interesting to note that the application of co-occurrences of the word have become a common phenomena in the area of concepts categorization and formation of semantic maps. The technique of co-word analysis also has been used for building thematic maps in the last years Callon 86, Callon91, Courtial 89, Law 92, and Whitaker 89. Based on these review of literature, the following research questions were generated pertained to the present study: (i) How to define organize knowledge structures in GSI in a principled way?; (ii) how to deal with the heterogeneous subject data in GSI? ; Which semantic relation types should we use and standardize in organizing the dataset in GSI? How to construct the knowledge maps and what could be inferred from the maps.

5 Methodology

Topic map creation is a multi-stage modularized process and the following steps are followed in designing the topic maps for GSI. They are (i) extraction of concepts from the keywords (ii) fixing their semantic relations and (iii) creation of topic maps. A concept, in its most generic sense, can be any "thing" whatsoever- a person, an entity, really anything-regardless of whether it exists or has an other specific characteristics, about which anything whatsoever may be asserted by any means whatsoever. (H.H. Rath). Concept extractions are carried out by means of text mining. The process involved in the text mining are (a) segmentation; (b) phrase detection; (c) calculation of collocations and (d) integration of external knowledge. This process is carried out for all word types in the corpus. Semantic relation refers to the 'collocation of words' or the 'concept association between two words' and it is computed by joint occurrence of two given words A and B within a context. Creation of topic maps involves (i) formation of co-occurrence matrix (ii) cluster formation and (iii) creation of maps. The following diagram represents the flow of activities in the formation of the topic maps.

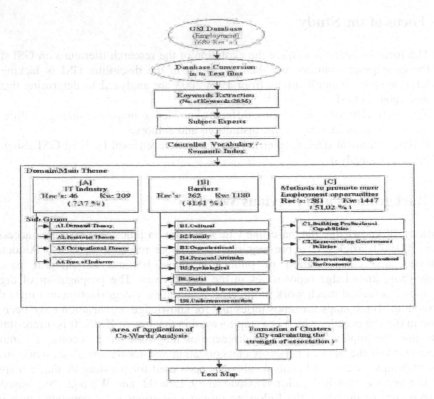

Fig. 1. Activities involved in building Topic Maps using Lexi maps & JCP techniques

5.1 Concept Extraction by Means of Keyword Analysis

For the purpose of the present study, about 689 documents dealing with the subject GSI were selected. The main concepts of these documents are identified by means text mining. Text mining, also known as document information mining, text data mining, or knowledge discovery in textual database is an apt technology for analyzing large domains of unstructured data in order to extract relevant patterns or knowledge. Here, the text mining tools like TexNet32 and Site Content Analyzer were applied on the GSI database to get the relevant words. These tools extract the words, word-phrases and context-relevant passages representing the contents of the publications by adopting the stemming procedure based on the context sensitive longest-match principle and a phrase recognition algorithm, The extracted word lists were standardized by involving the domain-experts. Due to the non-availability of subject thesaurus in the discipline GSI, the experts attempted to build a macro-thesaurus by collating the unique, unambiguous and concept-related words out of the pool of words. The homonyms were disambiguated and the synonyms were hooked to one hub term as the preferred term. The filtered keywords were organized into a database with their appropriate broader terms, narrower terms and associative terms. Once extracted, the words are standardized and stored in a database (thesaurus) in order to be queried, data mined, summarized in natural language.

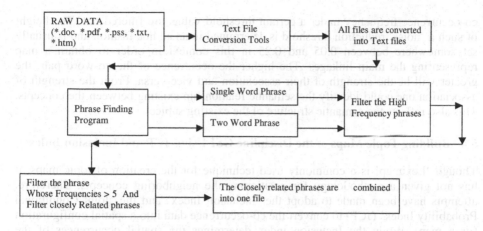

Fig. 2. Methods Used For Extraction of Keywords from the Textual Corpus on GSI

5.2 Co-occurrence of Semantically Related Concepts

Since single concept does not convey meaningful connotations of a topic, associations of semantically related concepts are identified to form the domains and sub-domains of the subject GSI. The Salton 's co-occurrence procedure is adopted to compute the cohesion between pairs of concepts in the given database and the results are presented in the co-occurrence matrix. Here, co-words are constructed by identifying the linkages or strength among the important concepts (keywords). The frequencies of the co-occurrences of concepts are ranked to form a matrix of co-word pairs. In this context, the occurrences of single concept in the whole sample were not taken into consideration for the formation of co-word matrix in order to avoid the spurious linkages. In the co-occurrence matrix, each cell in this symmetric matrix represents the number of times two concepts co-occur together (Cij). This method is followed by the 'co word clustering method' and its purpose is to create groups or clusters of associated keywords (co-words) as a means to trace the numbers of research topics in the GSI database.

5.3 Building Lexi-Maps Based on Co-occurrence Matrix

To understand the nature of relationship among the co-occurrence of concepts, lexi-map technique is adopted. In this method, each concept is considered as a node connected by the relation of co-occurrence to another node. Co-occurrences are the ties or the links. The lexi-map is formed out of the co-occurrence matrix. The strength of the linkage 'S' of the co-occurrences are measured by using the formula: $S(Ci,Cj, Cij) = Cij*Cij / CiCj$ $0 \leq S \leq 1$ Where 'Cij' is the number of co-occurrence of concepts i and j. Here, the occurrence of a single concept i within a set of publications is denoted as Ci. 2. The higher (1) or the lower (0) strength of the co-occurrence is determined by the number of times a co-word pair occurs together in a given document or in a database of a specific subject. As the strength of the co-occurrence ranges between 0 and 1, it is necessary to fix certain thresholds in order to filter the 'uninteresting co-occurrences'. This implies that the 'co-word pairs' with a co-occurrence frequency under a certain threshold value, are filtered out. The height of such a 'noise' reduction threshold is determined in an ad hoc fashion and is usually set somewhere between 0.05 and 0.25 in this context in order to obtain a map representing the main linkages .The higher the occurrence of the co-word pair, the greater will be the strength of their association and vice-versa. From the strength of association one could identify the semantic relationship existing between the concepts. This also reflects the semantic structure of the existing subject.

5.4   Building Topic Maps of the Discipline GSI Using JCP and Inclusion Index

Though 'Leximap' is a commonly used technique for the creation of topic maps, it has not given a methodology for positioning the neighboring concepts. Therefore, attempts have been made to adopt the 'Inclusion Index' and the 'Joint Conditional Probability Index' (JCP) to convert the co-occurrence data into a spatial configuration (or a map). While the Inclusion index determines the spatial occurrences of the concepts (distance) on the Topic maps, the JCP determines their strength of relations. Inclusion Index (I) is computed by using formula: $(C_{ij}/min(C_i, C_j))$ where C_{ij} is the count of all records in which the two concepts co-occur, and C_i and (C_j) are respectively counts of all records indexed. The degree of relatedness may vary between 0 to 1 where '0' indicates the state of no-co-occurrence; and '1' complete co-occurrence. The identification of relevant or master keywords can be fixed by setting a threshold value (≥ 5 occurrences). Only those nodes that have "I" values between 0.25 and above are taken for analysis. The distances on the map, in this study are not an indication of the intensity of relationships. The strength of inclusion between concepts is determined by their co-occurrences. In this context, Joint Conditional Probability is used to measure the strength of relationship between a given pair of entities. The JCP of the co-occurrences of the concepts in a GSI database is calculated using the formula: $((C_{ij} / C_i) + C_{ij} /C_j)) /2$ where C_{ij} is the count of all records in which two concepts co-occur, and C_i (C_j) are the count of all records indexed . The JCP is 0 when the two concepts are never assigned to the same record, and approaches 1 as a joint assignment of that two concepts increase proportionately in comparison of that frequency of assignment in the database as a whole. The higher the JCP values, the stronger the links between the concepts. While the spatial distribution of the nodes are determined by the inclusion index, their strength of relations are fixed by the JCP index. It is the links between the concepts that are of interest, rather than the spatial arrangement; thus the structure of GSI has been arranged keeping in mind the better graphic display of the links.

6   Analysis and Interpretation

6.1   Details of the Database Selected for the Present Study

The publication trend of the discipline 'Gender Studies in Informatics' has gained a momentum in the recent years. These publications have deliberated on a wide variety of topics viz. (i) gender situation in the IT labour market i.e. in the software, hardware, telecom, IT-enabled and business processing sectors; (ii) gender related barriers prevailing in the IT related industries; (iii) and the strategies to maintain gender equity in the field of informatics etc. Parallel to the growth of publications on this discipline, there is a corresponding demand for literature on this area of research. This situation has demanded data consolidation and topic map generation to meet the user requirements. For the purpose of this study a sample database of 689 records covering 2836 keywords have been selected . Topic map techniques were applied on this basic data.

6.2 Outline of the Semantic Structure of the Discipline GSI

The 'knowledge management system (KMS) ' of the discipline 'Gender Studies in Informatics' is built on three major inter-related activities viz: (i) building a dynamic knowledge repository; (ii) developing a comprehensive and interactive semantic index or thesaurus and (iii) creating a knowledge or topic maps. The 'knowledge repository' component of the KMS involves in acquiring domain-specific knowledge in diverse forms (xml, html, doc, ps., etc) from heterogeneous sources like WWW, Journals, Conference Proceedings, Reports and Projects. The 'semantic index' component of the KMS involves in organizing the heterogeneous knowledge on the basis of their epistemological and ontological structures. Such kind of organization results in dichotomous division of knowledge as 'conceptual model' and the 'representation paradigms' of the domain GSI. The following diagram explains the semantic structure of the discipline GSI. It is obtained by means of 'keyword extraction technique' and 'clustering technique' as suggested in the methodology part of this paper. It explains the organizational structure of the discipline GSI and enumerates the entities that form the domains, sub-domains, and facets.

6.3 Co-occurrence Matrix

It is noticed that themes or topics are formed not by a single concept represented through a keyword but through a collection or combination of concepts (keywords) . S. R. Ranganathan in his theory of 'Knowledge organization' has discussed the various modes through which words would combined together and generate a new themes or topics. In this study, the co-word method is adopted to trace the formation of new themes. Table 3 depicts the number of times each concept (i) co-occurs with another concept (j) in the database taken for analysis. The cell value in the co-occurrence matrix represents the co-word pairs (Cij) selected for the current study. For instance, the theme 'C3' in Table-3 co-occurs with theme 'B3' 143 times & with 'C1' 172 times within a database of 689 documents having 2836 descriptors or keywords. In the same manner the concept 'B3' co-occurs with concepts 'A1 & C1' 18 times and 110 times respectively. Similar is the case with concept 'A'. There is a closer correlation between the co-occurrence of the keywords and the formation of new themes. The more the co-occurrences of the keywords the higher will be the emergence of new themes in any given subject. Though co-occurrence of themes is a meaningful measure to identify the cohesion existing between two thematic groups, it will not show the type and intensity of the relationship between the thematic pairs. In other words, it is observed that absolute frequencies of co-occurrences are a biased measure, which is otherwise known as "scale effect" in the raw co-occurrence data and therefore a further analysis like leximap techniques are applied on the co-occurrence data to identify the specific relations between the nodes. The procedure used for the computation of the leximap is given below:

(i) Compute pairwise co-occurrence for high-frequency words.

(ii) If this co-occurrence is lower than a threshold, then do not consider the pair any further.

(iii) For pairs that qualify, compute the cohesion value.

$$\text{Cohesion}(Ci, Cj) = \text{co-occurrence-frequency}/(\text{sqrt}(\text{frequency}(Ci)*\text{frequency}(Cj))) \tag{1}$$

6.4 Leximap-Table Indicating the Strength of Relationship Between the Thematic Groups in GSI

Leximap table is based on the co-word pairs given in the co-word matrix (Table 7.3). The 15 thematic groups or sub-domains derived out of the 2836 keywords representing the concepts in the GSI database have formed a 15 X 15 matrix. Out of the 105 possible co-occurrences of themes formed from the above matrix, only 27 thematic pairs were chosen based on the threshold value prescribed (maximum>=5 co-occurences). Here, the words representing each theme is considered as a node and the combination of these nodes with other nodes is measured by their strength value. Based on the calculated strength value (S), the type of relation existing between the thematic pairs viz: high, medium and low is determined. The following table illustrates the type of relationship exists between the co-word pairs.

Table 1. Co-Word Pairs Showing the Strength of Relationship Between the Thematic Groups in GSI

Ord.	Node-i (ci)	Node-ti(cj)	Co-oc(cij)	Strength(s)	Range
1	Building Professional Capabilities(C1)[291]	Restructuring the Organisational Environment(C3)[105]	172	0.2718	High
2	Organisational Barriers(B3)[232]	Restructuring the Organisational Environment(C3)[105]	143	0.2357	High
3	Organisational Barriers(B3)[232]	Building Professional Capabilities(C1)[291]	110	0.1792	High
4	Reconstructing Government policies(C2)[172]	Restructuring the Organisational Environment(C3)[105]	105	0.1714	High
5	Organisational Barriers(B3)[232]	Underrepresentation(B8)[170]	81	0.1664	High
6	Underrepresentation(B8)[170]	Restructuring the Organisational Environment(C3)[105]	99	0.1542	High
7	Technical Incompetency(B7)[142]	Restructuring the Organisational Environment(C3)[105]	38	0.1393	High
8	Underrepresentation(B8)[170]	Building Professional Capabilities(C1)[291]	80	0.1294	High
9	Building Professional Capabilities(C1)[291]	Reconstructing Government policies(C2)[172]	79	0.1247	High
10	Organisational Barriers(B3)[232]	Technical Incompetency(B7)[142]	65	0.1233	High
11	Social Barriers(B6)[133]	Restructuring the Organisational Environment(C3)[105]	77	0.1161	High
12	Cultural Barriers(B1)[201]	Organisational Barriers(B3)[232]	56	0.1120	High

The above table shows the linkages between the thematic pairs. For instance, the association of the node C3 is strong with a set of nodes as C1, B3, C2, B7 and B6; it is medium with another set of nodes such as A3 & A4 and it is weak with respect to B2 & B5. Similarly, the association of B3 is strong with respect to C1, B8, B7 &B1; and it is weak with respect to A1, A3 and B4. Same is the case with the other nodes.

The association exiting between the nodes given in table be represented in a more vivid manner through a diagram. The following diagram or map explains the assocition of the nodes in a better manner.

6.5 Leximap

The leximap shows the degrees of nodes on the map. The degree of a node 'X' is defined as a number of links incident with X and is denoted by d (X). The strong degree, medium degree and weak degree of a node 'X' is defined as number of strong, weak and medium links incident with it and it is denoted by d s (X), d m (X), dw(X) respectively. It is easy to verify that d(X)=ds(X)+dm(X)+dw(X). The above lexi-map indicates that d (C3) = 10 , ds(C3) =6, dm(C3)=2, dw(C3)=2; d (B3) = 8 , ds(B3) =4, dm(B3)=1, dw(B3)=3; d(C1) = 8 , ds(C1) =4, dm(C1)=3, dw(C1)=1; d(B8) = 4 , ds(B8) =3, dm(B8)=1, dw(B8)=0; d(B1) = 3 , ds(B1) =0, dm(B1)=2, dw(B1)=1; d(C2) = 3 , ds(C2) =2, dm(C2)=1, dw(C2)=0; d(A4) = 3 , ds(A4) =0, dm(A4)=2, dw(A4)=1; d(A3) = 3 , ds(A3) =0, dm(A3)=1, dw(A3)=2; We declare a node X as a ', cluster' if ds (X) >= n, for a given n. We take n =4 in the present context.   Based on this criteria, it is observed that C1, C3 & B3 are clusters.Out of the 105 co-word combination for the 15 subject categories [n (n-1)/2], only 27 pairs have been taken for analysis filtering out the word-pairs fall below the threshold value (<5). It is observed from the Lexi-map that these 27 word pairs have lent themselves into three meaningful clusters. It is interesting to note that the subject C3 has linked with 9 other subject headings viz:A3, A4, B2, B3, B5,B6,B7,C1, C2 and formed the primary cluster. Similarly, the subject B3 has linked with 7 other subject headings viz; A1,A3,B1, B4, B7,B8, C1 and formed a secondary cluster. The tertiary cluster is formed by C1 in associated with other subject headings like A1, B1, B6, B8, C2. The following diagram illustrates the formation of the above mentioned clusters.

Core Theme   Intermediate Theme   Peripheral Theme

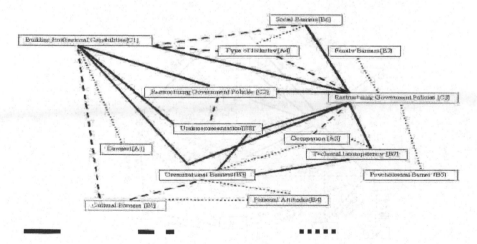

Fig. 1. Lexi-Map depicting the strength of relationship between the sub domain in the GSI

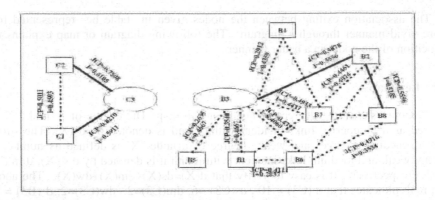

Fig. 2. Computation of Inter-relationship between the topics using JCP & Inclusion index

The inter and intra-relationship between the nodes have been calculated by using the Inclusion Index (I) and the Joint Conditional Probability Index (JCP). The inter-cluster relationships of the nodes   A1-A4; B1-B8 and C1-C3 have been analyzed. Based on the calculated values, the co-occurrence structure for the individual nodes are formed (Figure-4). While considering the individual nodes in the group A, it is identified that none of the nodes in this group has any meaningful co-occurrence. On the other hand in group B, the node B3, form a cluster because of its strong and medium co-occurrence relationship with other nodes within their groups. For example ds (B3)= 1 and dm(B3) =5. Similarly, in group C, the node C3 forms a cluster because of its stronger association with two other nodes C1 &C2. It is noted from the above analysis that the degree of potential nodes (d (X) = that form a cluster within groups are limited. Out of the 15 nodes taken for analysis only B3 &C3 have the potentiality to form a cluster.

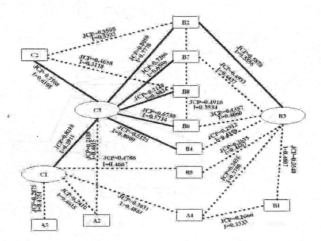

Fig. 3. Computation of Intra-relationship between the topics using JCP & Inclusion index

From figure 5, it is observed that out of the 15 nodes taken for analysis, only three nodes viz: C3, B3 & C1 forms the cluster because of their maximal degree. Out of these three clusters, the C3 has forms a larger cluster. For instance d (C3) = 8 where ds (C3) =7, and dm (C3) =1. In the same manner, d (B3) = 7; where ds (B3) =1, and dm (B3) =6. Similarly, d (C1) = 6 where ds (C3) =1, and dm (C3) =5. It is interesting to note that the intra relationship of the cluster C3 is stronger than the other clusters because of its stronger association both within (C1 & C2) and outside the clusters viz: B2, B4, B6, B7, B8 & A2.

7 Conclusion

In this paper an attempt has been made to map the structure of 'Gender Studies in Informatics' over a period of twenty years. This study has experimented with several techniques like the leximap, inclusion index, joint probability index etc in order to create topic maps of the given discipline. The inter and intra cluster maps applied here help to trace out the interactions among the sub-domains in the discipline GSI.

Managing Digital Repositories Through an Ontology-Based Design

Jian Qin[1] and Foster Zhang[2]

[1] School of Information Studies, Syracuse University, Syracuse, NY 13244, USA
jqin@syr.edu
[2] Digital Services Group, Stanford University, Stanford, CA 94305, USA
fjzhang@stanford.edu

Abstract. The conventional design of digital repository systems provides little flexibility and is often difficult to scale and customize. The authors analyzed the causes for inflexibility and difficulties in managing digital repository systems and proposed an ontology-based design in managing digital repository systems in this paper. The ontology focuses on the system controls that manage a wide array of functions such as object data, user access control, and rights management. The authors used an instance in the Object class to demonstrate how the ontology can be used to reduce the difficulties in conventional design of repository systems.

1 Background

Digital repository systems are becoming an increasingly important solution to preserving, storing, and providing access to digital content created by members of academic institutions. An institution-wide digital repository system reduces the need for individuals and departments to host their own digital content. Such effort is often costly because it requires expensive computer hardware, software, technical staff, and maintenance operations in order to provide users with uniform discovery services for all kinds of digital contents in the repository system.

It is extremely challenging to maintain digital assets in an institution-wide or a shared multi-institutional digital repository system without losing specialties of individual digital assets. A common practice is using metadata to manage and control such digital assets. For instance, DSpace (http://dspace.org/technology/features.html) uses qualified Dublin Core Metadata Element Set (DC) for owners to submit digital assets. Since DC provides only a simple set of metadata elements and no implementation model, adopting institutions or repositories often have to develop local elements to meet special needs for resource description. DSpace provides an open source API programming tool so that adopting institutions can customize the software to overcome the limitations of DC. Another example is Fedora, a project that uses a much more comprehensive metadata set—Metadata Encoding and Transmission Standard (METS, http://www.loc.gov/standards/mets/)—to describe digital objects. METS includes not only those elements from DC, but also has a behavior section about how to use the object. While DC is over simplified for

Z. Chen et al. (Eds.): ICADL 2004, LNCS 3334, pp. 300–309, 2004.
© Springer-Verlag Berlin Heidelberg 2004

repository systems, METS has a much larger number of elements, which generates long and complicated metadata records in XML format even for very simple digital objects. This makes implementation very difficult and time-consuming.

There are at least two problems associated with the metadata approach. The first problem concerns with metadata's ability to encompass complex data models needed for representing, organizing, and retrieving digital content. An example is that the digital content for a course would be very different from a digitized museum object, or from a faculty's collection on a specific topic that may contain electronic journals and pre-prints. These objects can vary widely in subject matter, content structure, and format. A digital repository system needs to deal with complex data models that can distinguish one type of objects from others while maintaining their knowledge associations. Metadata can not handle these problems alone even by using structured metadata standards such as METS.

Another problem lies in the programming needed to support customization in order for the complex content to work as if it were one-single type. Digital libraries can include virtually any type of digital objects, but the fixed programming can deal with only one type at a time. The current metadata approach requires programming to customize the system and its functions in order to be able to handle complex data models. Too much customization will not only make interoperability and sharing difficult and the common repository become a non-common platform, but also limit the usefulness of an institutional repository system. It will not be cost-effective but time-consuming if various digital assets are added to the repository and require customized codes to support the applications.

Finally, access control and rights management are too often entangled together and need heavy coding to establish associations between user types and individual digital assets. These requirements cannot be managed by metadata alone either.

To address problems associated with the metadata approach in developing digital content repositories, we propose an ontology-based design that will integrate representation, organization, retrieval, and management of digital assets in a repository system.

2 Relevant Research

Digital repositories face three main challenges as Lynch points out: preservable formats, identifier, and rights documentation and management [9]. While standards play a critical role in digital repositories for them to sustain the time and technology evolution, a deeper issue has been largely ignored, that is, how to achieve such sustainability. In other words, the semantic infrastructure such as metadata is as important as the technical infrastructure in creating interoperable and lasting digital repositories. There are two approaches currently used in establishing the semantic infrastructure for digital repositories: one is the metadata approach that applies Dublin Core or other metadata standards or locally developed metadata application profiles and the other the ontological approach.

A number of institutional digital repositories have been developed in the last few years, such as DSpace at MIT [14], Fedora developed through collaboration between University of Virginia and Cornell University [15], eSholarship at University of California [16], and the Digital Repository Services at Harvard University [3]. These institutional repositories perform functions including user registration, certification (peer review, associative certification and online response), awareness (interoperable open repositories and support services), and archiving (perpetual access) [1]. The metadata used in these repositories mainly deals with document information that is needed for searching, identifying, and locating a document. For example, DSpace uses qualified Dublin Core for document description including abstracts, keywords, technical metadata and rights metadata. They are also experimenting with METS to develop extension schemas for the technical and rights metadata for digital objects in various formats [14]. The Fedora project adopts the Open Archive Initiative (OAI) metadata schema [15].

The metadata approach is easy to implement and can provide familiar access points for users, including title, author, subject and keywords. However, metadata elements only define what data fields contain. Relationships between object types or data categories can only be established at the implementation time, which can result in a widely varying data structures and programs and make interoperability and extensibility very difficult to realize. One example is scientific papers that may contain links to raw data sets (such as a genome research paper containing DNA sequences and each of these sequences is related to a number of references). In this case, the metadata schema is limited in establishing associations between the data sets and their associated publications effectively and consistently in terms of system implementation.

The ontology-based approach is developed as a solution to tackle the limitations in metadata approach. The term "ontology" is often used to refer to the semantics of a data model in an information system. Because an ontology models the conceptual structure and defines the meaning of data elements, it is used as a tool to build the structure and vocabulary for a system. In this sense, the ontology-based approach looks at the repository system as a whole and models the data structures for all of its functions including metadata.

General ontology modeling related to metadata includes the <indecs> metadata framework [12] and the Functional Requirements of Bibliographic Records (FRBR) [10]. There have been quite a few publications discussing the models, but implementation of such models is still in experimental stage [4]. Lagoze and Hunter [7] built a conceptual model to facilitate interoperability between metadata ontologies from different domains. Their model uses *Entity* as the root class and assigns three categories—*Temporality, Actuality*, and *Abstraction*—as its subclasses. The next level of subclasses includes *Artifact, Event, Situation, Action, Agent, Work, Manifestation, Item, Time*, and *Place*. The properties of these concept classes are defined as a set of relations such as "isPartOf," "inContext," "contains," phaseOf," and "hasRealization." As the authors state, this model is syntax-neutral and they suggest to use the Resource Description Framework (RDF)/XML as the data binding language.

Other ontology projects attempt to build metadata models based on existing metadata standards and controlled vocabulary. Kamel Boulos et al [5] developed a Dublin Core (DC) metadata ontology for the health informatics domain, in which the *Subject* element in DC was populated with the Unified Medical Language System (UMLS) and clinical codes. Using controlled vocabulary to build ontology-based metadata schemas is another approach. Qin and Paling [11] analyzed the controlled vocabulary from the Gateway to Educational Materials (GEM) and constructed an ontology to represent the facets of subject, pedagogy, relation, audience, educational level, format, and language in learning objects. Their metadata model uses *Resource* as the root concept which has *Resource Type* as subclass (e.g., lesson plan is a subclass of resource) and the above mentioned facets are global properties that may be inherited by the subclasses of *Resource*. Khan et al [6] created a domain-dependent ontology to represent the context and meaning of audio objects' content. Other early projects in ontology-driven Web access, including the Simple HTML Ontology Extensions (SHOE) project, which provides users with easy access to machine-readable semantic knowledge on the Web by embedding ontologies in the HTML tags [8]; the OntoSeek experiment by Guarino and his colleagues [2].

Ontology-based approach has been mainly used to represent digital objects' subject content, but rarely in modeling the dynamic processes of managing a digital library or repository system. The complexities of digital objects and their requirements for use and management need a holistic modeling for the objects and system functions. Ontologies as a modeling tool can produce not only the conceptual model but the implementation model in desired encoding as well. We will discuss the ontology for digital repository systems in the following sections.

3   Components in a Digital Repository System

Let us use DSpace as an example to discuss the basic components in a digital repository system. Based on DSpace's functions as shown in Fig. 1, a digital repository system consists of a management component, a retrieval component plus the user interface, a data input/submission component, and a database maintenance/preservation component. These components form its functional layers presented in Fig. 2.

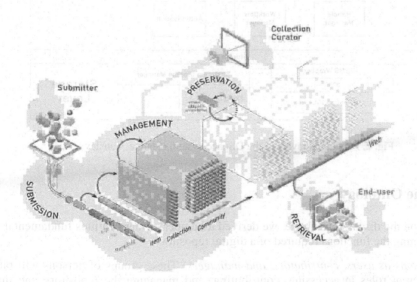

Fig. 1. The DSpace system function graphic chart (Source: Smith 2004)

As Tansley [17] indicates, the architecture shown in Fig. 1 and Fig. 2 has no flexibility, i.e., changing a particular aspect of functionality involves changing UI as well as underlying business logic module. Difficulties also exist in maintaining the system due to low-level APIs, which are somewhat ad-hoc, difficult to remain stable and implement enhanced/alternative functionality behind them. Tansley [17] points out that the heavy inter-dependence between modules and a lack of real "plug-in" mechanism makes it tricky to manage a modification alongside evolving core DSpace code.

The "traditional" design of a digital repository system will not be able to fulfill its mission without solving these issues. As a result of relevant research review and problem analysis to DSpace's model, we propose an ontology-based design for digital repository systems. The next sections will discuss what the ontology contains and how it can be used to solve the current problems in conventionally designed digital repository systems.

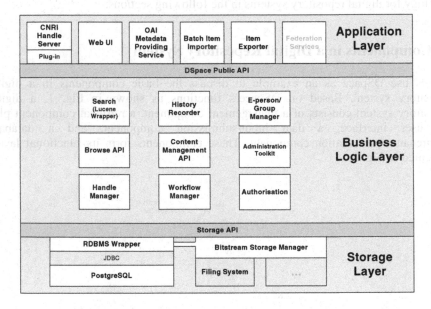

Fig. 2. Functional layers in the DSpace system (Source: Tansley, 2004)

4 The Ontology

Based on the discussions above, we derived a number of main entities fundamental to performing the functions required of a digital repository:

- *Persons as users, contributors, and managers:* These groups of persons will play different roles in accessing, contributing, and managing the repository and thus have different access rights and permissions. A person may play several roles, e.g., an author is a contributor and, at the same time, a user.

- *Participating organizations:* A digital repository may have multiple participating organizations, or may be in a specific domain with distributed participating organizations.
- *Digital objects*: This entity itself warrants a comprehensive model to cover the widely varying formats, subject contents, sizes, and applications that are needed to render the objects. What adds to the complexities of digital objects is that an object may be composite, i. e., consists of multiple digital objects. In this case, it is important to provide identification and sequencing for assembling the objects.
- *Rights*: The rights entity consists of conditions/permissions of use, owner(s) of digital objects, which in turn are associated with persons or organizations, and the objects the rights are referred to.
- *Vocabulary for data elements and values as well as for application methods and processes*: Vocabulary is a special entity that will be reused in many other entities to provide a consistent form for controlling different kinds of terms: preferred, synonymous, and related. In the case of application methods and processes, the vocabulary will also map the technical specifications at the backend with the standard or public display semantics at the front end.

The main classes in the preliminary ontology are listed in Fig. 3, which was created using the Protégé ontology editor from Stanford University. Each class has its own properties. Properties of a higher level class are inherited by the lower-level classes. For example, *Object* class has three subclasses, each of which will inherit the same properties of the *Object* class as shown in the right hand column in Fig. 3.

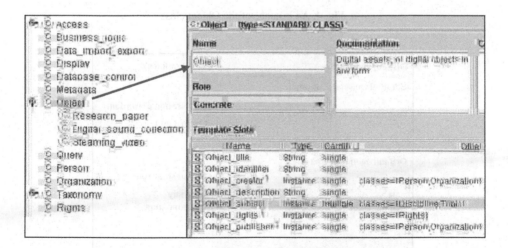

Fig. 3. Main classes and the properties for the *Object* class

We use a group of screenshots taken from our preliminary ontology to demonstrate how ontology-based design can be used to solve the problems mentioned in the discussions above. Fig. 4 presents an instance in the *Object* class: Monterey

Jazz Festival Tape Archive. The *Object* class has such template slots (properties) as creator, rights, description, identifier, publisher, and subject. Each of the properties in red rectangles represents a reuse of and association with another class's instance(s). Fig. 5, Fig. 6, and Fig. 7 show the details of associated instances with objects. In Fig. 4, the object creator property has an instance "Stanford University Library", which is an instance of the class Organization that has properties as shown in Fig. 5. The object rights are usually associated with an organization and digital objects. In this case, the instance of Stanford University Library is associated with rights properties as shown in Fig. 6. Finally, the object subject rectangle is backed by a Topic class that controls for preferred terms, related terms, and synonymous terms (Fig. 7).

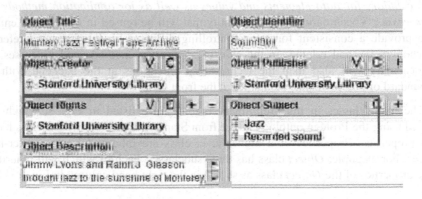

Fig. 4. An instance of the Object class

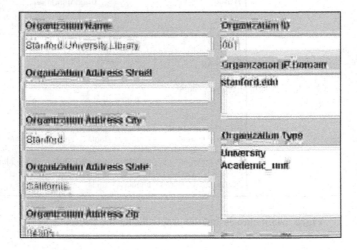

Fig. 5. An instance, Stanford University Library, in the *Organization* class is associated with and reused in the *Object* class

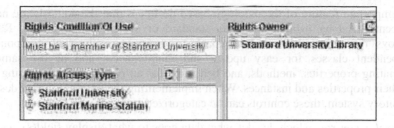

Fig. 6. An instance of *Rights* class is associated with the *Object* class

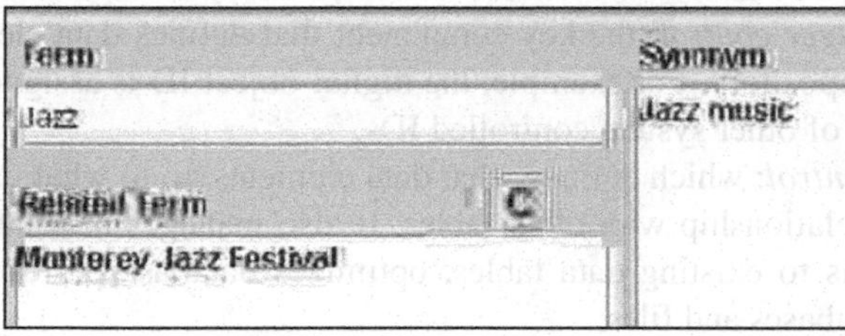

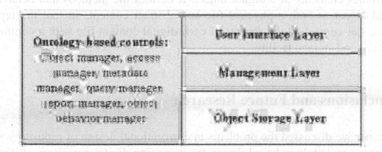

Fig. 7. An instance in the *Topic* class is associated with the *Object* instance

5 The Implementation

The architecture of a typical repository system has a management layer between user access and data storage layers (Fig. 8). The ontology models the components in the management layer and controls various object classes and relations among the classes.

Fig. 8. An ontology-based digital repository system

The management layer of the repository system can be categorized by the usage of digital objects, such as access, retrieval navigation, preservation, storage space requirement, and/or rights management. The various control managers will be maintained at the top level of the repository system with an ontology-based interface. Modifications and changes to the controls are table-driven and the links to each control manager uses a relational structure, as we have shown in the previous section.

One important feature of the ontology-based design is that the controls are not fixed nor centralized by using a metadata standard or system programming. Rather, it employs the objected-oriented approach to designing individual components as independent classes for easy update and maintenance, and at the same time, associating properties, methods, and behaviors for an object through reusing classes and their properties and instances. When implementing the ontology-based design in a repository system, these controls can be categorized into:

- *Display control:* which decides what data goes to what display field(s), and where the field is placed on the screen, sequence of screen events for a digital object;
- *Access control:* which controls access to each object through access control policies on who can see what content in compliance with rights management;
- *Object manager control:* the key component that defines data elements for digital assets in a repository. For example, the digital object ID is assigned here, which is independent of other system controlled IDs.
- *Database control:* which defines what data elements go to what database table and have what relationship with other tables. It also manages new table additions and modifications to existing data tables, optimizes database performance, and links between databases and files;
- *Data import/export control:* which performs data infusion and export as well as mapping table definitions for dataset import and export;
- *Metadata control:* which establishes associations between the object class and metadata standards used for record import and export;
- *Query control:* which executes predefined queries and creates indexes for performance;
- *Report manager control:* which generates statistics for the usage and administration of the repository; and
- *Object behavior control:* the intelligent part in a system that defines and determines elements of a digital object. It defines the methods and behavior of a digital object as both a physical file and abstract content, so that the repository system can control all the aspects of each digital content file with a common user interface and storage facility.

6   Conclusions and Future Research

In this paper we discussed the problems in conventional design of repository systems and proposed an ontology-based design for managing digital repository systems. The main contribution of our work is a conceptual model for the digital repository ontology that analyzes the relations among functional components and converts the ontology classes and relations into management controls. Although the ontology is still in its preliminary stage, we began to see its potential in tackling the problems existing in conventional systems. Our next phase of research will be to identify more concepts and relations and refine the ontology, as well as to identify methods for incorporating the ontology with existing repository management tools.

References

1. Crow, R. The case for institutional repositories: a SPARC position paper. 2002. http://arl. cni.org/sparc/IR/ir.html#dspm
2. Guarino, N., C. Masolo, and G. Vetere. OntoSeek: content-based access to the Web. IEEE Intelligent Systems, 14 (1999): 70-80.
3. Harvard University Office for Information Systems. Introduction to digital repository services. (2004). http://hul.harvard.edu/ois/systems/drs/introdrs.html
4. Hickey, T, and D. Vizine-Goetz. Implementing FRBR on large databases. Fall 2002 CNI Task Force Project Briefing presentation. http://staff.oclc. org/~vizine/CNI/OCLCFRBR_ files/frame.htm
5. Kamel Boulos, M.N., A.V. Roudsari, and E.R. Carson. Towards a semantic medical web: HealthCyberMap Dublin Core Ontology in Protégé-2000. In: Proceedings of the Fifth International Protégé Workshop, Sowerby Centre for Health Informatics at Newcastle, England, July 18, 2001, http://protege. stanford.edu/ontologies/dublincore/hcm_dc_in_ protege_newcastle.pdf
6. Khan, L., D. McLeod, and E. Hovy. Retrieval effectiveness of an ontology-based model for information selection. The VLDB Journal, 13 (2004): 71-85.
7. Lagoze, C. and J. Hunter. The ABC ontology and model. Journal of Digital Information, 2 (2001): http://jodi.ecs.soton.ac.uk/Articles/v02/i02/Lagoze/
8. Luke, S., L. Spector, D. Tanger, and J, Hendler. Ontology-based Web agents. In: ACM Autonomous Agents 1997, 59-66. New York: ACM Press.
9. Lynch, C. A. Institutional repositories: essential infrastructure for scholarship in the digital age. ARL, no. 226 (February 2003): 1-7. http://www.arl.org/newsltr/226/ir.html
10. Plassard, M.-F. (ed.) Functional Requirements for Bibliographic Records: Final Report. UBCIM Publications - New Series Vol. 19. K . München: G. Saur (1998).
11. Qin, J. and S. Paling. Converting a controlled vocabulary into an ontology: the case of GEM. Information Research, 6(2) (2001): http://InformationR. net/ir/6-2/paper94.html.
12. Rust, G. and M. Bide. The <indecs> metadata framework: principles, model and data dictionary. 2000. http://www.indecs.org/pdf/framework.pdf
13. Smith, M. DSpace: an institutional repository system. Presentation at Web-Wise 2004: Sharing Digital Resources. 2004.
14. Smith, M., M. Barton, M. Bass, M. Branschofsky, G. McClellan, D. Stuve, R. Tansley, J. H. Walker. DSpace: an open souce dynamic digital repository. D-Lib Magazine, 9(1) (2003): http://www.dlib.org/dlib/january03/smith/01smith.html
15. Staples, T., R. Wayland, and S. Payette. The Fedora project: an open-source digital object repository management system. D-Lib Magazine, 9(4) (2003): http://www.dlib.org/ dlib/april03/staples/04staples.html
16. Tennant, R. eScholarship infrastructure. (2003). http://www.cdlib.org/inside/projects/ escholarship/infrastructure.html
17. Tansley, R. DSpace 2.x Architecture Roadmap. (2004). http://www.dspace.org/conference/ presentations/architecture.ppt

Metadata Extraction from Bibliographies Using Bigram HMM

Ping Yin, Ming Zhang, ZhiHong Deng, and DongQing Yang

School of Electronics Engineering and Computer Science,
Peking University, Beijing, China
{yinping_, mzhang, zhdeng, ydq}@db.pku.edu.cn

Abstract. In recent years, we have seen huge volumes of research papers available on the World Wide Web. Metadata provides a good approach for organizing and retrieving these useful resources. Accordingly, automatic extraction of metadata from these papers and their bibliographies is meaningful and has been widely studied. In this paper, we utilize a bigram HMM (Hidden Markov Model) for automatic extraction of metadata (i.e. title, author, date, journal, pages, etc.) from bibliographies with various styles. Different from the traditional HMM, which only uses word frequency, this model also considers both words' bigram sequential relation and position information in text fields. We have evaluated the model on a real corpus downloaded from Web and compared it with other methods. Experiments show that the bigram HMM yields the best result and seem to be the most promising candidate for metadata extraction of bibliographies.

1 Introduction

Authors and publishers are beginning to make scientific publications available on the World Wide Web in increasing number. In order to search and exploit these disorganized digital documents, there is a growing need to organize them efficiently. Organizing articles by their metadata is a good way and becomes more and more popular. Accordingly, automatic extraction of metadata from vast number of papers and papers' bibliographies has been widely studied in recent years. We are interested in improving the metadata extraction from papers' bibliographies, which is, segmenting a bibliography into individual fields such as author, title, publisher, date and so on.

The field extraction from bibliographies is non-trivial because of the high variance in the structure of the current record-level search. Previous approaches have typically used rule-based system to do this. Citeseer [2] uses a heuristic method which first parses those fields that have relatively uniform syntax, position, and composition. In addition, it uses syntactic relationships between fields and dictionaries of author names and journal titles to help identify fields. There is also another rule-based bibliographic metadata extractor called DECITER (decoding citations) [3]. There are some problems in such systems which rely on hand-written rules. Firstly, rules have to be modified if an entry with a new style is added to the domain. Secondly, they only work for the regions they are developed and can't extend to other domains. A lot

Z. Chen et al. (Eds.): ICADL 2004, LNCS 3334, pp. 310–319, 2004.

of manual work has to be performed in rewriting these rules while shifting domains. In this paper, we adopt a bigram HMM to automatically extract bibliographic metadata with a seed set of example labeled bibliography entries.

The remainder of the paper is organized as follows. Section 2 describes Hidden Markov Models as background. Section 3 describes the key steps for extracting metadata from bibliographies via a bigram HMM. Section 4 experimentally evaluates the bigram HMM on a corpus. Section 5 discussed some related works. Section 6 summarizes the paper.

2 Hidden Markov Models

A Hidden Markov model (HMM) is a finite state automation comprising with stochastic state transitions and symbol emissions. The automation models a probabilistic generative processes whereby a sequence of symbols is produced by starting at a designated start state, transitioning to a new state, emitting a symbol selected by that state, transitioning again, emitting another symbol, and so on, until a designated final state is reached. Associated with each of a set of states, $S = \{S_1, ..., S_n\}$, are a probability distribution over the symbols in the emission vocabulary $V = \{w_1, ... w_m\}$, and a probability distribution over its set of outgoing transitions. [4, 5]

In this model, a symbol sequence can be generated through some state path with a probability which can be computed as the product of all transition and emission probabilities along the path. Given an output sequence, we can also recover the most probable state transitions that could have generated it.

HMMs, while relatively new to the structure extraction task, have been used with much success for speech and hand-writing recognition tasks and for natural language tasks like parts-of-speech tagging. In spite of the general principles being known, applying it to information extraction requires new enhancements to this model.

Next section we will see how to implement the metadata extraction using a modified HMM, bigram HMM.

3 Bibliographic Metadata Extraction with Bigram HMM

A bibliographic entry can be viewed as a sequence of fields (e.g. author, title, publisher, date, pages, etc.). Given an HMM, each state of which is marked with a label that is the name of some field., metadata extraction from bibliographies is performed by determining the sequence of states that was most likely to have generated the entire word sequence of the bibliography entry, and then putting each word to the corresponding field according to the state sequence.

To perform extracting we therefore require an algorithm for finding the most likely state sequence given a HMM model M and a sequence of symbols. Although a naïve approach for finding the most likely sequence would take time exponential in the sequence length, a dynamic programming solution called the viterbi algorithm [1, 4] solves the problem in just $O(TN^2)$ time.

To perform extracting we also need to build an HMM, including the structure and the parameters. Other work such as OOV problem, parameter smoothing and so on has to be dealt with as well to finish the extracting perfectly.

3.1 The Viterbi Algorithm

Given an output sequence $O = O_1 O_2 ... O_T$ of length T and an HMM having N states, we want to find out the most probable state sequence from the start state to the end state which generates O. [1, 4]

Let S_0 and S_{N+1} denote the special start and end states which don't emit symbols.

Let $\delta_t(j)$ denotes the highest probability along a single path, at time t, which accounts for the first t observations and ends in state S_j. Therefore $\delta_t(j)$ can be written as

$$\delta_t(j) = \max_{q_1 q_2 ... q_{t-1}} P(q_1 q_2 ... q_t = S_j, O_1 O_2 ... O_t \mid \lambda) . \tag{1}$$

We begin at the start state S_0. Thus, initially,

$$\delta_0(0) = 1, \ \delta_0(k) = 0, \ k \neq 0 . \tag{2}$$

By induction we have

$$\delta_t(j) = \max_{1 \leq i \leq N} \left[\delta_{t-1}(i) a_{ij} \right] b_j(O_t), \ 1 \leq t \leq T, 1 \leq j \leq N \tag{3}$$

where a_{ij} is the transition probability from state S_i to state S_j, $b_j(O_t)$ is the emission probability of emitting O_t at state S_j. The maximum is taken over all states of the HMM.

Finally, that is at time $T+1$, the state sequence will end at the end state S_{N+1}. So we have

$$\delta_{T+1}(N+1) = \max_{1 \leq i \leq N} \delta_T(i) a_{i(N+1)}, \qquad \delta_{T+1}(j) = 0, \ 1 \leq j \leq N . \tag{4}$$

The most probable path can be gotten by storing the argmax at each step. This formulation can be easily implemented as a dynamic programming algorithm running in $O(TN^2)$ time.

3.2 Learning Structure

In order to build an HMM for information extraction, first of all, we must decide how many states the model should contain and what transitions between states should be allowed. A reasonable initial model is to use one state per field, and to allow transitions from any state to any other state. However, this model may not be optimal in all cases. When a specific hidden sequence structure is expected in the extraction domain, we may do better by building a model with multiple states per field, with only a few transitions out of each state. This can be done by learning the structure automatically from the labeled training data consisting of labeled word sequences. [6]

Firstly an HMM is constructed which produces exactly the input word sequences. The start state has as many outgoing transitions as there are word sequences and each word sequence is represented by a unique path with one state per word. All paths end at the final state with probability 1. The probability of entering these paths from the start state is uniformly distributed. Within each path there is a unique transition arc whose probability is 1. The emission probabilities are 1 from each state to produce the corresponding word. This model is called as maximum likelihood model.[6]

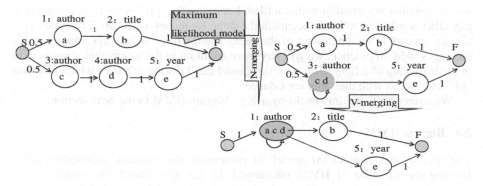

Fig. 1. Learning structure using labeled bibliography entries "<author>a</author><title> b</title>" and "<author>c d</author><year>e</year>"

Then "Neighbor-merging" and "V-merging" are used to merge some states that have the same label to generalize the maximally specific model. "Neighbor-merging" combines all states that share a link and have the same field label. "V-merging" merges any two states that have the same label and share transitions from or to a common state.

All of these can be illustrated in Fig. 1.

3.3 Learning Parameters

Once the structure of the HMM is fixed, we need to learn its transition and emission probabilities, which can be calculated using the Maximum Likelihood approach on all training sequences.

The probability of making a transition from state q to state q' is the ratio of the number of transitions made from state q to q' in the training data to the total number of transitions made from q. The probability of emitting symbol σ at state q is the ratio of the number of times σ is emitted in q to the total number of symbols emitted in the state. This can be written as

$$P(q \rightarrow q') = \frac{c(q \rightarrow q')}{\sum_{s \in Q} c(q \rightarrow s)} \qquad\qquad P(q \uparrow \sigma) = \frac{c(q \uparrow \sigma)}{\sum_{\rho \in \Sigma} c(q \uparrow \rho)} \qquad (5)$$

where $q \uparrow \sigma$ denotes state q emits word σ and $c(x)$ denotes the number of event x occurring in the training data. [6]

In this model, it is unreasonable that two words with the same frequency in the same state have equal importance because it ignores much helpful information. Firstly, it ignores any sequential relationship amongst words in the same filed. For example, phrases like "Technical Report" will be outputs of the same state. This state will accept "Technical Report" with the same probability as "Report Technical". In fact, it is very unusual that "Report Technical" appears. Secondly, it ignores the words' position information within a filed. For example, "pp." is more important than any other word (i.e. "w") that occurs in the same frequency with "pp.", because "pp." always appears in the beginning of the pages filed, while "w" always appears inside the pages field. In practice, we will pay more attention to the words that always occur in the beginning of a field. However, this model can't distinguish this, which will treat "pp" and "w" as with the same importance.

We overcome these drawbacks by using a bigram HMM in the next section.

3.4 Bigram HMM

The Bigram uses a modified model for computing the emission probability, while keeping the structure of HMM unchanged. In the new model, the probability of emitting symbol σ at state q composes of beginning emission probability and inner emission probability. The former is the probability that q emits σ as the first word, and the latter is the probability that q emits σ as the inner word (not the first word).

We will later see how to use the emission probability in the modified viterbi algorithm and understand that by this we can capture the words' position information in the state. The inner emission probability is computed using a bigram model, which can capture the words' bigram sequence relationship within the same filed.

We can write the new emission probability model as

$$P(\sigma \mid q) = \begin{cases} P(q \underline{\uparrow} \sigma), & \sigma \text{ appears in the beginning of q} \\ P(q \overline{\uparrow} \sigma) = P(\sigma \mid \sigma_{-1}, q), & \sigma \text{ appears in the inner of q} \end{cases} \quad (6)$$

where $q \underline{\uparrow} \sigma$ denotes state q emits word σ as the beginning word, $q \overline{\uparrow} \sigma$ denotes q emits σ as the inner word and σ_{-1} denotes the word before σ.

We can also use the ratio from the training data to compute $P(q \searrow \sigma)$ and $P(\sigma \mid \sigma_{-1}, q)$.

$$P(q \underline{\uparrow} \sigma) = \frac{c(q \underline{\uparrow} \sigma)}{\sum_{\rho \in \Sigma} c(q \underline{\uparrow} \rho)} \qquad P(\sigma \mid \sigma_{-1}, q) = \frac{c(q \uparrow \sigma_{-1}\sigma)}{c(q \uparrow \sigma_{-1})} \quad (7)$$

3.5 Viterbi for Bigram HMM

We make a little modification to the viterbi algorithm for the bigram HMM, where we will see how to use the beginning emission probability and the inner emission probability presented in last section.

$$\delta_t(j) = \max_{1 \le i \le N}\left[\delta_{t-1}(i)a_{ij}\right]b_j(O_t), \qquad 1 \le t \le T, 1 \le j \le N$$

$$\text{where}, \ b_j(O_t) = \begin{cases} P(S_j \uparrow O_t), & S_j \neq S_{j-1} \\ P(O_t \mid O_{t-1}, S_j), & S_j = S_{j-1} \end{cases} \qquad (8)$$

Only the formula in the induction has been modified, where the beginning emission probability is used if the current state S_j is not equal to the last state S_{j-1} which shows the current word O_t is the first word of state S_j, or else, the inner emission probability is used.

3.6 Smoothing

When the training data is insufficient, maximum likelihood estimation of emission probabilities will lead to poor estimates, with many words inappropriately having zero probability. So we need to smooth emission probabilities to prevent zero-probability estimates and improve estimation overall. There are many methods for smoothing. Both *Laplace smoothing* and *absolute discounting* calculate the word distribution in a state using only the training data in state q itself. In contrast, the third technique called *shrinkage* can leverage the word distributions in several related states in order to improve parameter estimation.[5]

An idea similar to *shrinkage*, a method which we call as *back off-shrinkage* [7] can be used here for the bigram HMM. Because of insufficient training data, bigram HMM may not see some bigrams or words, in which case the model backs off to a less-powerful, less-descriptive model. So we define a level of back-off models as below, from bigram model to unigram model, then to global model, and finally to uniform model.

Backing off of $P(q \uparrow \sigma)$: $P(q \uparrow \sigma) \rightarrow P(q \uparrow \sigma) \rightarrow P_{global}(\sigma) \rightarrow 1/m$

Backing off of $P(\sigma \mid \sigma_{-1}, q)$: $P(\sigma \mid \sigma_{-1}, q) \rightarrow P(q \uparrow \sigma) \rightarrow P_{global}(\sigma) \rightarrow 1/m$

where m is the size of vocabulary, $1/m$ is the emission probability of the uniform model, and $P_{global}(\sigma)$ is the emission probability in the global model, that is the probability of σ occurring in the training data.

We then combine the estimates with a weighted average, for example,

$$\overline{P}(q \uparrow \sigma) = \lambda_1 P(q \uparrow \sigma) + \lambda_2 P(q \uparrow \sigma) + \lambda_3 P_{global}(\sigma) + \lambda_4 / m,$$
$$\text{where } \lambda_1, \lambda_2, \lambda_3, \lambda_4 \ge 0, \text{ and } \lambda_1 + \lambda_2 + \lambda_3 + \lambda_4 = 1 \qquad (9)$$

The weights are adjusted in practice according to the actual importance of models. In the bibliographic metadata extraction, the words in the beginning of fields are very important, so λ_1 was assigned a large value in the experiment. Because the global emission probability $P_{global}(\sigma)$ is always non-zero, the uniform emission probability is meaningless. Therefore, we set λ_4 to 0.

3.7 OOV Problem

During testing we may encounter words that have not been seen during training. How we estimate the emission probabilities of these unknown words. This problem is known as OOV (out of vocabulary) problem. This paper uses a method which we call as *minimum frequency method* [6]. Let f denotes the minimum frequency. The vocabulary is constituted by the words whose frequency in the training data is not less than f, while other words whose frequency is less than f are mapped to the unknown word "<UNK>". Any word in the testing data that is out of vocabulary is also mapped to "<UNK>", so its emission probability is the emission probability of "<UNK>" which can be estimated via the training data.

4 Experimental Evaluation

4.1 Preliminaries

713 bibliography entries were stochastically extracted from 250 papers using the paper metadata extractor we have implemented before, which can extract title, author, abstract, keywords, the list of bibliographies and so on from PDF formatting papers. These entries were then hand-labeled as follows to construct our data set.

"<author>Andrew W. Appel. </author><title>A semantic model of types. </title><journal>In Twenty-Seventh ACM Symposium, </journal><pages>pages 243-253, </pages><location>Boston, </location><date>January 2000. </date>"

We use 4-level cross validation, splitting the dataset into four parts averagely, one part as testing set in turn, other three parts merged as training set, performing four times of experiments. The training set is used to train the HMM, and the testing set is used to evaluate the effect of extraction. The final result is the average of the four experiments' results.

We use both precision (P) and recall (R) borrowed from information-retrieval community to evaluate our result where

$$P = \frac{\text{number of tokens corrected tagged using HMM}}{\text{number of tokens tagged using HMM}} \quad \text{and } R = \frac{\text{number of tokens corrected tagged using HMM}}{\text{number of tokens tagged by expert}}$$

F1, the harmonic mean of P and R, i.e. $2/(1/P + 1/R)$, is used to balance P and R.

4.2 Results

We find the smoothing method *back off-shrinkage* makes better precision than other methods, so we choose it as the smoothing method in our experiment.

In Figure 2 we compare the precision, recall and F1 of three different models, bigram HMM presented in this paper, traditional HMM (unigram HMM) and DECITER mentioned in section 1 as a rule-based metadata extractor. We can make the following observations from these results.

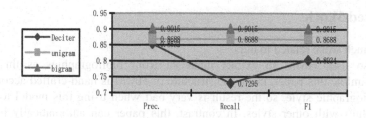

Fig. 2. Comparison of different models

Table 1. Results in Individual fields

Field	Tokens present	Prec.	Recall
title	2957	0.8959	0.9212
author	3144	0.9770	0.9587
date	616	0.9239	0.9447
pages	570	0.9552	0.9630
volume	162	0.8405	0.8997
issue	135	0.8860	0.8995
journal	2221	0.9052	0.8080
url	218	0.8770	0.9553
publisher	78	0.6436	0.8330
location	345	0.6689	0.7827
other	174	0.4288	0.6180
total	10620	0.9015	0.9015

1. The overall precision and overall recall are equal when using both traditional and bigram HMM because all tokens are tagged, while not equal when using DECITER because DECITER leaves many tokens untagged by not assigning them to any of the fields, which also causes the low recall 0.7295.
2. Bigram HMM makes an improvement in precision more than three percentages than traditional HMM, while DECITER gets the lowest precision and recall. The peak precision is more than 90%, which is satisfactory.

Finally, details of precision and recall in every field when using bigram HMM are shown in table 1. The precision and recall of most fields are acceptable except the three fields publisher, location and other which accepts tokens that don't belong to any other filed. Fortunately, these fields happen to be less important and occur infrequently in training and testing data. The scarcity of data prevents them from getting trained properly.

5 Related Work

There is much work related to ours.

[8] also uses HMM to extract metadata from bibliographies as this paper. However, unlike this paper, in [8] the structure of HMM is hand-crafted according to some bibliographic style, so the result is very bad when using this model to extract bibliographies with other styles. In contrast, this paper can automatically learn the HMM structure using the labeled training data in which there are bibliography entrics with as much styles as possible, and can achieve high precision in spite of the style of the testing data.

[7] presents a Nymble system to perform "named entity" extraction as defined by MUC-6 using a two-level hierarchical HMM in which the nested model is a full-connected model which can also overcome the shortcoming presented in section 3.3. All different fields to be extracted are modeled in a single HMM composed of some name-class states, and each name-class state is composed of m (the size of vocabulary) word-states each of which generates the corresponding word with probability 1 and can connect to any other word-state.

[1] presents a DATAMOLD system also using a two-level hierarchical HMM to segment text into structured records, an application of which is also the bibliographic metadata extraction. Unlike [7], the outer model and inner model can both be learned from the training data. The inner HMM can capture the finer structure of the corresponding filed, and it can also capture the length information of the field by a parallel path structure.

In contrast to [7] and [1], this paper keeps the structure of HMM unchanged, capturing part structures of fields by modifying the emission probability model and accordingly the viterbi algorithm.

6 Conclusions

This paper has dedicated to the problem of extracting metadata from bibliographic entries using a bigram HMM which uses a modified emission probability model to exploit additional cues from several sources, including words' sequential relation and words' position information within a filed. The structure and parameters of HMM is automatically learned from the labeled training data, alone with which is the *back-off shrinkage* smoothing. Experiments yield precision greater than 90%, considerably better than traditional HMM and a rule-based algorithm.

References

1. V. R. Borkar, K. Deshmukh, and S. Sarawagi. Automatic Segmentation of Text into Structured Records, Proc. ACM-SIGMOD Int'l Conf. Management of Data (SIGMOD 2001), ACM Press, New York, 2001, pp. 175-186.
2. S. Lawrence, C. Giles, and K. Bollacker, "Digital libraries and autonomous citation indexing," IEEE Computer, vol. 32, no. 6, pp. 67-71, 1999.

3. harvester.jar, http://www.cs.cornell.edu/cdlrg/Reference%20Linking/software/RefLink.tar. gz
4. L. Rabiner. A tutorial on hidden markov models and selected applications in speech recognition. Proceedings of the IEEE, 1989, 77(2), pp. 257-285.
5. Freitag D., McCallurn A. Information extraction with HMMs and shrinkage, Workshop Notes of AAAI-99 Conference on Machine Learning for Information Extraction, 1999, pp. 31-36.
6. Seymore K., McCallum A., Rosenreid R. Learning hidden Markov model structure for information extraction. AAAI-99 Workshop on Machine Learning for Information Extraction, 1999, pp. 37-42.
7. Bikel D.M., Miller S., Schwartz R. and Weischedel R. Nymble: a high performance learning namefinder. In Proceeding of the fifth Conference on Applied Language Processing, 1999, pp. 194-201.
8. J. Connan and C.W. Omlin. Bibliography Extraction with Hidden Markov Models, Technical Report US-CS-TR-00-6, 24 February 2000, Department of Computer Science, University of Stellenbosch.
9. Leek T. Information Extraction Using Hidden Markov Models, Masters Thesis, Department of Computer Science & Engineering, University of California, San Diego, 1997.
10. Freitag, D., McCallum, A. Information extraction with HMM structures learned by stochastic optimization. Proceedings of the Eighteenth Conference on Artificial Intelligence (AAAI-2000), 2000.
11. Stolcke, A. and Omohundro, S.M. Hidden Markov Model Induction by Bayesian Model Merging. Advances in Neural Information Processing Systems, 1992, Volume 5, S. J. Hanson, J. D. Cowan and C. L. Giles, editors, Morgan Kaufman, pp. 11-18, 1992.
12. Andreas Stolcke and Stephen M. Omohundro. Best-first model merging for hidden Markov model induction. Technical Report TR-94-003, Computer Science Division, University of California at Berkeley and International Computer Science Institute, 1994.
13. A. McCallum, D. Freitag, and F. Pereira. Maximum entropy Markov models for information extraction and segmentation, in Proc. 17th International Conf. on Machine Learning, 2000, pp. 591-598.
14. Probabilistic Logic Learning Seminar. Hidden Markov Models for Information Extraction.
15. Soderland S. Learning Information Extraction Rules for Semi-Structured and Free Text, Machine Learning: Special Issue on Natural Language Learning, 1999, 34, pp. 233-272.

Metadata Quality Evaluation: Experience from the Open Language Archives Community

Baden Hughes

Department of Computer Science and Software Engineering,
University of Melbourne,
Parkville VIC 3010, Australia
badenh@cs.mu.oz.au

Abstract. We describe the motivation, design and implementation of an infrastructure to support metadata quality assessment within a specialised Open Archives Initiative (OAI) sub-domain, the Open Language Archives Community (OLAC). While services for structural validation of metadata are widely used, there is little corresponding work regarding services which evaluate the semantic and syntactic content of metadata from a qualitative perspective. We posit that any measure of metadata quality benefits from both contextual and referential assessment - metadata on a per record and per collection basis is legitimately assessed against the baseline of broader community practice, as well as for compliance to any external standard. In this paper we describe the implementation of a metadata quality assessment scheme, and the corresponding interfaces to the evaluation tool.

1 Introduction

Much effort has been contributed to the design and implementation of metadata standards in the digital libraries community. The promotion of a distributed model of metadata creation and management, leveraged by central services for harvesting and aggregation of metadata, have resulted in a rapid expansion of the number of institutions and individuals who now contribute metadata to the digital libraries community as a whole. One consequence of the devolution of metadata creation and management has been that while metadata standards such as Dublin Core [1] are well accepted by the community as a whole, compliance with metadata standards and their domain-specific extensions is in fact highly variable.

While there are a number of structural validation tools available for metadata repositories within the Open Archives Initiative (OAI) [2] framework, relatively little effort has been expended on a framework for metadata quality assessment, a task which requires both structural and semantic validation and comparison.

In this paper, we report the motivation, design and implementation of an infrastructure to support metadata quality assessment within a specialised OAI sub-domain, the Open Language Archives Community (OLAC) [3]. We argue that the determination of metadata quality benefits from contextual and referential assessment: metadata on a per record and per collection basis is legitimately assessed against the baseline of broader community practice, as well as for compliance to external

Z. Chen et al. (Eds.): ICADL 2004, LNCS 3334, pp. 320–329, 2004.

standards. The combination of both these assessment models provides a significant incentive for archive managers to improve the quality of their metadata.

The structure of this paper is as follows: we contextualise the work within OLAC; describe our motivation in terms of the broader digital archives community; report the design of a metadata quality evaluation service; and review the implementation itself. Evaluation is followed by a brief discussion of items for future work. Finally we reflect on the broader implications of metadata quality evaluation for the digital libraries community as a whole.

2 Background

The Open Language Archives Community (OLAC) is a consortium of linguistic data archives, at the time of writing consisting of 29 archives and a corresponding catalogue of 27,000 objects described by metadata. (For a more detailed description of OLAC, we refer interested readers to [17] and [16]). OLAC metadata is based on Dublin Core, with a number of extensions [15] to the Dublin Core Metadata Set [4] for relevant conceptual domains such as language [10], linguistic type [7], subject language [8], linguistic subject [9] and linguistic role [11].

Derived from the model adopted within the OAI, the OLAC model has a two-tiered approach to implementation. Data providers are the institutional language archives which publish their XML-based metadata according to the OAI Static Repository standard [5]. Individual archives use a variety of software to manage their catalogues internally. Service providers leverage the OAI Protocol for Metadata Harvesting [6] to harvest the XML expressions of metadata catalogues. Within the OLAC community, typical practice is to aggregate these into an SQL database using the OLAC Harvester and Aggregator [12]. Service providers can then build services which utilise the union catalogue of OLAC metadata. (The work reported here is an example of exactly this type of service.)

As a metadata community and a virtual digital library, OLAC has motivated a number of developments at the OAI level, notably the need for supporting static repositories [5], the development of virtual service providers [13] and personal metadata creation and management tools [14].

3 Motivation

Our primary motivation in the work reported here is to establish infrastructural support at the service provider level to facilitate metadata quality assessment in an ongoing fashion. As mentioned earlier, one consequence of the devolution of metadata creation and management has been that while metadata standards such as Dublin Core are well accepted by the community as a whole, compliance with these metadata standards and their extensions is in fact highly variable.

While the structural validation tools for metadata (such as the OAI Repository Explorer [26]) are in use within OLAC, there is a notable absence of tools which are oriented towards both structural and semantic validation. Previous work within the OLAC context [27] has resulted in useful survey tools, although they lack a qualitative dimension. Spanne [29] provided a useful overview of the state of OLAC metadata after the first year of implementation experience, and in part motivates the work reported here. In the broader OAI context, there are few examples of metadata quality assessment services (see for example [24], [25]). In particular, we draw motivation from previous work of Ward [19], where a longitudinal evaluation of the quality of DC metadata based on element and attribute usage within the OAI community is described.

Our work differs from previous efforts in three areas. First, we seek to establish a baseline against which future metadata instances can be compared in order to evaluate the maturity of the metadata creation process within OLAC. Second, we desire to provide assistance to individual data providers within OLAC with the means of self-evaluation and self-improvement. A third, but not insignificant goal, is to evaluate a number of domain-grounded controlled vocabularies specifically with regard to their adoption.

4 Algorithm Design

The objective of the algorithm is to arrive at a per metadata record score of between 0 and 10, based on the adherence to best practice guidelines for the use of Dublin Core metadata elements and codes ("core elements"), and the OLAC domain-specific controlled vocabularies ("codes"). Operations here are on a per metadata record basis.

The main algorithm derives two values - a Code Existence Score and an Element Absence Penalty, and then weighted to provide a Per Metadata Record Weighted Aggregate. Subsequent derivative metrics are then obtained using this aggregate as a baseline.

4.1 Code Existence Score

The principle for the derivation of the Code Existence Score is that for each element which has an associated extension from an OLAC controlled vocabulary, there is a corresponding increase in the quality of the metadata (ie. it becomes more fine-grained). A nominal score of 1 point is thus attributed to the metadata record. In turn, this is converted into a proportion of elements which use codes against the number of total elements in a record which have an associated controlled vocabulary. Hence the Code Existence Score is equal to the number of elements containing the code attributes divided by the number of elements of a type associated with a controlled vocabulary in the record, a value between 0 and 1.

4.2 Element Absence Penalty

The principle of deriving the Element Absence Penalty is that the quality of metadata declines with the absence of core elements which have been shown to be important to any metadata record (based on findings of Ward [19], Spanne [29] and our own surveys). Thus the following core elements have been deemed necessary in every record: title, description, subject, date and identifier.

For each of these core elements which is absent from a metadata record, a score of 0.2 is deducted from the metadata record score. This implies equal weighting of all the core elements. Hence, the Element Absence Penalty is equal to the number of core elements absent divided by the total number of core elements in a record, a value between 0 and 1.

4.3 Per Metadata Record Weighted Aggregate

Now we have both a Code Existence Score and an Element Absence Penalty, we combine these to derive a Per Metadata Record Weighted Aggregate. Essentially our approach is to reduce the theoretical maximum metadata record score of 10 by a factor proportional to the product of the Code Existence Score and the Element Absence Penalty. Hence the Per Metadata Record Weighted Aggregate is equal to the maximum score multiplied by the weighted product of the Code Existence Score and the Element Absence Penalty.

This results in an integer score out of 10 for each metadata record. These scores are held in a table ranking each item with a score out of 10. Scores are re-calculated when incremental metadata harvesting by the OLAC Harvester and Aggregator updates the collection of metadata records.

4.4 Derivative Metrics

Following this, a number of different metrics pertinent to metadata quality within an archive can be derived:

- Archive Diversity metric: A calculation of the diversity of controlled vocabulary usage within an archive, calculated for both subject and type. Diversity is calculated as being equal to the number of distinct code values divided by the number of instances of a metadata element, multiplied by 100 to provide a percentage.
- Metadata Quality Score metric: Derived from the aggregation of Per Metadata Record Weighted Aggregate scores within an archive.
- Core Elements Per Record metric: The percentage of records which have n of the core elements present at least once.
- Core Element Usage metrics: The percentage of records which contain the named element(s) at least once.
- Code Usage metrics: The number of times an element which has an associated code attribute is used by the archive, and the percentage of those elements which actually use a code attribute.
- Code and Element Usage metrics: The number of times an element is used. Where applicable, the number of times that a code attribute is used with that element.
- "Star Rating": A gross indicator, derived based on the average item score for the archive. It is calculated by dividing the average Per Metadata Record Weighted Aggregate for an archive by a factor of 2 and then applying rounding.

On the basis of this algorithm we can compute a score for each metadata record within an archive, for each archive in total, and for the community as a whole.

5 Implementation

The metadata quality assessment service is built on top of the foundational layer provided by the OLAC Harvester and Aggregator [12]. The implementation uses the open source technologies MySQL [22] and PHP [23], and is able to be installed on a range of platforms. The operational instance of the metadata quality assessment service can be viewed online [21]. The software has been released under an open source license, and is freely available to interested parties from [20].

6 Evaluation

Using the metadata quality assessment infrastructure, we can now evaluate a number of different aspects of metadata quality within the OLAC context. We consider our findings in a number of areas: on a per data provider basis; across the whole community; trends and similarities between archives; and specifically within the OLAC context, the use of controlled vocabularies.

6.1 Evaluating Metadata Quality on a Per Data Provider Basis

It is immediately apparent that there is a high degree of variability between individual data providers within OLAC. Some archives have very high per metadata record scores, while others are very low. While we did not specifically set out to create an "archive ranking system", it is clear that some archives have significantly better quality metadata than others.

There appears to be no systematic correlation between the size of an archive and its corresponding average Per Metadata Record Weighted Aggregate. While the archive which at the time of writing has the largest number of metadata records also has the highest average Per Metadata Record Weighted Aggregate, and the smallest archives have the lowest average Per Metadata Record Weighted Aggregate, the mid-sized archives are apparently random in distribution in terms of average Per Metadata Record Weighted Aggregates.

There does however, appear to be a positive correlation between the size of an archive and the average number of elements per metadata record within the archive. This can be accounted for by the fact that larger archives typically export OLAC metadata as a derivative of a larger, much richer, metadata catalogue. OLAC metadata elements are optional and optionally repeatable, and it is clear that larger archives have a strong tendency to repeat elements such as subject and type, an approach inherited from the richer non-OLAC metadata natively used in such archives.

6.2 Evaluating Metadata Quality on a Community-Wide Basis

Across the entire community, metadata quality is averaged, and as such, broad measures of metadata quality are subject to some bias on the basis of the ratio between number of metadata records per archive and the corresponding Per Metadata Record Weighted Aggregate. If a large archive was to leave the community there would be a significant effect on the metadata quality metrics not simply owing to the number of records in any one archive, but their corresponding average metadata score.

We find evidence to reinforce the findings of Ward [19] in relation to the metadata elements which were most frequently used. Furthermore, we can see that in the context of OLAC fact element usage can also be classified into 4 distinct classes.

In the first class is a single element: subject, which is used twice as often as the members of the next class. The second class consists of five elements: title, description, date, identifier and creator, which are used around half as often as subject. A third class contains format, type, contributor, publisher and isPartOf. Beyond this, a fourth class of infrequently used elements accounts for the remaining 33 elements from the Dublin Core Metadata Set. This last class interestingly includes language, which we find suprising given the linguistic focus of the digital archives within OLAC itself.

6.3 Qualitatively-Based Archive Clustering

Archives which have high metadata quality scores overall can be characterised as larger archives with high degree of quality control in the metadata creation process (generally long-standing archives with extensive infrastructural support, and for whom OLAC metadata is automatically generated). These archives have a tendency to use only core elements, and utilise sub-domain specific controlled vocabularies focused around subject. These archives have average Per Metadata Record Weighted Aggregate scores of between 8 and 10 points.

A second group of archives, characterised as smaller in size, but still having access to automated metadata generation systems archives, and significantly increased use of controlled vocabularies, can also be observed. These archives have average Per Metadata Record Weighted Aggregate scores between 4 and 7 points.

A final group of archives with the lowest average Per Metadata Record Weighted Aggregate scores (0-3 points) are clustered at the bottom of the list. These archives which provide only minimal metadata for small numbers of records, and their metadata catalogues have a tendency to be manually maintained. However, these archives are distinguished by virtue of their specialised holdings.

Over time, our objective is to promote upward migration on this scale - increasing the average item scores for each archive. One of the advantages of the infrastructure reported here is the fact that we can derive a longitudinal perspective on the evolution of metadata quality, a point we return to in the next section.

6.4 Use of OLAC Controlled Vocabularies

Specifically within the OLAC context, we can also evaluate the use of the various controlled vocabularies which distinguish this community from other Dublin Core-based efforts. Significant effort has been invested in the development of these controlled vocabularies, and the return on investment in these areas can now be assessed. In addition to raw statistics, we can observe a number of interesting trends across all archives.

In reference to subject, the controlled vocabulary was used 56% of the time, largely for language identification where international standards such as ISO-639 [28] (the recommended Dublin Core approach to language classification) are insufficiently granular to account for linguistic diversity. This contrasts with the use of the code for language, which is only used 30% of the time.

An interesting comparison can be made between creator and contributor. The same controlled vocabulary, the OLAC Role vocabulary [11] is applicable in both cases as an extension. However, we see that the creator code is used less that 1% of the time, while the contributor code is used 78% of the time. We can attribute this distinction perhaps to the process of creating language resources - there is typically one creator (a linguist) but multiple contributors (informants, translators etc). An additional factor here is that the Dublin Core recommendation to use contributor rather than creator emerged just prior to 2 of the largest OLAC data providers joining the community.

Perhaps suprisingly, the type code is only used 33% of the time. The OLAC Linguistic Data Type vocabulary is only small (consisting of three elements), yet important from the perspective of linguists in distinguishing the various data types prevalent in language documentation and description. Despite the low volume of usage of this controlled vocabulary, we can adduce that much differentiation between linguistic data types can be performed based on the title and subject elements.

7 Future Work

Now we have established viable infrastructural support for metadata quality assessment within the OLAC domain, we now turn to a discussion of future work. We identify a number of natural extensions to the work reported here: an improvement to the algorithm; a longitudinal study of metadata quality; the need for new services which leverage the metadata quality assessment mechanism; possible new metrics; and an assessment methodology for human-agent collaboration in the metadata creation task.

One possible weakness in the algorithm used in the first instance is that no consideration is given to the size of the archive in determining its ranking. As an item of future work, we propose to extend the overall algorithm to derive a new metric, a weighted aggregate ranking, which will eliminate this possible weakness in the scheme as implemented currently.

A stable but dynamic infrastructure for metadata quality assessment allows us to conduct a longitudinal study of the changing nature of metadata implementation within OLAC. We propose to collate snapshots of the quality of metadata on a per data provider and the aggregate for the whole community on a monthly basis, and to archive these online as a precursor to trend analysis.

Based on the ranking system on a per record and per archive basis, we can conceive of integrating the metadata quality assessment data as a key part of a range of extended services. Perhaps the most immediately realisable of these is the use of metadata quality metrics to provide visual and logical ordering to search engine results. We have already commenced work on a general search engine for OLAC [18] which leverages domain specific knowledge, and we view the metadata quality assessment framework as an integral part of such a service.

A second generation of metadata quality evaluation metrics within the OLAC context is also emerging. While the instantiation reported here forms a useful starting point, other metrics which reflect the core values of OLAC (such as the availability of data online and the use of OLAC's fine-grained domain-specific vocabularies) are envisaged with subsequent alterations to the core algorithm. Additionally exploration of the consistency of application of metadata across a data provider's records could be considered, allowing insight at the level of individual records rather than through the Per Metadata Record Weighted Aggregate. Such a metric (which is oriented at the quality of an archive's metadata) could be contrasted with another which reflected the quality of an archive's collection.

Furthermore, we are conscious that in many cases, metadata creation is an human-intensive process, and as such any computational assistance which can be offered is welcome. To date, one limiting factor has been the absence of an objective metadata quality evaluation framework without which it is difficult to assess the contribution of pro-active metadata creation by computational agents. In the OLAC context, we can now explore the automated enrichment of existing metadata and the creation of new metadata based on web data mining approaches as discussed in [30], and assess the effectiveness of such approaches against baseline.

8 Conclusion

Our work here has resulted in the deployment of a scalable, dynamically-adjusted metadata quality evaluation infrastructure. In turn this allows a new perspective on the quality of metadata within digital archives. While the lack of infrastructural support for qualitative assessment of metadata within the digital archives community is notable, we believe that the provision of tools which assist metadata creators and managers to understand the qualitative aspects of metadata are of critical importance. Such tools enable archive managers to identify specific areas for metadata enrichment activity, and hence derive the greatest return on investment. Having now implemented of a framework for metadata quality assessment which is sustainable over an extended period, we hope that such a service will assist archive maintainers to focus their metadata improvement efforts, resulting in higher quality metadata across the whole Open Language Archives Community. We offer our approach and implementation to the broader digital libraries community in the hope that the model and implementation may benefit a larger range of institutional data providers, and ultimately, end-users.

Acknowledgements

We are grateful to Amol Kamat for his programming assistance; to Steven Bird for editorial comments on an earlier version of this paper; and to Gary Simons for informative discussions.

The work reported in this paper has been sponsored by the National Science Foundation Grant Numbers 9910603 (ISLE: International Standards in Language Engineering) and 0094934 (Querying Linguistic Databases).

References

1. Dublin Core. http://dublincore.org
2. Open Archives Initiative. http://www.openarchives.org
3. Open Language Archives Community. http://www.language-archives.org
4. Dublin Core Metadata Element Set, Version 1.1: Reference Description. http://dublincore.org/documents/dces
5. Patrick Hochstenbach, Henry Jerez, Herbert Van de Sompel, 2003. The OAI-PMH Static Repository and Static Repository Gateway. Proceedings of the IEEE/ACM Joint Conference on Digital Libraries 2003 (JDCL'03). pp. 210-220.

6. Carl Lagoze, Herbert Van de Sompel, Michael Nelson and Simeon Warner, 2002. The Open Archives Initiative Protocol for Metadata Harvesting. http://www.openarchives. org/OAI/openarchivesprotocol.html
7. Helen Aristar-Dry and Heidi Johnson, 2002. OLAC Linguistic Data Type Vocabulary. http://www.language-archives.org/REC/type.html
8. Gary Simons and Steven Bird, 2003. OLAC Subject Language Vocabulary. http://www. language-archives.org/REC/language.html
9. Helen Aristar-Dry and Michael Appleby, 2003. OLAC Linguistic Subject Vocabulary. http://www.language-archives.org/REC/field.html
10. Gary Simons and Steven Bird, 2003. OLAC Language Vocabulary. http://www.language-archives.org/REC/language.html
11. Heidi Johnson, 2003. OLAC Role Vocabulary. http://www.language-archives.org/REC /role.html
12. Gary Simons, 2003. A Query Facility for the Selective Harvesting of OLAC Metadata. http://www.language-archives.org/NOTE/query.html
13. Gary Simons, 2003. OLAC Virtual Service Provider. http://www.language-archives. org/viser
14. Kurt Maly, Mohammad Zubair and Xiaoming Liu, 2001. Kepler. An OAI Data/Service Provider for the Individual. D-Lib Magazine 7(4). http://www.dlib.org/dlib/april01/ maly/04maly.html
15. Gary Simons and Steven Bird, 2002. Recommended Metadata Extensions. http://www. language-archives.org/REC/olac-extensions.html
16. Gary Simons and Steven Bird, 2003. The Open Language Archives Community: An infrastructure for distributed archiving of language resources. Literary and Linguistic Computing 18, pp.117-128.
17. Steven Bird and Gary Simons, 2003. Extending Dublin Core Metadata to support the description and discovery of language resources. Computing and the Humanities 37, pp.375-388.
18. Baden Hughes and Amol Kamat, 2004. A Metadata Search Engine for Language Archives. Manuscript.
19. Jewel Ward, 2003. A Quantitative Analysis of Unqualified Dublin Core Metadata Element Set Usage within Data Providers Registered with the Open Archives Initiative. Proceedings of the IEEE/ACM Joint Conference on Digital Libraries 2003 (JDCL'03). pp.315-317.
20. Open Language Archives Community Project at Sourceforge. http://olac.sourceforge.net
21. OLAC Archive Report Card. http://www.language-archives.org/tools/reports/archive ReportCard.php
22. MySQL Database Engine. http://www.mysql.com
23. PHP Scripting Engine. http://www.php.net
24. Lloyd Sokvitne, 2000. An Evaluation of the Effectiveness of Current Dublin Core Metadata for Retrieval. Proceedings of VALA 2000. Victorian Association for Library Automation: Melbourne.
25. Jane Greenberg, Maria Cristina Pattuelli, Bijan Parsia, and W. Davenport Robertson, 2001. Author-Generated Dublin Core Metadata for Web Resources: A Baseline Study in an Organisation. Journal of Digital Information 2(2).
26. OAI Repository Explorer. http://oai.dlib.vt.edu/cgi-bin/Explorer/oai2.0/testoai
27. OLAC Archive Survey. http://www.language-archives.org/tools/survey.php4

28. ISO, 1998. ISO 639-2: Codes for the representation of names of languages -- Part 2: Alpha-3 code. International Organisation for Standardization.
29. Joan Spanne, 2002. OLAC: The State of the Archives. Proceedings of the IRCS Workshop on Open Language Archives. Institute for Research in Cognitive Science, University of Pennsylvania. pp.42-46.
30. Baden Hughes, 2004. Perspectives on Metadata. Proceedings of the LREC 2004 Workshop on Building the Language Resources and Evaluation Roadmap: Joint COCOSDA and ICCWLRE Meeting. European Language Resources Association: Paris.

New Feature Selection and Weighting Methods Based on Category Information

Gongshen Liu, Jianhua Li, Xiang Li, and Qiang Li

School of Information Security Engineering, Shanghai Jiaotong University,
Shanghai, 200030, China
{Lgshen, lijh888, xiangli, Qiangli}@sjtu.edu.cn

Abstract. The traditional methods of feature selection and weighting make the best of document information, but despise or ignore the category information. The new feature selection and weighting methods use category information as a factor, which make up the disadvantages of traditional methods. Using new methods, the features distributed equally on a single category are more important than using old methods. It is proved by the experiment that four famous classifiers based on new feature selection and weighting methods are more effective than those based on traditional methods.

1 Introduction

Text categorization is the problem of automatically assigning predefined categories to free text documents. While more and more textual information is available online, effective retrieval is difficult without good weighting and summarization of document context. Text categorization can help to increase the efficiency of information retrieval by organizing information orderly. Text categorization dates up to the early'60s, but only in the early'90s did it become a major subfield of the information systems discipline, thanks to increased applicative interest and to the availability of more powerful hardware. A growing number of statistical classification methods and machine learning techniques have been applied to text categorization in recent years, including support vector machine[1], rocchio method[2], regression models[3], nearest neighbor classification[4], Bayes probabilistic approaches[5], decision trees[6], neural network[7], symbol rule learning[8], inductive learning algorithms[9] and voted classification[10].

Generally speaking, a text categorization system is composed of three steps (see Fig. 1.): text presentation, training process and classification process. The first step in text presentation is preprocessing, which removes the interferential information. Subsequently, the vector presentation of text is given by features selection and weighting. In training process, the system constructs and trains a classifier which is used in classification process. In classification process, the system can assigns a category label to a new text according to the trained classifier. Although the training and classification process are keys to the system, text presentation is also very important because it's the foundation of the others.

The VSM (Vector Space Method) is popular method to present a text as a vector. A major difficulty of text categorization is that the high dimensionality of the feature

Z. Chen et al. (Eds.): ICADL 2004, LNCS 3334, pp. 330–338, 2004.

space brings the high computation complexity to the system. Now, feature selection is the most effective and popular dimensionality reduction method. The features used to present text are confirmed after feature selection. The function of feature weighting is to determine the weight of each feature. Thus far, the common feature selection methods include document frequency (DF), information gain (IG), χ^2-statistic method (χ^2), mutual information (MI), term strength (TS) and so on. There are six popular feature weighting methods, such as Boolean weighting, word frequency, term frequency inverse document frequency (TFIDF), term frequency collection (TFC), Length Term Collection (LTC) and Entropy weighting. After introducing these traditional methods, new feature selection and weighting methods are proposed in this paper. In order to prove these new methods, an experiment is given.

An important issue of text categorization is how to measure the performance of classifiers. Many measures have been used, each of which has been designed to evaluate some aspect of the category performance of a system. The *precision* and *recall* are the most common methods for multi-label category[16]. They are defined as follows:

$$precision = \frac{a}{a+b} \qquad recall = \frac{a}{a+c}$$

where a – the number of documents correctly assigned to this category.

   b – the number of documents incorrectly assigned to this category.

   c – the number of documents incorrectly rejected from this category.

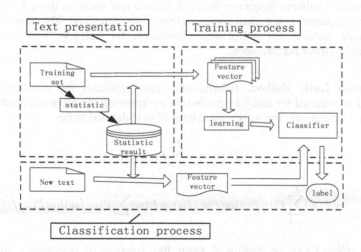

Fig. 1. A typical process of text category system

Firstly, this paper introduces the process of text category system and common feature selection and feature weighting methods. In section 2, we describe there feature selection methods and three feature weighting methods in detail. New methods for feature selection and weighting are given in section 3. Section 4 and 5 are experiment setting, experiment results and its analysis respectively.

2 Traditional Feature Selection and Weighting Methods

The vector space model is the most popular text presentation method. In this method, a text is presented by a vector (each item of the vector is the weight of corresponding feature) which is indexed by a feature set (According to the characteristic of different systems, feature may be word, string or conception). In order to describe easily, let $c_1, c_2, ... c_k$ denote K possible categories. w denotes a feature. a_{ik} is the weight of feature i in document k. f_{ik} is the frequency of feature i in document k. N is the number of documents in sample collection. n_i is the frequency of feature i in sample collection.

2.1 Feature Selection

Feature selection aims to remove some features which are non-informative for category prediction, increase the efficiency of category system and decrease time complexity. It is proved that, DF, IG and χ^2-statistic are three most effective methods in the five methods described above[11]. We describe these three methods as follows.

Document Frequency Method. The document frequency for a feature is the number of document in which the feature occurs. In Document Frequency method one computes the document frequency for each feature and removes those features whose document frequency is less than some predetermined threshold. The basic assumption is that rare features are either non-informative for category prediction, or not influential in global performance.

Information Gain Method. Information Gain measures the number of bits of information obtained for category prediction by knowing the presence or absence of a feature in a document. The information gain of w is defined to be:

$$IG(w) = -\sum_{j=1}^{K} P(c_j) \log P(c_j)$$

$$+ P(w) \sum_{j=1}^{K} P(c_j/w) \log P(c_j/w) + P(\overline{w}) \sum_{j=1}^{K} P(c_j/\overline{w}) \log P(c_j/\overline{w})$$

Here, $P(c_j)$ can be estimated from the fraction of documents in the total collection that belongs to class c_j and $P(w)$ from the fraction of documents in which the feature w occurs. Moreover, $P(c_j/w)$ can be computed as the fraction of documents from class c_j that have at least one occurrence of feature w and $P(c_j/\overline{w})$ as the fraction of documents from class c_j that does not contain feature w.

In feature selection process, the features whose information gain is less than some predetermined threshold are removed. As above formula shown, information gain take into account category information partially. There is a shortcoming of information gain: when feature w only occurs in one category, the value of IG is very small despite w is distributed equally in the category. In our own opinion, the value of IG must be comparatively big because w is a very strong feature of the category.

χ^2-**Statistic Method.** The χ^2-statistic measures the lack of independence between feature w and class c_j. It is given by:

$$\chi^2(w,c_j) = \frac{N \times (AD - CB)^2}{(A+B) \times (B+D) \times (A+B) \times (C+D)}$$

Here A is the number of documents from class c_j that contains feature w, B is the number of documents that contains w but does not belong to class c_j, C is the number of documents from class c_j that does not contain feature w, and D is the number of documents that neither belongs to class c_j nor contains feature w. Two different measures can be computed based on the χ^2 statistic.

$$\chi^2(w) = \sum_{j=1}^{K} P(c_j)\chi^2(w,c_j) \quad \text{or} \quad \chi^2_{max}(w) = \max_j \chi^2(w,c_j)$$

As above formula shown, along with increasing of χ^2, the independence of feature decreases and the dependence increase. Although the method also takes into account category information, there is the same shortcoming as information gain. When feature w only occurs in one category, the value of χ^2-statistic is zero despite w is distributed equally in the category. In our own opinion, the value of χ^2-statistic must be comparatively big because w is a very strong feature of the category.

2.2 Feature Weighting

The basic idea of Vector Space Model is to turn a text into a simple vector every element of which is the weight of corresponding feature. The features belong to vector confirmed after feature selection. The function of feature weighting is to determine the weight of each feature. There are six popular feature weighting methods, such as Boolean weighting, frequency weighting, term frequency inverse document frequency (TFIDF), term frequency collection (TFC), Length Term Collection (LTC) and Entropy weighting. Because of the demand of our experiment, frequency weight, TF-IDF and Entropy weighting are introduced as follows[12]:

Frequency Weighting. In this method, the weight is equal to frequency of feature.

$$a_{ik} = f_{ik}$$

TF-IDF Weighting. The previous scheme does not take into account the frequency of the feature throughout all documents in the collection. A well-known approach for computing weights is the TF-IDF weighting which assigns the weight to feature i in document k in proportion to the number of occurrences of the feature in the document, and in inverse proportion to the number of documents in the collection for which the feature occurs at least once.

$$a_{ik} = f_{ik} * \log(\frac{N}{dofw_i})$$

Here, $dofw_i$ is the number of documents in the collection for which the feature occurs at least once.

Entropy Weighting. Entropy weighting is based on information theoretic ideas and is the most sophisticated weighting scheme. In [13] it turned out to be the most effective scheme in comparison with the others. In the entropy weighting scheme, the weight for feature i in document k is given by:

$$a_{ik} = \log(f_{ik} + 1.0) * (1 + \frac{1}{\log(N)} \sum_{j=1}^{N} \left[\frac{f_{ij}}{n_i} \log(\frac{f_{ij}}{n_i}) \right])$$

Where, $\dfrac{1}{\log(N)} \sum\limits_{j=1}^{N} \left[\dfrac{f_{ij}}{n_i} \log(\dfrac{f_{ij}}{n_i}) \right]$ is the average uncertainty or entropy of feature i.

This quantity is -1 if the feature is equally distributed over all documents and 0 if the feature occurs in only one document.

There is not a factor in all above methods. Even if they make use of the factor, they only take into account the factor which is imposed on feature by document collection instead of category information. In our own opinion, the factor imposed by category information is more important than that imposed by document collection.

3 New Feature Selection and Feature Weighting Methods

In a text category system, a feature is expressed by word, string or conception. Due to the characteristic of Chinese language, there is a central problem for Chinese text category system: The dimensionality of feature space is very high because of the large number of Chinese word, string or conception. Feature selection aims to remove some features which are non-informative for category prediction, increase the efficiency of category system and decrease time complexity.

Definition 1. Feature Cluster
A feature cluster is a subset of feature set, which is the appropriate presentation of a category.

Definition 2. Feature Cluster of Category C.
The feature cluster which is the appropriate presentation of category C is the feature cluster of category C. It's denoted by $SofC(C)$.

Let T be the feature set after feature selection. The relation between all feature clusters and feature set T is: $T = SofC(C_1) \cup SofC(C_2) \cup \cdots \cup SofC(C_K)$. The aim of feature selection is to select a feature set, which satisfies the following two properties:

First, the intersection of feature clusters tends to be a null set. The less the intersection is, the less the interferential information among categories is, and the higher the precision of the category system is. The boundary of the intersection is null, i.e. $\theta = SofC(C_1) \cap SofC(C_2) \cap \cdots \cap SofC(C_K)$. When the intersection is null, there is not interferential information among categories and the feature space is the most appropriate.

Second, all features of a feature cluster are distributed equally in documents which belong to its corresponding category. The distribution of a feature reflects the extent of its presentation. When a feature occurs in every document of a category, its distribution is the most equal and its presentation to the category is the strongest. Whereas, when a feature occurs only in one document of a category, its distribution is the most unequal and its presentation to the category is the weakest.

Under the guidance of above theories, a new feature selection method and a new feature weighting method are proposed based on the analysis of old methods.

3.1 Feature Selection Function $s(w)$

Let $f(w, c_j)$ denote the relativity of feature w and category c_j. The feature selection function $s(w)$ is defined as follows:

$$s(w) = \max_{1 \le i < k}[f(w, c_i) - \sum_{1 \le j < k, j \ne i} f(w, c_j)]$$

The greater the value of $s(w)$ is, the stronger the presentation of feature w is. If we regard the samples in category c_j as a document set, i.e. c_j is composed of a group of documents d_x ($0 < i \le D_j$, D_j is the number of documents belonging to category c_j), the value of $f(w, c_j)$ should be in proportion to the occurrences of w in c_j, and in proportion to the equality extent of w's distribution in c_j. Let $finc_{ij}$ be the frequency of feature i in category c_j, $dofw_{ij}$ be the number of documents in category c_j in which feature i occurs. The definition of $f(w, c_j)$ is:

$$f(w, c_j) = \frac{\log(finc_{ij} + 1.0) * \log(\dfrac{dofw_{ij}}{D_j} + 1.0)}{\sqrt{\sum_{t=1}^{|T|}\left[\log(finc_{tj} + 1.0) * \log(\dfrac{dofw_{tj}}{D_j} + 1.0)\right]^2}}$$

3.2 Feature Weighting Function a_{ik} :

There is a shortcoming of traditional feature weighting methods. There is not a factor in some methods. Even if they make use of the factor, they only take into account the factor which is imposed on feature by document collection instead of category information. In our own opinion, the factor imposed by category information is more important than that imposed by document collection. Below is weighting function proposed in this paper:

$$a_{ik} = \log(f_{ik} + 1.0) * (1 + \frac{1}{\log(K)} \sum_{j=1}^{K} \left[\frac{finc_{ij}}{n_i} \log(\frac{finc_{ij}}{n_i}) \right])$$

Where, K denotes the possible category number in document collection. $finc_{ij}$ is

the frequency of feature i in category c_j. $\frac{1}{\log(K)} \sum_{j=1}^{K} \left[\frac{finc_{ij}}{n_i} \log(\frac{finc_{ij}}{n_i}) \right]$ is the factor.

When feature i is distributed equally in every category, the value of the factor is -1 and a_{ik} reaches its minimum value 0. When feature i occurs only in one category, the value of the factor is 0 and a_{ik} reaches its maximum value $\log(f_{ik} + 1.0)$.

4 Experiment Settings

In order to prove the new feature selection and feature weighting methods proposed in this paper, we use a few classifiers to compare new methods with the old ones.

Feature selection methods for comparison are document frequency, information gain and χ^2-statistic. They are denoted to S_1, S_2, S_3 respectively.

Feature weighting methods for comparison are frequency weighting, TF-IDF weighting and Entropy weighting. They are denoted to W_1, W_2, W_3 respectively.

There are four classifiers used in this experiment: Rocchio, KNN, Naïve Bayes (NB) and Support Vector Machine (SVM). The Naive Bayes method is modified from Laird Breyer's dbacl project [14]; The SVM method is the famous LibSVM software [15]; The Rocchio and KNN algorithms are coded by us.

The sample set is come from China Infobank (a famous company in HongKong). , It is enough to evaluate new classifier, although the sample set used in this experiment is not the standard collection (such as Reuters). The sample set is composed of 100 thousand documents which are Chinese news (written in Chinese apparently).

There are 116 possible category labels in the sample set. Because the sample set is large enough, there are many documents belonging to each possible category label. For a category C_i ($0 < i \leq 116$), the documents are split into a 70% training set (tr_i) and 30% testing set (te_i) randomly. At last, the training set of the sample set is Tr (Tr $= \sum_{i=1}^{116} tr_i$) and the testing set is Te (Te $= \sum_{i=1}^{116} te_i$).

The evaluation method is open test. We use *precision and recall* to evaluate them.

5 Experiment Results and Conclusion

New feature selection and feature weighting methods are measured with four classifiers respectively. As table 1 shown, the *precision* and *recall* of every classifier are all improved with new feature selection and feature weighting methods. The improvements of Roochio and KNN are remarkable, because these classifiers depend on text presentation very much. The improvements of NB and SVM are not so remarkable as that of Roochio and KNN, because the dependency of these classifiers on text presentation is less.

Table 1. Test results of control experiment

methods	NB		Rocchio		KNN		SVM	
	precision	recall	precision	recall	precision	recall	precision	recall
S_1+W_1	78.9	81.2	75.3	79.8	81.2	79.9	83.1	82.8
S_1+W_2	77.8	76.4	74.9	80.4	82.5	80.1	82.9	81.5
S_1+W_3	76.6	80.1	78.5	78.7	81.8	80.3	83.0	84.3
S_2+W_1	80.0	79.7	75.7	79.3	80.7	81.7	87.3	88.0
S_2+W_2	82.3	82.5	80.8	81.4	83.0	78.9	87.7	86.9
S_2+W_3	81.9	83.4	81.0	80.3	82.8	82.0	88.0	90.2
S_3+W_1	80.7	79.8	80.7	78.6	81.4	80.6	89.2	89.3
S_3+W_2	84.0	83.2	82.0	83.1	82.4	83.4	90.9	91.1
S_3+W_3	86.7	85.9	83.3	84.6	82.0	84.7	92.1	91.4
New	89.2	87.4	90.3	89.0	93.5	91.5	92.8	93.6

References

1. Joachims T. Text categorization with support vector machines: learning with many relevant features. In Proceedings of ECML-98, 10th European Conference on Machines Learning (Chemnitz, Germany, 1998), 137-142.
2. Hull D.A. Improving text retrieval for the routing problem using latent semantic indexing. In Proceedings of SIGIR-94, 17th ACM International Conference on Research and Development in Information Retrieval(Dublin, Ireland 1994), 282-289.
3. Fuhr N. Pfeifer U. Probabilistic information retrieval as combination of abstraction inductive learning and probabilistic assumptions. ACM Trans. Inform Syst. Vol.12, 1994(1), 92-115.
4. Greecy R. H., Masand B. M. Smith S. J. Waltz D. L. Trading mips and memory for knowledge engineering: classifying census returns on the connection machine. Comm. ACM, 1992(35), 48-63.
5. Lewis D. D. Naïve Bayes at forty: The independence assumption in information retrieval. In Proceedings of ECML-98, 10th European Conference on Machine Learning (Chemnitz, Germany, 1998), 4-15.
6. Mitchell T.M. Machine Learning. McGraw Hill, New York, NY 1996.

7. Dagan I, Karov Y, Roth D. Mistake-driven learning in text categorization. In Proceedings of EMNLP-97, 2nd Conference on Empirical Methods in Natural Language Processing (Providence, RI, 1997), 55-63.
8. Moulinier I, Raskinis G, Ganascia J. Text Categorization: a symbolic approach. In Proceedings of the 5th Annual Symposium on Document Analysis and Information Retrieval. 1996.
9. Lewis D. D, Schapire R. E, Callan J. P. Training algorithm for linear text classifiers. In SIGIR'96: Proceedings of the 19th Annual International ACM SIGIR Conference on Research and Development in Information Retrieval , 1996, 298-306.
10. Schapire R. E. Singer Y. BoosTexter: a boosting –based system for text categorization. Mach. Learn. Vol.39, 2000(2/3), 135-168.
11. Yang Y., Pedersen J. P. Feature selection in statistical learning of text categorization, In the 14th Int.Conf.on Machine Learning. 1997, 412-420.
12. Salton G., McGill M. J. An Introduction to Modern Information Retrieval, McGraw-Hill, 1983.
13. Dumais S.T. Improving the retrieval information from external sources, Behavior Research Methods, Instruments and Computers, Vol.23, 2(1991), 229-236.
14. Breyer L.A. The DBACL Text Classifier, http://www.lbreyer.com.
15. Chang C. C., Lin C. J. LIBSVM: a Library for Support Vector Machines, http://www. csie.ntu.edu.tw.
16. Yang Y. An evaluation of statistical approaches to text categorization. Journal of Information Retrieval, Vol.1, 1(1999), 67-88.

Metadata Quality Study for the National Science Digital Library (NSDL) Metadata Repository

Marcia Lei Zeng[1], Bhagirathi Subrahmanyam[1], and Gregory M. Shreve[2]

[1] School of Library and Information Science,
[2] Dept. of Applied Linguistics,
Kent State University, Kent, OH 44242-0001, USA
{mzeng, bsubrahm, gshreve}@kent.edu

Metadata repositories are loosely-controlled environments where each discrete metadata dataset retains its independent identity, multiple standards were applied, and records were contributed on a voluntary-based system. As more integrated digital libraries take such an approach in order to provide comprehensive collections, quality of the metadata records describing these collections' items has drawn increased attention, since they function as a 'window' of a digital library collection and its services and directly involve in the success or failure of any information seeing performance. This poster reports the preliminary findings from a project funded by the National Science Foundation to study the quality of the metadata records in the National Science Digital Library (NSDL)'s Metadata Repository. (Figure 1. Project work space).

Measurements were conducted based on two research samples as well as the complete datasets of the collections in the repository. Data was collected for the

Z. Chen et al. (Eds.): ICADL 2004, LNCS 3334, pp. 339–340, 2004.

analysis of sample level, collection level, record level, and element level. Measurement aspects include:

- Completeness;
- Correctness (content, format, input, browser interpretation, mapping/integration, and redundancy);
- Consistency; and
- Duplication (intra-collection and inter-collection).

Most of the completeness and consistency checking and part of the correctness checking were completed through automated process. Data of content correctness, duplication, and mapping/converting was colleted based on record-to-original-source analysis by human. This poster will display different levels measurement datasheets, as illustrated by the following figure: (Figure 2. Collection level analysis).

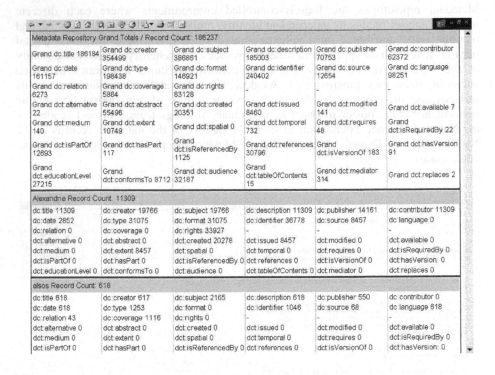

The project has made recommendations of quality control procedures and provided some quality checking tools.

Providing Parallel Metadata for Digital Libraries with Linguistically Heterogeneous Documents

Gregory M. Shreve[1] and Marcia L. Zeng[2]

[1] Dept. of Applied Linguistics,
[2] School of Library & Information Science,
Kent State University, Kent, OH 44242-0001, USA
{gshreve, mzeng}@kent.edu

Abstract. Discusses multilingual and culture-dependent metadata issues affecting the GREEN digital library and proposes a robust approach to internationalizing digital library collections.

1 Background: The GREEN Digital Library

The GREEN (Green's Functions Research and Education Enhancement Network) Digital Library (DL) is a member collection of the National Science Foundation's National Science Digital Library (NSDL). A unique aspect of the GREEN collection is that it was designed from the outset to include multilingual resources. The collection contains original documents from multiple languages, currently including English, French, German, Spanish, and Chinese.

GREEN metadata records are an XML version of the IEEE Learning Object Metadata specification (IEEE-LOM). The records describe a variety of electronic resources in the domain of computational materials science. These resources range from traditional journal articles to custom markup documents in MathML (Mathematical Markup Language) and MatML (Materials Markup Language).

2 Handling Linguistically Heterogeneous Documents

DLs like GREEN may contain resources in many languages. Accessible through the Internet, these resources may be consulted by individuals in other *cultural locales* seeking resources *in their own languages* or searching *across languages* for documents in languages other than their own. DLs must be properly engineered to accommodate cross-language and cross-cultural use.

Two important processes are involved in creating *culturally adapted* and *culturally adaptable* libraries: *internationalization*, a design process intended to enable subsequent linguistic and cultural adaptation; and *localization*, the preparation of locale-specific versions of a library's interface, metadata, and resources.

Localization is the preparation of locale-specific versions of an object or collection. It consists of the *translation* of textual material into the language and

Z. Chen et al. (Eds.): ICADL 2004, LNCS 3334, pp. 341–344, 2004.

textual conventions of the target locale and the *adaptation* of non-textual materials and *delivery / display* mechanisms to take into account the cultural requirements of that locale. Internationalization is an "upstream" engineering process that should precede localization. Its aim is to make subsequent localization easier, more efficient, and less costly. It may involve extensive use of *controls* (writing style, graphics and typography, vocabularies/terminologies) and *separation* of a *neutral kernel* from language/culture dependent resources.

The internationalization question in DL design involves (1) the languages of the resources described and (2) the languages used in descriptions of the resources. Preparing a digital library for multilingual usage means that a range of important issues have to be dealt with: different writing systems and character sets of resources; different display preferences (interface, resources); universal and localized metadata; cross-language restricted vocabularies; cross-language searching; and multilingual content of metadata elements.

While the issues of writing systems and display preferences are interesting, this paper focuses on metadata, restricted vocabulary value spaces for elements and metadata content.

3 Providing Metadata in Support of Localizing a DL

Technologically, there are two approaches to providing metadata in support of localizing a DL. Both approaches involve multilingually / multiculturally "parallel" metadata elements and value spaces.

The first approach is *inline parallel* and involves providing multiple local versions of, for instance, a title or keyword data element in a resource record. The data elements are flagged as "local" versions via the *lang* attribute. (Figures 1 and 2). This is the most common localization method. Note that "equivalence" is assumed via adjacency and no authority is provided.

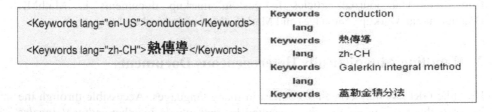

Figs. 1 and 2. Examples of parallel metadata values as they appear in an original metadata record (left) and on the web browser (right)

A second and more fruitful approach provides references to external localized objects. The external objects can be translation memories (for translations of titles, descriptions or other textual content, see Figure 3) or standard (e.g., ISO 12620) glossaries (for multilingual equivalents of data element names and their possible restricted vocabulary values). This is the *external parallel* approach.

Both inline parallel and external approaches can exploit the multilingual character of original sources included in the DL collection. We have found that many non-English theses, technical reports and specifications provide various levels of English translations, mainly the title, author, and sometimes, keywords and glossaries. These equivalent "pairs" of terms form a basic bilingual or multilingual terminology pool. They are usually provided by the authors who have done reading and research in the subject area, therefore terms are generally well-accepted translations in the community and therefore more accurate than machine or uninformed human translation. It would be a waste to let such useful information be wasted by creating English only metadata records. The inline and external parallel approaches can preserve this important data.

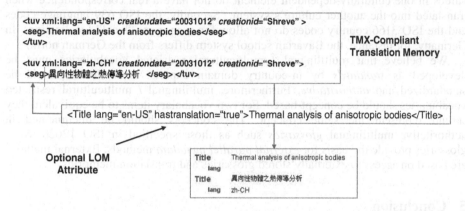

Fig. 3. A localization process based on a translation memory

Internationalizing a metadata schema involves determining the elements and element attributes that could affect the scheme's ability to be used for classification, search, retrieval, and reuse of learning objects in multicultural and multilingual contexts. Internationalization specifies elements that are *culturally and linguistically dependent*. Ideally, internationalization is a goal during initial schema development. It may be necessary to recommend additions and modifications to the elements and element sets of an existing metadata schema.

4 Understanding Issues of Culturally Dependent Metadata

Some "universal" metadata elements have values that may be very culturally dependent. These could be the elements of *Addresses, Calendar, Currency, Date, Numbers, Telephone, Time*, etc. International and national standards have been developed to guide and control of use of values for these elements. Some particular metadata elements value spaces in particular schemas may be pre-defined by the metadata schema producers. For instance, an American-based schema might control its *educational context* element value space with the terms *elementary school, middle school*, etc. These choices could be extremely limiting because they are derived from a single cultural context. As one can see from the following example. (Figure 4.)

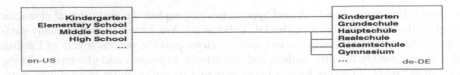

Fig. 4. Examples of different educational systems in different countries

In this example, some values have one-to-one equivalence. Others do not. The values imply different age ranges, different educational objectives and values and different social structures. There could be two potential problems here. First, the values in one culturally-dependent element do not have a real correspondence when translated into the another culture's system. Secondly, the ISO 639 language codes and the ISO 3166 country codes do not allow for even more "local" localization. In Germany, for instance, the Bavarian school system differs from the German norm.

We believe that multilingual / multicultural restricted vocabularies must be developed as *standards* by in-country domain experts. Equivalence should be standardized and *authoritative*. Furthermore, multilingual / multicultural restricted vocabularies should be concept-based. For two vocabulary items to be equivalent they should represent the same concept. The concepts should be documented in authoritative multilingual *glossaries* such as those specified in ISO 12620. Such glossaries provide the basis for *external parallel metadata* methods. External methods are based on access to externally stored glossaries and translation memories.

5   Conclusion

Adding multilingual and multicultural metadata to a DL involves:

1. Determining the metadata elements, attributes, value spaces and values that are culturally dependent and, if the display and interface are to be localized, those metadata elements that are to be rendered in multiple languages;
2. Providing an inline or external parallel mechanism for localization;
3. The external parallel mechanism is a more robust and scalable solution to digital library internationalization.

References

1. Baker, Thomas. 1997. Metadata Semantics Shared Across Languages: Dublin Core in languages other than English. http://dublincore.org/documents/multilingual-semantics/
2. European Committee for Standardization. 2003. CEN Workshop Agreement 14643. Internationalisation of the IEEE Learning Object Metadata. ICS 03.180; 35.060; 35.240.99.
3. European Schoolnet. Recommended data model format to be used as a standard by national systems to include national/local resources in the EU Treasury Browser. http://www.en.eun. org/etb/survey/d4.2.pdf

A Kind of Index for Content-Based Music Information Retrieval and Theme Mining*

Jianzhong Li, Chaokun Wang, and Shengfei Shi

Department of Computer Science and Engineering,
P.O.Box 318, Harbin Institute of Technology, 150001, Harbin, Heilongjiang, China
{lijzh, chaokun, shengfei}@hit.edu.cn

Abstract. Content-based music information retrieval and theme mining are two key problems in digital music libraries, where "themes" mean the longest repeating patterns in a piece of music. However, most data structures constructed for retrieving music data can not be efficiently used to mine the themes of music pieces, and vice versa. The suffix tree structure can be used for both functions, nevertheless its height is too large and its maintenance is somewhat difficult. In this paper, a kind of index structure is introduced, which adopts the idea of inverted files and that of N-gram. It can be used to retrieve music data as well as to mine music themes. Based on the index and several useful concepts, a theme mining algorithm is proposed. Also, two implementations of a content-based music information retrieval algorithm are presented. Experiments show the correctness and efficiency of the proposed index and algorithms.

1 Motivation

With the rapid progress of technologies for production, processing, and promulgation of music data, more and more attention has been paid to research and development of digital music libraries. Music information retrieval and music theme mining are two key problems in the field, where a repeating pattern is a sequence of notes appearing more than once in a music object and "themes" mean longest repeating patterns in a piece of music. There have been a lot of work for the first problem [e.g. 1], as well as many works for the second one [e.g. 2, 3].

However, methods for the two problems are almost detached, i.e., the data structures constructed for retrieving music data can not be efficiently used to mine the themes of music pieces, and vice versa. A lot of storage space and computational time are wasted for that. The suffix tree structure can be used for both functions, nevertheless its height is too large and its maintenance is somewhat difficult [4]. In this paper, the N-gram inverted index is proposed to partially bridge this gap. It adopts

---

* This work was supported by the National Grand Fundamental Research 973 Program of China under Grant No.G1999032704, the NSF of China under Grant No.60273082, the 863 Research Plan of China under Grant No.2002AA444110 and the Army Research Plan of China under Grant No.41315.2.3.

Z. Chen et al. (Eds.): ICADL 2004, LNCS 3334, pp. 345–354, 2004.

the idea of inverted files and that of N-gram, and can be used to retrieve music data as well as mine musical themes.

Our main contributions are as follows. Firstly, the N-gram inverted index structure is proposed. It can be used for both music theme mining and music information retrieval. Secondly, the complete difference, abbreviated as CD, between two integer sets is proposed. The properties of the operation are also presented. Thirdly, a music theme mining algorithm based on CD is given. Finally, two implementations of a content-based music information retrieval algorithm based on CD are given.

The rest of the paper is organized as follows. Related work is reviewed in Section 2. The structure of N-gram inverted index is described in Section 3. The applications of the index structure for theme mining and music information retrieval are respectively discussed in Section 4 and 5. Experimental results are reported in Section 6. Conclusions and future work are given in Section 7.

2 Related Works

Many works have been made in the field of indexing symbolic music data. Chou et al. investigated the music index structures based on chord-representation model and PAT-tree [5]. In [1], Chen et al. proposed techniques to retrieve music data on mubols (where a mubol is the rhythm pattern of measure in the song) and L-Tree index structure. Liu et al. stored positions of the same music notes into linked lists [6]. Only the notes involved in the query string will be retrieved. However the kind of index structure is not efficient when the query string includes nearly all characters of the alphabet. On the basis of suffix trees, Lee and Chen proposed four kinds of index structures for music information retrieval to process queries on different music features [7]. However, Combined Suffix Tree can not be used to process queries on single music feature. More time will be used by Independent Suffix Tree when queries are proposed on multiple music features. In addition, the scalability of Twin Suffix Tree is not good. The construction of Grid-Twin Suffix Tree is fussy, especially when there are 3 and more kinds of music features. Chen et al. considered the problem to retrieve songs by music segments and a kind of modified suffix trees [8]. A music segment is a triplet that consists of the segment type and the associated beat and pitch information. However the height of the tree is limited. It is suggested be no more than 30.

As an important music feature, the music theme can be used for both music data analysis and content-based music information retrieval. There is also some work on the problem of repeating pattern and theme finding of music data. Tseng proposed an algorithm to extract the key melody from music objects [2]. Hsu et al. presented two methods to extract non-trivial repeating patterns from music data [3]. One is based on correlative matrix computing, and the other is the combination of PR-Tree and string join operations.

Unfortunately, to our best of knowledge, there are few works on the combination of theme mining and information retrieval of music data, though the previous work can be used to deal with one of them. In detail, existing methods ignore the relation between the two problems. For example, one has to establish a PR-Tree for music theme mining although he or she has established a PAT-Tree for information retrieval. In order words, it will be better to use a same data structure to mine music themes and retrieve music information. It is said that suffix trees can be used to find music themes and retrieve music data in [7], however no effective solution is proposed to reduce the height of the tree structure.

3 The Structure of the N-Gram Inverted Index

In this section, the preliminary knowledge about music is provided. Then the distribution of feature substrings of a music dataset is discussed. Finally the structure of the N-gram index is presented.

3.1 Preliminary Knowledge

A piece of music is considered as a note sequence in much research work (e.g. [9]), thus a piece of music and a note sequence have the same meaning in this paper. According to the music theory and MIDI specification [10], the range of notes can be extended to $C_3 \sim G^6$. The algorithm used here for musical feature-extracting is applied widely, and the idea of it can be found in [11]. For instance, let a character set Σ be $\{R, U, W, D, B\}$. R means the latter note is same to the former note. U means the latter is higher than the former by at most 3 semi-tones. W means the latter is higher than the former by at least 4 semi-tones. D means the latter is lower than the former by at most 3 semi-tones. B means the latter is lower than the former by at least 4 semi-tones. Then a segment of melody $C^1C^1D^1AE^{1\#}F^1F^1$ is mapped into a string $RUBWUD$, which is called a feature string of the melody.

3.2 Distribution of Feature Substrings

HIT-DML is a digital music library prototype that adopts a novel framework [12]. There are currently 1,069 pieces of MIDI music in the library. The HIT-DML dataset, whose character set is the above Σ, is a set of real melody strings stored in HIT-DML. The average length of each melody is 511, and the maximum length is 3,839. There are 28% W, 15% U, 16% R, 15% D, and 26% B in it. The HIT-DML dataset is restored from a table in the database to a text file in the disk for experiments in this paper. In order to establish indices reasonably, the statistical information about music feature strings of a music dataset is collected firstly. Let i be the length of feature substrings, N_i be the number of feature substrings whose lengths are i, n_i be the number of distinct feature substrings whose lengths are i. The ratio between N_i and n_i, denoted as η_i, is called the average occurrence of feature substrings with length i. Intuitively, η_i represents the average usage frequency of each distinct substring with length i.

The statistical results on the HIT-DML dataset are listed in Table 1. It shows that the average occurrence decreases when the length of feature substrings increases. When i is more than 7, η_i is less than 10; when i is more than 12, η_i is less than 2.5. Thus it is not sensible to make indices on longer substrings. The same is for shorter feature substrings because their semantics are not clear, i.e., each of them corresponds to a lot of music objects and is not capable to distinguish various music objects, and a user hardly ever retrieves music data based on two or three notes. In a word, it is better to decide a basic unit for indexing the HIT-DML dataset by the N-gram method. The same is to other music datasets.

Table 1. Statistical results on the HIT-DML dataset

i	N_i	n_i	η_i
1	542,584	5	108,516.80
2	541,522	25	21,660.88
3	540,460	125	4,323.68
4	539,398	625	863.04
5	538,336	3,093	174.05
6	537,276	13,267	40.50
7	536,216	40,315	13.30
8	535,156	80,741	6.63
9	534,098	121,487	4.40
10	533,040	155,907	3.42
11	531,982	183,895	2.89
12	530,926	206,157	2.58

3.3 The Structure of the Index

The N-gram index structure is established based on the idea of inverted files and that of N-gram. The structure of the index can be described as an array. Each element of the array is a feature substring, called an indexed term, and a pointer to a linked list. A record in the linked list is a two-tuple (*midi_id*, *positions*), which shows that the indexed term occurs at these *positions* of the feature string whose identifier is *midi_id*. All indexed terms have the same length.

The process of creating the index of a music dataset is divided into two phases. A temporary table for a piece of music is created, and then it is inserted into the index. The temporary table used in the following algorithm is an array whose element has the format (*fss*, *positions*), where *positions* are the locations of a feature substring *fss* in the piece of music.

Table 2. A set of music feature strings

Id	string
1	UUBDWDDUDWWBR
2	WDDWUUBDWDDWUDWRBR
3	RDRUUUBDWDRUUDDWU

Based on the discussion in the previous subsection, a certain value should be decided to be the length of indexed feature substrings. Without loss of generality, in the rest of this paper, the number 4 is used as the length of indexed terms in the temporary file. It is because the tradeoff between the number of distinct feature substrings with length 4 and the average occurrence of such substrings is better.

Given a set of music feature strings (see Table 2) based on the feature character set Σ in Subsection 3.1, where *id* is the identifier of each feature string, and *string* represents the content of the feature string, then the temporary table of the second feature string is illustrated in Fig. 1. The index of the set is shown in Fig. 2.

$$
\begin{aligned}
\text{``WRBR''} &\longmapsto [14]\\
\text{``UDWR''} &\longmapsto [12]\\
\text{``WDDW''} &\longmapsto [0, 8]\\
\text{``WUUB''} &\longmapsto [3]\\
\text{``URDW''} &\longmapsto [5]\\
\text{``DWUD''} &\longmapsto [10]\\
\text{``WUDW''} &\longmapsto [11]\\
\text{``BDWD''} &\longmapsto [6]\\
\text{``UUBD''} &\longmapsto [4]\\
\text{``DWRB''} &\longmapsto [13]\\
\text{``DDWU''} &\longmapsto [1, 9]\\
\text{``DWUU''} &\longmapsto [2]\\
\text{``DWDD''} &\longmapsto [7]
\end{aligned}
$$

Fig. 1. The temporary table of a feature string

4 Theme Mining Based on *N*-Gram Inverted Index

In this section, the application of the N-gram index for music theme mining is proposed. The temporary table of a music feature string is used here. The mining process can be performed during or after the construction of the N-gram index. At first, several concepts are introduced.

Let A and B be two finite integer set, $A=\{p_1, p_2,..., p_i\}$, $B=\{q_1, q_2, ..., q_j\}$. The complete difference between A and B is defined as $\gamma(A, B) = \{d:[pd_1, ..., pd_t] \mid d = q_y - pd_x,\ 1 \le x \le t,\ \{pd_1, ..., pd_t\} \subseteq A,\ 1 \le y \le j\}$. The k-component of the complete difference between A and B is defined as $\gamma_k(A, B) = \{pd_1, ..., pd_t\}$, if $q_y - pd_x = k,\ 1 \le x \le t,\ 1 \le y \le j$; otherwise $\gamma_k(A, B) = \Phi$, where Φ means a null set.

For example, let $A=\{1, 2, 3\}$, $B=\{-2,-1,4\}$, then the complete difference between A and B is $\gamma(A, B)=\{1:[3], 2:[2], 3:[1], -2:[1], -3:[1,2], -4:[2,3], -5:[3]\}$. The -4-component of the complete difference between A and B is $\gamma_{-4}(A, B)=\{2,3\}$, and the 4-component of the complete difference between A and B is $\gamma_4(A, B)= \Phi$.

Let A and B be two finite integer set, $A=\{p_1, p_2, ..., p_i\}$, $B=\{q_1, q_2, ..., q_j\}$. If the complete difference between A and B is $\gamma(A, B) = \{d^1:[c^1_1, c^1_2, ..., c^1_{n_1}], d^2:[c^2_1, c^2_2, ..., c^2_{n_2}], ..., d^m:[c^m_1, c^m_2, ..., c^m_{n_m}]\}$, the complete difference between B and A is $\gamma(B, A) = \{-d^1:[d^1+c^1_1, d^1+c^1_2, ..., d^1+c^1_{n_1}], -d^2:[d^2+c^2_1, d^2+c^2_2, ..., d^2+c^2_{n_2}], ..., -d^m:[d^m+c^m_1, d^m+c^m_2, ..., d^m+c^m_{n_m}]\}$. This property is called the duality principle of complete difference. One of its applications is as follows.

Let A and B be two finite integer set, $\gamma(A, B)=\{1:[3], 2:[2], 3:[1], -2:[1], -3:[1,2], -4:[2,3], -5:[3]\}$. Then the complete difference between B and A can be achieved directly from $\gamma(A, B)$. That is $\gamma(B, A)=\{-1:[1+3], -2:[2+2], -3:[3+1], -(-2):[-2+1],$

- (-3):[-3+1,-3+2], -(-4):[-4+2,-4+3], -(-5):[-5+3]} = {-1:[4], -2:[4], -3:[4], 2:[-1], 3:[-2,-1], 4:[-2,-1], 5:[-2]}.

$$
\begin{aligned}
\text{"WDDU"} &\longmapsto (1, [14]) \\
\text{"WDDW"} &\longmapsto (2, [0, 8]) \\
\text{"WWBR"} &\longmapsto (1, [9]) \\
\text{"DWUD"} &\longmapsto (2, [10]) \\
\text{"WUDW"} &\longmapsto (2, [11]) \\
\text{"DWWB"} &\longmapsto (1, [8]) \\
\text{"DWUU"} &\longmapsto (2, [2]) \\
\text{"WDRU"} &\longmapsto (3, [8]) \\
\text{"RUUU"} &\longmapsto (3, [2]) \\
\text{"WUUB"} &\longmapsto (2, [3]) \\
\text{"UUDD"} &\longmapsto (3, [11]) \\
\text{"RDRU"} &\longmapsto (3, [0]) \\
\text{"UUBD"} &\longmapsto (1, [0]) \longrightarrow (2, [4]) \longrightarrow (3, [4]) \\
\text{"RUUD"} &\longmapsto (3, [10]) \\
\text{"DRUU"} &\longmapsto (3, [1, 9]) \\
\text{"WRBR"} &\longmapsto (2, [14]) \\
\text{"UUUB"} &\longmapsto (3, [3]) \\
\text{"UBDW"} &\longmapsto (1, [1]) \longrightarrow (2, [5]) \longrightarrow (3, [5]) \\
\text{"UDDW"} &\longmapsto (3, [12]) \\
\text{"DWRB"} &\longmapsto (2, [13]) \\
\text{"UDWW"} &\longmapsto (1, [7]) \\
\text{"UDWR"} &\longmapsto (2, [12]) \\
\text{"DDUD"} &\longmapsto (1, [5]) \\
\text{"DWDR"} &\longmapsto (3, [7]) \\
\text{"BDWD"} &\longmapsto (1, [2]) \longrightarrow (2, [6]) \longrightarrow (3, [6]) \\
\text{"DDWU"} &\longmapsto (2, [1, 9]) \longrightarrow (3, [13]) \\
\text{"DUDW"} &\longmapsto (1, [6]) \\
\text{"DWDD"} &\longmapsto (1, [3]) \longrightarrow (2, [7])
\end{aligned}
$$

Fig. 2. The index for a set of feature strings

The complete difference based mining algorithm, abbreviated as *cdm* algorithm consists of four main steps. The first step is constructing the temporary table. The second is cleaning the table, i.e. deleting any element whose occurrence is less than 2. The third is computing the candidate theme set. A candidate theme means a substring, whose length is as long as possible, generated by connecting the existing two equal-length substrings. The last is computing the theme set. The main differences between *cdm* algorithm and string-join algorithm [3] are that *cdm* only computes the selected pairs instead of all pairs when computing the candidate theme set, and the application of the duality principle of complete difference speeds up the computation.

Let a music feature string be "ABCDEFGHABCDEFGHIJABC", the application of the *cdm* algorithm on it can be illustrated in Fig. 3. After four steps, the theme set of the given feature string is achieved.

"ABCD" ⟼ [0, 8]
"BCDE" ⟼ [1, 9]
"CDEF" ⟼ [2, 10]
"FGHI" ⟼ [13]
"GHIJ" ⟼ [14]   "ABCD" ⟼ [0, 8]
"IJAB" ⟼ [16]   "BCDE" ⟼ [1, 9]   "ABCDEFG" ⟼ [0, 8]
"DEFG" ⟼ [3, 11] ⟹   "CDEF" ⟼ [2, 10]   "BCDEFGH" ⟼ [1, 9]   "ABCDEFGH" ⟼ [0, 8]
"FGHA" ⟼ [5]   "DEFG" ⟼ [3, 11]
"EFGH" ⟼ [4, 12]   "EFGH" ⟼ [4, 12]
"GHAB" ⟼ [6]
"JABC" ⟼ [17]
"HABC" ⟼ [7]

Fig. 3. A *cdm* example

5 Music Information Retrieval Based on *N*-Gram Inverted Index

In this section, the application of the *N*-gram index for content-based music information retrieval is discussed. Firstly, the position list of a substring is introduced. In a set of strings, the position list of a substring β is a linked list, denoted as P_β. P_β can also be considered as a relation. Each element of P_β is a two-tuple (*string-id, positions*), which means that β occurs in the string whose identifier is *string-id* and each address is included in *positions*. For example, the position list of the substring "UUBD" in the string set shown in Table 2 is ((1, [0]), (2, [4]), (3, [4])).

Let $P_{\beta_1} = (E, A) = \{(e, a)\} = \{(e, [a_1, a_2,..., a_x])\}$, $P_{\beta_2} = (D, B) = \{(d, b)\} = \{(d, [b_1, b_2,..., b_y])\}$, the *c*-operation between them is $P_{\beta_1} \propto_c P_{\beta_2} = \{(d, \gamma_c (\{a_1, a_2,..., a_x\}, \{b_1, b_2,..., b_y\})) \mid \exists (e, a) \in P_{\beta_1} \wedge (d, b) \in P_{\beta_2} \wedge e=d \wedge \gamma_c(a, b) \neq \Phi\}$, where the value domain of E and that of D are the set of *string-id*. For instance, when the position lists of substrings β_1 and β_2 are respectively illustrated in Fig. 4(a) and Fig. 4(b), some *c*-operations between them are shown in Fig. 4(c) (where *c*=7) and Fig. 4(d) (where *c*=2). It means that the *positions*es with same *id* are computed to get the *c*-component of their complete difference.

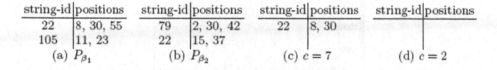

string-id	positions		string-id	positions		string-id	positions		string-id	positions
22	8, 30, 55		79	2, 30, 42		22	8, 30			
105	11, 23		22	15, 37						

(a) P_{β_1} (b) P_{β_2} (c) $c = 7$ (d) $c = 2$

Fig. 4. The *c*-operations between P_{β_1} and P_{β_1}

The *c*-operation is very important because the retrieval can be easily carried out via it. In this paper, two algorithms are proposed to implement the *c*-operation. Their ideas come from the implementations of the join operation in the relation algebra. One is the NestedLoop-*c* algorithm in which the *c*-operation is performed in the nested loop fashion. For example, in Fig. 4, four *string-id* pairs (22, 79), (22, 22), (105, 79), and (105, 22) are compared one by one. When two elements in a pair are equal, the *c*-component of the complete difference between the corresponding *positions*es is computed. The other is the SortMerge-*c* algorithm, in which the two position lists are sorted firstly according to the *string-id* field and then the computation is performed. For example, in Fig. 4, $P\beta_1$ and $P\beta_2$ are sorted in the ascending order. Thus only two comparisons, (22, 22) and (105, 79), are needed.

Based on the complete difference and *c*-operation, the retrieval algorithm can be gotten. Let L_u be the index used, and u be the length of feature substrings in the index. *divmod*(*w*, *u*)=(*m*, *n*) means $m=\lfloor w/u \rfloor$ and $n=w$ modulo u. q_i is a substring of q. $q_i= a_{(i-1)*u+1}a_{(i-1)*u+2}...a_{(i-1)*u+u}$} when $i=1, ..., m$, and $q_i=a_{m*u-(u-n-1)}\} ... a_{m*u}... a_{m*u+n}$ when $i=m+1$. If n is zero, the retrieval result is $Pq_1\propto_u Pq_2\propto_u ...\propto_u Pq_m$, otherwise it is $Pq_1\propto_u Pq_2\propto_u ...\propto_u Pq_m\propto_n Pq_{m+1}$.

Let $u=4$. The query string q is "UUBDWDD", and the feature string set is shown in Table 2. *divmod*(7, 4)=(1, 3), then q_1="UUBD", and q_2="DWDD". $P_{UUBDWDD} =P_{UUBD} \propto_3 P_{DWDD}=\{(1, [0]), (2, [4]), (3,[4])\} \propto_3 \{(1, [3]), (2, [7])\} = \{(1, [0]), (2, [4])\}$. It means that q occurs at the position "0" in the string whose *id* is 1, and occurs at the position "4" in the string whose *id* is 2.

6   Experiments

Our experiments are divided into two parts. We will first run experiments to evaluate the response time of the complete difference based theme mining algorithm. Comparisons with the string join algorithm [13] will be made. Afterwards, we will test the efficiency of retrieval on the NestedLoop-*c* algorithm comparing with that on the SortMerge-*c* algorithm. The experiments are performed on a PC with a Pentium IV 1.7 GHz processor and 256MB of memory, running Windows XP. All codes are written in ANSI C++ and complied with all optimization options.

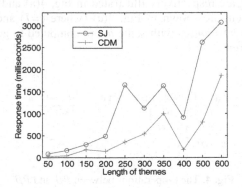

Fig. 5. Mining time in the HIT-DML dataset

As a previously proposed method, the string join algorithm was proposed for finding all non-trivial repeating patterns. It has the best performance in [3]. Obviously, it can also be used to mine themes. For fairness, the RP-tree 2^2 is constructed for string-join before the testing.

The experimental result of theme mining on the HIT-DML dataset is shown in Fig. 5. It shows that the time used to mine themes of a music object doesn't always increase when the length of the theme increases. It is because that the retrieval time is affected by the length of the theme, the length of the feature string, the number of themes, and other factors. Obviously, however, the performance of the complete difference based theme mining algorithm is better than that of the string join algorithm. The main reason is that the *cdm* algorithm computes the certain component of complete difference only when it is necessary.

In the second experiment, given a number *l*, five different substrings whose lengths are *l* are randomly selected from the data file. Each query is processed three times and the response times are all recorded. Then the average of these 15 values is used as the response time for query strings with the length *l*. The experimental results are illustrated in Fig. 6. It shows that the retrieval algorithm based on NestedLoop-*c* needs more time than that based on SortMerge-*c* when a query string is given.

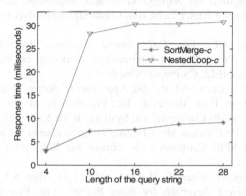

Fig. 6. Retrieval time in the HIT-DML dataset

In NestedLoop-*c* based retrieval, when the length of the query is 4, the response time is low because the results are directly selected from the index structure. The response time increases along with increasing of the length of the query string. Also, it shows that the increasing trend becomes slow when the length of the query string is more than 10. In SortMerg-*c* based retrieval, the previous conclusion still exists.

When there is no exact answer, approximate query processing can be considered. One or more feature characters will be replaced by certain characters, or some characters are inserted or deleted. Then the exact query processing will be implemented one by one. We do not make experiments on approximate query processing in this paper because it can be considered as the repetition of a sequence of exact query processing.

7   Conclusions and Future Work

The *N*-gram inverted index is proposed in this paper. It can be used to retrieve music information and mine music themes. Experiments show the correctness and efficiency of the proposed index structure and algorithms. Other applications of the N-gram inverted index and the complete difference will be studied in the future.

References

1. Chen, J.C.C., Chen, A.L.: Query by Rhythm: An Approach for Song Retrieval in Music Databases. In: Proceedings of 8th International Workshop on Research Issues in Data Engineering, Continuous-Media Databases and Applications, New York, USA, IEEE CS Press (1998) 139-146
2. Tseng, Y.H.: Content-Based Retrieval for Music Collections. In: Proceedings of the 22nd International ACM SIGIR Conference on Research and Development in Information Retrieval, Berkley, CA, USA, ACM Press (1999) 176-182
3. Hsu, J.L., Liu, C.C., Chen, A.L.P.: Discovering Nontrivial Repeating Patterns in Music Data. IEEE Transactions on Multimedia 3 (2001) 311-325
4. Gusfield, D.: Algorithms on Strings, Trees and Sequences: Computer Science and Computational Biology. Chapter 7. 1st edn. Cambridge University Press, New York, NY, USA (1997)
5. Chou, T.C., Chen, A.L., Liu, C.C.: Music Databases: Indexing Techniques and Implementation. In: Proceedings of International Workshop on Multimedia Data Base Management Systems, IEEE CS Press (1996) 46-53
6. Liu, C.C., Hsu, J.L., Chen, A.L.P.: An Approximate String Matching Algorithm for Content-Based Music Data Retrieval. In: Proceedings of the IEEE International Conference on Multimedia Computing and Systems (ICMCS). (1999) 451-456
7. Lee, W., Chen, A.L.P.: Efficient Multi-Feature Index Structures for Music Data Retrieval. In: Proceedings of SPIE Conference on Storage and Retrieval for Image and Video Databases. (2000)
8. Chen, A.L.P., Chang, M., Chen, J., Hsu, J.L., Hsu, C.H., Hua, S.Y.S.: Query by Music Segments: An Efficient Approach for Song Retrieval. In: Proceedings of the IEEE International Conference on Multimedia & Expo., IEEE CS Press (2000) 873-876
9. Tang, M., Yip, C.L., Kao, B.: Selection of Melody Lines for Music Databases. In: Proceedings of the IEEE COMPSAC, Taipei (2000)
10. MIDINOTES. (http://www.argonet.co.uk/users/lenny/midi/notes.html)
11. Dowling, W.J.: Scale and Contour: Two Components of a Theory of Memory for Melodies. Psychological Review 85 (1978) 341-354
12. Wang, C., Li, J., Shi, S.: HIT-DML: A Novel Digital Music Library. In: Proceedings of the 6th International Conference on Asian Digital libraries, Kuala Lumpur, Malaysia (2003) 265-274
13. Liu, C.C., Hsu, J.L., Chen, A.L.P.: Efficient Theme and Non-Trivial Repeating Pattern Discovering in Music Databases. In: Proceedings of the 15th International Conference on Data Engineering, IEEE Computer Society Press (1999) 14-21

An Implementation of Web Image Search Engines

Zhiguo Gong, Leong Hou U, and Chan Wa Cheang

Faculty of Science and Technology, University of Macau,
P.O.Box 3001 Macao, PRC
{zggong, ma36575, ma36600}@umac.mo

Abstract. This paper presents our implementation techniques for an intelligent Web image search engine. A reference architecture of the system is provided and addressed in this paper. The system includes several components such as a crawler, a preprocessor, a semantic extractor, an indexer, a knowledge learner and a query engine. The crawler traverses web sites in multithread accesses model. And it can dynamically control its access load to a Web server based on the corresponding capacity of the local system. The preprocessor is used to clean and normalize the information resource downloaded from Web sites. In this process, stop-word removing and word stemming are applied to the raw resources. The semantic extractor derives Web image semantics by partitioning combining the associated text. The indexer of the system creates and maintains inverted indices with relational model. Our knowledge learner is designed to automatically acquire knowledge from users' query activities. Finally, the query engine delivers search results in two phases in order to mine out the users' feedbacks.

1 Introduction

In recent years, huge amount of information is published on WWW and it continues to increase with an explosive speed. However, we cannot access to the information or use it efficiently and effectively unless it is well organized and indexed. Only after that, people can be possible to perform efficient browsing, searching and retrieving on the resources. Nowadays, we know that "Google" is accepted as the biggest and fastest search engine on WWW. Web users are becoming more and more reliable on this tool. Although "Google" has also provided image-searching function based on its existed technology, such as indexing and ranking, it still has some space for improvement. For instance, a Macau resident wants to find some images about the University of Macau with a keyword--"umac" in his image searching of "Google", we can find a "Luna" at the first page of the result, and it is not relevant to the query. Therefore, there may be much improvement space for web image retrieval technologies.

Image Retrieval has been a very active research area ever since 1970's, with the thrust from two major research communities, Database Management and Computer Vision. These two areas address image retrieval techniques in different ways. One is text-based and the other is visual-based. On the web, most of popular Image Search Engines (For example: Google) are text-based. The reason is due to the fact that

Z. Chen et al. (Eds.): ICADL 2004, LNCS 3334, pp. 355–367, 2004.

visual-based image retrieval can only work fine in some specific application domains. That means the web images are needed to be classified with respect to different domains before visual processing. Two methods can be used for the classification— manually or automatically. The former requires vast amount of labor and even impossible since the huge size of the web. Our system adopts the latter model.

In this paper, we are going to describe the implementation techniques in our text-based image retrieval system. We provide a reference architecture for web image retrieval systems, which includes a crawler, preprocessor, semantic extractor, indexer, knowledge learner and a query engine. We implement the crawler in a multithread model, therefore it can dynamically control its access load to a Web server based on the corresponding capacity of the local system. The preprocessor is used to clean and normalize the information resource downloaded from Web sites. In this process, stop-word removing and word stemming are applied to the raw resources. The semantic extractor derives Web image semantics by partitioning then combining the associated text. The indexer of the system creates and maintains inverted indices with relational model. Our knowledge learner is designed to automatically acquire knowledge from users' query activities. Finally, the query engine delivers search results in two phases in order to mine out the users' feedbacks.

In section 2, we describe our reference architecture of the system. And in section 3 to section 7, we will address our implementation technologies on the crawler/preprocessor, semantic extractor, indexer, knowledge learner and search engine respectively. And finally, we conclude this paper in section 8.

2   System Architecture

Figure 1 shows the fundamental working principles of our system. Firstly, web pages are collected by the crawler and delivered as a stream to the preprocessor of the system. After parsed by the preprocessor, the intermediate results, including all the web images, associated text, links and their relationships, are loaded into the document database. And the new links are passed back to the crawler for recursively web page gathering.

The semantic extractor takes the associated texts as input and represents them into DOM tree format. Then, it tries to partition the associated texts formally into a sequence of semantic blocks based on the element structures as well as their distances to the embedded images. In our system, the semantic relevant factor of each semantic block is measured with respect to its relative position to the corresponding image. For each pair of analytic image and its associated text, the semantic extractor parses the document and produces a set of postings, where each posting is an entry which shows the term's semantic relevance to the web image. The indexer sorts all the postings, then, creates an inverted index to support fast accesses to the images.

In terms of the knowledge base in our system, we consider users search activities as important resources to improve the retrieval performances of the system. Most of current web image retrieval systems can only provide static schemas, which are based only on limited sample data or experts' experiences, in their indexing the web images. Thus, such systems can not evolve to catch the dynamic changing of the WWW.

From users' query log, the knowledge learner in our system tries to mine out the semantic relevances between web images and query terms. In this way, retrieval performance of the system can be well improved. Furthermore, the system can recalculate the semantic distribution schemas of the web images by using extended sample space.

Our knowledge base also captures and maintains frequently used phrases or concepts in the user queries. And they can be used in the future semantic extraction processing and indexing.

For the query engine, it provides two phase deliveries of the query results. In the first phase, only indexing images (the small thumb images generated from the original images) are delivered to the users. And the second phase presents the original images or its owner web pages with users' further requests. In this way, users' searching activities can be captured and passed to knowledge learner. We will introduce each process in detail in the following sections.

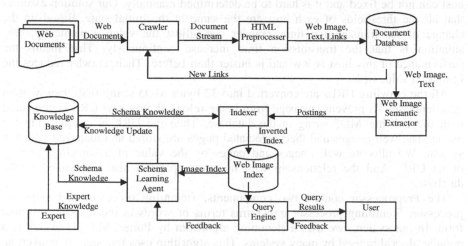

Fig. 1. The System Architecture Overview

3 The Crawler and HTML Preprocessor

Crawler is one of the important components in web information retrieval system. It gathers web pages from WWW and recursively fetch the new pages with the new URLs which are contained in the load documents. Generally, two strategies exist for web page traversing—BFS(breath first search) and DFS(depth first search). And BFS is exploited by our crawler.

In order to work, the crawler needs to maintain a queue of URLs, and it always selects URL from the top of the queue to start a new page traversing. And the newly gathered URLs are appended to the end of the queue. Because the web sites are autonomous and independent in nature, they may have different workloads and response capabilities to the crawler. For example, if the accesses received are more than the limitation of the host being accepted, the host may shut down (just like the host is attacked by Distributed Denial of Service attack).Therefore, it is not wise if the crawler only work on one site at one time. To solve this problem, our crawler is designed to employ I/O multiplexing or multithreading to allow web pages to be fetched from multiple sites at the same time. It is obvious that more threads being run at the same time can raise the system throughput. And this model can also leave more processing capabilities of the local sites for their local requests.

For this reason, the crawler needs to control the thread number at each accessed host. To reach this destination, our system separates the global URL queue into subqueues according to different hosts. Each subqueue of a individual host has a running count variable that records number of the running threads at the site. If the running count of a queue is less than the threshold N (For example: N=10), the crawler will pop up the top URL from this subqueue and goes on fetching state. Otherwise, it will try the next host's queue. The worst case occurs when all the hosts' running counts are more than the limitation, then crawler must switch to sleep state.

Because the network traffic keeps dynamic changing, the access threshold of each host can not be fixed and it is hard to be determined manually. Our solution assumes that all the thresholds of each host are the same at the initial state. Based on the change of the transmission time, crawler can adjust the value dynamically. One situation is that the transmission time increase continuously. That means the performance of this host is low and is busier than before. Then, crawler reduces the limitation value of N.

All the crawling URLs are converted into 32 bytes MD5 string first, then, written into database. To prevent any page from being reloaded, any new URL is compared with the existing MD5 string in the database. Then the URL is inserted into the queue. The web images and their associated pages are stored and managed with file system. We allocate web images and pages by the value of a harshing function of its URL. And the relationship with its parent page is also maintained in the database.

The Preprocessor contain two components: stemming processor and stopword processor. Stemming processor transforms terms or words in the texts into normal form. In our system, we uses a stemming algorithm by Porter, M.F [4], which is a popular algorithm used by many systems. This algorithm uses five steps to convert an informal English word into a formal one. For more detail, refer to [4].

Stop word processor is used to remove meaningless words, such as 'the', 'a', 'and', from the documents. In our implementation, we use the list provided by [2] as our set of stopwords. Of course, this list may not be the optimal one and we may extend it in the future.

Crawler is the fundamental component for web information retrieval systems. It takes charge of the document gathering. Besides universal crawlers, there are also many specific crawlers available in both the commercial market and academic communities [6,12]. For such kind of crawlers, topic relevance of each URL should also be taken into account when scheduling.

4 The Semantic Extractor

The semantic extractor takes the associated text of an image as input and tries to mine out the semantics of the image. The retrieval performance of the system is closely related to the correct extracting work of the semantic extractor. In this section, we address our implementation techniques for our extractor in detail.

4.1 The Problem

Images on the web can be classified into different types according to their purposes, such as (1) icon, (2) site logo, (3) realistic photo, and (4) cartoon pictures.

To simplify the problems, our system tries to removes stop-images (meaningless images) such as icon, web site logo before performing the image semantic extractions. In our approach, we use some measurements, such as the sizes of the images and the ratios between the width and the height of the images, as the criteria to discriminate whether an image is a stop –image or not.

Even though other solutions, such as link based, visual feature based, are also used for web image semantic extraction, text based methodology is the most fundamental one. Our semantic extractor is based on the associated texts of the images. Many TBIR researches [3, 6] use *title*, *alt of the analytic image*, *filename*, and ***surrounding text*** as the sources for the semantic extractions. However, we should pay attention to some problems in using the texts.

- How to determine the optimal range of the surrounding text?
- In general, we know that the terms which has the smaller distance to the image have higher relevances to the image. But this linearization distance method shows some defect as that the linearization distance inside the HTML document is different from what we can view with web browser.

4.2 Text Fragmentation

We know that many HTML documents often present information with a lot of HTML tags, however the traditional HTML document model is hard to be used to mine out such layout structures automatically. We need to use other document object model to replace the traditional one. One favorite model for representing the HTML structure is document object model tree (DOM tree) [5]. Based on the result by [9], we build the DOM tree using <TABLE> template tags: <TABLE>, <TR> and <TD>. After this transformation, the HTML structure becomes more easily to process. In general, the distance between the blocks and the analytic image rendered by the browser well match with that organized in the DOM tree. So we assume that the nearer blocks are more related to the analytic image. To formalize the distance between the analytic image and the associated text blocks, the DOM tree will be partitioned properly (Fig. 2).

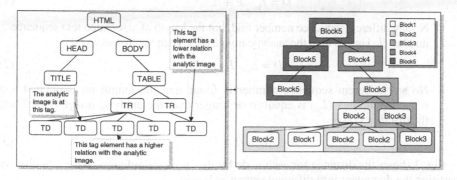

Fig. 2. DOM tree split into different blocks

Our Semantic Extractor uses MSHTML library, which is one of the Microsoft COM interface, to parse the HTML document into DOM tree. It builds the tree only by using these three tags: <TD>, <TR> and <TABLE>. Each tag contains its inner text and the relationship with its parent and child elements. For the characteristic of HTML document, we use Depth First Search (DFS) to build the tree. It scans the document from start to end. The inner text which contains between two of these tags is determined by this scan. Each node and its inner text will be grouped into difference blocks later. The following is the pseudo code for this processing:

```
STRING Trace_Dom_Tree (ParentNode)
{
    ExtractInnerText=ParentNode.GetInnerText();
    ForEach (NewChildNode) in ParentNode
    {
        If (NewChildNode.TagName == (<TABLE>||<TR>||<TD>))
        {
            ParentNode->ChildNode.Add(NewChildNode);
            ExtractInnerText.Remove(
                Trace_Dom_Tree(ParentNode->ChildNode));
        }
    }
    ParentNode.SetInnerText(ExtractInnerText);
    Return ExtractInnerText;
}
```

Our system uses a set of sequence numbers to determine the distance between the analytic image and the associated text elements. The sequence number is set by Semantic Extractor during building the tree. (Fig. 3) Each sequence number of the nodes is based on its parent and its sibling order under the same parent tag. In Fig. 3, the sequence number of analytic image's parent is 00 and its own order is 1, so the sequence number of analytic image is 001. After assigning the sequence number for each node, our system compares the analytic image sequence with others. The comparison checks the difference of the position of sequence number only. All the situations are showed as follows:

- The position of different sequence number (P) is equal to or less than the length of the associated text sequence number (L_{at}). Then the distance (D) is

$$D = L_{at} - P + 1 \tag{1}$$

- No any different sequence number find, but the length of associated text sequence number (L_{at}) is less than the analytic image (L_{ai}). Then the distance (D) is

$$D = L_{ai} - L_{at} \tag{2}$$

- No any different sequence number is found and the length of associated text sequence number (L_{at}) is equal to or longer than the analytic image (L_{ai}). Then, the distance (D) is

$$D = 0 \tag{3}$$

Fig. 3 shows the distance for each node by the above calculation. Based on this, we partition the document into different semantic blocks.

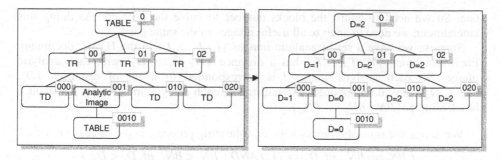

Fig. 3. Giving Sequence Number to each node

4.3 Distance Adjustment of Semantic Blocks

If the partitioning is only based on the absolute distance captured from the DOM tree as in last subsection, we find that the fragmentation can not properly reflect the visual rendering in many cases. As a matter of the fact, the same visual distances may tagged in the file differently by different authors. For instance, one author may like to write the nearest associated text within the same block as the analytic image block but others may not. Using the absolute approach as in section 4.2, the associated text of the first one is more related than the second one. However, they look the same when rendering in the browser. Since this confusion, in our approach we measure the position by relative distance (Fig. 4). We assume that the associated text appeared at the first block is the nearest block. So the above example will consider both of the associated texts to be the most related text.

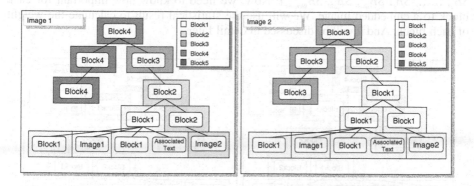

Fig. 4. DOM tree split into different blocks based on relative position

The above approach only works fine if the document only contains one image. However, there are quite a lot o documents containing more than one images. If the above images are in the same document, our approach considers that the importance between the associated text and the two analytic images is the same. But we know that the first image is closer to the associated text than the second one. It means that the relationship of the first image and the associated text is higher than the second one. So we need to adjust the blocks number to solve the problem. As doing this amendment, we need to analyze all useful images in the same page.

Suppose we have a set of analytic images $\{I_1, I_2......I_n\}$ in the HTML document. Each text block $\{T_1, T_2......T_m\}$ has a distance $\{D_1, D_2......D_n\}$ with each analytic image. So each analytic image I_i is corresponded to a set of distances $\{D_{i1}, D_{i2}......D_{im}\}$. Based on the order of the distance, each analytic image I_i has a sequence block number $\{BN_{i1}, BN_{i2}......BN_{im}\}$.

We define the semantic blocks with the following property in the same document:

$$(BN_{ik} == BN_{jk} \ iff \ D_{ik} == D_{jk}) \ AND \ (BN_{ik} < BN_{jk} \ iff \ D_{ik} < D_{jk})$$

In the same document, the blocks number is the same if and only if these blocks have the same value of the distance. And the smaller blocks number also have a smaller value of the distance. In Fig. 4, we know that the block number between the associated text and the two analytic images is the same, but their distances to the associated text are difference. Because of this property, we need to make following adjustment.

The adjustment has three steps: (1) Sort the sequence block number first. That means BN_{ik} is smaller than or equal to $BN_{i(k+1)}$ (2) If ($BN_{ik} == BN_{jk}$ AND $D_{ik} > D_{jk}$), then we adjust BN_{ik} to $BN_{ik}+1$. (3) Then, we continue to find all BN_{il} ($l>k$) and adjust all BN_{il} to $BN_{il} + 1$. Go back step (2) until no any ($BN_{ik} == BN_{jk}$ AND $D_{ik} > D_{jk}$). After these adjustments, we get a more reasonable distance measurement in splitting the DOM tree. The result shows on the Fig. 5.

With the approach above, we partition the inner text of HTML document into different blocks successfully. We combine these blocks with other semantic blocks: **title**, *alt of the analytic image* and *filename* to generate a set of semantic blocks $\{SB_1, SB_2, ..., SB_n, SB_{title}, SB_{alt}, SB_{filename}\}$. Now, we need to know how important for each block to a embedded image. We will use the statistical result to calculate the weight of each block. And it will be discussed in detail later.

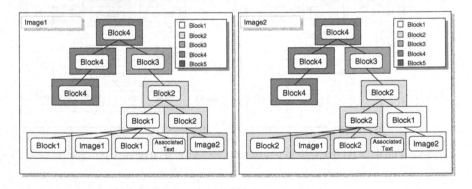

Fig. 5. The modified method for splitting the DOM tree

4.4 Term Weight Calculation

After we split the document into semantic blocks, Semantic Extractor finds out the weight of each term. In TFIDF model, the term of t's semantic relevance to page p is inverted document frequency of term t. In our system, we use terms (or concepts) of p to derive semantics of the Web image i. However, the above TFIDF approach can not be directly applied to index the embedded image.

In this paper, we modify TFIDF model as the following equation:

$$ntf(t)\,|_{SB_j} = \frac{tf(t)\,|_{SB_j}}{|\,SB_j\,|} \tag{4}$$

where $ntf(t)\,|_{SU_j}$ is called normalized frequency of term t over SB_j, $tf(t)\,|_{SB_j}$ is the frequency of term t over SB_j, and $|SB_i|$ is the size of SB_i. Thus, the total term frequency over the whole p is obtained as

$$ttf(t)\,|_p = \sum_{1 \leq i \leq N-1} w_j * ntf(t)\,|_{SB_j} \tag{5}$$

where N is the total number of the semantic blocks, and w_j is the weight of SB_j in implying the semantics of the embedded image i. Without loss of generality, we suppose w_j's are normalized, such that $\sum_{1 \leq i \leq N-1} w_j = 1$.

In our approach, $ttf(t)|_p$ indicates the semantic relevance level of term t to the embedded image i of page p. Then the indexer creates an inverted index based the values of $ttf(t)|_p$. We will discuss how to determine the values for w_j later.

5 The Indexer

Semantic Extractor passes the relation between the analytic image, the relationship of associated text and all the term frequency to Indexer. Like many other information retrieval systems, we use inverted index in our system. For performance, the table is built of a one-to-many relationship. Like the following table:

Term	Index
TERM1	DOC_ID_1, DOC _ID_2,., DOC_ID_N
TERM1	DOC _ID_N+1, DOC_ID_N+2
TERM2	DOC_ID_1, DOC_ID _2, DOC_ID _3

To increase the database performance, the length of the index has an optimal upper bound – N. If one term is corresponding to more than an upper bond documents, it will use more than one row to store the document ids. In our system, the index does not store only the document id but also stores some related information, such as the frequency of the term for each semantic block ($ntf(t)\,|_{SB_j}$).

For performance, we know that the cost of I/O access is higher than the cost of memory access, so our system stores the inverted index into memory first. When the index number is up to upper bound value, it writes the index from memory to database and clears the memory content. In order to reduce the total disk capacity, it stores inverted index to database in binary format. (Fig. 6)

6 The Knowledge Base

Knowledge Base is a subsystem which tries to capture the knowledge from experts and user feedbacks. In section 4, we have not determined the values of w_j yet. As we discuss before, our system use the statistical result to determine their values.

In the area of information retrieval, precision/recall is well accepted evaluation method which indicates the performance of the systems. In order to calculate the precision/recall value, our system needs the expert to provide some training set. Our system provides a user-friendly interface, to let the experts define the corresponded meanings for each image easily by using the mouse.

Since the result of a retrieval are usually long in size, especially in the World Wide Web environment, a figure of precision versus recall changing is commonly used as a performance measurement for a retrieval algorithm. However, this metric can not be used as an objective function in determining those weight values. We use the average precision concept instead of the above metric. The average precision is defined as

$$AP_{jk} = \frac{1}{R_{jk}} \sum_{k=1}^{R_{jk}} \frac{k}{N_k} \tag{6}$$

where R_{jk} is the total number of all relevant results with respect to $ntf(q_i)\,|_{SB_j}$ and N_k is the number of results up to the k-th relevant result in the image result list. As a matter of the fact, AP_{jk} is the single value metric which indicates the performance of querying q_k by only referencing semantic block SB_j. The optimal value of w_j is determined by the overall average precision objective defined as:

$$AP = \frac{1}{N} \sum_{i=1}^{N} AP_i(w) \tag{7}$$

where $AP_i(W)$ is the average precision for each semantic block. Because the higher value of AP represents the higher quality of the result. So we try to adjust the value of w_j for each semantic block to get a higher AP value. After this step, we get the optimal value of w_j. This is an iterative improvement. After we add some new record to our result set, we calculate the new optimal value of w_j based on the old one.

Knowledge base also handle the user's feedbacks. It uses a two steps model to handle about it. Like most of the current image retrieval systems, we display the search results in two steps: (1) indexing thumbs of the original images are delivered to the users (2) original images or the web pages which contain the original images are sent to users with users' further request command. The promise of using our users' feedbacks is that the second activity is performed by a user implies the result is likely to be the correct answer of the query. We store the users' feedbacks into Knowledge Base and display the result with the new rank function:

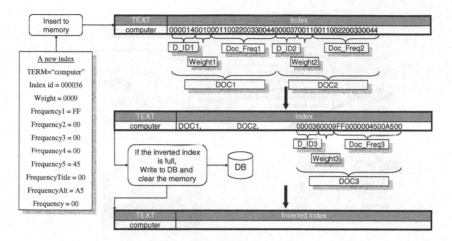

Fig. 6. Example of indexing

$$adj(t,i)=w_d \cdot ttf(t,i)+w_u \cdot srl(t,i) \tag{8}$$

where $ttf(t,i)$ is the term frequency for each semantic block which is discussed in equation 5, $srl(t,i)$ is term-image relevant values obtained from user query activities (its details addressed in our other papers, w_d and w_u are weights for objective function ttf and srl respectively, and $w_d+w_u=1$. We can use the same method as to calculate the w_j by average precision to determine these two values.

7 The Query Engine

Query Engine supports concept based searching function to the user. When it accepts a term from the user, it presents the relevant images to the user. For performance, the index is sorted by Indexer first. For one term searching, the system delivers the thumbs to user directly. But this sorting can not be satisfied with two terms or more. For two-term searching, the result set R is the intersection of those term result. We need to sort R for each searching because R is an unsort set. The sorting operation is time consuming even if we have already exploited a good sorting algorithm. So the sorting operation must decrease the system performance. One method to solve the problem is to store the i-term concept which may be from 1 to N to database. But we know that the number of two-term concept has already been very large. It is impossible to store all of these into database because since the physical limitation and the performance of the system.

In our approach, the database only stores some important N-term concepts which are captured by the user feedback. Because our system records all user queries, we will know which concept is more likely to search. Our system just stores the N-term concept, which frequency is higher than the predefined value, into database. How to balance the physical storage size and the performance is the problem of database management. But it is out of the range of this paper, we will not discuss in detail. Fig 7 shows an example of our retrieval interface.

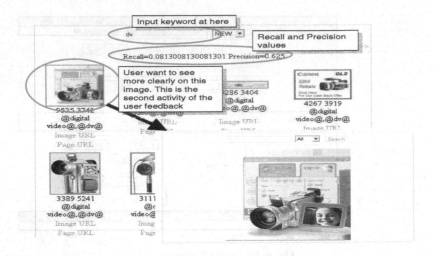

Fig. 7. One example of Search Interface

8   Conclusions and Future Work

In this paper, we provide a comprehensive survey on our implementation technologies of the text based image retrieval system. This paper introduces our methodologies on each essential components of our system, such as Crawler, HTML Preprocessor, Semantic Extractor, Indexer, Knowledge Learner and Query Engine in detail.

In our system, we partition the HTML document into a set of semantic blocks. It means our method only focus on analyzing the text which is inside one HTML document. We consider this model as a single level analysis of link structure. In web environment, the parents and the child nodes of HMTL document may have significant meanings to the extract the semantics of the analytic image. For this objective, we can try to expand the analysis to multiple levels.

Some link structure algorithms have developed on web environment, such as Hyperlink Induced Topics Search (HITS) or Google's Pagerank. And there existed some excellent surveys on link structure image retrievals already[7]. In our future work, we will try to combine our existed method with the link structure to get a better result.

The other improvement of our system is to use an electronic thesaurus (WordNet™) to expand both the user queries and the meta-data associated with the images. We want to get a model based on objects, attributes and relationships to allow us to use WordNet™ in a comprehensive automatic manner and to improve retrieval effectively.

References

1. S. Chakrabarti, M. V. D. Berg and B. Dom: Focused Crawling: a New Approach to Topic-Specific Web Resource Discovery. *Computer Networks* 31(11-16), 1999, pp. 1623-1640.

2. S. Chakrabarti, M. V. D. Berg and B. Dom: Focused Crawling: a New Approach to Topic-Specific Web Resource Discovery. *Computer Networks* 31(11-16), 1999, pp. 1623-1640.

3. Shi-Kuo Chang and Arding Hsu: Image information systems: Where do we go from here?. *IEEE Trans. on Knowledge and Data Eng.*, 4(5), Oct. 1992, pp. 431-442.

4. Chen, Z. et al.: Web Mining for Web Image Retrieval. To appear in *the special issue of Journal of the American Society for Information Science on Visual Based Retrieval Systems and Web Mining*.

5. DOM: http://www.w3.org/DOM/

6. Zhiguo Gong, Leong Hou U and Chan Wa Cheang: Web Image Semantic Extractions from its Associated Texts. *The 8th IASTED International Conference on Internet & Multimedia Systems & Applications*, Kauai, Hawaii, USA, August 16-18, 2004.

7. V. Harmandas, M. Sanderson, M.D. Dunlop: Image Retrieval By Hypertext Links. In: *Proceedings of SIGIR-97, 20th ACM International Conference on Research and Development in Information Retrieval* 1997.

8. Mingjing Li, Zheng Chen, Hongjiang Zhang: Statistical Correlation Analysis in Image Retrieval., *Pattern Recognition* 35, 2002, pp. 2687-2693.

9. Lin, Ho: Discovering Informative Content Blocks from Web Documents. *ACM SIGKDD 2002*, Edmonton, Alberta, Canada, July 23 - 26, 2002.

10. Porter, M.F.: An Algorithm For Suffix Stripping. *Program 14 (3)*, July 1980, pp. 130-137.

11. Stop Word List: http://www.searchengineworld.com/spy/stopwords.htm

12. Hideruki Tamura and Naokazu Yokoya: Image database systems: A survey. *Patt. Recog.*, 17(1), 1984, pp. 29-43.

A Relevance Feedback Model for Fractal Summarization

Fu Lee Wang[1] and Christopher C. Yang[2]

[1] Department of Computer Science, City University of Hong Kong,
Kowloon Tong, Hong Kong SAR, China
flwang@cityu.edu.hk
[2] Department of Systems Engineering and Engineering Management,
The Chinese University of Hong Kong, Shatin, Hong Kong SAR, China
yang@se.cuhk.edu.hk

Abstract. As a result of the recent information explosion, there is an increasing demand for automatic summarization, and human abstractors often synthesize summaries that are based on sentences that have been extracted by machine. However, the quality of machine-generated summaries is not high. As a special application of information retrieval systems, the precision of automatic summarization can be improved by user relevance feedback, in which the human abstractor can direct the sentence extraction process and useful information can be retrieved efficiently. Automatic summarization with relevance feedback is a helpful tool to assist professional abstractors in generating summaries, and in this work we propose a relevance feedback model for fractal summarization. The results of the experiment show that relevance feedback effectively improves the performance of automatic fractal summarization.

1 Introduction

There is an increasing need for automatic summarization in the wake of the recent information explosion. Many summarization models have been proposed, of which the fractal summarization model is the first to apply the fractal theory to document summarization [29][30]. This model generates a summary by a recursive deterministic algorithm that is based on the iterated representation of a document. Traditionally, automatic summarization systems have extracted sentences from the source document according to predefined rules [7][18], but rule-based extraction does not function properly in some extreme cases, and cannot truly reflect the actual circumstances of every individual document. For example, the thematic feature of summarization systems does not always reflect the significance of a term accurately. In addition, the position of key sentences varies from document to document, and can be very difficult for a summarization system to detect. As a result of these problems, the quality of the summaries that are generated by the extraction of sentences by machine is not high.

In most cases, ordinary users will be satisfied with reading the sentences of a document that have been extracted by machine, as it can help them to decide whether a document is useful. Ordinary users are also reluctant to provide explicit feedback, and therefore most summarization techniques are fully automated. Automatic

Z. Chen et al. (Eds.): ICADL 2004, LNCS 3334, pp. 368–377, 2004.
© Springer-Verlag Berlin Heidelberg 2004

summarization by sentence extraction is desirable due to the large volume of information that is available today, but the quality of the summaries that are generated by fully automated summarization systems is not good enough. Human professionals are the best summarizers because of their incredible summarization capabilities, and thus automatic summarization systems are best employed as a tool to aid summarization. This entails the extraction of important sentences from the source document by machine, and the synthesis of the summary by a human being based on the sentences that have been extracted [5][6]. With such a method of summarization, relevance feedback models are very helpful, because they provide a mechanism for the abstractor to specify the content that is important and that needs to be extracted, and also what is irrelevant and should be excluded. A relevance feedback model for fractal summarization is proposed in this work, and relevance feedback for each summarization feature is also discussed.

The rest of this paper is organized as following. Section 2 reviews the techniques of automatic text summarization. Section 3 presents a fractal summarization model, Section 4 proposes a relevance feedback model for fractal summarization, and Section 5 discusses the results of the experiment. Section 6 provides some concluding remarks.

2   Traditional Automatic Summarization

Traditional summarization models consider a document as a sequence of sentences, and the traditional method of automatic text summarization involves the selection of sentences from the source document based on their significance to the document as a whole [7][18] without consideration of the hierarchical structure of the document. The selection of sentences is based on the salient features of the document, with thematic, location, heading, and cue phrase features being the most widely used summarization features.

- The *thematic feature* was first identified by Luhn [18]. Edmundson proposes the assignment of a thematic weight to keywords that is based on term frequency, and allocates a sentence thematic score that is the sum of the thematic weights of the constituent keywords [7]. The *tfidf* (Term Frequency, Inverse Document Frequency) score is the score that is most widely used to calculate the thematic weight of keywords [22].
- The significance of a sentence can be indicated by its *location* [2] based on the hypotheses that topic sentences tend to occur at the beginning or the end of a document or paragraph [7]. Edmundson proposes the assignment of positive scores to sentences according to their ordinal position in the document, which is known as a location score.
- The *heading feature* is based on the hypothesis that the author conceives the heading as circumscribing the subject matter of the document [7]. A heading glossary is a list that consists of all of the words that appear in the headings and subheadings that have positive weights. The heading score of a sentence is calculated by the sum of the heading weights of its constituent words.
- The *cue phrase feature* that is proposed by Edmundson [7] is based on the hypothesis that the probable relevance of a sentence is affected by the presence of

pragmatic words. A pre-stored cue dictionary of terms with cue weights is used to identify the cue phrases, and the cue score of a sentence is calculated by the sum of the cue weights of its constituent terms.

Typical summarization systems select a combination of summarization features [7][15][17], and the total sentence score ($W_{sentence}$) is calculated as the weighted sum of the scores that are computed by each of the features, for example,

$$W_{sentence} = a_1 \times w_{thematic} + a_2 \times w_{location} + a_3 \times w_{heading} + a_4 \times w_{cue},$$

where $w_{thematic}$ is the thematic score, $w_{location}$ is the location score, $w_{heading}$, is the heading score, and w_{cue} the cue score of the sentence, and a_1, a_2, a_3, and a_4 are positive integers that adjust the weighting of the four features. Sentences with a sentence score that is higher than a given threshold value are selected for the summary. It has been proved that the weighting of the different summarization features has no substantial effect on the average precision [15]. Thus, in our experiment, the maximum score for each feature is normalized to 1, and the total score of each sentence is calculated as the sum of the scores of all of the summarization features without weighting.

3   Fractal Summarization

Of the many automatic summarization models that were proposed in the past, none of was developed based entirely on document structure, and none took into account the fact that human abstractors extract sentences according to the hierarchical structure of a document. The structure of a document can be described as a fractal [26][29][30]. In the past, fractal theory was widely applied in the area of digital image compression, which is similar to text summarization in the sense that both techniques involve the extraction of the most important information from a source and the reduction of the complexity of the source. The fractal summarization model represents the first effort to apply the fractal theory to document summarization [29][30], in which a summary is generated by a recursive deterministic algorithm that is based on the iterated representation of a document.

Many studies of the human abstraction process have shown that human abstractors extract topic sentences according to the structure of a document from the top level to the bottom level until they have extracted sufficient information [8][9]. Advanced summarization techniques take document structure into consideration to compute the probability that a sentence should be included in the summary, but most traditional automatic summarization models consider the source document as a sequence of sentences and ignore its structure. By contrast, fractal summarization generates a summary that is based on the hierarchical document structure [29][30].

The fractal summarization model is based on fractal theory [19], and applies the techniques of fractal view [14] and fractal image compression [1][12]. In fractal image compression, an image is evenly segmented into sets of non-overlapping square blocks, which are known as range blocks, and each range block is subdivided into sub-range blocks until a contractive map can be found that represents the sub-range block. In fractal text summarization, the original document is partitioned into range blocks according to the document structure, which is represented as a fractal tree structure (Figure 1). The important information is captured from the source document by exploring the hierarchical structure and the salient features of the document, and the summarization system then computes the number of sentences to be extracted based on the compression ratio. The system then assigns the number of sentences to the root as the quota of sentences, and the fractal value of the root node is taken to be 1. The system then calculates the sentence score for each sentence in each range block using traditional summarization methods, and the fractal values are propagated to the range blocks according to the sum of the sentence scores. The sentence quota is then shared out among the range blocks according to their fractal value. The system repeats the procedure for each range block to allocate the sentence quota to the sub-range blocks recursively until the quota that is allocated is less than a given threshold value, and the sub-range block is then transformed into key sentences by traditional summarization methods.

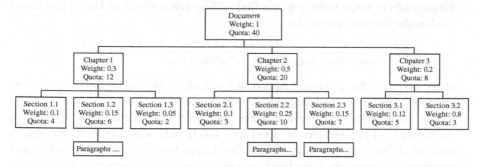

Fig. 1. An Example of a Fractal Summarization Model

The fractal value of each range block is calculated using traditional extraction features. However, traditional extraction features consider the document as a sequence of sentences, and thus are not entirely compatible with the fractal structure. We present a method for the modification of the extraction features to allow them to fully use the fractal structure of a document.

- The *tfidf* score is the most widely used thematic feature approach, but it does not consider document structure. Most researchers assume that the weight of a term remains the same over the entire document, but Hearst claims that a term carries different weights in different locations in a full-length document [11]. We define the ith term in a document as t_i. In fractal summarization, the *tfidf* of the term t_i in a range block is defined as the term frequency within that range block inverse the frequency of the range block that contains the term, i.e.,

$$w_{ir} = tf_{ir} \times \log_2(\frac{N' \times |t_i|}{n'}),$$

where tf_{ir} is the frequency of term t_i in range block r, N' is the number of range blocks in the document, n' is the number of range blocks that contain the term t_i in the document, and $|t_i|$ is the length of the term t_i. The Fractal Sentence Thematic Score, FSS_T, of the kth sentence (s_k) in range block r is calculated as the sum of the modified *tfidf* score, w_{ir}, of the constituent terms t_i of the sentence s_k, i.e.,

$$FSS_T(k,r) = \sum_{t_i \in s_k} w_{ir} .$$

The Fractal Thematic Score FTS_T of range block r is calculated as the sum of the Fractal Sentence Thematic Score FSS_T of all of the sentences in range block r, i.e.,

$$FTS(r) = \sum_{s_k \in r} FSS_T(s_k, r) .$$

- Traditional summarization methods assume that the location score of a sentence is static, but fractal summarization calculates the location score based on the document level that is being looked at. A location score is assigned to range blocks according to their position by traditional methods, and the sentences that are inside the range block are hidden. In the fractal summarization model, we consider the location score at the level below the level that is being looked at. The Fractal Location Score FLS of range block r is calculated as the reciprocal of the minimal distance of the range block r to the first sibling range block or last sibling range block under the same parent, i.e.,

$$FLS(r) = \frac{1}{\min(d(r,\ first\ sibling\ of\ r), d(r, last\ sibling\ of\ r))} ,$$

where $d(r, x)$ is the distance function that calculates the number of range blocks between range block r and range block x, inclusively.
- At different abstraction levels, some headings are hidden and some are emphasized. For example, at document level, only the document heading is considered, but if we look at the chapter level, then both the document heading and the chapter heading are considered, and the latter is more important because the main concept of the chapter is represented by its heading. Therefore, the significance of the heading is inversely proportional to its distance. The propagation of fractal value [14] is a promising approach for the calculation of the heading scores for a sentence. If a summarization is being conducted at the internal node x (range block x) with m_x child nodes, then there is a unique path that connects node x to the document root. If the sentence z under the branch of node x contains a term t_i that appears in the heading of node y in the path from the root to node z, then the Fractal Sentence Heading Score FSS_H of sentence k should be the weights w_{ij} of the term t_i divided by the product of the degree of nodes m_{node} in the path from node y to node x, i.e.,

$$FSS_H(k,r) = \sum_{y \in\ path\ from\ root\ to\ x} \frac{\sum_{t_i \in\ y \cap s_k} w_{iy}}{\prod_{i \in\ path\ from\ y\ to\ x} m_i} .$$

The Fractal Heading Score FHS of range block r is calculated as the sum of the Fractal Sentence Heading Score FSS_H of all of the sentences in range block r, i.e.,

$$FHS(r) = \sum_{s_k \in r} FSS_H(s_k, r) .$$

- When human abstractors extract sentences from a text, they pay more attention to range blocks with headings that contain bonus word such as "conclusion", because they consider them to be more important parts of the document, and thus contain more sentences that should be extracted. In a document tree, the heading of each range block is examined, and its quota is adjusted accordingly. The Fractal Cue Score *FCS* of range block *r* is calculated as the sum of the cue weight of all the terms in the heading of that range block, i.e.,

$$FCS(r) = \sum_{t_i \in heading(r)} cue(t_i),$$

where *heading(r)* is the heading of range block *r* and $cue(t_i)$ is the cue weight of term t_i.

In our system, the maximum score for each feature is normalized to 1, and the Range Block Significance Score *RBSS* of a range block is calculated as the sum of the normalized scores of each feature for that range block, i.e.,

$$RBSS(r) = NFTS(r) + NFHS(r) + NFLS(r) + NFCS(r),$$

where *NFTS*, *NFHS*, *NFLS*, *NFCS* are the normalized fractal thematic, heading, location, and cue score, respectively, of range block *r*. The fractal value F_v of the root of the document is 1, which is propagated to the child nodes according to the formula

$$Fv(child \ of \ x) = C \bullet Fv(x) \left(\frac{RBSS \ (child \ of \ x)}{\sum_{y \in children \ of \ x} RBSS \ (y)} \right)^{-1/D} .$$

C is a constant between 0 and 1 that controls the rate of decay and *D* is the fractal dimension, both of which are taken as 1, identically to fractal view experiment [14]. The sentence quota of a summary is calculated based on the compression ratio, and is shared among the child nodes according to their fractal values. The optimal length of a summary that is generated by the extraction of a fixed number of sentences is 3 to 5 sentences [10], and thus if the quota of a node exceeds the default threshold value of 5 sentences, then it will be propagated to grandchild nodes iteratively.

We conducted an experiment that compared the fractal summarization and traditional summarization of annual reports in Hong Kong [29][30], and found that fractal summarization produces a summary with a wider coverage of information subtopics than traditional summarization. A user evaluation by ten participants was conducted to compare the performance of the fractal summarization and the traditional summarization which doesn't consider the hierarchical document structure. The results show that all of the participants considered the summary that was generated by the fractal summarization method to be the better summary. The fractal summarization method achieved a precision of up to 91.3% and of 87.1% on average, but the traditional summarization only achieved a maximum precision of 77.5% and an average of 67.0%. The results also show that fractal summarization outperforms traditional summarization at a 99.0% confidence level.

4 Relevance Feedback

Many studies have shown that relevance feedback can greatly improve the performance of information retrieval systems [22][24]. However, relevance feedback for automatic summarization systems, which is a special application of these systems, has not been well studied. There are two types of relevance feedback models – the vector processing relevance feedback model, which makes use of term weights, and the probabilistic retrieval relevance feedback model, which uses purely probabilistic methods. We propose a relevance feedback model for fractal summarization that is based on these two existing relevance feedback models.

- As information is stored as vectors in most systems, the vector processing relevance feedback model is the most widely used. The system uses a query vector to specify relevant and irrelevant information, and relevance feedback is used to modify the query vector accumulatively, with documents being ranked subsequently according to their distance from the query vector. The best-known vector feedback algorithm is the Rocchio model [22], which measures similarity by using the inner product.
- Some researchers believe that documents should be extracted based on the theory of probability. Using this theory, documents are extracted based on the probability that each term will occur in relevant or irrelevant documents. This system uses relevance feedback to adjust the probability function of each term, and then recalculates the relevance probability of each document [24].

Relevance feedback models have been previously proposed for the four extraction features of fractal summarization that are discussed in detail in Section 2, but such a model that includes relevance feedback for the location, heading, and cue features is new to the field.

- The thematic feature displays a list of terms with thematic weight, which is equivalent to the query vector in the vector relevance feedback model. The summarization system extracts a set of sentences such that the inner product of the term list and the summary is maximized, and the list is constructed automatically. The weights of the terms are initialized as the *tfidf* score, which is adjusted accumulatively based on the relevance feedback to reflect the user's actual assignation of weight to the terms. The system increases the weights of the terms that appear in the sentences that have been selected, and decreases the weights of the terms that appear in the sentences that have been rejected [22][24]. The term list at the $n+1^{th}$ round (T^{n+1}) is constructed by the previous accumulated term list (T^{n}) and the accepted and rejected sentences in the nth round feedback, i.e.,

$$T^{n+1}_i = \alpha T^n_i + \beta P\left(t_i \middle| n^{th} \; round \; accepted \right) - \gamma P\left(t_i \middle| n^{th} \; round \; rejected \right),$$

where α, β, γ are constants and $P(t_i)$ is the probability of term t_i. The thematic score of the sentence is the sum of *tfidf* score with relevance feedback, i.e., the score for the accumulated term list (T^n).
- In fractal summarization, documents are represented by a hierarchical tree structure. If many sentences under a given branch are accepted, then this branch is deemed to be more important, and its location score is increased. However, if many sentences under a given branch are rejected, then the location score of the branch is decreased. By using a conventional probabilistic relevance feedback model [4][24], the location score of a range block r is multiplied with a probability function $P(r)$ of range block r.

$$P(r) = \log\left(\frac{P(r|accepted)(1 - P(r|rejected))}{P(r|rejected)(1 - P(r|accepted))} \right),$$

where,

$$P(r|accepted) = \frac{no \ of \ sentences \ accepted \ in \ r + 0.5}{total \ no \ of \ sentences \ accepted + 1}, \ \text{and}$$

$$P(r|rejected) = \frac{no \ of \ sentences \ rejected \ in \ r + 0.5}{total \ no \ of \ sentences \ rejected + 1},$$

The relevance feedback on the location score is considered only for the calculation of the fractal value of a range block. When the system is extracting sentences inside a range block, it is disabled.

- The heading feature is an extension of the thematic feature to some extent because it represents a string of matching keywords in the corresponding heading. The heading weight of each term is the thematic weight with relevance feedback, which is propagated along the fractal structure, that is, the thematic weight of the term in the Fractal Sentence Heading Score is replaced with the weight of the accumulated term list that is constructed in the thematic feature.

- The cue feature has a dictionary with cue weights that have been defined by linguists. However, this may not truly reflect the user's preference, and therefore the cue weights are updated based on the sentences that are accepted or rejected in a similar manner as for the thematic feature.

5 Results

An experiment with ten participants was conducted to measure the performance of the summarization system with relevance feedback. The results show that relevance feedback greatly improves the precision of the summarization.

Usually, the performance of information systems is measured according to precision and recall. However, the performance of summarization systems is usually measured in

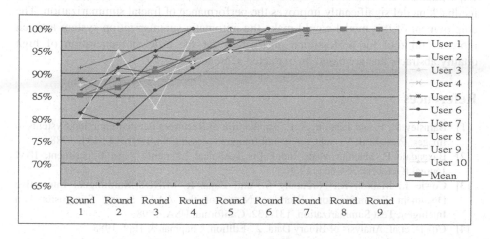

Fig. 2. Precision of Fractal Summarization with Relevance Feedback.

terms of precision only, as the measurement of recall is limited by the compression ratio of a summarization system. In addition to precision, the performance of relevance feedback can be measured by the time that is taken for the user to find information, and thus we measure the number of rounds that the summarization system takes to reach and retain its peak performance. First, a summary that was generated by generic fractal summarization was presented to the participants. The participants accepted or rejected the sentences based on whether they would include the sentence as part of the summary, and the precision of the summary was measured by the ratio of sentences that were accepted by the participants. The system then used the data of the users' feedback to update the sentence score, and generated another summary. This procedure was repeated until there was no further improvement. The results are shown in Figure 2.

As is shown in Figure 2, the average precision increases very quickly after the first few rounds. The mean precision in the first round is 85%, and increases significantly to 95% after three rounds of feedback. After that, the precision keeps increasing steadily, and reaches and retains 100% after the eighth round. By a t-test analysis of the precision, we found that there was no significant improvement in precision in the first and second rounds. The precision improved significantly at a 95% confidence level in the third to seventh round, and improved at an 80% confidence level in the eighth and ninth rounds. In other words, the performance is nearly saturated in the seventh round, after which the improvement in precision is not as significant as it in the previous rounds. In summary then, relevance feedback greatly improved the performance of the summarization system, and thus by using a fractal summarization model with relevance feedback, the professional abstractor can quickly extract important information from a document. This saves a lengthy read through the whole document, and allows the abstractor to generate a summary that is based on extracted sentences very quickly.

6 Conclusion

In this paper, a relevance feedback model for fractal summarization is proposed. Experiments were conducted with this model, and the results show that the relevance feedback model significantly improves the performance of fractal summarization. The employment of this model would make the automatic summarization system a much more useful tool for professional abstractors for the efficient generation of high quality abstracts that are based on extracted sentences.

References

[1] Barnsley M. F. and Jacquin, A. E. Application of Recurrent Iterated Function Systems to Images. Proc. SPIE Visual Comm. and Image Processing'88, 1001, 122-131, 1988.
[2] Baxendale P. Machine-Made Index for Technical Literature - An Experiment. IBM Journal (October), 354-361, 1958.
[3] Cowie J., Mahesh K., Nirenburg S., and Zajaz R. MINDS-Multilingual Interactive Document Summarization. Working Notes of the AAAI Spring Symposium on Intelligent Text Summarization. 131-132. California, USA, 1998.
[4] Cox D. et al. Analysis of Binary Data. 2nd Edition, Chapman & Hall, 1988.
[5] Craven T. C. Human Creation of Abstracts with Selected Computer Assistance Tools, Information Research, 3(4), 4, 1998.

[6] Craven T. C. Abstracts Produced Using Computer Assistance. J. of the American Soc. for Info. Sci., 51(8), 745-756, 2000.

[7] Edmundson H. P. New Method in Automatic Extraction. J. ACM, 16(2) 264-285, 1968.

[8] Endres-Niggemeyer B., Maier E., and Sigel A. How to Implement a Naturalistic Model of Abstracting: Four Core Working Steps of an Expert Abstractor. Information Processing and Management, 31(5) 631-674, 1995.

[9] Glaser B. G. and Strauss A. L. The Discovery of Grounded Theory: Strategies for Qualitative Research. Aldine de Gruyter, New York, 1967.

[10] Goldstein J. et al. Summarizing Text Documents: Sentence Selection and Evaluation Metrics. Proc. SIGIR'99, 121-128, 1999.

[11] Hearst M. Subtopic Structuring for Full-Length Document Access. Proc. SIGIR'93, 56-68, 1993.

[12] Jacquin. A. E. Fractal Image Coding: a Review. Proc. IEEE, 81(10), 1451-1465, 1993.

[13] Kendall M., and Gibbons J.D. Rank Correlation Methods, 5th ed. New York: Edward Arnold, 1990.

[14] Koike, H. Fractal Views: A Fractal-Based Method for Controlling Information Display. ACM Tran. on Information Systems, ACM, 13(3), 305-323, 1995.

[15] Kupiec J. et al. A Trainable Document Summarizer. Proc. SIGIR'95, 68-73, Seattle, USA. 1995.

[16] Lam-Adesina M. and Jones G. J. F. Applying Summarization Techniques for Term Selection in Relevance Feedback. Proc. SIGIR 2001, 1-9, 2001.

[17] Lin Y. and Hovy E.H. Identifying Topics by Position. Proc. of Applied Natural Language Processing Conference (ANLP-97), Washington, DC, 283-290, 1997.

[18] Luhn H. P. The Automatic Creation of Literature Abstracts. IBM Journal of Research and Development, 159-165, 1958.

[19] Mandelbrot B. The Fractal Geometry of Nature. W.H. Freeman, New York, 1983.

[20] Morris G., Kasper G. M., and Adams D. A. The Effect and Limitation of Automated Text Condensing on Reading Comprehension Performance. Info. Sys. Research, 17-35, 1992.

[21] Ogden W., Cowie J., Davis M., Ludovik E., Molina-Salgado H., and Shin H. Getting Information from Documents You Cannot Read: an Interactive Cross-Language Text Retrieval and Summarization System. Joint ACM DL/SIGIR Workshop on Multilingual Information Discovery and Access, 1999.

[22] Rocchio J. Relevance Feedback in Information Retrieval. The Smart Retrieval System, 313-323, Prentice Hall, 1971.

[23] Salton G. and Buckley C. Term-Weighting Approaches in Automatic Text Retrieval. Information Processing and Management, 24, 513-523, 1988.

[24] Salton G. et al. Improving Retrieval Performance by Relevance Feedback. J. America Soc. for Info. Sci., 41, 288-297, 1990.

[25] Teufel S. and Moens M. Sentence Extraction as a Classification Task. In Workshop of Intelligent and Scalable Text Summarization, ACL/EACL, 1997.

[26] Tsujimoto S. and Asada H. Understanding Multi-articled Documents, Proc. of the 10th Int. Conf. on Pattern Recognition, Atlantic City, N.J., 551-556, 1990.

[27] Wang F. L. and Yang C. C. Automatic Summarization of Chinese and English Parallel Documents, Proc. 6th Int. Conf. on Asian Digital Libraries, Kuala Lumpur, 2003.

[28] Yang C. C. and Li K. W. Automatic Construction of English/Chinese Parallel Corpora. J. of American Soc. for Info. Sci. and Tech., 54(8), 730-742, 2003.

[29] Yang C. C. and Wang F. L. Fractal Summarization for Mobile Device to Access Large Documents on the Web. Proc. 12th Int. WWW Conf., Budapest, Hungary, 2003.

[30] Yang, C. C. and Wang F. L. Fractal Summarization: Summarization Based on Fractal Theory, Proc. SIGIR 2003, Toronto, Canada, 2003.

A Query Analytic Model for Image Retrieval

Hsiao-Tieh Pu

Department of Adult & Continuing Education, National Taiwan Normal University,
162, Sec. 1, HoPing E. Rd.,Taipei, Taiwan 106
htpu@cc.ntnu.edu.tw

Abstract. Searching digital images on a networked environment is rapidly growing. Despite recent advances in image retrieval technologies, high-precision and robust solutions remain hampered by limits to knowledge about user issues associated with image retrieval. This paper examines a large number of queries from a Web image search engine, and attempts to develop an analytic model to investigate their implications for image retrieval technologies. The model employs the concepts of uniqueness and refinement to categorize successful and failed queries. The results show that image requests have a higher specificity and may often contain queries refined by interpretive, reactive, and perceptual attributes. Based on the proposed model, the study further investigates feasible technical solutions integrating both content-based and concept-based technologies to deal with real image query types. The initial study has provided useful results that enhance the understanding of digital image searching and suggests implications for the improvement of image retrieval systems.

1 Introduction

There has been a substantial increase in the availability of image collections in digital libraries. Searching digital images on a networked environment is rapidly growing. Though the design and technology of image databases have been extensively studied, high-precision and robust solutions remain hampered by limits to knowledge about user issues associated with image retrieval (Rasmussen, 1997). This indeed restricts the digital libraries to open up access to those non-text materials to a very broad user population. It is well assumed that existing large-scale image search engines are good sources to understand related problems in image searching due to its greater variety of images and users. Several Web search engines now attempt to index publicly accessible image files and offer image search capabilities ((Tomaiuolo, 2002). For example, as of this writing, Google claims to have more than 880 million indexed images. Currently, such Web image search engines provide keyword search options as in textual information retrieval (Smith & Chang, 1997). However, using text to search images may not prove successful in every case, especially when the images are not controlled collections and adequate annotations are not available for searching. It is not unusual for failed queries (defined as the searches that produce zero hits) to occur. For example, in the author's analysis of a 3-month log with over 2.4 millions real image queries, near 19% of the queries were found failed searches. Despite substantial efforts made on many image retrieval studies, the author thinks that the

Z. Chen et al. (Eds.): ICADL 2004, LNCS 3334, pp. 378–387, 2004.
© Springer-Verlag Berlin Heidelberg 2004

paramount challenge remains bridging the gap between research on image user studies and retrieval technologies. Undoubtedly, it is necessary to investigate characteristics of image queries before a more effective image retrieval system can be developed.

Image needs and seeking behaviors have been major concerns in the image retrieval field. Nevertheless, most of the research has focused on specific collections or specific groups of users (Choi & Rasmussen, 2003). With the rapid construction of multimedia digital libraries, a larger-scale investigation on understanding real users' image queries would be worthy to be conducted. So far there are few related studies, and mostly focused on analyzing textual queries. The results show that Web users tend to input short queries (Silverstein, et al., 1999; Jansen, et al., 2000; Pu, et al., 2002). However, the author's previous observation found that image queries are much longer and contain more unique searches than those of textual queries (Pu, 2003). This reveals that a higher level of specificity might exist in image queries and explain its higher failure rate than those in textual queries. Therefore, the purpose of this paper is to examine the differences between successful and failed image queries in a large-scale retrieval environment, to discover valuable features of the queries for consideration when designing an image metadata, and to develop an analytic model to investigate the relationship between image query types and feasible image retrieval techniques.

A 3-month dataset of over 2.4 millions successful and failed queries was collected from an image search engine. The study first analyzed and compared the factual characteristics of successful and failed queries, including their query length and query frequency. Human analysis was conducted in classifying top image queries into the proposed analytic model, which divides image requests into four dimensions employing uniqueness/refinement concepts. Further review of failed queries to induce and group various refiners into 3 categories of perceptual, interpretive, and reactive attributes was also conducted. Based on the above analysis, the distribution of image search patterns and important image attributes can be obtained. An investigation was conducted to understand the image query types and their problems in searching, and corresponding feasible image retrieval technologies were also discussed. It is proved that such model not just provides a better understanding of image search requests, but also has the value of providing shared perspectives and shared vocabularies among the researchers in different domains related to image retrieval.

The next section will first discuss the major assumptions and benefits of using image query analytic models. Section 3 is the research design. Section 4 and 5 show the results concerning the characteristics of successful and failed queries, and refined types of failed queries. In the final section 6, the study will discuss different characteristics of image query types, and to explore appropriate image retrieval technologies to overcome such a complex and variety of image needs.

2 Image Query Analytic Model

A "query" is a form of expression indicating a user's information need, and is often considered a compromised need when a user interacts with an information retrieval system (Taylor, 1968). A query analytic model, in other words, is a framework used to analyze users' queries. It can be effectively used to analyze the information needs expressed by the queries, and to compare characteristics of different types of queries. With the aid of a query analytic model, it is clearer to understand users' requests and their search patterns. Further, through the model, it may allow the discovery of problems and difficulties in searching, which provides significant implications and benefits to the design of an information retrieval system.

A number of studies have used query analysis to understand users' image needs and seeking behaviors. Various features of queries have been identified. Enser & McGregor (1993) employed the properties of uniqueness (unique/non-unique) and the concept of refinement (refined/non-refined) to map users' requests. In their study, uniqueness was a key attribute of image queries, with requests being for unique images (i.e., a specific person, place or event of which there is only one) or non-unique images (i.e., a certain type of person, item or place). They also noted that users further refined their queries based on time, location, action, event or technical specification attributes. Enser (1995) presented another conceptual framework to divide image retrieval into four models of query and search modes, based on linguistic and visual attributes. Jorgensen (1998) identified 3 image retrieval tasks (describing, searching, and sorting) and 12 classes of image attributes (literal object, people, people-related, art historical, color, visual elements, location, description, abstract concepts, content/story, external relationships, viewer response). Fidel (1997) assumed that retrieval tasks may affect searching behavior and described a continuum of use between a Data Pole and an Object Pole; i.e., each pole involves the retrieval of images for information and as objects. However, the related image user studies have been conducted mostly using written queries; little empirical research has examined users' queries in a digital environment.

According to Chen's study of the utility of the above models for the art history field, Enser & McGregor's categories of unique and non-unique received high degrees of matching image queries by human reviewers (2001). A possible explanation is that Enser & McGregor's study collected queries from real users with real image information needs, i.e., more user-centered. As Brown, et al. (1996) pointed out that experts were not a good source of terms preferred by users; instead, useful terms should be derived from users themselves. In the author's study, it was found that Enser & McGregor's scheme is particularly useful for identifying query types in the Web environment, and for establishing a common base to examine the differences between successful and failed queries. The proposed analytic model, therefore, extends this scheme to categorize Web image queries, and attempts to add more details to its refinement category. Several new refined types are deducted by analyzing the features of Web image requests.

3   Research Design

3.1   Datasets

This study used logs from VisionNEXT (http://www.visionnext.com/), which currently provides the largest image backend search service for several portals in Asia, such as Sina and Netease in China and PCHome in Taiwan. Their collection includes over 10 million Web thumbnail images crawled from the Web as of 2003/12, and over 100,000 images manually indexed using broad subject categories and assigned keywords. The engine allows users to search by term or to browse predefined subject categories of images; then, it returns 9 thumbnail images per page for users to view and select. Each thumbnail contains the URL of the image, the URL of the site where it resides, and some information about the image. Meanwhile, the engine implements a pornographic query filter, which is designed to filter out queries dealing with sexual content.

The logs were collected during a period of 3 months from July to September, 2002 containing 325,812 distinct query terms with a total frequency of 2,401,628. It was further divided to two subsets of successful (S-2002) and failed queries (F-2002). The 2 datasets contained distinct query terms and their corresponding aggregated frequencies. In this paper, a query denotes a query term exactly as entered by a user, which can be one or multiple words in English, or a sequence of characters in Chinese.

3.2 Methods

In this study, a failed query is defined as a query that produced zero hits, though a zero-hit search does not necessarily mean that the search was a failure and all failed queries are not necessarily zero-hit searches either. In addition, to avoid using only the VisionNEXT image query log as the experimental set, the contained queries were also submitted to the Google image search engine. It was found that most of the failed queries still produced zero hits in Google.

The study first analyzed and compared the factual characteristics of successful and failed queries. The major items for comparison consisted of query length and query frequency from S-2002 and F-2002. Next, the study developed an analytic model to categorize successful and failed queries, which was an extension of the uniqueness and refinement scheme developed by Enser & McGregor (1993). This scheme is popular due to the ease of identifying query types in a general-purpose searching environment like the Web and its practicality in examining the differences between successful and failed queries. The study then used the proposed analytic model to categorize the top 1,000 queries from S-2002 and F-2002. Finally, the study collected and reviewed 1,000 randomly selected failed queries using various refiners and grouped them into 10 refined types in 3 categories of perceptual, interpretive, and reactive attributes.

The categorization tasks, i.e., classifying the queries using the uniqueness/refinement scheme, was mainly done by 3 graduate students with substantial experience in Internet surfing and sufficient knowledge of image indexing and retrieval. During the categorization process, three principles were applied in this study. First, the judgment of uniqueness is based on the assumption that the image is a particular occurrence of an entity type. Thus, a query of "Triceratops" falls into the unique category since no other occurrence of the entity type Person has the same combination of required feature. A query of "dinosaur" falls into the non-unique category, then. All of the queries within the experimental set fell into either the unique or non-unique category, but both classes of queries were subject to refinement in terms of various specifications, like time, location, event, or technical attribute. Second, since a query may usually represent one feature, it was assigned to only one category. Third, each query was categorized by at least two analysts, and another analyst not previously engaged in the categorization process made the final decision if inconsistency occurred. Though the human analysts may have suffered from subjectivity, inconsistency, and lack of domain knowledge, they were only involved in classifying top query terms into appropriate categories. More importantly, the purpose of categorization was mainly to observe various trends of successful and failed queries, so the distortion caused by a few invalid human categorizations in fact would not seriously affect the accuracy of the experimental results.

4   Analysis of Successful and Failed Queries

4.1   Query Length

The average image query length in Total-2002 was 3.08 characters in Chinese (Table 2). According to general statistics on the Chinese language (Chien & Pu, 1996), the average word length is 1.5~1.6 characters; hence, 3.08 characters can be both treated as a word bi-gram or word pair. In addition, the average length of an English query was 1.40, mostly consisted of proper nouns like "IBM," "Microsoft," etc. Based on previous studies on Web searching, it appears that Web users type in short queries not only when searching for textual information, but also when searching for visual information. In addition, it is noted that a failed image query tended to be much longer (4.12 characters in Chinese) than the average length of successful queries (2.83 characters in Chinese), which indicates a higher level of specificity and the limitations of current Web image search engines. Further investigation will be discussed in a later section.

The average image query length in Total-2002 was 3.08 characters in Chinese. According to general statistics on the Chinese language (Chien & Pu, 1996), the average word length is 1.5~1.6 characters; hence, 3.08 characters can be both treated as a word bi-gram or word pair. In addition, the average length of an English query was 1.40, mostly consisted of proper nouns like "IBM," "Microsoft," etc. Based on previous studies on Web searching, it appears that Web users type in short queries not only when searching for textual information, but also when searching for visual information. In addition, it is noted that a failed image query tended to be much longer (4.12 characters in Chinese) than the average length of successful queries (2.83 characters in Chinese), which indicates a higher level of specificity and the limitations of current Web image search engines. Further investigation will be discussed in a later section.

4.2   Query Frequency

Figure 1 shows part of a histogram of query duplication, i.e., the frequency distribution of distinct query terms. Obviously the successful queries focused on popular queries or certain subject domains than those of failed queries. The top 5% of the successful image queries had over 80% of the total frequency, and the top 25 queries in the data set had fully 14.61% of the total frequency, despite representing only 0.00027% of the distinct queries. It appeared that there was a strong trend corresponding to Pareto's law in successful image requests. However, it needs to be noted that failed searches had a much higher rate of one-time query, 39.53% compared to 2% of successful queries. In fact, the distribution is very skewed toward the lower end of the number of failed queries, with a long tail of few users submitting a large number of unique queries. It is concluded that the variety of contents in failed queries may be greater in terms of query frequency than that in successful image queries, and warrants in itself a good source needed further investigation.

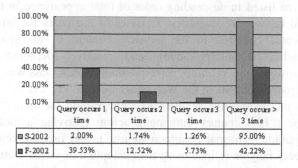

	Query occurs 1 time	Query occurs 2 time	Query occurs 3 time	Query occurs > 3 time
S-2002	2.00%	1.74%	1.26%	95.00%
F-2002	39.53%	12.52%	5.73%	42.22%

Fig. 1. Distribution of query frequency in successful and failed image queries

5   Analysis of Image Refined Types

Based on the proposed image query analytic model, the top 1,000 queries of F-2002 were mapped into four categories along two dimensions: unique/non-unique and refined/non-refined. Figure 2 shows the percentages of the four categories in terms of image successful and failed queries, which provides a practical way to examine their differences. Most of image queries were unique searches, particularly personal name searches, which may indicate a higher level of specificity as mentioned. In fact, the percentages of refined queries (15.73%) and unique queries (78.42%) among failed image queries were both higher than the overall percentages of image refined (6.24%) and unique (75.85%) queries. It is worth noting that refined queries occurred near 4 times more often in failed queries than in successful queries. Further investigation of the unique and refined query types may provide insight into the features of queries, which provides valuable source for image indexing and retrieval.

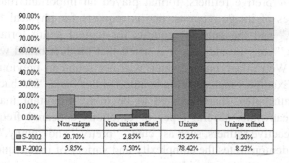

	Non-unique	Non-unique refined	Unique	Unique refined
S-2002	20.70%	2.85%	75.25%	1.20%
F-2002	5.85%	7.50%	78.42%	8.23%

Fig. 2. Successful and failed image query types within the experimental datasets

To induce the features of queries, this study collected and reviewed 1,000 refined queries from the failed image searches and grouped them into 10 refined types as listed in Table 1. The example queries are shown in the second column, and the refined types are listed in descending order of total appearance in the reviewed set. The 10 refined types were suggested 3 classes of attributes for image descriptions, namely, perceptual (related to the physical content of an image), interpretive (requiring intellectual interpretation), and reactive (demonstrating emotional responses). However, the attributes corresponding to each class were mainly deduced based on the ground analysis of the Web image queries. For example, a query may be refined based on interpretive features like geographic location ("national flag of Canada"), time ("19th century building"), action ("driving a motorcycle"), event ("New Year parade"), format ("cartoon mouse"), and product brand ("Nike sport shoes"). A query may be refined using the perceptual or visual features of an image, such as its shape ("shape of a hand"), color ("purple feather"), texture ("steel-made pan"), etc. A query may even be refined using reactive or abstract features like emotion ("cute cat").

Table 1. Refined types of failed image queries

Refined type		Example (translation in English)	%
INTERPRETIVE	Format	卡通老鼠(cartoon mouse); 漫畫魚(comic fish)	38.22%
	Geographic	日本寺廟(Japanese temple); 加拿大國旗(Canada flag)	21.64%
	Time	2000 奧運; 夏天的海邊(summer sea shore)	12.68%
	Brand	LV 背包(LV backpack); 耐吉球鞋(Nike sport shoes)	7.52%
	Event	中秋節月亮(moon in the Chinese Moon Festival)	3.43%
	Action	騎摩托車(riding a motorcycle)	0.22%
REACTIVE	Emotion	可愛的水果(cute fruit);好笑的臉(funny face)	9.25%
PERCEPTUAL	Shape	L型沙發(L-shaped sofa); 星星花邊(star grid)	4.81%
	Color	黑色柳丁(black orange);紫色羽毛(purple feather)	1.52%
	Texture	布紋(cloth texture)	0.71%

By and large, interpretive features were the most common refined types. Among these general interpretive refiners, format played an important role. Format may include two types of image requests: one is requests for physical file formats like "gif" and "jpeg," and the other is requests for logical genre formats like "logo," "map," "cartoon," etc. In addition, it is noted that product brand was an important refined type of Web image query, which was not found in previous related image query studies. Examples include "Honda automobiles" and "LV backpack." As for the perceptual attributes, shape seemed to be more important than the others in refinement. Meanwhile, several types of emotions appeared frequently in those queries having reactive refiners, such as "cute," "pretty," and "funny," etc. The above analysis further demonstrates the complexity and variety of image queries in terms of their refined types, and also provides a source for the features of image queries for further applications.

6 Image Query Types and Retrieval Technologies

As Enser (1995) noted the existence of parallel streams of research in image retrieval, divided into concept-based and content-based with little interaction between researchers and their literature. Enser (2000) argues for the continued importance of both concept-based and content-based research in image retrieval, and the development of hybrid retrieval systems. Therefore, based on the above analysis of features of image queries and investigations of current image retrieval technologies, this study has developed an analytic model to provide a common base to bridge the gap between research on image user studies and image retrieval technologies.

In Figure 3, the proposed analytic model took the form of a 4-quadrant (Q^1~Q^4) based on the refinement/uniqueness features of image queries and the corresponding image retrieval technologies investigated. Most of the image queries fit in the Q^1 quadrant, for example, 75.85% of image queries in the experimental datasets fall into this category. The A query set represents queries with a unique name search like "Arnold Schwarzenegger". It is obvious that simply using the content-based image retrieval (CBIR) technologies, which focus on perceptual image attributes like color or shape, cannot fully satisfy such requests. It is suggested that adequate image indexing is needed, such as to increase the number of annotations to images like utilizing automatic image annotation techniques A'. In fact, if the number of images is sufficiently large, each image may only need to be annotated one index term based on its most unique occurrence, which often appeared in its filename. The next most requested category is Q^2, for example, 17.91% falls into this category. In Q^2, the B query set represents queries with one broad search topic like "governor". In such case, if there are sufficient texts existed with the images like surrounding texts, these requests can be settled in some degree, which using current text information retrieval technologies A. is adequate.

Considering the 20/80 rule, most of image requests can be fulfilled using A' and B' technologies, either for successful or failed queries (84.72% and 95.95% in the experimental sets respectively). However, there are still 15.73% of failed queries rely on more advanced image retrieval technologies. In Q^3, the C query set contains refined topic searches like "governor Arnold Schwarzenegger". Since the search topic has been specified by various types of refiners (as discussed in the previous section), the query at least needs to be pre-processed using query processing technologies C', such as to identify the search topic and its refiner. If users are not so demanding in the images requested, the situation is basically similar to those in Q^1 or Q^2, i.e., to apply A' or B' technologies to handle those pre-processed queries. However, in the last Q^4, the D set consists of most complex requests, in each contains multiple topic searches with refiner like "Arnold, in black suites, kisses his wife at Tuesday night's celebration of his winning". In such case, both semantic and visual features of the images are necessary for effective retrieval, such as interpretive features of time, place, and action; and perceptual feature of color, etc. Therefore, besides using C' to pre-process the image query, there is also a need to understand the semantic meaning existed in the image using technologies D'.

It is suggested that any digital image service considers employing the above analytic model to understand characteristics of users' image requests, and investigate appropriate technological solutions, either in the direction of indexing or retrieval of image data, such as designing image metadata or applying automatic image annotation techniques.

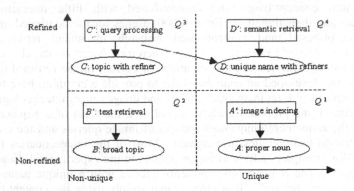

Fig. 3. The image query analytic model developed in this study

7 Conclusion

Searching digital images on a networked environment is rapidly growing. With the increase of digital image archives opening access to a broader population, it is important to understand users' image requests and design feasible solutions to deal with a greater variety of needs and uses on a large scale. This study examined the differences between successful and failed image requests using a large number of queries from a real Web image search engine. Overall Web users tend to input short queries in image searching. However, failed queries are much longer, have more distinct and unique queries made, which indicates a higher level of variety and specificity. From the analysis of refined types in failed queries, the features of image queries were grouped into three categories with ten different features. Among them, the interpretive attributes of refinement are the most commonly found than those of reactive and perceptual refiners. It is obvious that image metadata can benefit from such analysis, and consider the inclusion or priority of these image features. The paper also proposed a general-purpose image analytic model useful for describing the characteristics of users' query types and discovering feasible image retrieval technologies. Such model proves the value of providing shared perspectives and shared vocabularies among the researchers in different domains for further research on image user studies and image retrieval technologies.

References

1. Brown, P., Hidderley, R., Griffin, H., & Rollason, S. (1996). The democratic indexing of images. *The New Review of Hypermedia and Multimedia.* 2, 107-121.
2. Chen, H. (2001). An analysis of image queries in the field of art history. *Journal of the American Society for Information Science & Technology*, 52(3), 260-273.

3. Chien, Lee-Feng, & Pu, Hsiao-Tieh. (1996). Important issues on Chinese information retrieval. *Computational Linguistics and Chinese Language Processing*, 1(1), 205-221.
4. Choi, Y., & Rasmussen, E.M. (2003). Searching for images: The analysis of users' queries for image retrieval in American history. *Journal of the American Society for Information Science & Technology*, 54(6), 498-511.
5. Enser, P.G.B. (1995). Progress in documentation: Pictorial information retrieval. *Journal of Documentation*, 51(2), 126-70.
6. Enser, P.G.B. (2000). Visual image retrieval: Seeking the alliance of concept-based and content-based paradigms. *Journal of Information Science*, 26(4), 199-210.
7. Enser, P.G.M., & McGregor, C. (1993). Analysis of visual information retrieval queries. *British Library Research and Development Report*, 6104.
8. Fidel, R. (1997). The image retrieval task: Implications for the design and evaluation of image databases. *The New Review of Hypermedia and Multimedia*, 3, 181-199.
9. Jansen, B.J., Spink, A., & Saracevic, T. (2000). Real life, real users, and real needs: A study and analysis of user queries on the web. *Information Processing & Management*, 36(2), 207-227.
10. Jorgensen, C. (1998). Attributes of images in describing tasks. *Information Processing & Management*, 34(2/3), 161-74.
11. Pu, Hsiao-Tieh, Chuang, Shui-Lung, & Yang, Chyan. (2002). Subject categorization of query terms for exploring Web users' search interests. *Journal of the American Society for Information Science & Technology*, 53(8), 617-630.
12. Pu, Hsiao-Tieh. (2003). An analysis of Web image queries for search. *ASIST'2003*, 340-348.
13. Rasmussen, E. (1997). Indexing images. *Annual Review of Information Science and Technology*, 32, 169-196.
14. Sebe, N., Lew, M.S., Zhou, X.S., Huang, T.S., & Bakker, E.M. (2003). The state of the art in image and video retrieval. *CIVR 2003*, 1-8.
15. Silverstein, C., Henzinger, M., Marais, H,. & Moricz, M. (1999). Analysis of a very large Web search engine query log. *SIGIR Forum*, 33(1), 6-12.
16. Smith, J., & Chang, S. (1997). An image and video search engine for the world wide web, In Sethi, I., & Jain, R., *Proceedings of SPIE*, 3022, 84-95.
17. Taylor, R.S. (1968). Question-negotiation and information seeking in libraries: The process of asking questions. *College and Research Libraries*, 29, 178-194.
18. Tomaiuolo, N.G. (2002). When image is everything. *Searcher*, 10(1). http://www.infotoday.com/searcher/jan02/tomaiuolo.htm

Character Region Identification from Cover Images Using DTT

Lixu Gu

Computer Science, Shanghai Jiaotong University, Shanghai, China
gu-lx@cs.sjtu.edu.cn

Abstract. A robust character region identification approach is proposed here to deal with cover images using a differential top-hat transformation (DTT). The DTT is derived from morphological top-hat transformation (TT), and efficient for feature identification. This research is considered as a fundamental study for auto-classification of printed documents for organizing a Digital Library (DL) system. The entire procedure can be divided into two steps: region classification and character region identification. In the first step, a source gray image is segmented by a series of structuring elements (SE) into sub-images using the DTT. Since the widths of regions are relative to the scales of the characters, the different scales of characters are classified into the series of sub-images. The character region identification processing is composed of feature emphasis, extraction of candidate character regions and region reconstruction processing. Feature emphasis processing reduces noises and emphasizes characters in the sub-images, and then the candidate character regions are extracted from the gray scale sub-images by a histogram analysis. Lastly, a morphological image reconstruction algorithm based on conditional dilation is introduced to make the extracted character regions distinct from noises. To demonstrate the robustness of the proposed approach, 30 gray scale cover images were tested in the experiments, which revealed that an average extraction rate of 94% has been achieved.

Keywords: Optical Character Reader, Cover Image, DTT, Region Identification.

1 Introduction

An enormous amount of digital and printed documents are produced daily. The existing printed documents are gradually replaced by digital documents (i.e., digital magazines). To store and process these documents, efficient techniques of conversion from paper to digital documents are required. An Optical Character Reader (OCR) facilitates the conversion for organizing a digital library (DL) system. But there still have many difficulties in auto-processing these source printed documents. Among them, the most errors are considered come from the step of character region identification due to the increment of variety of printing styles, especially in the cover pages.

Many character region identification systems [1-7] are proposed in broad areas of different source documents. The main categories include:

Z. Chen et al. (Eds.): ICADL 2004, LNCS 3334, pp. 388–397, 2004.
© Springer-Verlag Berlin Heidelberg 2004

- Engineering Drawing (ED): to extract characters from design papers for the purpose of CAD/CAM.
- Texts: to segment text regions and figure regions with column structures from Newspaper, book and magazine for the purpose of the digital library.
- Maps: to extract and recognize characters from maps for the purpose of digital maps and digital navigation.
- Cover Images: to extract characters from covers of books, magazines or posters for the purpose of the digital library.
- Scene Images: to extract and recognize characters from scenes for the purpose of robotic navigation.

Comparing these researches, many similar features can be found between studies on EDs and texts [1-4], where character regions are usually separated from figures and characters usually have regular sizes, directions and positions. In these cases, feature extraction techniques (e.g. thresholding) can be efficient to distinguish character regions. Even if characters in maps [5] are in regular layout either, they usually mixed with figures, and more difficult to be extracted. The last two categories (cover images and scene images)[6-8] are even more complicated in the aspect of that character regions are composed in the figures with irregular sizes, directions and positions. More image processing techniques are required before the features can be extracted.

In this paper, we propose a novel character region identification approach using mathematical morphology. Since morphological operations are geometry basis, they can easily extract margins of characters with different shape. Several morphological approaches [9,10] are proposed for character identification where [9] are about character extraction from binary newspaper headlines, which have a patterned background. Some strict conditions are set up in these papers. For example, "background patterns are slenderer than the characters"; "background patterns are periodically arranged". Accordingly, we employ gray-scale and color images instead of binary images to extract characters from cover images of magazines without rigid preceding conditions.

The rest of the paper is organized as follows: in section 2, a brief review of DTT method and morphological reconstruction techniques are presented. In section 3, the novel segmentation algorithm is proposed. A demonstration of the proposed algorithm alone with a validation experiment is described in section 4. The robustness and finally accuracy of our approach are discussed in section 5.

2 Morphological Top-Hat and DTT

2.1 Top-Hat Transformation

The morphological "top-hat" transformation originally proposed by Meyer [11] provides an efficient tool for extracting bright (respectively, dark) objects from an uneven background. It is denoted by $T_i^{(i)}$, and defined as:

$$T_i^{(i)} = \begin{cases} T_i & \text{if } WTT; \text{ where, } T_i = F - F \circ_g r_i k \\ T^{(i)} & \text{if } BTT; \text{ where, } T^{(i)} = F \bullet_g r_i k - F \end{cases} \tag{1}$$

Where, F stands for source image. $r_i k = k \oplus k \oplus \cdots \oplus k$ (r_i times), when r_i denotes the scale of a structure element (SE, e.g. the radius of a disk).

The gray-scale original image F opened by a SE k can removes the bright areas which cannot hold the SE, and subtracting the opened image from the original one yields an image where the bright objects clearly stand out. This transformation is called "white top-hat" transformation (WTT). A closed original image in gray-scale subtracting original one allows us to extract dark objects from bright background, which is called "black top-ha" transformation (BTT), respectively.

2.2 Differential Top-Hat Transformation

For some complicated images, especially those in which the target objects are combined in the uneven background, the TT is difficult to segment interested particles satisfactorily since parts of noise regions are also holding the top gray regions which should be extracted with objective regions by the TT. Clues for detecting features were discovered when we concentrated on the TT with different sizes of disk SE. The difference between $T_i^{(i)}$, and $T_{(i-1)}^{(i-1)}$, includes our interested objects, and that image can be easily thresholded to make features stand out.

The new morphological segmentation algorithm named "Differential Top-hats" (DTT) corresponding to WTT and BTT is defined as follows:

$$F_i = |T_i - T_{i-1}|_B - F'_{i-1}; \quad F'_i = \bigcup_{1 \le j \le i} F_j; \quad F'_1 = \phi \tag{2}$$

or

$$F_i = |T^i - T^{i-1}|_B - F'_{i-1}; \quad F'_i = \bigcup_{1 \le j \le i} F_j; \quad F'_1 = \phi \tag{3}$$

Where F_i' denotes segmented images which hold different sizes i of objects. $| \ |_B$ stands for a threshold operation by a gray level B, which is determined experimentally. The differences of the neighbor TT results up to i are united together in Fi' with certain size of features.

As shown in Fig.2, the DTT is significantly improved from TT in the next aspects:

1. It can automatically select appropriate sizes of structuring elements satisfying different objects. Since the DTT operation does not only employ a single structuring element like the TT operation but also utilize a series of structuring elements. Appropriate sizes of structuring elements can easily be found to fit different objective regions in the studying image.
2. We can easily identify a satisfactory threshold value for DTT results. Since the DTT algorithm emphasized the differences between the regions with steep slopes and that with gradual slopes, a common threshold value can be easily found to all the steps of the processing.

3. The DTT can reduce more noises and emphasis the features of objects. Gray levels of most noises are greatly reduced due to their trivial gradients when gray levels of objects remain high. They are easily distinguished by a threshold operation as depicted in Fig. 2.

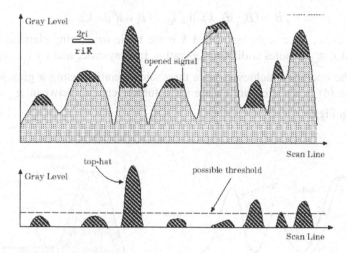

Fig. 1. The top-hat transformation. (upper) the result of opened signal and (lower) TT result T_i

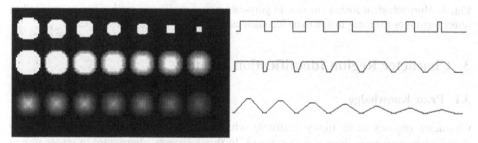

(a) Source testing image and its cross section lines

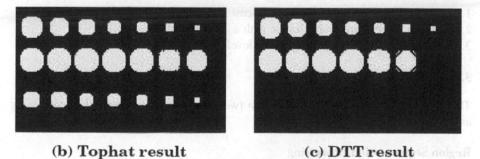

(b) Tophat result   **(c) DTT result**

Fig. 2. A test result comparing the TT and DTT algorithms

2.3 Morphological Reconstruction

Mathematical morphology is a powerful methodology for the quantitative analysis of geometrical structures where the Morphological Reconstruction is employed to reconstruct character regions. It is defined as:

$$B_i = (B_{i-1} \oplus_g k) \bigcap |f|_G \quad (B_i \in R^3, i = 1,2,...) \tag{4}$$

In the above, i is a scale factor and K is the basic structuring element (e.g. 1 pixel radius disk). $\oplus_{gray}$ denotes a dilation operation in grayscale, and $|f|_G$, represents the *mask* of the operation, achieved via a threshold operation using a gray level G. The iteration in (4) is repeated until there is no further change between B_{i-1} and B_i. It is depicted in Fig.3.

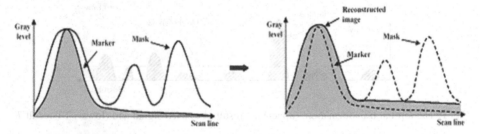

Fig. 3. Morphological Reconstruction in grayscale where regions in marker image are used to select regions of the mask image to be reconstructed

3 Character Region Identification Strategy

3.1 Prior Knowledge

Character regions have many features, which can be employed as restrictions to distinguish characters from a cover image. In this research, characters in cover image are considered satisfying the next conditions:

1. Character regions are composed of at least 3 characters;
2. Character regions are monochrome with a good contrast;
3. A character should be in a single gray level.

3.2 Identification Processing

The entire procedure can be divided into two steps: region segmentation processing and character extraction processing.

Region Segmentation Processing
The DTT algorithm is employed in this step. Where source image F is in gray-scale and the segmented sub-images are thresholded into binary images. Equation (2) and

(3) are performed respectively correspondence to different input images. In equation (2), all the regions which hold the same width as the disk shaped SE and brighter than the surrounding areas are detected into an image F_i. Consequently, the regions, which are smaller than specified SE and brighter than the surrounding areas (holding high gray levels) are collected together into a sub-image. F'_i. In the same way, equation (2) detects all the regions which are darker than the surrounding areas (holding low gray levels). The two equations are recurrently performed i_{max} times, which is determined in the width of the largest character lines $(2\ i_{max} + 1)$ in the source image. The mentioned threshold value is determined experimentally. The examples of resulting sub-images are shown in Fig. 4.

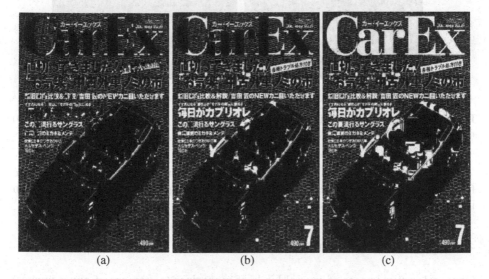

(a)	(b)	(c)

Fig. 4. The examples of resulting sub-images of DTT. (a) i = 4; (b) i = 10; (c) i = 30

Character Region Identification Processing
Since the character regions coexist with noises in the extracted sub-images, we firstly employ a morphological noise reduction algorithm based on dilation and opening operations to emphasize the character regions and suppress the noises. The resulted sub-images are transformed into gray-level images by an arithmetic multiplication between two same size images (source image and a sub-image).

Then, the character candidate regions are extracted by a histogram analysis technique. Since character regions hold peak gray values in the emphasized sub-images, the gray levels of character regions can be identified by detecting the peak values, which are bigger than the average value of all the peak values in their histogram curve. The detected peak value may be more than one because the character regions with different gray levels might coexist in one image. We employ all the peak values, which are bigger than the average one as the threshold levels. The sub-images are thresholded into binary images by the values.

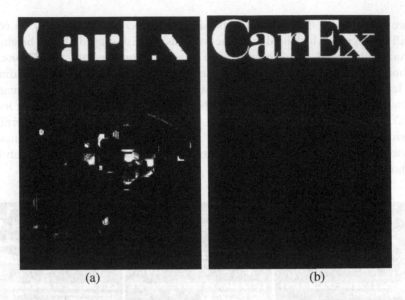

(a)   (b)

Fig. 5. The examples of identified character regions. (a) a sub-image with candidates; (b) reconstructed character region

Since there still remain some noises and part of character regions are lost, we finally reconstruct these sub-images using the morphological reconstruction algorithm in the last step. The examples are shown in Fig. 5.

4   Experimental Results

Gray-scale cover images of several kinds of magazines (a category of cover images) were employed to test our proposed algorithm. Although characters in some of them lay on a flat background, some of others are intricately composed of pictures and characters. They were regarded as a typical representative of covers with much variation.

A cover image database with 30 gray scale images were constructed and they were tested in the experiment to demonstrate the robustness of the proposed approach. They were scanned in 100dpi and 1170   848 pixels. Two examples are shown in Fig.6.

The procedure of the experiment was described fully in the last section. In the segmentation processing, we defined $i_{max} = 40$ because the largest character line in our source images was smaller than 81 pixels (diameter of a disk with radius of 40) according to a statistical inspection.

As shown in Fig.7, character regions were efficiently extracted using the proposed algorithm. Some inputs, which are quite simple similar to a text page, achieved significant high extraction rate (99%) except the extremely small character regions. Only increasing the scanning resolution can solve this common problem. There are

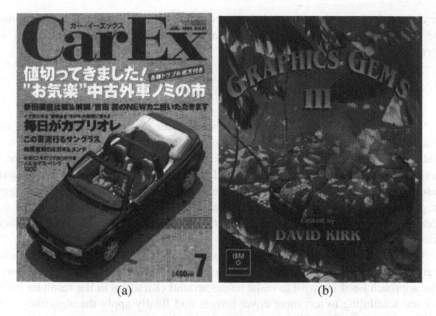

Fig. 6. Example of the source cover images. (a) CAREX; (b) Gems

Fig. 7. Example of the results. (a) CAREX; (b) Gems

many other inputs in our database, which are much complicated because the characters are mixed with their background such as the "Gems" shown in Fig.6 (b). A 92% extraction rate acquired for this case. The extraction rated is defined as the percentage between the extracted character regions and the total character regions in the inputs. Finally, among the database, an average of 94% character regions were correctly identified.

5 Conclusion

In this paper, a novel approach to identify character regions using DTT from cover images were proposed. The character regions in the cover images can be imagined as that they are ``floating on the background or sinking under it" with a flat texture. We devoted our attention to these features and proposed the characters extraction system based on the idea of detecting "thin and long" regions. As examples, cover images of magazines were employed in the experiment. The results show that even for some complicated images, good extraction results were achieved with an average extraction rate of 94%.

As the future work, the algorithm needs improvement to deal with some character regions in the complicated images, which could not be automatically identified so far. The approach need improve to resist noises around characters in the resultant images. We are scheduling to test more cover images and finally apply the algorithm into an OCR system to facilitate the conversion of printed documents to electronic document in organizing a digital library system.

References

1. S.Liang and M.Ahmadi, "A Morphological Approach to Text String Extraction from Regular Periodic Overlapping Text/Background Images", Computer Vision, Graphics, Image Processing, Vol.56, No.5, pp.402-413, Sep., 1994.
2. H.Goto, H.Aso. "Character Pattern Extraction Based on Local Multilevel Thresholding and Region Growing". Proc. of International Conference on Pattern Recognition (ICPR'00)-Volume 4: pp.4430–4433, 2000.
3. K.Marukawa, T.Hu, H.Fujisawa and Y.Shima, "Document Retrieval Tolerating Character Recognition Errors - Evaluation and Application", Pattern Recognition, Vol.30, No.8, pp.1361-1371, Aug. 1997.
4. A.K.Jain and Y.Zhong, "Page Segmentation Using Texture Analysis", Pattern Recognition, Vol.29, No.5, pp.743-770, May 1996.
5. P.Tofani and R.Kasturi, "Segmentation of Text from Color Map Images", Proc. of 14th International Conference on Pattern Recognition(ICPR'98), pp.945-947, August 1998.
6. X.Ye, M.Cheriet, and C.Y.Suen,, "Stroke-Model-Based Character Extraction from Gray-Level Document Images", IEEE Trans. on Image Processing, Vol. 10, No. 8, pp.1152-1161, August, 2001.
7. L.Gu, T.Kaneko, and N.Tanaka, "Morphological Segmentation Applied to Character Extraction from Color Cover Images", Mathematical Morphology and Its Applications to Image and Signal Processing, Kluwer Academic Publishers, pp.367--374, 1998.
8. J.Ohya, A.Shio and S.Akamatsu, "Recognizing character in scene images", IEEE Trans. on Pattern Anal. Machine Intell., Vol.16, No.2, pp.214-220, 1994.

9. S.Liang and M.Ahmadi, "A Morphological Approach to Text String Extraction from Regular Periodic Overlapping Text/Background Images", Computer Vision, Graphics, Image Processing, Vol.56, No.5, pp.402-413, Sep., 1994.
10. M.-Y.Chen, A.Kundu and S.N.Srihari, "Variable Duration Hidden Markov Model and Morphological Segmentation for Handwritten Word Recognition", IEEE Trans. on Image Processing, Vol. 4, No. 12, pp.1675-1688, Dec., 1995.
11. F.Meyer, "Contrast Feature Extraction", Quantitative Analysis of Microstructures in Material Sciences, Biology and Medicine, J.-L. Chermant, ed., Special issue of Practical Metallography}, Riederer Verlag, Stuttgart, Germany, 1978.

Multilingual Story Link Detection Based on Event Term Weighting on Times and Multilingual Spaces*

Kyung-Soon Lee[1] and Kyo Kageura[2]

[1] Division of Electronics and Information Engineering, Chonbuk National University,
664-14 Duckjin-gu Jeonju Jeonbuk 561-756 Korea
selfsolee@chonbuk.ac.kr
[2] National Institute of Informatics, 2-1-2 Hitotsubashi Chiyoda-ku Tokyo 101-8430 Japan
kyo@nii.ac.jp

Abstract. In this paper, we propose a novel approach for multilingual story link detection. Our approach uses features such as timelines and multilingual spaces for giving distinctive weights to terms that constitute linguistic representation of events. On timelines term significance is calculated by comparing term distribution of the documents on a day with that of the total document collection. Since two languages can provide more information than one language, term significance is measured on each language space, which is then used as a bridge between two languages on multilingual (here bilingual) spaces. Evaluating the method in Korean and Japanese news articles, our method achieved 14.3% improvement for monolingual story pairs, and 16.7% improvement for multilingual story pairs. By measuring the space density, the proposed weighting components are verified with a high density of the intra-event stories and a low density of the inter-events stories. This result indicates that the proposed method is helpful for multilingual story link detection.

1 Introduction

A story link detection system determines whether or not two randomly selected stories discuss the same event. Link detection is a component technology which can be used for topic detection and tracking. For example, detecting stories can be done by comparing each incoming story to the on-topic stories. Recent researches on story link detection focus on document representation, decision threshold and similarity metrics to make more accurate the determination of decision boundaries for the same event stories.

For this study, we propose the term weighting components in viewpoint of events in news articles such as timelines and multilingual spaces. Here event terms mean the essential terms to describe the event of a document. We represent the terms of a document on the collocation map to reflect co-occurrence information of terms, and to give an effect on the weight of a term based on co-occurrence relation with neighbors

---

* This study is partly supported by "Information Utilization for Heterogeneous Contents" (13224087), Japanese Grant-in-Aid Scientific Research on Priority Area "Informatics" (Area #006).

Z. Chen et al. (Eds.): ICADL 2004, LNCS 3334, pp. 398–407, 2004.

on the map. Then story link detection system determines whether two documents deal the same event by relevance degree.

In weighting event terms, we use the following information, based on our observations of event expressions:

- Internal properties: An event is most typically described with elements: who, where, when, what, why and how. So event terms represent these information. As such, recognition of named entity such as person, organization, location, country, time, and activity is helpful to give confidence to event term candidates.
- Behaviors in a document: Relevant event terms tend to occur throughout the story. In news articles, an event is basically announced as a declarative sentence. Therefore event terms tend to co-occur within a sentence throughout the story. Since an event expression tends to consist of two or more event terms, representing co-occurrence of terms is a useful way to obtain reliable event expressions.
- Distributional properties on timelines: Significant term shifts and rapid changes in the term frequency distribution are typical of stories reporting a new event on time. An aspect of term significance therefore can be calculated by the documents on a day and the total document collection.
- Contrastive properties on multilingual spaces: The amount of articles reported on an event would be different depending on the interest of societies, nations, cultures or languages. It has an effect on term significance on multilingual spaces. Since two language spaces provide more information than one language space, term significance is measured on each language space and can be used as a clue for event terms on the other language space instead of mixing multilingual spaces into one.

We have evaluated the proposed method on multilingual story link detection test set with Korean and Japanese news articles.

2 Related Researches

Traditional information retrieval is useful for content-based queries when a user knows more precisely the nature of the events or facts, but deficient for generic queries when a user does not have any knowledge of recent events to generate specific queries. The study of topic detection and tracking (TDT) [5] enables a user to obtain the event-oriented information. TDT works with chronologically ordered news stories from broadcasts or newswire sources to detect new events and stories which describe the same event.

Many researches on topic detection and tracking are not very different in dealing the event-oriented tasks from the subject-oriented problem such as document clustering and categorization although the tasks are defined differently. Carbonell et al. [2] tested different combinations of similarity metrics for story link detection in TDT. The best performance was achieved not with a combination of the N best individual metrics, but with a mix of best and second-tier metrics. Chen and Chen [3] showed that nouns, verbs, adjectives and compound nouns are useful to represent story, and story expansion used by information retrieval approach is helpful. They showed the results by testing several thresholds for monolingual and multilingual link detection.

Some researches have considered the event term properties to track events or to capture major events on timelines. Fukumoto and Suzuki [6] considered the behaviour of event terms called domain dependency of terms for event tracking by assuming that an event associated with a story appears throughout paragraphs, but a subject term does not. This method was applied to event tracking with some training stories and the event defined to track. Swan and Allan [15] showed term significance on timelines was useful to get major topics. They suggested a method to generate clusters of terms that capture the information corresponding to major news topics covered in the corpus. Atlam et al [1] proposed an evaluation method of word's popularity with time-series based on the frequency change by assuming that the word's popularity can be used for calculating the degree of similarity like term frequency and document frequency in traditional information retrieval. However, these studies tackled topics not for the document but for the document collection. Eichmann [4] considered named entities as event features.

On multilingual topic detection and tracking researches, Arabic and English link detection were conducted by an Arabic-English bilingual dictionary and translation probability [9]. Levow et al [11] and He et al [7] showed that the two-best translation selection based on a statistical lexicon and post-translation document expansion outperforms over one translation by machine translation system in Mandarin and Arabic to English multilingual topic tracking. After language translation based on a dictionary or a machine translation, multilingual detection methods concentrate language source specific normalization of similarity with lower thresholds compared to monolingual story pairs [9,3,10].

3   Link Detection Based on Event Term Weighting

In this paper, we adapt the features such as timelines and multilingual spaces as the weighting components to give distinctive weights to the terms which describe an event.

For multilingual story link detection, a machine translation system is used to make multilingual spaces to one language space. Terms are weighted based on event term properties. A document is represented on a collocation map to reflect co-occurrence information of terms by giving an effect on the weight of a term by relation with neighbors since event terms appear through the document. Then a story link is detected based on the relevancy between two stories.

3.1   Language Translation for Multilingual Event Detection

For multilingual event detection, we deal news articles in two languages: Korean and Japanese. To detect events from Korean and Japanese news, we use an ezTrans Japanese-to-Korean machine translation system [16]. Korean news articles are translated to Japanese by a machine translation system.

In a similar language pair like Korean and Japanese, the use of machine translation system might be more effective due to its relatively high translation quality [8]. In application, it would be helpful to provide translated stories for the same event to users. Then a user can see the translated multilingual stories and how different countries deal the same event in different views.

3.2 Term Significance on Timelines and Multilingual Spaces

To represent a document, terms are selected such as noun, proper noun, adjective and verb by part-of-speech tagging. To identify main objects of an event, named entities are recognized such as 'person', 'organization', 'country', 'location' and 'time'. A term tagged as verbal noun or verb is assigned to 'action' to represent an action or status. A noun phrase is chunked and all possible n-gram words are generated as indexing terms since event terms tends to be written in noun phrases in Japanese news.

Term Significance on Timelines. The term significance on timelines is calculated by the χ^2-statistic which measures the lack of independence between term t and class $t0$. Here the class is time which has the documents reported during certain time period as members (Swan and Allan, 2000). Table 1 gives a 2×2 contingency table. On the contingency table, time $t0$ is each day, which means the total number of documents on a focal day is equal to the sum of a and b.

Table 1. Contingency table to calculate term significance on timelines

	# of docs containing term t	# of docs *not* containing term t
# of docs on *time t0*	A	b
# of docs off *time t0*	C	D

$$\chi^2(t,t0) = \frac{(a+b+c+d)(ad-cb)^2}{(a+c)(b+d)(a+b)(c+d)} \quad (1)$$

$$wTime(t,t0,l) = \chi^2(t,t0) \quad (2)$$

where $wTime(t,t0,l)$ represents significance of a term t on the language space l on the time $t0$.

The term changes in significance on timelines are shown in the left of Fig. 1 for two events happened in Korean news articles. The event 'Kim Il Sung death'

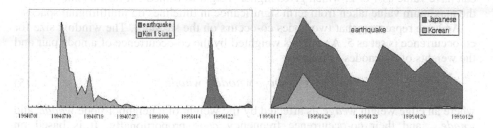

Fig. 1. The changes of term significance on times and multilingual spaces. Left figure is for term significance of 'Kim Il Sung' and 'earthquake' in Korean news articles. Right figure is 'earthquake' in Korean and Japanese news articles

happened on July 10, 1994. The event 'Kobe earthquake' happened on January 18, 1995. Around the time period related to the event, the terms 'Kim Il Sung' and 'earthquake' have significant values.

Term Distribution on Multilingual Spaces. A term of Korean location, 'Inchon', appeared in 261 days on Korean language space and in 31 days on Japanese language space in one year news articles. A Japanese term, 'Osaka', appeared in 312 days and in 60 days on Japanese and Korean language space, respectively. Since it is a location name of a country, the term tends to frequently occur in documents on its own country/language space. The number of documents reporting the same event on a focal day depends on a national interest for the event.

The term significance on timelines is separately calculated depending on each language space to reflect the term distribution of each language. Then lookup the weight on other language space and take higher weight. If the term weight is high in one space, it is possible to be reported to other country. The term occurring in multilingual space play a role as a bridge to link multilingual spaces if it is significant.

$$wTimeSpace(t, t0) = \max \arg_l wTime(t, t0, l) \tag{3}$$

The term changes in significance on multilingual spaces are shown in the right figure of Fig. 1. The term has higher values in Japanese news articles since Japanese articles reported about the event 'earthquake' which happened in Japan much more than Korean news. It indicates the event term is affected on time and lingual space. Therefore using term information in other language space would be helpful.

3.3 Event Term Weighting on Collocation Map

Each document is represented on a collocation map which has nodes and directed edges to consider the co-occurrence relation of a term with neighbors on the same sentence. Highly weighted nodes and edges on the collocation map would be the candidates of event terms to describe an event of the document. A node has a weight which is calculated based on the event term properties as follows:

$$wnode_i = tf_i \cdot wNE_i \cdot wTimeSpace_i \tag{4}$$

where $wnode_i$ means the weight of node i. tf is term frequency in a document. wNE_i can have value as 1 or 2, which gives higher weight to named entities. $wTimeSpace_i$ is the maximum value taken from term significance in timelines on multilingual spaces.

An edge represents that two nodes co-occurs on the sentence. The window size for co-occurrence is set as 5. An edge is weighted by the co-occurrence of a node pair and the weights of two nodes as follows:

$$wedge_{ij} = cooc_{ij} \cdot wnode_i \cdot wnode_j \tag{5}$$

where an edge weight $wedge_{ij}$ is affected by the weight of a neighbor node $wnode_i$ and $wnode_j$, and their co-occurrence frequency $cooc_{ij}$ proportionally. It is based on assumption that some of key event terms will be co-occurred throughout the document. To reflect the context of edges to the nodes, a node weight is re-calculated by edge weights for highly weighted edges $wedge_{ik}$:

$$wnode_i{}' = wnode_i \cdot \alpha \sum_k wedge_{ik} \tag{6}$$

A document vector is represented with a pair of a node and its weight calculated by Equation (6). To decide whether a pair of documents deals the same event, the documents link is determined based on the relevance degree by cosine coefficient.

4 Experiments

We have constructed a test collection and evaluated the effectiveness of proposed method on the multilingual test collection of Korean and Japanese news articles.

4.1 Experimental Set-Up

Documents consist of Korean news articles from the website of Hankyoreh and Japanese news articles from Mainichi newspaper, spanning from January, 1998 to June, 1998. The number of documents is 40000 and 61637 for Korean and Japanese, respectively. Korean documents are translated to Japanese by a machine translation system. Japanese documents and translated Japanese from Korean documents are tagged by ChaSen system [13]. The number of terms from the documents is 193730 and 353210 for Korean and Japanese, respectively, which have more than 3 in the document frequency from documents spanning from July, 1994 to May, 1995. For test documents, the document frequency is applied incrementally to calculate the weight of a term. To recognize named entities, NExT system [12] is used.

To evaluate a story detection system for Korean and Japanese news articles, we developed the test collection, which consists of 13 events which are taken from TDT2 test collection, and the evaluation set judged by two human assessors for each event on each language of Korean news and Japanese news articles. Table 2 shows the event list, which is a subset of TDT2 events. For the 13 events, 5902 documents are judged by two human assessors for each language with the rules used by Linguistic Data Consortium, and 3875 documents are on the events.

The numbers of target and non-target pairs for story link detection are 1731419 and 5224891, respectively.

We used evaluation metrics defined using contingency table, including precision, recall, miss alarm, false alarm, and micro-average F1 measure [5].

4.2 Experimental Results

To observe the effectiveness of the proposed weighting method based on event term properties, we have evaluated multilingual story link detection by thresholds of relevancy.

Table 2. Event list on the test collection for Korean and Japanese news articles

Upcoming Philippine Elections
1998 Winter Olympics
Current Conflict with Iraq
China Airlines Crash
Tornado in Florida
Asteroid Coming
Viagra Approval
India, A Nuclear Power?
Israeli-Palestinian Talks (London)
Anti-Suharto Violence
Anti-Chinese Violence in Indonesia
Afghan Earthquake
Clinton-Jiang Debate

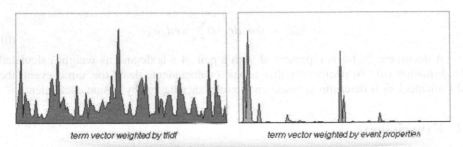

term vector weighted by tfidf   term vector weighted by event properties

Fig. 2. Term weights on a document vector. Terms are more distinctive in the weighting by the event term properties

We have compared the tfidf weighting scheme by term frequency and document frequency, and the proposed weighting method by Equation (6). The term vector of a document is shown in Fig. 2 according to the weighting methods. Some terms are more distinctive in the weighting method by event properties. The similarity is calculated by the cosine coefficient between two document vectors for the weighting methods.

Table 3. The performance comparisons for story link detection according to the event term weighting schemes

	Monolingual pairs				Total pairs (mono- and multi-)	
	Korean story pairs		Japanese story pairs			
	tfidf	*proposed*	*tfidf*	*proposed*	*tfidf*	*proposed*
Precision	0.3865	0.4240	0.2899	0.3313	0.3025	0.3559
Recall	0.8506	0.9042	0.9808	0.9131	0.9657	0.8970
Miss alarm	0.1494	0.0958	0.0192	0.0869	0.0343	0.1030
False alarm	0.2983	0.3298	0.6929	0.5765	0.5870	0.4601
Micro-avg F1	0.6593	0.7735	0.7349	0.8040	0.6896	0.7880

Table 4. Story link detection for Korean-Japanese story pairs with/without considering multilingual space

	Korean-Japanese cross language story pairs		
	tfidf	not considering multilingual space	considering multilingual space
Precision	0.3468	0.3678	0.3769
Recall	0.8799	0.7560	0.8324
Miss alarm	0.1201	0.2440	0.1676
False alarm	0.3992	0.3466	0.3734
Micro-avg F1	0.6566	0.6719	0.7665

Table 3 shows the performance comparisons by selecting the best results for each weighting scheme on thresholds, by applying thresholds from 0.005 to 0.35. The proposed weighting method based on event term properties achieved 17.3% improvement for Korean story pairs, 9.4% improvement for Japanese story pairs, and 14.3% improvement for multilingual story pairs over the tfidf weight method in the micro-averaged F1. Table 4 shows the effect by applying multilingual spaces component of terms which appear in two language spaces. Whether multilingual space is considered or not depends on applying equation (3) in the term weight. The proposed weighting method considering timelines and lingual spaces achieved 16.74% over the tfidf weighting scheme for Korean-Japanese news pairs. For multilingual pairs the weighing method without considering lingual spaces does not improve the performance over the tfidf weighting scheme. This result indicates that considering lingual spaces is effective for multilingual story link detection.

The performance changes depending on decision thresholds showed that the proposed method outperforms over conventional weighting in all thresholds.

4.3 Verification of the Results

To verify the performance of the weighting methods, we have measured the document space density. In correlation between indexing performance and document space density, Salton et al [14] showed that the best retrieval performance can be obtainable with a clustered space exhibiting tight individual clusters, but large inter-cluster distances. It can be applicable to link detection to verify our performance improvement whether the proposed method could make the intra-event stories tighter and the inter-event stories looser in distance. The higher intra-event stories density and the lower inter-event stories density can produce the better performance.

To calculate similarity, cosine coefficient measure is used. For a given event class K comprising m documents, each centroid C_k is defined as the average weight of the documents which belong to the event class E_k. The main centroid C_{main} for all documents is defined as the average weight of all N documents.

$$C_K = \frac{1}{M} \sum_{i \in E_k} d_i \tag{7}$$

$$C_{main} = \frac{1}{N} \sum_{i=1}^{N} d_i \tag{8}$$

We measured document space density as follows:

- Intra-event density (*DensityIntraC*): by averaging similarity between documents d_i and their cluster centroid C_k within a single cluster (factor x).

$$DensityIntraC = \frac{1}{N} \sum_{k=1}^{K} \sum_{i \in E_k} d_i \cdot C_k \tag{9}$$

- Inter-event density for main centroid (*DensityInterByCmain*): by averaging similarity between cluster centroids C_k and main centroid C_{main}.

$$DensityInterByCmain = \frac{1}{K} \sum_{k=1}^{K} C_{main} \cdot C_k \tag{10}$$

- Inter-event density on clusters (*DensiyInterC*): by averaging similarity between pairs of cluster centroid (C_i and C_j) (factor y).

$$DensityInterC = \frac{1}{K(K-1)} \sum_{i=1}^{K} \sum_{\substack{j=1 \\ i \neq j}}^{K} C_i \cdot C_j \qquad (11)$$

- Space density ratio: to measure the overall document space density by y/x.

Table 5. The effect of space density by each weighting method

	Intra-event density (x)		Inter-event density: centroid based		Inter-event density: cluster based (y)		Space density Ratio (y/x)	
	tfidf	*proposed*	*tfidf*	*proposed*	*tfidf*	*proposed*	*tfidf*	*proposed*
Korean	0.371	0.551	0.302	0.245	0.060	0.046	0.060/ 0.371 = .161	0.046/0.551 = 0.084 **-47.73%**
Japanese	0.303	0.481	0.302	0.262	0.076	0.050	0.076/ 0.303 = .251	0.050/0.481 = 0.105 **-58.30%**
Multi-lingual	0.229	0.482	0.312	0.264	0.077	0.049	0.077/ 0.229 = .258	0.049/0.482 = 0.101 **-60.87%**

All density measures are smaller for the proposed weighting scheme compared to the tfidf weighting scheme. The distances of the clusters are greater than the distance of documents inside each cluster. The proposed weighting scheme reduced the space density by maximizing intra-event density and by minimizing inter-event density, as shown Table 5. The results of Table 3 and Table 4 are supported by the notion that improved performance is associated with decreased density in the document space.

5 Conclusions

We have described the features such as timelines and multilingual spaces in weighting to give event terms distinctive weights. Evaluation on Korean and Japanese story link detection test collection showed that the proposed features are effective by achieving 14.3% improvement. The proposed method is verified by measuring the space density. This result indicates that the proposed weighting method is helpful to detect multilingual event story link.

For future works, the event terms can be extracted from the collocation map of a document, and can be provided to describe events for detected story links. Users could then decide for themselves how to treat stories which contain the event.

References

1. Atlam, E., Okada, M., Shishibori, M. and Aoe, J. 2002. An evaluation method of words tendency depending on time-series variation and its improvements. Information Processing and Management, 38 (2).
2. Carbonell, J., Yang, Y., Brown, R., Zhang, J. and Ma, N. 2002. New event & link detection at CMU for TDT 2002. Proc. of Topic Detection and Tracking (TDT-2002) Evaluations.
3. Chen, Y. and Chen, H. 2002. NLP and IR approaches to monolingual and multilingual link detection. Proc. of 19th International Conference on Computational Linguistics.
4. Eichmann, D. 2002. Tracking & detection using entities and noun phrases. Proc. of Topic Detection and Tracking (TDT-2002) Workshop.
5. Fiscus, J., Doddington, G., Garofolo, J. and Martin, A. 1999. NIST's 1998 topic detection and tracking evaluation (TDT2). Proc. of DARPA Broadcast News Workshop.
6. Fukumoto, F. and Suzuki, Y. 2000. Event tracking based on domain dependency. Proc. of 23rd Annual International ACM SIGIR Conference on Research and Development in Information Retrieval.
7. He, D., Park, H-R., Murray, G., Subotin, M. and Oard, DW. 2002. TDT-2002 topic tracking at Maryland: first experiments. Proc. of Topic Detection and Tracking Workshop.
8. Kwon, O.-W., Kang, I.-S., Lee, J.-H. and Lee, G. 1998. Conceptual cross-language text retrieval based on document translation using Japanese-to-Korean MT System. Computer Processing of Oriental Languages, 12(1).
9. Lam, W. and Huang, R. 2002. Link detection for multilingual new for the TDT2002 evaluation. Proc. of Topic Detection and Tracking (TDT-2002) Workshop.
10. Leek, T., Jin, H., Sista, S. and Schwartz, R. 1999. The BBN crosslingual topic detection and tracking system. Proc. of Topic Detection and Tracking (TDT-1999) Workshop.
11. Levow, G-A. and Oard, DW. 2000. Translingual topic detection: applying lessons from the MEI project. Proc. of Topic Detection and Tracking (TDT-2000) Workshop.
12. Masui, F., Suzuki, N. and Hukumoto, J. 2002. Named entity extraction (NExT) for text processing development. Proc. of 8th time annual meeting of The Association for Natural Language Processing (Japan). http://www.ai.info.mie-u.ac.jp/~next/next.html
13. Matsumoto, Y., Kitauchi, A., Yamashita, T., Hirano, Y., Matsuda, H., Takaoka, K. and Asahara, M. 2002. Morphological analysis system ChaSen version 2.2.9. Nara Institute of Science and Technology.
14. Salton, G., Wong, A. and Yang, C.S. 1975. A vector space model for automatic indexing. Communications of the ACM, 18(11).
15. Swan, R. and Allan, J. 2000. Automatic generation of overview timelines. Proc. of 23rd Annual International ACM SIGIR Conference on Research and Development in Information Retrieval (SIGIR 2000).
16. ChangshinSoft. 2003. ezTrans Korean-to-Japanese/Japanese-to-Korean machine translation system.

PaSE: Locating Online Copy of Scientific Documents Effectively

Byung-Won On[1] and Dongwon Lee[2]

[1] Department of Computer Science and Engineering &
[2] School of Information and Sciences and Technology,
The Pennsylvania State University, PA 16802, USA
on@cse.psu.edu, dongwon@psu.edu

Abstract. The need for fast and vast dissemination of research results has led a new trend such that more number of authors post their documents to personal or group Web spaces so that others can easily access and download them. Similarly, more and more researchers use online search for accessing documents of interest in Web, instead of paying a visit to libraries. Currently, to locate and download an online copy of a particular document D, one typically (1) uses Search Engines with the citation information and browses through returned web pages (e.g., author's homepage) to see if any contains D, or (2) uses searching facilities of an individual Digital Library (e.g., CiteSeer, e-Print) looking for D, and if not found, repeats the search in another Digital Library. However, the scheme (1) involves human browsing to get to the final online copy, while the scheme (2) suffers from incomplete coverage. To remedy these shortcomings, in this paper, we present a system, named as *PaSE*, which can effectively locate online copies (e.g., PDF or PS) of scientific documents using citation information. We consider a myriad of alternatives in crawling and parsing the Web to arrive at the right document quickly, and present a preliminary experimental study. Using some of the best alternatives that we have identified, we show that PaSE can locate online copy of documents more accurately and conveniently than human users would do at the cost of elongated search time.

1 Introduction

With the arrival of the World-Wide Web, authors often post their documents onto personal web space for others' easy access and fast dissemination of ideas. Recent study [19] also shows that online scientific documents are more likely to be cited than offline ones, boosting this phenomenon. As such a trend continues, the way researchers look for interesting documents changes as well; instead of searching through catalogues in the traditional library, researchers now search for online copies of documents via (1) Search Engines such as Google [11], or (2) Digital Libraries such as DBLP [13], CiteSeer [14], e-Print arXiv [15], research repositories [16]. Let us call the former as *SE-scheme* and the latter as *DL-Scheme*. For instance, to download the latest paper, one often enters citation data to Google to find author's home page, where a downloadable PDF version of the document may be found.

Z. Chen et al. (Eds.): ICADL 2004, LNCS 3334, pp. 408-418, 2004.
© Springer-Verlag Berlin Heidelberg 2004

Sometime, to find the scholar's home page, people even use a specialized Search Engine such as MOPS [1]. As another venue to look for documents, one may also search documents in some Digital Libraries, hoping to find an archived copy of the document.

Despite the excellent coverage of modern Search Engines or huge amount of archived documents of Digital Libraries, however, these schemes are not without problems. For instance, SE-Scheme assumes human users. That is, when Google returns a list of candidate pages (mostly HTML web pages) that are likely to contain the target document, a human must sift through the links and determine which one to follow further. Such a task can be trivial for human users, but no so trivial for software agents. Search Engines like Google can be advised to search for only specific document formats (e.g., PDF, PS, DOC) in advanced interfaces, but only so at the cost of decreased precision and recall. Similarly, in DL-Scheme, since the coverage of Digital Libraries is limited, when a document is not found in one Digital Library, one has to continue the search in next Digital Libraries. The limited access to Digital Libraries (e.g., subscription is required to access ACM or IEEE Digital Libraries) only exacerbates the problem.

To demonstrate our motivation, we ran a simple experimentation as follows. We first randomly gathered 200 real citations published from 1986 to 2004 and their corresponding PDF files (i.e., this is our solution set). Then, for each citation, we submit its "title" to Google using two interfaces – normal and advanced ones. Normal interface [11] would search any web pages (HTML, XML, XHTML, PDF, PS, PPT, DOC, etc.) that contain keywords of the title, while advanced interface [12] would search only PDF documents, excluding HTML web pages (the advanced search in Google can also be achieved by appending additional construct "filetype:pdf" to the normal search). For the normal search, if a PDF document identical to one of the solution set is found at web pages within at most 2 hops, starting from any of the top-10 links returned, we considered it as "Match." This is based on the recent study [9] that majority of people only look at the first returned page (i.e., 10 links) of Google. Therefore, if the first link returned from Google points to an author's home page that in turn points to the author's publication page that finally contains the PDF document with a matching citation, then it is considered to be a match.

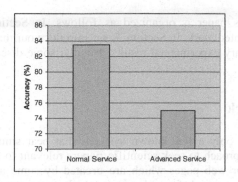

Fig. 1. Google accuracy

Fig. 1 shows the result of our experimentation. Note that normal service of Google can locate online copies of documents using its citation information with about 83% accuracy, where accuracy is #_of_match/200. Since the test data included some of the latest citations that may not be indexed by Google yet, the overall accuracy was not near 100%. Interestingly, the accuracy drops to 75% for the advanced service. That is, using Search Engines like Google, human users can locate online copies of documents fairly well (up to 83% accuracy) since one of the top 10 links returned from Google is likely to lead to the right URL (although the link itself does not point to the PDF directly). Therefore, just a little effort of sifting through and clicking a few returned links should be sufficient to get to the PDF document. However, since advanced service excludes all such possibilities and only focus on PDF documents, its accuracy degrades significantly. Note that it is this facility similar to the *advanced service* when a software agent needs to directly locate online copy of a document since it requires less human intervention. Therefore, the goal of this research is to build a function similar to the advanced search, only with a better accuracy:

$$[PDF_1, PDF_2, ...] \leftarrow PaSE(citation)$$

That is, given a citation information, we want to find the online copies of the documents (e.g., PDF or PS documents) more directly and effectively. Toward this goal, in this paper, we present a software system, named as *PaSE (Paper Search Engine)*, which can locate the publically-available online copies of documents, given proper citation information. More specifically, we use the normal search of Google to implement PaSE with the following challenges to cope with:

1. Given candidate pools (i.e., top-10 links) from Google's normal search, one needs good "crawling methods" to quickly get to the right web page that is likely to contain the online copy of documents. For this, we examine the *heuristic-based Random*, *BFS*, and *DFS* crawling algorithms.
2. Once arriving at the right web page, we need to identify the right *(citation, PDF)* pair among many candidates. This is important since typical scholar's web page contains a long list of publications, where often different publications share similar titles (e.g., conference and journal versions). To make the problem simple, instead of considering all the fields of citations (i.e., title, author, venue, year, etc), we only consider the "title" field since we believe that title has much less probability of being written in different formats (compared to author name or publication venue field).

The rest of this paper is organized as follows. In Section 2, we discuss the background and related work. In Section 3, we introduce our main ideas. In Section 4, we report preliminary experimental results. Finally, some discussion and conclusion follow in Section 5.

2 Related Work

System: There are only a few known systems that bear similarities to PaSE. The MOPS [1] is an approach to seek scientific papers relevant to a pre-defined research area. It searches for web pages which are created by some active scientists of the domain, but does not search for web pages which contain matching keywords. The name of these scientists is obtained from the DBLP server. Using HPSearch [20], MOPS first finds homepages, and research papers close to the homepages.

BibFinder [2] is an integrated bibliographic digital library on computer science domain, with links to online copies. However, it mainly focuses on citation data itself, not the online copies. Also, many times, links lead to web page near the online copies so that users have to sift through again. PaperFinder [3] is a tool that maintains user's personal profile, queries several digital libraries for new articles, and filters the results according to the profile. It is mainly designed as an add-on service to Digital Libraries.

Crawling Algorithms: Among many outgoing links in a given web page, choosing the right order of visit is an important issue for overall performance and accuracy of Search Engines. Toward this issue, [4] considers four approaches: (1) Similarity to a driving query Q, which is similar to TFIDF approach, (2) *Backlink Count*, where the priority of a visit is favored toward the link that is contained by more pages, (3) *PageRank*, that recursively defines the importance of a page to be the weighted sum of backlinks to it, and (4) *Location Metric*, in which importance of a page is a function of its location, not its contents (e.g., URLs with fewer "/" are more useful than otherwise). Fish-Search algorithm [5] is based on the assumption that relevant documents have relevant neighbors, and determines to pursue the exploration in that direction based on the relevancy. Shark-Search algorithm [6] uses a similarity engine which returns a fuzzy score between 0 and 1. Finally, an incremental crawling algorithm [7] continuously updates and refreshes the local collection of documents retrieved to have better results.

Citation Matching Algorithms: Citation matching problem is a specialization of a more general problem known as Record Linkage problem; i.e., given two lists of strings, find all pairs a and b whose distance is within some threshold. In our setting, the problem can be summarized to: given an input citation a and a list of citations b_1, ... b_n, found in a web page, determine b_i with the smallest $distance(a, b_i)$. As the citation matching algorithm, [8] examined (1) word matching – token based matching, (2) word and phrase matching – variation of n-gram, (3) Edit distance, and (4) subfield algorithms – citation is broken into each field (author, title, etc) and compared separately.

3 Paper Search Engine (PaSE)

3.1 The Architecture

Fig. 2 illustrates the overall architecture of PaSE. As shown at the top of the figure, *a Web services client* to Google [10] uses the keyword search in the Google's normal service [11]. Since the Google Web service supports Simple Object Access Protocol (SOAP), which is a technology to allow for Remote Procedure Call (RPC) over the Web, the client program creates a SOAP request message that contains citation information entered by a user, and then sends it to Google's Web services server. After the client receives a SOAP response message from the server, it parses the SOAP response, and then extracts the top-10 links. The links would be the URLs of web pages that are likely to contain the target document.

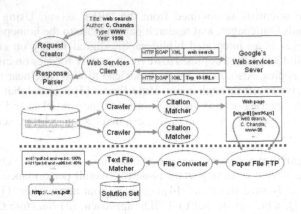

Fig. 2. Overview of PaSE

The *Crawlers* and *Citation Matcher (CM)* are shown in the middle. After ten Crawlers are created simultaneously, they start at their initial pages of top-10 links and stop if one of Citation Matchers finds the right web page that is likely to contain the online copy of the target document.

At the bottom, the *File Matcher (FM)* is illustrated. The FM is not part of PaSE system, but added for experimental validation purpose. That is, once the CM finds the candidate online copies, the FM downloads PDF or PS documents from the web page, converts them into text files using the Sherlock program [18], and compares them with solution set. Since the solution set contains the correct PDF document for each citation, we can estimate how good/bad the PaSE is.

3.2 The Crawler

Given a link to a web page, there are various orders to visit the link and its descendents: for instance, Breadth First Search (BFS), Depth First Search (DFS), Backlink Count (BC), Page Rank (PR), and Random schemes. Among these, we do not consider BC and PR since they were shown to be ineffective in a small domain [4]. Since our candidate pool contains only top-10 links and some of their descendents, our context is also a small domain, where most web pages have only a small number of backlinks.

To the rest of three BFS, DFS, and Random schemes, we add a simple but very effective heuristics – if words like *"research"*, *"publication"*, *"paper"*, *"group"*, *"laboratory"*, *"citation"*, or *"proceeding"* appear in anchors or URLs, then those links are favored.

In the BFS scheme, to give such a priority to web pages including the words, each crawler keeps two queues of URLs to visit. The first queue stores URLs with the words in anchors or URLs while the second queue keeps the rest of URLs to visit. Crawlers always prefer to take URLs to visit from the first queue. Algorithm 1 is *our heuristic-based BFS* crawling algorithm.

Algorithm 1. The heuristic-based BFS crawling algorithm

```
Procedure:
  enqueue(SecondQueue, startingURL)
  while (not empty(FirstQueue))
    if (not empty(FirstQueue))
      then URL = dequeue(FirstQueue)
      else URL = dequeue(SecondQueue)
    Page = crawlPage(URL)
    URLlist = extractURLs(Page)
    for each u in URLlist
      if (u is not in FirstQueue and SecondQueue)
        if (u contains topic words in anchor or url)
          then enqueue(FirstQueue, u)
```

Other schemes are similar and omitted due to space constraint.

3.3 The Citation Matcher (CM)

Next, when the Crawler visits a web page that has many citations in it, one needs to find out (1) which citation in the page matches the most with what a user specified; and (2) which PDF or PS is the corresponding online document of the matched citation? The CM does this job of finding the right (citation, PDF) pair that matches the given citation. Often, different users use different citation format to refer to the same document (e.g., "ICADL" vs. "Int'l Conf. on Asian Digital Libraries", or "J. Ullman" vs. "Jeffrey D. Ullman"). Therefore, it is not trivial to match what user specified with what is found on Web. In our setting, to make the problem simple, we assume that the user specified "title" of the citation, which is less likely to have different formats. That is, the CM uses the given title of the citation, finds the most similar citation of the page, and identifies the "start" and "end" of the citation. (called a citation block).

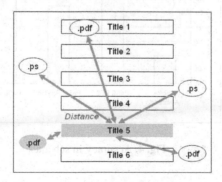

Fig. 3. The shortest distance title matching

Once the right citation block is identified, we may still have a problem, as illustrated in Fig 3. In the given web page, the "Title 5" is found to be the closest one to the input citation. However, there are various PDF or PS links near the "Title 5" block in the web page, and it is not always easy to find the right one. This often occurs since not all citations have matching links to online copies in a web page. To make matters worse, links to online copies may be found in front of, in the middle of, or after the matching citation. For instance, in Fig 3, the shaded PDF is the corresponding document of "Title 5".

Since the way to link a citation to PDF or PS document in HTML varies by persons and by pages, to remedy this problem, we use the notion of *distance*. That is, once the right citation block (e.g., "Title 5") is found in a web page, the CM measures the distance (i.e., word count, byte, etc) from the citation block to each neighboring PDF or PS document, and pick the one with the shortest distance with some threshold. In Fig 3, the shaded PDF will be chosen. It is also important to set proper threshold to this distance to avoid the chase of matching far-away citation and online copy (e.g., "Title 2" and shaded PDF).

4 Experimental Results

We first made a solution set with 1,000 pairs of "(citation, PDF)", randomly collected from CiteSeer [14]. An example of our input file is as follows:

```
NUM: 7
AUTHOR 1: jun yang
AUTHOR 2: Jennifer widom
TITLE: incremental computation and maintenance of temporal aggregates
TYPE: icde
YEAR: 2001
```

Fig. 4 shows the accuracies of Google Advanced Search and PaSE's *heuristic-based* BFS, Random, and DFS schemes.

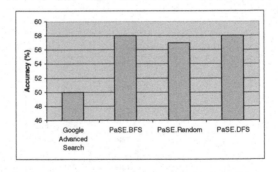

Fig. 4. Accuracy in schemes

In the graph, all the schemes of PaSE show higher accuracy than Google Advanced Search. It is mainly because PaSE can find online copies of documents hidden to Google during its crawling process. The relatively low accuracy compared to one of Fig. 1 is due to the fact that test set has many of the latest citations in 2004 that might not have been indexed by Google yet. Since the test data are drawn from CiteSeer, all of the corresponding online copies can be found in the CiteSeer. Interestingly, however, in our experimentations, Google Advanced Search did not include any links to CiteSeer. This is different from our previous experimentation done on 2004/April, where most of top ranked links to online copies are toward CiteSeer (see Table 1).

Table 1. An example of top-10 links returned from Google's Web services

Citation	NUM: 4 AUTHOR 1: george karypis AUTHOR 2: eui-hong (sam) han TITLE: concept indexing a fast dimensionality reduction algorithm with applications to document retrieval & categorization TYPE: university of minnesota YEAR: 2000
2004/4	1. http://citeseer.ist.psu.edu/karypis00concept.html 2. http://citeseer.ist.psu.edu/article/yang99reexamination.html 3. http://www-users.cs.umn.edu/~karypis/publications/Papers/Abstracts/CI.html 4. http://www-users.cs.umn.edu/~karypis/publications/ir.html 5. http://portal.acm.org/citation.cfm?id=354772&dl=ACM&coll=GUIDE&CFID=11111111&CFTOKEN=2222222 6. http://www.cs.rutgers.edu/~mlittman/courses/lightai03/keller.pdf 7. http://www710.univ-lyon1.fr/~hassas/gjan/Divers/liens_classif.html 8. http://davis.wpi.edu/~xmdv/docs/tr0314_mds_som.pdf 9 http://www.isse.gmu.edu/~carlotta/teaching/INFS-795-s04/info.html 10. http://www-a2k.is.tokushima-u.ac.jp/~kita/eprint/ICCPOL01.ps
2004/6	1. http://www.cs.rutgers.edu/~mlittman/ courses/lightai03/keller.pdf 2. http://www-users.cs.umn.edu/~karypis/publications/Papers/Abstracts/CI.html 3. http://www-users.cs.umn.edu/~karypis/publications/ir.html 4. http://portal.acm.org/citation.cfm?id=354772&dl=ACM&coll=GUIDE&CFID=11111111&CFTOKEN=2222222 5. http://portal.acm.org/citation.cfm?id=963661&dl=ACM&coll=portal&CFID=11111111&CFTOKEN=2222222 6. http://dx.doi.org/10.1145/354756.354772 7. https://wwws.cs.umn.edu/tech_reports/index.cgi?selectedyear=2000&mode=printreport&report_id=00-016 8. http://sie.mimuw.edu.pl/literature.php 9. http://www.iturls.com/English/TechHotspot/TH_DocCluster.asp 10. http://www.di.uniovi.es/~dani/ publications/presentaciones/icwe.ppt

Fig. 5 illustrates the individual accuracies of top-10 ranks. Google Advanced Search returns the online copies of the target document as #1 rank more than 80%. Also, when it cannot find the right match up to rank 3, it is very unlikely that a matching document can be found in the remaining ranks of top-10. We believe this is due to the effectiveness of PageRank algorithm. Interestingly, however, all of the PaSE schemes find target documents evenly across all top-10 ranks. We believe this illustrates the reason why PaSE schemes were able to achieve higher accuracy that Google Advanced Search. That is, when target documents cannot be found by Google, PaSE follows some of the middle-ranked links such as rank #4-#6, and was able to recover the hidden matching documents, at the cost of elongated search time.

Fig. 6 shows overall result of citation matching after file comparisons. Most matching results are 90% or more. However, small amount of matching results are 90% or less because of the possible errors during file download and/or conversion.

We ran several cycles of experimentations, and found that the matching threshold of 20% gave acceptable results.

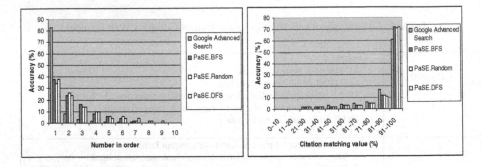

Fig. 5. Accuracy in rank   **Fig. 6.** Accuracy in citation matching

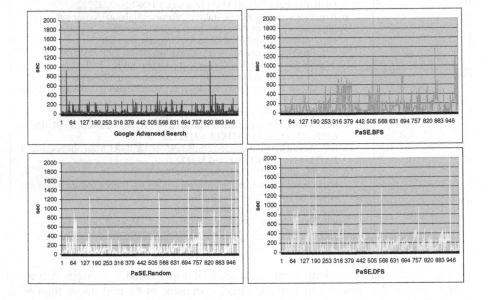

Fig. 7. The elapsed time per citation

Although PaSE can find target documents when Google cannot, it does so at the cost of time. To see how much additional time is needed for PaSE, we also check the time. Fig. 7 shows the elapsed time per citation. Clearly, Google Advanced Search takes a shorter time (on average) than the other three schemes of PaSE, which need to spend time on additional crawling and citation matching. The average crawling time of three PaSE's schemes is about 22 sec. per citation. However, in many cases, PaSE's crawling time is substantially smaller than 22 sec. As shown in Table 2, about

65% of the total citations take only 2 sec. of average crawling time regardless of the chosen crawling algorithms.

Table 2. The average crawling time

PaSE schemes	65%	14%	21%
BFS	2.33 sec	6.82 sec	90.58 sec
Random	2.18 sec	7.02 sec	99.24 sec
DFS	2.18 sec	6.93 sec	87.25 sec

For 21% of citations which took 80-100 sec, a large amount of time was wasted because of abnormal conditions (e.g., web server down). Such case can be avoided by setting some threshold on waiting time or by implementing more sophisticated error handing. We leave this as future work.

5 Conclusion and Future Work

We have developed PaSE to find online copies of scientific papers more effectively, and studied the heuristic-based crawling and distance-based title matching algorithms. Our preliminary experiments show that PaSE can deliver better accuracy than conventional approaches.

There are many rooms for future research. First, more thorough study on the effects of different crawling and citation matching algorithms (and their interplay with other factors such as domain) are needed. Second, by extending the PaSE with web services based interface, machine programs can communicate and retrieve online copies of target documents, making PaSE available for more applications.

References

1. G. Hoff, M. Mundhenk, "Finding Scientific Papers with HPSearch and Mops", SIGOC '01 (2001)
2. Z. Nie, S. Kambhampati, T. Hernandez, "BibFinder/StatMiner: Effectively Mining and Using Coverage and Overlap Statistics in Data Integration", 29th VLDB (2003)
3. A. E. Papathanasiou, E. P. Markatos, S. A. Papadakis, "PaperFinder: A tool for scalable search of digital libraries", WebNet 98, (poster paper) (1998)
4. J. Cho, H. Garcia-Molina, L. Page, "Efficient Crawling Through URL Ordering", 7th WWW (1998)
5. P. De Bra, R. Post, "Information Retrieval in the World Wide Web: Making Client-based Searching Feasible", 1st WWW (1994)
6. M. Hersovici, M. Jacovi, Y. S. Maarek, D. Pelleg, M. Shtalheim, S. Ur, "The Shark-Search algorithm – an application: tailored Web site mapping", 7th WWW (1998)
7. J. Cho, H. Garcia-Molina, "The evolution of the web and implications for an incremental crawler", 26th VLDB (2000)
8. S. Lawrence, C. L. Giles, K. Bollacker, "Autonomous Citation Matching", The 3rd Int'l Conf. on Autonomous Agents, Seattle Washington (1999)

9. B. J. Jansen, A. Spink, "An Analysis of Web Documents Retrieved and Viewed", The 4th Int'l Conf. on Internet Computing, Las Vegas Nevada (2003)
10. Google Web APIs, http://www.google.com/apis
11. Google normal service, http://www.google.com
12. Google advanced service, http://www.google.com/advanced_search?hl=en
13. DBLP Bibliography, http://www.informatik.uni-trier.de/~ley/db/
14. CiteScer.IST Scientific Literature Digital Library, http://citesser.ist.psu.edu
15. arXiv.org e-Print archive, http://arxiv.org
16. F, Burchsted, "Finding Personal Papers in United States Repositories", http://www.people.fas.harvard.edu/~burchst/FPPiUSR.htm
17. Amazon.com, http://www.amazon.com/
18. The Sherlock Plagiarism Detector, http://www.cs.usyd.edu.au/~scilect/sherlock
19. Lawrence, S., "Online or Invisible?," Nature 411(6837):521 (2001)
20. Homepage Search, http://hpsearch.uni-trier.de/hp/

Temporal Versioning of XML Documents

Vilas Wuwongse[1], Masatoshi Yoshikawa[2], and Toshiyuki Amagasa[3]

[1]Computer Science and Information Management Program, Asian Institute of Technology,
P.O. Box 4, Klong Luang, Pathumthani 12120, Thailand
vw@cs.ait.ac.th
[2] Information Technology Center, Nagoya University,
Furo-cho, Chikusa-ku, Nagoya 464-8601, Japan
yosikawa@itc.nagoya-u.ac.jp
[3] Graduate School of Information Science, Nara Institute of Science and Technology,
8916-5 Takayama, Ikoma, Nara 630-0101, Japan
amagasa@is.aist-nara.ac.jp

Abstract. A data model supporting the unification of the management of temporal XML document databases and version control, i.e., a *Temporal Version Data Model (TVDM)*, is proposed. TVDM is temporally change-centric and represents the change between two consecutive versions by means of *temporal delta (tDelta)*. A tDelta employs a *temporal XML expression (tXex)* which is an extension of ordinary XML elements by incorporation into them temporal as well as ordinary variables. In addition to valid time, TVDM introduces version time and associates it with each version. All versions including the base or the current one can be uniformly represented by tDeltas. A technique to implement TVDM is also presented.

1 Introduction

XML has now become an indispensable technology for digital libraries. It is used in encoding for the exchange and representation of metadata schemas, metadata, digital objects, their collections as well as management-related information. A basic unit representing all this information is XML elements a set of which forms an XML document. XML documents are related to time in two aspects: they contain temporal information and/or their contents evolve with time. Examples of the former case include history documents, digital versions of cultural heritage [7] and temporal relational databases published in XML [13]. This class of time-dependent information is normally managed by means of temporal databases in which a timestamp is attached to each object. A number of time types have been proposed, e.g., valid, transaction, decision and user-defined times, but only the first two are important and have widely agreed-upon semantics. A valid time of an object shows the time point or the duration when the object is true in the modeled reality. A transaction time of an object is a logical realization of physical insertion and deletion, and indicates the duration when the object is available in the storage and can be retrievable. Incorporation of one or both of these time types into XML databases leads to their various temporal data models [1], [5], [14], [15], some of which also aim at serving data warehouses of web contents [11].

Z. Chen et al. (Eds.): ICADL 2004, LNCS 3334, pp. 419–428, 2004.
© Springer-Verlag Berlin Heidelberg 2004

Normative texts, software documents and product catalogs are examples of documents with evolving contents. A traditional approach to handling this kind of documents is version management. In version management, a document that evolves into multiple versions is called a versioned document. Based on the observation that all versions of a versioned document share some common part and differ with respect to specific parts, the version management uses a delta to represent the difference between two successive versions. A delta normally contains an editing script describing how the difference is generated. Moreover, a delta has a direction, forward or backward, depending on whether it is new version minus old version or old version minus new version. A new version is constructed by applying a sequence of forward (respectively, backward) deltas to some base (respectively, latest) version. Depending on how documents evolve, versions are classified into revisions and variants. Revisions are sequential versions that evolve along the time dimension with new versions superceding old ones; hence their version times are linear. On the other hand, variants are parallel or alternative versions coexisting at a given time with no replacement, resulting in branching version times. A few version models have been developed for the management of multi-versioned XML documents [3], [10].

Although temporal data and versions are different concepts, they are related. Some real applications such as cultural heritage and webpage management systems demand the storage and retrieval of the information about their relationships. For example, information on how words and writing styles of a language change along historical time may be required by students. Accurate record keeping of multi-versioned webpages with respect to time is an important instrument for the management of current websites. Therefore, there is a need to develop a framework that unifies these two concepts of temporal data and versions in order to better manage evolving XML documents.

A data model supporting the framework, i.e., Temporal Version Data Model (TVDM), is proposed. TVDM is temporally change-centric and represents the change between two consecutive versions by means of temporal deltas (tDeltas). tDeltas employ temporal XML expressions (tXexes) which is an extension of ordinary XML elements by incorporation into it temporal as well as ordinary variables. In addition to valid time, TVDM introduces version time and associates it with each version. All versions including the base or the current one can be uniformly represented by tDeltas.

Sections 2, 3 and 4 present required preliminaries, a description and an implementation of TVDM, respectively. Section 5 reviews related previous work, and Section 6 draws conclusions as well as discusses future work.

2 Basic Concepts

2.1 Temporal XML Expressions

The basic construct used to describe TVDM is *tXex* which is an extension of XML elements. tXexes can turn all parts of XML elements into variables, i.e., their tag names, attribute names, attribute values, sets of their sibling elements as well as sets of ancestor or descendant elements, can become variables. The temporal values of some attributes will be specially turned into temporal variables. Intuitively, such a variable means *unknown*, but it could also indicate *don't care*.

Definition 1. A temporal XML expression (tXex), whose set is denoted by S_{TX}, takes one of the following forms:

1. *evar*
2. $<tag \ \ a_1=v_1 \ \ ... \ \ a_m=v_m \ \ pvar_1 \ \ ... \ \ pvar_k />$
3. $<tag \ \ a_1=v_1 \ \ ... \ \ a_m=v_m \ \ pvar_1 \ \ ... \ \ pvar_k > v_{m+1} </tag>$
4. $<tag \ \ a_1=v_1 \ \ ... \ \ a_m=v_m \ \ pvar_1 \ \ ... \ \ pvar_k > es_1 \ \ ... \ \ es_n </tag>$
5. $<ivar> e_1 \ \ ... \ \ e_n </ivar>$

where: N is a set of names; C^* is a set of character strings; $evar \in V_E$; $tag \in N \cup V_N$; $a_i \in N \cup V_N$; $v_i \in C^* \cup V_S \cup V_T$; $ivar \in V_I$; $pvar_i \in V_P$; $es_i \in S_{TX} \cup C^* \cup V_S$; $e_i \in S_{TX}$; $k, m, n \geq 0$; and all the variable sets used are defined in Table 1.

The table also shows the types of constants into which each variable type is to be instantiated.

Form 1 states that a variable denoting a sequence of zero or more tXexes alone without any tag is a tXex. Forms 2, 3, and 4 correspond to empty, simple and nested/mixed XML elements, respectively. Form 5 represents a sequence of n tXexes which is a descendant of a certain element whose structure, nesting pattern as well as list of attribute-value pairs are not fully known. Like ordinary XML elements, the order of the attribute-value pairs $a_1=v_1 \ \ ... \ \ a_m=v_m$ and the order of the P-variables $pvar_1 \ \ ... \ \ pvar_k$ are immaterial, while the order of the expressions $e_1 \ \ ... \ \ e_n$ or the mixed expressions $es_1 \ \ ... \ \ es_n$ is important. Note that a value v_i can stand for both a character string or a time point.

Table 1. All the variable sets used in Definition 1

Variable Type	Set of Variables	Variable Names Beginning with	Instantiation to
N-variables: Name variables	V_N	$N	Element types or attribute names
S-variables: String variables	V_S	$S	Strings
P-variables: Attribute-value-pair variables	V_P	$P	Sequences of zero or more attribute-value pairs
E-variables: Temporal XML expression variables	V_E	$E	Sequences of zero or more temporal XML expressions
I-variable: Intermediate expression variables	V_I	$I	Parts of temporal XML expressions
T-variables: Time variables	V_T	$T	Time points

Example 1. The tXex in Fig. 1 represents a product catalog document whose version ID is 2 and which has been derived from Version 1. This version of the document was created on August 11, 2004 and is still current until now. The document contains a number of existing and unchanged product descriptions (variable *$E:unchangedElement*), product#050 with certain product description (variable *$E:unchangedSubElement*), as well as a concrete description of the last product in the catalog, product#100.

```
<tDelta id="2" from-id="1">
    <versionTime start="2004-8-11" end="Now"/>
    <catalog>
        $E:unchangedElement
        <Product pid="050">
            $E:unchangedSubElement
        </Product>
        <Product pid="100">
            <Price>500</Price>
            <Name>DVD</Name>
        </Product>
    </catalog>
</tDelta>
```

Fig. 1. An example of temporal XML expressions: tDelta(2, 1)

2.2 Time Dimensions

Conventional version models treat a version of a versioned document as its snapshot and do not pay much attention to the temporal information associated with it. By explicit inclusion and employment of their associated temporal information, versioned documents can help access and maintain the history of the enterprise owning them. Two important time types for temporal versions are *version* and *valid times*.

Definition 2. The *version time* of a version of a document is the period of time which starts from the creation time of the version and lasts until it is replaced by its successive version.

A version of a document has only one version time which can be linear or branching depending on whether it is a revision or a variant of the document.

Definition 3. A *valid time* of an element is a time when the element is *true* in the modeled reality.

An element may have more than one valid time. Valid times are normally supplied by the user. The word *true* in Definition 3 can be interpreted differently depending on the applications being modeled. For example, a valid time of a record in an employee database could be an employment period of the employee in the record. A valid time of a statement in a regulation document could mean an effective time of the statement. A valid time of a part of a webpage could indicate a duration when users can access the part. Finally, multiple valid times of an element in an XML document might represent the element's re-effectiveness, re-activation or reuse in multiple periods of time.

These two types of time are related but orthogonal. Their relationships reflect physical properties as well as the characteristics of the modeled reality. For example, the starting time of the version time of a version must not be preceded by the starting time of a valid time of a new element in that version since a document version must be created before any employment of its new element. These time relationships are normally expressed as temporal constraints.

There are three distinguished temporal values which will be employed in TVDM: *Beginning*, *Forever* and *Now*.

Definition 4. The distinguished value *Beginning* is a special time point preceding the earliest time point in the modeled reality.

Definition 5. The distinguished value *Forever* is a special time point following the latest time point in the modeled reality.

Definition 6. The distinguished value *Now* is a special time point representing the ever-increasing current-time value of the modeled reality.

3 Temporal Versioning Data Model (TVDM)

Aiming at unifying the two approaches of temporal database and version management, TVDM incorporates temporal information into deltas yielding *temporal delta (tDelta)*. A tDelta has a unique *id* corresponding to the version identification number of the version it represents. In addition, instead of editing scripts, TVDM employs a tDelta to directly express the difference between two successive versions in a declarative manner. A change is declared in a tDelta in terms of ordinary XML elements with temporal extension whereas the unchanged parts in terms of appropriate variables, possibly interpreted as *don't care* parts in the tDelta.

```
<!ELEMENT tDelta (versionTime, (#PCDATA | mElement)*)>
<!-- The above #PCDATA is a placeholder for variables.
A tDelta is hence mixed content of variables and mElement to be defined below -->
<!ATTLIST tDelta id ID #REQUIRED>
<!ATTLIST tDelta from-id IDREF>
<!-- This from-id is the version ID of the previous version from which this version is derived. -->
<!ELEMENT versionTime EMPTY>
<!ATTLIST versionTime start NMTOKEN #REQUIRED
                      end NMTOKEN "Now">
<!-- The creation time of a version must be given whereas its replacement time is Now
by default and will be changed when a successive version is cretaed -->
<!ELEMENT mElement (#PCDATA | tElement)*>
<!-- mElement is mixed content of variables and Element, elements with temporal information. -->
<!ELEMENT tElement (oElement, validTime)>
<!-- oElement is an original element without temporal information -->
<!ELEMENT validTime EMPTY>
<!ATTLIST validTime start NMTOKEN "Beginning"
                    end NMTOKEN "Forever">
```

Fig. 2. tDelta DTD

If the schema of a versioned document is fixed, a change in a new version can take place at the content value, attribute value and element levels. However, as elements are an important and basic construct of XML documents, TVDM assumes that the minimal granularity to be dealt with is an XML element. In other words, if the content value or an attribute value of an element has been altered, the whole element is assumed to be changed without any specific part indication.

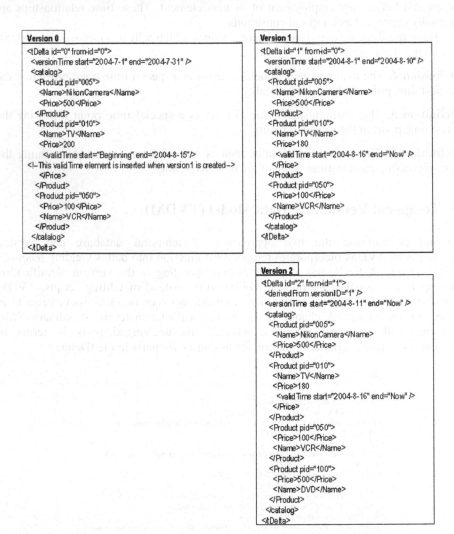

Fig. 3. Three versions of a product catalog document

TVDM attaches version and valid times to the components of tDeltas. A version time is attached to the root element of a tDelta as its child element. A tDelta has exactly one version time. Every element of a tDelta has as its child element(s) one or more valid times. The valid times whose starting and ending times are, respectively, *Beginning* and *Forever* can be omitted. The elements with such valid times could be considered to be time-invariant. An element with multiple valid times indicates that it is true, active or effective during multiple periods of time. An element without explicit valid time is assumed to be time-invariant. However, as a general, accepted constraint, the duration of a valid time of an element must be within that of the element's parent element. Therefore, the default times *Beginning* and *Forever* will actually be replaced by some appropriate specific times in order to satisfy the constraint. As time variables are also available in XML expressions, other temporal constraints can be readily expressed by employment of proper logical formulae or algebraic equations.

Finally, it should be noted that a change in this temporal information should not lead to a new version. A new version of a document is created only when its real content or structure has been modified.

A tDelta is defined in terms of DTD as:

Definition 7. A tDelta is an XML expression conforming to the DTD in Fig. 2.

Example 2. Consider the three versions of a product catalog document shown in Fig. 3. The base version, Version 0, was created on July 1, 2004 and lasted until July 31, 2004 when it was replaced by its successive version, Version 1, on August 1, 2004 with the reduction of the price of product#010 from 200 to 180, effective from August 16, 2004. Furthermore, Version 3 replaced Version 2 on August 11, 2004 when the description of DVD was appended. Forward tDelta(1, 0) and tDelta(2, 1) are shown in Fig. 4 and Fig. 1, respectively. These two tDeltas are more compact than the versions they represent. Note that the valid time of the price of TV in Version 0 can go beyond its version time. In addition, the reduced price in Version 1 can be planned to be valid after the starting time of the version, indicating a proactive action.

```
<tDelta id="1" from-id="0">
    <versionTime start="2004-8-1" end="2004-8-10" />
    <catalog>
        $E:unchangedElement1
        <Product pid="010">
            $E:unchangedSubElement1
            <Price>180
                <validTime start="2004-8-16" end="Now" />
            </Price>
            $E:unchangedSubElement2
        </Product>
        $E:unchangedElement2
    </catalog>
<tDelta>
```

Fig. 4. tDelta(1, 0)

4 Implementation

An XML-Diff tool [4] can be employed to detect the difference between a pair of successive XML documents from which a forward or backward tDelta for the pair can be derived. Assuming the availability of the base document version and forward tDeltas, the two basic operations required by TVDM are: reconstruction of a particular version from the base version and composition of *tDelta(i, j)* from a sequence of tDeltas between Versions *i* and *j*. The former operation is materialized by successively matching all variables in a tDelta to the ground parts or constants of the tDelta's preceding version. If i is the base version, the first matching will be between *tDelta(i+1, i)* and Version i, resulting into Version $i+1$, and so forth. The latter requires unification of two tDeltas where more specific information will substitute its less specific counterpart, yielding a more (or equally) specific tDelta than the two given tDeltas. Note that if the storage of the latest versions is desirable, then backward tDeltas will be generated, stored and utilized.

Since tDeltas are well-formed XML elements, existing XML tools could be used to process them. However, their variables demand efficient matching and unification mechanisms. *XML Equivalent Transformation (XET)*[2] is an engine that has the capability to manipulate XML expressions; hence it can be employed for version reconstruction and tDelta composition.

5   Related Work

There have been a lot of works on data models for temporal relational and object-oriented databases as well as models for version management of non-XML documents. However, this section will mainly focus on XML-related works.

Temporal Data Models. A number of data models have been proposed for temporal XML databases [1], [5], [6], [14], [15]. Most of them treat temporal information only as timestamps of valid times and express them as multiple child elements [1] or as an attribute-value pair [15] of an element with evolving contents. Transaction time was introduced into XML data models by [5] and was later combined with valid time yielding a bitemporal data model[14]. TVDM is the first data model that explicitly establishes version time. It does not deal with transaction time as the time is a temporal concept related mainly to data-oriented database operations and TVDM focuses more on documents than data. However, if required, transaction time, modeled as XML elements, can be readily incorporated into TVDM as another time dimension orthogonal to both valid and version times.

Version Management. Version management of XML documents has recently gained increasing attention [3], [10]. The change-centric method proposed in [10] employs a new representation of changes by means of *completed deltas* and *persistent identifiers*. Instead of edit-scripts, a completed delta contains a set of operations similar to a log in database systems, and can be inverted and composed from other completed deltas, though book-keeping of node positions is required. The *Reference-Based Versioning Model (RBVM)* [3], which concentrates on representing the common unchanged parts between two consecutive versions, has been shown to be superior to the edit-based approach which focuses on representing changes. Combining the strengths of both completed deltas and RBVM, tDeltas have unique version *ids*, use variables to refer to the unchanged parts and declaratively express changes, resulting in a well-balanced representation. Although tDeltas cannot be inverted, changes are declaratively visible and composition can be readily realized.

Temporal Versioning. Attempts to combine data models for temporal databases and version management have been carried out for object-oriented databases but have not yet been extend to cover XML documents. Lu et al. [9] was the first to extend their object-oriented data model to allow the representation of temporal and alternative versions and to support multiple dimensional time. A more formal approach to the union of object-oriented technology with temporal and versioning concepts appears in [12] where temporal and versioned types together with their valid values are formally defined and the notion of object versioning, version consistency and object equality proposed. A formal temporal versioning model has also been developed in [8] to support evolving schemas of object-oriented databases. TVDM has demonstrated that a uniform view of temporal database and version management concepts is also applicable to and useful for XML document databases. It seamlessly combines the two concepts in a flexible way allowing both revisions and variants, linear and branching version times as well as multiple time dimensions to be represented. Moreover, it can also handle evolving schemas as XML document schemas themselves are normally XML documents.

6 Conclusions

In addition to unifying temporal databases with version management and version time with valid time, TVDM can be considered to combine the existing three approaches to modeling evolving XML documents: timestamp-based, change-centric and reference-based. The version and valid times in tDeltas are timestamps attached to the whole and parts of a changing document. The ordinary XML elements in a tDelta normally represent the changed parts of a document; hence change-centric; whereas the variables refer to the unchanged parts; thus reference-based. Since TVDM models all time types as XML elements with start and end times, it can readily accommodate additional new time types required by specific applications, e.g., transaction and user-defined times. Moreover, time values can be expressed as variables; thus complex relationships and constraints between time values as well as between time and content can also be asserted.

TVDM can be implemented by means of XET, a rule-based language which can match, unify and manipulate temporal XML expressions. In fact, XET can perform computation too, enabling it to be used for reasoning on temporal relationships and constraints. Modeling and computation of complicated temporal relationships and constraints form part of future work.

Acknowledgement

The authors would like to thank Nimit Pattanasri for his help in the implementation of the data model.

References

1. Amagasa, T., Yoshikawa, M., Uemura, S.: A Data Model for Temporal XML Documents. In: Lecture Notes in Computer Science, Vol. 1873. Springer-Verlag, Heidelberg New York (2000) 334-344
2. Anutariya, C., Wuwongse, V. and Wattanapailin, V.: An Equivalent-Transformation-Based XML Rule Language. Proc. Int. Workshop Rule Markup Languages for Business Rules in the Semantic Web, Sardinia, Italy (2002)

3. Chien, S., Tsotras, V., Zaniolo, C.: Efficient Schemes for Managing Multiversion XML Document.VLDB J. 11 (2002) 332-353
4. Cobena, G., Abiteboul, S., Marian, A.: XyDiff Tools Detecting Changes in XML Documents. http://wwwrocq.inria.fr/cobena
5. Dyreson, C.: Observing Transaction-Time Semantics with TTXPath. Proc. 2nd Int. Conf. Web Information Systems Engineering (WISE2001), Kyoto, Japan (Dec. 2001) 193-202
6. Dyreson, C., Lin, H., Wang, Y.: Managing Versions of Web Documents in a Transaction-time Web Server, Proc. WWW2004, New York, USA (May 2004) 422-432
7. Grandi, F.: XML Representation and Management of Temporal Information for Web-based Cultural Heritage Applications. Data Science Journal 1 (2002) 68-83
8. Grandi, F., Mandreoli, F.: A Formal Model for Temporal Schema Versioning in Object-Oriented Databases. Data and Knowledge Engineering, 46 (2003) 123-167
9. Lu, J., Barclay, P., Kennedy, J.: On Temporal Versioning in Object-Oriented Databases. MoBIS '96 Modelling Business Information Systems, Cottbus, Germany, (Oct. 1996)
10. Marian, A., Abiteboul, S., Cobena, G. and L. Mignet. Change-Centric Management of Versions in an XML Warehouse. Proc. 27th VLDB Conf., Morgan Kaufmann (2001) 581-590
11. Norvag, K.: V2: A Database Approach to Temporal Document Management. Proc. 7th Int. Database Engineering and Applications Symposium (IDEAS) (2003) 212-221
12. Rodriguez, L., Ogata, H., Yano, Y.: TVOO: A Temporal Versioned Object-Oriented Data Model. Information. Information Science 114 (1999) 281-300
13. Wang, F., Zaniolo, C.: Publishing and Querying the Histories of Archived Relational Databases in XML. In WISE, 2003
14. Wang, F., Zaniolo, C.: XBiT: An XML-based Bitemporal Data Model. Technical Report, Department of Computer Science, University of California, Los Angeles. (2004)
15. Zhang, S., Dyreson, C.: Adding Valid Time to XPath. In Database and Network Information Systyms. Lecture Notes in Computer Science, Vol. Springer-Verlag, Heidelberg New York (2002)

Text-Based P2P Content Search Using a Hierarchical Architecture

Junjie Jiang[1] and Weinong Wang[2]

[1] Department of Computer Science and Engineering,
[2] Network and Information Center,
Shanghai Jiaotong University, Shanghai 200030, P.R. China
{jjj, wnwang}@sjtu.edu.cn

Abstract. As a scalable alternative to traditional server-based architecture, peer-to-peer (P2P) computing has become a popular distributed computing paradigm. However, efficient content search is absent, which hinders the wider deployment of the peer-to-peer systems. Earlier peer-to-peer systems such as Napster and Gnutella suffer from unscalability. Structured peer-to-peer networks achieve good scalability and high reliability, and yet they can only support a single-key based lookup instead of content search by means of DHTs (Distributed Hash Tables). In this paper, we propose a text-based peer-to-peer content search solution, which uses a hierarchical architecture. The heterogeneity of the popularity of terms both in documents and queries and the heterogeneity of hosts are both examined herein. There some techniques are employed to cope with the troubles arising from these heterogeneities. The experimental results show that the solution is feasible and efficient.

1 Introduction

In the information explosive era, there a huge amount of information in digital form has been published on Internet via WWW and so on. It's incredible by sifting through this massive information database to find desirable contents. Thus, an efficient content search mechanism, which helps users retrieve their interested information, is desired. The Web search engines allow a large amount of Web information to be efficiently searched, however the amazing quantity and growth rate of information on Internet are beyond the capability of any single Web search engine. Users look forward to a distinct and more efficient means for Internet content search.

As a scalable alternative to traditional server-based architecture, peer-to-peer computing has become a popular distributed computing paradigm. Many peer-to-peer systems, e.g. Gnutella and KaZaA, are gaining popularity quickly. Peer-to-peer file sharing has become a popular way to share huge amount of data and a major source of Internet traffic. There many other peer-to-peer applications have been proposed such as distributed storage system, application layer multicast and content distribution network. To achieve the wide deployment of such systems, efficient content search is absolutely necessary.

Z. Chen et al. (Eds.): ICADL 2004, LNCS 3334, pp. 429–439, 2004.

However current peer-to-peer systems still cannot provide satisfying content search mechanism. Napster uses a centralized directory while Gnutella employs query flooding to serve the content search needs. They both suffer from the unscalability and some other deficiencies. Structured peer-to-peer networks, such as CAN, Chord [1], Pastry and Tapestry, achieve good scalability and high reliability by means of DHTs (Distributed Hash Tables). DHTs systems can provide a hash table-like functionality on Internet-like scale and guarantee the location of an object if it exists anywhere in the network, whereas they can support only a single-key based lookup instead of content search. Providing efficient content search mechanism for a large scale peer-to-peer network remains a challenging problem.

The rest of this paper is organized as follows. In Section 2, Chord is introduced briefly. And in this section the system architecture of our solution is presented. In Section 3, vector space model is reviewed shortly. The heterogeneity of the popularity of terms both in documents and queries and the heterogeneity of hosts are examined. Also, a distributed combined indexing strategy and the content publishing/query processing solution are both described in this section. In section 4, results from simulation experiments are provided. Section 5 refers to the related work shortly and section 6 concludes the paper.

2   System Architecture

In this section, we first provide a brief overview of Chord, which is a popular structured peer-to-peer network protocol and we will take it as the substrate of our system. Then we propose our hierarchical system architecture.

2.1   Chord Overview

Chord is one of typical structured peer-to-peer networks. There is just one operation provided by Chord, that is lookup the node storing a given key's value.

The algorithm used for lookup through Chord is based on binary search. Chord defines a name space as a sequence of m bits and arranges the name space on a scaled virtual ring modulo 2^m called Chord ring. Both data objects and nodes are assigned an m bits identifier (i.e. key or node id) by using a consistent hashing and thus they are both mapped to the Chord ring according to their identifiers. In Chord, a node maintains a routing table with m entries, called the finger table. The ith entry (finger) in the table at a node contains the identity of the first node whose identifier follows its by at least 2^{i-1} along the Chord ring clockwise. Each data item is stored at the first node whose identifier is equal to or follows its key along the Chord ring clockwise. By using the finger table and such arrangements, Chord can resolve a lookup within at most $\lceil \log_2 N \rceil$ hops, where N is the number of nodes in the network. For more details about Chord, please refer to the reference [1].

Chord does provide just a lookup service instead of content search and however our solution can provide efficient content search based on the lookup service. Our work may be regarded as an extension to the existing structured peer-to-peer networks and herein Chord forms the backbone of our proposed hierarchical peer-to-peer network architecture. We choose Chord just because of the simplicity of the protocol and in practice our system does not rely on the specifics of Chord.

2.2 The Hierarchical System Architecture

Structured peer-to-peer (P2P) networks such as CAN, Chord, Pastry and Tapestry organize peers into a flat overlay network and provide lookup service by means of DHTs. Herein, we propose a hierarchical peer-to-peer system, in which peers are organized into clusters according to their network positions and the peers in the same cluster are topologically close to each other; for example, the nodes in a campus network or a autonomous domain form a cluster. We take Chord as the backbone of our system. Within each cluster, there are several superpeers that participate in the backbone surrogating the cluster and the superpeers within the same cluster may have the same peer id in the backbone, which maybe derived by hashing the IP address prefix of these nodes or the autonomous system number (ASN) of the autonomous domain using a consistent hash function such as SHA-1. Certainly the superpeers should be chosen from those powerful nodes, which have long online time, high CPU power and network connection bandwidth. In other words, all the superpeers in a cluster conceptually aggregate as a peer node in the backbone Chord system and we refer to such a peer node as the virtual node of the cluster. Accordingly a finger in the Chord system points to a virtual node, which has several IP addresses.

The operation in the backbone is almost same as the Chord and each virtual node is taken as a common Chord node. The only exception is that for each finger there are several IP addresses (i.e. superpeers) to be chosen while routing a message. Thus the workload is shared among the several superpeers within a cluster. Also the system is more stable and reliable. During the maintenance of the finger table in Chord, a node may contact just one of the superpeers for a finger and the superpeer can return the information about other superpeers with the same peer id together.

Within a cluster, except for superpeers, the other nodes are referred to as normal peers. The normal peers within a cluster maybe also organized along a separate scaled virtual ring with the superpeers together. More simply, the normal peers may register them at the superpeers while joining in the system. In this scheme, the superpeers should monitor the living of the normal peers periodically and allocate the tasks to them centrally. In this paper, we employ the latter scheme. The superpeers may send the maintenance message to all the normal peers within the same cluster by IP multicast to reduce the communication overhead. Also, the superpeers within a same cluster should exchange the information about the state of themselves periodically.

Figure 1 shows the hierarchical architecture of our system. Details about content search in the hierarchical system will be described in the next section. More detailed scenarios of the system operation are discarded herein.

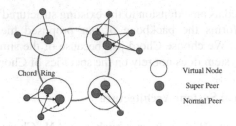

Fig. 1. The hierarchical architecture

3 Content Search Details

In this section, we will first introduce the vector space model, a widely used method in the information retrieval field. Then we present a distributed combined indexing strategy. Subsequently, the heterogeneity of terms and hosts will be examined and the query processing solution is proposed. Lastly we discuss the flash crowds and load balance in our system.

3.1 Vector Space Model

The vector space model (VSM) [2] has been widely used in the traditional information retrieval field. Though it has been criticized for being ad hoc, most Web search engines still use the similarity measures based on VSM to rank Web documents.

The VSM represents documents and queries as term vectors in k-dimensional space, where k is the number of unique terms in the document collection. Each term in a document or query is assigned a weight, which indicates the importance of the term in the document or query. The weight of a term in a document or query vector can be determined in many ways. The so-called $TF \times IDF$ (term frequency times inverse document frequency) method is the most common choice. Equation 1 is a popular formula for computing $TF \times IDF$ weight.

$$W(t, \bar{d}) = \frac{tf(t, \bar{d}) \times \log(N / n_t + 0.01)}{\sqrt{\sum_{t \in \bar{d}} \left[tf(t, \bar{d}) \times \log(N / n_t + 0.01) \right]^2}} \tag{1}$$

where $W(t, \bar{d})$ denotes the weight of term t in document $\bar{d}$, $tf(t, \bar{d})$ denotes the frequency of term t in document $\bar{d}$, N is the size of the document collection and n_t is the number of the documents containing the term t.

VSM measures the similarity between a query and a document as the cosine of the angle or Euclidean distance between their vector representations. Equation 2 is a common formula for the similarity computing.

$$Sim(Q,D) = \cos(\overline{Q},\overline{D}) = \frac{\overline{Q}^T \times \overline{D}}{\sqrt{\overline{Q}^T \times \overline{Q}} \times \sqrt{\overline{D}^T \times \overline{D}}} \tag{2}$$

where $\overline{Q}$ and $\overline{D}$ are the vector presentation of query Q and document D.

Usually, documents are ranked according to the similarity between the document vector and the query vector and only those documents with relative high similarity are returned and presented to users.

In our system, we use the Equation 1 to identify the importance of terms both in documents and queries. Equation 2 is used to evaluate the similarity between documents and queries.

3.2 Distributed Combined Indexing

Inverted files [3] have been traditionally the most popular indexing technique used along these years. An inverted file is an index structure, which has two main parts: a search structure or vocabulary, containing all of the distinct values being indexed (e.g. the index terms); and for each distinct value an inverted list, storing the identifiers of the records (e.g. the documents) containing the value.

In a distributed environment, there are two generic indexing strategies for distributing the inverted files over a set of hosts. One strategy is to partition the document collection among the hosts so that each host maintains a local inverted file for those documents it responsible for, which is called local inverted files [4]. The other one is to partition the index based on index terms so that each host maintains the inverted lists only for a subset of terms it responsible for in the document collection, which is called global inverted files [4].

We use a distributed combined indexing strategy, which combines the global inverted files and the local inverted files. That is to say, we first build the global inverted files for the documents, and then at each host, the local inverted files for the documents that occurring in the global inverted files the host responsible for are built. In our indexing strategy, as the first step, segmentation is done to the published document to extract all the unique terms occurring in the document while the stop words (i.e. those words that are too common and frequently used, such as "this", "that") are filtered out. By now, we can use the VSM to present the document as a term vector and compute the weights associated with each term using Equation 1.

From Equation 2, we can discover that those terms with very low weights in a document contribute few to the similarity between the document and any queries. Therefore it's unnecessary to take each term occurring in a document as an index term for the document. In other words, we need not distribute the metadata of the published document to all the nodes responsible for any terms occurring in the document. Accordingly, only the terms with relative high weights occurring in the published document are chosen as the index terms for the document. The index terms maybe identified by analyzing the skew distribution of the terms' weights for a document. There arc some terms with significantly higher weights relative to the others.

3.3 Heterogeneity of Terms and Hosts

The popularity of terms varies widely in both documents and queries. We call this phenomenon the heterogeneity of terms. The popularity of query terms derived from the IRCache trace is shown following a Zipf distribution [5]. There the most common term is involved in about 5% to 10% queries. The popular query terms dominate others, which indicates that the nodes responsible for popular terms maybe queried much more frequently and become hot spots. Also, some studies show that the document frequency of terms follows a Zipf-like distribution too. Thus we can deduce that some index terms have significantly larger inverted lists than others and so those nodes responsible for these index terms are placed much more load. In summary, the heterogeneity of terms incurs highly unbalanced load across peer nodes.

Most of the existing structured peer-to-peer networks make implicit or explicit assumptions about the homogeneity of all the nodes and treat them equally. In reality, the nodes usually are extremely heterogeneous in CPU power, storage capacity, network connection bandwidth and so on. Obviously placing equal load over all peer nodes will bring some bottleneck and vulnerabilities into the systems. However, most of the existing DHTs systems ignore the heterogeneity among the peer nodes.

3.4 Content Publishing/Query Processing

As described in Section 2, our system adopts the hierarchical architecture. In our system, each data item is stored at the first cluster whose virtual node identifier is equal to or follows the key along the Chord ring clockwise instead of a sole Chord node. Within the cluster, the data item is reassigned to a normal peer further according to the distribution scheme employed by the cluster. Each cluster may independently adopt different distribution schemes, such as a centralized assignment or the assignment based on a consistent hash space.

In this paper, we employ the centralized assignment scheme. Each superpeer maintains a directory on the data item assigned to the cluster it belonging to. While publishing or retrieving a data object, the key of the data object is first computing by using a consistent hash function, and then the message is submitted to any one superpeer in the same cluster as the request originator node belonging to. Subsequently along the backbone of our system, the message is routed to one superpeer of the cluster that is responsible for the data object. Finally the receiver superpeer will directly forward the message to the appropriate normal peers in the cluster that is actually responsible for the data object.

As to content publishing, each document is published under each index term of it. That is to say, the metadata information of each document is distributed to all the clusters responsible for any index terms of the document. Within these clusters, the metadata information is distributed across part of the normal peers actually and these peers may serve the search parallelly. The superpeers maintain the directory which indexing the locations of such information. Table 1 illustrates an example of such a directory at one superpeer.

Table 1. An example of the directory at one superpeer

Normal Peer #	IP Address	Indexing Terms
01	202.*.*.11	T_1, T_5, T_9
07	202.*.*.69	T_1, T_3
19	202.*.*.23	T_3, T_9, T_{10}, T_{12}
22	202.*.*.92	T_7

Considering the fault tolerance, each normal peer may choose another one or more normal peers in the same cluster to act as its replication peers and the superpeers should also append the replication peers into the directory. Because all these peers are in the same clusters, the communication is restricted in the campus network or the autonomous domain. Therefore the cost of replication operation is negligible.

While receiving a message for publishing or retrieving documents, the superpeer extracts the index terms included in the message first. Then it will examine the directory and look up the normal peers responsible for these index terms in the cluster, whereupon it forwards the message to these normal peers. To reduce the communication overhead, the superpeer could forward these messages by IP multicast also. As the message arriving at the destination peers, these normal peers will build index for the published document or return the results for the query. While serving a query, the normal peers computing the similarity between the documents and the query and give the rank to the documents according to the similarity. Only those with high similarity are returned. These results from multiple normal peers aggregate at the superpeers and maybe given a rank again to discard some documents with low relevance. Then the results are returned to the request originator node and it aggregates the documents from different clusters once more. Herein a global rank maybe given to all these returned documents also. Only those documents with highest similarity are presented to users.

Due to the adoption of the hierarchical architecture, there most of communication is restricted in cluster. Thereby the communication overhead is reduced significantly. Most of the maintenance messages are also restricted in each cluster so that the maintenance overhead is also reduced remarkably. The $\lceil \log_2 N \rceil$ bound of average routing path length of Chord ensures a reasonable query transmission time. And the parallelization of search can help to speed the search further.

3.5 Flash Crowds and Load Balance

A flash crowd is a billow in traffic to a specific node. After the exploration of the heterogeneity of terms, we can deduce that there flash crowds may come out in peer-to-peer systems due to the extreme heterogeneity of query terms and some nodes will become hot spots. Different from the traditional load unbalance problem, the hot spots herein only last for a short amount of time. Therefore, traditional static load balance techniques could not perform well under this condition. Backslash [6] is a proposal for a P2P caching scheme to address flash crowds at a host. Request redirection and result caching are the two powerful techniques for this problem. Due to the limitation of space, we omit the details of these techniques here.

As to the load unbalance arising from the heterogeneity of terms in documents and the heterogeneity of hosts, we can run a simple centralized schedule scheme at the superpeers to balance the load among nodes. For example, the superpeers may monitor the performance and spare resource of normal peers, and then they can allocate more tasks to the nodes with more spare resource, and also they can migrate the tasks from overloaded nodes to the light loaded nodes. More simply, the superpeers may distribute requests to normal nodes in the round-robin fashion.

4 Experiments and Results

To evaluate the performance of our solution, we implement a simulator for our hierarchical system in Java and extend it to support the content search solution. NPL corpus is used as the test document collection and the attached queries in the corpus as the test queries.

One main advantage of our solution is the decrease in total index size. For a document, there are few terms with relative high weights that account for a large fraction of the document vector length. These terms play more important roles in distinguishing contents of documents. Herein, we publish documents only under the terms with relative high weights, which account for a certain fraction of the document vector length, and then compute the total size of the index. When the fraction equals one, it means each document is published under all terms (except stop words) occurring in the document. We use the normalized index size, i.e. the index size normalized to that of publishing each document under all terms, to measure the index size. Figure 2 shows the experimental results. The index size decreases significantly as we reduce the number of index terms of each document, which indicates that our distributed combined indexing scheme is very efficient.

Recall and precision are two common metrics to evaluate the performance of information retrieval. Recall is the number of relevant documents retrieved divided by the total number of relevant documents. Precision is the number of relevant documents retrieved divided by the total number of documents retrieved. The computing formulas for recall and precision are shown as Equation 3 and Equation 4 respectively.

$$\mathrm{Re}\, call = \frac{\text{Number of relevant documents retrieved}}{\text{Total number of relevant documents}} \tag{3}$$

$$\mathrm{Pr}\, ecision = \frac{\text{Number of relevant documents retrieved}}{\text{Total number of documents retrieved}} \tag{4}$$

$$Relative \quad Recall = Relative \quad Precision$$
$$= \frac{\text{Recall/Precision of distributed combined indexing}}{\text{Recall/Precision of centralized indexing}} \quad (5)$$

We use relative recall and precision, namely the ratio of the recall and precision of our distributed combined indexing scheme to that of the centralized inverted files indexing scheme, to evaluate the performance of our solution. According to the definition, apparently the relative precision and recall are always equal. The computing formula for relative recall and precision is shown as Equation 5. In the experiments, while processing each query, we retrieve the top 10, 20 and 30 documents with highest similarity to the query. First, each cluster queried returns the most similar 10, 20 and 30 documents respectively. The query originator node emerges the results from different clusters and then gives them a global rank. Finally, the top 10, 20 and 30 documents with highest global scores are presented respectively. The results are shown in Figure 3, which indicate that there are little effects on the precision and recall when we publish documents only under the terms with relative high weights, i.e. discard some terms with low weights while identifying the index terms. So we can discard more terms with low weights until there is a sharp drop in the relative precision and recall. There is a tradeoff between precision/recall and indexing cost and also a proper threshold for terms' weights for users, which helps identify the index terms.

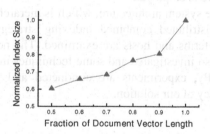

Fig. 2. Normalized index size

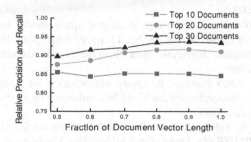

Fig. 3. Relative precision and recall

5 Related Work

Our idea is inspired by the observation on the heterogeneity of terms and hosts, and the recent studies on multiple keywords search in peer-to-peer networks [5], [7]. Li et al. [7] discuss the feasibility of keyword based web search in structured peer-to-peer networks and explore the p2p text search. Reynolds and Vahdat [5] discuss a search infrastructure using distributed inverted indexing. Different from their work, we employ a novel indexing strategy, which combines the global and local inverted files.

The most significant difference between other work and ours is that our system uses a hierarchical architecture, which could help us reduce the communication overhead and enhance the reliability and stability of the system. There are some other work [8][9] that involved in the nodes clustering and hybrid architecture in peer-to-peer networks. Our design of virtual node is quite different from them. The virtual node design achieves high fault tolerance for routing at a very low cost of additional maintenance.

6 Conclusion

Content search in peer-to-peer networks is a very active research area currently and still remains a challenging problem. In this paper, we propose a text-based content search solution for large scale structured peer-to-peer networks. In our solution, a hierarchical architecture is employed.

First, we present the system architecture, which is hierarchical and based on nodes clustering. Next, a distributed combined indexing strategy is described and the heterogeneity of both terms and hosts are examined. The nodes' overload and flash crowds problem are also investigated and some techniques maybe employed to tackle these problems. Finally, experiments are conducted and the results approve the feasibility and efficiency of our solution.

References

1. Stoica, I., Morris, R., and Liben-Nowell, D. et al. Chord: a scalable peer-to-peer lookup protocol for Internet applications. IEEE/ACM Transactions on Networking, Vol. 11, No. 1, pp. 11-32, Feb. 2003.
2. G. Salton, A. Wong, and C. Yang. A vector space model for automatic indexing. Communications of the ACM, Vol. 18, No. 11, pp. 613-620, Nov. 1975.
3. Salton, G. Information Retrieval: Data Structures and Algorithms. Addison-Wesley, Massachussetts, 1989.
4. Ribeiro-Neto, B. AND Barbosa, R. Query performance for tightly coupled distributed digital libraries. In Proceedings of the 3rd ACM Conference on Digital Libraries, New York, NY, pp. 182-190, Jun. 1998.
5. P. Reynolds and A. Vahdat. Efficient Peer-to-Peer Keyword Searching. In Proceedings of the 4th ACM/IFIP/USENIX International Middleware Conference, Rio de Janeiro, Brazil, LNCS 2672, pp. 21-40, Jun. 2003.

6. Tyron Stading, Petros Maniatis, and Mary Baker. Peer-to-peer caching schemes to address flash crowds. In Proceedings of the 1st International Workshop on Peer-to-Peer Systems (IPTPS02), Cambridge, MA, LNCS 2429, pp. 203-213, Mar. 2002.

7. LI, J., LOO, B. T. and HELLERSTEIN, J. On the feasibility of peer-to-peer web indexing and search. In proceedings of The 2nd International Workshop on Peer-to-Peer Systems, Berkeley, CA, LNCS 2735, pp. 207-215, Mar. 2003.

8. Lakshmish Ramaswamy, Bugra Gedik and Ling Liu. Connectivity Based Node Clustering in Decentralized Peer-to-Peer Networks. In Proceedings of the 3rd International Conference on Peer-to-Peer Computing, Linköping, Sweden, pp. 66-73, Sep., 2003.

9. B. Yang and H. Garcia-Molina. Comparing hybrid peer-to-peer systems. In Proceedings of the 27th International Conference on Very Large Data Bases, Roma, Italy, pp. 561-570, Sep., 2001.

A Document Image Preprocessing System for Keyword Spotting

C.B. Jeong and S.H. Kim

Department of Computer Science, Chonnam National University,
300 YongBong-dong, Buk-Gu, Gwangju 500-757, Korea
cbjeong@iip.chonnam.ac.kr
shkim@chonnam.ac.kr

Abstract. This paper presents a system for the segmentation of a printed document image into word images, which can be used effectively for document image retrieval based on keyword spotting. The system is composed of three image manipulation modules: skew correction, document layout analysis, and word segmentation. To enhance the practical applicability and flexibility of our research results, we test the system with 50 images of Korean papers and 50 images of English papers provided through full-text image retrieval services by the Korea Information Science Society and the Pattern Recognition Society, respectively. Currently, the accuracy of word extraction ranges from 90 to 95%, depending on the language of the document.

1 Introduction

Two approaches for document indexing and retrieval have been developed. One reads the document image by an optical character recognition (OCR) system and converts it into an adequate electronic format, and then applies both indexing and retrieval with this format. The other approach is based on keyword spotting where the document image is first segmented into words, and the user keywords are located in the image by a word-to-word matching [1].

Fig. 1. Block diagram of the proposed system

In this paper, we propose a preprocessing system for the segmentation of a printed document image into word images. The system is composed of three image manipulation modules: skew correction, document layout analysis, and word segmentation. Two major purposes of this research are (1) to make each module

Z. Chen et al. (Eds.): ICADL 2004, LNCS 3334, pp. 440–443, 2004.

superior to traditional methods, and (2) to make our system practical as well as reliable for the real-world document images. The remainder of this paper is organized as follows: In Section 2, we describe the detail of each module of the proposed system. An experimental results and a statement for future work are given in Section 3. Fig. 1 shows a block diagram of the proposed system.

2 Proposed System

The skew estimation module adapts the Hough transform algorithm using a BAG(Block Adjacency Graph) representation of document images. The BAG is an efficient data structure for extracting both the contours of the connected components in the images, and the lower and upper center points of the surrounding bounding boxes. The skew correction algorithm also uses the block in the BAG. Since the rotational transformations for skew correction are performed on the blocks, rather than individual pixels, the processing speed of our method is faster than that of traditional pixel-oriented methods [2].

The document layout analysis (DLA) segments the skew-corrected document into various regions by analyzing the geometrical layout, and then the regions are classified into either text or non-text. The DLA algorithm combines top-down and bottom-up approaches. To reduce the physical segmenting time, we first create multi-resolution images by halving the size of the document image. In the coarse segmentation, we execute a rough segmentation by analyzing connected components from the lowest resolution images. In the refine segmentation, we precisely segment the document image using projection profiles analysis upon the original image. Region classification process assigns each region into either text or non-text by a rule-based scheme [3].

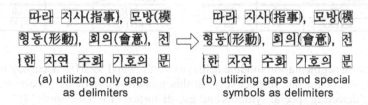

(a) utilizing only gaps
as delimiters

(b) utilizing gaps and special
symbols as delimiters

Fig. 2. An example of the word segmentation utilizing gaps and special symbols as delimiters

The word segmentation module separates the text region, which is segmented from a document image by the DLA, into the unit of words. It uses a horizontal projection profile cut method to segment a text block into lines, and utilizes gaps and special symbols as delimiters between words in order to separate a text line into word units. A gap clustering technique, which is an average linkage clustering method, is used to differentiate the between-word gaps and within-word gaps. In addition, it detects two types of special symbols lying between words using their morphological features. The first one is for the special symbols which are elongated horizontally such as dash ('-') or tilda ('~'). The second one is for the vertically elongated symbols such as various kinds of parentheses ('{', '[', '('). These symbols can be used for further decomposition over the result of gap-based segmentation as in Fig. 2 [4].

3 Experimental Results and Future Work

The proposed system has been implemented on a Pentium-4 2.0GHz PC, and tested with 50 images of Korean papers and 50 images of English papers scanned at a resolution of 300 dpi. These images are provided through full-text image retrieval services by the Korea Information Science Society and the Pattern Recognition Society.

The performances of the skew correction module can be evaluated in terms of speed and accuracy. The average processing time of the skew estimation and correction are 0.16 and 0.34 seconds, respectively. The average error of skew estimation is ± 0.06 degrees [2].

Table 1 shows a confusion matrix of the DLA for the sample documents. Most of the segmentation errors occur in single line captions, that is, single line captions were classified into a part of image or table. The average processing time of layout analysis for Korean and English images is about 0.23 and 0.35 seconds, respectively. Although more than 10% of TRs are incorrectly identified as NTRs for both Korean and English images, there are only 1.24% and 1.3% of all words in the miss-identified TRs, respectively.

Table 1. The result of the DLA for Korean and English images, respectively: TR denotes a text region, NTR denotes a non-text region

Input \ Output	#TRs	#NTRs
#TRs	313	52
#NTRs	3	88

Input \ Output	#TRs	#NTRs
#TRs	550	69
#NTRs	4	137

The word segmentation module achieves 99.87% and 99.51% accuracy for Korean and English documents, respectively. In this module, most of the errors are due to a failure of detecting special symbols and gap distortions for italic fonts [4].

The performance of the whole preprocessing system is summarized in Table 2. In Table 2, WTR and WNTR have been counted using gap and special symbols as delimiters between words. STR and SNTR are the numbers of words extracted by the proposed system from TRs and NTRs, respectively. The overall accuracy of word segmentation for Korean and English documents is 90.84 and 95.27%, respectively.

There are three causes of errors in the system: error of DLA, error of word segmentation, and incapability of word extraction from non-text regions. For the 50 Korean documents, as an example, 23,287 out of 25,636 are correctly extracted. Among the 2,349 words which could not be extracted, 322 words are due to the error of DLA, 30 words are due to the error of word segmentation, and the remaining 1,997 words are due to the incapability of our system for handling non-text regions. Considering only the text regions in the original documents, the accuracy of word segmentation is 98.51%. Similar analysis can be drawn for the English documents.

As can be seen from the table, the most significant cause of error is the incapability of word extraction from non-text regions. Therefore, the future work of our research is to develop a word extraction algorithm from non-text regions (table, figure, etc).

Table 2. The results of word segmentation of the proposed system on the images of Korean and English papers: WTR denotes the number of words in TRs, WNTR denotes the number of words in NTRs, AWDI (WTR+WNTR) denotes the number of all words in the document image (DI), STR denotes the number of extracted words in TRs, SNTR denotes the number of extracted words in NTRs, SDI (STR+SNTR) denotes the number of extracted words in all regions. Accuracy for text regions ($=$STR$\div$WTR$\times 100$) and accuracy for the whole document ($=$SDI$\div$AWDI$\times 100$) show the performance of the proposed system

		#words(input)			#extracted words(output)			Accuracy(%)	
		WTR	WNTR	AWDI	STR	SNTR	SDI	For TRs	For the DI
K O R	1	474	0	474	472	0	472	99.58%	99.58%
	2	707	0	707	707	0	707	100.00%	100.00%
	3	564	32	596	519	0	519	92.02%	87.08%
	48	491	10	501	486	0	486	98.98%	97.01%
	49	477	15	492	470	0	470	98.53%	95.53%
	50	402	98	500	378	0	378	94.03%	75.60%
	Total	23639	1997	25636	23287	0	23287	98.51%	90.84%
E N G	1	199	0	199	199	0	199	100.00%	100.00%
	2	792	0	792	764	0	764	96.46%	96.46%
	3	637	38	675	629	0	629	98.74%	93.18%
	48	262	80	342	247	0	247	94.27%	72.22%
	49	814	6	820	774	0	774	95.09%	94.39%
	50	908	0	908	887	0	887	97.69%	97.69%
	Total	26842	787	27629	26321	0	26321	98.06%	95.27%

Acknowledgement. This work was supported by grant No. R05-2003-000-10396-0 from the KOSEF.

References

1. Doermann, D.: The indexing and retrieval of document images: a survey, Computer Vision and Image Understanding, Vol. 70 N. 3 (1998) 287-298
2. Kwag, H.K., Kim, S.H., Jeong, S., Lee, G.S.: Efficient Skew Estimation and Correction Algorithm for Document Images, Image and Vision Computing, Vol. 20 N. 1 (2002) 25-35
3. Park, D.Y., Kwag, H.K., Kim, S.H.: Document Layout Analysis using Coarse/Fine Strategy, Proceedings of the Conference on Korea Electronics Engineers Society, Vol. 23 N. 1 (2000) 198-201 (text in Korean)
4. Kim, S.H., Jeong, C.B., Kwag, H.K., Suen, C.Y.: Word Segmentation of Printed Text Lines Based on Gap Clustering and Special Symbol Detection, Proceedings of the International Conference on Pattern Recognition, Vol. 2 (2002) 320-323

A Gaussian-Fuzzy Content Feature Recognition System for Digital Media Asset Objects

Sanxing Cao and Rui Lu

School of Computer Science and Software, Communication University of China,
No.1 Dingfuzhuang Dongjie, Beijing, 100024, P.R. China
{c3x, lvrui}@bbu.edu.cn

Abstract. One of the key issues within the research of Media Assets is the description and intelligent recognition of content-based features. Upon the basis of massive fundamental research, we present in this paper a configurable content description and recognition model based on a Gaussian-Fuzzy membership system. Multiple and partial memberships and compatibility for various algorithms are supported in this architecture.

1 Introduction

In digital resource platforms designing, the key issue is to set up a content description system that could, within a specific application environment, represent reasonably and effectively the content features that users are interested in. Upon it, a content feature extraction system should be implemented, providing semi-automatic metadata annotation. ISO/IEC JTC1/SC29/WG11 (MPEG) has proposed MPEG-7 (M6155, M6156, N3575)[1], a general architecture based on Ds, DSs and XML-Schema-based DDL. DCMI [2] (ISO TC46/SC4 N515) sponsored by OCLC has been employed as a well-operable standard for DL content description. RDF [3] designed by W3C on the basis of XML has taken on the role of modeling Internet resources into semantically retrievable entities. Schemes above are, in certain sense, not considering much about content features' personalization, uncertainty and complexity in membership, thus leaving considerable vacancy for researches related to these issues.

2 The Gaussian-Fuzzy Content Description Scheme

In this paper we introduce a content description scheme that deals with the uncertainty of content categorization and feature evaluation. Buckley [4], Negota [5] and Sanchez [6] have raised a number of schemas that focus on the description and manipulation of uncertainty in Expert Systems. We add Confirmation constraint (cf_value) to content feature values and retrieval rules, so as to model the uncertainty of the content object in reality.Fuzzy mathematical solutions, including the Fuzzy Sets Theory [7], Rough Sets Theory [8] and Fuzzy Decision Models [9], have been widely applied since the 1970s. To set up the fuzzy model, we use the Gaussian Distribution defined below:

Z. Chen et al. (Eds.): ICADL 2004, LNCS 3334, pp. 444–448, 2004.
© Springer-Verlag Berlin Heidelberg 2004

$$f(x) = \frac{1}{\sigma\sqrt{2\pi}} e^{-\frac{1}{2}\left(\frac{x-v}{\sigma}\right)^2} \qquad -\infty < x < \infty \tag{1}$$

For a vector $\mathbf{x} = (\xi_1, \xi_2, ... \xi_N)^T$ in the N-dimension L^2 space, we

have $\|\mathbf{x}\| = \left(\sum_{i=1}^{n} \xi_i^2\right)^{\frac{1}{2}}$. Let the Membership Function be $\hat{\mu}_x = \mu(\mathbf{x}) = \lambda f(\mathbf{x})$,

take $\lambda = \sigma\sqrt{2\pi}$, we have the convex regular campanulate fuzzy model shown in (2).

$$\hat{\mu}_{1x} = \mu(\mathbf{x}) = e^{\frac{-\|\mathbf{x}-v\|^2}{2\sigma^2}}, \text{ where } \|\mathbf{x}-v\| \in [0, +\infty), \hat{\mu}_{1x} \in (0,1] \tag{2}$$

Architecting of Mass Media Resource Platform [10][11], we formulate the concept hierarchies and feature sets of resource content objects (Res objects) in 3 dimensions, namely, Content, Data and Subject. Lim et. al. [12] used a hierarchical event taxonomy in a home photo content model. Lu et. al. [13] introduced a concept hierarchy based on relevance feedback. But these hierarchies do not support multiple memberships. In our approach, a Res object's membership in the Data hierarchy is definite and singular, but those in the Content and Subject hierarchies would support uncertainty and multiplicity. Suppose the following content concept hierarchy would be applied.

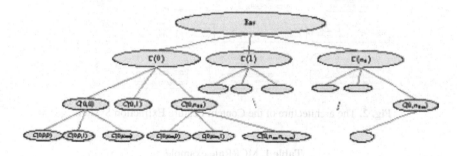

Fig. 1. Content concept hierarchy

$$\begin{cases} \mu_{C_1}(\hat{R}) = \hat{\mu}_{\hat{R}C_1} \\ \mu_{C_2}(\hat{R}) = \hat{\mu}_{\hat{R}C_2} \\ ... \\ \mu_{C_n}(\hat{R}) = \hat{\mu}_{\hat{R}C_n} \end{cases}, \text{ where } \begin{cases} C_1 = C(i_{11}, i_{21}, i_{k_1 1}) \\ C_2 = C(i_{12}, i_{22}, i_{k_2 2}) \\ ... \\ C_n = C(i_{1n}, i_{2n}, i_{k_n n}) \end{cases} \tag{3}$$

Suppose Res object $\hat{R}$ owns Content memberships indicated in (3), and $\hat{R}$ also belongs to Data category $C_D(i_{D1}, ..., i_{Dk_D})$ and Subject categories $C_S(i_{S1j}, ..., i_{Smj}), m = 1, 2, ..., k_{Sj}$, $j = 1, 2, ..., n_s$ We have complete feature in (4).

$$\tilde{F}(\hat{R}) = \tilde{F}_{CONT}(\hat{R}) \cup \tilde{F}_{DATA}(\hat{R}) \cup \tilde{F}_{SUBJ}(\hat{R})$$

$$= \left\{ \bigcup_{j=1}^{n} \bigcup_{m=1}^{k_j} \tilde{F}_{CONT}[C(i_{1j},...,i_{mj})] \right\} \cup \left\{ \bigcup_{m=1}^{k_D} \tilde{F}_{DATA}[C_D(i_{D1},...,i_{Dm})] \right\} \cup \left\{ \bigcup_{j=1}^{n_s} \bigcup_{m=1}^{k_{sj}} \tilde{F}_{SUBJ}[C_S(i_{S1j},...,i_{Smj})] \right\} \quad (4)$$

3   The Content Feature Extraction System

The Content Feature Extraction System analyzes the Data features of a Res object, matches their values with nominal values that characterizes specific Content features on certain confirmation degree, and relate Data and Content features across the semantic gap. A content feature extraction rule, or MCRRule Γ, is composed of the source feature expression E_Γ, the destination feature $F_{\Gamma d}$ and its value $V_{F\Gamma d}$, and the nominal confirmation degree $cf_{\Gamma 0}$. E_Γ is composed of the source feature $F_{\Gamma s}$, the matching operator $\Theta_{\Gamma s}$, the source feature nominal value $V_{F\Gamma s0}$ and the matching Gaussian variance $\sigma_{E\Gamma}$. Given E_Γ, $F_{\Gamma d}$, $V_{F\Gamma d}$ $cf_{\Gamma 0}$, and the source feature actual value $V_{F\Gamma s}$, we can get the rule confirmation degree cf_Γ via a Gaussian fuzzy matching model.

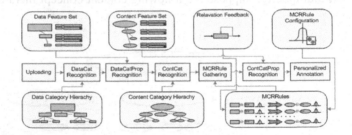

Fig. 2. The architecture of the Content Feature Extraction System

Table 1. MCRRule example

$F_{\Gamma d}$	$V_{F\Gamma d}$	$cf_{\Gamma 0}$	$F_{\Gamma s}$	$\Theta_{\Gamma s}$	$V_{F\Gamma s0}$	$\sigma_{E\Gamma}$
Keyword	Sky	0.85	ColorRegion(#238aff)	Higher than	0.3200	0.1207

We designed and implemented an experimental Gaussian-fuzzy content feature extraction system during the development of the AV Library Platform for broadcasting companies. Typical of the MCRRules in the system are the rules that recognizes visual content features via Gaussian-fuzzy HSV-space ellipsoid color region matching. An example of the MCRRule is shown in Table 2. We implemented an MCRRule configuration module so as to facilitate manual adjusting of MCRRule parameters. Its interface is indicated in Fig. 3. Auto-annotation experiment based on the MCRRule is performed. 8 images are analyzed and cfs are calculated to stand for their relevance with the keyword "sky". Deviations of cfs from manual-annotated values are shown in Table 3. Although it produces a larger difference on color-deviated occasions, the rule is still able to return a non-ignorable *cf* to indicate the possible content feature.

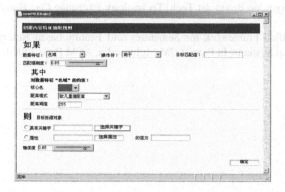

Fig. 3. Interface of MCRRule Configuration Module

Table 2. Results of the Automatic Annotation Experiment

Image								
$V_{\vec{\mathcal{A}}_T}$	0.1702	0.2262	0.6865	0.0935	0.2133	0.4127	0.2026	0.0980
cf_T	0.5365	0.7040	0.8500	0.2209	0.6725	0.8500	0.6432	0.2393
$\tilde{\mu}$	0.40	0.60	0.90	0.35	0.95	0.95	0.90	0.55
$\lvert cf_T - \tilde{\mu} \rvert$	0.1365	0.1040	0.0500	0.1291	0.2775	0.1000	0.2568	0.3107

References

1. IEC JTC1/SC29/WG11: Multimedia Description Schemes. La Baule (2000)
2. ISO TC 46/SC 4 N515: Information and documentation — The Dublin Core metadata element set. ISO Copyright Office, Geneva (2003)
3. Frank Manola, Eric Miller, Brian McBride: RDF Primer - W3C Recommendation. http://www.w3.org/TR/REC-rdf-syntax (2004)
4. J. Buckley: Managing uncertainty in a fuzzy expert system. Intl. J. Man-Machine Studies (1988) 29 129–148
5. C. Negota; Expert Systems & Fuzzy Systems. Menlo Park, CA: Benjamin-Cummings (1985)
6. L. Zadeh and E. Sanchez: Artificial Intelligence. Applications of quantitative reasoning, Oxford, Pergamon Press (1987)
7. L. Zadeh: Fuzzy Sets. Information and Control 8 (1965) 338–353
8. Z. Paulak: Rough Sets. Intl. J. of Computer and Information Sciences, 11 (1982) 341–356
9. A. Kaufman and M. Gupta: Fuzzy Mathematical Models in Engineering and Management Science, North-Holland, Amsterdam (1988)
10. Cao Sanxing, Lu Rui: Large-Scale TV Station OA Application Systems based on Intranet and Web. In Proc. CIEYC2001, Beijing Broadcasting Institute Press (2001) 234–237

11. J. H. Lim, Q. Tian and P. Mulhem: Home Photo Content Modeling for Personalized Event-based Retrieval, IEEE Trans. Multimedia, Vol. 5, No. 3(2003) 28–37
12. Cao Sanxing, Xu Jun and Gao Fu'an: Media ERP: Concept and Application Framework. In Proc. Intl. Sym. on Broadcast Tech, Technology Exchange Co.: Hongkong (2003) 234–237
13. Y. Lu: A Unified Framework for Semantics and Feature-based Relevance Feedback in Image Retrieval Systems, In Proc. ACM Multimedia, ACM Press (2000) 31-37

A Novel Watermarking Scheme Based on Video Content

Guomin Wu, Yueting Zhuang, Fei Wu, and Yunhe Pan

College of Computer Science, Zhejiang University, Hangzhou 310027, China
wuguomin@263.net, yzhuang@cs.zju.edu.cn

Abstract. In this paper, we propose a novel blind MPEG video watermarking technology to hide copyright information by a slight modification of discrete cosine transformation domain in I-frames. It takes full advantage of both stillness and motion information of video content to guarantee the high perceptual invisibility. An effective characteristic extractor of block is delicately designed based on the properties of stillness and motion information, namely the texture, the luminance and the difference between adjacent frames. An eigenfunction is proposed to modify the extracted block characteristic. We illustrated the robustness of the scheme to several video distortions.

Keywords: Copyright protection, perceptual masking, video watermarking.

1 Introduction

Watermarking of digital video serves a number of purposes including copyright protection, tracking and tamper detection etc. Many existing video watermarking algorithms are based on the idea of spreading the watermark energy over all of the pixels in each of the frames ([1-2]). Some approaches proposed that the watermark energy is conditional spatially localized ([2-3]). They are often based on MPEG coding structures rather than the visual content. Others are content-dependent, but they may be constrained to some regular patterns or cannot effectively solve some distortions special for video such as frame dropping, averaging and swapping.

A stillness feature and motion estimation based blind MPEG video watermarking scheme is proposed in this paper. The algorithm describes a mixed perceptual model based on texture masking, luminance masking and motion masking.

2 Watermark Embedding Scheme

2.1 Feature Analyse and Calculation Based on Video Content

Intuitively, psycho-visual studies indicate that human cannot see the detail of the fast moving objects. So motion masking is also important for video masking. This paper presents a mixed perceptual model that can be used to incorporate the texture masking, luminance masking and motion masking properties into compressed MPEG video with only a small computational overhead.

Z. Chen et al. (Eds.): ICADL 2004, LNCS 3334, pp. 449–452, 2004.
© Springer-Verlag Berlin Heidelberg 2004

The perceptual model is improved on the model proposed by Tong et al. [4], and the computation of the motion masking factor is based on the difference of DC in value range of 0.9 to 1.1. The model computes a local multiplying factor m_k that is used to scale the potential embedding intensity: $m_k = TextMask_k \times LumMask_k \times MotionMask_k$. From lots of experiment results, we set a *Threshold* $T_M = 0.99$ for ignoring plain blocks.

2.2 Feature Correction

m_k means the maximum scaling of embedding intensity without destroying the invisibility. For highly textured or bright regions, the scaling m_k is excessive for intensity embedding than that of relative plain blocks. Here we use the minimum principle to construct an eigenfunction m_{gk} to cut the excessive energy:

Let us assume there are n blocks for embedding (i.e. n DC coefficients). The absolute values of DC are regarded as a series $L_{dc} = [dc_1, dc_2, \cdots, dc_n]$. We construct:

$$f(x) = a_1 \times e^{-\left(\frac{(x-b_1)}{c_1}\right)^2} + a_2 \times e^{-\left(\frac{(x-b_2)}{c_2}\right)^2} + a_3 \times e^{-\left(\frac{(x-b_3)}{c_3}\right)^2}. \tag{1}$$

Then $m_{gk} = f(DC_k)$. Let us denote λ_k is the corrected multiplying factor: $\lambda_k = m_k \times m_{gk}$.

Through lots of experiments, when we assign a1=1.2,b1=–18, c1=146, a2=0.3, b2= –340, c2=620, a3= 0.18, b3=–1321, c3=1423 the algorithm shows solidity and robustness to different videos.

2.3 Watermark Embedding

Let assume a watermark of $L = M \times N$ bits is embedded into M I-frames and N bits each frame: $w_k(i) = w(k \times N + i) = w_{k \times N + i} \in \{-1,1\}$. $k = 0, \cdots M - 1$. $i = 0, \cdots N - 1$. . By the λ_k and scaling factor $\alpha = 0.1$, the watermark signal w_k is embedded in the original signal x_k to produce the watermarked signal y_k: $y_k = x_k + \alpha \lambda_k w_k x_k$.

3 Watermark Detection

A blind detection is presented in the algorithm. During the detection we read the watermarked signal y in frame model. Let us denote S by the following sum:

$$S = \frac{1}{L} \sum_{i=0}^{L-1} y(i)w(i) = \frac{1}{L}\left(\sum_{i=0}^{L-1} x(i)w(i) + \sum_{i=0}^{L-1} (\alpha\lambda(i)w(i)x(i))w(i) \right) \tag{2}$$

For L sufficiently large, we denote by B a set of $L_B = |\Delta w|$, $\Delta w = \sum_{i \in B} w(i) = \sum_{i=0}^{L-1} w(i)$.

Obviously, $L_A = L - |\Delta w|$ and $\sum_{i \in A} w(i) = 0$. If $S_1 = \frac{1}{L}\sum_{i \in A} x(i)w(i)$., $S_2 = \frac{1}{L}\sum_{i \in B} x(i)w(i)$.,

and $S_3 = \frac{1}{L}\sum_{i=0}^{L-1} \alpha\lambda(i)x(i)$. We can conclude: ①if the signal is not watermarked, then

$S_3 = 0 : S \approx S_2 \approx \frac{\Delta w}{L}m_x$. ② if the signal is watermarked: $S \approx \frac{\Delta w}{L}m_x + \frac{1}{L}\sum_{i-0}^{L-1} \alpha\lambda(i)x(i)$.

For watermark detection we construct the ratio R: $R \cong \frac{S - S_2}{S_3}$.

x required for evaluation is replaced by y without significant error. We first detect the watermark in frame mode, and then the maximum result is used for full detection.

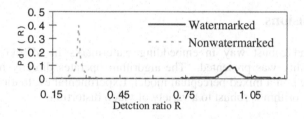

Fig. 1. Empirical pdf of the detection ratio in 1000 watermarked versions signal and nonwatermarked signal with using 1000 watermark keys

In the case that the signal is watermarked, R will be approximately equal to one. Or else, R will be zero. To decide whether a certain watermark exists in the video can be taken by comparing R against a suitable threshold T_r. We do experiments for confirming the empirical threshold of the detection ratio R. The result is shown in Fig. 1. Based on the result, we can assume $T_r = 0.5$.

4 Experimental Results

We test our algorithm to lots of videos. *PSNR* (43.4dB of Forman video) is computed between the original and watermarked frame. The watermark almost causes no degradations to the host video.

We perform several distortions including colored noise, MPEG coding (0.08bpp), multiple watermarks (0.25bpp, 3 layers) and temporal processing (dropping B or P frames or swapping) to verify the robustness of our algorithm. For each distortion, the test was repeated 100 times with a new noise sequence for each run. The maximum, mean, minimum detection ratios are computed over all 100 runs of each attack. The results of Forman video (8bpp, 352×288) are shown in Table 1. Obviously, a video signal with or without watermark can be clearly detected under all distortions.

Table 1. Detection ratios and PSNR of Forman video (8bpp) under a series of video distortions

Attack Type	PSNR (dB)	With watermark			No watermark		
		Max	Mean	Min	Max	Mean	Min
Unattacked	43.4	-	0.94	-	-	0.20	-
Colored noise	20.61	1.07	0.89	0.65	0.35	0.29	0.22
Coding (0.08bpp)	21.44	1.04	0.87	0.62	0.33	0.28	0.21
Frame dropping	21.09	1.11	0.93	0.69	0.26	0.22	0.17
Multiple3 (0.25bpp)	21.36	1.10	0.90	0.67	0.37	0.30	0.22

5 Conclusions

A novel and robust way in embedding watermarks in MPEG video with high imperceptibility was presented. The algorithm operates directly in the compressed domain based on a mixed perceptual model. Experimental evaluation showed that the proposed algorithm is robust to a variety of video distortions.

Acknowledgements

This work is supported by the National Natural Science Foundation of China (60272031), 973 Program (2002CB312101), Technology Plan Program of Zhejiang Province (2003C21010), Doctorate Research Foundation of the State Education Commission of China (20010335049), Zhejiang Provincial Natural Science Foundation of China (M603202)

References

1. Cox I. J., Kilian J., Leighton T., and Shamoon T.: Secure spread spectrum watermarking for multimedia. IEEE Transactions on Image Processing, Vol. 6. (1997) 1673–1687
2. Hartung F., Girod B.: Watermarking of uncompressed and compressed video. Signal Processing, Vol. 66. (1998) 283–301
3. Agung I. W., and Sweeney P.: Video scene characteristic detection to improve digital watermarking transparency. IEE Proceedings - Vision, Image and Signal Processing, Vol. 151. (2004) 146-152
4. Tong H. H. Y., and Venetsanopoulos A. N.: A Perceptual Model for JPEG Applications based on Block Classification, Texture Masking and Luminance Masking. Proceedings of International Conference on Image Processing (ICIP), Chicago (1998) 428-432.

Subjective Relevance: Implications on Digital Libraries for Experts and Novices

Shu-Shing Lee, Yin-Leng Theng, Dion Hoe-Lian Goh,
and Schubert Shou-Boon Foo

Division of Information Studies, School of Communication and Information,
Nanyang Technological University, Singapore 637718
{ps7918592b, tyltheng, ashlgoh, assfoo}@ntu.edu.sg

Abstract. Traditional information retrieval (IR) systems are developed based on the "best match" principle which assumes that users can specify their needs in a query and documents retrieved are relevant to users. However, this objective measure of relevance is limited as it does not consider differences in experts' and novices' knowledge and context. This paper presents initial work towards addressing this limitation by investigating subjective relevance (that can include topical, pertinence, situational, and motivational relevance) features that can be incorporated into digital library interfaces to help experts and novices search and judge relevance more effectively. A pilot study was conducted to elicit initial subjective relevance features from experts and novices. The paper concludes with a discussion of elicited design features and their implications for user-centered digital libraries.

1 Introduction

Traditional IR systems are developed based on the "best match" principle assuming that users can specify their needs in a query [1]. Using this principle, the system retrieves documents "matching closely" to the query and regards these documents as relevant to the user. However, this objective measure of relevance is limited as it does not consider differences in experts' and novices' knowledge and context.

Experts and novices have different skills. Experts have experience with IR systems and domain knowledge that allow them to search and judge relevance more effectively than novices who do not possess such skills [2]. To address experts' and novices' needs, and limitations of objective measure of relevance, user-centered digital libraries can attempt to incorporate additional features such as support for subjective relevance in an attempt to further improve document retrieval to suit users' needs and contexts.

This paper presents initial work towards user-centered digital libraries by investigating features prompting subjective relevance of documents that can be incorporated into digital library interfaces to address experts' and novices' needs.

Z. Chen et al. (Eds.): ICADL 2004, LNCS 3334, pp. 453–457, 2004.
© Springer-Verlag Berlin Heidelberg 2004

2   Types of Subjective Relevance

Relevance is a relation between some entity and the information object [7]. Subjective relevance considers relevance from the perspective of users' knowledge and information needs [3]. This subjective approach sees relevance judgment as a product of personal perception that is closely connected to task and context [8]. Four types of subjective relevance are highlighted in [7]:

- Topical Relevance: Here, information objects are relevant if the topic covered by the assessed information object is "about" the topic specified in the query or information need [4].
- Pertinence Relevance: This relevance is measured based on the relation between user's knowledge state and retrieved information objects as interpreted by the user [7]. Hence, this relevance is dependent on user's conceptual knowledge, perceptions and intentions to assess relevance of retrieved information objects.
- Situational Relevance: This is measured in terms of the relation between perceived situation/task at hand and usefulness of retrieved information objects for that situation/task. Hence, relevance is determined based on whether the user can use retrieved information objects to address a particular situation/task [4].
- Motivational Relevance: Here, relevance is assessed based on whether the user is able to use the retrieved information object for the task/context [7]. Moreover, in motivational relevance, the broader community (context/environment) in which the user operates in is also responsible for measuring success of the relation.

3   Pilot Study

A pilot study was conducted to elicit initial subjective relevance features. The study aimed to elicit "desired" and "expected" design features from novices and experts for digital library interfaces supporting subjective relevance.

Subjects
Four subjects were selected to participate. Subjects were divided into two groups, Group A and Group B, to represent the needs of both expert and novice users respectively. Group A was made up of two PhD students with IR (information retrieval) training. Group B consisted of two Masters students without IR training. IR training in this context was defined as users who had undergone a module on IR in the course of their post-graduate studies.

Methodology
The study was conducted in two sessions, one for Group A and another for Group B. The methodology for both sessions was the same. To ensure subjects understood the concept of subjective relevance, they were first briefed about the objective of study and were given definitions of subjective relevance. After that, they were given 20 minutes to complete a task. The task was to gather information for a discussion on "The social impact of the Internet" using the ACM Digital Library (http://www.acmdl.org). The purpose of this task was to set a context to get them thinking about what design features might be important to help them assess relevance

of documents. After completing the task in each session, subjects came together to brainstorm features that they thought were useful to help assess document's relevance. Brainstorming is a technique used to generate creative ideas whilst suspending judgment of ideas [6]. During brainstorming, all features suggested by subjects were recorded. After brainstorming features, subjects were asked to indicate among the suggested features which ones were most important.

4 Findings and Analysis

A list of subjective relevance and usability features for experts and novices was gathered as findings. Features elicited from each session were matched with characteristics of each type of subjective relevance. For features that could not be categorized under a subjective relevance type, further examination showed that these were usability features. Hence, remaining features for each session were organized based on characteristics of the ten heuristics outlined by Nielsen [5] for heuristic evaluation. This resulted in a list of usability features for experts and novices.

Due to space constraints, we can only provide examples from the lists of subjective relevance features and usability features for novices and experts to demonstrate how features in each list were coded and organized. Table 1 illustrates examples of features elicited, from novices and experts, for each type of subjective relevance. Table 2 illustrates examples of usability features elicited, from novices and experts, corresponding to five of the ten heuristics outlined by Nielsen [5]. Most important features for Tables 1 and 2 are indicated with an asterisk.

Table 1. Subjective relevance features for novices and experts

Type of Subjective Relevance	Feature (experts)	Feature (novices)
Topical relevance	Provide taxonomy of documents*.	Provide recommendation of related documents*.
	Provide artificial intelligence agents*.	Provide visualization of search results.
	Rank retrieved documents by relevance.	-
Pertinence relevance	Provide selected references used in documents.	Provide selected references used in documents*.
Situational relevance	Provide abstract of documents retrieved*.	Provide search option to search abstracts*.
Motivational relevance	Provide recommendation of what others have looked at.	Provide details of other people the author has worked with*.

In Table 1, experts and novices suggested interesting features for situational relevance. The features seemed to indicate that both experts and novices felt digital libraries had limited ability in retrieving documents for their contexts and tasks. Hence, they preferred to evaluate relevance of documents by going through abstracts.

Novices indicated more subjective relevance features in their list of most important features. This could be because novices did not possess as much domain knowledge and hence required more subjective relevance features to help them search and perform relevance judgments more effectively.

Subjective relevance features provided by experts tended to focus more on *topical* relevance. This might suggest that experts preferred to personally judge relevance of documents for their tasks but they would appreciate system support by indicating if the document was about the topic they were interested in. Among experts' most important features, a large portion was *usability* features. This might be because experts had the domain knowledge to evaluate relevance of documents for their tasks. Hence, they were more concerned with having a pleasant experience using the interface and that the interface allowed them to search and browse easily.

Usability features in Table 2 seemed to indicate that experts understood the information seeking process and that the results list was essential for relevance evaluation. At the same time, they also understood that a query was needed before a results list was returned and that users had problems constructing queries. Hence, they had suggested features to facilitate query formulation.

Table 2. Usability features for experts and novices

Heurisitc Guidlines	Feature (Experts)	Feature (Novices)
Match between system and the real world.	Provide natural language searching*.	-
Consistency and standards.	Display results list*.	Allow preview of abstract before downloading PDF file.
Recognition rather than recall.	Provide search fields to facilitate searching*.	-
Flexibility and efficiency of use.	Provide search options, such as author, title, keyword search*.	Provide direct download of documents in PDF format*.
User control and freedom.	-	Provide "clear query" button*.

5 Discussion and Conclusion

The pilot study aimed to elicit a set of subjective relevance features for experts and novices. In general, the findings (of which only a subset is presented here) seemed to indicate that although subjective relevance features were important, experts were more concerned with the usability of interfaces supporting subjective relevance.

Results presented here are preliminary and part of on-going research to elicit subjective relevance features for user-centered digital libraries. Elicited features need to be further refined and tested before they can emerge as features and principles for the design of better digital library interfaces to address experts' and novices' needs. Future work could focus on expanding the pilot study to larger groups of experts and novices to elicit a comprehensive set of important usability and subjective relevance features for user-oriented digital libraries.

References

1. Belkin, N. J., Oddy, R. N., & Brooks, H. (1982). ASK for information retrieval: Part I. background and theory. *The Journal of Documentation, 38*(2), 61-71.
2. Chen, H., Houston, A. L., Sewell, R. R., & Schatz, B. R. (1998). Internet browsing and searching: Use evaluations of category map and concept space techniques. *Journal of the American Society for Information Science, 49*(7), 582-603.
3. Ingwersen, P. and Borlund, P. (1996). Information transfer viewed as interactive cognitive processes. In Ingwersen, P. and Pors, N. O. (Eds.). *Information Science: Integration in Perspective* (pp. 219-232). Copenhagen, Denmark: Royal School of Librarianship.
4. Janes, J. (1994). Other people's judgments: A comparison of users' and others' judgments of document relevance, topicality, and utility. *Journal of the American Society for Information Science, 45(3),* 160-171.
5. Nielsen, J. (1994). Heuristic evaluation. In Nielsen, J. & Mack, R. L. (Eds.), *Usability Inspection Methods*, John Wiley & Sons, New York.
6. Osborn, A. (1993). *Applied imagination: Principlse and procedures of creative problem-solving.* Creative Education Foundation.
7. Saracevic, T. (1996). Relevance reconsidered '96. In Ingwersen, P. and Pors, N. O. (Eds.). *Information Science: Integration in Perspective* (pp. 201-218). Copenhagen, Denmark: Royal School of Librarianship.
8. Tang, R. and Soloman, P. (1998). Toward an understanding of the dynamics of relevance judgment: An analysis of one person's search behavior. *Information Process and Management, 34,* 237-256.

Visual Information Retrieval Based on Shape Similarity

Jong-Seung Park

Dept. of Computer Science and Engineering, University of Incheon,
177 Dohwa-dong, Nam-gu, Incheon, 402-749, Republic of Korea
jong@incheon.ac.kr

Abstract. An effective and fast shape description and retrieval method is presented for huge image databases. As a shape representation for deformable objects, a multi-scale skeleton representation is proposed in order to preserve the consistency of the skeletons and to reduce the effect of the structural changes. Incorrect matches due to the boundary noise in a segmentation process are avoided by including multiple coarse skeletons of different scales. A fast computational method for the similarity of skeletons is also proposed by using the moment invariants. Experimental results on animal databases showed that the proposed method gives prominent accuracy in retrieval.

1 Introduction

The indexing and retrieval of digital photographs is becoming relevant for many applications, including in multimedia libraries, art galleries and museum archives, in picture and photograph archiving and communication, and in medical and geographic databases. The problem of content-based image retrieval in an image archiving system is to obtain a list of images from a huge database which are most similar to the query description. Two critical issues of a content-based image retrieval system are feature extraction for indexing and similarity computation for retrieval. Feature extraction is for automatic characterization of an image. Based on the similarity measure, relevant images are retrieved. Most of the previous image retrieval systems were based on the image feature analysis such as colors, textures, and regions. Such features do not represent shape properties of a query object quite well hence irrelevant images are frequently retrieved. Recently, there has been works to handle shape features effectively [1][2][3].

In this paper, to improve the retrieval effectiveness of a content-based image retrieval system, a shape-based similarity comparison method is presented. A new multi-scale skeleton-based invariant feature representation is proposed as a shape representation. The method of multi-scale skeletons is not a new one [4][5]. In contrast to their approaches, our method extracts invariant features from the multiple skeletons and keeps only the feature vectors to the database. The moment invariants are used to compute the similarity of two images.

Z. Chen et al. (Eds.): ICADL 2004, LNCS 3334, pp. 458–461, 2004.
© Springer-Verlag Berlin Heidelberg 2004

2 Multi-scale Skeleton Representation

There are two different processes for the image archiving system: image archival process and image retrieval process. The image archival process is related to registration of collected images to the database. For the registration of an image to the archive system we first obtain the region segmentation data using our specialized segmentation utility. From the segmentation data, multiple skeletons are computed according to the level of details for the boundary representation. Also a feature vector is computed for each skeleton representation. The image and the set of feature vectors are saved to the database in the image registration process.

The image retrieval process is related to the search and retrieval of similar images to the given query description. The user should provide a region boundary of the object to be searched in the query image. Then, the system constructs a skeleton structure for the specified region and also computes the feature vectors for the structures. The feature vectors for the structures are compared to the feature vectors stored in the database and the most similar results are retrieved.

Skeleton representation is a natural way of shape description especially for deformable objects such as human beings, animals, fishes and insects. Beside its naturalness, the shape can be reconstructed from the skeleton representation by taking an inverse skeleton transform. The major drawback of skeleton representation is that it is sensitive to noise. For an example, approaches of medial axis may cause spurious branches and shape distortions for the jagged boundaries. To prohibit the sensitivity to boundary noises we propose a method of skeleton structure by employing a multi-scale representation. The multiple skeletons describe coarse boundaries as well as fine details.

The skeleton of an object shape is defined as the locus of the centers of the maximal disks that are contained within the shape. Among several methods of skeleton extraction, we use a fast two-pass algorithm [6] to compute the skeleton using a distance transform. By limiting the minimal size of maximal disks multiple skeletons with different scales are obtained. For each skeleton an invariant feature vector is computed and the set of feature vectors is registered to the database together with the image.

3 Invariant Features for Similarity Measure in Retrieval

Moment invariants are useful measures for 2-D shape matching. Moments are defined on a continuous image intensity function. For a discrete binary image, a simple approximation is possible using summation operation. For each region, a 7-D feature vector of seven moments is computed where each moment is invariant to translation, scale changes and rotation for the case of continuous functions. The invariants are still strictly invariant under image translation and are approximately invariant under rotation and scale changes due to sampling, digitizing, and quantizing of the continuous image for digital computation [7].

In the case of articulated objects such as human beings or animals, the shape transformation due to the motion of articulations causes the shape matching to an original shape to fail and the system may regard them as a different object. In our multi-level structure representation, the shape deformation of a deformable object due to a small articulation movement is less affected since scale reduced skeletons could be matched. The similarity between two feature vectors is computed as the Euclidean distance. Note that some values of feature vectors are quite small or vary a lot. So they need to be normalized for comparison.

4 Experimental Results and Conclusion

We tested the proposed method on several databases. Fig. 1 shows intermediate data for the invariant feature computation. Fig. 2 shows the multi-scale skeletons and their shape boundaries. For a query image the system retrieves the most relevant eight images from the database images. Fig. 3 shows two examples of image retrieval from a fish image database which was originally used in the work of Mokhtarian et al. [2]. The left-most images are the query images and the remains are the retrieved images in order of similarity measurements. The query processing time is less than one millisecond in most cases for the database of 1,100 animal images. For each query, there are only vector length operations for 1,100 feature vectors and one array sorting operation.

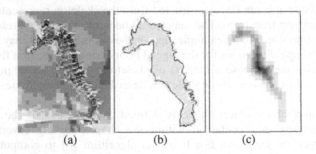

(a)   (b)   (c)

Fig. 1. (a) A sea horse image; (b) the region boundary; (c) the distance image

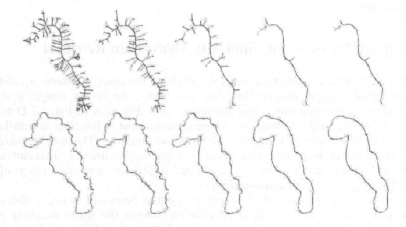

Fig. 2. Multi-scale skeletons (upper row) and corresponding region boundaries (lower row)

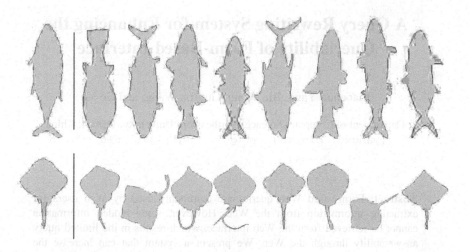

Fig. 3. Examples of image retrieval using the multi-scale skeleton feature vectors

This paper presented a shape-based image retrieval scheme which represents an object as a set of multi-scale skeleton structures. Invariant features which were obtained from multiple skeleton representations are insensitive to small boundary deformations. Hence the method overcomes the shape deformation of animated object. As future works of our research, we are developing a motion-based image segmentation algorithm which extracts objects in motion regardless of the complexity of the environment where the object is located in.

References

1. Sclaroff, S., Pentland, A.: Model matching for correspondence and recognition. IEEE Trans. Pattern Analysis and Machine Intelligence 17 (1995) 545–561
2. Mokhtarian, F., Abbasi, S., Kittler, J.: Robust and efficient shape indexing through curvature scale space. Proc. British Machine Vision Conf. (1996) 545–561
3. Celenk, M., Shao, Y.: Rotation, translation, and scaling invariant color image indexing. Storage and Retrieval for Image and Video Databases VII. SPIE 3656 (1999) 623–630
4. Ogniewicz, R.: Skeleton-space: a multiscale shape description combining region and boundary information. CVPR (1994) 746–751
5. Telea, A., Sminchisescu, C., Dickinson, S.: Optimal Inference for Hierarchical Skeleton Abstraction. IEEE ICPR (2004)
6. Arcelli, C., di Baja, G. S.: Euclidean skeleton via centre-of-maximal-disc extraction. Image and Vision Computing 11 (1993) 163–173
7. Teh, C.H., Chin, R.T.: On digital approximation of moment invariants. CVGIP 33 (1986) 583–598

A Query Rewriting System for Enhancing the Queriability of Form-Based Interface

Xiaochun Yang, Bin Wang, Guoren Wang, and Ge Yu

Department of Computer Science, Northeastern University, 110004, China
{yangxc, binwang, wanggr, yuge}@mail.neu.edu.cn

Abstract. Form-based Web queries are commonly used by Web users for extracting information from the Web. However, some hidden information cannot be retrieved from the Web interface, which results in the limited query answerability through the Web. We present a system that can increase the amount of information to answer users' queries. The design of our system includes (i) the introduction of a Web query rewriting model that handles any form-based query, and (ii) the evaluation of input queries using answers to previous, relevant queries. Experimental data shows that our query rewriting approach achieves more expected answers.

1 Introduction

With the popularity of the Internet, through a form-based Web query interface, most users can enter a query by filling in the contents or keywords of different fields (entries) specified in a form. We treat each field in any form as an *attribute descriptor*, whose content, along with the contents of other attribute descriptors, yield an input query. In some cases, a user cannot get expected answers to her query, a close examination, however, reveals that the result is existed. Therefore, using search engines exhibits the necessity of enhancing the mechanism in answering query straightly based on keyword search.

In this paper, we introduce an approach for enhancing the answerability of a form-based query with the intention to achieve high recall ratio [11] by considering the set of previous related queries and their answers and then rewriting the query according to these additional information. Using existing query rewriting techniques [1, 2, 5, 10, 12], it is required that the schema of the underlying database and mapping between the interface and the underlying database be known in advance; however, these constraints do not apply to our query rewriting approach. Query rewriting using views is one of the design issues in data management and is applicable for optimizing queries [4], maintaining physical data independence [9, 14], data integration [13], data warehouse[3], and designing Web-site query processing strategies [3, 15]. Some approaches for querying data from the Web is by using "database-like" query languages. Two types of these query languages have been proposed in the literature. One of them is structure-sensitive, i.e., the one that exploits structures of Web data. These languages include SQL-like WebSQL [7] and W3QS [6]. For WebSQL, however, the internal structure of data objects in hypertext documents is not implicitly

Z. Chen et al. (Eds.): ICADL 2004, LNCS 3334, pp. 462–472, 2004.

exploited at all or only limited extend is considered, and thus querying these documents using these languages is restricted.

Differ from typical query rewriting techniques, our rewriting approach works with form-based queries. We analyze previous submitted queries and their answers off-line and classify their answers into different clusters. Each of these clusters contains a set of records or documents and their linked pages extracted from answers to previous queries. Using the constructed clusters, we develop different query cases, each of which is a combination of a previous query and a set of knowledge that was learned from the corresponding query answers. We identify two kinds of knowledge: extracted knowledge and associated knowledge. *Extracted knowledge* is derived from keywords extracted from an answer to a previous query, whereas *associated knowledge* is inferred from the contents of attribute descriptors in the previous query and keywords extracted from its answers. We adopt information retrieval and data mining techniques in generating extracted knowledge and associated knowledge. According to extracted and associated knowledge, we create three rewriting rules to enhance query answerability. Since different query cases are individually treated as different training sets and their data are extracted from previous query answers, extracted and associated knowledge could conflict within a query case or among different query cases.

The rest of this paper is organized as follows. In Section 2, we introduce our Web query rewriting system, and propose a Web query rewriting model. In Section 3, we present two kinds of knowledge, extracted knowledge and associated knowledge. In Section 4, we derive three rewriting rules based on query cases. Furthermore, we will justify the set of knowledge selection strategies. In Section 5, we discuss our experimental data, and in Section 6 we provide concluding remarks.

2 Web Query Rewriting System

We present the overall architecture of the proposed query rewriting model (as shown in Figure 1) that can be adopted by any query processing system with a form-based query interface. By using a Web query engine, a user query Q can be submitted through the interface I and its corresponding answer R can be retrieved. In our model, a *query processor* (as shown in Figure 1) is attached to the original query system. The query processor rewrites Q to Q' and proceeds the rewritten query to obtain the corresponding answer R', where $R' \supseteq R$ and R is the answer to Q.

We use *conjunctive query expressions* in expressing user queries submitted to a form-based Web interface. The logical view of a *conjunctive query q* is presented in the form $q(X):- g_1(X, v_1), \ldots, g_n(X, v_n)$, where $g_1, \ldots, g_n$ are attribute descriptors specified under a query interface, variable X denotes a record included in the answer to q extracted through the interface, and constants $v_1, \ldots, v_n$ are values specified under the corresponding attribute descriptors respectively. The union of a set of conjunctive query expression, each of which has the same head predicate, denote union predicate. Note that join predicates, which denote attribute descriptors, are expressed by multiple occurrences of the same variable X. An attribute descriptor can only appears at most one time in a conjunctive query expression. The query expression $Q(X):- title(X, "answer queries"), year(X, "2000")$ denotes the query that request all the publications in the year of 2000 with the tile "answer queries."

Figure 1 depicts the reference architecture of our Web query processing system. The system consists of four major components: *Query-Answer-Analyzer, Query-Reformulator, Case-Manager*, and *Answer-Compositor*, where

- *Query-Answer-Analyzer*. The analyzer creates query cases using previous queries and their respective answers. Query cases are maintained in the *Knowledge-Manager*, which includes a database, to facilitate the construction of rewritten queries. The sub-components of this analyzer include
  - *filter* that eliminates "non-representative" words, such as 'the,' 'a,' and 'for,' in a previous query answer.
  - *classifier* that classifies the filtered "representative" words into clusters, each of which contains closely-related answers to previous queries.
  - *extractor* that uses words in a cluster to identify a previous query answer that is relevant to the keywords.
  - *miner* that constructs the relationships among contents of attribute descriptors and extracted words from previous queries and their results. The constructed relationships assists the system in rewriting queries.

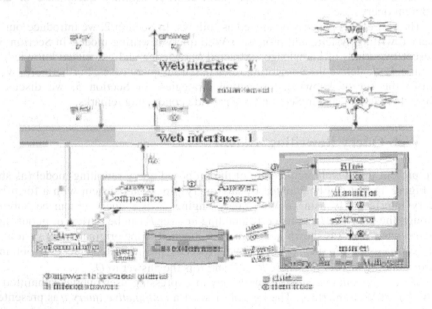

Fig. 1. The System architecture

- *Query-Reformulator*. The reformulator analyzes a form-based user query Q and rewrites Q using query cases to generate an optimized Q, called Q', such that Q' can retrieve more relevant answers to Q.
- *Case-Manager* manages a case base, which is a collection of query cases. Using *indexes*, which link each query answer to its query case, the manager can retrieve their corresponding (previous) query answers from the *Answer-Depository*, which

can be used by the Answer-*Compositor* to generate the enhanced query answers to a given query Q.

3 Learning from Previous Query Answers

Different from the traditional query rewriting approaches, our query rewriting approach rewrites a query using knowledge, *extracted knowledge* and *associated knowledge*, that have been inferred from previous query answers.

3.1 Knowledge for Answering Queries

In this section, we discuss two types of knowledge, which are *extracted knowledge* and *associated* knowledge. Extracted knowledge is generated from linked information of previous query answers. Extracted knowledge is presented as a set of triple $< t, k, r_{ID}>$, where t is a root tree that captures the result of a query q, k is an assigned data value of an internal node, which is the keyword of the subtree rooted by the internal node, and r_{ID} is the data value of a leaf node, which is the identifier of the corresponding extracted record. If there is a path between k and r_{ID} in t, then record r_{ID} can be expressed by k, which is denoted by *path* (k, r_{ID}). The values of all internal nodes in between can be described by the meaning of r_{ID}.

According to the extracted knowledge, we determine any implicated constraints between attribute descriptors of a Web interface and existing clusters, if there are any. We call these implicated constraints extracted knowledge. The definition of associated knowledge between attribute descriptors and extracted keywords is captured by the following expression: $r[q(X)]: g_1(X, v_1), \ldots\ldots, g_n(X, v_n) \rightarrow keyword(X, v)$ where r is the associated knowledge name, the predicate *keyword(X, v)* forms the tail of the associated knowledge which indicates that record X is related to the keyword v in the previous query $q(X)$.

3.2 Mining Knowledge

Previous query answers can be treated as a set of training data. Based on a set of training data, the QueryAnswerAnalyzer mines extracted knowledge and associated knowledge for rewriting a new query.

Mining Extracted Knowledge. To generate extracted knowledge from linked information, we construct a similarity matrix, $Sim_{m \times n}$, of all the records in a query answer. The similarity matrix is a $m \times n$ matrix in which each value $S_{i,j}$ in $Sim_{m \times n}$ is the similarity value between records r_i and r_j. $S_{i,j}$ is calculated according to the vector-space model [11]. As shown in Figure 1, this step includes filtering stem and stop words, in addition to calculating the term weight of each term in a filtered record by using TD-IDF [11]. The similarity value calculation is given in Equation 1, where $w_{k,i}$ is the term weight of term k in record r_i.

$$s_{i,j} = \frac{\sum_{k=1}^{m} w_{k,i} \times w_{k,j}}{\sqrt{\sum_{k=1}^{m} w_{k,i}^2} \times \sqrt{\sum_{k=1}^{m} w_{k,j}^2}} \tag{1}$$

We categorize records in a query answer into several clusters. Note that a similarity matrix can be converted into an undirected graph, where each record is denoted as a vertex in the graph, and $s_{i,j}$ ($1 < i, j \leq n$) is denoted as an edge between vertices r_i and r_j. If $s_{i,j} \neq 0$ in $Sim_{m \times n}$, an edge is constructed from r_i to r_j to capture the similarity between r_i and r_j. We use a threshold value λ to determine which vertices are assigned to which clusters by removing paths that do not satisfy the constraint $s_{i,j} \geq \lambda$ in $Sim_{m \times n}$.

Mining Associated Knowledge. Mining associated knowledge based on a set of training data is an area of study in machine learning. The query answer of each case can be treated as training data. In our rewriting approach, we derive the associated knowledge by using *decision trees* since they provide good performance in discrete-valued applications, and a decision tree is a robust method to noisy data and capable of learning disjunctive expressions [8]. We adopt the C4.5rules for mining associated knowledge between attribute descriptors and query cases.

4   Web Query Rewriting Using Learned Knowledge

Now, we describe how the learned knowledge can be used for rewriting a user query to enhance the answerability of a query through the query interface.

4.1   Query Rewriting Rules

Since any previous query and its derived knowledge constitute a query case, we consider three types of rewriting rules (*Rule 1, Rule 2, and Rule 3*) in determining the rewriting rules from a set of query cases to yield a new query as defined below.

Rule 1 can be applied to answer a new query based on existing query cases. Given a new query Q, the rewriting expression of Q is a query over a set of query cases. Since any extracted, linked information of a materialized query answers must have been analyzed in advance, it is possible to retrieve all the closely related answers to the query. Rule 1 is suitable for archiving data where the incremental problem is easy to be maintained, e.g., retrieving data to be included in the archives. Rules 2 and 3 are established for retrieving query answer through a query interface. According to the extracted knowledge in a query case, Rule 2 uses keywords of nodes in the extracted knowledge to rewrite a query, whereas Rule 3 rewrites queries by using associated knowledge between attribute descriptors posted under the interface and the corresponding keywords in a query case.

Given a query Q with a number of attribute-value pairs $AV = \{\langle a_1, v_1 \rangle, \langle a_2, v_2 \rangle, \ldots, \langle a_m, v_m \rangle\}$, where a_i ($1 \leq i \leq n$) is an attribute descriptor in the query interface, v_i ($1 \leq i \leq m$) is the filled-in value of a_i, and $Q(X) :- a_1(X, v_1) \ldots, a_m (X, v_m)$ is a rewriting rule.

Rule 1. *Rewriting a query over query cases.* Given a set of query cases $Q_{case} = \{Q_{c1}, Q_{c2}, Q_{c2}\}$ and a query Q, the following steps derive the answer to Q using Q_{case}.

Step 1. For each query case $c_{qi} \in C_q$ $(1 \leq i \leq n)$, where c_{qi} has attribute-value pairs $AV_{qci} = \{\langle g_{ci1}, v_{ci1}\rangle, \langle g_{ci2}, v_{ci2}\rangle, \ldots\ldots, \langle g_{cik}, v_{cik}\rangle\}$, the following cases derive different conjunctive expressions of q':

1.1 If $AV_q \in AV_{qci}$, then a conjunctive expression $q_{i'}$ over c_{qi} is q_{ci}, i.e.,

$$q_{i'}(X) :- q_{ci}(X)$$

1.2 Else according to the previous query q_{ci} over c_{qi}, $q_{i'}$ is

$$q_{i'}(X) :- \bigwedge\nolimits_{\langle g, v\rangle \in AVq-AVqci,\ \langle g, v'\rangle \notin Avqci} g(X, v) \wedge q_{ci}(X)$$

Step 2. The rewritten query of q is $q'(X) :- \bigcup_{i=1}^{n} q_i'(X)$

Rule 2. *Rewriting queries over a query interface using extracted knowledge.* Given a Web interface I and a query case Q_c over I, query Q is rewritten according to the following condition:

– If $\forall \langle a, v\rangle \in AV - AV_{cj}$, $\exists \langle a, v_l\rangle \in AV_{cj}$ such that $k_1, \ldots\ldots, k_n$ are child nodes of $v - v_l \in t(Q_c)$, i.e., $k_i \in t(Q_c).child(v - v_l)$, $1 \leq i \leq n$, then $k_1, \ldots\ldots, k_n$ can be used to rewrite Q over I to yield the new query Q'.

$$Q'(X) :- \bigcup\nolimits_{ki \in t(Qc).child(v-vl)} (a(X, v-v_l+k_i), \bigwedge \langle a', v'\rangle \in AV, a' \neq a\ a'(X,v'))$$

Rule 3. *Rewriting queries over a query interface using associated knowledge.* Given a Web interface I, a query case Q_c over I with attribute-value pairs $AV_c = \{\langle a_1, v_1\rangle, \langle a_2, v_2\rangle, \ldots\ldots, \langle a_p, v_p\rangle\}$ and a set of associated knowledge $R_1, R_2, \ldots\ldots, R_k$ in Q_c such that $R\_i[Q(X)]$ is $a_{i,1}(X, v_{i,1}), \ldots\ldots, a_{i,u}(X, v_{i,u}) \rightarrow keyword(X, k\_i)$, the following steps rewrite Q:

– If $\forall \langle a, v\rangle \in AV - AV_{cj}$, $\exists \langle a, v_l\rangle \in AV_{cj}$ such that $v - v_l = k_i$, then the query rewriting expression Q' of Q over I is $Q'(X) :- a_{i,1}(X, v_{i,1}), \ldots\ldots, a_{i,u}(X, v_{i,u}), Q_c(X)$

Finally, a rewritten query $Q'(X)$ for $Q(X)$ is the union of the three rewriting expressions discussed above, i.e., $Q'(X) = Q_1'(X) \cup Q_2'(X) \cup Q_3'(X)$.

4.2 Selection of Learned Knowledge

Note that extracted knowledge and associated knowledge are derived from different query cases. Since different query cases are treated as different training sets and different query cases have different biases of data, the learned knowledge can be conflicted with one another among different cases and the combination knowledge could be more useful than any individual knowledge in a case. Hence, it is necessary to provide a selection criteria to determine what knowledge should be selected to construct rewriting expressions for a new query. The problem of knowledge selection includes selection of knowledge within a case and inter cases.

Selection of Knowledge Within a Case. In a query case, we classify the relationships among associated knowledge as *mutual benefit*, *conflict*, and *unrelated relationships*.

– *Mutual* benefit *relationship.* If keywords $k_i = k_j$, then R_i and R_j have mutual benefit relationship.
– *Conflict relationship.* If $k_i \neq k_j$, and k_i is the ancestor node of k_j in the extracted knowledge $t(Q_i)$, then R_i and R_j have conflict relationship.

– Unrelated *relationship*. If $k_i \neq k_j$, and the common ancestor of k_i and k_j is the root node of extracted knowledge $t(Q_i)$, then R_i and R_j have unrelated relationship.

We use probability $P_{Qi(X)}(R_i)$ to express the accuracy of each associated knowledge R_i that satisfies all the records related to keyword k_i in a query case $Q_i(X)$. If R_i and R_j have conflict relationship in query case $Q_i(X)$ and $P_{Qi(X)}(R_i) > P_{Qi(X)}(R_j)$, R_i is selected to construct the rewriting expression with respect to a new query. Otherwise, if R_i and R_j have mutual benefit relationship, we can combine them into one associated knowledge. By using the *probability theorem*, the probability of R in query case $Q_i(X)$ is shown in Equation 2.

$$P_{Q_i}(R) = P_{Q_i}(R_i \vee R_j) \times P_{Q_i}(R_i) + P_{Q_i}(R_j) - P_{Q_i}(R_i) \times P_{Q_i}(R_j) \tag{2}$$

Solving Inconsistence of Knowledge Inter-Cases. The inconsistence of associated knowledge created from different cases can be conflicted with each other because they are mined from different cases with different set of training data. We classify the inconsistence between associated knowledge into four categories which are *target conflict*, *source conflict*, *source containment conflict*, and *source overlap conflict*. Furthermore, *source overlap* can be classified as source-overlap conflict with the same target and source-overlap conflict with different targets.

– *Target* conflict. Given associated knowledge from query cases Q_1 and Q_2, if $k_1 \neq k_2$, then $R_1[Q_1(X)]$ and $R_2[Q_2(X)]$ are target conflict with each other.

Associated knowledge mined from individual query case is the main reason of target conflict. Different query cases are treated as different training data sets. If the training data set cannot represent the whole hypothesis, e.g., data in the underlying data source, the associated knowledge cannot represent the associated knowledge in the underlying data source. Therefore, target conflict could be derived.

– *Source* conflict. Given associated knowledge from query cases Q_1 and Q_2, if $a \neq b$, then $R_3[Q_1(X)]$ and $R_4[Q_2(X)]$ have source conflict with each other.
– *Source* containment *conflict*. Given associated knowledge from query cases Q_1 and Q_2, $R_5[Q_1(X)]$: $a(X,v_a) \rightarrow$ keyword(X,k_1) source contains $R_6[Q_2(X)]$: a (X, v_a), b(X,v_b) $\rightarrow$ keyword(X,k_1).
– *Source*-overlap *conflict*. Source overlap is classified as *source overlap conflict with the same target* and *source overlap conflict with different targets*.

In order to handle the above conflicts, we propose a generic selection method: Given two associated knowledge R_i from query case $Q_1(X)$ and R_j from query case $Q_2(X)$, the probabilities of R_i and Rj that independent to any query cases are given in Equation 3, where $P(R_i)$ is the probability of R_i that is independent to any query cases. The rule with higher probability is selected to construct the query rewriting expression.

$$R_i[Q_1(X)]: a_{i1}(X,v_{i1}),\ldots\ldots, a_{i1}(X,v_{im}) \rightarrow \text{keyword}(X,k_i)$$
$$R_j[Q_2(X)]: a_{j1}(X,v_{j1}),\ldots\ldots, a_{j1}(X,v_{jn}) \rightarrow \text{keyword}(X,k_j)$$

$$P(R_i) = P_{Q_i}(R_i) \times \prod_{a_{jl} \neq a_{ih}, v_{jl} \neq v_{ih}, l=1, h=1}^{l=n, h=m} P_{Q_j(X)}(a_{ih}(X, \neg v_{ih}) \mid k_j) \tag{3}$$

5 Experimental Data

Our proposed system is suitable for enhancing documents retrieval through form-based Web interface because it uses item trees and inferred rules to derive the implicate constraints of the retrieved documents. To better evaluate the effectiveness and efficiency of our query rewriting system, we have tested a range of queries on it, which includes the following two aspects.

5.1 The Effectiveness of the System

In this section, a series of experiments were conducted to evaluate the proposed approach and the related issues were studied. The documents used in the experiment come from ACM SIGMOD Anthology. We use five queries to evaluate our approach, which are $Q_1(A)$:- title(A, "transaction"), $Q_2(A)$:- title(A, "index"), $Q_3(A)$:- title (A, "transaction model"), $Q_4(A)$:- title (A, "index schema"), and $Q_5(A)$:- title(A, "object-oriented"). The following parameters for evaluating our approach are listed in Table 1.

Table 1. The parameters for evaluating the approach

$|R|$	Number of *correct* answers to the query in a sampling document collection.
$|I|(|C|)$	Number of answers retrieved by Web interface (our system).
$|R_I'|(|R_c'|)$	Number of *correct* answers retrieved by Web interface (our system).
$P_I(P_c)$	Precision ratio using Web interface.
P_c	Precision ratio using our system.
R_I	Recall ratio using Web interface.
R_c	Recall ratio using our system.
F_I	Harmonic mean using Web interface.
F_c	Harmonic mean using our system.

The comparison results are summarized in Table 2. We discuss the experimental results of the test queries below.

Applying our rewritten Q_1 (i.e., Q_1'), and the only incorrectly retrieved article, "A New Framework For Itemset Generation," published in Proceedings of PODS'98, introduces a framework for generating itemsets based on a large database of *sale transactions*, which are different from *database transactions*.

Using Q_2', twelve relevant articles were retrieved. Applying Rule 3 based on the representative keywords and using the mapping rule r(A):- title(A, "tree")→ item (A, "index"), Q_2 is rewritten as Q_2' (A):- title (A, "tree"), for example, to obtain a relevant article, "I/O Complexity for Range Queries on Region Data Stored Using an R-tree," which is one of articles not retrieved by direct mapping. Both direct mapping and direct mapping, however, failed to retrieve the article "Finding data in the neighborhood," published in Proceedings of VLDB'97, because each term in the title of the article is *nonrepresentative*.

In retrieving answers to the rewritten Q_5 (i.e., Q_5'), we missed one of the relevant articles "Concurrent Garbage Collection in O2," published in Proceedings of VLDB'97, since we did not treat "O2" and "object-oriented database" as synonyms, which was overlooked by us. Our approximate mapping approach also missed another relevant article to the rewritten Q_5 "Data Manager for Evolvable Real-Time Command and Control System," published in Proceedings of VLDB'97, since the article is classified as a "distribute management" article. Compared with direct mapping, however, approximate mapping performs significantly better.

Table 2. The comparison results

Query	$|R|$	$|I|$	$|R_I'|$	$|P_I|\%$	$|R_I|\%$	$F_I\%$	C	R_C'	$P_C\%$	$R_C\%$	$F_C\%$
Q_1	47	31	31	100	66	79.5	48	47	97.9	100	98.9
Q_2	54	29	29	100	53.7	70	53	49	98.1	92.5	95.2
Q_3	12	6	6	100	50	66.7	12	12	100	100	100
Q_4	20	10	10	100	50	66.7	15	15	75	75	85.7
Q_5	27	12	10	83.3	44.4	57.9	28	23	85.2	85.2	83.6

5.2 Effectiveness of the Rewriting Rules

To verify the effectiveness of using the three types of rewriting rules, Rule 1, Rule 2, and Rule 3 in Table 3, we modified the system so that it can be configured to apply only one type of rewriting rule in the process of query rewriting.

Table 3. The results of applying Rule 1, Rule 2 and Rule 3

Type	$|R|$	$|C|$	$|R_C'|$	P_C	R_C	F_C
$Rule_1$	56	25	25	100%	44.6%	61.8%
$Rule2$	56	18	18	100%	32.1%	48.6%
$Rule3$	56	28	11	39.3%	19.6%	26.2%
$Total$	56	60	48	80%	85.7%	82.8%

Type	$|R|$	$|I|$	$|R_I'|$	$|P_I|$	R_I	F_I
$Interface$	56	19	19	100%	33.9%	50.6%

It can easily been seen that when our query rewriting system employs both rewriting rules, it provides the best performance. To analyze the reasons for the poor performance of using only one type of rewriting rules, we considered different rewriting rules in Table 4. Note that the larger the size of query cases, the higher the performance is anticipated when the rewritten queries are constructed by Rule 1 since Rule 1 constructs rewritten queries straightly based on the answers stored in the *Answer-Depository* (in Figure 1), and that causes the precision of answers to each rewritten query derived by Rule 1 to be high. On the other hand, the recall ratio is low when Rule 1 is used by itself because the answers to a previous query are a small subset of all the articles of the underlying data source. Rule 3, however, can handle this problem since each inferred rule derived from previous queries can further be used to retrieve all relevant articles in the underlying data source. It is not required to have a large number of query cases if we rewrite queries using Rule 3. Furthermore, using Rule 3 for query rewriting increases the recall ratio.

Table 4. Comparison only using one of the rules

Type	$|R|$	$|C|$	$|R_c'|$	P_c	R_c	F_c
$Rule_1$	18	11	11	100%	61.1%	75.9%
$Rule2$	18	8	7	87.5%	38.9%	53.8%
$Rule3$	18	10	3	30%	16.7%	21.4%
$Total$	18	18	17	88.8%	94.4%	91.5%
Type	$|R|$	$|I|$	$|R_I'|$	$|P_I|$	R_I	F_I
Interface	18	10	9	80%	44.4%	57.1%

6 Conclusions

Our query rewriting system has been implemented as a tool for mining information from an unknown data source through Web interfaces. Furthermore, the experimental data shows that our case-base query rewriting method can enhance the answerability of the Web queries and achieve high recall ratios. The main contributions of our work include (i) proposing a simple model for querying Web hypertext data, (ii) using previous answers to determine what relevant query answers should be, and (iii) presenting a new query rewriting approach that can retrieve query answers with high recall ratio through a query interface.

References

1. S.Abiteboul, L.Segoufin, and V.Vianu. Representing and querying XML with incomplete information. InProceedings of PODS 2001, pages 40–50, May 2001.
2. F. N. Afrati, et al,. Generating Efficient Plans for Queries Using Views. In SIGMOD, 2001.
3. G. M. Bierman. Extracting Structured Data from Web Pages. In Proc of SIGMOD Conference 2003, pages 337–348, 2003.
4. S. Chaudhuri et al. Optimizing queries with materialized views. In ICDE, 1995.
5. G. Grahne and A. Thomo. Query containment and rewriting using views for regular path queries under constraints. In Proc. of PODS 2003, pages 111–122, 2003.
6. D. Konopnick, et al. W3QS: A Query System for the World-Wide Web. In VLDB, 1995.
7. A. O. Mendelzon and T. Milo. Formal Models of Web Queries. In PODS, 1997.
8. T. M. Mitechell. Machine Learning. McGraw-Hill, 1997.
9. L. Popa, A. Deutsch, et al. A chase too far? In Proceedings of SIGMOD, 2000.
10. R. Pottinger and A. Levy. A Scalable Algorithm for Answering Queries Using Views. In Proc. of VLDB, pages 484–495, 2000.

11. R. Raeza-Yates et al. Modern Information retrieval. ACM Press, 1999.
12. J. D. Ullman. Information Integration Using Logical Views. In ICDT, 1997.
13. C. Yu and L. Popa. Constraint-Based XML Query Rewriting For Data Integration. In Proc. of SIGMOD Conference 2004, pages 371–382, 2004.
14. X. Yang, C. Li. Secure XML Publishing without Information Leakage in the Presence of Data Inference. In Proc of VLDB Conference, 2004.
15. X. Yang, G. Wang. Mapping Referential Integrity Constraints from Relational Databases to XML. In Proc of WAIM Conference, pages 329–342, 2001.

Digital Library Retrieval Model Using Subject Classification Table and User Profile

Seon-Mi Woo and Chun-Sik Yoo

Division of Electronic and Information Engineering, Chonbuk National University,
664-14 1ga Duckjin-Dong, Duckjin-Gu, Jeonju, Jeonbuk, 561-756, Republic of Korea
{smwoo, csyoo}@chonbuk.ac.kr

Abstract. Existing library retrieval systems present users with massive results including irrelevant information. Thus, we propose SURM, a Retrieval Model using "Subject Classification Table" and "User Profile," to provide more relevant results. SURM uses Document Filtering technique for the classified data and Document Ranking technique for the non-classified data in the results from keyword-based retrieval system. We have performed experiment on the performance of filtering technique, updating method of user profile, and document ranking technique with the retrieval results.

1 Introduction

Because existing information retrieval systems are using the exact matching technique with user's query, they present users with massive results including irrelevant information. So, a user spends extra effort and time to get the relevant information to one's need in the results. Therefore, research about user-centered information retrieval is gone to offer the retrieval convenience to user.

In this paper, we propose SURM, a Retrieval Model using Subject Classification Table and User Profile, to provide more relevant results. SURM uses document filtering technique for the classified data and document ranking technique for the non-classified data in the results from the keyword-based retrieval system. Filtering technique uses SCT (Subject Classification Table), and ranking technique uses user profile and SVD (Singular Valued Decomposition). SCT consists of "classification number list" created by librarian. The values of MARC (MAchine Readable Cataloging)'s 090 field of data are compared with SCT according to user's subject. Then data matched with 090 fields of MARC are included in the area about subject classification numbers. User profile consists of log-in information, subjects, term array, and preference vector according to the interest field of him. And the user profile is updated by "user access" and "user relevance feedback". The latent structures of documents in same domain are analyzed by SVD, a statistical analysis method used in Latent Semantic Indexing. And the rank of documents is decided by comparison of user profile with document analyzed on the basis of relevance. We have performed experiments on the performance of filtering technique, method of user profile updating, and technique of document ranking with the results of information retrieval system used in digital library of our university.

Z. Chen et al. (Eds.): ICADL 2004, LNCS 3334, pp. 473–482, 2004.

2 Related Studies

2.1 User-Centered Information Retrieval

Researches for user-centered information retrieval has involved technique of document ranking [3], [7], [8], [11], technique of information filtering [5], [9], and the method to endow adaptation using machine learning theory [1], [7], [10]. Recently, the researches for filtering using statistical analysis are studied, and this method can find an relevant document that don't retrieved by an exact matching method. In this paper, we create subject classification table to filtering and create user profile to store user's preference. And we analyze documents by SVD for document ranking.

2.2 SVD (Singular Valued Decomposition)

To find relevance score of each document with regard to user's preference, LSA (Latent Structure Analysis) is used. Analysis of relationship of document is as follows (see *step 1~3*) [4].

Step 1. Makes a term-document matrix X, the values of matrix is term frequency.
Step 2. Decompose X into three matrixes (see formula 1).
Step 3. Does Reduced SVD (see formula 2).

$$X = T_0 S_0 D_0 \tag{1}$$

for, T_0 : orthogonal, $T_0' T_0 = I$, D_0 : orthogonal, $D_0' D_0 = I$,
S_0 : diagonal, D_0' : transpose of D_0

$$\hat{X} = T_0 S_0 D_0 \tag{2}$$

for, $\hat{X}$: analytic matrix (t×d), T : orthogonal, $T'T = I$ (t×k),
D : orthogonal, $D'D = I$ (t×d), S_0 : diagonal, (k×k),
k : reduced rank of matrix $(k \leq m)$.

Pseudo document is used to obtain the similarity between the user's preference and the retrieved documents. Pseudo document is variant form of a user profile (see formula 3). We use formula 4 to calculate the similarity between $\hat{X}$ and a pseudo document. Finally, similarity is relevance score (see formula 4). Formula 3 and 4 are defined in our previous study [7].

$$DP = P_i T_0 S_0^{-1} \tag{3}$$

for, P_i : preference vector of ith interest in user profile,
T_0 : orthogonal matrix by SVD,
S_0^{-1} : inverted matrix of diagonal matrix S_0 .

$$Rscore = ES^2 E' \tag{4}$$

for, E : reduced E_0 , E_0 : extended matrix combined D and DP.

3 Design of SURM

Retrieval flow of SURM (Retrieval Model using Subject classification table and User profile) proposed in this paper is shown in figure. 1.

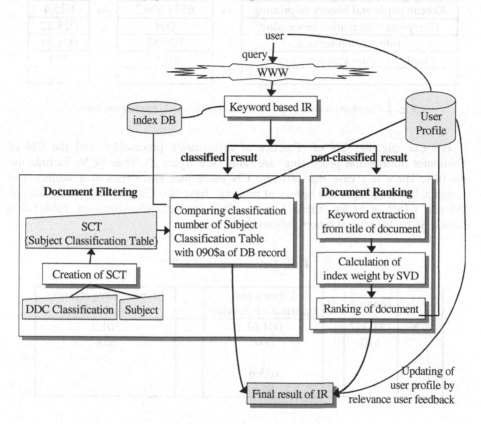

Fig. 1. Retrieval flow of SURM

We use filtering for classified data and we use document ranking for non-classified data in the results from the keyword-based retrieval system. Detailed explanation about method is described in next section.

3.1 Filtering of Classified Data

In case of classified documents among retrieved document, we offer documents that don't include irrelevant documents to user using SCT (Subject Classification Table).

First, a librarian selects CN (Classification Number) that correspond to the subject using DDC classification table. Figure 2 shows the process that librarian creates CN and SCNs (Subject Classification Numbers) belonging to the subject. We decide CN using classification system that is used in Chonbuk National University digital library. Then, we find numbers that is not overlapped in CN and we create SCNs.

Subject	CN	SCNs
Practice of information processing	004	004
History of library culture	020.9	020.9
Information document structure	025.3 / 025.4	025.3
Korean paper and history of printing	655 / 676.2	025.4
Computer information processing	004	025.52
Information service	025.52	001.61
Analysis of information system	001.61	384
:	:	:

(arrows: Subject → CN → SCNs)

Fig. 2. Creation process of SCNs about 'Library and information service'

For example, the CN of 'Practice of information processing' and the CN of 'Computer information processing' are same (see figure 2). Thus SCNs include the one 004. There is a case that different CN more than two exists to a subject. For example, "Korean paper and history of printing" have two CN(655 and 676.2), we put 655 and 676.2 in SCTs. Table 1 shows SCT (Subject Classification Table) that include SCNs for several school subject.

Table 1. An example of SCT

Subject	Nursing	...	Library and Information Service	...	Chemical engineering and technology
SCNs	131.322 610 :	...	001.61 004 : 655.6 951	...	301.3 628 :

The subject of user is stored in user profile. After compare SCNs about subject with classification number of record, we offer document that is included to SCT to user.

3.2 Ranking of Non-classified Document

In the case of non-classified document, we present documents according to the order similar to user's preference among retrieval result. Therefore, a user can reduce efforts that must examine all great many of retrieved result.

3.2.1 Creation and Updating Of User Profile

For document ranking, the preference of user should be reflected. We create user profile to reflect information of user. User profile consists of user ID, user password, subjects, term array, and preference vector. Term array and preference vector are constitute according to the subject. Term array is consisted of terms (extracted from title of the document) and preference vector stands for the user's preference to correspond to term array. The user's preference begins with 0 and represents a value between 0 and 1 accomplishing updating.

Updating by User's Access

When the user gives the importance to a specific term, he or she directly alters the value of the preference vector and thus reflects a user's preference.

Updating by User Relevance Feedback

By user's relevance feedback, user profile is modified. We define updating formula as follows (see formula 5 and formula 6).

i) Weight of term is high $(0.5 \le w_{ik})$

$$\vec{P}_i = \left| 2p_{ij} + (\sum_{k=1}^{n} w_{ik} / n) \right| j = 1,...,n \tag{5}$$

ii) Weight of term is medium $(0.2 \le w_{ik} < 0.5)$

$$\vec{P}_i = \left| p_{ij} + (\sum_{k=1}^{n} w_{ik} / n) \right| j = 1,...,n \tag{6}$$

for, D_i : ith relevant document by user evaluation,

w_{ij} : weight of jth term of D_i , $\vec{P}_i$: ith preference vector,

w_{ij} : weight of jth term of D_i , n : the number of term extracted

3.2.2 Weighting of Index

To find the relevance score of each document with regard to user's preference, we compute the weight of index by SVD. We explain analysis process by using documents in table 2. The query and the title of document are written in Korean originally. We transform it in English, so it maybe strange.

In analysis process, first we create term-document matrix X like figure 3; the value of cells be the term frequency. After matrix X is formed, it is decomposed into three matrixes to describe the characteristics of factor by formula 1. Then we can get T_0 (5×18), D_0 (5×5), and S_0 (5×5). To determine the analytic matrix $\hat{X}$, we accomplish the analysis using the representative matrix indicating tendency of values among results by SVD. That is, to reduce the dimension at the expression space, we execute reduced SVD by formula 2.

Matrix $\hat{X}$ is equal to matrix X approximately ($X \approx \hat{X} = TSD'$), though the rank of matrix is just reduced to k. We select one representative factor among a tendency of the documents and execute reduces SVD. The reason is that data to be analyzed are the retrieved document about a one subject of user. As a result of reduced SVD, we can have T (5×1), S (1×1), D(5×1), and D' (1×5), and we can obtain the final result, matrix $\hat{X}$ (18×5) by computing TSD' . The values of $\hat{X}$ indicate the degree that terms(18 rows) represent the document(5 columns). Because this paper is analyzed by one factor, the value of matrix $\hat{X}$ shows relevance of a user's demand, that is, a tendency being common to 5 documents.

Table 2. Retrieved result of query "evaluation system"

Doc	Title
D1	An implementation of the system for interactive web-based education and effect of learning achievement
D2	Design and implementation of the web-based computerized adaptive testing system
D3	A design and implementation of evaluation system for Web-based instruction
D4	Evaluation system of assembly efficiency of manual assembly process in the shoes manufacturing
D5	Web-based evaluation system for level learning of computer practicum

$$X = \begin{bmatrix} 0\,1\,0\,0\,0 \\ 0\,0\,0\,0\,1 \\ 1\,0\,0\,0\,0 \\ 0\,1\,1\,0\,0 \\ 1\,0\,0\,0\,0 \\ 1\,1\,1\,0\,0 \\ 0\,0\,0\,1\,0 \\ 0\,0\,0\,0\,1 \\ 1\,1\,1\,1\,1 \\ 1\,1\,0\,0\,1 \\ 0\,0\,0\,0\,1 \\ 0\,0\,0\,1\,0 \\ 0\,0\,0\,1\,0 \\ 0\,0\,0\,1\,0 \\ 1\,1\,1\,1\,1 \\ 0\,0\,1\,0\,1 \\ 0\,1\,0\,0\,0 \\ 1\,0\,0\,0\,0 \end{bmatrix} \qquad \hat{X} = \begin{bmatrix} 0.255\ 0.270\ 0.223\ 0.165\ 0.235 \\ 0.222\ 0.235\ 0.194\ 0.144\ 0.205 \\ 0.241\ 0.255\ 0.210\ 0.156\ 0.222 \\ 0.465\ 0.492\ 0.407\ 0.301\ 0.430 \\ 0.241\ 0.255\ 0.210\ 0.156\ 0.223 \\ 0.705\ 0.747\ 0.617\ 0.456\ 0.652 \\ 0.156\ 0.165\ 0.136\ 0.101\ 0.144 \\ 0.222\ 0.235\ 0.194\ 0.144\ 0.205 \\ 1.083\ 1.147\ 0.947\ 0.701\ 1.001 \\ 0.717\ 0.759\ 0.627\ 0.464\ 0.663 \\ 0.222\ 0.235\ 0.194\ 0.144\ 0.205 \\ 0.156\ 0.165\ 0.136\ 0.101\ 0.144 \\ 0.156\ 0.165\ 0.136\ 0.101\ 0.144 \\ 0.156\ 0.165\ 0.136\ 0.101\ 0.144 \\ 1.083\ 1.147\ 0.947\ 0.701\ 1.001 \\ 0.433\ 0.458\ 0.378\ 0.280\ 0.400 \\ 0.255\ 0.270\ 0.223\ 0.165\ 0.235 \\ 0.241\ 0.255\ 0.210\ 0.156\ 0.222 \end{bmatrix}$$

Fig. 3. A term-document matrix   **Fig. 4.** Result of analysis $\hat{X}$

3.2.3 Ranking of Document

We decide the rank of the document using user profile and the analysis result in the previous stage. Pseudo document is used to obtain the similarity between the user's preference and the retrieved documents. Pseudo document is variant form of user profile. Thus pseudo document is computed by formula 3. If the values of preference vector are (0.8 0.5 0.9 0.2 0.8 0.1 0 0.6 0.1 1.0 0 0 0 0 0.9 0.9 0.9 0.95), we can get pseudo document DP (1×5) by formula 3 (see figure 5).

$$DP = \begin{bmatrix} 0.4173117 \end{bmatrix}$$

$$DR = \begin{bmatrix} 4.311 & 4.564 & 3.770 & 2.789 & 3.983 \\ 4.564 & 4.831 & 3.991 & 2.953 & 4.217 \\ 3.770 & 3.991 & 3.297 & 2.439 & 3.483 \\ 2.789 & 2.953 & 2.439 & 1.804 & 2.577 \\ 3.983 & 4.217 & 3.483 & 2.577 & 3.681 \end{bmatrix}$$

Fig. 5. A pseudo document   **Fig. 6.** Similarity between preference of user and documents

We use formula 4 to compute the similarity between $\hat{X}$ and a pseudo document. In figure 6, the values in italics show the similarity among documents, that is, relevance degree, so the rank of the document is decided in order D2, D1, D5, D3, and D4.

4   Experiments and Evaluation

We performed experiment on the DB of our university digital library (search engine: Fulcrum 3.x, DBMS: Oracle) and 50 researchers (10 researcher in proportion to 5 subjects) participate in our experiments. We estimate performance our technique by filter ratio that precision ratio is modified (see formula 6). And terms are extracted from a title of document using Automatic Indexing System [2] developed by our research team, and we use SAS 6.12 and IML (Interactive Matrix Language) for statistical analysis.

4.1   Performance of Filtering

To evaluate our filtering method, we modify 'precision ratio' to 'filter ratio' (see formula 7), and modify 'snobbery ratio' to 'filter snobbery ratio' (see formula 8).

$$filter\ ratio = \frac{the\ number\ of\ relevant\ document\ of\ filtering}{the\ number\ of\ relevant\ document} \quad (7)$$

$$filter\ snobbery\ ratio = \frac{the\ number\ of\ relevant\ document\ of\ filtering\ be\ missing}{the\ number\ of\ relevant\ document} \quad (8)$$

Figure 7 shows the result of filtering experiment. As a result of this experiment, the average of filter ratio is maximum 98% and minimum 96%. Filter snobbery ratio occurs some but, is less than user's effort that user must examine retrieved results.

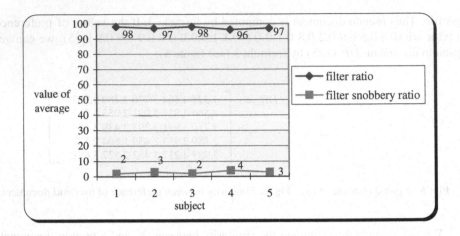

Fig. 7. Performance of filtering

4.2 Performance of Ranking

In the performance evaluation of document ranking, we perform experiment and evaluations in two ways; one way is to consider the user's preference and another way is to estimate a technique of document ranking. We use the relevance ratio to evaluate performance of ranking [7] (see formula 9). In figure 8, folded-line indicates the average relevance ratio for 5 subjects. As a result of this experiment, we can reflect the user's preference sufficiently in the small number of retrieved tries and performance is also over 98%. And the relevance ratio was over 90% by 6 times updating. If "updating by user's access" and "updating by user's feedback" are used together, the relevance ratio was over 90% by 3 times updating [see figure 9].

$$relevance\ ratio = \frac{\sum_{i=1}^{n} R_{score}}{\sum_{i=1}^{n} R_{max}} \times 100 \qquad (9)$$

for, R_{score} : relevance score estimated by user, [0..8],

R_{max} : a value of 8

n : the number of document belong in 10% of ranked document

After training 10 user profile in each subject at 20 retrieval tries, we decided the rank of documents. The result of experiment is presented in Table 3. We used formula 8, n is the number of document in interval of rank. For example, n belong in the 1st ~5th is 5 and n belong in the 11th ~20th is 10. As a result of this experiment, with regard to the result of the 1st~15th, the relevance ratio is over 97.8%, within 100th, the relevance ratio is over 90%.

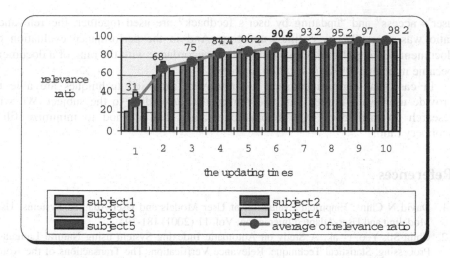

Fig. 8. Updating result of user profile by user relevance feedback

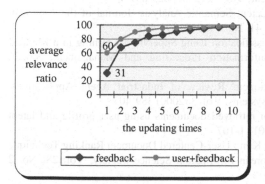

Fig. 9. Updating of user profile

Table 3. Relevance ratio per rank interval

order subject	15	30	100	200
subject 1	99	99	93	90
subject 2	98	97	91	89
subject 3	97	97	92	90
subject 4	99	97	90	89
subject 5	96	95	85	80
average	97.8	97	90.2	87.6

5   Conclusion and Future Works

In this paper we create SCT (Subject Classification Table) to filter classified document, and we constructed user profile to reflect the user's preference for document ranking of non-classified document. And we compute the weight of term using SVD in ranking process. In the performance evaluation of filtering, the filter ratio was over 98%, and the filter snobbery ratio was less then 4% (in 1st~50th ranked documents). In the performance evaluation of document ranking, we did experiment and evaluations in two ways; one way is to consider the user's preference and another way is to estimate a technique of document ranking. In the experiment of user profile updating, the relevance ratio was over 90% by 6 times updating. If "updating by user's access" and "updating by user's feedback" are used together, the relevance ratio was over 90% by 3 times updating. And in the performance evaluation of document ranking, the relevance ratio was in accordance with the rank of a document became maximum 99.4%(1st 30th ranking).

In case that many documents are retrieved, proposed techniques are able to provide users with filtered data and ranked data according to the subject. We will research on method of SCT automatic creation, and method to minimize filter snobbery ratio.

References

1. David N Chin : Empirical Evaluation of User Models and User-Adapted Systems, User Modeling and User-Adapted Interaction, Vol. 11 (2001) 181-194
2. Chun-Sik Yoo, et al.: A Study on Automatic Indexing System using Natural Language Processing, Statistical Technique, Relevance Verification, The Transactions of the Korea Information Processing society, Vol. 5, NO. 6 (1998) 1552-1562
3. Czeslaw Danilowicz, Jaroslaw Baliski : Document Ranking based upon Markov Chains, Information Processing and Management, Vol. 37 (2001) 623-637
4. Deerwester, Scott et. : Indexing by Latent Semantic Analysis, Journal of the American Society for information Sciences, Vol. 41, No .6 (1990) 391-407.
5. Mostafa, J., Lam, W. : Automatic Classification using Supervised Learning in a Medical 5Document Filtering Application, Information Processing and Management, Vol.36 (2000) 415-444
6. Parunak, H. Van Dyke : A Practitioners' Review of Industrial Agent Applications, Autonomous Agent and Multi-Agent Systems, Vol. 3 (2000) 389-407
7. Seon-Mi Woo : Ranking technique of retrieved documents using user profile and latent structure analysis, Ph. Doc. Thesis (2001) 1-107
8. Seon-Mi, Chun-Sik Yoo, Yong-Seong Kim : User-Centered Document Ranking Technique using Term Association Analysis, Korean Information Science Society, Vol. 28, No. 2 (2001) 149-156
9. Shepherd, Michael et. : The Role of User Profiles for News Filtering, Journal of the American Society for Information Science and Technology, vol.52, No.2 (2001) 149-160
10. Geoffrey I. Webb, Michael J. Pazzani, Daniel Billsus : Machine Learning for User Modeling , User Modeling and User-Adapted Interaction, Vol. 11 (2001) 19-29
11. Wechsler, Martin and Schauble, Peter : The Probability Ranking Principle Revisited, Information Retrieval, Vol.3 (2000) 217-227
12. Yung-Mi Jung, Iinformation retrieval, Gumi (1993)
13. Zukerman, Ingrid and Albrecht, David W : Predictive Statistical Models for User Modeling, User Modeling and User-Adapted Interaction, Vol. 11 (2001) 5-18

Hot-Spot Passage Retrieval in Question Answering

Jian Huang, Xuanjing Huang, and Lide Wu

Dept. of Computer Science and Engineering,
Fudan University, Shanghai, 200433, P.R. China
lukehj@vip.sina.com
{xjhuang, ldwu}@fudan.edu.cn

Abstract. Question Answering has been the recent focus of information retrieval research; many systems just incorporate a search engine as a black box and most effort has been devoted to the question analyzer and the answer identifier. In the context of QA, however, passage provides an ideal medium between the document collection and an exact answer. And passage retrieval is a finer-grain approach than the traditional document retrieval both for the answer identifier and a human reader. In this paper, distinctions are first made between document retrieval and passage retrieval. And the Hot-Spot Passage Retrieval algorithm, which takes into account the measures of *blurred BM25*, *coverage* and *height*, is examined in detail. For evaluation, an isolated test is conducted and the algorithm gains 18.3% better answer redundancy and 4.8% better coverage rate than Okapi's original passage retrieval algorithm.

1 Introduction

In traditional Information Retrieval tasks, a human user feeds in a keyword-based query to the search engine, which returns a ranked/unranked list of relevant documents (depending on the underlying IR model). The recent Question Answering (QA) task is much more user-friendly and 'intelligent' in that, the user asks a natural language question and the QA system returns a single terse answer, minimizing human efforts for forming good queries and extracting an exact answer.

Reviewing the existing QA systems, most of them can be decomposed into three components: a question analyzer, a search engine and a post-retrieval answer identifier [1;2;3;4]. The search engine, located in the middle, has fundamental impact on the overall performance of the system: when its precision is low, the answer identifier would suffer from false or irrelevant snippets; when its recall is low, it would again suffer from low answer redundancy to justify a correct answer.

Briefly, passage retrieval better addresses the QA problem than the traditional document retrieval in the following aspects:

First, traditional retrieval methods take into account the query terms while other terms are seldom considered. The underlying idea is that, the more the document and query terms co-exist and the closer they are, the higher the score. But for QA, *surrounding texts* are very important: query terms are good hints for where the answer locates, but we expect to locate answer terms which are typically surrounding query terms but they themselves are not query terms.

Z. Chen et al. (Eds.): ICADL 2004, LNCS 3334, pp. 483–490, 2004.

Second, a document retrieval engine that retrieves a collection of full-length documents is inappropriate since that would be a heavy load upon the answer identifier, which typically incorporates a variety of advanced NLP techniques. Even when response time is less important in experimental environments, the answer identifier implicated in answer redundancy would suffer from low signal-to-noise rate.

Third, a 'bad' document might contain a specific part that provides an explicit answer to the question, though the document as a whole is about something else; also, a 'good' document might be too general to extract an answer, or it is too 'hard' to do so due to the elaborate language typically used in newspapers.

What's more, in [5], Lin argued that providing a context instead of an exact answer would be much easier for users to justify a correct answer. A highly relevant passage would be suitable for this case.

Given all the reasons above, we desire a finer-grain approach than document retrieval in the QA context, and passage retrieval provides a good intermediate between a document and an exact answer.

Passage retrieval has been looked into in the past few decades, but its main idea is substituting or combining the best passage weight with the document weight, aiming at either improving document retrieval or lessening human effort for finding the supporting documents [6;7]. Passage retrieval has not been widely studied in detail until 2002, when a few TREC[1] participants tried some density-based features to boost the passage retrieval results [8]. For example, IBM's passage retrieval algorithm [4] calculates five measures: the matching words measure, the mis-match words measure, the dispersion measure, the cluster words measure and the thesaurus measure.

In this work, we propose three features that are specifically related to the QA task in the hot-spot passage retrieval algorithm. For evaluation, we conduct an isolated test that tries to untangle the efficacy of the passage retrieval algorithm with the QA system.

2 Hot-Spot Passage Retrieval – The Algorithm

In this section, we discuss our Hot-Spot Passage Retrieval (HSPR) algorithm with its three measures: the blurred BM25 measure, the *height* measure and the *coverage* measure, and then we discuss how these measures relate to the QA task.

2.1 The Blurred BM25 Measure

Among many *tf-idf* (term frequency-inverse document frequency) weighing schemes, Okapi's BM25 term weighing scheme [7] represents the state of the art of in document retrieval. And it is paraphrased as follows:

---

[1] Beginning in 1999, the Text REtrieval Conference (TREC) of NIST (National Institute of Standard and Technology, U.S.A.) incorporates the Question Answering track, evaluating systems that retrieve small snippets of text, which contained an answer for open-domain, closed-class questions. For example, the answer to the question 1898 "What city is Disneyland in?" could be Paris, Tokyo or Anaheim. Please refer to http://trec.nist.gov/ for details.

For a given term T_t that coexists with a query term in document D_s, it's given the *Robertson-Sparck Jones* weight (R and r being zero):

$$w_{s,t}^{(1)} = \log \frac{N-n+0.5}{n+0.5} \qquad (1)$$

In (1), N is the number of documents in the corpus; n is the document frequency. This formula can be regarded as the *idf* part.

And then a simplified BM25 weight is calculated for a term T_t:

$$w_{s,t}^{(2)} = w_{s,t}^{(1)} \frac{(k_1+1)tf}{k_1+tf} qtf \qquad (2)$$

In (2), *tf* is the term frequency and *qtf* is the corresponding query term frequency[2].

All above is adopted from traditional document retrieval, and we may substitute it with any other term weighing schemes. Next we'll define the blurred BM25 measure.

Term T_t is referred to as the hot-spot because it coexists with a query term. We choose a window of size τ with T_t being the centre. The surrounding term weights are blurred according to their distances with the hot-spot. That is, for a specific term T_u in the window with distance d to the hot-spot, it is given the following weight[3]:

$$w_{s,t,u}^{(3)} = w_{s,t}^{(2)} [k_2 - \log(1+d)]/k_2 \qquad (3)$$

Because there may be quite a few hot-spots near a term T_u, summing all these contributions gives term T_u the blurred BM25 weight:

$$w_{s,u}^{(4)} = \sum_{T_t} w_{s,t,u}^{(3)} \quad \text{where } T_t \text{ is a hot-spot} \qquad (4)$$

The blurred BM25 measure strengthens the weight of the hot-spot and the surrounding text, especially when query terms coexist in some part of the text; also, it implies the distance metric when blurring.

2.2 The Height Measure

When a window slides across a document, a sequence of terms $(T_i, T_{i+1}, ..., T_j)$ make up a window passage[4] $P_{i,j}$.

The measure of height is defined with respect to the passage window, as follows:

$$H_{i,j} = \max \{ w_{s,u}^{(4)} \} \quad \text{where term } T_u \text{ belongs to passage } P_{i,j} \qquad (5)$$

The quality of the passage $P_{i,j}$ is justified when there exists a great height in it: when more query terms coexist close to each other, they will reinforce one another's weights and the weights of the surrounding texts too, hence greater height is formed.

---

[2] k_1 is given Okapi's recommended value 1.2.

[3] As a matter of fact, k_2 is chosen $\log (1 + \tau)$ so that the scale factor is positive and less than one.

[4] Though one might suspect that a discourse passage provides natural semantic boundaries, [6] demonstrated that inconsistency of passage lengths by different writers could be a problem.

If a passage is about general terms, their weights will hardly overlap so we anticipate lower height. The height measure is a good measure for how specific a passage is about, with respect to the query.

2.3 The Coverage Measure

Although vector space model and probability model outperform traditional Boolean IR model, many QA systems still favor the Boolean model because it explicitly supports the Boolean operations. Yet it has its pros and cons: operator AND provides the most specific snippets but its recall is very low; operator OR retrieves even the most lenient snippets but it may result in low precision. To address such problems, the coverage measure goes between these two extremes and gives a numeric measure:

$$C_{i,j} = {nq_{i,j}} \Big/ {nq} \tag{6}$$

In (6), nq denotes the distinct query terms, and $nq_{i,j}$ denotes the distinct query terms that exists in the passage $P_{i,j}$.

Thus, the coverage measure takes the advantage of both the AND operator and the OR operator: it rewards the most specific snippets and punishes those with partial occurrence of query terms. This should help assuage the deficiency of the probability or vector space model in the context of QA.

2.4 Best Passage Selection and Passage Ranking

After the aforementioned measures are calculated, they are normalized and summed to get the weight of a window passage. To calculate the weights efficiently, a revised tournament algorithm is used and the complexity of the algorithm is $O(|N|*logk)$, where N is the number of words in the document, and k is the constant size of the passage. This is an improvement over Okapi's original passage retrieval algorithm, which according to [7] is $O(|A|^3)$, |A| being the number of the passages in the document.

In [8;9], Okapi's passage retriever suffers from extracting a single discourse passage from a document. Thus, it's reasonable to adopt two or a few more passages as candidates. But too many passages from a document could dominate the ensuing process. The passages are ranked by their final passage weight.

For human readers, it might be helpful to trim the beginning and the end of the best passages whose term weights are zero to lessen human effort.

3 Experiments and Evaluations

3.1 Test Set

For evaluation, part of the TREC's QA corpus (AQuaint1, New York Times 1998 to 2000, 1.5GB) was used for testing. 200 questions were taken from the TREC 2003's QA question set (question 2194 to 2393), and they were divided into six categories, as shown below[5].

---

[5] In [7], however, Okapi passage retriever has 3.5% average precision improvement over Okapi document retriever.

Table 1. Question classification and example questions

Question Type	Total	Example
People (P)	16	Who is Anwar Sadat? (Q2349)
Number (N)	43	How many times a day do observant Muslims pray? (Q2293)
Location (L)	26	What city hosted the 1936 Summer Olympics? (Q2344)
Time/Date (T)	16	When was the Titanic built? (Q2338)
Manner (M)	13	How did Harry Chapin die? (Q2335)
Noun Basic (NB)	37	What instrument did the jazz musician Art Tatum play? (Q2340)

To untangle to performance of the question analyzer and the passage retriever, the questions are fed in without any modification. To be objective, we used the standardized answers developed by TREC to match the 200 retrieved passages. Note that among the 200 test questions, only 151 have at least one standardized answer.

3.2 Test Metrics

In traditional IR, precision and recall are the most important metrics. In QA, however, answer redundancy should be of priority (Especially when supporting documents are few, redundancy is even more important than precision) [9; 10]. TREC uses the MRR and percentage of incorrect as the evaluation metrics, which reveal the overall performance of the QA system; however, we would like to know how the passage retriever alone performs in order to untangle the efficacy of other components.

Thus, in [9], two other metrics – *redundancy* and *coverage* – are advocated instead of the traditional precision and recall metrics for evaluating the performance of passage retrieval approaches.

These two metrics are adopted here for evaluation:

1. *Coverage Rate*. The proportion of the questions for which correct answers could be found among the passages retrieved.

2. *Redundancy*. The number of times answers exist per question.

These are neat measures for passage retrieval in the QA task: the coverage rate metric is the maximum possible rate for the answer identifier to extract an answer; the redundancy reveals the chance it can do so. So these measures provide an isolated approach to test the efficacy of the passage retrieval algorithm.

3.3 Test Results

The following figure shows a sample run, which should clarify the situation.

In Fig. 1, the dots denote the weight distribution and the horizontal line outlines the *height* measure in different positions; the two vertical lines are the boundaries of the best passage in the document, where concentrations of hot-spots are located and greatest height and coverage is achieved.

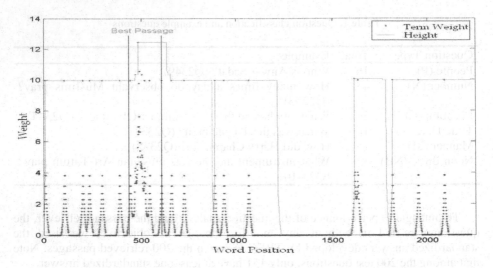

Fig. 1. A sample run against question 1122 "Where is the Grand Canyon" for the document NYT19980714.0362

In the results below, system A denotes Okapi's original passage retrieval engine, which represents the state of the art of document retrieval; system B denotes the HSPR algorithm that works upon Okapi's document retrieval engine.

First, for each question, a sign test is performed between the redundancies of the two systems to eliminate the situation that a single result dominates the overall one.

Table 2. Sign test for comparison of answer redundancy

Question type	#Total	#System A better	# Tie	#System B better
P	16	4	3	9
N	43	11	9	23
L	26	9	3	14
T	16	2	7	7
M	13	3	5	5
NB	37	13	12	12
(All)	151	42	39	70

According to Table 2, letting n_+=70 and n_-=42, we may perform a sign test whose result is p=0.0104, which is lower than the level of significance of 5%. Hence we reject the null hypothesis that the values larger and smaller than the medians are equally likely. In other words, system B performs significantly better than system A.

Moreover, HSPR did better than Okapi's original PR in all question categories except the Noun Basic type. This is within our expectation, because we expect an answer to the questions of people, number, location and time, to exist close enough to the hot-spot; while for the Noun Basic type which contains a variety of unclassified noun phrases, the assumptions in the HSPR might not work as well.

Table 3. Comparison of answer redundancy and coverage rate

Metrics	System A	System B	Percentage Improved
Redundancy	15.33	18.14	18.3%
Coverage Rate	80.9%	85.7%	4.8%

Table 3 reveals that the answer redundancy of the answer in the TREC QA corpus (i.e., AQUAINT) is not high compared to that of Google, and the HSPR algorithm should be helpful for the answer identifier with its 18 percent higher answer redundancy. Also, the 4.8 percent uncovered questions could be regained by the answer identifier, when HSPR was used as the passage retriever.

Table 4. Comparison of the contribution of the three features to the overall performance

Metrics	Height + Coverage	Blurred BM25 + Height	Blurred BM25 + Coverage	HSPR
Redundancy	17.01	17.44	17.50	18.14
Coverage Rate	80.1%	81.6%	82.3%	85.7%

From Table 4, it is straightforward to observe that removing any of the three features will cause the deterioration of performance. The most important feature here is the blurred BM25 feature.

4   Conclusion and Future Work

This paper investigates three features: the blurred BM25 measure, the coverage measure and the height measure. And these features are incorporated in the framework of the Hot-Spot Passage Retrieval algorithm. An isolated test is conducted to untangle the efficacy of the algorithm with other components of the QA system, and it achieves 18.3% better answer redundancy and 4.8% better coverage rate, than Okapi's original passage retrieval engine, as was shown in table 3.

In the future, we plan to investigate other features that could characterize the surrounding text. And pseudo-feedback using surrounding text terms might be helpful in PR. Also, better combination of the features should help boost the efficacy of the algorithm.

Acknowledgements

This work was partly supported by NSFC under contract number 60103014, as well as the 863 National High-tech Promotion Project (Beijing) under contract number 2001AA114120 and 2002AA142090.

This work was also supported by the Chun-Tsung Scholar program. We would like to thank Dr. Tsung Dao Lee, and to commemorate Jeannette Lee, for their long-standing devotion to university education in China.

References

1. Ellen M. Voorhees. Overview of the TREC 2003 Question Answering Track. In Proceedings of the Twelfth Text Retrieval Conference (2003)
2. Dan Moldovan, Marius Pasca, Sanda Harabagiu, and Mihai Surdeanu. Performance Issues and Error Analysis in an Open-Domain Question Answering System. ACM Transactions on Information Systems, Vol. 21, No. 2, April 2003, Pages 133-154 (2003)
3. Cody Kwok, Oren Etzioni and Daniel S. Weld. Scaling Question Answering to the Web. ACM transactions on Information Systems, Vol. 19, No. 3, July 2001, Pages 242-262 (2001)
4. Ittycheriah, M. Franz, and S. Roukos. IBM's statistical question answering system at TREC 10. In Proceedings of the Tenth Text Retrieval Conference (2001)
5. J. Lin, D. Quan, V. Sinha, K. Bakshi, D. Huynh, B.Katz and D.R. Karger. What makes a good answer? The role of context in question answering. In Proceedings of the Ninth IFIP TC13 International Conference on Human-Computer Interaction (2004)
6. James P. Callan. Passage-level evidence in document retrieval. In Proceedings of the 17th Annual International ACM SIGIR Conference on Research and Development in Information Retrieval (1994)
7. Stephen E. Robertson, S. Walker, S. Jones, M.Hancock-Beaulieu, and M.Gatford. Okapi at TREC-3. In Proceedings of the 3rd Text Retrieval Conference (1994)
8. Stefanie Tellex, Boris Katz, Jimmy Lin, Aaron Fernandes and Gregory Marton. Quantative Evaluation of Passage Retrieval Algorithms for Question Answering. In Proceedings of the 26th Annual International ACM SIGIR Conference on Research and Development in Information Retrieval (2003)
9. Ian Roberts and Robert Gaizauskas. Evaluating Passage Retrieval Approaches for Question Answering, University of Sheffield, U.K. (2003)
10. Susan Dumais, Michele Banko, Eric Brill, Jimmy Lin, Andrew Ng. Web Question Answering: Is More Always Better? In Proceedings of the 24th Annual International ACM SIGIR Conference on Research and Development in Information Retrieval (2002)

Query Formulation with a Search Assistant

Lin Fu, Dion Hoe-Lian Goh, Schubert Shou-Boon Foo, and Yohan Supangat

Division of Information Studies, School of Communication and Information
Nanyang Technological University, Singapore 637718
{p148934363, ashlgoh, assfoo}@ntu.edu.sg,
fyohans@pmail.ntu.edu.sg

Abstract. Information overload has led to a situation where users are swamped with too much information, resulting in difficulty sifting through the material in search of relevant content. In this paper, we address this issue from the perspective of collaboration in query formulation. We describe a search assistant that helps users with query formulation by finding related previously submitted queries through mining query logs. The search assistant runs as a reusable software component and can be incorporated into various search engines. We report our approach to designing and implementing the software and evaluation results.

1 Introduction

With the proliferation of online search engines, more attention has been paid to assist the user in formulating an accurate query to express his/her information needs. A number of approaches have been proposed. One approach is to use interactive query reformulation systems which aim to detect a user's "interests" through his/her submitted queries and give users opportunities to rephrase their queries by suggesting alternate queries.

There are two approaches to obtaining the recommended query terms: (1) through analyzing the results returned by the search engine corresponding to the initial query and using the most frequently occurring terms as recommendations [2, 3]; (2) through mining query logs and using similar queries issued by other users as recommendations, which is also known as collaborative querying [4, 8]. A common technique in collaborative querying is known as query clustering, which groups similar queries automatically without using predetermined class descriptions. A query clustering algorithm could provide a list of suggestions by offering, in response to a query Q, the other members of the cluster containing Q. In this way, there is an opportunity for a user to take advantage of previous queries and use the appropriate ones to meet his/her information need.

Since similarity is fundamental to the definition of a cluster, measures of similarity between two queries are essential to the query clustering procedure. We have developed a hybrid query similarity measure that exploits both the query terms and query results URLs. Experiments reveal that using the hybrid approach, more balanced query clusters can be generated than using other techniques. We have developed a search assistant which exploits the hybrid similarity measure to cluster

Z. Chen et al. (Eds.): ICADL 2004, LNCS 3334, pp. 491–500, 2004.
© Springer-Verlag Berlin Heidelberg 2004

queries and a graph visualization approach to represent the query clusters. The system gives users the opportunity to rephrase their queries by suggesting alternate queries.

The rest of this paper is organized as follows. In Section 2, we review the literature related to this work. We then present the design and implementation of the search assistant, the Query Graph Visualizer (QGV). Next, we report a user study to assess the usefulness and usability of the QGV. Finally, we discuss the implications of our findings for collaborative querying systems and outline areas for future work.

2 Related Work

There are several useful strands of literature that bear some relevance to this work. This section briefly reviews literature from these fields. Firstly, a survey of interactive query reformulation is provided as the background for this research. Next, a review of different query clustering approaches is presented.

Several techniques have been used to incorporate aspects of interactive query reformulation systems into the information retrieval process. One technique to obtain similar queries is to use terms extracted from the search results documents. Examples include HiB [3], Paraphrase [1] and Altavista Prisma [2], which parse the list of result documents and use the most frequently occurring terms as recommendations. Another approach is collaborative querying. Related queries (the query clusters) may be calculated based on the similarities of the queries in the query logs [9] which provide a wealth of information about past search experiences. The system can then either recommend the similar queries to users [9] or use them as expansion term candidates to the original query to augment the quality of the search results [5]. Here, calculating the similarity between different queries and clustering them automatically are crucial steps.

Traditional information retrieval research suggests an approach to query clustering by comparing query term vectors (content-based approach) [12]. Raghavan and Sever [11] determine similarity between queries by calculating the overlap in documents returned by the queries (results-based approach). Fitzpatrick and Dent [7] further developed this method by weighting the query results according to their position in the search results list. Glance [9] uses the overlap of result URLs as the similarity measure instead of the document content.

3 Query Graph Visualizer: A Search Assistant

We have designed a search assistant, the Query Graph Visualizer (QGV) based on the query clusters generated using a hybrid query similarity measure [8]. In our system, the query clusters can be explored using a graph visualization scheme.

3.1 System Architecture

Figure 1 sketches the architecture of the QGV. After capturing a new query, the system will identify related queries and use them as recommended queries to users.

The recommended queries are displayed in HTML format, similar to [1, 2, 5]. Users may further explore the recommended queries by visualizing the query clusters as a graph which contains the initial query and recommended queries. The QGV is designed to be an independent agent and can be incorporated into different information retrieval systems.

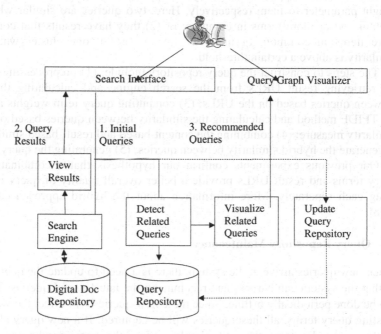

Fig. 1. Architecture of the collaborative querying system

It can be seen from the architecture that there are three essential processes to accomplish collaborative querying. The first is the query repository construction procedure which involves query cluster generation. The second process is the maintenance of the query repository. The third process is the query recommendation phase that includes related query detection and query graph visualization.

3.2 Query Repository Construction

As mentioned previously, the content-based approach uses overlap between query terms as the similarity measure to cluster the queries. However the content-based approach might not be appropriate for query clustering since most queries submitted to search engines are quite short [13, 14]. Thus query terms can neither convey much information nor help to detect the semantics behind them since the same term might represent different semantic meanings, while on the other hand, different terms might refer to the same semantic meaning. For the results-based approach, the same document in the search results listings might contain several topics, and thus queries with different semantic meanings might lead to the same search results. Thus, we hypothesize that using both query terms and the corresponding results may compensate for the drawbacks inherent in each method. The hybrid approach is a linear combination of the content-based and results-based approaches [8]. The effect of each individual approach on the hybrid approach can be controlled by assigning a weight parameter to them respectively. Here, two queries are similar when (1) they contain one or more terms in common; or (2) they have results that contain one or more items in common. Further, two queries are in one cluster whenever their similarity is above a certain threshold.

The steps to construct the query repository include: (1) preprocessing the queries; (2) retrieving result URLs from the search engine and calculating the similarity between queries based on the URLs; (3) computing query term weights according to the TFIDF method and calculating the similarity between queries based on the cosine similarity measure; (4) combining the content-based and result-based similarity values to generate the hybrid similarity between queries; (5) generating the query clusters.

Our previous experiments confirm our hypothesis that a combination of both query terms and result URLs provide a better overall quality of query clusters than using each separately. More information about the hybrid approach can be found in [8].

3.3 Query Repository Maintenance

When new queries arrive at the system, there is a need to update the query repository so that the system can harness and recommend the latest useful queries. This process can be done periodically offline. Since these new queries will affect the weights of the existing query terms, all these queries will be captured. If a new query already exists in the query database, then we simply update the corresponding query weights (TFIDF) and similarity values. For those that are unique, the new queries incorporated into the query database similar to the query repository construction process (see Section 3.2).

3.4 Query Recommendation

This process involves identifying related queries in the query repository constructed in the previous step and visualizing the related queries.

3.4.1 Detecting Related Queries

Given a query submitted by a user, we search the query repository for related queries and then recommend these to the user. Here, a recursive algorithm is implemented to search for query clusters in the query repository with the initial query regarded as the root node. First, the system will detect the query cluster G(Qi) containing the initial query Qi. Given the definition of a query cluster (Section 3.2), all its members are directly related to Qi. Therefore G(Qi) can be regarded as the first level in the graph structure of all queries related to Qi, as shown in Figure 2. Besides the query cluster G(Qi), the system will further find query clusters containing the members of G(Qi). For example since Q1 is a member in the cluster G(Q1), the system will locate the query cluster G(Q1) which forms the second level of the graph structure as shown in Figure 2. This recursive process will stop at the user-specified maximum level to be searched. In our algorithm, the default maximum value is 5 which means the algorithm will only detect the top five levels of query clusters related to the root node. Thus the final set of related queries to Qi might go beyond the members within G(Qi), giving a range of recommended queries directly or indirectly related to Qi. If a query is not found in the repository, the system will split the query terms and provide statistical information on each individual term. For example, for the query "data mining", the QGV will tell the user how many queries are related to the term "data" and the term "mining". At the same time, the query repository will be updated with this new query.

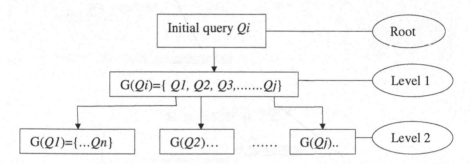

Fig. 2. Detecting related queries

3.4.2 Query Cluster Visualization

Our system, the QGV, displays query clusters in a graph (Figure 3). The graph edges show the relationship between two graph nodes, with the value on the edge indicating the strength of the relationship. For example, 0.1 on the edge between the nodes "data mining" and "predictive data mining" indicates the similarity weight between these two nodes is 0.1. In addition, the system offers a control tool bar to manipulate the graph visualization area including zooming, rotating and locality zooming. The zooming function allows users to shrink or enlarge the graph visualization area. The rotating function allows users to view the visualization area from different directions. Finally, locality zooming refers to the number of levels of related queries to be displayed.

By right clicking on an individual node, a popup menu appears, offering a variety of options. Firstly, users can use the selected query node and post it to a search engine (e.g. the Digital Library at Nanyang Technological University, Google, etc.). Recall that the QGV is running as an independent agent and can be incorporated into various search engines. Secondly, users may use this query to carry out a new search across the query repository and locate queries related to the selected one. Further, users can expand and collapse each query node on the graph. The QGV is implemented using "Touchgraph" which is an open source component to visualize information in graph formats (http://toughgraph.sourceforge.net).

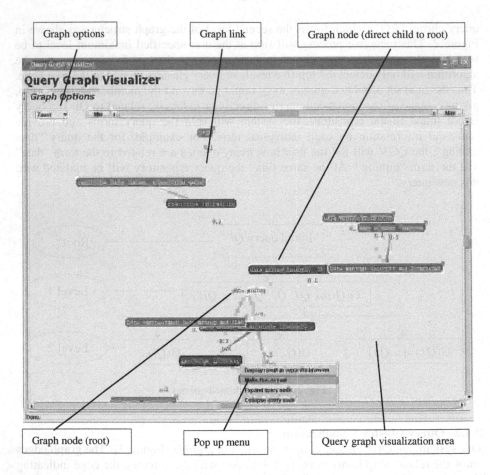

Fig. 3. Query graph visualizer

4 Evaluation

An evaluation was conducted on the QGV through a questionnaire in a controlled environment to assess its usefulness and usability. Here, we adopt Nielsen's heuristic evaluation approach [10]. This technique is used to find usability problems by getting a small number of evaluators to examine an interface and judge its compliance with ten recognized usability principles. The goal is to obtain the most useful information for guiding re-design with the least cost. In this section, we report our evaluation design and results.

4.1 Evaluation Design

Twelve participants were involved in this evaluation. Among the twelve, seven participants have a Bachelor's degree and five subjects have a Master's degree. Seven participants had a computer science background, four were from various areas in engineering and one was from communication studies. All of participants used computers everyday and said they had good skills in using online search engines.

The twelve participants were randomly divided into two groups of six participants each. Group A used the QGV to finish two search tasks while group B used the Google search engine to finish the same tasks as group A. Participants in group A were given a ten minute introduction to the QGV followed by a practice session before carrying out the tasks. Participants in group B were introduced to the QGV after they finished the tasks using Google and asked to try the system. The first task was to "find information on a semantic web seminar held in 2002 which discussed and explored various rule system techniques that are suitable for the web". The second task was to "find information about a web project which aims to represent mathematical documents in a form understandable by humans and interpretable by machines on World Wide Web". The time taken to accomplish the tasks was recorded. At the end of the evaluation, the participants were asked to complete a preference questionnaire on the QGV.

4.2 Evaluation Results

Table 1 shows a noticeable difference between groups in the time required to complete the tasks accurately. Participants in group A exhibited a major reduction in terms of average time to complete the tasks. This suggests that the QGV helped the participants find the desired information more quickly than Google alone. In other words, it appears that the QGV can help users formulate better queries by harnessing other information seekers' knowledge and reduce the time needed to sift through search result documents in search of relevant content.

Table 1. Average Time to Complete Tasks for Each Group

	Group A	Group B
Task 1	3 min	13.6 min
Task 2	3 min	23.4 min
All tasks	6 min	37 min

With regard to the usability issue, we evaluated the QGV in terms of Nielsen's 10 heuristic principles. In our evaluation, each heuristic principle is reflected by one or more questions concerning the design of the QGV. Each question is rated along a five-point scale – "strongly disagree", "disagree", "neutral", "agree" and "strong agree". Due to space limitations, we only report the number of participants who rank "agree" or "strongly agree" (see Table 2). As shown, the QGV satisfies most of ten heuristic principles according to our participants. For example, in "visibility of system status", 10 participants agreed that the status bar at the bottom was informative enough to reflect the action status of the system. As far as "consistency and standards" is concerned, 10 participants were comfortable with the graphic and layout design in the QGV and agreed that the font size, color, buttons, text box and popup menu were consistent; etc. The results thus indicate that the QGV performs well in terms of usability issues.

Table 2. Heuristic Evaluations Result Summary

Heuristic principles	Corresponding questions	Number of participants who rank "agree" or "strongly agree"
Visibility of system status	The status bar at the bottom has enough information to reflect the action status of the system.	10
Match between system and real world	The language used in the system is phrased in Standard English instead of technical terms.	10
	The language used in the system is easy to understand.	10
User control and freedom	The zoom graph menu function under the graph navigation option is easy to use.	12
	The rotate graph menu function under the graph navigation option is easy to use.	8
	The locality graph menu function under the graph navigation option is easy to understand and useful in reducing the complexity of graphical display.	6
	Overall, it is easy and convenient to navigate within the query graph.	10
Consistency and standards	The font size, type, color, buttons, text box and dropdown box menu are consistent.	10
	There are informative tool tips on each button, text box and dropdown box control menu.	12
Error prevention	The system prompt when a searched query list cannot be found is useful.	8
Recognition rather than recall	The graph option dropdown box containing zoom, rotate and locality messages are easily understood	8
	The Query Node click and drag feature is noticeable.	10
	The Query Node popup menu that appears when right-clicking is noticeable.	10
	The use of gradation color to differentiate query node level and edge weight helps the user understand the relatedness between query nodes better.	10
Flexibility and efficiency of use	In overall, the Query Graph Visualization system speeds up the search process compares to other conventional search engines, eg. Google.	12
Aesthetic and minimalist design	The screen elements are not cluttered and placed appropriately on the screen.	10
	The dropdown boxes, buttons and text labels provide adequate information to perform the task.	12
Help user recognize, diagnose and recover from errors	The "Query search not found" error message displayed is helpful in rectifying any errors	8
Help and documentation	This system can be operated and navigated with little / no instruction and help documentation.	2

Responses towards the overall impression of the QGV show that the positive features of the QGV focused on the recommended query lists which gave users more ideas on what query terms to use, and the graph visualization scheme which specifies the relationship between queries with varying weights. Participants also liked the options to control the visualization area. For example, one participant said that the QGV was "really useful in speeding up the searching process and to better understand the relation between queries, since the weights between queries are clearly shown. It also made searching process more fun because of the graph and the zooming features. The system is also easy to use and the functions are self explanatory, which can be followed with minimum instruction". The negative comments go to the lack of detailed documentation which was needed to support the successful use of the QGV by some participants. This was due to the fact that some technical terms were used in the system, such as "weight", "locality zooming". Further, three participants complained that the QGV was time consuming to load and execute because it needed to be downloaded into client's browser before it could be run. Despite the fact that there are some drawbacks in the current version of QGV, all 12 participants expressed strong interest in it, and indicated that they would use the QGV if it became available in the future.

5 Conclusions and Future Work

In this paper, we introduced a search assistant, the QGV, which utilizes the hybrid query similarity measure to generate query clusters for each submitted query. Our work can contribute to research in collaborative querying systems that mine query logs to harness the domain knowledge and search experiences of other information seekers found in them. Firstly we propose a hybrid query clustering approach which differs from [7, 9, 11] since all them do not use the query content itself. Secondly, we employ a graph-based approach to visualize the recommended queries which differs from [1, 9] since all them only adopt text or HTML to display the recommended queries.

Our evaluation examined the effectiveness of the QGV from the perspectives of usefulness and usability. The time to complete tasks and the subjective preferences of the participants were used as metrics in our study. Results show that the system offers a viable option for online information seeking. The QGV appears to help users complete information seeking tasks faster and our participants expressed a preference for using the system. However the QGV might not be useful for all types of information seeking tasks since the tasks in our study are open-ended and required some amount of exploration. Whether users can benefit from the QGV for well-defined search tasks remains unknown.

In addition to the initial development in this work, alternative approaches to detecting related queries will also be attempted. In the existing algorithm, if a new query does not exist in the query repository, the QGV will display statistical information regarding with each term in the query. Possible solutions to improve this basic approach include using other query clustering algorithms, such as K-means, to detect related queries. Further, our evaluation also highlighted several areas for further improvement. For example, because the graph-based mode of interaction is unfamiliar to many users, online help will need to be incorporated into the QGV. Finally, due to the small sample size of this initial evaluation, our findings cannot be generalized. Instead, a comprehensive evaluation will be conducted to further assess the performance and effectiveness of the QGV involving more users and a greater variety of task types.

Acknowledgements

This project is partially supported by NTU with the research grant number: RCC2/2003/SCI. Further we would like to express our thanks to the NTU Library and the Centre for Information Technology Services for providing access to the queries.

References

1. Anick, P.G. & Tipirneni, S. (1999) The paraphrase search assistant: Terminological feedback for iterative information seeking. *Proceedings of SIGIR 99,* 153-161.
2. Anick, P. G. (2003) Using terminological feedback for web search refinement: A log-based study. *In proceedings of SIGIR'03,* 88-95.
3. Bruza, P.D., Dennis, S. (1997) Query reformulation on the Internet: Empirical data and the Hyperindex search engine. *Proceedings of the RIAO 97 Conference,* 488-499.
4. Churchill, E.F., Sullivan, J.W. & Snowdon, D. (1999) Collaborative and co-operative information seeking, *CSCW'98 Workshop Report* 20(1), 56-59.
5. Crouch, C.J., Crouch, D.B. & Kareddy, K.R. (1990) The automatic generation of extended queries, *Proceedings of the 13th Annual International ACM SIGIR Conference,* 269-283.
6. Ester, M., Kriegel, H., Sander, J., Xu, X., (1996) A density-based algorithm for discovering clusters in large spatial databases with noise. *Proceedings of second International Conference on Knowledge Discovery and Data Mining,* 226-231.
7. Fitzpatrick, L. & Dent, M. (1997). Automatic feedback using past queries: Social searching? *Proceedings of SIGIR'97,* 306-313.
8. Fu, L. Goh, D. & Foo, S. (2003). Collaborative querying through a hybrid query clustering approach. *Proceedings of Sixth International Conference of Asian Digital Libraries,* 111-122.
9. Glance, N. S. (2001). Community search assistant. *Proceedings of Sixth ACM International Conference on Intelligent User Interfaces,* 91-96.
10. Nielsen, J. 1992. Finding usability problems through heuristic evaluation. *In Proceedings of the ACM CHI'92 Conference,* 373-380.
11. Raghavan, V. V., & Sever, H. (1995). On the reuse of past optimal queries. *Proceedings of the Eighteenth International ACM SIGIR Conference on Research and Development in Information Retrieval,* 344-350.
12. Salton, G. & Mcgill, M.J. (1983). *Introduction to Modern Information retrieval.* McGraw-Hill New York, NY.
13. Silverstein, C., Henzinger, M., Marais, H., & Moricz, M. (1998) Analysis of a very large Altavista query log. *DEC SRC Technical Note 1998-14.*
14. Wen, J.R., Nie, J.Y., & Zhang, H.J. (2002) Query clustering using user logs. *ACM Transactions on Information Systems,* 20(1), 59-81.

Semantic Query Expansion Based on a Question Category Concept List*

Hae-Jung Kim, Bo-Yeong Kang, Seong-Bae Park, and Sang-Jo Lee

Department of Computer Engineering, Kyoungpook National University, Sangyuk-dong,
Puk-gu, Daegu, 702-701, Korea
hjkim325@hanmail.net

Abstract. When confronted with a query, question answering systems endeavor to extract the most exact answers possible by determining the answer type that fits with the query and the key terms used in the query. However, the efficacy of such systems is limited by the fact that the terms used in a query may be in a syntactic form different to that of the same words in a document. In this paper, we present an efficient semantic query expansion methodology based on a question category concept list comprised of terms that are semantically close to terms used in a query. The semantically close terms of a term in a query may be hypernyms, synonyms, or terms in a different syntactic category. The proposed system first constructs a concept list for each question type and then builds the concept list for each question category using a learning algorithm. When a new query is given, the question is classified into the node in question category, and the query is expanded using the concept list of the classified category. In the question answering experiments on 42,654 Wall Street Journal documents of the TREC collection, the traditional system showed in 0.223 in MRR and the proposed system showed 0.50 superior to the traditional question answering system. The results of the present experiments suggest the promise of the proposed method.

1 Introduction

Question answering (QA) systems assign relevance degrees to words, paragraphs or clauses based on a given query, and then provide answers ranked according to relevance. However, the efficacy of such systems is limited by the fact that the terms used in a query may be in a syntactic form different to that of the same words in a document. Consider, for example, the following query and sentences:

- Who is the inventor of paper?
- S1: C is the inventor of knives
- S2: A devised paper

When analyzing this query, the traditional QA system would classify the sample query into "NAME" as a subcategory of "PERSON", and then keywords such as

---

* The research was supported by Kyoungpook National University Research Fund, 2004.

Z. Chen et al. (Eds.): ICADL 2004, LNCS 3334, pp. 501–509, 2004.
© Springer-Verlag Berlin Heidelberg 2004

"inventor" and "paper" would be extracted. Therefore, the items that are used in answer analysis would be the category "Person_Name" and the keywords "inventor" and "paper". In this example, however, S1 contains the keyword "inventor" and S2 contains the keyword "paper", and hence their relevance degrees for the query will be the same. As a result, we cannot extract exact answers from sentences S1 and S2, even though S2 is obviously the correct answer. Moreover, even if we expand the keywords to "inventor", "discoverer", and "paper", the ranking of the sample sentences will remain unchanged because the term "devise" in S2 belongs to a syntactic category different to that of "inventor" in the query. However, if we were to expand the keyword "inventor" to include related words such as "discoverer", "devise", "invent", "develop", and "creator", then we could represent the same concept over a range of syntactic and semantic categories, and thereby reduce the number of answer candidates and extract more exact answers.

In this paper, we present an efficient semantic query expansion methodology based on a question category concept list comprised of terms that are semantically close to terms used in a query. The concept list associated with a particular query includes most possible representations of the concept of the question. The semantically close terms of a term in a query may be hypernyms, synonyms, or terms in a different syntactic category. The proposed system first constructs the question category of each question type after analyzing question patterns and information request type for 117 who_questions in TREC collection, and then builds the concept list for each question category using a learning algorithm. When a new query is given, the question is classified into the node in question category, and the query is expanded using the concept list in the classified category. This paper is organized as follows. Section 2 describes related work on question categorization and expansion. In Section 3, we present our concept list based semantic query expansion methodology, and in Section 4, we present the results of experiments using the proposed methodology. Our conclusions are given in Section 5.

2 Previous Work

Answer type of QA system can be called semantic category of the query that a user requested, and it had an influence on a QA system performance enhancement to express answer type as the small classification of semantic category[1-7].

Cardie et al. [1] modified the traditional approach to question type classification by dividing the answer type into 13 subcategories, thereby creating more specific question categories. This modification significantly improved the performance of the traditional QA system. Hovy et al. [2] proposed an automatic learning method on the regular pattern of question types on Web, but the expansion range of this method was very narrow. Kazawa et al. [3] developed a QA system called SAIQA-e and applied support vector machines (SVM) to named entity recognition that is used for answer type classification in the system.

Prager et al. [4] proposed an alternative methodology for finding the semantic class that covering all possible semantic classes that may be used in a query; specifically, they determined a synset of question terms by using an inventory such as a hypernym tree from WordNet. However, their method entails the derivation of the synset-class mapping, which is a labor-intensive task that results in incomplete coverage.

In contrast to the above methods, which focus on question category construction for the answer type annotation and answer type matching when calculating the relevance of documents to a particular query, we have devised an efficient question category construction method for semantic query expansion. In our method, the question category contains a concept list that can be used to expand query terms into semantically close terms.

3 Semantic Query Expansion Based on a Question Category Concept List

Queries in the form of information requests by users typically have sentence patterns that are much less complex than those of the documents being searched. In addition, the type of information that a user is attempting to find through an information request can be categorized. We exploit these characteristics of user queries to create an efficient semantic query expansion methodology based on question category concept lists.

3.1 System Description

The proposed method first constructs the question category of each question category by analyzing the question sentence patterns and query information type, which will be explained in the following Section 3.2.1, and then builds the concept list for each question category using a learning algorithm. If a new query is given, the question is classified into the node in question category, and the query is expanded using the concept list in the classified category.

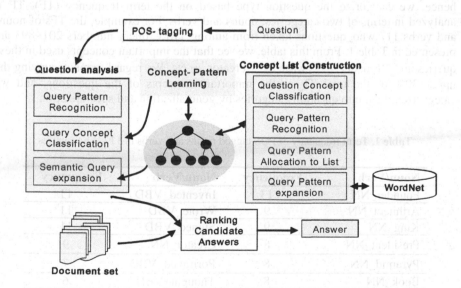

Fig. 1. Overall System Configuration

Figure 1 shows a flow diagram of the overall system configuration. The system contains three main components: concept list construction, concept learning, and question analysis modules. In the question category concept list construction module, the concept list of each question category is constructed for semantic query expansion. First, the question categories are established according to important question concepts by the question concept classification module. Then, the concept list for each question category is constructed by query pattern recognition, allocation to a list, and expansion by WordNet. In the concept pattern learning module, the system builds the constructed concept list of each question category using a learning algorithm. Finally, in the question analysis component, the system classifies the given query into the corresponding question category based on learned data, and then expands the query into the semantically close terms using the concept list of a classified category node.

3.2   Question Category Concept List Construction

To construct the question category concept list for a given user query, we extract the pattern of the question and augment the question terms with frequently used concept keywords of the question. For example, " inventor" , " invent" , " devise" , " develop" , " create" , and " creator" fall within various syntactic categories, but may all be in the same concept list constructed by query pattern recognition, allocation to a list, and expansion by WordNet.

3.2.1   Question Category Classification

In formulating the proposed method, we assume that the important concept of a question will be embodied in the terms that are most frequently used in the question; hence, we categorize the question type based on the term frequency (TF). TF is analyzed in terms of two categories, nouns and verbs. For example, the TFs of nouns and verbs 117 who_questions taken from among TREC query numbers 201~893 are presented in Table 1. From this table, we see that the important concepts used in these queries are " founder" , " write" , " creator" , etc. We regard terms occupying the upper 30% of the total TF as the important concepts of the questions, and we categorized them into question categories by generalization and specialization.

Table 1. Term frequency of POS tagged nouns and verbs in 117 Who-queries

Noun/Verb	Frequency	Noun/Verb	Frequency
Founder_NN	13	Invented_VBD	11
Arthitect_NN	9	Wrote_VBD	11
King_NN	9	Signed_VBD	11
President_NN	8	Creator_NN	9
Pyramid_NN	8	Portrayed_VBD	7
Book_NN	8	Thought_VBD	6

The question categories based on TF are shown in Table 2. The queries in the Who_question query set usually ask the name of the person related with a certain event; thus we can more specifically categorize these queries into subcategories such as " INVENTOR" , " WRITER" and " LEADER" by examining the important concepts of the queries based on TF.

Table 2. Question subcategories for Who-terms

Question Category			Examples
W h o	PERSON	INVENTOR	Who invented television?
	_NAME	KILLER	Who killed Martin Luther King?
		WRITER	Who wrote the Farmer's Almanac?
		LEADER	Who is the Prime Minister of Australia?
		PLAYER	Who is the fastest swimmer in the world?
		FOUNDER	Who is the founder of the Wal-Mart stores?
		OWNER	Who is the owner of CNN?
		OTHERS	Who is Coronado?

3.2.2 Concept List Construction

To construct the concept list of each question category, we first extract the terms that represent the concepts of each question category, and then assign the extracted terms to each question category. Then, to increase the terms of each question category concept list, the assigned terms are expanded semantically by using WordNet.

Because the sentence patterns of a query are much less complex than those of a document, we extract the pattern of the query to facilitate extraction of the concept of the query. For instance, in the query "Who is the inventor of paper?", we can ascertain the question category of the query from two words, "Who" and "inventor", just as we can ascertain the question category for the query "Who invented paper?" from the words "Who" and "invented". Question patterns for question category management are defined as in Definition 1. For example, the question pattern from the query "Who is the inventor of paper?" is <Who, null, is_BE, inventor_NN>, and the pattern from the query "who invented paper" is <Who, null, invented_VBN>.

[Definition 1: Question Pattern]
Question patterns are defined as the following two types based on the noun (N) and verbs (BE_V, V) around Wh_term, where, BE_V is the verb "to be" or one of its conjugated forms. Noun N1 is the first noun before verb V and noun N2 is the first noun after verb V.

Question pattern 1 = [Wh_term, N1, BE_V, N2]
Question pattern 2 = [Wh_term, N, V]

The patterns extracted from a query by the defined format are assigned to the corresponding question category. The patterns assigned to each question category make up the "concept list" that represents the concept of a question category. The patterns in each concept list are additionally expanded semantically by using WordNet to increase the number of terms in each question category concept list.

Figure 2 presents an example concept list; in this figure, the final concept list of the question category "INVENTOR" is the expanded version of the allocated patterns.

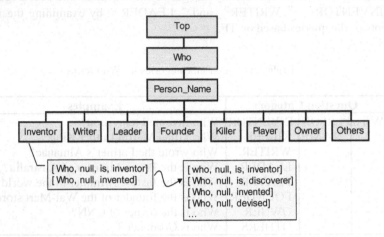

Fig. 2. Concept List: Question pattern allocation and expansion

3.3 Question Category Concept Learning

This section illustrates the question category and concept list learning and classification method. For concept learning and classification, we use the Naïve Bayes theorem. The learning algorithm is as follows:

$$P(v_j \mid S_k) = \frac{C(v_j, S_k)}{C(v_j)} \quad, P(S_k) = \frac{C(S_k)}{C(w)}$$

where w represents the term to be classified into a question category, S_k represents question category k, and v_j is terms around w in the constructed concept list in each question category.

When a new query is given, the following classification algorithm is used to classify the query into a question category: For wh_term w and other terms v_j in a pattern, we calculate the S_k for all categories k and select the S_k that has the highest probability as the question category S' of the given query.

$$Decide \ S' \ if \ S' = \arg\max_{S_k} [\log P(S_k) + \sum_{v_j \ in \ C} \log P(v_j \mid S_k)]$$

3.4 Semantic Query Expansion

In this section, we outline the semantic query expansion process based on the learned data when a new query is given. For a new query, the proposed system first extracts the query pattern and then classifies the concept of the query into the corresponding question category based on the learned data. The system then acquires the expansion terms from the concept list in the classified question category, which can represent and share the concept of a question category. The query expansion process is depicted in detail in Figure 3 for the sample query "Who is the inventor of paper". In analyzing this query, the pattern of the query is first extracted for the convenience of concept comprehension. Based on the learned knowledge, the concept of the query is classified into the question category "inventor". From the question category "inventor", we then obtain semantic expansion terms such as "inventor", "discoverer", "invent", and "devise", and the query is expanded into "Person_Name, paper, inventor, discoverer, invent, devise".

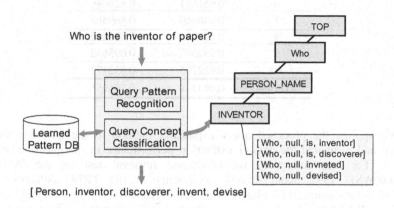

4 Evaluation

To test the proposed method, we conducted two experiments on the TREC collection. In the first experiment, we tested the learning and classification performance of the constructed question category concept list. In the second experiment, we applied the proposed query expansion method to the question answering system and evaluated the answer extraction performance.

For the query set, we used 117 who_questions from among the 692 queries numbered 201~893 in the TREC collection, and for the question answering experiment we conducted a retrieval test on the 42,654 Wall Street Journal (WSJ) 1991 documents.

We used precision as measures of the accuracy, which are the ratio of correctly classified patterns to total patterns.

When we constructed the question category and concept list for the selected query set, the total number of patterns in the constructed concept list was 117, and the total pattern number in the concept list including expanded patterns was 221. When the system learned the constructed question category and concept list by Naïve Bayes theorem, the performance characteristics were 94.44% precision for the learning data and 78.70% for the validation data by 10-fold cross validation. The break-down of the precisions obtained for each pass in the 10-fold cross validation is illustrated in Table 3.

Table 3. Precision in 10-fold cross validation for concept list learning

	Traning set	Validation set
1	0.917874	0.695652
2	0.966184	0.782608
3	0.966184	0.869565
4	0.917874	0.826086
5	0.951691	0.826086
6	0.951691	0.826086
7	0.946860	0.869565
8	0.971014	0.826086
9	0.932367	0.695652
10	0.922705	0.652173
Average	0.944444	0.786955

We applied the proposed query expansion method to the question answering system and evaluated the answer extraction performance in the question answering system. For test collection, we conducted retrieval test on the Wall Street Journal(WSJ) 1991 about 42,654 documents in the TREC collection and 6 who_questions among 117 who_queries numbered 201~893 in the TREC collection that have WSJ 1991 document as answer set. Similarity measure between a question and documents was defined in this experiment as follows.

$$Sim(Q, D) = \sum_i \sum_j \alpha * d(q_i, d_j), \quad \text{where} \quad d(q_i, d_j) = 1 \text{ if } q_i = d_j \text{ otherwise } 0$$

Table 4 shows the Mean Reciprocal Ratio(MRR) results for the comparison of the traditional QA system and the proposed. We set the sentence boundary as three sentences. As shown in Table 4, the traditional system showed in 0.223 in MRR and the proposed system showed 0.50 superior to the traditional system. Therefore, The proposed method showed the potential to improve the performance of question answering system.

Table 4. MRR of the traditional QA system and the proposed system

	Traditional	The proposed
Three sentences	0.223	0.50

5   Conclusion and Future work

In this paper, by assuming that the important concepts of a query are embodied in the most frequently used terms in the query, we constructed a question category concept list that contains an expanded collection of query terms related to the concept of a query. We evaluated the performance of the proposed method as a question answering system by applying it to questions from TREC.

The question category and concept list for each question category were constructed by analyzing and classifying the patterns of 117 who_questions taken from among TREC query numbers 201~893. The system learned the constructed question category and its concept list by using Naïve Bayes theorem. The learning performance, as evaluated by 10-fold cross validation, was a precision of 94.44% for the learning data and 78.70% for the test data. Moreover, the traditional system showed in 0.223 in MRR and the proposed system showed 0.50 superior to the traditional system. The results of the present experiments suggest the promise of the proposed method, and we plan to carry out more extensive experiments on other question categories to further test its potential.

References

[1] C., Cardie, V., Ng, D., Pierce and C., Buckley, Examining the Role of Statistical and Linguistic Knowledge Sources in a General-Knowledge Question-Answering System, In Proceeding of the 6th Applied Natural Language Processing Conference(2000), pp.180-187

[2] E. Hovy, et al., Learning Surface Text Patterns for a Question Answering system, In Proceedings of the ACL conference(2002), pp.180-187.

[3] H. Kazawa, T. Hirao, H. Isozaki, and E. Maeda, A machine learning approach for QA and Novelty Tracks:NTT system description, In Proceedings of the Eleventh Text Retrieval Conference (TREC-10),(2003).

[4] J. Prager and D. Radev, E. Brown and A. Coden, The Use of Predictive Annotation for Question-Answering in TREC8, In Proceedings of the TREC-8 Conference NIST(2000), 309-316

[5] R. Mandela, T. Tokunaga and H. Tanaka., Combining Multiple Evidence from Different Types of Thesaurus for Query Expansion, In Proceedings of the 22nd Annual International ACM SIGIR Conference on Research and Development in Information Retrieval(1999), August 15-19.

[6] U. Hermjakob, Parsing and Question Classification for Question Answering, In the Proceedings of Workshop on Open-domain Question Answering at ACL-2001.

[7] E. Voorhees, Query Expansion using Lexical Semantic Relations, In Proceedings of SIGIR Conference(1994), pp.61-69.

Multilingual Collection Retrieving
Via Ontology Alignment*

Liang Zhang[1], Guowen Wu[2], Yanfei Xu[1], Wei Li[1], and Yang Zhong[3]

[1]Department of Computing and Information Technology , [3]School of Life Science,
Fudan University, China
[2]Academy of Changjiang Computer (Group) Company, China
{zhangl, 032021154, 022021149, yangzhong}@fudan.edu.cn,
wuguowen@hotmail.com

Abstract. As parts of global information infrastructure, digital libraries will likely be accessed by people all over world. Ontologies and their association can alleviate the heterogeneity and particularly the diversity of languages. This paper proposes a solution to cross-lingual information retrieval problem via ontology alignment. We elaborate two original techniques, i.e. primitives' association based on CL-LSI and mapping configuration optimization, to augment existing ontology mapping technology. As a result, multilingual collections can be bridged by this mapping, and searching across them can be achieved by three tractable steps: querying against local ontology, routing to target ontologies, and harvesting contents there online.

1 Introduction

The Internet is bringing us a global information society. As its essential parts, digital libraries (DLs) are involved in this globalization tide. Meanwhile, there is no doubt that people will continue to hold on to the values and beliefs of their native cultures and languages. In order to realize the cross-fertilization of multi-cultures, it is necessary to develop effective means to remove the language barriers.

Unicode has laid a foundation for character encoding, but the matter goes far beyond the coding issue, and calls for more sophisticated processing. Among all the endeavors, *Cross-Lingual Information Retrieval* (*CLIR*) is an active research topic.

CLIR based on lexical and syntactic information was extensively studied in last decade, e.g. [1]. Recently, impelled by the *Semantic Web*[2], there has been an increasing trend of using semantic information for this task[3, 4]. Related with the work here, OBSERVER[4] exploits a set of inter-ontology relationships to link multiple pre-existing ontologies, then to access heterogeneous data repositories via them. However, it does not treat the multiliguality in the mapping construction. Whereas Chen and Fung[3] proposes an automatic algorithm to construct an English-

---

* This work is partially supported by the NSFC key project under grant No. 69933010, the Chinese Hi-tech (863) Project under grant No. 2002AA4Z3430, and No. 2002AA231041, as well as Shanghai S&T Commission key project under grant No. 02DJ14013.

Z. Chen et al. (Eds.): ICADL 2004, LNCS 3334, pp. 510–514, 2004.

Chinese bilingual FrameNet, but it heavily relies on the trans-lingual lexicon in its initial step, which hampers its applicability in general settings. With regard to underlying techniques for ontology merging and alignment, Noy and Musen have developed a series of techniques. Their latest method Anchor-PROMPT[5] enhances the detection of matching terms using non-local context. Except lacking of the optimization of mapping configuration and the difference in anchors construction, Anchor-PROMPT is a good choice for contextual alignment.

In this paper, we propose a solution to CLIR via ontology alignment. The main contribution of this work includes: (1) a novel CLIR solution via ontology alignment, (2) a practical primitives' association algorithm, and (3) the original concept of configuration optimization for ontology alignment. To the best of our knowledge, there is seldom research result on the last topic.

The paper is organized as follows: section 2 gives the problem definition and the rationale of proposed solution. In section 3, we elaborate algorithms for primitives' association and configuration optimization. Finally, section 4 draws conclusions.

2 Problem Definition and Our Solution

We deal with the issue of CLIR. For simplicity, we ignore issues here pertaining to multimedia, and focus on the extensions to traditional Information Retrieval (IR). First, we introduce some definitions.

Definition 1. *Information Source.* A information source S is characterized as a triple $<O, C, A>$, where C is a collection of documents in one specific language, O is an ontology, and A is the access mechanism to the source S.

As usual, assume that O governs A, i.e. people can but issue queries against O to get items in C.

Definition 2. *CLIR.* CLIR refers to the process of information retrieval across two or more information sources in different languages.

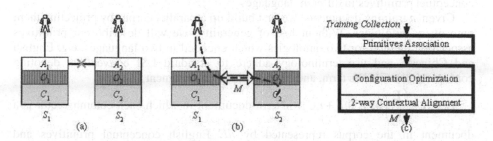

Fig. 1. Cross-Lingual Information Retrieval (CLIR). (a) Direct IR to other sources, (b) CLIR via ontology alignment (dashed line), and (c) Proposed procedure for aligning ontologies

Without loss of generality, assume there exist two information sources $S_1 =< O_1$, $C_1, A_1>$ and $S_2 =< O_2, C_2, A_2>$, C_1 and C_2 are collections in different languages, O_1 and O_2 are two ontologies with some semantic overlap but differ in structure, coverage and granularity. Due to this heterogeneity, a user can not get relevant information from S_1 and S_2 unless she afford both A_1 and A_2 (illustrated by Fig. 1-a).

We present a CLIR solution via ontology alignment. Concretely, once O_1 and O_2 were related each other through an ontology mapping M, multilingual collections C_1 and C_2 can be bridged by it, and searching across them can be achieved by three coherent steps: querying against local ontology (say A_1), routing to target ontology (via M), and harvesting contents. The solution is illustrated by Fig.1-b.

Obviously, the cornerstone here is the ontology alignment. We believe it is feasible in respect that:

- *formal nature of ontology,* compared with general thesauri, meaning of ontology is entirely captured in its structure and formal semantics, it is easier for a machine to understand it
- *tools availability*, this is owe to fruitful achievements in the Semantic Web research, and
- *economy*, the mapping is constructed once and offline, and is paid off by many times online CLIR.

The ontology alignment procedure is depicted in Fig.1-c. Two steps with broad border will be elaborated in the next section.

3   Alignment Algorithms

This section elaborates the two algorithms that will augment existing ontology alignment technology.

3.1   Associating Conceptual Primitives

We associate conceptual primitives based on CL-LSI [1]. We believe that taking an analytical course instead of traditional linguistic similarity could yield a more effective and robust mechanism to discover underlying correspondence between conceptual primitives in different languages.

Given m training documents, we first build up a parallel corpus by projecting them onto every ontologies. Without loss of generality, we will describe our primitives association method for two ontologies which encoded in two languages, e.g. English and Chinese, and use terminology adhere to standard LSI convention, denoting conceptual primitive as term, and item in corpus as document.

Let $\mathbf{A} = \begin{pmatrix} \mathbf{E} \\ \mathbf{C} \end{pmatrix}$ be a $(nE + nC) \times m$ term-document in which each column vector is a document in the corpus represented by nE English conceptual primitives and nC Chinese conceptual primitives. Apply singular value decomposition (SVD) on $\mathbf{A}$ and take only the k-largest singular values, it will yield its representation $\mathbf{A}^k$ in the reduced k-dimension future space:

$$\mathbf{A}^k = \mathbf{U}\mathbf{S}_k\mathbf{V}^\mathrm{T}, \text{ where } \mathbf{U}^\mathrm{T}\mathbf{U} = \mathbf{I}_n, \mathbf{S}_k = \mathrm{diag}(\sigma_1, \cdots, \sigma_k, 0, \cdots, 0)_{n \times n}, \mathbf{V}^\mathrm{T}\mathbf{V} = \mathbf{I}_m \quad (1)$$

The dot product between two row vectors of $\mathbf{A}^k$ reflects the extent to which **two** terms have a similar pattern of occurrence across the set of documents, $\mathbf{A}^k\mathbf{A}^{kT}$ is a square symmetric matrix containing all these term-to-term relationship. Since $\mathbf{S}$ is diagonal and $\mathbf{U}$ is orthonormal, we have:

$$\mathbf{R} = \mathbf{A}^k\mathbf{A}^{kT} = \mathbf{US}^2\mathbf{U}^T \tag{2}$$

The element r_{ij} of $\mathbf{R}$ represents the association strength between term i and term j. In our setting to associate conceptual primitives from two languages parts, we can simply extract the term-term relationship from English and Chinese parts, respectively. This gives the association algorithm below.

Algorithm Associating_conceptual_primitives
1. Prepare a parallel corpus by projecting training collection onto the two ontologies, respectively;
2. Make the matrix **A**, then apply the LSI on it as Equ.(1), Calculate the matrix **R** as Equ.(2);
3. Scan the upper right part of **R**, for each row i, find a j such that $r_j = \max_p r_p$ ($i < p \le n$, and i, j belong to the two languages, respectively);take r_j as the strength of connection between primitives i and j;
4. Normalize the strength.

3.2 Optimizing the Mapping Configuration

As for the mapping configuration optimization, we have noticed that even variety of methods for ontology alignment have been proposed, the issue of optimal mapping configuration under certain constrains is almost neglected. Most algorithms treat mapping between *two* ontologies, but as we know, in the worst case, it will produce $O(n^2)$ mappings for n ontologies. Now, assume the constraint is that only $O(n)$ mappings are allowed, we will seek an algorithm to produce a better configuration than those produced by conventional alignment algorithms. Ideally, it should give n-1 mappings for n ontologies.

Our modus operandi is encapsulating an existing 2-way-alignment algorithm (e.g. the Anchor-PROMPT) by our configuration optimizer (as in Fig.1-c). Once primitives are associated, all primitives in one ontology with some outer associations, together with inner roles among them can be modeled as a *directed acyclic graph* (DAG), any subgraphs of such a DAG can be regarded as a context. The following algorithm will produce a better mapping configuration under certain constrains (e.g. with n-1 mappings here). We assume that all ontologies involved have some semantic overlap.

Algorithm Optimizing_the_mapping_configuration
1. Put all ontologies in to the set TO-BE-ALIGNED, except the one user chosen as the *current* context; Let ALIGNED be NULL;
2. Repeat until TO-BE-ALIGNED is NULL
   a) Search for each context whose distance to the *current* is less than a threshold, move all those

ontologies that contain selected contexts to set ALIGNED, and remove them from TO-BE-ALIGNED;

b) Use encapsulated 2-way-alignment algorithm to map each of selected context with the *current*

c) Choose ontology in ALIGNED and select a context of it as *current*

The distance of two DAGs, G_1 and G_2, is measured by their maximal common subgraph (MCS)[6]:

$$d(G_1, G_2) = 1 - \frac{|\operatorname{mcs}(G_1, G_2)|}{\max(|G_1|, |G_2|)} \tag{3}$$

Here $|G|$ denotes the number of nodes in G, and $|\operatorname{mcs}(G_1, G_2)|$ is the number of MCS of G_1 and G_2. The identity of nodes between two graphs is judged by the primitives' association. All other methods, including the MCS judgment, are omitted here due to the length limit. We refer reader to [7] for details.

4 Conclusion and Future Work

In this paper, we proposed a solution to CLIR via ontology alignment. Besides its novel framework, our work has other two features: an analytical primitives' association algorithm which gains better applicability than that of lexicon-based methods; a brand-new concept of configuration optimization can produce better configuration under certain constrains for ontology alignment Our future work includes intensive testing of proposed method against larger scale problems.

References

1. Dumais, S.T., Landauer, T.K., Littman, M.L.: Automatic Cross-Linguistic Information Retrieval Using Latent Semantic Indexing. In SIGIR'96 – Workshop on Cross-Linguistic Information Retrieval(1996) 16–23
2. Berners-Lee, T., Hendler, J., Lassila, O.: The Semantic Web. Scientific American, 284(5) (2001)34–43
3. Chen, B.F., Fung, P.: Automatic Construction of an English-Chinese Bilingual FrameNet. In: Proceedings of Human Language Technology conference 2004 (HLT/NAACL-04). Boston, Mass: May (2004)
4. Mena, E., llarramendi, A., Kashyap, V., Sheth, A.P.: Observer: An Approach for Query Processing in Global Information Systems Based on Interoperation across Pre-existing Ontologies. Distributed and Parallel Databases, 8(2)(2000)223–271
5. Noy, N.F., Musen, M.A.: Anchor-Prompt: Using Non-local Context for Semantic Matching. In Proceedings of the Workshop on Ontologies and Information Sharing at the Seventeenth International Joint Conference on Artificial Intelligence (IJCAI-2001), Seattle, WA, USA(2001)
6. Bunke, H., Shearer, K.: A Graph distance metric based on maximal common subgraph. Pattern Recognition Letter 19(2/3)(1998)255-259
7. Lu, Y., Zhang, L., Wang, W., Duan, Q.Y., Shi, B.L.: DTD Ranking in the Smart XML Query. Journal of Computer Research and Development. 40(11)(2003)1579-1585 in Chinese

Using Content-Based and Link-Based Analysis in Building Vertical Search Engines

Michael Chau[1] and Hsinchun Chen[2]

[1] School of Business, The University of Hong Kong, Pokfulam, Hong Kong
mchau@business.hku.hk
[2] Department of Management Information Systems,
The University of Arizona, Tucson, Arizona 85721, USA
hchen@bpa.arizona.edu

Abstract. This paper reports our research in the Web page filtering process in specialized search engine development. We propose a machine-learning-based approach that combines Web content analysis and Web structure analysis. Instead of a bag of words, each Web page is represented by a set of content-based and link-based features, which can be used as the input for various machine learning algorithms. The proposed approach was implemented using both a feedforward/backpropagation neural network and a support vector machine. An evaluation study was conducted and showed that the proposed approaches performed better than the benchmark approaches.

1 Introduction

The number of indexable pages on the Web has exceeded three billion and it has become increasingly difficult for search engines to keep an up-to-date and comprehensive search index. Users often find it difficult to search for useful and high-quality information on the Web using general-purpose search engines, especially when searching for specific information on a given topic. Many vertical search engines, or domain-specific search engines, have been built to alleviate his problem to some extent by providing more precise results and more customized features in particular domains. However, these search engines are not easy to build. There are two major challenges for vertical search engine developers: (1) How to locate relevant documents on the Web? (2) How to filter irrelevant documents from a collection? This study addresses the second issue, the Web page filtering problem, and proposes new approaches.

2 Related Work

Web page filtering is important in the process of vertical search engine development. In general, the filtering techniques can be classified as follows: (1) domain experts manually determine the relevance of each Web page (e.g., Yahoo); (2) the relevance

Z. Chen et al. (Eds.): ICADL 2004, LNCS 3334, pp. 515–518, 2004.

of a Web page is determined by the occurrences of particular keywords (e.g., *computer*) [6]; (3) TFIDF (term frequency * inverse document frequency) is calculated based on a lexicon created by domain-experts and Web pages are then with a high similarity score to the lexicon are considered relevant [1]; and (4) text classification techniques such as the Naive Bayesian classifier are applied [3, 9]. Among these, text classification is the most promising approach. Techniques such as Naïve Bayesian model, neural networks, and support vector machines have been widely used in text classification. It has been shown that SVM achieved the best performance among different classifiers on the Reuters-21578 data set [7, 10].

When applied to Web page filtering, few of the text classifiers, however, have made use of the special characteristics of the Web, such as its unique hyperlink structure which has been increasingly used in other Web applications. For example, the PageRank score, computed by weighting each in-link to a page proportionally to the quality of the page containing the in-link, has been applied in the search engine Google for search result ranking [2]. In addition, since Web pages are mostly semi-structured documents like HTML, useful information often can be used to derive some important features of a Web document. Such metrics and other characteristics of Web pages could possibly be applied to improve the performance of traditionally text classifiers in Web page filtering.

3 Proposed Approach

One of the major problems of traditional text classifiers is the large number of features, which result in long processing time. To address this problem, we propose to represent each Web page by a limited number of content and link features rather than as a vector of words. This reduces the dimensionality of the classifier and thus the number of training examples needed. The characteristics of Web structure also can be incorporated into these features easily.

Based on our review of the literature, we determined that, in general, the relevance and quality of a Web page can be reflected in the following aspects: (1) the content of the page itself (similarity of the document's title and body text to a domain lexicon); (2) the content of the page's neighbor documents (including parents, children, and siblings); and (3) the page's link characteristics (including PageRank, HITS, number of in-links, and anchor text information). A set of 4 to 6 features , calculated based on metrics such as those mentioned above, are defined for each aspect. A total of 14 features are defined and used as the input values to machine learning classifiers. We adopt a feedforward-backpropagation neural network (NN) [8] and a support vector machine (SVM) [7] as our classifiers.

4 Evaluation

An experiment was conducted to compare the proposed approach with two traditional approaches: a TFIDF approach (Benchmark 1); and a keyword-based text classifier approach using SVM (Benchmark 2), in the medical domain. The proposed Web-feature-based approaches are codenamed Approach 1 (for the neural network classifier) and Approach 2 (for the SVM classifier) in our experiment. A set of 1,000 documents were randomly selected from a medical testbed created in our previous research [4, 5]. A medical lexicon, created based on the metathesaurus of the Unified Medical Language System (UMLS), was also used in our experiment. A 50-fold cross validation testing was adopted. Testing was performed for 50 iterations, in each of which 49 portions of the data (980 documents) were used for training and the remaining portion (20 documents) was used for testing.

Accuracy and F-measure were to measure the effectiveness of the proposed approaches. The macro-averages for each approach are shown in Table 1. In general, the experimental results showed that the proposed approaches performed significantly better than the traditional approaches in both accuracy and F-measure ($p < 0.005$), especially when the number of training documents is small. When comparing the two proposed methods, we found that the NN classifier performed significantly better than the SVM classifier ($p < 0.05$). In terms of efficiency, the proposed approaches also performed better than the traditional keyword-based approach.

Table 1. Experiment results

	Accuracy	F-measure
Benchmark 1	80.80%	0.6005
Benchmark 2	87.80%	0.6646
Approach 1	89.40%	0.7614
Approach 2	87.30%	0.7049

To study the efficiencies of the different approaches, we also recorded the time needed for each system to perform the 50-fold cross validation, including both training and testing time. We found that Benchmark 2 (the keyword-based SVM) took the longest time (382.6 minutes). The reason is that each document was represented as a large vector of keywords, which created a high dimensionality for the classifier. The classifier had to learn the relationships between all these attributes and the class attribute, thus requiring more time. Benchmark 1 (TFIDF) used the least time, as it only had to calculate the TFIDF score for each document and determine the threshold, both of which did not require complex processing. Approach 1 (103.5 minutes) and Approach 2 (37.6 minutes) are in the middle. Approach 1 required a longer time than Approach 2 because the neural network had to be trained in multiple epochs, i.e., in each iteration the training data set had to be presented to the network thousands of times in order to improve the network's performance.

5 Conclusion

The experimental results are encouraging and show that the proposed approach can be used for Web page filtering by effectively applying Web content and link analysis. We believe that the proposed approach is useful for vertical search engine development, as well as other Web applications. We also plan to apply the techniques to Web page filtering in other languages, such as Chinese or Japanese.

Acknowledgement

This project has been supported in part by the following grants: NSF Digital Library Initiative-2, "High-performance Digital Library Systems: From Information Retrieval to Knowledge Management" (IIS-9817473, Apr 1999-Mar 2002), NIH/NLM Grant (PI: H. Chen), "UMLS Enhanced Dynamic Agents to Manage Medical Knowledge" (1 R01 LM06919-1A1, Feb 2001-Jan 2004), and HKU Seed Funding for Basic Research, "Using Content and Link Analysis in Developing Domain-specific Web Search Engines: A Machine Learning Approach" (Feb 2004-Jul 2005). We also thank the medical experts who participated in the user studies.

References

1. Baujard, O., Baujard, V., Aurel, S., Boyer, C., and Appel, R. D.: Trends in Medical Information Retrieval on the Internet. Computers in Biology and Medicine 28 (1998) 589–601.
2. Brin, S. and Page, L.: The Anatomy of a Large-Scale Hypertextual Web Search Engine. In: Proceedings of the 7th International World Wide Web Conference, Brisbane, Australia (1998).
3. Chakrabarti, S., Dom, B., and Indyk, P.: Enhanced Hypertext Categorization Using Hyperlink. In: Proceedings of ACM SIGMOD International Conference on Management of Data, Seattle, Washington, USA (1998).
4. Chau, M. and Chen, H.: Comparison of Three Vertical Search Spiders. IEEE Computer 36(5) (2003) 56–62.
5. Chen, H., Lally, A. M., Zhu, B., and Chau, M.: HelpfulMed: Intelligent Searching for Medical Information over the Internet. Journal of the American Society for Information Science and Technology, 54(7) (2003) 683–694.
6. Cho, J., Garcia-Molina, H., and Page, L.: Efficient Crawling through URL Ordering. In: Proceedings of the 7th International World Wide Web Conference, Brisbane, Australia (1998).
7. Joachims, T.: Text Categorization with Support Vector Machines: Learning with Many Relevant Features. In: Proceedings of the European Conference on Machine Learning, Berlin (1998)137–142.
8. Lippmann, R. P.: An Introduction to Computing with Neural Networks. IEEE Acoustics Speech and Signal Processing Magazine 4(2) (1987) 4–22.
9. McCallum, A., Nigam, K., Rennie, J., and Seymore, K.: A Machine Learning Approach to Building Domain-specific Search Engines. In: Proceedings of the International Joint Conference on Artificial Intelligence (1999) 662–667.
10. Yang, Y. and Liu, X.: A Re-examination of Text Categorization Methods. In: Proceedings of the 22nd Annual International ACM Conference on Research and Development in Information Retrieval (1999) 42–49.

wHunter: A Focused Web Crawler – A Tool for Digital Library*

Yun Huang and YunMing Ye

Department of Computer Science, Shanghai Jiaotong University
{Huangyun, Ycyunming}@cs.sjtu.edu.cn

Abstract. Topic-driven Web Crawler or focused crawler is the key tool of on-line web information library. It's a challenging issue that how to achieve good performance efficiently with limited time and space resources. This paper proposes a focused web crawler wHunter that implements incremental and multi-strategy learning by taking the advantages of both SVM (support vector machines) and naïve Bayes. On the one hand, the initial performance is guaranteed via SVM classifier; on the other hand, when enough web pages are obtained, the classifier is switched to naïve Bayes so that on-line incremental learning is achieved. Experimental results show that our proposed algorithm is efficient and easy to implement.

1 Introduction

Topic-driven Web search engine [1] is a new and promising technology to overcome the drawbacks of general-purpose search engine in Web information retrieval community. To achieve the goal of crawling the Web selectively for specified topics, the topic-driven crawler, or focused crawler, has a page classifier to determine the relevance of crawled pages to the target topics and a link predictor to select the candidate URLs that have high probability of being relevant. The precision and robustness of the page classifier and the link predictor determine the performance of a focused crawling system.

Chakrabarti and et al [1] first coined the notion of focused crawler and conducted a comprehensive study on focused crawling based on the linkage sociology analysis. In recent years, several methods have been proposed to build focused crawlers. Good examples include the keyword based similarity method [2, 3], the crawling strategy based on the PageRank values[4], the reinforcement learning method[5], evolutionary multi-agent systems[6], the context graph[7], statistical interest model[8, 9] and the 'critic-apprentice' learning paradigm[10]. These methods do not have the incremental learning capability that can improve the classification accuracy of the page classifier during the crawling process.

In this paper, we propose an incremental learning framework for building focused crawlers. Under this framework, SVM classifier guarantees the initial performance. When enough web pages are obtained, the classifier is switched to naïve Bayes so that on-line incremental learning is achieved and high efficiency is held. The rest of the

---

* This paper has been supported by China NSF project (No.60221120145).

Z. Chen et al. (Eds.): ICADL 2004, LNCS 3334, pp. 519–522, 2004.

paper is organized as follows: Section 2 describes our wHunter system. Experimental results and analysis are presented in Section 3. Section 4 concludes our work in progress.

2 wHunter: A Focused Web Crawler Based on Incremental and Multi-strategy Learning

From an agent perspective, a focused crawler is an intelligent agent that interacts with the environment (the Web) and attains goal states (picks up relevant pages). Focused crawling is a dynamic and incremental process inherently. In AI community, it has been testified that incremental learning is very useful for incremental tasks [11]. As the crawled pages D increase, it is natural for the focused crawler to learn incrementally from them. Based on these ideas we define an incremental learning framework. It has four main components: (1) a crawling module to get URLs from the URL queue and downloads the corresponding Web pages, (2) a page classifier that learns from Sample and classifies the crawled pages as relevant or irrelevant, (3) a link predictor that computes and assigns the link score (i.e. the probability of being relevant) to each URL in the URL queue. The URLs with higher link scores will be crawled preferentially, and (4) a on-line sample detector that analyzes the crawled pages to seek for new samples for the page classifier. In this framework, the incremental learning capability is enabled by the online sample detector.

The page classifier is one of the key components to ensure the crawling process being focused. After the success of SVM in solving small sample size non-linear high sample dimension problems [12], it has shown that SVM can yield good generalization performance in both text classification problems and hypertext categorization tasks. So far, SVM is a better choice for constructing hypertext categorization systems [13]. But for SVM, the incremental learning ability is intractable and the time complexity for training depends quadratic on the sample size. As a classical classifier, naïve Bayes has the incremental learning ability and is suitable to the large sample size. (According to Vapnik's theory, a sample size is considered to be small if $\ell/h < 20$ (the ratio of sample size to the sample dimension is less than 20) [14].

In our system, the initial performance is guaranteed by SVM classifier; when enough web pages are obtained, the classifier is switched to naïve Bayes so that on-line incremental learning is achieved and high efficiency is held.

The link predictor directly controls the 'focus' of the crawling process since it determines the visit priority of candidate URLs in the URL queue. The link score of each candidate URL p is calculated based on the link context and the relevance of its parent pages (the pages which link to p), and is defined as:

$$LS(p) = LCS(p) + \varepsilon/n + (1-\varepsilon) \sum_{(q,p)\in G} LS(q)/outlink(q) + \sum_{(q,p)\in G} PRS(q)/outlink(q) \qquad (1)$$

3 Experiments

wHunter was implemented in Java. Target topics were defined in keywords and page samples. The page samples were obtained through meta-searching the Yahoo! search engine. Three strategies were implemented for performance comparison: (1) Only SVM used for page classifier, (2) Only naïve Bayes used for page classifier, and (3) both SVM and naïve Bayes used for page classifier.

We employed the precision metric to evaluate the crawled pages. Precision often called 'harvest rate' is used as a major performance metric in the focused crawler community.

We have tested 60 topics covering a variety of domains. For each topic, crawlers started with 10 seed sample URLs, and crawled about one thousand Web pages. Both English and Chinese topics were tested.

Table 1 shows the final harvest rates of six topics after crawling one thousand pages. The more important demonstration is that wHunter with incremental learning got a harvest rate higher than other. This testifies that our incremental learning method could indeed improve the performance of focused crawling.

Table 1. The Final Harvest Rate of Some Topics

Topic	Topic Language	SVM	NB	SVM and NB
History	English	0.52	0.16	0.672
American History	English	0.61	0.19	0.71
African American History	English	0.56	0.121	0.69
China travel	English	0.456	0.166	0.534
Beijing travel	English	0.537	0.26	0.612
Huang mountain travel	English	0.474	0.17	0.756

4 Conclusion

In this paper we have proposed an incremental learning framework for focused crawling under which an online sample detector is constructed to incrementally distill new positive and negative samples from the crawled Web pages. New samples are feeded back to the page classifier and the link predictor to update their learning models online. With the incremental learning capability, the system can start from a few page samples and gain more integrated knowledge about the target topic over time so that the precision and robustness of the page classifier and the link predictor are improved.

We have presented the focused crawler system wHunter implemented based on this framework. Our experiments on several topics, including topics in Chinese, have shown that our incremental learning method indeed improved the harvest rate with a few samples.

References

1. Chakrabarti, S., M., V.D.B., Dom, B.: Focused crawling: a new approach to topic-specific web resource discovery. In: Proceedings of the 8th International WWW Conference. (1999)
2. P., D.B., G., H., Y., K.: Information retrieval in distributed hypertexts: Making client-based searching feasible. In: Proceedings of the ¯rst International WWW conference. (1994)
3. Hersovici, M., Jacovi, M., Maarek, Y.S., Pelleg, D., Shtalhaim, M., Ur, S.: The shark search algorithm-an application: Tailored web site mapping. In: Proceedings of the 7th International WWW Conference. (1998)
4. Cho, J., Garcia-Molina, H., Page, L.: E±cient crawling through url ordering. In :Proceedings of the 7th International WWW Conference. (1998)
5. Rennie, J., McCallum, A.K.: Using reinforcement learning to spider the web efficiently. In: Proceedings of the 16th International Conference on Machine Learning.(1999)
6. Menczer, F., Belew, R.K.: Adaptive retrieval agents: Internalizing local context and scaling up to the web. Machine Learning 39 (2000) 203{242
7. Diligenti, M., Coetzee, F.M., Lawrence, S., Giles, C.L., Gori, M.: Focused crawling using context graphs. In: Proceedings of the 26th International Conference on Very Large Databases. (2000)
8. Aggarwal, C.C., Al-Garawi, F., Yu, P.S.: Intelligent crawling on the world wide web with arbitrary predicates. In: Proceedings of the10th International WWW Conference. (2001)
9. Aggarwal, C.C., Al-Garawi, F., Yu, P.S.: On the design of a learning crawler for topical resource discovery. ACM Transactions on Information Systems, 19 (2001) 286-309
10. Chakrabarti, S., K., P., M., S.: Accelerated focused crawling through online relevance feedback. In: Proceedings of the 11th International WWW Conference. (2002)
11. Giraud-Carrier, C.G.: A note on the utility of incremental learning. AI Communications 13 (2000) 215-224
12. Peter Bartlett, John Shawe-Taylor, Generalization performance of support vector machines and other pattern classifiers, Advances in kernel methods: support vector learning, MIT Press, Cambridge, MA, 1999
13. Dennis Decoste, Bernhard Schoelkopf, Training Invariant Support Vector machines, Machine Learning, 46, 161–190, 2002
14. V. N. Vapnik,, An overview of statistical learning theory, IEEE Transactions On Neural Networks, 10(5)988-999, 1999

Extending Your Neighborhood-Relationship-Based Recommendations Using Your Personal Web Context

Avaré Stewart, Claudia Niederée, Bhaskar Mehta,
Matthias Hemmje, and Erich Neuhold

Fraunhofer IPSI, Darmstadt, Germany,
{stewart, niederee, mehta, hemmje, neuhold}@ipsi.fraunhofer.de
http://ipsi.fraunhofer.de/delite

Abstract. The people, documents, and other entities from a domain persons know, or are in other ways associated with, influence their decision making and the types of recommendations that serve them best. For example, recommending persons to meet in a conference or a paper to read from a digital library collection does not only depend on the task, interests, and skills of a user, but also on the persons and works they are already familiar with. In order for personalization services to reflect this dependency, extended user models that consider users' network of related domain entities in addition to other user characteristics, are required. Based on a unified context model, we present the Personal Web Context approach that models the typed relationships a user is involved in. Based on a Resource Network which can, for example, be built from the information collection and the associated meta data managed by a digital library, domain-specific rules are used to suggest valuable extensions of this "neighborhood" of a user. Such work can form the basis for new types of digital library services.

1 Introduction

Personalization is an important method for digital libraries to take a more active role in dynamically tailoring its information and service offer to individuals in order to better meet their needs [1]. The most prevalent models of digital library users to date limit their representation of users to aspects of the cognitive pattern dimension, like interests or skills. Studies have shown, however, that one of the main hindrances to successful personalization in digital libraries is the limited representation of users and their information needs [2, 3]. In addressing these challenges, we consider a Unified User Context Model (UUCM [4]), i.e. an advanced and extensible model of the user and his context of use, covering additional dimensions beyond the cognitive patterns, like a user's tasks and environment. One central dimension of this model, the Relationship Dimension, discussed in this paper, takes into account a person's context within a community, describing it in terms of their ties within a web of domain resources.

This web, which we refer to as Personal Web Context (PWC), is defined and affected by the work persons do, the things and people they know, and the activities

Z. Chen et al. (Eds.): ICADL 2004, LNCS 3334, pp. 523–532, 2004.

they engage in. Extended user and context modeling, such as PWC, go beyond cognitive patterns by relying on a more comprehensive picture of the user, but also raises new challenges with respect to: 1) collecting information for user models and for 2)extending the matchmaking methods employed in exploiting these models. For the PWC we use an information infrastructure, which we refer to a Resource Networks (RN), describing relevant entities in an information collection and their typed relationships. These relationships are used for rule-based extension of the PWC by proposing new domain elements for consideration, e.g. persons to meet on a conference or documents to read. In implementing this approach, digital libraries can play an important role. Resource Networks, can be provided as a value-added service based on an analysis of information collections and the related bibliographic meta data.

The rest of this paper is structured as follows: Section 2 discusses related work. The PWC approach is presented in Section 3 together with a set of relationship rules and the underlying domain ontology. An overview of a first experimental implementation and results of the PWC approach can be found in Section 4. The paper concludes with a summary of the most important issues of the paper and some ideas for future work.

2 Related Work

A wide range of personalization methods is applicable in digital libraries [5]. Most of the work so far focuses on user models that cover aspects of the cognitive pattern dimension, i.e. interests, skills, etc. There is a consensus, however, that an improvement of personalization services can be achieved by relying on more extended user models that provide a better coverage of the characteristics of the users and their tasks [6, 1]. These more comprehensive models are sometimes called user context models [7]. Property-based information filtering provides a basis for such contextual approaches because they do not just use a person's interest, but also take into account the personal and organizational context of an individual within a community. The status of the user (profession, position), interrelationships within an organization or stereotypical community roles are used to support recommendations or information filtering of documents, email messages, etc. [8, 9]. In our work, the PWC, captures the relationships a user is involved in, and is related to property-based filtering [4]. Additionally, however, the PWC is embedded in a Unified User Context Model (UUCM) approach, that provides an RDF-based schema for an extensible user context model covering others dimensions as well; such as, user tasks and environmental issues like location. Our work on the PWC is also influenced by research in the area of Social Network Analysis (SNA) which uses graph-based structures to model salient interactions between human beings in a cooperation or community context [10].

In this respect, our work is similar to the approaches described in [11, 12], which consider properties of people linked by professional activity (i.e. co-authorship, co-participation, and citations) for filtering information. Additionally, we consider the sub-area of SNA, ego-centric analysis, which focuses on the individual (or ego) and uses the individuals' network of relations to understand the diverse factors contributing to their behavior and attitude [13] and in our case, their context. More general than social networks, relationships between entities other than persons, as well relationship types, are considered of high significance in modeling users and information [14, 15]. An important trend is the use of ontologies to model relationship types as well as concepts in a given domain [16, 17]. Our work builds upon the ontologies described in [18--20]. Further, ongoing research includes examining relationship types that apply to a relationship built from either the composition of several relationships or the co-occurrences of relationships [21, 5]. The PWC approach for extending the Personal Web is building upon this work.

3   The Personal Web Context

Within our extended user modeling approach the PWC covers the relationship dimension. A PWC represents the relevant entities in the domain a user is directly related with and the kind of relationship that exists between the user and the respective entity. The focus of our work is in suggesting extensions to the PWCs that would be helpful for the users in completing a task. Examples of such recommendations would be persons to meet or talks to visit at a conference. Such recommendations are based on analysis of information spaces or more precisely RNs that describe information spaces. Digital libraries could offer new forms and models of services by lending their information spaces to the construction of RNs as well as offering recommendation services for extending a user's PWC.

3.1   Relationship and Domain Ontologies

The structure underlying the RN and the PWC is a domain ontology describing relevant entities in a domain and the types of relationships that exist between these entities. We have chosen the scientific community domain as a starting point but the PWC can, in general be applied to other domains. An important factor in the use of ontologies is their ability to support the reuse of domain knowledge [22]. For this reason, we examined three (KA, Science, AKT) existing ontologies [18--20] as a basis for a modeling the scientific domain. Of the three, AKT most extensively defines the domain of our interest. This ontology describes, for example, people, event and publications. We build upon it by integrating additional concepts and relations from the other ontologies. Such integrations include the incorporation of what we consider to be stereotypical roles of academics and students from parts of the Science Ontology in addition, we associate keywords and subject areas with events and publications.

3.2   Building Resource Networks

The domain ontology provides the basis for creating graph-based structures which we refer to as Resource Networks (RNs). RNs are information models in which the nodes represent types resources in a domain and the labeled, directed edges indicate typed relationships between connected resources. RNs also provide the basis for expanding the PWC.

In general, RNs do not pre-exist but have to be extracted from information from different sources. Information collections (together with the related meta data) that are representative of a community are valid and promising starting points for the extraction of RNs. In addition to automatically analyzing information collections like DBLP [23], information about community events, such as conferences, can be added manually or extracted automatically from other sources in order to further enrich the RN. The RN construction we used is de- scribed in Section 4.

3.3   Targeted Extension of the Personal Web Context

The aim of the PWC approach is to help the user in the context of an information related task by suggesting (recommending) information objects that could be valuable extensions for his/her PWC. An example task that could be supported by this approach is "'Find potentials collaborators at this conference for a proposal in Grid computing'". For this purpose, a systematic process is required.

The PWC Extension Process. The process to suggest extensions for a PWC starts from an existing PWC and a relevant RN and is driven by the task of the user. The core part of the PWC Extension Process is a match-making process that supports discovering sequences of relationships from which a single weighted relation can be compositionally inferred. For this purpose, composition rules are used to: 1)decide which compositions candidates to use, 2) determine the type of composed relationships, and 3) compute the weight of the composed relationship. Such a weight reflects the likelihood that the composed relationships holds. The measure for a composed relationship is determined by: 1) the type of composed relationships, and 2) the weights of the composing relationships. The composed relationship acts as a surrogate for the sequence it replaces.

Before the composition rules are iteratively applied to the RN, the RN is first reduced to a subset that is relevant for the specific user task. In our case a subject-based approach is used, that filters out all nodes that are more than four steps away from the topic(s) related to the task 1 As an additional result of this step a Subject Web Context (SWC) is created for each task-relevant subject, which is very similar to the PWC but revolves around specific subjects.

The application of rules to the reduced RN brings resources nearer together. If one of the resources involved in the composition is part of the PWC, the 1 This assumes that every user task is related to one or more subjects of the RN. composition links portion of the users existing PWC with entities in the information space. This does not necessarily mean that the PWC is automatically extended; rather these entities are proposed to the user (the PWC owner) for further consideration.

Extension Rules. Using the relationship types of the domain ontology discussed in Section 3.1 as a starting point, we have defined a set of rules for the first phase of the PWC extension process [4]. Within these rules, the relationships are represented as quadruples of the form (Subject, Predicate, Object, weight). Subject, Predicate and Object are represented as RDF statements [24]. Predicate represents the relationship types and weight assigned to the relationship. Some example rules are discussed in more detail below to illustrate our approach. For each rule, we make the following assumptions: all a_i are persons, all d_i are documents, all p_i are probabilities, all e_i are events, and all s_i are subject areas. Furthermore, we assume that an event, e_i , is a serial or periodic event devoted to a given subject matter - typical serial events are annual conferences.

Rule 1 aims to identify influential community members. A domain specific criterion, to determine influence, is the type and amount of publications a person has in events devoted to a given subject. Additionally, rules for identifying influential persons in the community could use the has-editor relationship as a determinant within the community. Rule 2 shows details of the publication-amount predicate from Rule 1.

Rule 1: DETERMINANT-AUTHOR

RULE: $(a_1, publication\text{-}amount, s_1, p_1) \wedge (a_2, publication\text{-}journal, s_2, p_2) \wedge$
$(d_3, publication\text{-}editor, a_3, p_3) \wedge (a_1 = a_2 = a_3) \wedge (s_1 = s_2 = s_3)$
$\longrightarrow (a_1, determinant\text{-}author\text{-}for, s_1, p_5)$ where $p_5 = MIN(p_1, p_2, p_3)$

Rule 2: PUBLICATION-AMOUNT

RULE: $(d_1, has\text{-}author, a_1, p_{1,1}) \wedge (d_1, published\text{-}for, e_1, p_{1,2}) \wedge (e_1, has\text{-}subject\text{-}area, s_1, p_{1,3}) \wedge (p_{1,2} > 0.5) \wedge (p_{1,3} > 0.5)) \wedge$
. . .

$(d_5, has\text{-}author, a_5, p_{5,1}) \wedge (d_5, published\text{-}for, e_5, p_{5,2}) \wedge (e_5, has\text{-}subject\text{-}area, s_5, p_{5,3}) \wedge (p_{5,2} > 0.5) \wedge (p_{5,3} > 0.5))$
$\wedge (d_1 \neq d_2 \neq d_3 \neq d_4 \neq d_5) \wedge (a_1 = a_2 = a_3 = a_4 = a_5) \wedge (s_1 = s_2 = s_3 = s_4 = s_5)$
$\longrightarrow (a_1, publication\text{-}amount, s_1, p_4)$ where $p_4 = AVG_i(\prod_{j=1,..3} p_{i,j})$

3.4 PWC and Digital Libraries

The provision of valid and expressively annotated RNs is in the core of the PWC approach. Digital libraries managing a preselected and quality controlled information collection for a user community may provide such networks extracted from their information collection as value-added service to other parties, e.g. conference organizers, that want to implement the PWC approach as an additional service to their clients (e.g. conference participants). RNs extracted and maintained by digital libraries provide a representative coverage of the domain related to the library user community and can be based on the library meta data managed by the digital library as well as on additional analysis of the library's information collection. The digital libraries can also implement the PWC approach as part of their own services. Again, this requires the creation of a RN.

4 Experimental Implementation of the Personal Web Context

The PWC approach has been prototypically implemented and first experiments have been performed. Figure 1 depicts an overview of the major components of the implemented PWC Environment.

A digital library implementing the PWC approach as part of their own services, would interact with the user via the PWC User Subsystem. The Domain Model Manager manages the different domain models and the RN created from them. Part of this includes the maintenance of domain-specific rules and the assignment and update of probability information (weights) associated with the rules as well as validating instances against ontology schema. The Data Analyzer Subsystem maintains representations of a number of information sources and is responsible for the class mappings between the Domain Subsystem and these external information sources. The information used by the Data Analyzer Subsystem can be obtained either explicitly, or semi-automatically from a variety of sources [25, 26, 23].In the experiment in this work uses the DBLP and IEEE/ACM information sources. Additionally, technologies employed in the experimental environment is built using the ontology support within the a Jena 2.1 API. The domain ontology was instantiated using the SAX, event driven XML parser. The rules were implemented using the Jena Rule class and probabilities are implemented by extending the built-in procedures of Jena Inferencing component and using unique rules names as a hash map to link each rule with the RDF-reified, graph-based data structure representing the associated weights.

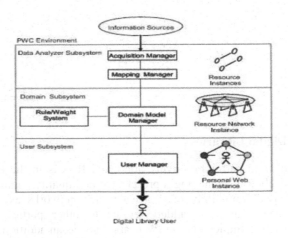

Fig. 1. Overview of PWC Environment

4.1 Sample Data

The first domain we consider in building the PWC is scientific research in computer science. We used a subset of DBLP that corresponded to publications produced from four serial digital library events as well as a subset of IEEE/ACM subject classification. The data sets were initially chosen as they provide a source of information that is mutually distinct, yet complementary and contains a set of resources which can be used in describing some important aspects of scientific community involvement. 2a) summaries the DBLP data used for the ECDL, European Conference on Digital Libraries; ICADL - International Conference of Asian Digital Libraries; JCDL - Joint Conference on Digital Libraries and IJODL - International Journal of Digital Libraries. The zeros represent unavailable DBLP data. Further, the data shown for JCDL prior to the year 2001 reflects the available ACM-DL Conference data only.

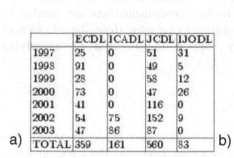

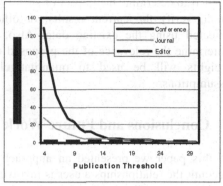

a)

	ECDL	ICADL	JCDL	IJODL
1997	25	0	51	31
1998	91	0	49	5
1999	28	0	58	12
2000	73	0	47	26
2001	41	0	116	0
2002	54	75	152	9
2003	47	86	87	0
TOTAL	359	161	560	83

b)

Fig. 2. a) Publication Data Set   b) Filtering of Determinant Persons

4.2 First Experimentation and Results

The goals of the first experiments was to validate the working environment whereby we could get initial results on the rule system's capabilities to support a value added service in a digital library that suggests a potential, subject-determinant persons who would be recommended as part of targeted expansion of a PWC. Such a service should be capable of filtering for example, the determi-nant persons based on subject matter. The initial experiments are summarized in the Figure 2b) and reflect the application of the "Determinant-Author" rule mentioned in Section 3.3. The rules were applied to a RN to test the subject-based approach to reducing the RN to a relevant subset for a specific task. We assumed that the task required: a) a need for collaboration with persons who shares common research (subject) interests and b) a consideration of the level of community involvement of the potential collaborator. In phase one, labeled in the graph as "Conference", we identified all potential collaborators by calculating each author's conference publication. A range of publication threshold values were examined and only authors having publications greater than the given publication threshold were considered and used in the subsequent phases. Threshold values below 4 represent extremities and were eliminated for clarity. In phase two (Journal), the results from phase one were used to determine which candidates also had journal publications. Finally, in phase three (Editor), those candidates from phase two who also had editors roles were considered.

Based on initial experiments with publication data, we were able to test domain specific rules as they contribute toward reducing the RN to items that can be potentially relevant in expanding a PWC. We found that for the range of threshold values examined, the number of potential determinant authors diminished. However, for all publication threshold values, the results of applying the editor filtering, remained the nearly the same. This can possibly be explained by the fact that not all events had available editor information. Further experiments are still needed to determine the impact of such PWCs. Manually completing the editor data could verify the current results, or other determinant criteria may need to be selected using the existing data. Also, further experimentations are needed to determine the relevance of the proposed entities to the user. Here, the adoption of weights will be used to quantitatively support the revision of underlying assumptions.

5 Conclusions and Future Work

In this paper we presented an approach for extended user modeling taking into account the relationships a user is involved in within a domain. The PWC approach enables personalization services that recommend how users can best extend their personal neighborhood within the domain to complete a specific task. After discussing the conceptual foundation of the PWC approach we gave an overview of a first experimental implementation and results of a PWC that uses the DBLP data in constructing a RN. The presented PWC approach is work in progress that still requires further investigation in several areas. Some important issues for further research and development activities in supporting relationship based recommendation services are:

– Further validation and refinement of the existing composition rules as well as the definition of further rules; In this area we especially plan to investigate in more systematic approaches for the definition of composition rules that rely on common properties of groups of relationship types;
– The PWC is also subject to information decay; Some relationships may become obsolete or loose their significance over time. In this area ideas of information aging as discussed in [27] will be investigated to ensure that the PWC adequately adapts to changes in the real world context of the user.
– Validation of other information collections as a basis for the RNs; In addition to using other information collections like e.g. the one offered by CiteSeer we also plan to combine information from different sources in order to get more robust and multifaceted RNs; This raises the special challenge of mapping relationship types used in different information collections to each other;

Acknowledgments. The research reported in this paper funded in part by the VIKEF Integrated Project (FP6, IST-507173) and by the DELOS Network of Excellence on Digital Libraries (FP6, G038-507618).

References

1. Callan, J., Smeaton, A.: Personalization and recommender systems in digital libraries. Technical report, DELOS-NSF Workshop on Personalization and Recommender Systems in Digital Libraries (2003) Further Contributors: Beaulieu M., Borlund P., Brusilovsky P., Chalmers M.,Lynch C.,Riedl J., Smyth B., Straccia U., Toms E.

2. Hanani, U., Shapira, B., Shoval, P.: Information filtering: Overview of issues, research and systems. User Modeling and User-Adapted Interaction 11 (2001) 203--259

3. Madle, G., Kostkova, P., Mani-Saada, J., Weinberg, J.: Evaluating the changes in knowledge and attitudes of digital library users. In Koch, T., Solvberg, I.T., eds.: Research and Advanced Technology for Digital Libraries 7th European Conference on Digital Libraries (ECDL 2003). Volume 2769 of Lecture Notes in Computer Science (LNCS)., Springer Verlag (2003) Trondheim, Norway, ISBN: 54040726X.

4. Niederée, C.J., Stewart, A., Mehta, B.: A multi-dimensional, unified user model for cross-system personalization. In: Proceedings of Advanced Visual Interfaces International Working Conference (AVI 2004) - Workshop on Environments for Personalized Information Access, Gallipoli (Lecce), Italy, May 2004. (2004)

5. Neuhold, E.J., Niederée, C., Stewart, A.: Personalization in digital libraries: An extended view. In: Proceedings of ICADL 2003. (2003) 1--16

6. Kaplan, C., Fenwick, J., Chen, J.: Adaptive hypertext navigation based on user goals and context. In: User Modeling and User-Adapted Interaction 3. Kluwer Academic Publishers, The Netherlands (1993) 193--220

7. Goker, A., Myrhaug, H.: User context and personalization. In: Proceedings of the European Conference on Case Based Reasoning (ECCBR 2002) - Workshop on Personalized Case-Based Reasoning, Aberdeen, Scotland, 4-7 September 2002. Volume LNCS 2416 of Lecture Notes in Artificial Intelligence., Springer-Verlag (2002)

8. Shapira, B., Shoval, P., Hanani, U.: Stereotypes in information filtering systems. Information Processing and Management 33 (1997) 273--287

9. Malone, T.W., Grant, K.R., Turbak, F.A., Brobst, S.A., Cohen, M.D.: Intelligent information-sharing systems. Communications of the ACM 30 (1987) 390--402

10. Wasserman, S., Galaskiewicz, J., eds.: Advances in Social Network Analysis. Sage, Thousand Oaks, California (1994)

11. McDonald, D.: Recommending collaboration with social networks: A comparative evaluation. In: Proceedings of the ACM Conference on Human Factors in Computing Systems (CHI'03), 2003. Volume 5., ACM Press (2003) 593--600

12. Tomobe, H., Matsuo, Y., Hasida, K., Ishizuka, M.: Social network extraction of conference participants. In: WWW. (2003) 13. McCarty, C.: Structure in personal networks. Journal of Social Structure 3 (2002)

13. Sowa, J.F.: Knowledge Representation: Logical, Philosophical, and Computational Foundations. Brooks Cole Publishing Co., Pacific Grove, CA (2000) 15. Trigg, R.H., Weiser, M.: Textnet: A network-based approach to text handling. ACM Transactions on Office Information Systems 4 (1983) 1--23

14. Liana Razmerita, Albert A. Angehrn, A.M.: Ontology-based user modeling for knowledge management systems. User Modeling (2003) 213--217

15. O'Hara, K., Alani, H., Shadbolt: Identifying communities of practice: Analysing ontologies as networks to support community recognition. In: In Proceedings IFIP World Computer Congress. Information Systems: The E-Business Challenge. (2002)

16. Middleton, S., Alani, H., Shadbolt, N., Rource, D.: Exploiting synergy between ontologies and recommender systems. In: Proceedings of the Eleventh International World Wide Web Conference - Semantic Web Workshop, Hawaii, USA, 2002. (2002)
17. Freitas, F.: Ontology of SCIENCE (2001) Protégé Project, Stanford University.
18. Erdmann, M., Staab, S., Angele, J., Decker, S., Hotho, A., Maedche, A., Schnurr, H.P., Studer, R., Sure, Y.: The KA ontology. http://www.aifb.uni-karlsruhe.de/ (2000)
19. Anyanwu, K., Sheth, A.: The p operator: Discovering and ranking associations in the semantic web. SIGMOD Record 31 (2002) 42--47
20. Noy, N.F., McGuinness, D.L.: Ontology development 101: A guide to creating your first ontology smi technical report smi-2001-0880. (2001)
21. Ley, M.: (Computer science bibliography) 24. Klyne, G., Carroll, J.J.: Resource Description Framework (RDF): Concepts and abstract syntax, W3C recommendation - 10 February 2004. http://www.w3.org/RDF (2004)
22. Berners-Lee, T., Hendler, J.and Lassila, O.: The semantic web. In: Scientific American. (2001)
23. Patel, C., Supekar, K., Lee, Y.: Ontogenie: Extracting ontology instances from the www. In: Workshop on Human Language Technology for the Semantic Web and Web Services 2nd International Semantic Web Conference. (2003)
24. Nieder'ee, C., Ste#ens, U., Schmidt, J.W., Matthes, F.: Aging links. In Borbinha, J., Baker, T., eds.: Research and Advanced Technology for Digital Libraries, Proceedings of the Third European Conference, ECDL 2000, Lisbon, Portugal, September 2000. Volume LNCS 1923 of Lecture Notes in Computer Science., Springer-Verlag (2000) 269--279

Interest-Based User Grouping Model for Collaborative Filtering in Digital Libraries

Seonho Kim and Edward A. Fox

Virginia Tech, Department of Computer Science, Blacksburg, Virginia 24061, USA
{shk, fox}@vt.edu

Abstract. Research in recommender systems focuses on applications such as in online shopping malls and simple information systems. These systems consider user profile and item information obtained from data explicitly entered by users. - where it is possible to classify items involved and to make recommendations based on a direct mapping from user or user group to item or item group. However, in complex, dynamic, and professional information systems, such as Digital Libraries, additional capabilities are needed for recommender systems to support their distinctive features: large numbers of digital objects, dynamic updates, sparse rating data, biased rating data on specific items, and challenges in getting explicit rating data from users. In this paper, we present an interest-based user grouping model for a collaborative recommender system for Digital Libraries. Also, we present several user interfaces that obtain implicit user rating data. Our model uses a high performance document clustering algorithm, LINGO, to extract document topics and user interests from documents users access in a Digital Library. This model is better suited to Digital Libraries than traditional recommender systems because it focuses more on users than items and because it utilizes implicit rating data.

1 Introduction

One of the most anticipated roles of a Digital Library (DL) is to support a variety of user classes, such as researchers and learners, who are interested in similar research and learning topics. Another expected role for DLs is the active support of social communities. In order to implement these complex functions of DLs, more research should be carried out on the users rather than the system. Many studies of collaborative filtering (CF) and adaptive techniques for recommender systems have been conducted for online shopping malls and personalized websites [1, 4]. However, those techniques focus on exploring learning methods to improve accuracy instead of focusing on 1) scalability, 2) accommodating new data and 3) comprehensibility - three important aspects of recommender systems in DLs [5]. We propose a user grouping technique to improve these aspects by concentrating on user interests.

2 Previous Studies

Recommending has been studied with regard to Ungar's system [4] for online media shopping malls; GroupLens [13] for Usenet netnews systems; and for DLs: PASS [2],

Z. Chen et al. (Eds.): ICADL 2004, LNCS 3334, pp. 533–542, 2004.

Renda's system [3], and DEBORA [15]. The main idea of these studies is the sharing of user profile and preference information, which was entered explicitly by users, with other users within the system, to provide them with more productive service. PASS provided personalized service by computing similarity between user profiles and documents in pre-classified research domains. Renda's system emphasized collaborative functions of DLs by grouping users based on their profiles.

Unlike other systems, GroupLens employs a time consuming factor, which is a type of implicit rating data, together with explicit rating data. Nichols's research [11] emphasized the potential of the implicit rating technique and suggested the use of implicit data as a check on explicit ratings. Gonçalves' research defined an XML based log standard for DLs [16] which paved the way for the study of implicit ratings in DLs. This research emphasized the interoperability, reusability and completeness of the log system. However, without extension, this log suggestion is not suitable for recommender systems, that use the standard HTTP log system, because it initially focused on extracting system rather than content information.

3   Recommending Through Interest-Based User Grouping

In our system, users that share a research or learning interest are placed in the same group. Users' interests are collected from their implicit ratings, based on browsing and selection of clustered document sets, rather than explicit ratings such as from questionnaire responses. One hypothesis of our model is that high performance document clustering algorithms, such as LINGO [7], can be used to extract topics from documents. We also can use document clustering algorithms to overcome data sparseness problems. Document topics are stored in the user model and are used for grouping the users and making recommendations. Since we integrate item information into the user model, we can concentrate on the user side and make it easier to formulate recommendations. Because of these features, our model is especially suitable for DLs.

Our system employs LINGO to extract topics from documents. Document clustering also is used to overcome the bias caused by sparse ratings in most research areas and highly-duplicated ratings in very narrow areas. LINGO was selected because of its ability to discover descriptive names for clusters. Unlike most other algorithms, LINGO first attempts to find descriptive names for future clusters and only then proceeds to assign matching documents to clusters [7]. The names found by LINGO are treated as "document topics". When a user performs a search and gets a set of result documents, a selection of topics is provided to the user. Topics which are rated positively are treated as user "interests". Thus, user ratings are made implicitly.

Our system uses implicit user rating information collected by tracking user interactions with the interface: sending a query, expanding a dynamic tree, selecting a document cluster, and selecting a document to read or download. When a user rates document topics in a DL, the document topics are saved in temporary storage by the client. The saved user interests are sent to the server and stored in the user profile database for use by the recommender system when the user returns to the DL. Unlike GroupLens [12], our system doesn't use a time-consuming factor because it causes so much noise in real world use and distracts experiment participants.

Our recommender system is based on collaborative filtering; to make a user recommendation, the system refers to other users that have similar interests. User grouping is based on similarity. In the field of information retrieval, there are two general methods (which we employ) to calculate similarity between documents: correlation and vector similarity. Thus we compute:

$$w(a,i) = \frac{\sum_j (v_{a,j} - \bar{v}_a)(v_{i,j} - \bar{v}_i)}{\sqrt{\sum_j (v_{a,j} - \bar{v}_a)^2 \sum_j (v_{i,j} - \bar{v}_i)^2}} \qquad (1)$$

$$w(a,i) = \sum_j \frac{v_{a,j}}{\sqrt{\sum_{k \in I_a} v_{a,k}^2}} \frac{v_{i,j}}{\sqrt{\sum_{k \in I_i} v_{i,k}^2}} \qquad (2)$$

$$\bar{v} = \frac{total\ number\ of\ topics\ selected\ by\ the\ user}{total\ number\ of\ topics\ proposed\ to\ the\ user\ by\ the\ system} \qquad (3)$$

(1) represents the correlation of user 'a' and user 'i'. 'v_{aj}' is the rating value of item 'j' of user 'a' which means the number of positive ratings on 'j' made by 'a'. 'j' represents common items which are rated by user 'a' and 'i'. '$\bar{v}$' is the average probability of positive rating of the user which is obtained by (3). (2) represents vector similarity between two users. 'I_a' is a set of interests of user 'a', and 'k' is an element of the interests set. Either formula can be used to calculate the similarity between two users. In these calculations, we treat user interests as atomic terms that are strings. Thus, the strings "digital library" and "digital camera" are not considered similar even though they share the common term "digital".

A recommendation is triggered either when an item in a DL attains a rating greater than a certain value defined by the system manager, or when a newly arrived item gets a positive rating, after reading or downloading, from any user that has mentor level status in his/her group. The recommendation process of our model consists of two phases. In phase one, the recommender system decides which user groups will be recommended by a new positive rating. These groups are determined based on the probabilities that each of its users makes the same rating. R_k is the probability that user group 'k' is affected by the rating, which is made by a user 'a' to an item 'j'.

$$R_k = P_k^{\frac{1}{N} \sum_{i:C_i = k} v_{i,j}} (1 - P_k)^{\frac{1}{T-N} \sum_{i:C_i \neq k} (1 - v_{i,j})} \qquad (4)$$

where T is the total number of users registered in the system, C_i is the group that user 'i' belongs to, $v_{i,j}$ is the probability that user 'i' rates item 'j', N is the total number of users in group 'k' and P_k is the base rate of group 'k' observed from the database (which is calculated by dividing the number of users in group 'k' by 'T', the total number of registered users in the system).

The second phase of the recommendation process is individual recommendation. Once the groups are selected for a new rating, individual users in highly ranked groups are checked for eligibility to get a recommendation for the rating that evoked the recom-mendation. We compute $P_{a,j}$, the probability that a user 'a' in group 'k' likes item 'j'.

$$P_{a,j} = \bar{v}_a + \kappa \sum_{i=1}^{n} w(a,i)(v_{i,j} - \bar{v}_i) \qquad (5)$$

where 'n' is the number of users in the group. This formula is derived from the Memory-Based Algorithm [14] but we use average probability of positive rating of user 'a' for $\overline{v_a}$ instead of the mean rate value of the user. By only calculating this formula for users in the selected groups we decrease the cost of the recommendation.

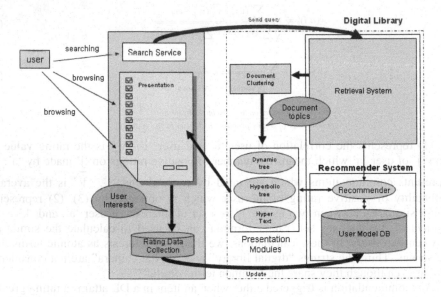

Fig. 1. A schematic drawing of the components in the interest-based recommender system for DLs. Document topics are extracted by the naming algorithm of the document clustering system, LINGO, and are presented to the user to be rated by way of hyperbolic tree, dynamic tree, and normal HTML pages. While using the DL, the user gives implicit ratings, such as by sending queries, browsing result documents, and reading some documents. User interests are gathered from these implicit ratings and stored into a "rating data collection" which will affect the user's profile that is stored in the "user model DB" in the DL

Generally, user models are implemented with user profile data such as name, ID, sex, major, interests, position, hobby, etc. Our system, illustrated in Figure 1, which is based on the Carrot2 system [6], uses XML formatting for all messages exchanged and stored among the DL components. Once the temporary user rating data is transferred to the DL server, it is processed by the recommender and added to the user model database as XML. Unfortunately, the standard HTTP log protocol cannot extract the title of an anchor, which is treated as a document topic in our system. Specially designed user interfaces implemented in JavaScript (see Figure 2) or Java (see Figure 3) [9, 10, 17], are required. For instance, when a user selects the anchor "Statistics for Librarians" on a web page, we need the title "Statistics for Librarians" to be stored in the log file along with the data gathered by the standard HTTP protocol such as URL, current time, error codes, IP addresses, etc. The interests of the current user are stored in a cookie at the client and are transferred to the server the next time the user accesses the DL. The cookie size limit of 4000 bytes is large enough to store the user's behavior for a single login session.

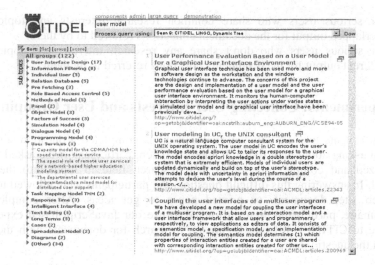

Fig. 2. A JavaScript based user interface. The left (dynamic tree) and right (HTML page) frames present a clustered result set efficiently. Data on user interactions such as opening clusters or selecting a document are stored temporarily in a cookie

4   Hypotheses

With our system, which extracts user interests for user grouping, we may test three hypotheses about proper document clustering algorithm behavior:

1. For any serious user who has his own research interests and topics, show consistent output for the document collections referred to by the user.

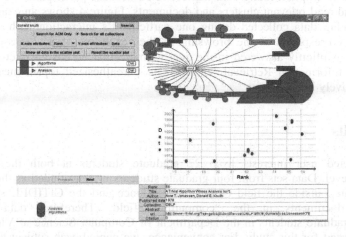

Fig. 3. CITIVIZ: An Interactive Visualization Interface for CITIDEL. Search result clusters are presented as nodes in a hyperbolic tree. Users can select relevant nodes to see detailed information of the document in clusters [17]

2. For serious users who share common research interests and topics, show overlapped output for the document collections referred to by them.
3. For serious users who don't share any research interests and topics, show different output for the document collections referred to by them.

5 Experiments: Collecting User Interests and User Grouping

Our experiments test the hypotheses. Participants completed a questionnaire with a question asking about their research interests. Then, participants were asked to list 10 specialized and complex queries in their research field to input into the DL for retrieval. In answering this difficult question, the participants were allowed to refer to any web site, document, or printed paper to get ideas. After completing the questionnaire, participants were instructed to use our JavaScript-based experimental interface to CITIDEL [8] (see Figure 2), to search for documents with the queries listed in the questionnaire.

<Semi Structured Data <Cross Language Information Retrieval CLIR <Translation Model <Structured English Query <TREC Experiments at Maryland <Structured Document <Evaluation <Learning <Web <Query Processing <Query Optimisers <QA <Disambiguation <Sources <SEQUEL<Fuzzy <Indexing <Inference Problem <Schematically Heterogeneity <Sub Optimization Query Execution Plan <Generation <(Semi Structured Data) (Cross Language Information Retrieval CLIR) (Structured English Query) (TREC Experiments at Maryland) (Evaluation) (Query Processing) (Query Optimisers) (Disambiguation)

Fig. 4. Implicit rating data collected from one user

After CITIDEL displayed the search results, the participants were asked to browse through them. Implicit rating data was collected because participants were supposed to open and read relevant clusters and documents. Figure 4 shows an example of the implicit rating data collected during one participant's interaction with our system. This data corresponds to the browsing of the result set of a single query. This participant explicitly answered in the questionnaire that he has an interest in Cross Language Information Retrieval (CLIR). The parenthesized topics mean they are rated positively by the user.

6 Results

We collected user interests from 22 graduate students at both the Ph.D. and Master's level. Data sets from four graduate students were excluded as their research domains are outside the field of computer science and the CITIDEL system only contains documents in the "computing" field. Therefore, data from 18 selected graduate students in the Department of Computer Science at Virginia Tech were analyzed for this study. For convenience, we named each subject according to their research interests, which were obtained from the questionnaires, as shown in Table 1.

User grouping was based on vector similarity as in (2). User similarities among all subjects are shown in Figure 5. A longer column in the graph represents greater similarity. Columns are either high or very low. This means the document clustering algorithm is able to distinguish a user from others who have different interests.

Table 1. Symbols of participants of this experiment and their profiles. They were obtained from explicit ratings made by their answering the questionnaire

	User Symbols	User profiles collected from questionnaire
1	dlmember	The one who belonged to the Digital Library Research Laboratory
2	softeng	The one who has an interest in Software Engineering
3	bio	The one who has an interest in Bioinformatics
4	vr_hci	The one who has an interest in Virtual Reality and Human Computer Interaction
5	clir_1	The one who has an interest in Cross Language Information Retrieval
6	clir_2	The one who has an interest in Cross Language Information Retrieval
7	nlp_1	The one who has an interest in Natural Language Processing
8	nlp_2	The one who has an interest in Natural Language Processing
9	vr_1	The one who has an interest in Virtual Reality
10	vr_2	The one who has an interest in Virtual Reality
11	EC_agent	The one who has an interest in E-Commerce and Agent
12	CybEdu_agt	The one who has an interest in Cyber Education and Agent
13	dlandedu_1	The one who has an interest in Digital Library and Education
14	dlandedu_2	The one who has an interest in Digital Library and Education
15	person_1	The one who has an interest in Personalization
16	person_2	The one who has an interest in Personalization
17	se_me	The one who has an interest in Software Engineering
18	fuzzy	The one who has an interest in Fuzzy Theory

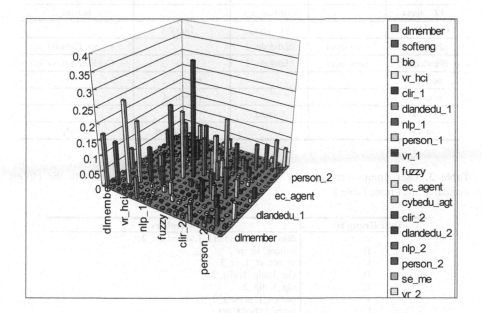

Fig. 5. User similarities among the users

Hypothesis 1 is supported by the results of Figure 5, which shows that similarities among users are distinctive according to their research topics. Hypotheses 2 and 3 are supported in Table 2. Several pairs of users with the same interests, such as "person_1 and person_2", "nlp_1 and nlp_2", "clir_1 and clir_2", "dlandedu_1 and dlandedu_2", and "softeng and se_me" show high similarities, which indicates that the document clustering algorithms generated highly overlapped outputs. Further support and clarification is given in Table 3, which shows nine user groups from eighteen participants in the experiment, based on our interest-based user grouping model.

Table 2. Similarities levels, sorted & grouped between each user & the other (Level 5) users

User ID	Level 1	Level 2	Level 3	Level 4
dlmember			dlandedu_1, dlandedu_2	
softeng			se_me	person_2
bio				
vr_hci			vr_2, vr_1	person_1, person_2
clir_1	nlp_1, clir_2		nlp_2	
clir_2	clir_1, nlp_1		nlp_2	
nlp_1	nlp_2		clir_1, clir_2	
nlp_2	nlp_1		clir_1, clir_2	
vr_1				vr_2, vr_hci
vr_2		vr_hci	vr_1	person_1, person_2
EC_agent		CybEdu_agt		person_2
CybEdu_agt		EC_agent	fuzzy	
dlandedu_1	dlmember	dlandedu_2		vr_hci, CybEdu_agt
dlandedu_2	dlmember	dlandedu_1		CybEdu_agt, vr_hci
person_1			person_2	
person_2			person_1	
se_me		softeng		
fuzzy			CybEdu_agt	bio, nlp_1

Table 3. User groups generated by merging a user and other members with the closest similarity level from Table 2

User Group ID	Members
A	dlmember, dlandedu_1, dlandedu_2
B	softeng, se_me,
C	vr_hci, vr_1, vr_2
D	clir_1, nlp_1, clir_2
E	nlp_1, nlp_2
F	person_1, person_2
G	fuzzy, cybedu_agt
H	EC_agent, cybedu_agt, fuzzy
I	Bio

7 Conclusions and Future Work

We proposed an interest-based user grouping model for collaborative filtering recommender systems. These are suitable for systems such as DLs which have sparse rating data and dynamically increasing contents. This model focuses more on users than items. Also, it actively finds user communities. A document clustering algorithm and specially designed user interfaces are employed to extract document topics and user interests by way of implicit ratings. Results of experiments to test the hypotheses support our approach. Future work will include detailed analyses of this model for accuracy, scalability, and efficiency. Other work will seek further confirmation of our hypotheses by way of wider deployment of the visualization front-ends for CITIDEL.

Acknowledgements

We thank the: people and organizations working on CITIDEL, student participants in our experiments, developer of the LINGO algorithm, and developers of the CITIVIZ visualization tool. Thanks go to the National Science Foundation for its support of grants NSF DUE-0121679, DUE-0121741, IIS-0307867, and NSF IIS-0325579.

References

1. Georgios Paliouras, Vangelis Karkaletsis, Christos Papatheodorou, Constantine D. Spyropoulos: Exploiting Learning Techniques for the Acquisition of User Stereotypes and Communities. In Proc. Int. Conference on User Modelling, UM '99 (1999) 169-178.
2. Chun Zeng, Xiaohui Zheng, Chunxiao Xing, Lizhu Zhou : Personalized Services for Digital Library. In Proc. 5th Int. Conf. on Asian Digital Libraries, ICADL (2002) 252-253.
3. M. Elena Renda, Umberto Straccia: A Personalized Collaborative Digital Library Environment. In Proc. 5th Int. Conf. on Asian Digital Libraries, ICADL (2002) 262-274
4. Lyle H. Ungar and Dean P. Foster: A Formal Statistical Approach to Collaborative Filtering. CONALD '98, Carnegie Mellon U., Pittsburgh, PA (1998).
5. John S. Breese, David Heckerman and Carl Kadie: Empirical Analysis of Predictive Algorithms for Collaborative Filtering. In Proceedings of the 14th Conference on Uncertainty in Artificial Intelligence (1997) 43-52.
6. Carrot2 Project, A Research Framework for experimenting with automated querying of various data sources, processing search results and visualization, http://www.cs.put. poznan/ pl/dweiss/carrot/ (2004)
7. Stanisław Osiński and Dawid Weiss: Conceptual Clustering Using Lingo Algorithm: Evaluation on Open Directory Project Data, Advanced in Soft Computing, Intelligent Information Processing and Web Mining, Proceedings of the International IIS: IIPWM'04 Conference, Zakopane, Poland (2004) 369-378
8. CITIDEL project, Computing and Information Technology Interactive Digital Educational Library, http://www.citidel.org/ (2004)
9. Abdelmoumin Ghada, Alafaliq A. Ahmad, Nithiwat Kampanya, Seonho Kim: Virginia Tech report, at http://infovis.cs.vt.edu/cs5764/Fall2003 /projects.html (2003)

10. Saverio Perugini, Kathleen McDevitt, Ryan Richardson, Manuel Perez-Quinones, Rao Shen, Naren Ramakrishnan, Chris Williams, Edward A. Fox: Enhancing Usability in CITIDEL: Multimodal, Multilingual and Interactive Visualization Interfaces, in Proc. of the Fourth ACM/IEEE Joint Conference on Digital Libraries (2004) 315-324

11. David M. Nichols: Implicit Rating and Filtering. In Proceedings of 5th DELOS Workshop on Filtering and Collaborative Filtering (1997) 31-36

12. Paul Resnick, Neophytos Iacovou, Mitesh Suchak, Peter Bergstrom, John Riedl: GroupLens: An Open Architecture for Collaborative Filtering of Netnews. In Proceedings of Conference on Computer Supported Cooperative Work (1994) 175-186

13. Joseph A. Konstan, Bradley N. Miller, David Maltz, Jonathan L. Herlocker, Lee R. Gordon, and John Riedl: GroupLens: Applying Collaborative Filtering to Usenet News. Communications of the ACM, Vol. 40 (1997) 77-87

14. Kai Yu, Anton Schwaighofer, Volker Tresp, Xiaowei Xu, Hans-Peter Kriegel: Probabilistic Memory-based Collaborative Filtering. IEEE Transactions on Knowledge and Data Engineering (2003) 56-69

15. David M Nichols, Duncan Pemberton, Salah Dalhoumi, Omar Larouk, Clair Belisle, Michael B. Twidale: DEBORA: Developing an Interface to Support Collaboration in a Digital Library. In Proceedings of the Fourth European Conference on Research and Advanced Technology for Digital Libraries (2000) 239-248

16. Marcos A. Gonçalves, Ming Luo, Rao Shen, Mir Farooq, and Edward A. Fox: An XML Log Standard and Tools for Digital Library Logging Analysis, in Proc. of Sixth European Conference on Research and Advanced Technology for Digital Libraries (2002) 16-18

17. Nithiwat Kampanya, Rao Shen, Seonho Kim, Chris North, Edward A. Fox: Citiviz: A Visual User Interface to the CITIDEL System, in Proceedings of Fourth European Conference on Digital Libraries, ECDL 2004 (2004)

Leveraging Enterprise Technology for the Library Portal at the National University of Singapore

Lee Shong Lin Cecelia[1] and Yulin Yang[2]

[1] Library Automation, Central Library, National University of Singapore
cybrarian21@yahoo.com
[2] BEA Systems Singapore Pte Ltd
yuliny@bea.com

Abstract. In large academic libraries, the organization and management of diverse digital content for easy access has always posed a challenge. Users have varying information needs and are often confounded by having to access information residing on disparate systems via different interfaces and authentication credentials. To improve the user experience, the new Library Portal was implemented using enterprise portal technology to deliver personalization and single sign-on capabilities. It leverages the widely-adopted J2EE standard for application integration using an industry-leading application server and award-winning portal framework on low cost Linux platform. By utilizing standard-based technologies, the library is able to manage a scalable and highly-configurable portal which integrates with INNOPAC, the library`s automated system, and the campus LDAP directory servers to provide convenient single sign-on to library services. Personalized access to INNOPAC, library contents and digital library resources is delivered through user profiling, group-based entitlements and a rule engine.

1 Introduction

The organization and management of diverse digital content for easy access has always posed a challenge. In large academic libraries, users tend to have varying information needs and are often confounded by having to access information residing on disparate systems via different interfaces and authentication credentials.

The National University of Singapore (NUS) Libraries comprises six libraries which support teaching and research for various departments, faculties and their graduate divisions. To improve the user experience, the NUS Libraries implemented the library portal using enterprise portal technology to deliver personalization and single sign-on capabilities. The portal was released in June 2004 and serves as a one-stop gateway to library information and resources for more than 50,000 users, including faculty, staff and students of the university. It provides a single sign-on, branded and pervasive access to personalized library applications, services and digitized collections for the campus community.

Z. Chen et al. (Eds.): ICADL 2004, LNCS 3334, pp. 543–552, 2004.

Jointly developed with BEA Systems and Greenhouse, the library portal marks a significant milestone in the library's computerization journey by introducing an array of enterprise-grade technologies, namely J2EE, RDBMS and Linux. It leverages industry-leading products such as WebLogic Server^{TM}, WebLogic Portal^{TM}, WebLogic Workshop^{TM}, Oracle^{TM} Database and Redhat^{TM} Linux. The adoption of standard-based technologies will cater to future needs of application integration across university departments.

2 A New Generation Library Portal on Enterprise Technology

The new generation library portal was built on the following technology foundations:

a. *Linux* – the library portal is one of first on campus to adopt a Linux and Intel-based architecture to lower the entry cost without comprising on scalability, reliability and performance.
b. *Oracle Database* – The Oracle database server has been selected as a proven SQL and RDBMS implementation. It delivers faster response time, provides a higher level of concurrent data retrieval, and also caters to plans for future increases in the volume of information storage.
c. *J2EE and WebLogic Server* - Java 2 Platform, Enterprise Edition (J2EE) defines the standard for developing component-based multi-tier enterprise applications. Weblogic Server is the leading product that implements the J2EE standard.
d. *WebLogic Portal & Workshop IDE* - BEA WebLogic Portal and Workshop provide the unified industry strength framework for developing, deploying and managing custom-fit portals.

The following diagram depicts an architectural view of the library portal:

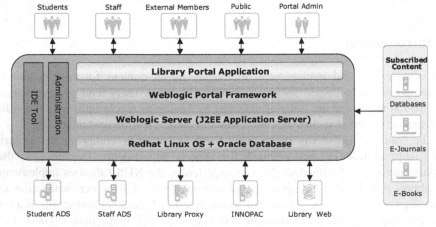

Library Applications & Content Campus Infrastructure

Fig. 1. Library Portal Architecture

3 Key Features

3.1 Single Sign-On Eliminates Multiple Username/Password Pairs

A key feature of the library portal implementation is the simplicity and convenience provided by the single sign-on service. Before the portal was implemented, users were required to log in with different sets of usernames and passwords to authenticate to the various services provided by the library. For example, when accessing their library record via the library's OPAC called LINC (Library Integrated Catalogue), they would log in with their staff or matriculation number and library PIN, which are managed locally at the LINC application on INNOPAC. However, when accessing electronic forms or logging into the library's proxy server to access electronic resources, they were required to login with their campus network ID and password, which are stored in the campus-wide LDAP directory servers.

To overcome the inconvenience and confusion caused by multiple username / password pairs, single sign-on was implemented for the library portal. It provided seamless integration to INNOPAC, the library's automated system, as well as to the campus LDAP directory servers for staff and students.

As depicted in Figure 2, single sign-on was achieved by:

- Using an LDAP server, in this case Microsoft Active Directory Server, as a unified user identity store
- Configuring Microsoft IIS Web Server to support Windows NT Challenge/Response (NTLM)
- Developing a custom IdentityAsserter based on Weblogic Server's SSPI (Security Service Provider Interface) security framework to achieve perimeter authentication to Weblogic
- Synchronization of user authentication data for INNOPAC via batch data exporting/importing and storing such data in the user profile
- Automatically signing users into INNOPAC via the library portal using session cookies

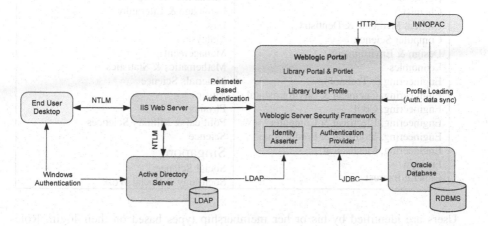

Fig. 2. Single Sign-On Solution for NUS Library Portal

The ubiquitous ID and password for the campus network, NUSNET, enables user login to Windows-based desktop. Upon desktop login, users are seamlessly logged in to the library system to retrieve their library records in LINC and automatically receive library notifications reminding them of overdue loans or pick-up notices for items reserved by them. Users can also customize their own preferences to view a list of new book arrivals pertaining to their areas of interest.

In addition, the portal login enables users to access electronic forms as well as subscribed electronic resources via the library proxy without the need for additional login. With single sign-on, there is no need for users to keep multiple username / password pairs from disparate systems and applications.

3.2 Personalization Through User Profiles

Personalization is the capability of a web application to tailor its content and behavior according to user characteristics. It empowers users by enabling them to create their own information and research environments based on the available library resources [5]. By providing adaptive content services, the library portal delivers the right information and services to the user based on his roles, privileges, requirements and interests. To cater to the diverse information needs of staff and students from various faculties and departments, users have the option to subscribe to a choice of 30 subject-based interest groups (see Table 1) to view library news, events, and new book arrivals for their selected categories. For ejournals and ebooks, these broad interest groups are further categorized into 228 subcategories to enable users to filter out resources which are not in their preferred interest groups. They can also customize their listing of electronic resources to view or search only the reference databases, ejournals and ebooks in their areas of interest.

Table 1. List of subject-based interest groups which users can subscribe

Biological & Life Sciences	History & Geography
Business	Humanities & Art
Chemistry	Language & Literature
Clinical Medicine & Dentistry	Law
Computer Science	Malaysia
Design & Environment	Management
Economics	Mathematics & Statistics
Engineering & Technology	Materials Science
Engineering, Chemical & Environmental	Music
Engineering, Civil	Physics
Engineering, Electrical & Computer	Political & Military Sciences
Engineering, Industrial & Production	Science
Engineering, Mechanical	Singapore
Finance	Social Sciences
General Interest	Sociology & Social Work

Users are identified by his or her membership types based on their login. Role-based access rules ensure that restricted services such as access to the Examination

Papers database or a listing of relevant electronic forms are displayed only to the authorized users. An undergraduate or honors student, for example, can only access the electronic forms for library services which they are entitled. Library staff can also access administrative functions via a separate portal administrator interface.

Ease of use and time savings are important factors in encouraging user adoption. As Ketchell commented, "Libraries must move from customization to personalization to simplify workflow for their users."[4] To facilitate requests, electronic forms for library services are auto-populated with user particulars such as name, email address and staff or student identification number. Requests for certain services which require approval are automatically routed to the relevant person via email as part of the requesting workflow.

3.3 Branded Library Resource and Service

The need to make portal use "intuitive and convenient" cannot be overstated [8]. The library portal adopts a user-centric approach by unifying content from multiple repositories and consolidating service delivery across channels. It features a unique library branding with a consistent look and feel. Users are no longer confounded by the myriad of interfaces they encounter as they navigate from one site to another.

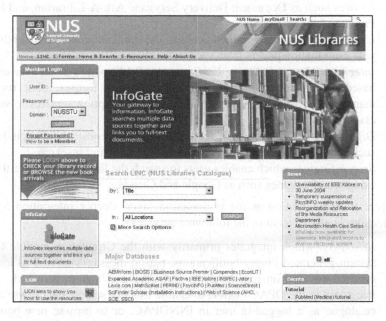

Fig. 3. The NUS Library Portal combines vibrant design with seamless application integration to deliver one-stop access to library services

Diverse applications are unified in a single point of entry and presented to users in an attractive interface. The WebLogic Portal™ Framework provides a versatile environment to customize the look and feel using themes, skins and skeletons.

Together with the use of Cascading Style Sheets (CSS), these components define how the portal desktop is rendered to achieve a consistent look and feel.

3.4 Application Integration

A wide range of resources and services are unified with the library portal as the single point of entry. Different types of services call for varying levels of integration. Sullivan describes the three levels of application integration based on the three-tier architecture of portals: presentation layer, application layer, and data services layer [8]. In the context of the library portal implementation, most of the application integration is evident at the presentation layer. This layer consists of services which are presented as portlets linking to multiple applications. Some examples include:

a. *Search LINC* which enables users to search the library OPAC using predefined indexes such as author, title, keyword, ISBN/ISSN and limit the search to specific collections.
b. *InfoGate* which is the federated search engine that enables users to perform simultaneous searches on electronic databases, electronic journals and library catalogues through a single interface.
c. *Electronic Forms* which enables users to submit requests online for library services such as Document Delivery Services, Ask-A-Librarian, and Request to Purchase Library Materials.
d. *Exam Papers Database* which contains the digitized copies of over 20,000 past year examination papers from various faculties of the university.
e. *Integrated Virtual Learning Environment (IVLE)* which contains a set of Web-based tools and resources such as discussion forums, chat rooms, quiz management, assignment repositories, and subscription services to supplement classroom learning.
f. *Digital Media Gallery* which serves as a central repository of digital resources such as video, audio and images used for teaching and research.
g. *Search Engines* which enables users to search the library website or the Internet using search engines such as Google and Cicada.

Apart from integration at the presentation layer, deeper integration to backend applications is also evident in the following services:

a. *INNOPAC* which integrates primarily with the Circulation module to retrieve system-generated library notifications, patron messages as well as loans, fines, checked-out and on request items from the user's library record. It is also integrated to the OPAC module to enable users to search and browse the library catalogue as a logged-in user in INNOPAC, or to browse new book arrivals based on the user's preferred interest groups.
b. *LDAP integration* to provide authentication for the campus community using the staff and student Active Directory Server (ADS)
c. *Digital Library / E-Resources* which provides access to electronic resources subscribed by the NUS Libraries. It features a comprehensive listing of

reference databases, electronic books and journals browsable by title, subject and publisher as well as title search capability.

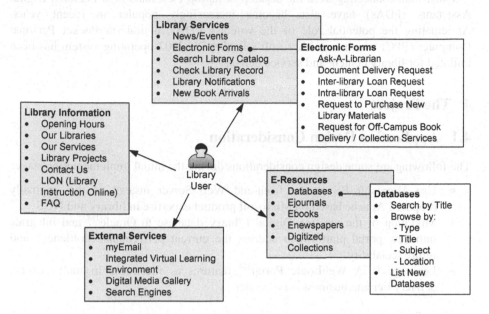

Fig. 4. Use Case Diagram - Services and Resources available to library user

3.5 Managing Information Using Web Content Management

For any website, it is important to keep information manageable and up-to-date. To achieve this, the library portal features a database-driven content management system to automate the publishing, retirement and archiving of time-sensitive web content such as library news and events.

When publishing a news item or event to the portal, library staff simply inputs the necessary information using a form-based template, specifying the expiration date and relevant metadata to classify the content, e.g. title, event type, subject category, etc. Post-publishing tasks such as retiring and archiving of the content is handled by the Content Management System.

To facilitate further collaboration between content contributors from the various libraries, the TeamSite® Content Management system implemented campus-wide is also used to manage and deploy content to the portal server.

3.6 Pervasive Access – Anytime, Anywhere

Since July 1999, staff and students at the National University of Singapore have been able to access the campus network (NUSNET) and the Internet using Wireless LAN technology. To make anytime, anywhere access a reality, the campus is equipped with

400 wireless access points to provide both indoor and outdoor wireless connections for the campus community.

Other than connecting from the desktop or laptop PCs, hand-held Personal Digital Assistants (PDAs) have also become increasingly popular in recent years. Anticipating the potential role of the wireless PDAs, a trial on Pocket Personal Computer (PPC) which uses Microsoft's Pocket PC 2002 operating system has been initiated for library content and service delivery.

4 The Project

4.1 Application Design Consideration

The following are some design considerations during the initial implementation stage:

- Use Microsoft IIS as the front-end Web Server instead of the originally proposed Apache based on Microsoft product expertise in library and NUS.
- Migration of the existing Digital Library database to Oracle^{TM} and integrate into new portal platform to address the current performance bottleneck and future scalability.
- Leverage BEA WebLogic Portal^{TM} features as illustrated in multi-channel delivery tier and business services tier.

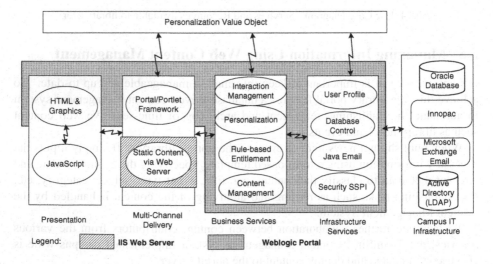

Fig. 5. Library Portal Application Design View

4.2 Timeline and Project Committee

Aiming for unified, responsive web site to support rich learning user experience over library information and services, tenders are called for building the new library portal in the first half of year 2003. Major requirements include integration of the current library backend systems and applications, providing single sign-on and website customization and tailoring capabilities to logon users for "My Libraries", as well as designing a one-stop consistent user interface for library branded services.

The library portal project committee went through a careful evaluation process, including a POC (proof-of-concept) exercise covering key functions, namely single sign-on, integration to library system (INNOPAC) and wireless PDA access. Key selection criteria are vendor's solution delivery capability, compliance to mandatory requirements, technology and product strength and, of course, cost.

The contract was awarded to Greenhouse and BEA joint team in Oct 2003. During the project kick-off meeting, implementation strategy was to coordinate the effort and maximize the strength of all stakeholders as stated below to ensure quality and timely delivery:

- Library Automation Department will drive the requirement and provide expertise of the library system, IT environment and onsite development.
- BEA will undertake the solution architecture, design and implementation and rollout.
- Greenhouse will design the user interface and customize the look and feel.
- NUS Computer Center will conduct the performance and load testing on library portal

5 Best Practices and Lessons Learned

The project team adopted the following best practices to ensure a well-coordinated effort within the short implementation timeframe:

- Web-based project documentation and message sharing using SharePoint™ document library to facilitate collaboration between team members
- Use of SteelThreads implementation methodology to incorporate experience-based best practices to deliver projects with lower cost, reduced risk, higher quality, and shorter time to market
- Divide-and-Conquer approach to leverage technical and domain expertise among team members
- Onsite development to foster greater communication between the "external" design and implementation teams and in-house library team
- Knowledge transfer via mentoring to enable library staff to achieve a high level of self-sufficiency at maintaining the portal

6 What's Next

In June 2004, the initial release of the library portal targeted staff and students at the National University of Singapore. Essential portal features such as integration with the campus LDAP and INNOPAC, a personalized Digital Library and role-based access to electronic forms for library services were introduced.

Additional features will be incorporated progressively to enhance the usability and value of the portal. Upcoming enhancements for the library portal include:

- Leveraging Service Oriented Architecture (SOA) and Web Services to share and reuse business logic between multiple technologies
- Incorporating workflow capabilities to increase the efficiency and accuracy of processing electronic forms for library services
- Introducing more personalization features such as enabling users to save search strategies and bookmarks, or displaying a student's course list
- Greater collaboration with other university departments such as the Centre for Instructional Technology (CIT) to deliver curriculum integration
- Creating administrative portlets for library staff to add, delete or modify entries for ejournal or ebook information in the E-Resources database

As emerging standards and technologies evolve, new possibilities pave the way for greater collaboration between university departments and the ease of application sharing and reuse. User needs and expectations also change over time. Therefore, the usability and appeal of the library portal must be constantly reviewed to ensure that it delivers the right information to the right people at the right time.

References

1. Borgman, Christine L.: Challenges in Building Digital Libraries for the 21st Century. In E.-P Lim et al. (eds.): ICADL 2002. *Lecture Notes in Computer Science,* Vol. 2555. Springer-Verlag, Berlin Heidelberg (2002) 1–13.
2. Jordan, William: My Gateway at the University of Washington Libraries. *Information Technology and Libraries*, 19(4) (2003): 180–185.
3. Katz, Richard N. and Associates. *Web Portals and Higher Education: Technologies to Make IT Personal.* Jossey-Bass, San Francisco (2002).
4. Ketchell, Debra S.: Too Many Channels: Making Sense out of Portals and Personalization. *Information Technology and Libraries*, 19(4) (2003): 175–179.
5. Lakos, A., Gray C.: Personalized Library Portals as an Organizational Culture Change Agent. *Information Technology and Libraries*, 19(4) (2003): 169–174.
6. Neuhold, E., Niederee, C., Steward, A.: Personalization in Digital Libraries – An Extended View. In T.M.T. Sembok et al (eds.): ICADL: 2003. *Lecture Notes in Computer Science*, Vol. 2911, Springer-Verlag, Berlin Heidelberg (2003) 1–16.
7. The Open Group. Security Forum: Introduction to Single Sign-On. http://www.opengroup.org/security/sso_intro.htm. (2001)
8. Sullivan, Dan. *Proven Portals: Best Practices for Planning, Designing, and Developing Enterprise Portals.* Pearson Education, Boston MA (2004).
9. Tschang, F.T., Senta, T. Della (eds.): *Access to Knowledge: New Information Technologies and the Emergence of the Virtual University.* Elsevier Science, Oxford UK (2001).
10. Yin, Leng Theng et. al.: Design Guidelines and User-Centred Digital Libraries. In S. Abiteboul, A.-M. Vercoustre (eds.): ECDL '99. *Lecture Notes in Computer Science*, Vol. 1696, Springer-Verlag, Berlin Heidelberg (1999) 167–183.

Supporting Field Study with Personalized Project Spaces in a Geographical Digital Library

Ee-Peng Lim[1], Aixin Sun[1,2], Zehua Liu[1,5], John Hedberg[2], Chew-Hung Chang[3], Tiong-Sa Teh[3], Dion Hoe-Lian Goh[4], and Yin-Leng Theng[4]

[1] Centre for Advanced Information Systems, Nanyang Technological University,
Nanyang Avenue, Singapore 639798
liuzh@pmail.ntu.edu.sg
[2] Centre for Research in Pedagogy and Practice, National Institute of Education,
1 Nanyang Walk, Singapore 637616
[3] Humanities and Social Studies Education Academic Group
[4] National Institute of Education, 1 Nanyang Walk, Singapore 637616
{jhedberg, axsun, chchang, tsteh}@nie.edu.sg
[4] School of Communication and Information, Nanyang Technological University,
Nanyang Avenue, Singapore 639798
{aseplim, Tyltheng, ashlgoh}@ntu.edu.sg
[5] Institute of Systems Science, National University of Singapore,
25 Heng Mui Keng Terrace Singapore 119615

Abstract. Digital libraries have been rather successful in supporting learning activities by providing learners with access to information and knowledge. However, this level of support is passive to learners and interactive and collaborative learning cannot be easily achieved. In this paper, we study how digital libraries could be extended to serve a more active role in collaborative learning activities. We focus on developing new services to support a common type of learning activity, field study, in a geospatial context. We propose the concept of personal project space that allows individuals to work in their personalized environment with a mix of private and public data and at the same time to share part of the data with team members. To support the portability of the resources in our digital library, the selected resources can be exported in an organized manner.

1 Introduction

1.1 Motivation

Compared to traditional libraries, information stored in digital libraries can be easily accessed without time and location restrictions. With the rapid growth of information in digital form, digital libraries are playing more and more important roles in our daily activities including study and research. On one hand, digital libraries have been rather successful in supporting these activities by providing users the desired information. On the other hand, the level of the support is passive to the users in many ways as illustrated below:

Z. Chen et al. (Eds.): ICADL 2004, LNCS 3334, pp. 553–562, 2004.
© Springer-Verlag Berlin Heidelberg 2004

- Digital library accesses is a standalone task separate from other applications or systems that support the remaining learning tasks. Often times, digital libraries provide very little or no interface mechanism to share services and content with the other applications and systems. The only exceptions are those that support some query and data dissemination services over the internet through the various protocols, e.g., Z39.50[7] and OAI[5]. Even when these services and content are available, they are usually made available only to other digital library systems instead of an integrated e-learning environment.
- Digital libraries are not designed to cater to the needs of the different learning activities. Unlike e-learning environments where different learning activities such as lectures, laboratory experiments, field studies, etc., provide structured experiences for student learning, digital libraries usually focus on a narrow set of generic tasks, i.e., cataloging/classifying content and metadata, searching and browsing. They are clearly inadequate to independently support the various learning activities.
- Digital libraries are less personalized to meet the learning needs of different users. A user centric or user group centric view to create, organize and deliver content and metadata is lacking in the existing digital library designs. This leaves an impression that digital libraries are created for a mass public and are not friendly to learning individuals and groups.
- Single-directional delivery of information in digital libraries prevents collaborative learning. In most digital libraries, information is delivered to the user upon users' queries including both browsing and searching. However most of the users are unable to share their findings with other users. One reason is that the information to be shared may not match the format requirement of the digital library. Another reason is that information needs to be carefully evaluated before it can be made available to other users.

1.2   Research Objectives and Contributions

In this paper, we adopt a holistic approach to design a digital library portal for supporting interactive and collaborative learning activities to address the above shortcomings of digital libraries. We introduce the concept of **personalized project space** to the design of G-Portal, a digital library portal providing both map-based and classification-based interfaces to geography metadata resources. We specifically describe the use of personalized project and its services in the field study learning activity. Within a user-owned personalized project, a specialized collection of metadata resources can be assembled from existing projects and freshly created to meet the needs of a field study project. The G-Portal services that are useful for field study include:

- Metadata resource gathering and creation for personalized projects;
- Classification and visualization of both geographical and non-geographical resources;
- Annotation of resources; and
- Exportation of project resources for report writing;

To justify the use of personalized project space in G-Portal, we examine a field study exercise that involves students studying beach erosion at the East Coast of Singapore. We will show that G-Portal personalized project services can support the various learning tasks in the field study, integrating them in a flexible manner.

1.3 Paper Outline

The remaining portions of the paper are structured as follows. Section 2 gives an overview of the G-Portal project as a whole. We introduce field study as a general learning activity in Section 3 . This is followed by a description of a personalized project and its services in Section 4 . In Section 5, a working field study example is given. Before the paper concludes in Section 7 , the work related to our project is surveyed (see Section 6).

2 G-Portal Overview

G-Portal is a Web-based digital library that collects and manages metadata of geospatial and geo-referenced resources on the Web and provides digital library services to access them [6]. The information maintained by G-Portal are mainly metadata records that describe raw resources, such as Web pages, images and other objects that are accessible on the Web. Other types of information managed by G-Portal include semi-structured data records and annotations. These metadata records, data records and annotations are known as *resources* in G-Portal.

Every resource contains among other attributes, a location attribute storing its geospatial shape and position, and a link to the corresponding raw resource if it is a metadata resource. For non-geospatial resources, the location attribute is left unused. Similarly, G-Portal leaves the link attribute unused for the semi-structured data and annotation records that do not have their corresponding Web-based raw resources.

All resources are stored as XML records, and we adopt a common basic resource schema specifying the set of basic attributes to be used for all resources. Other extended resource schemas can be derived from the basic schema to allow some controlled heterogeneities among resources by having each type of resources to include attributes in addition to the basic ones.

Annotations are special types of resources that store useful remarks or supplementary information about some other resources. Besides having all characteristics of ordinary resources, each annotation record contains the id(s) of the annotated resource(s). In other words, annotations provide a flexible mechanism to let users actively augment the existing resources within the digital library.

G-Portal organizes resources into projects where each project contains a collection of resources that are relevant to a specific topic or learning activity. Within each project, resources are further grouped into layers for finer grained organization. Each layer serves as a *category* to hold logically related resources. For example, a project for field study might include rivers, mountains and targeted objects of the study; the rivers and mountains can be grouped into *map* layer and other objects into another.

G-Portal provides a map-based interface that visualizes resources with geographical attributes on a map (see Figure 3). This interface makes resources with known geographical locations easily and intuitively accessible and helps users discover the spatial relationships between resources. Other user interfaces used to access resources in G-Portal include a classification-based interface that classifies and organizes resources into taxonomies and a query interface that permits queries on resources based on keywords and spatial operators.

3 Field Study Activity

In this section, we describe the tasks to be performed in a field study for the geography domain. The purpose is to examine the tasks before we present the G-Portal services supporting them in Section 5.

Field study refers to research conducted in the real environment where data are collected from live situations. Often times, field study is preferred over laboratory work because of the realism the former provides for learning of topics such as geography, history, business, etc..

Consider a field study for secondary school geography students. Before the field study is conducted, a teacher is responsible for:

- Defining clearly the field study objectives and tasks;
- Providing reading materials including reference books, maps, photos, etc.;
- Equipping the students with devices necessary for taking measurements in the field study task, and instructions of using these devices; and
- Briefing on the requirement of a field study report for final assessment.

Nowadays with much of the reading materials digitized, a digital library can host this information organizing it in a way convenient for searching and browsing throughout the field study. Since G-Portal can accommodate different projects, each representing an organized collection of resources, the reading materials for field study can be placed in a G-Portal project and thus be visualized, browsed and queried. While in a G-Portal project, the resources can be easily updated and probably be reused in other field study projects.

From the student's perspective, it is possible to:

- Read the materials and understand what to do in the field study;
- Learn to use the device(s);
- Make trips to the designated areas;
- Document the necessary measurements and notes;
- Analyze the data obtained; and
- Write a report with supporting materials.

Starting from accessing reading materials, students need to plan for the field study by knowing the designated field trip areas. A digital library providing a map view of the field trip areas and related geographical objects is essential. G-Portal clearly meets this requirement.

A field trip usually involves teams of students. Students in a team are expected to collaborate in data collection, data analysis, and report writing. To facilitate collaborative learning, a digital library should allow a new collection of resources to be constructed and maintained by each team of students, along with the one defined by the teacher. Services that facilitate resource creation, annotations, and customized resource organization will be extremely important. For example, a student team may need to compile a large list of references related to the field study task. The references include textbooks, reading materials given by the teacher, online information sources and others arranged in a topic hierarchy.

Furthermore, to prepare a good report, the selected resources including map and other geographical objects will need to be made available in an online report which can be a set of inter-linked Web pages documenting the field study findings. Such an online report can be made publicly available for general consumption.

A G-Portal project provides the excellent space for students to manage information. However, there are several limitations. The previous version of G-Portal assumes that project is created by experienced information experts. The project services are therefore not geared towards supporting individual or group learners.

In the following section, we will present the *personalized project management* module in G-Portal which offers hopefully most if not all answers to the requirements of a field study activity.

4 Personalized Project Management

The personalized project management module is a new extension to the project services of earlier version of G-Portal to provide better support to learning activities such as field study.

In G-Portal, a personal workspace is provided to each user (or group of users) to build his/her (or their) own collections of resources and annotations in form of personalized projects. A personalized project has the same basic attributes as any project in G-Portal including *name* and *description*. The unique attribute of a personalized project is the *accessibility*, which can be *private* or *public*. A private project is visible and accessible to the creator only and a public project is accessible to all the users.

Personalized project management module in G-Portal enables the users to create, manipulate, export and delete their own projects. Functions of the personalized project management module can be further classified into five groups:

– **Project Management**
To create a new project, user specifies the basic attributes of the project including *name*, *description*, and whether the project is *private*. The creator can also alter these attributes or delete a personalized project.

– **Layer Management**
Within a project, layers can be defined to maintain resources in different logical groupings. Properties including *name*, *description* and *type* (resource layer or annotation layer) are specified for each layer. Within a personalized project,

appropriate layers can be defined to group resources logically. Note that the layers and the assignment of resources to layers can only updated by the corresponding project owners.

– Schema and Resource Management

Every resource in G-Portal is created using a resource schema that serves as a template. In a personalized project, schemas can be user-defined to meet the needs of a learning activity for a user (or team of users). In a personalized project, resources are either entirely created by the user or copied from the other public projects, e.g. the master project created by a teacher for students' reference. In a collaborative learning setting, it is also quite likely to have multiple users exchanging resources among their personalized projects.

– Resource Classification

The resource classification function gives users the freedom to define the classification criteria to group resources under different categories deem relevant to the field study. In other words, the same resources could well be classified differently when they appear in different personalized projects.

– Resource Presentation

The resource presentation function allows users to configure the HTML representation of the resources when they are displayed within a personalized project. Note that the resources are stored as XML records in G-Portal. By customizing the resource presentation, users of the personalized project can decide to format the resource content appropriately.

– Personalized Project Export

By providing each user a personalized workspace in G-Portal, the management of the resources (information) becomes much easier for each learning activity. Nevertheless, if the access to personalized project is always confined to the G-Portal server, there will be several serious shortcomings. Firstly, G-Portal server will always be the bottleneck for data access especially in cases where high speed network access to the server is not available. Secondly, users will find it extremely difficult to extract the personalized project content for report writing. To make the resources much more portable, G-Portal provides a project export module, which can: (i) export all resources in the project to one or more Web pages that can be easily saved to a local storage device; (ii) export the resource organization information, i.e., the layers and the schemas; and (iii) export an Applet as the map-based interface and for accessing the resources. All these Web pages exported are stored in a zip file downloadable from the G-Portal Web server.

5 A Working Example

In this section, we discuss the field study support in G-Portal using a working example. We consider a field study of beach erosion at the East Coast Park (ECP) area in Singapore. East Coast beach is a popular recreation spot for Singapore residents as it has a long swimming area, well located eating places, and several other water sports facilities. Nevertheless, this beach has been prone to erosion as sea waves wash away large amounts of the beach sand which must be regularly replenished with new sand.

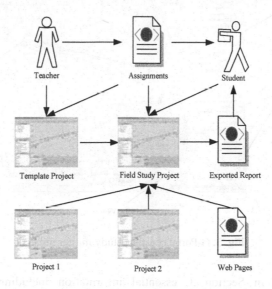

Fig. 1. Sample Field Study Process

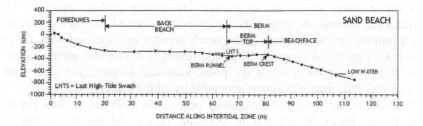

Fig. 2. A Sample Beach Profile

The objectives of the beach erosion study are: (i) to understand what beach erosion is and what causes beach erosion; (ii) to assess current state of the beach; (iii) to compute a rough rate of erosion based on historical records; and (iv) to document the process of field study and findings. The devices used in beach erosion study are: transit rods; line; sight marker; GPS device; and a digital camera [8]. The GPS device is used to locate the beach profiles[1] where the previous measures have been taken. The digital camera is to visually document the current state of the beach that is being assessed. A sample beach profile is reproduced[2] in Figure 2.

---

[1] A beach profile is a cross-section taken perpendicular to a given beach contour; the profile may include the face of a dune or sea wall; extend over the backshore, across the foreshore, and seaward underwater into the near shore zone.

[2] Available [online] http: //response.restoration.noaa.gov/shor_aid/profile.html

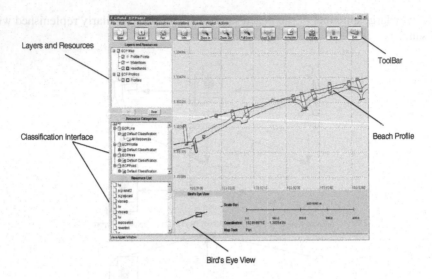

Layers and Resources

ToolBar

Classification Interface

Beach Profile

Bird's Eye View

Fig. 3. G-Portal coastline study master project

As discussed in Section 3, essential information including instructions for measuring beach profiles, instructions for using the GPS device, report format, etc., can be defined in an "assignment" Web page (see Figure 1). This assignment serves as a raw resource in the *master project*. The master project, shown in Figure 3, provides the students the map of the beach to be accessed, the GPS positions of the beach profiles and so on. Each of the beach profiles is associated with a Web page known as a profile description. A profile description provides photos taken at the point to help the student locate the point, historical records, and other supporting information. This master project is accessible by all the students.

Students create their own field study projects in G-Portal as their personalized project workspaces. Recall that in G-Portal, layers and resources from existing projects can be easily added to a personalized project. Students may selectively add resources from the master project or other relevant projects (e.g., similar field study projects done by another group of students) in G-Portal. These resources could be map objects and profile descriptions. The assignment Web page can be added to the personalized project for easy reference.

When all measurements are collected, the newly collected data can be added to the field study personalized project as resources or annotation to existing resources. For example, a student can create a Web page to contain each photograph taken at the beach, define the corresponding metadata resource in the personalized project describing the photograph, and provide a link from the metadata resource to the Web page. This Web page then serves as a raw resource in the field study project.

To prepare a field study report, the resources in the field study project can be exported to Web pages for easy analysis and reference. This is done by using the resource presentation and project export functions of personalized project. In the report, different map-based and classification-based visualization of the resources will be needed in the different report sections. G-Portal allows these different visualizations to be exported. On the other hand, a completed field study report may be also added to the field study project for future reference.

Due to the large number of beach profiles, each student (or each group of students) may be required to assess only a small number of beach profiles. By sharing the field study projects, the report and the findings of each student (student group) are accessible by the teachers and all the other students.

6 Related Work

Despite the great success of personalization systems in many areas (e.g., Amazon.com), personalization in digital library has yet been well supported.

Giacomo *et al.* proposed a personalized service for digital libraries named MyLibrary [3]. It provides digital library users (as individuals or groups) with personalized shared Web environment, recommender system integration, Web link checking mechanism and tools that extend the functionality of Web browsers. However, it has been commented that MyLibrary focuses on applying basic personalization and rudimentary recommender systems in a reasonably straightforward way and does not really add much value to the digital library [2].

A personalized information environment (PIE) for the digital library is proposed in [4] and the personalization is considered in two stages: material personalization and collection personalization. Material personalization is to provide facilities to use the digital library materials according to the user's personal requirements such as active reading and information gathering. Collection personalization is designed to provide facilities such as personalized retrieving and filtering based on both the user's interest and the user's working context. Nevertheless, interactive and collaborative learning are not supported in PIE.

CYCLADES envisages a digital library not only as an information space in which individual users may search for and organize the information, but also as a collaborative meeting place of people sharing common interests [1]. It provides personalized services such as notification and recommendations, which are lacking in G-Portal. However, G-Portal is also unique in that it has an exporting function and other standard DL services such as annotation and classification that can be seamlessly applied to personalized projects.

7 Conclusions

Digital libraries have been successful as information sources for learners. Nevertheless, the support of interactive and collaborative learning has not yet been achieved. In this paper, we show that learning activities can be supported in the G-Portal digital library using the concept of personalized project space. We first give an overview of G-Portal and its key concepts followed by a detailed discussion on the personalized project functions in G-Portal. We show that a common type of learning activity, field study, in a geospatial context, can be supported using the personalized project management. The process is illustrated with a working example. We believe that one of the most interesting functions in personalized project management is exportation. Exporting resources from a project to a set of Web pages while preserving the resource organization gives the users great flexibility in using the resource independent of the G-Portal digital library. The development of this exportation function is currently ongoing. As a part of future work, we would like to examine other types of learning activities and extend the G-Portal functions to meet the corresponding requirements. We would also like to evaluate the personalized project management and its usefulness in supporting field study.

Acknowledgements

This research is partially supported by the Ministry of Education, Singapore, under the grant CRP 40/03 LEP.

References

[1] H.Avancini and U.Straccia. Personalization, collaboration, and recommendation in the digital library environment CYCLADES. In *Proceedings of IADIS Conference on Applied Computing*, Lisbon, Portugal, March 2004.

[2] J.Callan, A. Smeaton, M. Beaulieu, B., P.Borlund, P. Brusilovsky, M.Chalmers, C.Lynch, J.Riedl, B.Smyth, U.Straccia, and E.Toms. Personalisation and recommender systems in digital libraries, May 2003. Joint NSF-EU DELOS Working Group Report Available[online]: http: //www.ercim.org/publication/ws-proceedings/Delos-NSF/ Personalisation.pdf.

[3] M.Di Giacomo, D.Mahoney, J.Bollen, A.Monroy-Hernandez, and C.M.Ruiz Meraz. Mylibrary, a personalization service for digital library environments. In *In Proceedings of Joint DELOS-NSF Workshop on Personalisation and Recommender Systems in Digital Libraries*, Dublin, Ireland, June 2001.

[4] C.Jayawardana, K.P. Hewagamage, and M.Hirakawa. A personalized information environment for digital libraries. *Journal of Information Technology and Libraries*, 20(4), December 2001.

[5] C.Lagoze and H.Van de Sompel. The Open Archives Initiative: Building a Low-Barrier Interoperability Framework. In *Proceedings of the First ACM+IEEE Joint Conference on Digital Libraries (JCDL 2001)*, Roanoke, VA, USA, 2001.

[6] Ee-Peng Lim, Dion Hoe-Lian Goh, Zehua Liu, Wee-Keong Ng, Christopher Soo-Guan Khoo, and Susan Ellen Higgins. G-Portal: A Map-based Digital Library for Distributed Geospatial and Georeferenced Resources. In *Proceedings of the Second ACM+IEEE Joint Conference on Digital Libraries (JCDL 2002)*, Portland, Oregon, USA, July 14–18 2002.

[7] C.A. Lynch. The Z39.50 Information Retrieval Standard. *DLib Magazine*, April 1997.

[8] Phyllis E. Rumpp and George W. Rumpp. Measuring beach profiles. Available[onine]: http: //mciunix.mciu.k12.pa.us/~seastar/beachdir.html.

Academic Digital Library Portal — A Personalized, Customized, Integrated Electronic Service in Shanghai Jiaotong University Library

Wei Pan, Youhua Chen, Qiaoying Zheng, Peifu Xia, and Ruxing Xu

Shanghai Jiaotong University Library, Huashan Road 1954,
Shanghai 200030, P.R. China
{wpan, yhchen, zheng, pfxia, xu}@lib.sjtu.edu.cn

Abstract. Recent years, electronic resources and electronic services provided by academic libraries in the Chinese mainland are becoming ever-increasingly diverse and multiplex. Libraries patrons strongly expect to obtaining one kind of more quicker, more easier, one-stopped, and personalized service to access libraries collections and use libraries services. Under the condition, Library of Shanghai Jiaotong University initiated the portal project. Shanghai Jiaotong University Library portal project defines its portal as a personalized, customized and integrated service of all kinds of resources and services provided by library. This article details the project background, general understanding of this portal service, functional requirements, design strategies, and some key and difficult problems in developing such a service in China.

1 Introduction

Academic libraries provide information resources and services to students, faculty and researchers in an environment that supports learning, teaching and research. Recent a few years, both the numbers and the types of electronic resources and web-based services provided by academic libraries in the Chinese mainland have been growing rapidly. For the different accessing platforms of most electronic resources, library patrons often complained about difficulty to access their expected academic information easily and quickly. Such a situation is just same as that in most developed countries.

In 1999, the Library and Information Technology Association (LITA) has identified a number of important future trends for technologies in libraries[1]. They identified Trend 1 as "library users ... expect customization, interactivity, and customer support." They stated that "approaches that were library-focused instead of user-focused would be increasingly irrelevant". For Shanghai Jiaotong University Library, service-orientated digital library construction has been a key task recent a few years. So a customizable and personalized library portal project was initiated at the middle of last year in Shanghai Jiaotong University Library because we agree on this point of view that such a library portal service "addresses the modern library role

Z. Chen et al. (Eds.): ICADL 2004, LNCS 3334, pp. 563–567, 2004.
© Springer-Verlag Berlin Heidelberg 2004

directly by being customer focused, responding to customer needs, and empowering users to create personal information systems that are responsive to their individual needs."[2]

2 SJTUL Portal Functional Requirements

Due to lacking a single definition of a library portal, at the beginning of SJTUL (Shanghai Jiaotong University Library) portal project, we reviewed a large number of documents on this topic in Chinese and English, surveyed and compared some famous library portal services and products that have been implemented or used in China and other countries libraries so that we can gain a more clear understanding on a library portal. On the basis of this work and considering our long-term plan of building service-orientated digital library, we thought SJTUL portal should be a personalized, customized and integrated information service to aggregate all kinds of SJTU library resources and services through a single access and management point for our users. According to this understanding, we defined the preliminary functional requirements list of SJTUL portal. Then after discussing more than one times within a focus group that its members are from our librarians team, teachers and researchers from different departments who may be the primary users of SJTUL portal, we defined some core features of SJTUL portal as follows:

- Tools for resources and services discovery

In fact, these are a series of recommending tools for the users to navigate through available resources and services according to the users' profiles, e.g. by searching descriptions of services, browsing resources pre-clustered by subjects, or by analysis users' historic information usage behaviors.

- Personalisation and customization

Personalisation and customization by an individual user can help direct users to the most relevant resources to them, based primarily on the subjects of their research aeries, and also can help point up new resources to them.

Personalisation and customization should also offer current awareness services to the user, based on their profile or choice, e.g., alerts of relevant Tables of Content(TOCs), new acquisitions or re-runs of searches.

- Cross searching

Integrated searching is a key feature of a portal. For the users, the ability to target heterogeneous resources is required. This is also a most important characteristic to empower users' seeking information process to be quick and easy. The ability allows the user to do a searching in a simple and common interface and retrieve articles and needed information from multiple full-text and bibliographic databases (local catalogs, online journals, or locally digitized resources etc.) and web resources the user customized or selected simultaneously regardless of what formats they are.

- Cross-linking to document delivery and different information services

Cross-linking between resources enable the user find the full text of an article discovered through online citations. We think that the resolution should find the "appropriate copy": that is, the best of all document delivery options, for instance, go to library, online full text, interlibrary loan(ILL), document delivery, even possibly in multiple places, for that particular user, as determined by rules set by the library. The implementation of this feature allows the system to support for OpenURL resolver.

Cross-linking between services provided means that the user can switch seamlessly the different library information services whenever needed. For example, when the user is doing a searching, he can initiate a virtual reference service, submit an ILL request, and transfer into course management systems, all without leaving that web site. This feature will based on the web services.

- Citation management

The ability provides the user to effectively manage his searching results or those articles written by himself in his individual server space assigned to him by the portal service, including storage, searching or browsing, ranking, display and output citations according to his special need and format. This feature will target to be provided mainly to 200-300 teachers and researchers whose research areas are the key topics in Shanghai Jiaotong University. Also, the feature will be compatible with Endnote or RefWork-like products.

- Authentication/authorization

Another central requirement is that there be a single point of authentication. The user must not be constantly challenged for sign on. The system architecture should allows interacting with other local authentication (e.g. university) so that the user only has to log in once some where on the local system for authorization credentials for other systems to be activated, and allows the use of different methods for authenticating users and recognizing various user roles or classes of users(e.g., IP-address linked to external identification systems, refer URLs, passwords, etc.) This will achieve a "single sign on"[3]. This can ensure the full functionality of the portal system be available off campus.

- Statistics

Statistics about users and usage should be at the heart of improved library services. Currently, libraries have huge problems measuring the relative performance and value of services. Due to the portal service targets the individual user or specific subject, the statistics is more easier to be done and also make it more easier to export the integrated statistics results to spreadsheets for processing and cross analysis.

Certainly, SJTUL portal also has been defined some other detailed features as communication, searching results manipulating etc.. Through above core functional requirements descriptions, we can consider SJTUL portal as a syntheses of MyLibrary-like services, Metasearch tools, and Citation management tools. We agreed that such a definition can provide our users to access and use our digital library resources and services easily and quickly in deed.

3 SJTUL Portal Design

According to the three core features categories of SJTUL portal, MyLibrary feature, a powerful metasearch engine, and a citation management tool, we think of that the most difficult task is the development of metasearch engine. Unlike other countries(United States, UK), nowadays there are no perfect products of metasearch tools in the China marketplac. The devclopment on such a kind of products is only in trial using stage. Considering the limited human and financial resources, we choose the Shanghai Finegold Computer System Engineering Co. Ltd. to be our one of partners to collaboratively develop this portal system with us. Finegold's cross-searching product is being applied in our library. So it is easy for Finegold to embed its cross-searching technology in our portal system.

During the process of design, we strongly stress three important strategies:

• Platform independent: this means that such a system should work on any platform.

• Following standards: the system should be capable of interoperating with other system, based on open standards. For example, Z39.50, OpenURL, OAI-MPH, XML/XSL, ISO ILL, MARC, Z39.85(DC), etc.

• Easy for using: the one of main aims of a library portal itself is to resolve the difficulty for users in accessing library resources and using library services. So easy for using is the most important thing when we design a library portal.

4 Conclusion

SJTUL portal project is now just in the first phase for trial using in the middle of the year. In the stage, among those of three core features categories of SJTUL portal, only two of them -- MyLibrary feature and a powerful metasearch engine will be implemented. To ensure full functionality will be further work in next a few phases.

In the Chinese mainland, due to lacking the existing mature portal solutions, there are probably many new problems in case the service would be provided broadly in our university wide. For example, how users think about the new kind of service, how to further expand the interactive characteristics of the portal with our librarians and with many other systems, how to further improve the searching effect of cross-searching, how to integrate the library portal into many other portal-like systems of our university(e.g., university portal, the learning management systems, content and course management system), how to manage effectively this kind of service for librarians, etc.. These all need us to study during a long period of time.

References

1. LITA TopTech Trends. Technology and Libraries Users: LITA Experts Identify Trends to Watch. ALA Midwinter Meeting, Jan, 1999. Retrieved March 2004, from http://www.lita.org/committee/toptech/mw99.htm

2. Anamarija Rozic-Hristovski, Iztok Humar, Dimitar Hristovski. Developing a Personalised Medical Library Portal. Retrieved May 2004, from http://134.95.56.211/fileadmin/pdf_dateien/EAHIL_2002/rozic.pdf
3. Pinfield, S., Eaton, J. and Edwards, C. Realizing the hybrid library. D-lib Magazine, Oct. 1998. Retrieved May 2004, from http://www.dlib.org/october98/10pinfield.html
4. Andrew Cox, Robin Yeates. Library portal solutions. Aslib Proceedings, v55, n3, 2003, p155–165

A Digital Library of a Service-Orientated Architecture in SJTU – A Case Study*

Zongying Yang, Qiaoying Zheng, and Guojing Yuan

Shanghai Jiao Tong University Library,
Shanghai 200030, China
zyyang@mail.sjtu.edu.cn

Abstract. Through a research and development of some key techniques and related technologies of digital library for ten more years, an important technical foundation for developing a practical digital library has been established. A dozen of digital libraries are summarized in three main types as the following: a DL of special collection; a service-orientated DL; a DL with commercial database. The architecture of a service-orientated DL has been developed in Shanghai Jiao Tong University (SJTU): It consists of various E-resources and an information service platform. Generally, the E-resources for this type of DL includes three parts: a) digital special collections of their own; b) commercial online e-publications or databases (including locally mirror-sited databases); and: c) some selected information resources on the Internet. The information service platform consists of an unique information searching platform and a VRS platform. E-resources are searched through a unique interface. Using the virtual reference system patrons is given advice and guidance concerning their problems in searching resources or other problems.

The 21st century has seen a rapid emerging of a knowledge-economic era of high-tech with the rapid development in the fields of computer, information and communication sciences. The evolution in IT technology, symbolized by the Internet and the multi-media technologies, will prompt the automation and digitalization in library field. The development of digital library systems and its related databases are under way adopting the last IT technology in many countries and regions all over the world, with a number of DL prototypes appeared on the Internet as a result. Since 1996 a digital library has been researched and developed in Shanghai Jiao Tong University (SJTU). Through the research of a DL prototype and the development of a DL test-bed, a digital library of a service-orientated architecture has being built in SJTU since 2002 year[1].

1 The Emerging Three Main Models of DL

The research and development of some key technologies and related technologies of DL in recent couple of ten years has laid an important foundation for a practical DL

---

*This project was supported by National Natural Science Foundation of China. No 60221120145.

Z. Chen et al. (Eds.): ICADL 2004, LNCS 3334, pp. 568–573, 2004.
© Springer-Verlag Berlin Heidelberg 2004

technologically. A number of DL now in operation or under development could fall into three main categories:

• A DL with a digital special collection of its own

In this kind of a DL, the library's precious collections (rare books and/or ancient books) or special collections (including times of photo, sound, music, movie and collections in other media) have been digitized and made available on the Web. "American Memory" of the Library of Congress of the United States in one example.

• A service-orientated DL

Generally, the information resources for this type of DL consists of three parts: a) digital special collections of their own; b) commercial online e-publications or databases (including locally mirror-sited databases); and: c) some selected information resources on the Internet. All these resources could be made available through a unique interface. Examples are CDL in California and IDAL in Illinois, USA and academic DL in China.

• A DL with commercial databases

Some DLs have been developed for commercial purposes by publishers, documentation providers and vendors where full-text E-journal and E-books (including some music and movie materials), etc. are provided with a searching facility. Examples are Super-Star DL of China, which provides e-books, the Elsevier Publishing Co. of the Netherlands, which provides full-text E-journal of some 1500 titles it publishes and the NetLibrary in Colorado, USA, which provides tens of thousands of e-books.

2 The Architecture of a Service-Orientated DL

Based on the three main digital resources (example, digital special collections of a library, commercial online e-publications or databases and the selected information resources on the Internet), this type of a DL will provide efficiently information services through its unique searching platform and a VRS (Virtual Reference System) platform, which are indispensable for a practice. In the architecture, they are interconnected with each other somewhere.

Following is the diagram of it:

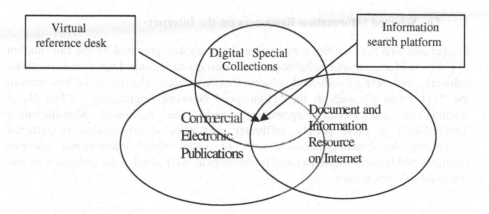

3 Digital Resources

The case of the development of a service-orientated DL of Shanghai Jiao Tong University Library is discussed below.

3.1 The Digital Local Special Collections

A bibliographic database of some 430,000 records with serials' holding information has been created covering monographs and serials as well as E-books and E-journals in both Chinese and foreign languages. Secondly, the full-text databases for the Ph.D dissertations of Shanghai Jiao Tong University and the journals published by the SJTU Press have been made including <Journal of the Shanghai Jiao Tong University> and <Energy Information Express> (both in Chinese), etc. An e-book database, covering <The Proceedings of the International Symposium on Academic Library in the 21st Century> and some reserved books, has also been created.

Based on the campus' 10GB/S backbone network, the development of a multi-media VOD system could now provide on synchronous online requests digital materials such as some selected video programs of inspiriting ideas of innovation, tuition demos, language teaching programs and some fantastic films. Besides, a multi-media computer room is built where a second bandwidth of 100MB/S is adopted for users to watch VOD within the library. A Chinese folk music database system has also been provided on the campus network.

Among these developments are the CALIS academic digital holdings information system, including a union list and a union catalogue in both Chinese and Western languages and an abstract database of the Master and Ph. Ds' thesis of Chinese colleges and universities, etc.

3.2 Commercial E-Publications

A number of databases on the Web has been subscribed including the Elsevier's full-text e-journals, the full-text Chinese Academic Journals of CNKI, Emerals, Ei Village, OCLC FirstSearch, Web of Knowledge, IEEE/IEE Electronic Library, PQDD, Netlibrary, ABI, NTIS, LISA, INSPEC and Dialog, etc.

3.3 The Selected Information Resources on the Internet

Cooperated with the faculties concerned and getting well prepared for the information of progress of science and technology, the librarians have created ten portals for those subjects and their subordinated subjects that have been selected as the key ones in the "211 Projects", such as the "High-speed Network Engineering", "The Naval Architecture and Ocean Engineering" and "The Advanced Manufacturing Technology". In these portals, infiltrated and selected information is gathered concerning the dynamic research work of some related international research institutes and famous specialists and researchers as well as related e-publications and international conferences.

All these three information resources could be accessed via a unique interface. If one wants to look for the above information, he or she could visit our library's Homepage (Website: http://www.lib.sjtu.edu.cn) where contents of sound, image and moving picture are available, which are allocated in different servers of the library.

4 The Information Service Platform

It consists of an unique information searching platform and a VRS platform.

4.1 The Unique Information Searching Platform

The existing prototypes of DL, or test-beds or of DL or DL is equipped with either digital local special collections databases or subscribed commercial abstracts and full-text databases, some of which are made locally mirrored and some are remote authorized-access, or subjects' portals to go and search selected information resources on the Internet. All these databases are allocated in different servers with different operating software, different database software and different searching facilities. The unique information searching platform is therefore developed to solve the primary problems in searching information at different platforms, provide users with one and easy searching interface and an inter-operation in different DLs and make it possible for users to carry on at only one searching platform searching in all databases however different their searching facilities are to acquire the needed information in the fastest time instead of getting access into different databases respectively.

Research has been done on the issue for several years in SJTU. Effort was made in installing a searching facility at the library's Website to realize the key word searching across the different systems at HTML level of different databases or files. And then a Z39.50 server and client system has been developed that could do broadcasting search at the client at one click in all different databases that support Z39.50 protocol. From 2001 on, we have been trying to compile the main indexes for the 14 foreign full-text databases subscribed with the "mid-ware" technique and users could therefore find which database holds the needed information through only one search and go further to locate the original document. More research will be done to develop a distributed relational system, which could search heterogeneous resources, where the OAI protocol is also adopted. One stop service using portal technology will be provided on campus network.

It is a hot subject being studied by computer and information specialists both at home and abroad. Some progresses have been made by some companies and manufacturers. Take ISI Company for example. It uses the "Web of Science" as the core ultra-platform to search all its' eight related databases and make various hype-linkages to the "citing and cited" references back and forth. It is believed that with the further application of XML language and Dublin Core, the searching problem on different system platforms will be better solved.

4.2   The VRS Platform

These years, Virtual Reference Systems are becoming one hot study by the world important libraries because the DL and the service of the electronic documents on the Webs are accepted in a larger scale while the requests via VRS are increasing greatly. A VRS has been developed in SJTU since 2002 year. We believe that a VRS is to become an indispensable part of a DL as a traditional reference segment does to a library.

At present, there will be some situations and trends in the development of a VRS:

- Descriptions and instructions on the Web on how to do the searching in information databases step by step. It is an online learning center.
- Summarization of frequently-asked questions on the Web, for example the 100-FAQ, which is tending to the creation of an independent FAQ database system where users could either check weather their questions already have existing answers or key in their questions and get feedback or receive answers via emails, etc. FAQ database will work in some extent as Knowledge database does.
- Development of a VRS system that has the functionality in interacting with users and answering their questions by adopting the expert system technology.
- A VRD system where subject specialists work "on site" and answer users' questions is used. Examples are the VRD system of the Shanghai Library, Shanghai China where sixteen specialists do the reference "on site" and the VRD system of the Library of Congress of the United States where a group of specialists, with their contact information on the Web, who are invited to answer questions via email, Web form or other tools. The library of SJTU is going to make it a real-time VRS, adopting tools such as Call Center and NetMeeting, conduct the reference work "face to face" on the Web (in the future, it could do it "face to face" using audio or video technology.) in dialog or talking in written form when reference specialists could view users' queries and questions as they conduct online searching and even could help and instruct them to solve the problems without interrupting their searching procedure like co-browsing.

5   Conclusion

Development of a DL is a huge and complicated system project with its techniques and contents, the tools it applies and the environment it operates, and the related standards, laws and rules, etc. needed to be improved further. Now coming up more and more are the different models of DL. Our objective is to improve the existing the DL system of our library by expending it in order to house more information, adopting more advanced information access technology, management and searching tools to provide more con-current users and move gradually into a practical and service-orientated DL in a great larger scale.

References

1. Arora, Jagdish, Network-enabled digitized collection at the Central library, IIT Delhi International Information Library review Vol.36 Issue: 1, March, 2004-3-31, pp1—11
2. Faiks, Angi Herold; Docherty, Karen J., Libraries as digital crossroads: a report on the 10th Annual Collection Development Symposium, Library Collection, Acquisition, and Technical Services. Vol. 27, Issue:4, Winter, 2003, pp.153—176
3. Lee, Ook, An action research report on the Korean national digital library, Information and management, Vol. 39 Issue: 4 Jan.2002
4. McFadden, T.G. Building a National Strategy for Digital Preservation: Issues in Digital Media Archiving, Serials Review , Vol.29, Issue:2 Summer,2003,pp157-159
5. Graham,T. Electronic access to and the preservation of heritage materials, Electronic Library (UK) 21(3):223-6 2003
6. Schwartz, Candy , Digital libraries: an overview, The Journal of Academic Librarianship Vol.26, Issue:6 Nov. 2000, pp385--393
7. Catherine CANDEE, California Digital Library, "E-Scholarship and CDL-ECAI Partnership", PNC 2001
8. Arms, W.Y. "Digital Libraries", MIT Press 2000
9. http://memory.loc.gov 2004-04-05
10. http://www.cdlib.org 2004-04-05
11. Liu Wei, etc. " Introduction to Digital Library" Shanghai Science and Technology Document Press 2000. 12
12. Zhu Qiang "Pre-Requirements of the Digital Library" Journal of Academic Libraries (Beijing) 2000 no.1
13. Marcia Lei Zeng , Foster Zhang, Yang Zongying. "Digital libraries: where to go? ---An analysis of the definitions, architectures, and projects of digital libraries" Journal of the China Society for Scientific and Technical Information 2000 no.1

A Research to Increase Users' Satisfaction and Loyalty Based on the Customer Satisfaction Index: A Case Study on the National Taichung Institute of Technology's Library

Tung-Shou Chen[1], Rong-Chang Chen[2], and Tsui-Yun Chang[3]

[1]National Taichung Institute of Technology, Department of Information Management, Taichung, Taiwan, R.O.C.
[2]National Taichung Institute of Technology, Department of Logistics Engineering and Management, Taichung, Taiwan, R.O.C.
[3]National Taichung Institute of Technology, Department of Information Management, Taichung, Taiwan, R.O.C.
{tschen, rcchens, s13903050, s18934101}@ntit.edu.tw

Abstract. A good library can make significant contributions to library users. These users are likely to return to the library again and again where service is excellent and materials are accessible easily. The research purpose for this paper is to adopt the European Customer Satisfaction Index (ECSI) on a survey performed on library users to measure users' satisfaction and loyalty factors. A questionnaire is designed to integrate measurement into the library's management system for visual analysis of what users expect from the library. Results from the survey show that users expect more improvement in the "library environment" and "collections of printed publications" section. Conclusions from the study, we were able to make the following suggestions to satisfy users' expectations: (1) increase seating areas for readers, (2) increase collections of printed publications and periodicals to meet readers' demands, and (3) increase the number of duplications on popular literatures.

1 Introduction

S. R. Ranganathan (1931) proposed a theory "the five laws of library science" which emphasized that the library exists because of utilizing. [6] Based on this theory, three features are noticed, the collections of printed publications should conform to the reader's demand, human side of user services should get the reader's affirmation, and the true kernel of the library is *reader*. Thus, the library should keep an eye on user services. But, which determinants in the library should have low priority or high priority for users? What is the effect of various improvement activities for user satisfaction and user loyalty? [2] There are several characteristics on survey using traditional method in the literature. First, there is no standard measurement system. It

Z. Chen et al. (Eds.): ICADL 2004, LNCS 3334, pp. 574–583, 2004.
© Springer-Verlag Berlin Heidelberg 2004

is difficult to do the comparison of the investigation results. Second, the complicated statistical analysis result is difficult to understand.

2 Review

Anne Martensen and Lars Grønholdt (2003) [2] provided a detailed case study of the development and application of a structural equation model which allows librarians to quantitatively measure library users' perceived quality, satisfaction and loyalty with a library as well as the degree to which specific elements of a library's services, collections and environment contribute to those perceptions. This study was inspired by the successful experiences from the European Customer Satisfaction Index (ECSI) pilot project in 1999.[1] ECSI is founded on structural modeling, based on validity and operationally requirements.[3] It was decided that this modeling approach, which would allow us to determine the degree of users' perceptions of library value, individual satisfaction and loyalty, the degree of interactions among these perceptions, and the degree to which basic elements of library services, collections and environment contributed to these perceptions, should form the foundation of the library performance measurement system.[2] But, this methodology has not been used on the internal library yet.

3 Methodology and Data Analysis

Our research focuses on Taiwanese library environment with features specific to National Taichung Institute of Technology (NTIT) Library. The conceptual model is based on Anne Martensen et al.'s study on measurement library users' perceived quality. Figure 1 is the path model.

The determinants to the left of Figure 1 represent six quality dimensions: Electronic resources (e.g., database search systems and electronic publications), printed publications (e.g., books, periodicals and newspapers), other library services (e.g., library user courses), technical facilities (e.g., computers and photocopiers), the library environment (e.g., space design, atmosphere and library hours) and the human side of user service (e.g., the library staff's knowledge ability and friendliness).

Main cause-and-effect relationships indicating in Figure 1 provide answers for what helps create user satisfaction and loyalty. [2] Each of the nine latent variables in Figure 1 is measured by a set of measurement variables and observed by survey questions to library users. In this study, we designed a questionnaire for NTIT Library, which consisted of fifty questions and the corresponding latent variables as shown in Table 1. Among these questions, twenty-four questions are designed in a generic way, meaning that they can be used in all libraries. The rest of the questions are interpreted the library specific, that is, they only capture specific dimensions of the six determinants.

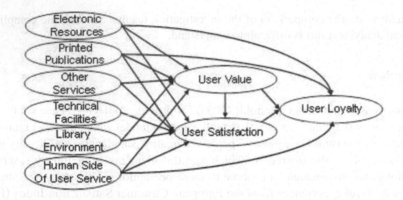

Fig. 1. The user satisfaction and loyalty model [2]

Table 1. Measurement Variables for the Nine Latent Variables

Latent Variable	S/G[1]	Measurement Variable
		A part of survey question
Electronic resources	S	The range of electronic resources in the library is adequate in my field of interest.
	S	The library web-site is easy to use.
	S	The library WebPAC is easy to navigate.
	S	The library uses e-mail automatic notice reader's relevant information is a good service.
	G	The general evaluation of electronic resources in the library is satisfactory.
	G	The electronic resources in the library meet my requirements.
Printed publications	S	The range of books in my field of interest is generally adequate.
	S	The range of periodicals in my field of interest is generally adequate.
	S	Normally the material I want is available in the library.
	S	The book volumes that can be lent out is suitable.
	S	Lending time is suitable.
	S	Materials from other lending libraries arrive quickly.
	S	It is easy to locate materials that I want on the shelves.
	G	The general assessment of the range of materials in the library is satisfactory.
	G	The materials in the library meet my requirements.
Other library services	G	Course of using resources organized by the library meet my requirements.
	G	Courses organized by the library meet my requirements.
	G	The quality of courses and events is high.

---

[1] The sign 'S/G' means that the questions are designed in a specific or generic way. S='specific way,' G='generic way.'

Table 1. *(continued)*

Latent Variable	S/G[1]	Measurement Variable / A part of survey question
Technical facilities	S	The quality of technical facilities (computers, printers, photocopiers, etc.) is satisfactory.
Technical facilities	S	The speed of the computers is satisfactory.
	S	The waiting time for access to the computers is acceptable.
	S	The waiting time for access to the printers and photocopiers is acceptable.
	G	The general assessment of the technical facilities is satisfactory.
	G	The technical facilities of the library meet my requirements.
Library environment	S	The library space design is satisfactory.
	S	The seats number of reading room are adequate.
	S	The reading room is peaceful enough to permit concentration and study.
	S	The library has a pleasant atmosphere.
	S	The library is clean enough.
	S	The indoor climate (lighting, noise, temperature, etc.) of the library is satisfactory.
	S	The library opening hours are adequate to my requirements.
	G	The general evaluation of library environment is satisfactory.
	G	The library environment meet my requirements.
Human side of user service	S	Staff can provide professional guidance.
	S	Staff is friendly and helpful.
	S	The waiting time at the lending counter to get assistance from staff is suitably short.
	S	The waiting time at the audio-visual division's lending counter to get assistance from staff is suitably short.
	G	Overall assessment of staff competence is satisfactory.
	G	Overall assessment of staff service provision is satisfactory.
	G	The service provided by staff meet my requirements.
User value	G	I use the library to keep up to date.
	G	The library helps me grow academically.
	G	The library's services satisfy my needs for knowledge and learning.
	G	Library services are of decisive importance to me.
User satisfaction	G	The library services meet my general requirements.
	G	The library can meet my expectations.
	G	Imagine a library which is perfect in all aspects. How far removed from or how close to this ideal is the library?[2]
User loyalty	G	I will be using more of the library services in the future.
	G	It is important for me to be able to use the library in the future.
	G	I will recommend the library to other users.

---

[2] Measured on a 5-point scale from 1='very far away' to 5='very close.' Others are measured on the 5-point scale from 1= 'definitely disagree' to 5= 'definitely agree.'

A 5-point scale is used to evaluate the users' degree of agreement with the questions. Besides, if user have no experience with the library or if they don't have an opinion, they can tick "don't know". The data was conducted from April 13, 2004 to May 4, 2004. A total of 281 NTIT Library users, including staffs and students, participated in the study, but only 232 respondents were left for further analysis. We use quota sampling and convenience sampling to collect data among the students, teachers and administrative staffs. Missing values in some cases or responses ticked "don't know" are represented by -1.

4 Results from a Strategic Perspective

The model in Figure 1 can be estimated by using the PLS-GUI 1.0 statistics software developed by Yuan Li (2003). The PLS statistical technique can calculate values for the performance level for each of the nine variables and values for the degree of relationship between the variables. [2]

Figure 2 shows the estimated model for the NTIT Library with performance indexes for each latent variable as well as impact scores between the latent variables (these are shown on the arrows). The model is able to explain 45% of what drives user satisfaction ($R^2 = 0.45$). The estimated model in Figure 2 shows that:

- 'User satisfaction' is created as an interactive result of 'electronic resources,' 'printed publications,' 'other services,' 'technical facilities,' 'library environment,' 'human side of user service,' and 'user value.'
- 'User loyalty' is created as an interactive result of 'electronic resources,' 'the human side of user service,' 'user value,' and 'user satisfaction.'

The performance index for a latent variable is estimated by a weighted average of scores from the corresponding measurement variables (questions), transformed from the original 5-point scale to a 0-to-100-point scale.

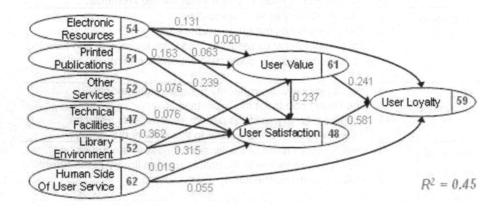

Fig. 2. The estimated model for the NTIT Library

E.g. 'human side of user service (62)' is only getting over 60 point scores in six quality dimensions and 'technical facilities (47)' get the lowest score. An impact score that shows on the arrows represents the effect of a change in the performance index of one point in a latent variable. E.g. if the 'human side of user service' is improved by 1 point, the loyalty index will rise by 0.066. This impact is calculated by adding the direct effect on 'user loyalty' and the indirect effect via 'user satisfaction'. Thus, a 1-point increase in the index for 'human side of user service' results in a 0.055 + 0.019 x 0.581 = 0.066 points' increase in the loyalty index. The total impact on 'user satisfaction' and 'user loyalty' can be calculated as shown in Table 2.

Table 2. Effect of a one point improvement in the determinants on user satisfaction and loyalty

Determinants	Effect on Satisfaction	Effect on Loyalty
Electronic resources	0.068	0.175
Printed publications	0.278	0.201
Other library services	0.076	0.044
Technical facilities	0.141	0.082
Library environment	0.401	0.320
Human side of user service	0.019	0.066

We find that 'library environment' affects 'user satisfaction' and 'user loyalty' most profoundly: if this variable is improved by one point, the satisfaction index will rise by 0.401 and the loyalty index will rise by 0.320. User satisfaction is thus created primarily via 'library environment' and 'printed publications.' But, the 'printed publications (0.278)' is only half the size of 'library environment.' Besides, 'human side of user service' only slightly affects on user satisfaction and user loyalty.

Anne Martensen et al.'s (2003) [2] study has provided a useful management system called a priority map. Such a map is appealing from a managerial viewpoint and useful in priority setting and strategy development. [2] A priority map contains two features/categories, total impact scores (from Table 2) and performance indexes (from Figure 2).

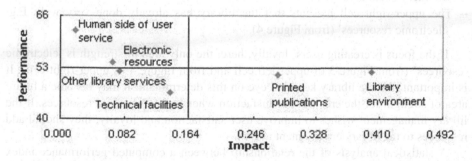

Fig. 3. Impact versus performance in driving user satisfaction: priority map

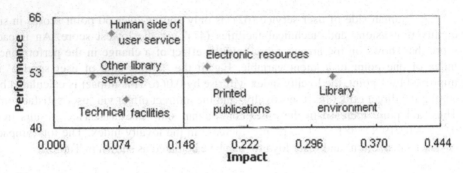

Fig. 4. Impact versus performance in driving user loyalty: priority map

If the library management wishes to improve user satisfaction significantly, they should plan and initiate activities through Figure 3. The lines separating the respective cells are based on the average of performance and impacts indexes. The four cells of a priority map can be interpreted in managerially useful ways. [5] Description of each cell:

– The upper-left cell is an area in which performance is strong, but the impact is low. At best, this suggests maintaining the status quo. E.g. 'human side of user service' and 'electronic resources' (from Figure 3) should be maintained, and when the library receives extra resources so that it may also become a future area of strength for the creation of satisfaction and loyalty.
– The lower-left cell represents the area that the library is not doing particularly well, although it does not matter. It should have a very low priority. That is to say, it is best to ignore 'other library service' and 'technical facilities' (from Figure 3 and 4) which slightly affects on user satisfaction and loyalty.
– The lower-right cell is important for the library users, and the library is not doing well. This area represents the greatest opportunity. E.g. the library should concentrate its effort on 'printed publications' and 'library environment' (from Figure 3 and 4) and add resources to these determinants to improve users' satisfaction and loyalty.
– The upper-right cell presents that the library has already done very well. E.g. 'electronic resources' (from Figure 4).

If the focus is creating users' loyalty, here, the only area of strength is 'electronic resources' (from Figure 3 of upper-left cell and from Figure 4 of upper-right cell). It is important that the library keeps an eye on this determinant. It may become a future area of strength for the creation of satisfaction when it receives extra resources. If the library management wishes to improve user satisfaction and loyalty, they should add resources to the library environment at first.

A statistical analysis of the relationship between a computed performance index and its specific indicators (e.g. seven specific questions of 'library environment' in Table 1) may be carried out by the use of regression analysis. [2][4] Figure 5 presents a detailed description of initiate activities that may improve the library environment.

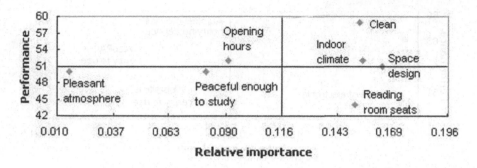

Fig. 5. Importance versus performance for library environment: priority map

As illustrated in Figure 5, the estimation of the specific questions related to 'library environment' has the following response. Respondents perceived that the library was clean enough, the space design of the library and indoor climate were satisfactory. But the seats of reading room are not available enough, so the library must increase seating areas for readers.

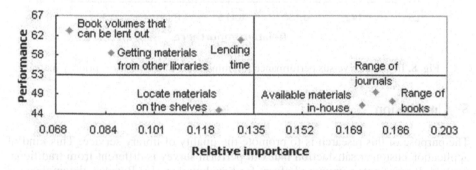

Fig. 6. Importance versus performance for printed publications: priority map

Figure 6 shows that the 'range of books', 'journals' and 'available materials in-house' are very important for the users, but the library is not doing well. Thus, the library must increase the duplicates of the collection and pay more attention to the field of printed publication that the library users are interested in. Specially, 'electronic resources' may also become a future area of strength for the creation of satisfaction. As it appears from Figure 7, the library does well in two areas today 'automatic e-mail' and 'WebPAC', but the library website is user inconvenient. Thus, the library has to improve on user satisfaction for easy access to website in the future.

We found the 'human side of user service (62)' got the highest scores in six quality dimensions (from Figure 2), but, unfortunately, it received little emphasis on categories of user satisfaction and loyalty. Finding from the analysis, the importance of 'friendly and helpful' should be strengthened in the future (from Figure 8).

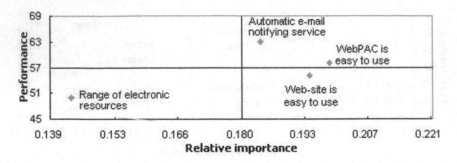

Fig. 7. Importance versus performance for electronic resources: priority map

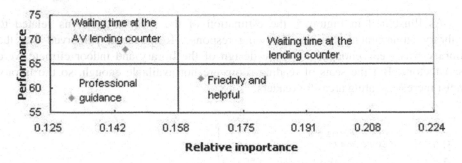

Fig. 8. Importance versus performance for human side of user service: priority map

5 Conclusion

The purpose of this research is to promote the quality of library service. This kind of application customer satisfaction index to perform survey is different from traditional method. It represents a unique platform for benchmarking.[1] Besides, the application of priority map provides clear guidelines for the library management. By further analytical study in the survey data, we were able to make the following suggestions to satisfy users' expectations: (1) increase seating areas for readers, (2) increase collections of printed publications and journals to meet readers' demands, (3) increase the number of duplications on popular literatures, (4) improve the convenience of using web-site, and (5) offer more friendly and helpful user service.

References

1. Anne Martensen, Lars Grønholdt & Kai Kristensen, "The drivers of customer satisfaction and loyalty: cross-industry findings from Denmark." *Total Quality Management,* 11 (July 2000): 544–553; Lars Grønholdt, Anne Martensen & Kai Kristensen, "The relationship between customer satisfaction and loyalty: cross-industry differences," *Total Quality Management* 11 (4, 5 & 6) (July 2000): 509–514; Kai Kristensen, Anne Martensen & Lars Grønholdt, "Measuring customer satisfaction: A key dimension of business performance," *International Journal of Business Performance Management* 2 (1, 2 & 3) (July 2000): 157–170.

2. Anne Martensen and Lars Grønholdt, "Improving Library Users' Perceived Quality, Satisfaction and Loyalty: An Integrated Measurement and Management System," *The Journal of Academic Librarianship*, Vol. 29, 3 (May 2003): 140-147.

3. ECSI Technical Committee, *European Customer Satisfaction Index: Foundation and Structure for Harmonized National Pilot Projects*, Report prepared for the ECSI Steering Committee (October 1998)

4. Kai Kristensen, Anne Martensen, & Lars Grønholdt, "Customer satisfaction measurement at Post Denmark: Results of application of the European Customer Satisfaction Index methodology," *Total Quality Management* 11(7) (September 2000): S1007–S1015.

5. Roland T. Rust, Anthony J. Zahorik & Timothy L. Keiningham, *Service Marketing* (New York, HarperCollins College Publishers, 1996), pp. 265–267; Michael D. Johnson, *Customer Orientation and Market Action* (Upper Saddle River, NJ: Prentice Hall, Inc.), pp. 119–120; Michael D. Johnson & Anders Gustafsson, *Improving Customer Satisfaction, Loyalty, and Profit: An Integrated Measurement and Management System*, University of Michigan Business School Management Series (San Francisco, CA: Jossey-Bass Inc., 2000), pp. 13–14, 142–144; Martin Christopher, Adrian Payne & David Ballantyne, *Relationship Marketing: Creating Stakeholder Value* (Oxford, UK: Butterworth- Heinemann), pp. 70–73.

6. S. R. Ranganathan, "The Five Laws of Library Science," *Madras: The Madras Library Association*, 1931.

Cross-Cultural Usability of Digital Libraries

Anita Komlodi[1], Nadia Caidi[2], and Kristin Wheeler[3]

[1] Department of Information Systems, UMBC,
1000 Hilltop Circle, Baltimore, MD, 21250, USA
komlodi@umbc.edu
http://www.research.umbc.edu/~komlodi
[2] Faculty of Information Studies, University of Toronto
Toronto, ON M5S 3G6, Canada
nadia.caidi@utoronto.ca
[3] Grambling State University

Abstract. The advent of digitization has enabled individuals, institutions, and communities to create and disseminate digital representations of their cultural heritage in digital libraries (DL). These digital collections are increasingly broader in scope and reach, spanning geographical and cultural boundaries. They serve users from their originating culture and often also play the role of cultural ambassadors by serving users from other cultures. While cross-cultural use of DLs is present, little research is available on the influence of culture as it pertains to the design and use of DLs. In this paper, we define cross-cultural usability guidelines for DLs and apply these to the heuristic evaluation of six "national" DLs. Results of a usability evaluation study of five of the DLs are also reported. The national DLs were selected based on their mission, funding model, and originating organization and they all represent their respective cultures. Results of the evaluation show that current DL UIs and content do not serve international users very well. These results were confirmed in a user study in which users were asked to browse "national" digital libraries from countries other than their own. Based on our results, we propose guidelines for the designers of DLs to support their international users and truly serve as "cultural ambassadors" for their originating countries. While the results of this study were gained through the evaluation of DLs using the Latin alphabet, the general design guidelines are proposed for DLs of all cultures.

1 Introduction

The advent of digitization has enabled individuals, institutions, and communities to create and disseminate digital representations of their cultural heritage in digital libraries (DL). These developments raise new and challenging issues around the representation of the vast collections of human cultural artifacts in digital forms. Important considerations include: the definitions of the targeted end users, biases in content selection to represent a given culture, access versus ownership issues, and the implications for information institutions in managing and organizing content [1].

Z. Chen et al. (Eds.): ICADL 2004, LNCS 3334, pp. 584–593, 2004.

Another important area is user interfaces (UI), as these connect users to the digitized collections and have a major impact on the user experience of the DL.

We examine and compare six DL initiatives aimed at representing the cultural and historical heritage of a country. The selected DLs attempt to serve as 'cultural ambassadors' by showcasing their national culture in their collections. The underlying goal of our research is to identify elements constitutive of this 'cultural ambassador' function of the DL, for instance, through the ways in which content is selected, information organized, and the UI is designed. To do so, we defined cross-cultural usability criteria for DLs and used these criteria to evaluate and compare the six national DLs.

While it is obvious that users who do not speak the language of a website will have serious difficulties in using the site, the goal of the present study is to identify international user interface design guidelines that are especially relevant for DLs and that can provide pointers for the designers of these DLs in the future.

2 Methodology: Evaluation of National DL User Interfaces

Six national DLs were selected for the usability study (Table 1). All satisfy at least one of the following criteria: 1) fully or partially funded by the government of the country, 2) housed at the national library or equivalent, 3) charged with the digitization of the country's "cultural heritage" (e.g., Americana, classic authors). Of the many DLs that could fulfill these requirements, the selected set represents languages spoken fluently by the authors and/or close collaborators. At this phase of the study, due to this limitation, all six DLs evaluated are from countries where the Latin alphabet is being used.

Table 1. Digital libraries evaluated

Digital Libraries:	Selection Criteria:	1	2	3
Biblioteca Italiana, Italy: http://www.bibliotecaitaliana.it/		●		●
Early Canadiana Online, Canada: http://www.canadiana.org/		●		●
Gallica, France: http://gallica.bnf.fr/		●	●	●
Library of Congress National Digital Library, USA: http://memory.loc.gov/		●	●	●
Neumann House, Hungary: http://www.neumann-haz.hu/		●		●
Proyecto Biblioteca Digital Argentina: http://www.clarin.com.ar/pbda/				●

First, the selected DLs were evaluated by the authors using an expert review UI evaluation methodology, heuristic evaluation [2, 3]. Next, five of the six DLs were evaluated in a usability evaluation, with the involvement of participants from the United States. Next, these two methods, along with the cross-cultural usability criteria used for the heuristic evaluation, will be described.

2.1 Heuristic Evaluation Methods

Heuristic evaluation [3] is a widely used method of usability evaluation in UI design whereby experts review interfaces "to determine the conformance with a short list of design heuristics" [2, p.126]. The method requires a thorough examination of all screens and usually identifies many usability problems at the beginning phases of the design.

The six DLs selected were examined by at least two evaluators, one of whom was a target language speaker and the other, without the target language skill, served as an international user representative. The homepage and all main pages were examined, with selected representative content pages from each DL. The websites were all accessed between February and April 2004. The evaluators completed their reviews separately, then discussed and combined their results.

2.2 Cross-Cultural Usability Criteria

Four usability design guidelines were used in the evaluation. Two of these –language and visual representations– are established guidelines for the design of international UIs, as described by Fernandes [4] and Del Galdo [5]. Two additional guidelines were included to address more specifically the information provision function of DLs: content selection and content organization [6]. These are detailed below:

Language: The site should provide support for at least one of the six official United Nations (UN) languages (Arabic, Chinese, English, French, Russian, and Spanish) in addition to the language of the country. The official UN languages are treated here as widely spoken languages that allow access for large international user groups. If the DL's native language is among these, second-language support is not as necessary, but a limited number of culturally-specific metaphors, vocabulary, and spelling should be used in the native language. Language support can exist at three levels in DLs: 1) the UI, 2) content, and 3) services. These levels translate into increasing language support for international users. For example, a Hungarian DL can provide English-language links in the UI to Hungarian content, which will only help users who speak both languages. At the content level, the English-language links can lead to English language content, or at the services level, English-language indexing can support searching in English as well.

Visual Representation: The images used for navigation and interaction with the content of the DL should be 'universalized' in order to allow international users to navigate even if they do not speak the language. For culture-specific images, text labels or other explanatory mechanisms should be included to help users who are not familiar with the culture, its meanings, and symbols. While it may be appropriate to include images highly specific to a culture for the collections, visual UI elements, such as menu and link representations, should be understandable by an international audience.

Content Selection: The content selected should be meaningful and representative of the culture for content providers, designers, and users. Adequate explanations for the content should be included for international users. The content selection of a culturally representative DL is often a sensitive issue and biases in the nature and scope of materials included (e.g., inclusive or exclusive of various voices, perspectives and communities' histories) can occur. Policies and the decision-making authority for content selection need to be clearly established and presented to users.

Content Organization: If the DL sets out to serve international users, the organization of the information should not rely exclusively on culturally-specific categories and classification schemes, but provide alternative access mechanisms. For example, access to a literary collection exclusively by author will benefit users familiar with the authors. However, cross-cultural users may not be familiar with author names and this access mechanism can be confusing for them. A solution to this is the provision of additional indices by genre or chronology. Whenever culturally-specific organization schemes are used, this should be clearly stated and explained to users who may not be familiar with this type of arrangement. The last two dimensions are closely related and the results will be reported together.

Taken together, these four guidelines serve as good starting points for evaluating the cross-cultural usability of DLs. Language is clearly the most important consideration for users from different cultures, because if users do not understand the textual information provided in a certain language, their use of the collection will be severely limited. Similarly, images can lead to usability problems if they represent culturally-determined physical objects or metaphors that cannot be readily understood by users from other cultures. However, assessing national language support and visual representations alone is not sufficient. When we deal with content-rich collections, such as DLs whose function is to showcase the cultural heritage of the country, the content and its organization is also essential to assess. Content selection and organization should be representative of the culture in question, but should also be usable and understandable by users from other countries [6]. In addition to these criteria, the usability evaluation identified additional areas of concern for the designers of internationally used DLs.

2.3 Usability Evaluation

Expert reviews are invaluable tools. However, observing and interviewing real-life users provide crucial insights. The goal of usability evaluation is to identify problems users encounter when interacting with software user interfaces [2, 3]. Usability evaluation methods are widely used techniques in the development of user interfaces. In these sessions, users are asked to interact with the user interface of the system and think aloud while doing so. They carry out predetermined tasks and they are interviewed about their experience and opinions afterwards.

Seven science major college students participated in our usability study from United States higher education institutions. All of them were science majors between the ages of 17 and 24. English was every participant's native language, with one participant having spent most of her life in Kenya. Four identified themselves with 'American', while three with 'African American' cultural background. All of them have used computers for more than six years and use them daily. They had varying levels of DL experience.

The participants in our evaluation were asked to come to our research laboratory and use the six digital libraries there. They were first asked to fill out a demographic questionnaire describing their cultural background, computer and DL use experience. Next, they were asked to use the digital libraries and think aloud while they were interacting with them. They used the Library of Congress National Digital Library first to practice the procedure and thinking aloud, then the other DLs. For each DL, they were first asked to explore the site, then find specific information. They were interviewed about their opinions and experience after each DL interaction and at the end of the session. The sessions were audio recorded along with a capture record of the screen during the interactions. The interviews were transcribed and coded to identify difficulties, likes, and dislikes of the participants.

Many of the findings of the heuristic evaluation were reinforced in the usability study, while some were newly identified. The results from the heuristic evaluation and the usability study are organized around five major themes.

4 Findings

4.1 Summary of the Heuristic Evaluation

Table 2 presents a summary of the results of the evaluation. The DLs did very poorly in the language support category, which excludes many international users and decreases the importance of the other guidelines. If language support is not present, content organization and the use of images become less crucial. The results are described in detail in the following sections.

Table 2. DL compliance with cross-cultural usability guidelines

Digital Libraries:		Language	Images	Content
Biblioteca Italiana		No support	Very good	Very good
Early Canadiana Online		Very good	Good (branding)	Limited support
Gallica, France		No support	No support	Very good
US Library of Congress NDL		No support	Good (branding)	Very good
Neumann House, Hungary		Good	Good (int'l use)	Limited support
Proyecto Bibl. Dig. Argentina		No support	Good (int'l use)	Good

4.2 Summary of the Usability Evaluation

Participants in the usability evaluation were discouraged early on from exploring the DLs by usability problems. All of them mentioned that they would have given up early had the researcher not asked them to continue. While using a DL site where the language is not familiar does not happen frequently, this scenario allowed the researchers to explore cross-cultural usability problems, as many DL sites do not have access in multiple languages. The data collected highlighted several usability problems and opportunities for improvement. The usability issues identified in this evaluation, but not examined in the heuristic evaluation revolve around user access to the collections, such as search and browse/navigate features.

4.3 Language Support

When it comes to language support, the DLs evaluated do not fare well. Four out of the six DLs only provide UIs in the language of the originating culture. The Canadian Early Canadiana Online site is fully bilingual (i.e. supports both English and French for the UI, indexing, and content), reflecting the two official languages of Canada. Because of its multilingual indexing, a user is able to enter terms in one language and find relevant documents written in another language. The Hungarian collection provides support in English at the UI level, however, the indexing and the content are only in Hungarian. France's Gallica uses French almost exclusively. The Argentinean, Italian, and US collections do not include any second-language support. Introductory information for international users would be helpful at these sites. Although full second-language support may be a distant goal for most DLs, samples of the content and descriptions of the site should be presented in other languages to give some insight for international visitors. Results from our heuristic evaluation show that multi-language support and multilingual indexing are lacking.

As expected, the most important stumbling block for users in the usability evaluation was the lack of language skills. Several participants mentioned that even rudimentary machine translation tools could have been helpful in exploring the sites. Limited familiarity with the target language did not help with exploring complex information spaces like DLs, in some cases it confused users even more. Vague familiarity with he language prompted users to guess meanings of words which were often wrong and led to more frustration. When an English-language version was provided for a DL, participants often had trouble finding the link to it.

4.4 Visual Language

Four out of the six DLs used very limited images in the UI. The French Gallica site uses the most, all of which are representative of the French culture and as such may be most likely unfamiliar to foreign visitors. While these images are aesthetically pleasing, informational labels could increase the usability of the site. The Italian DL provides an excellent example of image use: the navigational images offer simple designs with international reach (i.e., pages of a book to represent collections), while culturally-specific images with meaningful labels are used to provide highlights of the various collections. The presence of a maple leaf adorns many pages of the Canadian site (i.e. the welcome page, the logo of the DL itself, the background pages and alongside mentions of government agencies). This element is the only symbol of 'Canadianness' although certain projects (such as educational resources) have accompanying pictures, such as First Nation members, prominently displayed.

The US flag is prominently displayed and contributes to "brand" the US DL site. The affiliation with the Library of Congress is also clearly established. The American site uses a fair amount of images and graphics, which contributes a visually pleasing and seemingly content-rich DL. The light bulb depicted next to the 'Learning' section adds to its visibility. The Hungarian and Argentinean sites use very limited navigational visual elements and have no particular 'national flavors' or representations. Those used were easy to interpret (i.e., logos). The colors displayed in the main page of the Argentinean DL are reminiscent of the country's national colors (pale blue and white stripes), but the accompanying images in the opening page do not convey any additional information to those unfamiliar with that culture.

Most participants mentioned the need for more visual (icon) representation for navigation elements, as in the next quote:

"There should have been symbols next to the options to tell you what they were."

They viewed icons as a potential solution for international communication, a good way to express what certain functions and links on the website did. Participants also enjoyed the images representing the content and expressed a need for the inclusion of more content images, as an internationally better understood medium.

4.5   Content Selection and Organization

The content organization of a site is very important for international users, as it not only provides access to materials, but informs users about the structure of the content and the coverage available. If there is only one way to access a collection via browsing, this should be informative enough for all users. As described above, access through an author index may be useless for users who are not familiar with the culture of the country and cannot judge what they will find at the other end of the link. Genre translates across cultures better and gives international users a better idea of what to expect. Topical organization schemes may vary from culture to culture, and topical categories can be interpreted differently by users from different cultures. A telling example is that of the French DL, Gallica, which focus is on the 19th century. This choice may seem 'natural' to the creators of the DL, to French reviewers of the site, or to Francophiles who are aware that 19th century is considered by the French as the century of modern printing, of scientific and technical discoveries and other great intellectual pursuits (literature, history, philosophy, etc.), but this may not be clear or evident to outside users, especially non francophones, as the site is primarily about French culture. Another example of cultural confusion related to content organization can be found in the language used in the Italian DL. While the site provides access by author, time period, and genre, the labeling can be confusing for international users. A non-Italian speaker having a basic familiarity with the Arabic numbering format can browse the DL collections by time period. However, the centuries are represented by the Italian format (i.e., Italians abbreviate the 1800s to 800s), which can be confusing for a user unfamiliar with this norm. A more culturally-sensitive label would have enabled better browsability. In fact, none of the participants in the usability study could solve the mystery of the Italian period representation.

The organization of the content varies the most across our six DLs. The American DL provides access to materials via several organized lists: topic, time, format, place, library division. The French Gallica site allows access by time, topic, format (for the image collections), and an author index to the text collection. The Canadian DL allows access by collections, such as Canadian Women's History, along with New titles and Collection descriptions. The Argentinean site organized materials (text only) by genres and authors, while the Hungarian site organized content into collections accessible by author indices. Most sites also allow searching in the originating language. In general, multiple access methods will help international users not just find materials easily, but also gain a better understanding of the collection.

Participants in the usability study preferred well-organized and highly structured collections and they were in favor of search tools. While they often had difficulty describing the structure of the collection, they addressed many issues involved in finding their way in the DL. These will be described next.

4.5.1 Search

The participants in the usability evaluation were very enthusiastic about searching tools and saw search boxes as the solution to their problems in finding information. Several of them suggested that the search box should be presented on the home page of each site. This over-reliance on search, combined with the difficulty of providing foreign-language search and indexing on these sites misled the participants to many unsuccessful searches. Study participants were especially disappointed when using search tools on the websites without first realizing that they cannot search for English words.

4.5.2 Navigation

Participants in the usability study had serious problems with navigation of the sites. In addition to the lack of language skills, the pages did not follow design conventions that the North American students were used to. There were often no stable left-side menus, no logos in the upper left corner taking users back to the homepages, and as described above, no consistent visual navigation systems. In addition to navigation systems, participants often mentioned the advantages of clearly and systematically organized collections where it was easy to figure out how content was grouped, illustrated by the next example:

"Which site did you like the best?

The Argentinean one, because it was organized in several broad categories that were easy to find on start and they were pretty exhaustive."

All participants liked the Argentinean site, which was very clearly organized, while they deemed the Canadian site in need of a better organization scheme. Participants favored topical organization as an easy way to access the collections.

5 Conclusions and Suggestions for Improvements

National DLs can potentially serve a large number of international users and represent the culture of the originating country on the Web. In order to achieve cross-cultural usability of these DLs, it is very important to follow guidelines of usability, simple and functional design, and specific international design guidelines. The DLs evaluated in our study do not serve international users well. Our analysis identified several guidelines, which will help achieve this goal.

National language support in the DLs evaluated is severely limited, making them unusable by visitors who do not speak the originating language. Some of the DLs did well in terms of information organization and provided multiple indices for users to access; others did very poorly, simply organizing the access by collections or authors. Support for more languages at the UI level, and samples of the collection in other languages will help international users and so will presenting multiple, culturally–independent organization of the information access methods.

If these DLs are to serve a 'cultural ambassador' function, it seems important that they provide a brief introduction in at least one of the official UN languages to explain their mission and objectives. Several participants mentioned this need. It also seems important that any cultural assumptions about content selection be explained. For example, Gallica's rationale for choosing the 19th century should be explained for those unfamiliar with the historical context. Similarly, any national representations and symbols (e.g., maple leaf, etc.) need to be explained –at least in the introductory pages, by means of a text embedded in the graphic that provides a brief explanation of the rationale behind the choice of the logo and its signification.

Multiple content organization and access schemes should be provided to allow international users not just to find documents but also to learn about the culture through the collection. Simply providing author names will not help international users, but putting the authors into historical and cultural contexts will not only enrich access to cultural artifacts, but also educate about the culture. Moreover, the learning and instruction section of the site should be given more emphasis. Indeed, a balance between providing in-depth resources and materials in a digitized form is best combined with an educational component, and the Canadian's ECO is a good example of site that combines these two aspects and does it well. The American DL is also very successful in its integration of learning modules. While applying heuristics from the cross-cultural UI design field is a good idea, more research is needed on the behavior of culturally diverse user groups of information resources. These studies can form the basis for culturally sensitive design for DLs.

Acknowledgements. The authors would like to thank Wayne G. Lutters for his editorial help, Lola Stefanelli and Enrique Stanziola for their help in the selection and evaluation of the Italian and the Argentinean DLs.

References

1. Caidi, N.; Komlodi, A. (2003). "Digital Libraries Across Cultures: Design and Usability Issues." SIGIR Forum, 37(2). Fall issue. Pp. 62-64.
2. Shneiderman, B. (1998) Designing the User Interface, Addison Wesley Longman, Reading, MA.

3. Nielsen, Jakob. (1993) Usability Engineering, Morgan Kaufmann, San Francisco, CA.
4. Fernandes, Tony. (1995) Global interface design: A guide to designing international user interfaces. AP Professional, Boston, MA. p. 191.
5. Del Galdo, Elisa; Nielsen, Jakob (eds.). (1996) International user interfaces. John Wiley & Sons, Inc. New York, NY. p. 276.
6. Stanziola, Enrique; Komlodi, Anita (2003) Exploring ethnocentrism in the information architecture of World Wide Web sites. Latin American Conference on Human-Computer Interaction (CLIHC). Rio de Janeiro, Brasil, August 17-20, 2003. p. 283-285.

Design Lessons on Access Features in PAPER

Yin-Leng Theng[1], Dion Hoe-Lian Goh[1], Ming Yin[2],
Eng-Kai Suen[2], and Ee-Peng Lim[2]

[1] Division of Information Studies, School of Communication & Information
Nanyang Technological University,Singapore 637718
{tyltheng, ashlgoh}@ntu.edu.sg
[2] Center for Advanced Information Systems, School of Computer Engineering
Nanyang Technological University,Singapore 639798
{asmyin, aseksuen, aseplim}@ntu.edu.sg

Abstract. Using Nielsen's Heuristic Evaluation, this paper reports a user study
with six usability-trained subjects to evaluate PAPER's access features in
assisting users to retrieve information efficiently, part of an on-going design
partnership with stakeholders and designers/developers. PAPER (Personalised
Adaptive Pathways for Exam Resources) is an improved version evolving from
an earlier implementation of GeogDL built upon G-Portal, a geospatial digital
library infrastructure. After two initial evaluations with student and teacher
design partners, PAPER has evolved into a system containing a new bundle of
personalized, interactive services with four modules: mock exam; personal
coach (practice and review); trend analysis and performance review. This paper
highlights lessons learnt in the design of PAPER using Nielsen's heuristics, and
discusses implications for the design of access features in digital libraries in
general.

1 Introduction

Subject-based digital libraries (DLs) are beginning to emerge on the Web, and
promise opportunities we never had with traditional libraries or even the Web. Recent
work developing educational applications of DLs across all disciplines range from
primary schools through graduate schools. However, there are many design and
usability issues that remain unresolved. One of which is still the lack of more user
studies done on interactive systems to improve navigation and help, a concern voiced
in a keynote address by Ben Shneiderman at the 8th ERCIM Workshop on "Universal
Access for All" at Vienna (Austria) in June 2004 [5].

As part of an on-going design partnership with stakeholders and
designers/developers, in this paper, we report a third user study employing six
usability-trained subjects as design partners to evaluate PAPER's access features,
particularly on instructions or descriptions to assist better user navigation and
understanding of PAPER. PAPER is a DL of geography examination resources
designed with four main personalized, interactive services: (1) a mock exam; (2)
personal coach (practice and review); (3) trend analysis and (4) performance review.

Z. Chen et al. (Eds.): ICADL 2004, LNCS 3334, pp. 594–607, 2004.
© Springer-Verlag Berlin Heidelberg 2004

The paper concludes with lessons learnt in the design and development of PAPER, and discusses implications for the design of access features in DLs in general.

2 Design History and Philosophy of GeogDL and PAPER

PAPER, which stands for **P**ersonalised **A**daptive **P**athways for **E**xam **R**esources, was first conceptualized as GeogDL, a geospatial DL on geography examination resources, an application built upon G-Portal [3]. G-Portal aims to explore identification, classification and organization of geospatial and georeferenced content on the Web, and the provision of digital services such as searching and visualization. One of the main objectives of G-Portal is allowing authorized users to contribute resources to a common environment for knowledge sharing.

Since then, GeogDL has undergone several refinements, resulting from participatory design partnerships with prospective stakeholders and designers/developers. Prior to the study reported in this paper, two previous studies with student and teacher design partners were conducted and reported in [7, 2].

In the first study [7], student design partners gave feedback from the perspectives of prospective users on possible scenarios of use in GeogDL (predecessor of PAPER), and identified usability problems with positive and negative consequences employing Carroll's Claims Analysis, and grouped usability problems using Nielsen's heuristics. Based on their feedback, GeogDL was modified. In the second study [2], teacher design partners were employed, resulting in new, additional services or modules. GeogDL was renamed as PAPER.

In section 2.1, we briefly revisit our previous work on GeogDL to provide a background for the body of this paper and the issues explored within it. Section 2.2 describes PAPER, improved version of GeogDL. Section 2.3 reviews and compares related work.

2.1 GeogDL – Early Version

In GeogDL, past-year examination questions (with their solutions) are created as separate G-Portal projects. Each project consists of Web resources, at least one of which contains the solution to the question. Other resources contain information to related topics and are used as supplementary material for further exploration. Resources may be further organized into layers depending on the needs of the teacher. For example, the solution to an equatorial region question could appear as a resource in a layer while a separate layer might contain supplementary vegetation resources found in equatorial climates.

In the initial version of GeogDL, examination questions are first accessed through the classification interface that organizes questions by year. Upon selection of a question, the associated project, its resources, and the corresponding map are loaded. Resources are divided into three categories containing question, solution and supplementary resources, each of which is accessible separately via the classification interface.

To view the question, the user selects it using the classification interface, causing GeogDL to display metadata associated with it on the Resource Information Window. This includes information such as the year in which the question appears, type of question, keywords and URL of the question. The user then selects the URL and the question appears in a separate Web browser window. Viewing the solution and supplementary resources follows a similar process. The user first loads the desired category of resources on the classification interface and selects a resource from it. The URL of the resource is selected on the Resource Information Window and G-Portal will then display it in a separate Web browser window. More information may be found in [7].

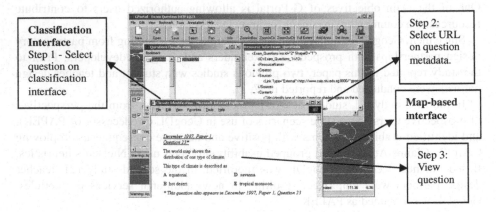

Fig. 1. Viewing an Examination Question

2.2 PAPER – Revised Version of GeogDL

Below are brief descriptions of the four modules implemented in PAPER, a revised version of GeogDL, based on the first two user studies:

1. *Mock Exam.* Provides a timed and scored test that reflects the structure and content of the actual geography examination. Presently, multiple-choice questions are available. Upon reading a question, users select an answer and proceed to the next question. Users may also revisit previous questions to modify their answers. PAPER monitors the time taken for each question to give an indication on how difficult a particular question is to a student. Upon completion of the mock exam, PAPER grades it and displays a performance report. The report contains a summary of the results and includes the total score and total time taken. Users may also review the solutions and explore supplementary resources from the report interface.

2. *Personal Coach (Practice and Review).* Provides recommendations of examination questions to attempt based on performance in previous mock exam sessions (see Figure 2). The personal coach may be invoked from the mock exam

report. The interface consists of two major sections with the panel on the left providing a list of recommended questions organized into topics as described in the geography syllabus, and the panel on the right presenting a question selected by the user and also allowing users to attempt it. Questions are recommended based on a user's past performance in the mock exams. Specifically, each question in a mock exam is associated with one or more topics in the geography syllabus. The personal coach calculates a competency level for each topic based on a user's performance for that topic in previous mock exam sessions. This is a weighted score involving the most recent mock exam and a cumulative score from previous sessions. Using this approach, the personal coach adapts to the student as he or she interacts with PAPER. Difficulty levels range from 1 (easiest) to 5 (most difficult) and are stored in each question's metadata. These are once again assigned by experienced geography teachers to ensure validity.

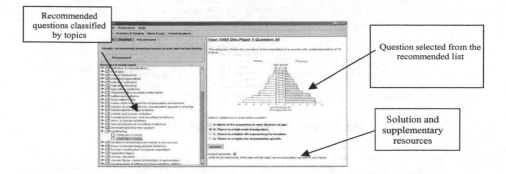

Fig. 2. The Personal Coach : Practice and Review

3. *Trend Analysis.* The idea is to give information on when and what questions are being set over the years (see Figure 3). This would help students identify trends in the types of questions asked and the topics covered. The tool provides statistics on topic areas that appear within a user-specified range of years. These are generated using metadata associated with each examination question. Once again, questions within each topic are classified as "very easy" to "very hard". Selection of a particular bar in either chart will cause PAPER to retrieve and list the associated questions. Upon selection of a particular question, PAPER will display that question together with its answer and supplementary content.

4. *Performance Review.* It provides diagnostic tools to help users gauge how well they fare in their attempts at questions in the mock exam (see Figure 4). It allows students and teachers to view individual or aggregate performance in examination questions. From a student's point of view, the performance review module allows the student to see how well he/she has done in answering questions in the mock exams. Teachers, on the other hand, can either view each student's performance in

mock exams as well as aggregate performance across all students in the class. Performance indicators are categorized by topics so that a student, for example, is able to determine which topics he/she are weak in and therefore pay amount attention to them during revision. Likewise, teachers are able to use this information to tailor their lessons according to the learning needs of the class [2].

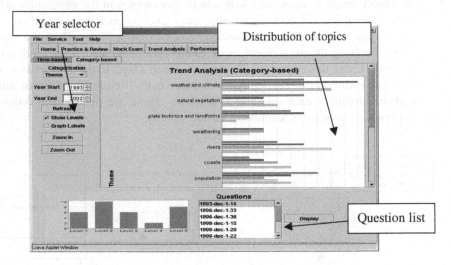

Fig. 3. Trends Analysis for All Topics Over Time

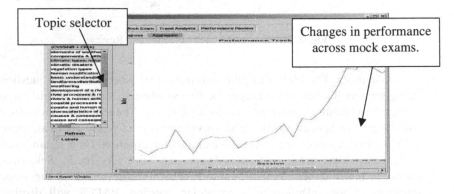

Fig. 4. Performance Review by Mock Exam Session

2.3 Comparison with Other Educational Digital Libraries

While PAPER shares the same education philosophy of active learning as existing education-oriented geography DLs, its design and implementation approach differs due to the importance of examinations in the Singapore education system. For example, the Alexandria Digital Earth Prototype System [6] provides students with "learning spaces", personalized collections of geospatial resources relevant to one or more concepts or hypotheses. Through the process of exploring, manipulating and interacting with the resources in these learning spaces, students' scientific reasoning skills in geography may be cultivated. These skills can then be applied to solve real-word problems as well as examination questions. In contrast, PAPER adopts a "bottom-up" approach in which students are first assisted with examination preparation. As students explore examination questions and solutions, PAPER provides related higher-level concepts for them to investigate, allowing them to draw associations between various geographical issues and developing their reasoning skills. Since requirements for the geography examination are broad, solutions and their associated supplementary resources are developed in cooperation with experienced geography teachers who know how much depth and breadth to provide for each question.

In addition, while the mock exam module shares similarities with existing online tools such as QUIZIT [8] and PILOT [1] in that all provide a Web-based environment for testing and grading, our approach differs in that the mock exam is integrated with PAPER's other modules thus offering various interrelated avenues for revision. For example, because the mock exam operates in conjunction with the Trend Analysis and Performance Review modules, students are not only able to ascertain their areas of weaknesses through their scores but also receive recommendations of important topic areas and hence, examination questions, that should be explored further.

3   Modified Heuristic Evaluation

3.1   Experimental Protocol

Since this study is part of an on-going design partnership with stakeholders and designers/developers, it is important that we obtain "quick" and frequent feedback on PAPER. Hence, in the user studies carried out so far, we made use of small numbers of subjects. In this study, six usability-trained subjects were recruited to evaluate PAPER using Nielsen's Heuristic Evaluation. Compared to other forms of usability evaluation techniques, Heuristic Evaluation is simple to conduct and common usability problems could be detected quickly [4]. These six subjects were graduate students at a local university trained in Heuristic Evaluation. They were frequent Web and DL users, and had been taught how to carry out Nielsen's Heuristic Evaluation.

The subjects were first given a quick tour of PAPER (see http://155.69.149.173:10001/geogdl/index.htm), and then another ten minutes to browse PAPER before they were asked to attempt four different tasks, with one task described for each of the four modules :

- Task 1 : Subjects were to use the *"Practice and Review"* module to practise and review exam questions from 2000-2001 on "rivers".
- Task 2 : Subjects were to take a mock exam using the *"Mock Exam"* module to retrieve papers from "Paper Year 2002 December".

- Task 3 : This involves getting the subjects to review "exam question trends" on "weather and climate" from 1999 – 2003, using the *"Trend Analysis"* module.
- Task 4 : Subjects reviewed performance for Tasks 1 and 2, as well as overall performance from other subjects using the *"Performance Review"* module. They were also asked to explore other features provided in the module on : (i) number of attempts; (ii) proficiency of subjects; (iii) progress of subjects; and (iv) aggregate scores.

In accomplishing these tasks, the subjects were also asked to interrogate PAPER using Nielsen's well-established heuristics focusing specifically on access features

Table 1. Nielsen's Ten Heuristics

H1 : *Visibility of system status*. The system should always keep users informed about what is going on, through appropriate feedback within reasonable time.
H2 : *Match between system and the real world*. The system should speak the users' language, with words, phrases and concepts familiar to the user, rather than system-oriented terms. Follow real-world conventions, making information appear in a natural and logical order.
H3 : *User control and freedom*. Users often choose system functions by mistake and will need a clearly marked "emergency exit" to leave the unwanted state without having to go through an extended dialogue. Support undo and redo.
H4 : *Consistency and standards*. Users should not have to wonder whether different words, situations, or actions mean the same thing. Follow platform conventions.
H5 : *Error prevention*. Even better than good error messages is a careful design which prevents a problem from occurring in the first place.
H6 : *Recognition rather than recall*. Make objects, actions, and options visible. The user should not have to remember information from one part of the dialogue to another. Instructions for use of the system should be visible or easily retrievable whenever appropriate.
H7 : *Flexibility and efficiency of use*. Accelerators -- unseen by the novice user -- may often speed up the interaction for the expert user such that the system can cater to both inexperienced and experienced users. Allow users to tailor frequent actions.
H8 : *Aesthetic and minimalist design*. Dialogues should not contain information which is irrelevant or rarely needed. Every extra unit of information in a dialogue competes with the relevant units of information and diminishes their relative visibility.
H9 : *Help users recognise, diagnose, and recover from errors*. Error messages should be expressed in plain language (no codes), precisely indicate the problem, and constructively suggest a solution.
H10 : *Help and documentation*. Even though it is better if the system can be used without documentation, it may be necessary to provide help and documentation. Any such information should be easy to search, focused on the user's task, list concrete steps to be carried out, and not be too large.

such as search and browse facilities. To ensure that the subjects had the same understanding of Nielsen's heuristics, they were also given a handout with the following descriptions on the ten heuristics (see Table 1).

In giving feedback on the different modules, the subjects were asked to complete four sets of evaluation forms, one for each module, to identify violations against the respective heuristics, and suggest possible recommendations to address these problems. All the subjects completed evaluations of the four modules in approximately two hours.

4 Findings

Although there were only a small number of subjects, using Nielsen's Heuristic Evaluation, we were able to obtain insightful feedback on PAPER. The heuristics

Table 2. Violations against Heuristic #1 and Suggestions for Improvement of the Four Modules

Modules	Violation against Heuristic H1 (Visibility of system status)	Suggestion(s) for Improvement
Personal Coach (Practice and Review)	- The current location is not easy to know. - Not sure what happened to system when entered query. No error message was given.	- Make the tab page more informative; users may feel confused where they are. - Provide some error messages after entering command.
Mock Exam	- No question number given. - I don't know when the exam is over. Don't know how many questions in total, how much is left, how much to be finished. - Not sure what review means.	- Question number should be given, so that students can move back to questions they are not sure of. - Should provide clear message and instructions. - Need to specify that "review" means review previous performance.
Trend Analysis	- No indication on what's going on. - No indication of progress. - User keeps clicking same option unanswered if processing is taking place	- Make the tab page more informative. - System should show a message box indicating the process of running when I click on the "refresh chat". - System takes time to process request. Hence, a display like "please wait…" would tell us system still working.
Performance Review	- If I choose one question bar, such as "rural settlements", there is no response. - No feedback from the system when I click on refresh for a user who has not taken a test before. - Not clear what the different charts mean	- Tell user their choices. Grey out options not available. - Provide feedback. - More informative labelling of charts.

helped the subjects to interrogate the four modules in PAPER, focusing on identifying "obvious" usability problems that came about because of violation against the ten heuristics.

In general, the subjects found PAPER useful in helping students prepare for geography examinations, and PAPER was sufficiently easy to navigate, once they got used to the interface. However, they highlighted that more could be done to assist navigation, and hence provide better user experience.

Due to space constraints, we will not be presenting all the tables highlighting usability problems of the four modules. As an illustration, we selected Table 2, which reports findings of the study with respect to violations against heuristic H1 "visibility of system status" (see Column 2), with suggestions for improvement (see Column 3) by the six subjects. The feedback given by the subjects showed that the modules in PAPER should comply with H1 to "always keep users informed about what is going on, through appropriate feedback within reasonable time". For example, in the Personal Coach module (see Table 2, Row 2, Column 2), subjects did not know where they were, and wanted messages to inform them of what PAPER was doing with their inputs. The subjects suggested making the tab page more informative, and provide messages informing them of errors made or status of PAPER (see Table 2, Row 2, Column 3).

Similar tables such as Table 1 were compiled for all the ten heuristics and four modules. The heuristics were useful in helping subjects to focus on common usability problems highlighted by Nielsen's heuristics, initial efforts made in this project to ensure a good, usable PAPER before implementation and deployment in schools.

5 Discussions on Usability Problems and Recommendations

In this section, owing to space constraints, we will only identify some areas of design recommendations in the four modules based on violations against Nielsen's ten heuristics (see Table 1) detected by students described in tables similar to Table 2, to illustrate that useful recommendations by students serve as on-going design lessons for us in addressing and "fixing" design flaws in PAPER.

5.1 Personal Coach : Practice and Review

Design Violations Against

- *Heuristic H1*. Subjects were confused with regard to where they were. PAPER did not provide enough messages or cues.
- *Heuristic H2*. The subjects did not like the grey background colour, and thought PAPER should be more attractive. The "search" button in the advanced search seems to be in the "wrong place" as the subjects needed to move the mouse down to select the parameters then up again to submit the search. Search's submit box is not next to query field, e.g. "because I expected search results to be displayed on right window but it is in left window, at the bottom", etc.

- *Heuristic H3*. Subjects indicated that they did not know how to switch between the simple and advanced searches.
- *Heuristic H4*. Subjects could not understand what "show annotation" meant. They thought the interface was more like a traditional database system, but it did not comply with established web design conventions.
- *Heuristic H5*. No keywords stemming provided, and some results were not relevant.
- *Heuristic H6*. Not able to distinguish between search and simple search. Annotation feature does not match with prior experience.
- *Heuristic H7*. "Simple search" and "advanced search" were not easy to find. Did not know they should click the text. Feature did not allow submission of search by using "enter" on keyboard.
- *Heuristic H8*. No violation. Generally, subjects were happy with the minimalist design.
- *Heuristic H9*. No good help given. "When entered with invalid characters, no message except sorry! No exam question..."
- *Heuristic H10*. No documentation provided for subjects if they were unsure how to proceed.

Some Recommendations

Recommendations include making the tab page more informative to give context of where they are (see H1). Some error messages should be given, for example, if server is down (see H1). "Search button" should be placed next to query search box, following normal conventions (see H2). Make simple and advanced searches obvious (see H6). Instead of "show annotation", it might be changed to "discussion board of questions" (see H6). The subjects also indicated that better improve information retrieval performance through stemming (see H7). There should also be multiple ways to submit search query (see H7).

5.2 Mock Exam

Design Violations Against

- *Heuristic H1*. Question numbers should be given, so that students can move back to questions they are not sure of. "I don't know when the exam is over. Don't know how many questions totally, how much left, how much finished." The subjects were not sure what review means.
- *Heuristic H2*. "When I get zero scores. It is "00" I think "0" is better. The subjects were confused with this interface, not a conventional one
- *Heuristic H3*. Need to first specify answer, next question appears. The question should not already have a predefined checkbox at the answer. Don't replicate an exam setting. Users should be allowed to stop exam, a cancel option should be given. Linear form of navigation from first question to last and vice versa restricts flexibility. Test papers could be loaded by double-clicking on the exam paper list displayed. No "back button" to return to select a new exam.

- *Heuristic H4*. Loading exam and starting exam seemed like the same function. But their functions are supposed to be different. Not consistent with "practice & review" module.
- *Heuristic H5*. User must click on "load paper" before all the papers show up. Seems like an extra step. Not sure what "Pre" button means, and no explanation given when clicked. It had a default answer from the second question onwards, so users might make mistakes if they did not know what to choose.
- *Heuristic H6*. Numbering of questions should be provided.
- *Heuristic H7*. PAPER did not prompt to "save" work done in other modules.
- *Heuristic H8*. Subjects were satisfied with the simple design.
- *Heuristic H9*. No indication on how to proceed when errors occurred.
- *Heuristic H10*. Proper paper instructions should be given on the structure of PAPER. No "help" feature is available on-line.

Some Recommendations

Should provide clear message and explain what "review" means (see H1). The next question icon should be available all the time (see H2). Checkbox should not be ticked before the user selects the answer (see H2). Give timing as well as cancel options (see H2). Perhaps, a feature should be added to allow users to mark questions they are not sure of, so they could navigate back to the question when they have extra time (see H3). Allow exam papers to be loaded by double clicking the list (see H3). Give a workflow of how this function works, or offer the same search interface similar to "practice & review", or directly display two mock papers, so there is no need to click "load" (see H7). Make help more prominent at present (see H10). System should explain the difficulty levels of the questions (see H10).

5.3 Trend Analysis

Design Violations Against

- *Heuristic H1*. "No indication on what's going on." System should show a message box indicating the process of running when subjects clicked on the "refresh chat".
- *Heuristic H2*. "Trend analysis" option is not intuitive. Normally, the convention is from left to right. But displayed questions on PAPER are from right to left.
- *Heuristic H3*. User may feel confused because lots of options are available. Not clear if users can have multiple choices from list. Display functions cannot be displayed by double-clicking.
- *Heuristic H4*. Category type field is grey. Users may think it is invalid. Time based & categories based are different interfaces. Year in "practice & review", for example, is a dropdown list but it is not in this module.
- *Heuristic H5*. Not sure what "levels" mean.
- *Heuristic H6*. "Refresh chart" icon is not very intuitive. For category-based, there is no indication on the meaning of colours. The choices and design are not very interactive.

- *Heuristic H7.* Not clear about what's difference between domain, theme and topic.
- *Heuristic H8.* The design is complex. The user should not have to scroll horizontally to read the category name under category list as well.
- *Heuristic H9.* The response time is long, and subjects not certain whether it encountered error or working. Not clear what this module can achieve. Should provide intuitive display of error messages, when users do something wrong.
- *Heuristic H10.* No help available.

Some Recommendations

Make the tab page more informative so users may not feel confused where they are (see H1). PAPER takes time to process request. Perhaps, a display like "please wait..." would tell users whether PAPER is still working (see H2). Should provide help and make the options more informative (see H3). More informative labelling of features should be available. Provide on-line help to assist user (see H10).

5.4 Performance Review

Design Violations Against

- *Heuristic H1.* The interface and fonts were not clear. No feedback from the system when subjects clicked on refresh. Not clear what the different charts mean.
- *Heuristic H2.* Yes. The message box use "Error" as title. Confused by the interface. The use of "Ctrl+click" to select user is not conventional.
- *Heuristic H3.* Clicking on the blue bar did not show list of question attempted already. The various themes should be displayed as rule-headings under :
  main domain-> theme->topic
- *Heuristic H4.* No violation.
- *Heuristic H5.* Not sure what "save as" do. Attempts, proficiency, and aggregate have no data at times.
- *Heuristic H6.* Subjects did not know they had to click bar to retrieve question lists.
- *Heuristic H7.* No violation.
- *Heuristic H8.* Had to scroll both horizontally and vertically to read topics. The meaning of each review should be stated
- *Heuristic H9.* In the "attempts< when user did not choose a question bar, firstly and click "show questions", the error message just tells users should choose one question. No explanation given.
- *Heuristic H10.* Simple instructions should be given so that users can find questions of interest. Subjects did not see the purpose and benefit of each sub category.

Some Recommendations

More informative labelling for charts should be provided (see H1). Allow display list of questions by clicking on the blue bar (see H3). Provide documentation and help so that users will know what each function does (see H10).

6 Conclusions and On-Going Work

Using Nielsen's Heuristic Evaluation, this paper reported a third user study with usability-trained subjects on PAPER, following the first two studies with stakeholders such as students and teachers, to improve the access features, in particular the search and browse facilities. With six subjects, usability problems as a result of violations against Nielsen's heuristics were highlighted, and recommendations were made to address the problems.

Design ideas for PAPER could go on. However, in seeking improvements, it is sometimes tempting to propose the implementation of new features which, in the end, may or may not enhance the system. Whether it be an aesthetic make-over or a re-design of the underlying information structure, there will be a need to find out whether the changes suggested do, in fact, have the desired outcome prior to implementation, and this is where future work needs to be performed. In spite of this, the evaluation findings using Nielsen's heuristics suggest a few broad recommendations for PAPER.

In the three studies on PAPER, we carried out participatory design with a small group of stakeholders, designers/developers and usability-trained subjects to help us obtain "quick" feedback through testing and retesting initial designs. On-going work with PAPER involves deploying it in an actual school environment with "real" user students and teachers working in their "natural" settings.

Acknowledgements. The authors would like to thank the subjects for their participation and ideas. The project is partially supported by the SingAREN 21 research grant M48020004.

References

1. Bridgeman, S., Goodrich, M.T., Kobourov, S.G., and Tamassia, R., PILOT: An interactive tool for learning and grading, ACM SIGCSE Bulletin, Vol. 32, No. 1, 2000, pp. 139-143.
2. Goh, D., Theng, Y.L., Ming, Y., and Lim, E.P.: PAPER for an Educational Digital Library. The 6th International Conference on Asian Digital Libraries - Digital libraries: Technology and Management of Indigenous Knowledge for Global Access, pp. 493-504. Springer-Verlag. (2003).
3. Lim, E.P., Goh, D., Liu, Z., Ng, W.K., Khoo, C., Higgins, S.E. G-Portal: A Map-based Digital Library for Distributed Geospatial and Georeferenced Resources. Proceedings of the Second ACM+IEEE Joint Conference on Digital Libraries. pp. 351-358. (2002).
4. Nielsen, J. Heuristic Evaluation. Retrieved July 12, 2004 from http://www.useit.com/papers/heuristic/.
5. Shneiderman, B. Interface Design Strategies to Promote Learnability for All. 8th ERCIM Workshop. Retrieved July 10, 2004 from http://www.ui4all.gr/workshop2004/keynote/shneiderman.html.
6. Smith, T., Janee, G., Frew, J., & Coleman, A., The Alexandria Digital Earth ProtoType system, Proceedings of the 1st ACM+IEEE Joint Conference on Digital Libraries, pp. 118-119. (2001).

7. Theng, Y.L., Goh, H.L., Lim, E.P., Liu, Z., Pang, L.S., Wong, B.B. and Chua, L.H. Intergenerational Partnerships in the Design of a Digital Library of Geography Examination Resources, in Lim, E.P., Foo, S., Khoo, H.C., Fox, E., Urs, S. and Constantion, T. (Eds.), ICADL2002, pp. 427-439, LNCS 2555, Springer-Verlag, (2002).
8. Tinoco, L., Fox, E., and Barnette, D., Online evaluation in WWW-based courseware, Proceedings of the 28th SIGCSE Technical Symposium, 1997, pp. 194-198.

Information and Communication Technologies, Libraries and the Role of Library Professionals in the 21st Century: With Special Reference to Bangladesh

Md. Anisur Rahman[1], Md. Hanif Uddin[2], and Ragina Akhter[3]

[1] Senior Information Officer, Library and Information Services Unit,
and Acting Programme Librarian, Poverty and Health Resource Centre,
ICDDR, B: Centre for Health and Population Research,
(GPO Box 128, Dhaka 1000), Mohakhali, Dhaka 1212, Bangladesh
anis@icddrb.org
[2] Department of Information Science and Library Management,
University of Dhaka, Ramna, Dhaka 1000, Bangladesh
[3] Bangladesh Shishu Academy, Old High Court Area, Ramna, Dhaka 1000, Bangladesh
{mhuddin, raginaakhter}@yahoo.com

Abstract. Information and communication technologies (ICT) facilitate the process of identification, collection, storing, processing and disseminating of information. The library and information science professionals are utilizing ICT to keep pace with the problem of information explosion. The benefit of instant access to digital information is the most distinguishing attribute of the information age. In this paper, the authors tried to highlight the libraries/information centers in the 21st century, the different components of providing digital information services, and Information and Communication Technology's role in modernizing libraries. In Bangladesh, the use of ICT is yet to take off. In absence of strong telecommunication the Internet facility is not spread out successfully. Financial constraints are the major hindrance for its growth at the national, local and organizational levels. As a result, the implementation of ICT facilities for libraries is not receiving adequate support from their parent body. Most of the libraries in Bangladesh do not have computer facilities. The print media is still a major source of information in libraries. However, the situation is changing, and the library professionals should be ready for everything to cope with the new ICT used in libraries/information centers. In this paper, the authors intended to emphasize the expected change in libraries/information centers in respect of user services and how to cope up with.

1 Introduction

The 21st century is the age of electronic communication; knowledge and technology have become borderless, and have become the basis for all appropriate decisions in relation to socioeconomic development of people. Electronic formats dominate all spheres of life, including education, employment, agriculture and industrial

Z. Chen et al. (Eds.): ICADL 2004, LNCS 3334, pp. 608–617, 2004.
© Springer-Verlag Berlin Heidelberg 2004

environment, and even in personal life. The coming together of computers and telecommunication led to the prevalence of IT. Digital technology and audio video are providing us multimedia, and Electronic Data Interchange (EDI) facilities, which leaded totally new dimension in international trade. In this changing environment, modern libraries are no longer mere depositories of conventional knowledge but these are becoming increasingly information oriented.

2 Electronic/Digital Information Services

Digital services are the services those are delivered digitally through computer networks. It maintains all, or a substantial part of its collection in computer accessible form as an alternative, supplements, or complements to the conventional printed and microforms materials currently dominated library collection. Electronic/Digital information services are providing: CD-ROM facilities; Electronic transmission of documents; Maintaining of on-line subscriptions and purchase; Access to online periodicals, including free online journals; E-mail and electronic alerts from publishers of journals and Handling of websites and databases.

3 Digital Materials

Digital materials are the items that are stored, processed and transferred via digital devices and networks. Different components of digital information dissemination/services are: Telephone, telex and fax, including e-fax; CD-ROM; Scanner; World Wide Web (WWW) and Internet.

3.1 Compact Disc Read-Only Memory

The discovery of CD-ROM provided a major change in the process of the storage, retrieval and dissemination of information. The CD-ROM has data encoded in a spiral track beginning at the center and ending at the outermost edge of the disc. The spiral track holds approximately 700 MB data or 320,833 A4 size pages of text. CDs and other computer readable media are influencing to replace the traditional form of publications in print media. There are three types of CD-ROM: Read only; Write once, Read many times (WORM) and Erasable optical disc. Some widely used CDs for information dissemination are:

- The new Grolier Multi-media Encyclopedia;
- The Random house unabridged Dictionary;
- AHED (Asian Health, Environmental and Allied Databases);
- DEVINSA (Development Information Network for South Asia);
- AGRIS (Current Agricultural Research Information System);
- Tuberculosis, CABI Publishing;
- Sexually Transmitted Diseases, CABI Publishing;
- HIV/AIDS, CABI Publishing;

- Leprosy, CABI Publishing;
- Sickle Cell Disease, CABI Publishing;
- Diarrhoeal diseases, CABI Publishing;
- Malaria, Royal Perth Hospital, etc.

3.2 Scanner

A scanner captures images from photographic prints, posters, magazine pages, and similar sources for computer editing and display. Scanners come in hand-held, feed-in, and flatbed types and for scanning black-and-white or color. Scanners usually attach to the personal computer with a Small Computer System Interface (SCSI). An application such as Photoshop uses the TWAIN program to read in the image. Some major manufactures of scanners are Epson, Hewlett-Packard, Microtel, and Relays, etc.

3.3 World Wide Web (WWW)

WWW is a browsing and searching system originally developed by the European Laboratory for Particle Physics. WWW is the most-widely-used part of the Internet. The WWW is the universe of network-accessible information and a set of server on the Internet that are interconnected through hypertext.

3.4 Internet

The Internet is a WWW of interconnected university, business, military, and science networks. It is a *network of networks*. The Internet is made up of little Local Area Networks (LANs), City Wide Metropolitan Area Network (MANs), and huge Wide Area Networks (WANs) connect computers for organizations all over the world.

These networks are hooked together with everything from regular dial-up phone lines to high-speed dedicated leased lines, satellites, microwave links, and fiber optic links.

The Internet was not born full-blown in its present world wide form of thousands of networks and connections. It had a humble-but exiting-beginning as one network called the ARPANET (Advanced Research Project Agency), the "Mother of the Internet". In 1969 this computer networking system was developed by the U.S. Government aiming at creating a network that allow users of a research computer at one university to be able to communicate with computers at other universities.

4 Libraries and Information Technologies

Most of the people have experience in using a library– perhaps at school, at college, at work, or in the place where they live. There are seven basic roles that most of the libraries are trying to fulfill. They provide various mechanisms for:

a) knowledge archival;   b) the preservation and maintenance of culture; c) knowledge dissemination; d) knowledge sharing; e) information retrieval; f) education; g) social interaction.

This paper is concerned with the use of new technologies within library systems and how such technologies might shape the future of libraries.

The impact of the information technology on society is also being felt in the library community. Libraries meet the educational, cultural and leisure and general information needs of the present and future society. They are one of the most heavily used institutions in managing, disseminating and preserving knowledge.

The shift from printed to digital publications are affecting the way of processing library materials. In the past, materials were published in print; thus, only printed materials were collected by the libraries and, users used to come to the library to make use of these books and journals. But now a days, the advent of a new format for information resources and infrastructures has been enabled libraries and users to access multimedia information from remote locations anywhere in the world and the users also can reserve their items through Online Public Access Catalogue (OPAC) using their user name and password. Now learning can be obtained from non-conventional courses and in non-traditional ways. The new information society demands that libraries become learning centers with collections or services available electronically over the Internet as well as other online services used in the office or at home. With continuing developments in ICTs and publications in electronic media several scenarios for libraries of the future can be depicted. According to user's demand a computer-based systems will required to manage the library and move towards it to a digital library. Thus, in the future, four types of libraries will be emerged:

4.1 Polymedia Libraries

The term 'polymedia' is used to denote the use of several different independent media for the storage of information and knowledge. For example, they will have a wide range of media—paper, microfilm, print, electronic, etc. for the storage of information and knowledge, and will be able to manage manually. They will continue to acquire hard copies—books, periodicals and other materials necessary to maintain the collection but they will also have to contend with the management of electronic information materials using manual systems of organizing and servicing the collection.

4.2 Electronic Libraries

The expression 'electronic library' is one which has a range of different meanings associated with it. Electronic library is 'a complicated inter-disciplinary system with its own specific features, requirements and problems.' Electronic libraries will have a core collection of materials in various formats for immediate response to the basic information needs of users. They will have integrated library systems for more efficient library operation. Access to the collection will be through electronic indexes either on a local file server, a CD-ROM server or online directly to the host via

Internet. Electronic libraries will also have full text information databases, collection of journals and other materials in electronic format. This library may have interoperability and interconnectivity with other electronic libraries for resource sharing.

4.3 Digital Libraries

Digital libraries differ from the two above types of libraries. A digital library is a collection of documents, which are organized in electronic format, available on the Internet, or on CD-ROM discs. A digital library allows the users to search and retrieve the required information as easily as possible, there will be no human intermediary in the information search and retrieval process. Depending on the specific library, a user may be able to access magazine, articles, books, papers, images, sound files and videos. Some institutions have begun the task of converting classic books to electronic format for using on the Internet. Some files can be viewed directly in HTML format; other can be downloaded in PDF format, and others. Social, economic and political aspects will influence the development and use of digital library, of them the most prominent ones being intellectual property, privacy and security.

4.4 Virtual Libraries

A virtual library is defined in terms of its collection. It has no collection of its own. It is a library dependent on the collection of other libraries. It is a "library without walls". The virtual library is not concerned with managing a collection. But it is concerned with selecting, acquiring, and organizing information for a particular user's request. A library without collection of its own could be a referral or switching center with only guides, indexes, abstracts and other tools to improve access to information resources. It could be an information storehouse of the most relevant and recent electronic resources downloaded and provided to its user community. A library of this nature will organize and make available to its users for different levels of accessibility. Some will be available in the library only, others will be distributed to the users automatically and others will be distributed on demand. In this type of library, the users provide information about his profile and needs so that the librarians can crafty relevant search strategies, collect relevant information for his needs and forward them to his personal database. Future systems are envisioned to have online filtering systems for the information to be delivered directly to the individual's personal computers.

Whatever the form of library is, the libraries are important resources both for individuals and for community people who are interested in gathering knowledge. Libraries will, therefore, continue to play an important social, cultural, technical and pedagogic role in the future. Indeed, for the majority of people, libraries will act as a powerful multimedia window on the outside world, particularly through the use of computer network systems and broadcast channels.

5 Changing Role of the Librarians/Library Professionals in an Information Age

The computer and other information technologies have brought about dramatic changes in the way to libraries function, in the nature of services offered, and the organizational structured of libraries, these technologies enabled libraries and users to access multimedia information from remote locations anywhere in the world. Learning can now be obtained from non-traditional ways. The new Information society demands that libraries become learning centers with collections or services available electronically over the Internet as well as other online services used in the office or at home. As a result, it also demands that librarians will have to learn new roles and new skills in order to meet users needs.

Possessing the library and information science educational background, the professionals are an information intermediary between the needs of users and the larger world of information. He/she acts in a multi-role of negotiator, identifying needs; facilitator, providing effective search strategies; educator, familiar with the literature in all of its various formats; and information broker, providing current awareness services for the user to be served.

The Internet presents an interesting dilemma for librarians. For while only about 5000 books are published each year in the United States, the WWW contains about 320 million web pages. When a book is published, it has been assessed by editors and publishers, and hopefully has some worthiness. When a web page is published, it has been uploaded to a server somewhere. There are no guidelines for the Internet. Anyone can publish—and does. Here the librarians can play an important role in weeding through the drop out and establishing annotated lists of links that patrons can feel comfort it's using. Thus the librarians have to take opportunity to serve as guides for users and patrons who are overwhelmed by the vast quantity of web sites out there. So, their role will be a navigator and monitor. Librarians, too, should be designed their libraries' own web sites that serve as portals to interesting sites that have been reviewed and annotated by them, and they will continue to play an important role as information professionals in the Information Age. If we take our brief, however, and analyze the situation from the perspective of the role of the librarians/information professionals, the situation is much less clear–it all depends upon what we consider the role of the librarians to be. We can see a future for the librarians/information professionals as network navigator and individual information consultant, and we can also see their role as network learning support agents.

To cope with this information age, the librarians/Information professionals have to acquire:

- sharing ideas with faculty and other specialists for dissemination of information and instruction;
- teaching users how to access information, whatever its formal and location, and how to select and evaluate what they find;
- serving as consultants on information resources, issues and problems;
- developing and implementing information policy;

- creating information access tools and techniques;
- selecting, organizing and preserving information in all formats;
- digitizing and document management skills;
- basic networking skills; web design and development skills;
- skills for designing and evaluating digital library architecture, system and software;
- information collection, management and retrieval skills;
- digital reference and information services skills;
- skills related to various types of user studies, user education, etc.
- general management skills such as vision, leadership qualities, strategic decision- making qualities, interpersonal communication skills;
- personnel and financial management skills
- Information marketing and customer/user relation's management skills;
- research design and management skills; fund management skills
- publication and reporting skills;

From above, it becomes clear that in the changing technological environment, today we require that kind of information professionals, who are experts in handling information technologies and who have ICT skills, management skills, and research and project management skills in order to be able to undertake and successfully accomplish library projects. So, the information professionals/librarians will have to develop themselves to cope with this information age.

6 Bangladesh Scenario

The automation process in Bangladesh began with the installation of a second-generation computer at the Bangladesh Atomic Energy Center in 1964. The government allowed the private companies to install VSATs and provide ISP services beginning June 1996. Since then libraries have been slowly and steadily going for computerization and Internet facility, and the libraries and information centers also started to automate its functions, and began to create databases.

The ICT sector of Bangladesh is one of the fastest growing sectors of its economy. The Government has declared ICT as the thrust sector. Bangladesh Computer Council (BCC), an apex body for promotion of all kinds of ICT activities in the country, works under the Ministry of Science and Information & Communication Technology. For the development of ICT sector within the framework of overall national development, the Government has approved the National ICT Policy in October 2002. The vision of this Policy aims at building an ICT-driven nation comprising of knowledge-based society by the year 2006. In view of this, Bangladesh Telegraph and Telephone Board (BTTB) have already established fiber optic links in most of the cities of the country (50 out of 64 districts) areas. BTTB signed a contract on 27 March 2004 to connect Bangladesh with the Information Superhighway through submarine fiber-optic cable project 'South East Asia-Middle East-West Europe (SEA-ME-WE-4)' with a landing site at Cox's Bazar. It will be built using DWDM (Dense Wavelength Division Multiplex) technology with 1.28 terabits per second speed. The facility is to be operational by June 2005. Based on this, all 64 districts and about 35% (165) of upazillas of Bangladesh have been brought under Internet coverage by BTTB through dial-up connections. BTTB increased its backbone bandwidth from 10.0 Mbps (download and upload capacity) to 12.0 Mbps by June 2004 and 24.0 Mbps by December 2004.

At present the total number of telephone lines is 0.92 million and the number of cellular phones offered by 4 private operators is about 2 million. The teledensity is about 2%. It is targeted to increase teledensity to 3.3% by 2005. BTTB has been given the responsibility by MOPT to register and maintain Country Code Top Level Domain (ccTLD) of Bangladesh (.bd). BTTB registers domain as .com.bd, .net.bd, .edu.bd, .ac.bd, and .gov.bd. Up to April 2004, total of 363 domains has been registered under .bd. The following table shows the ICT status of Bangladesh at a glance:

Table 1. ICT status of Bangladesh

Number of Telephone (land-lines)	0.92 million
Number of Cellular phones	2 million
Telephone density (Landline and cellular combined)	2% (approx.)
Paging and Radio Trunk subscribers	7000
Telex subscribers	1600
International Trunk Exchanges	3
Total International Circuits	3700
International Internet Backbones	12 MB
VSAT providers	31
VSAT users	70
Number of ISPs	195
Fiber optic Cable Network (under Railway)	100 KM
Satellite Earth Stations	4
Internet users	2.0 million
Registered Dial-Up user accounts	0.25 million
Broadband subscribers accounts	0.15 million

In an article published in The Independent, Prof. Jamilur Reza Choudhury concluded that Information Technology played a great role in changing the methods of collection, collation, processing, production and dissemination of information in all fields significantly. He stated that the printed materials are changing rapidly in to digital formats, which emphasize the information-seekers' behavior dramatically. Information-seekers are using various search engines to reach the remote host. Thus, our National Information Infrastructure is changing its shell.

In Bangladesh there are no adequate library automated services. Some of the special libraries, public and private universities libraries are using various types of software. Some of them are serving their catalogue services through Internet. It is found that only financially rich libraries are providing the automated library services.

Comparatively, private universities are ahead compared to the public universities. Among public universities, University of Dhaka, Bangladesh University of Engineering and Technology (BUET) are providing automated library facilities. Some universities, like Rajshahi University, Chittagong University, Jahangirnagar University, Shahjalal University of Science and Technology, Khulna University and Islamic University, are using computers but they do not yet introduce computers for automated library services. Among the 52 private universities, most are not using library management software. But a few private universities, like North South University (NSU), Independent University, Bangladesh (IUB) and East West University (EWU), are providing automated library services. BRAC University Library is going to launch automated library services within a short time.

The time is ripe now, and we have to take a keen interest to adopt IT in libraries, and have to proceed with a clear and appropriate vision without losing any more time. We should try to keep our public informed of the resources in the web for easy and fast access and for wider dissemination, it may organize our business to earn revenues. There is also an immediate need to make a decision to ensure an appropriate electronic-communication environment in the country to facilitate the use of Internet to disseminate information, building communication, marketing products and publications, and earn revenue through e-commerce.

7 Conclusion

Since access to information is becoming more end-user-oriented through the use of the Internet, the role of Information professionals is becoming more vulnerable. It is high time that information managers, educators, researchers, and planners have concentrated on revising information science programmes to produce trained professionals who could shape and properly manage the world of information. We as librarians, information scientists and educators do better than any one in the world to make information manageable and accessible to those who need it.

References

1. Ahmed, S.M.M., Rahman, A.K.M.H.: ICT's: leading the way to sustainable development. (www.bttb.net.bd/home/main/download/wtd-2004/theme.pdf)
2. Anderson, K.H.: The librarians in the electronic age. Paper presented at BIDS library seminar, Dhaka, September 1996
3. Barker, P.: Electronic libraries: vision of the future. The Electronic Library, 12 (4) (1994) 221-229
4. Bashar, S.A.: Fiber-optic telecommunication & better ICT in Bangladesh. (2002) (http://www.betelco.com/bd/bdstel/dstar.pdf)
5. Borgman, C.L.: Will the global information infrastructure be the library of the future? Central and Eastern Europe as a case study example. IFLA Journal, 22(2) (1996) 121-227
6. Chowdhury, C.G., Chowdhury S.: Introduction to digital libraries. Facet Publishing, London (2003) 284-92

7. Deane, J.: Information, knowledge and development. (www.oneworld.org/panos)
8. Edwards, C.: Global knowledge: a challenge for librarians, 66th IFLA   Conference. Jerusalem, (2000) (www.ifla.org/IV/ifla66/papers/153-154e.htm)
9. International Telecommunication Union. (2004) (http://www.itu.int/ITU-D/ict/statistics/0/)
10. Khan, M.O.F.: Information and communication technology (ICT) status, issues and future development plans of Bangladesh. (www.adb.org/Documents/Events/2004/SASEC/First_Mtg_ICT/Bangladesh_Country_Paper.pdf)
11. Khan, M.S.I.: Electronic communication and information dissemination, Lecture delivered in the workshop on Population Information Network, IEM/BCC unit, Dhaka, 29 Oct 2000
12. Khan, M.S.I.: Preparing Bangladesh libraries and librarians for the 21st century: the case of library education. Eastern Librarian, 17(1&2) (1992) 49-58
13. Librarians in the 21st century: libraries and the Internet. (http://istweb.syr.edu/21stcenlib/where/internet.html)
14. Malavya, V.C.: Electronic libraries. Ess Ess Publications, New Delhi (1999) 251-261
15. Rahman, A.K.M.H.: Data and Internet service: BTTB scenario. (http://www.bttb.net.bd/home/main/download/wtd-2004/services.pdf)
16. Rahman, S.: An overview of ICT and OSS in Bangladesh. Paper presented at 3rd Asia Open Source Software Symposium, Hanoi, Vietnam, March 2004 (http://www.banglait.org/banglaict.htm)
17. Rahman, S.: An overview of ICT sector in Bangladesh. Paper presented at FOBANA 2003 Convention. Washington, DC, August 2003 (http://www.banglait.org/ICTBANGLADESH.pdf)
18. Sharon, T.: Digital libraries on the Internet. 66th IFLA Conference. Jerusalem, (2000) (http://www.ifla.org/IV/ifla66/papers/029-142e.htm)
19. Shivalingaiah, D., Manjunatha, K.: Digital libraries in the networked world. In: Sirurmath, S.S., Kumbar, B.D., Koganuramath, M.M. (eds.): Electronic libraries. Allied Publishers, Mumbai (2002) 48
20. Stueart, R.D.: Educating information professionals for the 21st century. (http://web.simmons.edu/~chen/nit/NIT'89/89-389-stuart.html)
21. Sun Microsystems. Digital library technology trends. (2002) (www.sun.com/products-n solutions/edu/whitepapers/pdf/digital_library_trends.pdf)
22. Uddin M.S.: ITC's issues and illusions. (http://www.bttb.net.bd/home/main/download/wtd-2004/issues.pdf)
23. Wattegama, C.: Digital divide: a South Asian case study. (2004) (E-mail alert from chanuka1986@yahoo.co.uk through bangla_ict@yahoogroups.com)
24. Wilson, T.: The role of librarians in the 21st century. (www.informationr.net/tdw/publ/papers/21stcent.html)
25. University Grants Commission of Bangladesh. Annual report 2002. Dhaka: University Grants Commission of Bangladesh (2003)

Integrating Electronic Pathfinders in Digital Libraries: A Model for China

Hanrong Wang[1] and William J. Hubbard[2]

[1] Assistant Professor, Houston Cole Library, Jacksonville State University,
700 Pelham Road North Jacksonville, Alabama, 36265-1602 U.S.A.
[2] Professor, Houston Cole Library, Jacksonville State University,
700 Pelham Road North Jacksonville, Alabama, 36265-1602 U.S.A.
{hwang, bhubbard}@jsucc.jsu.edu

Abstract. Electronic pathfinders/subject guides help library patrons learn about library resources and develop research strategies. By reviewing the existing literature and the current status of reference service in digital libraries in China, the authors suggest that integrating subject specific pathfinders in digital libraries would benefit both users and librarians. This paper also offers a format and a construction guide to aid librarians in preparing readable and usable electronic pathfinders. An appendix presents pathfinder format guidelines and a sample pathfinder.

1 Introduction

Significant changes in digital libraries in China had been brewing for some time before the introduction of the China Digital Library in 2000. As the first Internet based full-function digital library system in China, Tsinghua University has been active in the design and development of digital library service since September 1995. The initial version of the Chinese National Petroleum Corporation Digital Library has been operational since April 1996 [1]. The growing number of Internet users has also contributed to speeding the development of digital libraries. With 170,000 e-books, and more than 200,000 pages of information digitized daily, China Digital Library is attracting an increasing number of users, from 2,700,000 readers a year in 1999, to almost 200,000 readers per day in 2000 [2]. At present, state and county level digital libraries are also helping the development and construction of the information network.

Like ever-extending bookshelves, digital libraries provide information and service access in electronic format without time and space limitations. Much has been done to build digital library systems in China. Online public catalogs, electronic books & articles, and online audio-visual materials are examples of this trend. But as digital resources are proliferating at an astonishing rate, users are confused and frustrated by their inability to find useful information [3]. Navigational and search difficulties persist whenever they use the digital resources. Virtual reference service, online FAQs, and online listings of new arrivals ease some of the difficulties, but will never completely satisfy some readers, especially those who are doing research. Creating electronic pathfinders in digital libraries has been shown to be a very efficient way to

Z. Chen et al. (Eds.): ICADL 2004, LNCS 3334, pp. 618–625, 2004.
© Springer-Verlag Berlin Heidelberg 2004

aid library users in academic, research and public libraries in developing information retrieval and life long learning strategies.

Developing electronic pathfinders is still new to most Chinese digital libraries. Informational, technical, and professional directions are needed when placing a pathfinder on the web. By reviewing the existing literature, the authors constructed a model for developing virtual pathfinders for Chinese digital libraries. A template for integrating a pathfinder is also included.

2 Literature Review

An electronic pathfinder is a subject-specific resource guide in electronic format. It can be an organized introductory checklist of various types of sources and materials on a specific topic [4]. It is developed to help patrons locate published information in a particular subject, and includes indexes, bibliographical lists, audio-video materials, related subject headings, web sites, related indexes, core journal titles, and web sources. Pathfinders also offer users essential information and technology skills, guide and promote reading, and provide information and technology services.

Librarians have long been familiar with the paper pathfinder. With the development of network technology, uploading pathfinders on the web seemed natural. A librarian, in cooperation with teaching faculty, may design a guide around a college course. Alternatively, a librarian may develop a guide on a very specific subject for the local community or the global Internet community. As Dahl [5] mentioned, although pathfinders had existed traditionally in the form of paper handouts, they are becoming increasingly popular in electronic format as additions to library web pages. Sloan [6] also found that students actually used virtual pathfinders and the number of electronic pathfinders exceeded the number distributed in paper format in one month at the University of New Brunswick.

The electronic pathfinder adds another dimension to using the Internet as a research tool. The links created on a subject-specific pathfinder result in a more dynamic and interactive tool [7]. Birmingham (Alabama) Public Library [8] created a "Subject Guide" web page with interactive links to the library catalog and referred websites. New York Public Library [9] even links reference librarian contact information under the Subject Guide page. Nuttall and McAbee [10] from Jacksonville (Alabama) State University described the value and styles of pathfinders that are used as subject guides, and advised the inclusion of pathfinders in online catalogs (see Fig.1.).

Fig. 1. The catalog portion of the pathfinder searches the library's subject fields (Yellow Wallpaper) and prompts the user with terms from the Library of Congress Subject Headings. In this way, a user can obtain a pathfinder on any subject by using the hyperlinks, and access the electronic pathfinder by clicking the "Electronic version" Internet Link.

Some universities in China have already developed virtual pathfinders termed "Navigation by Subject". Reference source titles, related subject headings, call number ranges, and related web sites are listed on some "Navigation by Subject" web pages from Tsinghua University Library [11]. A collection of links to related web sites, databases, electronic journals and catalog records is the main feature of "Navigation by Subject" from Fudan University library [12]. Shanghai Jiaotong University library [13] lists links to related association, production & market, electronic publication, and conference information on the "Navigation by Subject" page. China Digital Library provides links to related library science, laws from all countries, China studies, and other country government departments.

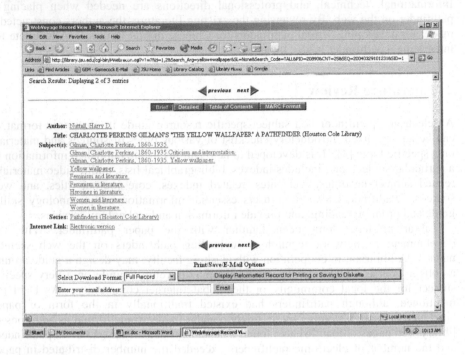

The increasingly common practice of making pathfinders available electronically has raised the need to assess current guidelines for creating pathfinders in general. Unfortunately, no guidelines pertaining specifically to electronic pathfinders have been established, even though their unique format renders existing guidelines inadequate. Principles and instructions are needed before developing an electronic pathfinder.

3 Integrating Web Pathfinders

Creating an electronic pathfinder requires close collaboration between the librarian and the user in order to precisely target the most useful materials. Formats and contents of pathfinders might vary due to the different missions of individual libraries, but the basic principles and the steps for integrating a pathfinder are the same for all.

3.1 Setting Up Service Mission

This is the very first step before actually writing a pathfinder. Of course, the mission of creating a pathfinder is to provide an overview of a topic and sort out the basic information for the topic so patrons can have a good starting point to locate needed information on it.   Academic and research libraries' pathfinders may be closely curriculum and research related with a lot of authoritative research sources. On the other hand, public libraries' pathfinders may be community-interest related and include general reference sources.

3.2 Defining Target Audience

Knowing your audience is the key for creating a successful pathfinder. Choosing the right topic, the right sources, or even the right language style will all depend upon the target audience. Working closely with departments and instructors may be a very good starting point in an academic library.   Understanding what they need and determining the best sources to support the course and research projects will be of great help. College course catalogs can be used as a good reference. Defining the target audience is a little harder in a public library. Knowing the population structure and the needs of the community by using surveys or past experience will help. Browsing the local newspaper and other media can also help identify hot topics in the community. For example, if there are many school-aged children in the community, preparing a homework guide is necessary.

3.3 Integrating the Contents

This is most important when making a pathfinder. A digital pathfinder usually contains an introduction; a catalog call number range with some useful subject headings; lists of core print sources; major electronic databases; and some links to good web sites. A typical electronic pathfinder can be created like this:

Introduction: The purpose of the pathfinder and a general discussion on the topic from an authoritative source may be included. Who are the target audiences and what is not included in the pathfinder can also be specified;

Subject Headings & Call Number Range: Pertinent subject headings with links to the library's online catalog may be provided. Call number ranges can also be displayed for the areas in the stacks where browsing may be profitable;

List of Core Sources: Encyclopedias, dictionaries, journals, databases, and evaluated Internet sources can all be listed with possible hyperlinks. Sources with annotations will be more useful than a simple title list. It is also important to explain that a pathfinder is just a starting point for further research. It is not an exhaustive subject guide or bibliography.

Reference Librarian's Contact Information: Always list a reference librarian's contact information for further requests. The latest update may also need to be specified so that users can determine the currency.

An electronic pathfinder can be a little bit longer than a paper one. Usually 2-5 pages are adequate. Too many works or links may overwhelm users, yet too little information will not help them at all. Sharing information with other subject specialists and viewing other guides on the same subject will also help.

3.4 Uploading and Evaluation

Uploading the created pathfinders on the library's web site and placing them in an easy to access location is important. A print version of the pathfinders also may be available for on-site access.

Pathfinder access can be evaluated by viewing the script control statistics and users' feedback. It is the information specialists' duty to add latest information to the pathfinder and keep all the links active.

4 Conclusions

Building an electronic subject-oriented Internet resource guide is a challenging and time-consuming, yet highly rewarding experience. Identifying the library's mission and target audience can help the subject specialist follow the right direction when making this kind of resource guide. Sorting out the basic references for a pathfinder is an art which requires the librarian's familiarity with the library collection, databases, and Internet resources as a whole. Ongoing evaluation is a tool for improving existing pathfinders.

Today's users need to quickly find information that is usable, relevant, authoritative, and verifiable. Electronic pathfinders offer a unique way for the subject specialist to meet users' needs by adapting to an environment that is not constricted by time or physical place. By integrating the electronic pathfinder and leveraging their traditional information management skills in this new environment, librarians can provide a valuable service to their universities and to the global Internet community.

Topical guides will become increasingly valuable in helping users find information resources on the Internet. They serve as a gateway to a variety of information on the topic via links to other web sites and sources by making them available around the clock for both users and librarians. By taking the lead today in the development of subject-oriented guides, librarians are demonstrating the value of their skills in the era of networked information retrieval.

References

1. Wang, G.: The Digital Library in China. ERCIM News. 27 (1996). (Accessed http://www. ercim.org/publication/Ercim_News/enw27/wang.html)
2. China Education and Research Network: China Digital Library Aims to Be Biggest DCP (2001). (Accessed http://www.edu.cn/20010101/22085.shtml)
3. Morville, P. S., Wickhorst, S. J.: Building Subject-Specific Guides to Internet Resources. Internet Research: Electronic Networking Applications and Policy 6 (1996) 27-32
4. Harbeson, E. L.: Teaching Reference and Bibliography: The Pathfinder Approach. Journal of Education and Librarianship 13 (1972) 111-115
5. Dahl, C.: Electronic Pathfinders in Academic Libraries: An Analysis of Their Content and Form. College & Research Libr. 62 (2001) 227-37
6. Sloan, S. M.: The Virtual Pathfinder: A World Wide Web Guide to Library Research. Computers in Libr. 16 (1996) 53-4
7. O'Sullivan, M. K., Scott, T. J.: Pathfinders Go Online. Library Journal 125 (2000) 40-2

8. Birmingham Public Library: Subject Guides. (1996-2003). (Accessed http://www.
   bplonline.org/resources/subjectguides.asp)
9. New York Public Library: Where to Go for More Help. (2003). (Accessed http://www.
   nypl.org/research/chss/grd/resguides/biography/help.html).
10. Nuttall, H. D., McAbee, S. L.: Pathfinders On-line: Adding Pathfinders to a NOTIS ON-
   LINE System. College & Undergraduate Libr. 4 (1997) 77-101
11. Tsinghua University Library: http://www.lib.tsinghua.edu.cn/chinese/infoguide/user-
   guide1.html(2004)
12. Fudan University Library: http://202.120.227.59/navigator/navigator.asp(2000)
13. Shanghai Jiaotong University: http://www.lib.sjtu.edu.cn/chinese/network_navigation/
   subindex.htm(2004)

Appendix

The Following is an example of an electronic pathfinder for an academic library.

Restaurant and Foodservice Management
Library Research Guide
The basic elements for restaurant and foodservice management are customers, products, distribution, equipment and personnel. The concentration in Restaurant and Foodservice Management from the Family and Consumer Sciences Department (http://www.jsu.edu/depart/edprof/fcs/) of Jacksonville State University offers academic background and field experience for people interested in commercial foodservice. Most print sources (such as books, periodicals) related to restaurant and foodservice management are located on 4th or 10th floor in Houston Cole Library (http://www.jsu.edu/depart/library/). Electronic sources (such as databases) can be accessed via computer stations on each floor.

Books
Books are important sources of basic information on a topic, providing necessary definitions, background information, and statistics. Books provide a foundation for research which can be supplemented by more current information from periodical articles. Books may also contain useful bibliographies which may lead to additional sources of research. When looking for books, consult the Library of Congress Subject Headings to select the proper term(s) to use as subjects under "Find Books (Library Catalog)" (http://library.jsu.edu/cgi-bin/Pwebrecon.cgi?DB=local&PAGE=hbSearch).

The following table shows the call number ranges and the subject headings of "Restaurant and Foodservice Management" in the Library of Congress System:

G154.9-180	Tourism	HF5387-5390	Business etiquette
TX353	School lunchrooms, cafeterias, etc. management	TX642-820	Cookery
TX820	Food service	TX900-945	Restaurant management
TP 368-456	Food processing and manufacture	TP 500-660	Fermentation industries. Beverages. Alcohol

Other subject headings can be: Food service Equipment and supplies, Food service Personnel management, Food service Research, Food service Law and legislation, Food service management, Restaurants decoration, Wine tasting and etc.

A detailed list of reference books related to the topic can be accessed at http://www.jsu.edu/depart/library/personal%20web%20pages/HW_WEB/home.html

Periodical Articles

Current print issues of periodical articles to which the Library subscribes can be found at the Current Periodical Section on 10th floor. Older print issues of magazines and journals, usually bound into complete years or volume numbers, are located in the 10th floor Bound Periodical Section. You can also use Library subscribed electronic databases (http://www.jsu.edu/depart/library/graphic/articles.htm) to identify articles on particular topics in magazines, journals, and newspapers. The following are commonly used databases for restaurant and foodservice management: Academic Search Elite, Business and Company Resource Center, Business Index ASAP, Business Source Premier, CQ Researcher, Expanded Academic ASAP, MasterFILE Premier, ProQuest, Standard & Poor's NetAdvantage, Regional Business News, ValueLine Investment Survey, Vocational & Career Collection, and netLibrary. A detailed e-journal list is available upon request.

Internet Sources

American Culinary Foundation (http://www.acfchefs.org/) Official web site for the American Culinary Federation (ACF), Inc., a professional, not-for-profit organization for chefs and cooks, offering news and sources for professional development.

Hotel and Motel Management (http://www.hotelmotel.com): Provides the latest headline news and trends in the hospitality industry. Includes the current issue of the magazine plus human resources information and upcoming events.

HospitalityNet(http://www.hospitalitynet.org): All of Hospitality on the Web Provides industry news, job listings, and an index to other hospitality web sites.

Hotel Online (http://www.hotel-online.com/Neo/): A news service for the hospitality industry. Includes news, discussion forums, employment opportunities, classified advertising, and information on product pricing and trends.

International Council on Hotel, Restaurant, and Institutional Education (http://www.chrie.org/): Offers information on programs in hotel and restaurant management, foodservice management and culinary arts and helps students facilitate exchanges of information, ideas, research, training and resource development for the hospitality and tourism industry.

National Restaurant Association (http://www.restaurant.org/): Offers career advice, information on training seminars, products, and research.

Restaurants and Institutions (http://www.rimag.com/): Includes the current table of contents and the full text of several articles from the current issue with recipes, food safety information, details on foodservice products, and access to stock quotes for restaurant stocks.

Restaurant Report (http://www.restaurantreport.com/): The online version of the monthly magazine "Restaurant Report." Offers business news and feature articles. Provides access to classified ads and suppliers of restaurant equipment. Contains a buyer's guide and information on management issues. For more Internet sites, please visit *http://www.jsu.edu/depart/library/graphic/subjlist.htm*

Core Reference List

Pan Am's World Guide: The Encyclopedia of Travel *(Call Number: REF G 153.4 .P36 1982): A travel guidebook by Pan American World Airways, inc.*

Occupational Outlook Handbook (Call Number: REF HF5381.A1O36): Career information for specific types of jobs including pay scales, educational requirements, growth and other information. Also accessible at: *http://www.bls.gov/oco/home.htm*

The Dictionary of American Food & Drink (Call Number: REF TX349.M26 1983): Explores and Chronicle the vast array of American food, wine, and drink and the way we speak of it, consume it, and have changed it over the centuries.

The Cook's Dictionary and Culinary Reference (Call Number: REF TX349.B355 1996): Offers concise, accurate, and enlightening definitions and clarifications of common and obscure phrases, methods, tools, and ingredients.

The Cambridge World History of Food (Call Number: REF TX353.C255 2000): The History of food and nutrition through the span of human life on earth

The Oxford Companion to Food (Call Number: REF TX349.D38x 1999): *Definitions and historical aspects of food plants, food and dish preparation, and everything else.*

Encyclopedia of Food Science, Food Technology and Nutrition (Call Number: REF TX349.E47 1993): *All aspects of the science of food, at all stages along the food chain.*

Cornell Hotel and Restaurant Administration Quarterly *(Call Number: TX 901.C67): A journal publishing articles that help hospitality managers work smarter and do their jobs better. Also accessible via ScienceDirect Database.*

International Journal of Hospitality Management: *A Journal covers topics including Human management, marketing and planning, operational management, financial management, training, legislation. Also assessable via ScienceDirect Database.*

Journal of the International Academy of Hospitality Research (http://scholar.lib.vt.edu/ejournals/JIAHR/jiahr.html): *Offers access to full-text issues of the journal from 1990-1998 and abstracts for issues from 1997-1999.*

Copyrighting Digital Libraries from Database Designer Perspective

Hideyasu Sasaki[1,2] and Yasushi Kiyoki[3]

[1] Keio University, Graduate School of Media and Governance,
252-8520, 5322 Fujisawa, Japan
[2] Attorney-at-Law, New York State Bar
h-sasaki-7@alumni.uchicago.edu
[3] Keio University, Faculty of Environmental Information,
252-8520, 5322 Fujisawa, Japan
kiyoki@sfc.keio.ac.jp

Abstract. In this paper, we discuss current issues on the copyright of digital libraries from a database designer perspective, and present a scheme for copyright protection of indexed digital contents stored in digital libraries that are associated with keyword-based retrieval operations.

1 Introduction

Digital library is a global information infrastructure in the networked society [1]. The copyright protection of digital libraries is a critical issue in the digital library community, which demands a scheme for recouping their investment in database design and implementation. In this paper, we would describe the technical and legal issues on digital library as the object of copyright from a database designer perspective that has not been discussed with sufficient attention at the present.

The scope of this paper is restricted within the current standard of laws and cases in transnational transaction and licensing of digital copyright regarding digital library. Cultural diversity in the Asia-Pacific region is a source of legislative differences in copyright laws, though those countries join international trade agreements for intellectual property rights including copyright. We discuss the harmonized copyright standard regarding digital library with which the Asian-Pacific countries are able to keep up with the foregoing countries.

2 Background

Copyright gives incentive to advance proper investment in database design and implementation for the digital library community [2]. However, present legal studies are not satisfactory as the source of technical interpretation of the copyright regarding digital library. Content creators enjoy copyright enforcement over their works under the current legal scheme. Meanwhile, the database designers in the area of digital library have not found any satisfactory foundations for their copyright protection over their works.

Z. Chen et al. (Eds.): ICADL 2004, LNCS 3334, pp. 626–629, 2004.

Databases are different from mere collection of individual contents. The problem is that which component identifies an independent object of copyright protection in a database. That component should differentiate the entire content of each digital library from its copyrightable individual contents while the latter contents belong to content creators. Content creators create copyrightable individual contents, *e.g.*, pictures and images. Database designers integrate the entire content of each digital library with indexes or metadata under their specific blueprints or perspectives. The copyright protection for database designers should be discussed on the indexed digital libraries.

3 Indexed Digital Libraries

A compilation or assembling of individual contents, *i.e.*, preexisting materials or data, is a copyrightable entity as an original work of authorship [3]. Fig. 1 outlines that indexes including metadata are *statically* assigned to individual contents that are stored in databases as objects of keyword-based retrieval operations. The collection of static indexes and individual contents forms a component of contents-plus-indexes as an independent entity from its contents. That component identifies the entire content of each database as is a static and copyrightable compilation.

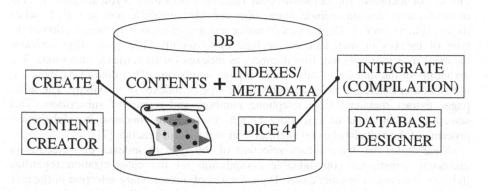

Fig. 1. The copyrightable component of a digital library

A compilation is copyrightable as far as it is an "original work of authorship that is fixed in tangible form" [4], [5]. A database is copyrightable in the form of a component of contents-plus-indexes while static indexes or metadata are fixed in a tangible medium of repository, database. In keyword-based retrieval, static indexes or metadata represent a certain kind of categorization of the entire content of each database. The originality on the categorization makes each database copyrightable as is different from the mere collection of its individual contents.

What kind of categorization should be *original* to constitute a copyrightable compilation? Minimal creativity in compilation is considered to be enough in satisfying this requirement of originality on databases [6]. It is not clear in technical sense. A uniform scheme on the categorization regarding indexes or metadata must be formulated in engineering manner.

4 Copyrighting Indexed Digital Libraries

We technically interpret a scheme for copyrighting the indexed digital libraries with keyword-based retrieval operations into a set of conditions. Those conditions determine which type of database for digital library design should be copyrightable in the form of a component of contents-plus-indexes.

Copyrightable compilation is to be of sufficient creativity, *i.e.*, originality in the form of a component of contents-plus-indexes. Its original way of categorization is represented in the selection of the type of indexes or metadata that are assigned to individual contents, or the type of taxonomy regarding indexes or metadata that integrate the individual contents into the entire content of each database.

The set of conditions on the original categorization regarding indexes or metadata is formulated as below: A categorization regarding indexes or metadata on digital library design is original only when

(1) The type of indexes or metadata accepts discretionary selection in the domain of problem database; otherwise,
(2) The type of taxonomy regarding indexes or metadata accepts discretionary selection in the domain of problem database.

We describe five typical cases of original or non-original categorization regarding indexes or metadata for keyword-based retrieval operations. Typical cases of non-original categorization include photo film cartridge database and so-called "white pages" (phone books). Those cases do not accept any discretion in the selection of the type of indexes or metadata, or the type of taxonomy. The photo film cartridge database uses its respective film numbers as indexes for its retrieval operations. The taxonomy of the indexes is only based on page numbering. That kind of database has not any other discretion in its selection of the type of indexes or taxonomy. The white pages extract metadata from telephone numbers and names of subscribers. That selection of the type of taxonomy is not discretionary because its alphabetical ordering of the metadata has no alternative in that field of practice [7].

Meanwhile, the discretionary selection of the type of indexes or metadata, or taxonomy constitutes copyrightable compilation on the categorization regarding indexes or metadata in other cases. Typical cases of discretionary selection of the type of indexes or metadata include the Web document encyclopedia and the other type of telephone directory, *i.e.*, "yellow pages". The latter yellow pages satisfy minimal creativity as a copyrightable compilation. The white pages list telephone numbers of subscribers in alphabetical order, while the yellow pages list business phone numbers by a variety of categories and feature-classified advertisements of various sizes. In the case of discretionary selection of the type of taxonomy, even numerical indexing, *e.g.*, page numbering, could form an original compilation, when page indexes work as categorization identifiers of a specific type of taxonomy in the domain of problem database. For example, lawyers often identify individual cases by citing their page numbers without any reference to case titles or parties. Mere page numbers work as categorization identifiers as far as the selection of page numbers is based on a specific type of taxonomy, and still allows other discretionary selection of the type of indexes, here, different ranges in paging or indexing of case numbers. The component of contents-plus-indexes, here, cases-plus-pages, constitutes an original work of authorship as a copyrightable compilation [8].

Giving an example, suppose that a database restores pictures of starfish that are manually and numerically numbered by day/hour-chronicle interval based on their significant life stages from birth to death. That database is to be an original work of authorship as a copyrightable compilation in the form of a component of contents-plus-indexes, here, pictures-plus-numbers.

We have formulated the set of conditions that determine which type of database is copyrightable as a digital library by assessing its original categorization regarding indexes or metadata whose collection identifies the entire content of a database as the referent of copyright protection. That condition set is effective in protecting the indexed digital libraries that are associated with keyword-based retrieval operations.

5 Conclusion

In this paper, we have discussed the copyright issues on digital libraries, and technically interpreted the legal schemes for protecting digital libraries. The protection of copyright is a critical issue in the digital library community. We have presented the scheme for copyrighting the indexed digital libraries with keyword-based retrieval operations from a database designer perspective.

References

1. Borgman, C.L.: From Gutenberg to the Global Information Infrastructure: Access to Information in the Networked World. Digital Libraries and Electronic Publishing. Cambridge, MA: MIT Press (2000)
2. Jakes, J.M., Yoches, E.R.: Legally Speaking: Basic Principles of Patent Protection for Computer Science. Comm. of the ACM **32(8)** (1989) 922-924
3. U.S. Copyright Act. 17 U.S.C. §§ 101, & 103 (1976)
4. Gorman, R.A., Ginsburg, J.C.: Copyright for the Nineties: Cases and Materials (4th Ed.). Contemporary Legal Education Series. Charlottesville, NC: The Michie Company (1993)
5. Nimmer, M., Marcus, P., Myers, D., Nimmer, D.: Cases and Materials on Copyright (4th Ed.). St. Paul, MN: West Publishing (1991)
6. American Dental Ass'n v. Delta Dental Plan Ass'n. 126 F.3d 977 (7th Cir. 1997)
7. Feist Publications, Inc. v. Rural Telephone Service. 499 U.S. 340, 111 S.Ct. 1282, 113 L.Ed.2d 358 (1991)
8. West Publishing Co. v. Mead Data Central, Inc. 799 F.2d 1219 (8th Cir. 1986), cert. denied, 479 U.S. 1070 (1987)

Design and Development of Internet Resource Navigation Database on Key Disciplines in CALIS Project

Xiya Zhang, Huijun Zhang, and Xiaobo Xiao

Xián Jiaotong University Library, Xián, 710049, P.R. China
xyzhang@mail.lib.xjtu.edu.cn

Abstract. With the rapid development of technology and the wide dissemination of information, many universities and institutions suffer from information overload and have to apply information management to deal with this information chaos in the digital world. During the 9th National 5-year Plan, CALIS started the project of Internet resource navigation database. In this paper, the goal, principle and contents for constructing an Internet resource navigation database on key disciplines are presented. The resource selection criteria and standards for web-based resource description are also described. The progress of the navigation database construction is introduced.

1 Introduction

It is well documented that the amount of information available on the Internet is increasing dramatically. Now one of the greatest challenges for users in the digital age is to learn how the Internet can be used to meet their information needs and to conceptualize how the different Internet search and retrieval tools can help them to do this [1]. As the intermediate between Internet resources and users, many academic libraries and institutions are currently looking for ways to help their users discover high quality information on the Internet in a quick and effective way. Subject gateways can provide a solution.

Subject gateways are a tool for Internet resource discovery. A user served by a subject gateway can get access to a quality-controlled collection of Internet resources and can enjoy the benefits such as searching and browsing through the collection [8].

During the 9th 5-year Plan, in April 2000, China Academic Library & Information System (CALIS) started the project of Subject Gateway (we called it CSG Phase I) which is a subject-based information gateway to quality-assured resources on the Internet. By the end of 2001, about 48 libraries had joined in the project and established several Internet resource navigation databases covering 217 subjects (some of them are duplicated). The creation of the project has benefited many researchers and students of the universities and institutions, but there were some shortages found in the development of CSG Phase I. For example, the main shortages are:

- Lack of uniform standards
- Some subjects developed were duplicated

Z. Chen et al. (Eds.): ICADL 2004, LNCS 3334, pp. 630–635, 2004.

- Lack of uniform publishing platform for the users
- Lack of collection maintenance mechanism

The above shortages will be overcome during the 10th National 5-year Plan along with the development of CSG Phase II.

2 Objectives and Principle

In October 2003 the project of CSG Phase II started. Since the CALIS Phase I CSG has been funded by Chinese Ministry of Education and directed by CALIS. Xi'an Jiaotong University Library (XJTU-Lib) is the executive institution of CSG during CALIS Phase II and collaborates with other university libraries to contribute to the development of the project.

2.1 Aim

The CSG Phase II is to develop an information gateway to evaluate and qualify Internet resources, with a focus for users such as students, researchers, academic and practitioners. The gateway is subject-based and will provide service mainly for the Chinese higher education. Of course it will also hope to be of benefit to a wide range of individuals, groups and organizations [9].

2.2 Objectives

Our aim is to produce a service that best meets the needs of the relevant academic communities. CSG is created by a team of core librarians and subject experts based in the universities of China. By the end of 2005 XJTU-Lib and its partners will fulfill the following tasks [2]:

- Developing a platform which contains three main function modules: resource discovery and catalogue, user service, collection management.
- Formulating policies and guidelines relevant to the project, which include selection policy, metadata formats, cataloguing guidelines and classification scheme.
- Creating a navigation database of high quality Internet resources which will cover at least 50 subjects.
- Exploring ways of sustaining the service after the 10th National 5-year Plan.

2.3 Execution Principle

In order to accomplish the above objectives, we have established the following execution principles [2]:

- General guideline: unified platform, unified standards, integral development, separate maintenance, focused service, and sharing all over the country.
- General principle: quality is of the first importance, application should be emphasized, quantity should be considered within measure.
- The classification scheme promulgated by the Ministry of Education P.R.C is adopted.

- The resource quality is fundamental and we should do our best to insure that every record is useful to the users.
- The platform should be applied first, and it should be advanced secondly.
- Avoiding duplication during the creation of the navigation resources.
- Making adequate use of the collection of CSG Phase I.

3 Policies and Guidelines

Developing and maintaining a high quality gateway is time-consuming and laborious, therefore it is necessary to define a set of policies clearly at the early stage to ensure smooth cooperation among all the partners in resource selection, resource cataloguing, etc. since the partners are distributed all over the country [2].

3.1 Resource Selection Policy

Gateways are characterized by the focus and quality of their collections. They aim to provide their users with a quality-controlled environment in which information can be searched on the Internet, and this can be completed by building selective collections where each resource that the gateway points to has been carefully selected for its quality.

In an information environment, a selection policy defines the criteria used for selecting resources to be added to a collection. It will typically outline the scope of the collection and the criteria used when new resources are selected for the collection. The scope policy relates to the need of the target user groups, while the selection criteria relate to the inherent features of the Internet resource. [3]

CSG has created selection quality criteria. A list of possible selection quality criteria is given below.

1) Content criteria (50%)
   - Applicability
   - Authority
   - Practicality
   - Accuracy
   - Leading edge
   - Uniqueness
   - Objectivity
2) Form criteria (20%)
   - Ease to use
   - Being reputable
   - Aesthetics
   - Use of recognized standards
   - Stability
3) Statute of limitations (10%)
4) Assessment of experts (20%)

Quality of the resources is the key to the success of CSG. No matter how sophisticated the search engine may be, if the resources it identifies are of poor quality then the information is of little use [4].

3.2 Metadata Format and Cataloguing Guideline

Subject gateways are characterized by their creation of the third-party metadata records – individual descriptions of Internet resources held in a database that have separate fields for different attributes of the resources, such as title, author, URL etc. These resource descriptions are used to help users learn more about the Internet resources (from a trusted third-party) and support information search and retrieval [3].

We have made decision about which metadata format to use. The metadata format we have formulated is based on the national standard "Web Resources Metadata Formats" (which was funded by Ministry of Science and Technology of P.R.C and executed by Shanghai Library) [5]. We have adopted its core metadata and have extended it in order to meet the needs of CSG.

One of the key roles of Internet subject gateways is the creation of descriptive metadata about networked resources that can be used as a basis for searching and browsing the gateway.

The role of cataloguing guidelines is to specify how the content of a metadata format is entered. Once a metadata format has been identified, consideration should then be given to how this metadata should be entered into the subject gateway database and how a set of cataloguing rules is prepared.

In line with the metadata format solution, we also use the national standard "Web Resources Metadata Formats: Cataloguing Guidelines" (which was funded by Ministry of Science and Technology of P.R.C and executed by Shanghai Library) [6].

3.3 Subject Classification Scheme

The attraction of subject gateway is based not only on the guaranteed high quality of the selected resource, but also on the facilities for subject-based access to the collection. So when we make decision about which classification scheme to use, we will give consideration to [2]:

– Systematicness
– Scientificity
– Maturation and equableness
– Conversant to the users
– Adequate of the levels

Based on the above, we have chosen the classification scheme formulated by the Chinese Ministry of Education. This classification scheme can meet all the needs mentioned above. It is especially important that the scheme is conversant to its users.

The classification scheme is a three–level structure. The first level has a general category and 12 subcategories that cover philosophy, economics, jurisprudence, education, letters, history, science, engineering, agriculture, medical science, military science, management science. Every general category contains several subjects, and every subject is composed of sub-subjects. This three–level structure forms a subject tree. We can provide for the users browsing by means of this kind of tree structure.

4 Progression

At the time of writing, we have accomplished these tasks and their deliverables are below:

Time	Content	Deliverables
10.2003	1th Conference of Project Management Team	– The project started
10.2003-12.2003	Investigation	– Practicability Report
01.2004 - 04.2004	Research of relevant standards	– Resource Type table – Quality Selection Policy – Metadata Formats – Cataloguing Guidelines – Management Regulation
01.2004 - 04.2004	Drafting out bid document	– System Statement of Requirements – System Software Supply Contract
04.2004	2th Conference of Project Management Team	– Criticism from the experts about the document
04.2004	Reviewing Conference of Partners	– Making choice of partners
05.2004	Modifying the relevant document	– Deliverable Policies and Guidelines
06.2004	Modifying the bid document	– Deliverable bid document
05.2004 –06.2004	Inviting bids of software	– Contracting

In September 2004, a training program for the cataloguers will be held in XJTU-Lib. By the end of 2004, the framework of CSG will be completed. All resources included in it will be catalogued in records that assess the resource's content, origin, and nature. This means that users can access CSG for the knowledge that they are looking for in a quality-controlled collection of resources.

5 Organizational Structure

CSG is funded by the Chinese Ministry of Education. CALIS is the leading institution and XJTU-Lib is its executive university. The project management team is composed of Beijng University Library, Nanjing University Library, Tsinghua University Library, Shanghai Jiaotong University Library, Wuhan University Library and Xiamen University Library.

As the Internet continues to expand it is clear that no single library can hope to identify, catalogue and organize all the available Internet resources to support the academic and research communities. Collaboration is needed to secure sustainable, high quality services.

At the beginning of CSG Phase II we intended to work with 30 libraries to develop the service, and made a decision that the amount of the subjects included in the navigation database would be 50. But over 80 libraries entered for the project with great ardor. In the end we have chosen 53 libraries as our copartners , every partner will be in charge of 1or 2 subjects. Almost all subjects are assigned to the partners. By the end of 10th 5-year Plan, we will establish an integrated, systematic information gateway to provide a trusted source of selected, high quality Internet information for students, academics, researchers and practitioners.

The partner libraries will work together to establish a mechanism for sharing information that will support the future development. This will ensure the most effective and sustainable use of resources in providing maximum possible coverage of the available material.

CSG provides an ideal starting point for end users in the higher education and research community, leading them to subject experts' descriptions of highly relevant, high quality resources available on the Internet.

References

1. Emma Worsfold: Subject gateways: fulfilling the DESIRE for knowledge. Computer Networks and ISDN Systems. 30(1998) 1479-1989
2. Zhang, Huijun, etc.: Thoughts on the Development of Web resources Navigation System. Journal of Academic Libraries. 135(2004) 34-37
3. DESIRS Information Gateways Handbook. http://www.desire.org/handbook
4. Lin, Jia: Web Resource Selection and Evaluation Policy of CSG. http://202.117.24.24/html/CALIS/calis.htm
5. Zhang, Chunhong.: Web Resource Metadata Formats of CSG. http://202.117.24.24/html/CALIS/calis.htm
6. Tony Gill: ADAM Annual Report 1997. http://adam.ac.uk.adam/reports/ar/1997
7. David Bawden, Lyn Robinson: Internet subject gateways revisited. International Journal of Information Management. 22(2002) 157-162

Live Digital Reference Service: Its Present and Future

Paul W.T. Poon

Education and Manpower Bureau Library, Hong Kong
paul_poon_wt@yahoo.com

"A Library that is not accessible out of business hours is of as little value as gold horded in a vault and withdrawn from circulation"
-- Alexander Graham Bell (Letter to Mabel Hubbard Bell, 17 November 1896)

Abstract. Information technology presents a challenge as well as an opportunity to reference service. This paper examines the reasons for the declining patronage of reference service, and outlines the benefits of offering live digital reference service. While covering the present status of this service, this paper also attempts to look ahead of its future development.

1 Introduction

Reference service is one of the more visible parts of the service that the library delivers to its users. It addresses the users' questions directly and on many occasions users' impression of the library service standard is based on the quality of reference service offered. Reference service has undergone many phases of development, but basically, its mode of operation is either synchronous or asynchronous. In general, reference librarians would prefer the synchronous service in the form of face-to-face encounter. Face-to-face reference has the benefit of understanding the users' questions more clearly because it affords an opportunity for a proper reference interview, which enables the reference librarians to tell from the users' tones and body language the unspoken intention, and to clarify the users' questions. The downside of this type of reference service is that the users have to physically visit the library and only during the hours when the library is open. Also, they may sometimes have to wait in the queue if the reference staff is busy with other users. Asynchronous mode of reference service is the reference assistance given to questions coming in via letters and emails. It is therefore not instant and lacks direct human interaction.

2 Present Status

Although reference librarians prefer synchronous type of service, statistics have consistently shown that the patronage of this type of reference service has been in the decline in recent years. A look at the reference statistics compiled by the Association of Research Libraries in USA bears out this point. For example, as cited by Steve Coffman, Ohio State University Library had about a million reference questions answered in 1995, and by 2000 the figures were down by nearly 50% to 500,000.[1]

Z. Chen et al. (Eds.): ICADL 2004, LNCS 3334, pp. 636–639, 2004.
© Springer-Verlag Berlin Heidelberg 2004

The reasons for this fairly general trend are (1) in this day and age when the pressure from work and family is greater than before, people have had less time to physically visit the library, and (2) just around this time, a number of searching tools have emerged on the Internet and these tools, e.g., Google, Yahoo, Ask Jeeves, in a certain way substitute the role of the reference library, and people who find it inconvenient to visit a library would turn to them for reference assistance.

However, the reference assistance offered by these search engines is not entirely satisfactory.   If libraries, with their professionally trained reference staff, rich collections of electronic databases as well as print materials, can also go on to the Web to offer reference service, the results would be more satisfactory.   Diane Kresh, Director of the Public Services at the Library of Congress put across this point very well when she was quoted by Scott Carlson in an article in the Chronicle of Higher Education as saying that "why not have libraries be really visible on the Web, so that people can go to library-based search systems and networks and get information that's credible, accurate, and objective, which you can't necessarily get from Ask Jeeves?"[2].

This new type of reference service makes use of the information technology to allow library users to interact with reference librarians, in real time, regardless of the boundaries of time and space.   The technology used is originally designed for call centers or customer support service that has been adopted by quite a number of commercial companies.   Different names such as chat-based, real-time digital, live digital, have been used to describe this kind of reference service.   It has been included as part of the library service for only a few years.   According to Buff Hirko, "the number of libraries experimenting with chat reference in 1999 could be counted on one hand." [3] But, since then, the number has definitely grown because of the following benefits that it offers.

- Any time and anywhere reference service.
- Great help for distance learners and homebound people as users do not need to physically visit the library.
- Meeting users on the Web because Web surfing is many people's daily activity today.
- Satisfying the rising expectations of users for immediacy and convenience.
- In tune with the next generation who are more at home with instant messaging and chat technologies than face-to-face interaction.
- A good training ground for reference librarians who need to keep abreast of the latest technology.

It is therefore not surprising to find that libraries that have implemented this service report positive responses from their users. For example, the statistics gathered by the Ryerson University Library in Canada that has used live digital reference service since the end of 2001 has shown that the use of the service has surpassed its email reference service.   Also, these statistics reveal that "the majority of questions asked ... were reference in nature, 56%, and the next largest category was technical assistance at 24%. In contrast the majority of questions asked of our email service involved technical assistance, 43%, with reference queries running at about 30%".[4]

Having outlined the benefits of live digital reference service, it is only fair to point out that there are some practical problems in its implementation. Basically, as with the introduction of any new facilities or services, chief obstacles are usually time involved, generating support of the staff, and technical know-how. Initially, a great deal of time has to be invested in planning, writing funding proposal, setting up operation policy, choosing hardware and software, and subsequently training of library staff and marketing of the service once the service is up and running. As live digital reference service uses the cutting-edge technology, not all library staff would be enthusiastic about it because running the service means having to spend time and energy to learn a new skill. Also, managing this service calls for a different type of reference staff who have to be agile on the PC and sometimes even have to carry out two kinds of reference work at the same time – one face-to-face and another via the Web. Getting the relevant staff interested and enthusiastic in this service, library management has to find ways to persuade them and to galvanize their support. Also, technically competent personnel have to be found for installing software, maintaining equipment and seeing that any technical hitches is smoothed out.

3 Future Development

Despite its implementation problems, it is safe to predict that live digital reference service is here to stay and will become more popular with libraries and their users. Looking into its future, the following issues are worthy of consideration and further study.

- **Technical Aspect**
There are still some technical glitches and limitations. For example, the co-browsing (or, escorting) – an attractive feature of the new technology – may sometimes not work perfectly with the result that users at the receiving end have to wait quite a while for the pages. Users with little patience would then quit the service in the middle of it. A greater technical limitation is that this service lacks the human touch that is present in the face-to-face reference service because the librarian and user do not see each other. A remedy to this shortcoming, as some have suggested, is sound and video contact over the Internet. But, then, this might present another psychological barrier to the librarians, as some are reluctant to appear on camera.

- **Copyright of Databases**
In the collaborative model, information and data from the licensed databases are provided to users who may not be the intended and legitimate users of a certain library that is doing the answering. It may therefore violate the letters and spirit of the contract entered into by the library and the database vendors.

- **Future of the Physical Library**
The purpose of having a successful live digital reference service is to make users satisfied in their information-seeking endeavor. But, will this service accelerate the trend of making users stay away from the library because their needs can be met satisfactorily when they are at home or in the office? If this trend continues and accelerates, what about the magnificent library buildings that we have invested so much resources on?

- **Future of the Librarian**
In conducting this service, librarians can work from home so far as they have access to the proprietary databases. A good example of this is the Librarians' Index to the Internet (http://lii.org). Therefore, an interesting question arises as to whether librarians who are not working in a library can still be called "librarians". Some

interesting analogies would be with doctors and teachers. Doctors who have their private practice are still called 'doctors". Teachers who may not teach in a school are still called "teachers" if they are still teaching. Will librarians who work from home still be called "librarians" ?

• **Privacy**

As live digital reference service collects personal data and records the reference transaction during the process, privacy has become an issue. To start with, libraries have to adhere to the confidentiality and should not disclose any information about the users if it is not for a good reason. Furthermore, if libraries wish to use the information collected later in reports or articles, users' consent has to be obtained. Therefore, in most libraries, a privacy policy statement has to be drawn up and made known to users before they start using the service.

References

1. Kenney B: Live, digital reference [J]. Library Journal, 2002, 127(16) : 46-50.
2. Carlson S: New service allows the public to pose reference questions without visiting the library [J]. The Chronicle of Higher Education, 2002 May 31.
3. Hirko, B.: Live, digital reference marketplace [J]. Library Journal, 2002, 127(17).
4. Granfield D: A digital reference service for a digital library : chat technology in a remote reference service. http://www.ryerson.ca/library/ask/McConnell.pdf, 2004-07-3.

3D Object Retrieval by Bipartite Matching

Xiang Pan, Yin Zhang, Xiuzi Ye, and Sanyuan Zhang

Institute of Computer Science,
Zhejiang University, 310027, Zhejiang, P.R. China
wzpx@zju.edu.cn

Abstract. This paper proposes a structural matching algorithm for 3D retrieval. It decomposes the 3D object into meaningful patches, and performs similarity calculation by bipartite matching. The retrieving performance of the proposed algorithm will remain almost no any decreasing for connected objects. While the performance will be a great improvement if the database contains disconnected objects.

3D object usually consists of some meaningful patches, and recent researches about 3D retrieval is emphasizing on performing structure matching from such patch set[1,2,3]. These algorithms will work well if the given object is connected while lots of 3D objects containing disconnected parts can not be matched by these algorithms. This paper proposed a structure matching algorithm for 3D retrieval, which is suitable for comparing disconnected objects as well as connected objects.

A bipartite graph is defined by decomposed patch sets representing the two 3D objects, and the edge cost of the graph is the local similarity of two patches belonging to different 3D objects. The global similarity between the two objects can be obtained by finding a maximum weight matching in the bipartite graph.

There are two DataSets for performance evaluation in experiments: DataSet1 only consists of connected objects, and DataSet2 also includes disconnected objects as well as connected objects. The comparison of retrieving performance is showed in Figure 1(ARG: the algorithms proposed by [2]. MWG: our algorithm).

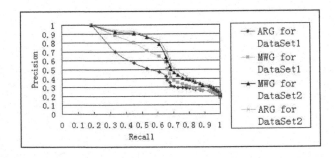

Fig. 1. Comparison of retrieving performance

Notice the performance of the out algorithm will improve greatly for DataSet2.

Z. Chen et al. (Eds.): ICADL 2004, LNCS 3334, p. 640, 2004.

A Hybrid Neural Network for Web Page Classification

Yukun Cao, Yunfeng Li, and ZhuZheng Yu

Department of Computer Science, Chongqing University, Chongqing, 400044, P.R. China
marilyn_cao@sina.com

1 Overview of the Architecture

Web page classification is one of the essential techniques for Web mining. The approach proposes a framework for Web page classification, that is a hybrid architecture using the PCA features selection approach and the SOFM with a combination of some conventional statistical methods. The proposed hybrid architecture consists of four modules as following:

The page-page-preprocessing module is used to extract textual features of a document, what is divided into *stopping* and *stemming*. The *stemming* is a process of extracting each word from a document by reducing it to a possible root word. The *stopping* is a process of deleting the high frequent words with low content discriminating power in a document, such as 'to', 'a', 'and', 'it', etc.

In the feature-weighting module, the vector obtained from the pre-processing module should be weighted using ameliorated TF-IDF algorithm. Because each sentence in a document has different importance for identifying the content of the document, we use WTF_i replace TF_i in TF-IDF, which is calculated as follows: each time a word occurs in the title its WTF_i is increased by ten, each time a word occurs in the heading its WTF_i is increased by six, each time a word occurs in the boldface type its WTF_i is increased by three, each time a word occurs its WTF_i is increased by one.

To improve the accuracy of categorization, the feature-selecting module uses the principal component analysis (PCA) neural network to reduce the original term-weight vectors with high dimensionality to a small number of 'effective' features and yet retains most of the intrinsic information content of the data.

In the approach, the page-categorization module employs a SOFM neural network. And the inputs of SOFM are the outputs of the PCA. The SOFM's objective in document clustering is to group the documents, which appear similar, close to one another and place the very different ones distant from one another.

2 Experiments and Conclusion

Through the comparison of categorization accuracy using Naïve Bayes classifier, K-NN classifier, and the proposed system, our experiments indicate that if the feature vectors are selected carefully, the improvement of web page classification using the combination of the PCA and SOFM in the approach could increase the classification accuracy.

Z. Chen et al. (Eds.): ICADL 2004, LNCS 3334, p. 641, 2004.
© Springer-Verlag Berlin Heidelberg 2004

A Metasearch Engine with Automatic Resource Binding Ability[*]

Guowen Wu[1], Liang Zhang[2], Yin Kang[2], Jun Yin[1], Xiangdong Zhou[2], Peiyi Zhang[1], and Lin Zhao[1]

[1] Academy of Changjiang Computer (Group) Company, China
[2] Department of Computing and Information Technology, Fudan University, China
{wuguowen, yinjun, peiyi_z, zhao_lin}@hotmail.com
{zhangl, kangy, xdzhou}@fudan.edu.cn

Metasearch has been proved to be a quite effective method to integrate information spaces provided by underlying search engines. But how to admit new resources dynamically was almost neglected. Current solutions include software recoding or resource rebinding by metasearch engine developers. Besides extra cost in time and money, both tactics might be futile for resources in a controlled network (e.g. a campus network using virtual IP address) or fail to keep pace with the emerging of new resources.

To deal with this issue, we have developed an automatic binding technique for Web resources in light of *proxy* design pattern. Taking note of the regularity of information access pattern and the variety of parameters, tools trace the interaction between a browser and a new Web resource at HTTP level, formulate a typical template, extract the user's feedback as parameters, and produce a *wrapper* for the resource. Here parameters include target URL, item name and data type, default value, as well as result indices. Each wrapper is a XML document that specifies one kind of information collecting process for the resource and all necessary term mappings between underlying resource and global schema.

Once wrappers for a resource are ready, our metasearch engine FU-Findgold can carry out metasearch across all bound resources, including the new one we have just treated. The next stage is to extract information from returned HTML files. This is fulfilled by the *extractor* which exploits HTML Tidy to transform HTML into XHTML, and applies XSLT on it to get required information. The extracting rules are also prepared in the wrapper building stage.The automatic binding technique was implemented in the FU-Findgold Metasearch Engine. Thanks to the technique, new resources can be added and maintained more easily by the searching service provider, instead of the software developer. The process of binding is almost automatic and needs little intervention of system administrator. Above automatic binding technique has been successfully used in many real applications, and the FU-Findgold has been boomingly deployed in several organizations, including Shanghai Library, East China Normal University, and Shanghai Jiaotong University. We are going to improve the FU-Findgold further by enhancing the query ability, incorporating personalization into the system, and supporting community collaboration.

[*] This work is partially supported by the NSFC key project No. 69933010, the Chinese Hi-tech (863) Project under grant No. 2002AA4Z3430, and No. 2002AA231041, as well as Shanghai S&T Commission projects No. 02DJ14013, No. 03ZR14005.

Z. Chen et al. (Eds.): ICADL 2004, LNCS 3334, p. 642, 2004.
© Springer-Verlag Berlin Heidelberg 2004

Certificate-Based Authentication and Authorization Architecture in Digital Library*

Lin Chen, Xiaoqin Huang, and Jinyuan You

Department of Computer Science and Engineering,
Shanghai Jiao Tong University, No.1954, Huashan Road, Shanghai, 200030, China
{chenlin, huangxq}@sjtu.edu.cn

In this paper, we design and implement a certificate-based authentication and authorization architecture in digital library. Our certificate-based authentication architecture consists of resource server, directory server, policy engine and log server. The heart of this system is the policy engine, which gathers and verifies certificates and then evaluates the user's right to access to the requested resource based on these certificates. Our system uses two types of persistent certificates: X.509 user identity certificates and attribute certificates. The identity certificates are generated and managed by certificate authorities, such as the Netscape CA server. These certificate authorities provide a Web interface that allows the creation or revocation of certificates. A directory server can be used to provide the certificates for use by applications and Web browser to manage the certificates for the user. The resulting certificates can be stored in directories chosen by the user that are accessible via a Web server, a directory server, or an MSQL database. The client first has to pass the Kerberos authentication. He has to provide the identity and the password. If he has passed the authentication, then the certificate authority issues the certificate for him. We implement the Kerberos algorithm and DES algorithm in the architecture. When we have got certificates and want to get services from service provider, we have to get authorization. In our model, authentication and authorization is separated. The authorization architecture consists of browser, service provider and authorization directory server. When an individual within the consumer community requests information from a remote service provider, the browser sends the individual's digital certificate. The service provider validates the individual's certificate and uses it to locate the institution's authorization server. The authorization server checks the validity of the service provider's certificate. If valid, it returns attributes concerning the individual's status to the provider in the form of a list of attribute names and values. From the authorization server's response, the service provider decides to whether deliver the service to the individual. Finally we compare the difference of certificate-based architecture and the user identity-password architecture. The excellence of the certificate-based architecture and the shortcomings of IP address, identity-password architecture are analyzed.

---

* This paper is supported by the National Natural Science Foundation of China under Grant No.60173033.

Z. Chen et al. (Eds.): ICADL 2004, LNCS 3334, p. 643, 2004.

Culture Grid and Its Key Technologies*

Zhendong Niu[1,2], Mingkai Dong[1], and Jie Zhang[1]

[1] National Library of China, Beijing, China, 100081
[2] Beijing Institute of Technology, China, 100081
zniu@nlc.gov.cn

The China Culture Grid is proposed to effectively organize, classify, and integrate the heterogeneous resources for the purpose of providing pervasive, proactive, on-demanded, and personalized services for various people with different backgrounds, capabilities and expectations, under different time and venue. This paper describes the architecture and key technologies of the China Culture Grid, including Uniform Content Locator, Ontology and Personal Content Locator. An experiment study and a prototype system are also presented.

The architecture of China Culture Grid is mainly composed of the following components.

Resource Integration Module. It is responsible for collecting and organizing heterogeneous resources. Based on the shared ontologies, the accumulated resources from large web sites (portal or professional websites) or other resources are classified, and the Uniform Content Locator (UCL) is also included in this component.

Resource Transmission Module. It fulfils the task of transmitting the well-organized resources to the client terminals in several ways, including Internet, and satellite broadcasting, etc.

Resource Receiving Module. By matching the UCL of the resources with the customization of users, it is to filter the resources and store the useful resources in the local repositories.

Resource Exploitation Module. It takes the charge of recommending the useful or interesting resources to users according to their PCL (Personal Content Locator). Users customize their interests by specifying the terms and related constraints.

By representing the features of different kinds of resources, UCL is used to identify and locate the content of resources in a uniform way. The UCL also corresponds to the users' preferences, which facilitates the content filtering and thus provides better personalized services. Each resource on the Web has a unique UCL code. UCL code includes 16 bytes, which is composed of two parts: manual classification code for 10 byes and ontology classification code for 6 bytes. The manual classification code represents the category of resource content in terms of manual classification, which is comprised of four parts: type, website, channel and temporal. The ontology classification code is used to provide the universal mapping

---

* This work was supported by National Library of China.

Z. Chen et al. (Eds.): ICADL 2004, LNCS 3334, pp. 644–645, 2004.

for each classification, which realizes the resources sharing and exploitation according to the uniform classification standard.

In the China Culture Grid, resources are classified based on ontologies and the existing manual constructed categories are also mapping to the ontologies. In this way, resources can be managed and shared on a global scale and thus facilitates the resource retrieval and filtering. On the other hand, ontology can enhance the resource locating and recommendation with semantic extensions. Based on the versatile semantic relationship between concepts and other semantic information, the system periodically checks users' profiles and recommends more semantic associated resources.

PCL is mainly composed of two parts: user modelling and personalized delivery. As for user modelling, each user has a profile to describe his interests and preference, which are composed of three components: interested classifications, preferred keywords, and suitability. Interested classifications are selected from ontology classifications. Personalized delivery is a kind of proactive service provided for different users. Based on users' profiles, the delivery module is responsible for filtering these resource candidates and recommending suitable content to suitable users. It is necessary to compute the suitability of resource candidates based on ontology and decide whether a resource is suitable according to user's profile.

We conducted an experiment to empirically evaluate the usefulness and effectiveness of the service provision. We selected 32 media websites (including portal websites and professional website) and 32 college courses as the resource origin. The network transmission takes 2-mege bytes bandwidth (32k bandwidth per website/course) and realizes 24 hours broadcasting. When the resources reach the client terminal, the system determines the corresponding UCL according to the users' pre-specified classification, then performs the UCL decoding of resource, and then determines whether to store the resource or not. The selected resources are stored in the resource repository of users. Following that, PCL fulfils the task of personalized content delivery. Although a rich data has been collected, only preliminary evaluation of the data has been accomplished. To provide personalization services, the client system is composed of three modules:

- PCL customizing module will assist user to build his/her PCL model by selecting and defining profile based on ontology classification.
- Content filtering module will select and filter suitable resources according to PCL model.
- Content service module will provide many kinds of service, such as category search, full-text search, latest recommendation, expert recommendation, similar content link, dynamic report, history analysis, and so on.

By incorporating users' characteristics, heterogeneous resources, and machine-understandable semantics, the China Culture Grid provides pervasive, proactive and personalized services for users. It aims to construct a platform for emerging applications in fields of digital library, distant education, E-Science, E-learning, etc. The prototype system of the China Culture Grid has been developed at the National Library of China, and the test experiments have shown the advantages of the Culture Grid.

The authors would like to thanks academician Youping Li and other members of the China Culture Grid Project and acknowledges the funding of National Library of China.

Face Region Detection on Skin Chrominance from Color Images by Facial Features

Jin Ok Kim[1], Jin Soo Kim[2], and Chin Hyun Chung[2]

[1] Faculty of Multimedia, Daegu Haany University, 290,
Yugok-dong, Gyeongsan-si, Gyeongsangbuk-do, 712-715, Korea
bit@dhu.ac.kr
[2] Department of Information and Control Engineering,
Kwangwoon University, 447-1, Wolgye-dong, Nowon-gu, Seoul, 139-701, Korea
chung@kw.ac.kr

Abstract. Face detection algorithms have primary factors that decrease a detection ratio: variations in lighting effect, location and rotation, distance between objects, and complex background. Variations in illumination, background, visual angle and facial expressions make the face detection difficult [1], [2]. We propose a face detection algorithm for color images in the presence of varying lighting conditions as well as complex background. Our method detects skin regions over the entire image, and then generates face candidate based on the spatial arrangement of these skin patches. The algorithm constructs eyes, mouth, nose, and boundary maps for verifying each face candidate.

1 Conclusion and Future Work

We have presented an approach that detects facial regions in color images and calculates facial features. Facial parts are determined on the basis of color and shape information. Therefore, we first extract regions with skin-like chrominance and luminance values and then compute the best fit ellipse for each of these regions. Based on the observation that eyes and mouth differ from the rest of the face because of their lower brightness and different response to chrominance, we first enhance the eye and mouth regions inside the ellipse by applying morphological operations. Then we determine the position of facial features by evaluating the horizontal and vertical projection and topographic grey level relief. The success of this method is verified on a large number of color images.

Z. Chen et al. (Eds.): ICADL 2004, LNCS 3334, p. 646, 2004.
© Springer-Verlag Berlin Heidelberg 2004

Image Assisted Remote Visualization of Volume Data

Xubo Yang

Shanghai Jiao Tong University, 1954 Hua Shan Road, 200030, Shanghai, P.R. China
yangxubo@cs.sjtu.edu.cn

Abstract. Three-dimensional volume data as a new type of resources for digital library poses a challenge for user to visualize the data remotely with ordinary network and user terminal. This paper presents a decoupling architecture with a front-end viewer and a back-end server. Multiple reference images are produced by the server and warped and composed by the front-end. This approach enables remote visualization at interactive speed and also protects original data.

1 Introduction

As more and more CT and MRI data being produced, it becomes a necessary digital library service to archive them and provide remote visualization service. This poses a challenge for user terminals and network. An ideal approach for remote visualization should both keep high quality images and support interactive viewing.

2 The Approach

We proposed a decoupling architecture, where the rendering engine is decomposed into two parts: a front-end viewer and a back-end renderer. The front-end viewer is responsible for changing view interactively by deriving new images from several high-quality reference images rendered and transmitted from the back-end renderer.

The front-end viewer is based on image warping techniques. It warps multiple reference images to current view, and the warped images are composed together to produce the final result. By using a predefined configuration of the reference images, we select a primary reference image to warp and then use other neighboring reference images to fill holes. The overlapped visible regions of multiple reference images are detected and clipped in advance to avoid unnecessary computation. A ray-casting volume renderer is used for the server and produces eight 400x400 size reference images with depth values for iso-surfaces. The volume data can be viewed from 360 degree surrounding angles with about 30ms per frame on a Pentium 4 1.6GHz PC.

To conclude, our approach has several advantages. Its performance depends on image resolution rather than on data complexity. It provides protection for the archived data - the original data is not disclosed to the user, instead, only the images of it is sent to the user. Our future work will include controlling the error between warped result and the rendered result, and using graphics hardware to accelerate.

Z. Chen et al. (Eds.): ICADL 2004, LNCS 3334, p. 647, 2004.
© Springer-Verlag Berlin Heidelberg 2004

Improving Multimedia Delivery Performance for Digital Library Applications

Yunpeng Wang, Xiulin Hu, and Hui Guo

Department of Electronic and Information Engineering,
Huazhong University of Science and Technology, Wuhan 430074, China
wyp@jhpa.com.cn

Abstract. Nowadays an educational digital library usually contains instructional materials such as class lectures, seminar presentations, and various training materials. These materials accompany video and audio media. In this case, multimedia streaming and delivery techniques are concerned in the construction of a novel multimedia digital library. In this paper, we focus on multimedia streaming techniques in digital library applications. To achieve scalability and deliver high quality streams, we present the multimedia proxy caching scheme between the server and client path, and a prototype design and implementation of a proxy caching system is proposed. By validate our implementation, the experimental results show that our proxy system can contribute to improve streaming media quality, reduce network transferring latency and decrease streaming service response time.

Because currently multimedia digital library applications consume network bandwidth along the client-server path for the entire session, the traditional client-server architecture for streaming continuous media objects could not scale to a large number of clients. To achieve scalability and deliver high quality streams, proxy caching is a client-oriented solution for large-scale delivery of high quality streams over the Internet. A proxy cache stores recently accessed resources in the hope of satisfying future client requests without contacting the server, which in turn reduces the load on the network and server, and also accommodates the scalability. Furthermore, since a proxy is located close to its clients, caching of popular streams at a proxy can effectively avoid network bottleneck and then substantially reduces service response time.

This paper presents the design and implementation of a multimedia proxy caching system, some issues and challenges in the design of proxy system are detailed discussed and our solutions are presented. From experimental results, streaming proxy can reduce overall client start-up latency and the possibility of adverse Internet conditions disrupting video playback. From the point of view of the server, streaming proxy dramatically reduces network load by intercepting a large number of server accesses, which ensures a large number of video requests and also accommodates the scalability.

Z. Chen et al. (Eds.): ICADL 2004, LNCS 3334, p. 648, 2004.
© Springer-Verlag Berlin Heidelberg 2004

Multi-document Summarization Based on Link Analysis and Text Classification

Jiangqin Wu, Yizi Wu, Jian Liu, and Yueting Zhuang

The Institute of Artificial Intelligence, Zhejiang University, Hangzhou, 310027, P.R. China
{wujq, ken3300}@zju.edu.cn, daniel_fox@263.com,
yzhuang@cs.zju.edu.cn

Abstract. This paper describes a multi-document summarizer in Chinese, ACRUX, which contains three new techniques: a fuzzy classification method based on KNN (FAMKNN), Subject-Oriented Multi-document Summarization (SOMS), and Multi-document Summarization with Link Analysis.

1 Introduction

Digital libraries have the prevailing problem of information overloading. It will be very helpful if a short summary of the required documents can be built automatically.

In this paper, we first propose a new *Fuzzy Classification Method based on KNN* (FAMKNN). Then we go a further step to analyze the link structure in multiple documents. In this way we come up with Subject-Oriented Multi-document Summarization (SOMS).

2 FAMKNN, Link Analysis and SOMS

In KNN classification, every document has a value of relevance to a class. We define fuzzy classification as: Assume that the maximal relevance value is D_{max}, if a relevance value $D > \alpha D_{max}$, or D is above a constant d_0 then we say this document also belongs to this class. By adjusting α and d_0, FAMKNN can do better than KNN.

Since digital texts have hyperlinks that binds them together, we can use these links to find there significance. We define a document Ranking Weight (**DRW**) denoted as $T_i . v_p$ (T_i for document i when choosing the sentence to include in the summarization).

We concentrate on the goal of retrieving and digesting useful material on certain subjects from mass information. So we calculate how much important a sentence is for a particular subject using Document Category Weight (**DCW**) denoted as $T_i . v_c$. We also consider the topic to be meaningful, so we define $d_{i,j}$ as the cosine distance between the feature vector of the sentence and the title. The calculation is like this:

$$S_{c,i,j}.v = (T_i.v_p)^\alpha \; \square \; (T_i.v_c)^\beta \; \square \; (1+d_{i,j})^\theta \; \square \sum_{k=1}^{m} W_{i,j,k}.v$$

Z. Chen et al. (Eds.): ICADL 2004, LNCS 3334, p. 649, 2004.
© Springer-Verlag Berlin Heidelberg 2004

Query Between Heterogeneous Ontology-Based Information Sources Using Association Matrix*

Jianjiang Lu[1,2], Baowen Xu[1], Wenxian Zhang[2], and Dazhou Kang[1]

[1] Department of Computer Science and Engineering, Southeast University,
Nanjing, 210096, China
[2] PLA University of Science and Technology, Nanjing, 210007, China
jjlu@seu.edu.cn

Abstract. This paper proposes a simple method of querying between heterogeneous Ontology-based information sources using association matrix. It introduces the definition and calculation of association matrix and presents a method using concept vector and association matrix to rewrite query.

Different information systems may use different ontologies, and cannot access each other directly. Therefore, it needs to find relations between concepts in different ontologies, and rewrite queries based on these relations. Learning methods can discover relations between concepts in different ontologies automatically. Current methods are often based on the similarity measures between concepts. They can mainly find the one-to-one mappings. When handling no equivalent concepts and ambiguous concepts, it is impossible to determine an accurate match. Moreover, it cannot find all the subsumption relations.

We use a simple association matrix to represent the relations between concepts. This matrix uses the known knowledge of the instances of concepts to learn relations between concepts in two ontologies. The category knowledge is often done by separate users and systems manually or automatically. Checking more instances will give results that are more exact. When using it to rewrite and answer users' queries, new results can be used to update the matrix to be more precise.

As we use association matrix to translate queries between different systems, we should first translate query expressions to the vector form, and then calculate them with the association matrix in order to query in different systems. The user sends a query requirement including the query expression and the keywords to the system. We use the concept vector to represent a query expression, it shows the probabilities of answers to this query belonging to each concepts. If an information source uses another ontology, the query expression has to be transformed to concept vectors.

System can now searches the keywords in the answers to the query. The results are returned to the user. The results can also be used to update the association matrix. Though it cannot rewrite the query expressions as precisely as manual mapping, this method is simple to be implemented and expected to run quite fast. We will go on study on the instances classifying and more precise mapping in the future.

---

* This work was supported by NSFC (60303024), National Grand Fundamental Research 973 Program of China (2002CB312000).

Z. Chen et al. (Eds.): ICADL 2004, LNCS 3334, p. 650, 2004.

Research and Development of Digital Library Platform

Jing Peng and Dake Wang

Computer Department of Shen Zhen Library,
1011 Hong Li Road, Shen Zhen, 518027, P.R. China
{pp334, dkwang}@szlib.szptt.net.cn

The project *Digital Library Architecture and Application Platform* (DLAAP) is a state hi-tech project approved by the State Planning Commission in 2001 and undertaken by the Project Team of Shenzhen Library. The General Plan and Technical Implementation Plan of the project had gained the experts' recognition in 2002 and the research of the architecture of the system and application platform development had made some achievements. At present a distributed digital library application platform had been developed, which includes digital resources process and inquiry system, library business processing system, reader service and management system, which will be fully put into use at the opening of the new Shenzhen Library.

The paper introduces the general target of DLAAP and content of research which includes the structural model of the digital library system, functions and features of the system, system implementation process and the application in network environment.

DLAAP is on going. The research of some parts and the realization of application technology need further practice.

We will continue the research on the several technical topics involved in the digital library, further optimize the model structure of the digital library system, deepen the research on the data resource management on WAN, image processing, hypermedia search technique, information search technique, copyright management and payment methods so as to make DLAAP technically optimized and functionally improved.

Z. Chen et al. (Eds.): ICADL 2004, LNCS 3334, p. 651, 2004.
© Springer-Verlag Berlin Heidelberg 2004

Understanding the Semantics in Reference Linkages: An Ontological Approach for Scientific Digital Libraries

Peixiang Zhao, Ming Zhang, Dongqing Yang, and Shiwei Tang

Department of Computer Science and Technology, Peking University
{pxzhao, mzhang, ydq}@db.pku.edu.cn
tsw@pku.edu.cn

In resent years, several digital libraries have established large repositories of scientific literature, such as ISI SCI®, CiteSeer.IST [2] and CORA[1] etc. These projects pay much attention on how to interlink scientific articles via reference indexes. However, few of them richly utilize the semantics behind reference links and people get limited supports in searching, reviewing and analyzing scientific literature from scholarly perspectives.

In this paper we investigate the usage of a domain-specific ontology to improve semantic linking ability in scientific literature via reference information. We utilize heuristic methods and regular expression matching techniques to extract metadata from scientific articles. The detailed reference information in the bibliographic section and citation anchor context (the sentences occurring near the citation tag) of citing articles are also extracted and matched with each other. An extraction rule database is used to guide metadata extraction process and we also use author name database, journal name database, and domain name database to help identify metadata. We develop a domain-specific ontology that models scientific literature and interlinked reference indexes in order to identify the semantics behind reference links. The ontology is consisted of concepts extracted from content of cited articles and reference motivations derived from citation anchor context. As to a specific scientific article, we use automatic summary generation algorithm to produce descriptions derived from citation anchor context of citing articles which include research theme and motivation, research topics, research background, research impact and applied fields etc. Compared with the abstract written by authors themselves, the summary is an objective description for the cited paper from different scholars' perspectives. Thus it is quite helpful for researchers to understand the literature better. Further reasoning upon the ontology is also provided as semantic query forms to reveal new facts in scientific libraries. In this way, users can perceive a comprehensive understanding of the specific research domain, not solely a scientific article.

Z. Chen et al. (Eds.): ICADL 2004, LNCS 3334, p. 652, 2004.
© Springer-Verlag Berlin Heidelberg 2004

Usage of Hybrid Model Based on Concepts Correlations in Adaption to Changes of User's Interest*

Lizhe Song[1], Zhendong Niu[2,3], Hantao Song[1], Zhengtao Yu[1], and Xuelin Shi[1]

[1] Department of Computer Science & Engineering,
Beijing Institute of Technology, Beijing, China 100081
[2] School of Software Engineering, Beijing Institute of Technology, Beijing, China 100081
{songlz, songhantao, shixuelin, zniu}@bit.edu.cn
[3] Beijing National Library Digital Technology Corp. LTD., Beijing, China 100083

In digital library, the provided personalized service responds to the user's interests. Therefore, it is important to trace and understand the changes of the user's interests, so as to supply pertinent service. This paper depicts a hybrid model, which is based on concepts correlations, to deal with users' interest change. Using this model, the change of the user's interest can be quickly found and combined with previous user's interests. So, a better personalized service can be provided.

The hybrid model consists of long-term interests model and short-term interests model, which adopts different algorithm to deal with the interest changes. Short-term model use sliding window algorithm to deal with the sequence of the user's interest samples, the samples appeared in window mean the current short-term interests of the user. Long-term model use gradual forgetting algorithm based on concepts correlations to calculate the weight of each interest sample, and the interests with larger weight are considered as the long-term interests of the user. The formula $c_j = \sum_{i=1}^{n} w_i a_i^j + \theta \xi$ is defined to calculate the weight of each interest when new interest appears. Here, w_i represents the decline of interest weight as time goes along and it is calculated by forgetting function $w = f(t)$. a_i^j depends on the correlations of interests. We give a function $(U = f(U, D, I))$ to calculate the interest correlations for each user based on a pre-defined matrix of concept correlation in one domain. The value of I includes the instances that new interests appear, already existing interests appear, and interests are deleted. This paper introduces the calculation of interest correlations for each user (U) at above three circumstances.

Experiment on this method is encouraging, not only can it trace the interest change of the user exactly, but also predicts the interest of the users.

* Funded by National Major Project of Social Sciences (01ATQ001).

Z. Chen et al. (Eds.): ICADL 2004, LNCS 3334, p. 653, 2004.

WEBDL: A Specific Digital Library for Web Data

Zhiqiang Zhang, Chunxiao Xing, and Lizhu Zhou

Department of Computer Science and Technology,
Tsinghua University, 100084, Beijing, China
{zqzhang, xingcx, dcszlz}@tsinghua.edu.cn

Abstract. This paper introduced a system-WEBDL (Web data Digital Library) which addressed the problems of effectiveness and efficiency of searching from the Web with the hope of making full use of available information on the Web The user could search the web information just like query in a local traditional Digital Library.

1   The Architecture of WEBDL

WEBDL's architecture consists of interface layer, service layer, and storage layer. It especially focuses on the web data searching, extracting and querying (see Fig. 1).

The **Interface layer** consists of Query interface, User management interface, Personalized Services interface, Z39.50 client. We also could plug in diverse browser-based viewers very easily, such as video, e-book etc. This layer provides an access to the digital libraries collections and is optimized for different users and different purpose effectively.

The **Service layer** is composed of major management and service components by Application Server. These components include System Management, User Management, Configure Management, Personalized Services, Search Agent, Ontology Manager, Extracting Agent, Index Manager, Query Processor, Virtual Collection Management, Access Controller and Data Format Converter. With regard to interoperability, we have developed a lightweight interoperable protocol based on the OAI PMH v2.0 (the Open Archives Initiative Protocol for Metadata Harvesting) for cross-library information discovery and retrieval. The services are performed by intelligent agents that can collaborate with each other.

The **Storage layer** consists of a group of data access managers, such as RDBMS Manager which is in charge of accessing against on the relational database. XML Repository Manager is responsible for operating the XML data. And the File Manager is focus on the file management. This layer provides the services and functions for the storage, maintenance and retrieval of the metadata, digital objects, and knowledge rules for the long-term preservation.

As shown in Fig. 1, comparing with the traditional digital libraries, WEBDL covers all the aspects that traditional digital libraries deal with, and it especially provides services for the web data. WEBDL has four special key components for web data searching, extracting and querying: Data Search Agent, Extracting Agent, Ontology Agent and Query Processor. It captures richer semantics based on domain

Z. Chen et al. (Eds.): ICADL 2004, LNCS 3334, pp. 654–655, 2004.
© Springer-Verlag Berlin Heidelberg 2004

ontology that are extensible, and provides a platform to find, extract, organize the specific domain data available from multiple web sources, and supports user to query the data and their relationships among the domain concepts [1, 2]. WEBDL can be customized to different domain by change of domain ontology. Now we have encapsulated the functions of above specific components into a series of web services which could be integrated into any traditional Digital Library or other systems.

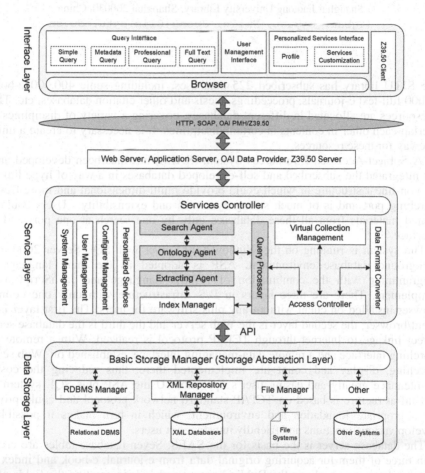

Fig. 1. The Architecture of WEBDL

References

1. Z. Zhang, C. Xing, L. Zhou and J. Feng, "A New Query Processing Scheme in a Web Data Engine", DNIS 2002, Lecture Notes in Computer Science, Vol. 2544. Springer-Verlag, Berlin Heidelberg New York (2002), pp 74-87, Japan, 2002.
2. Z. Zhang, C. Xing, L Zhou and J. Feng, "An Ontology-based Method for Querying the Web Data". Proceedings of IEEE 17th International Conference on Advanced Information Networking and Applications, IEEE Computer Press, pp 628-631, Xi'an, China, 2003.

A Practice in the Integration of e-Resources at SJTU Library

Yongge Bai, Guojing Yuan, Haoming Lin, and Jia Peng

Shanghai Jiaotong University Library, Shanghai 200030, China
{Ygbai, Gjyuan, Hmlin, Jpeng}@lib.sjtu.edu.cn

The SJTU library has subscribed 225 databases, including some 400,000 e-books, 1,7000 full-text e-journals, proceedings, thesis and other citation databases, etc. These e-resources are allocated in different databases, covering a variety of disciplines and overlap each other in contents in certain disciplines. It is necessary to create a unique gateway for these resources.

A Subject-Accessed E-resources System (SAES) has thus been developed and it has integrated the subscribed and self-developed databases in a way of hype linkage, the non-linear structure of which could provide multi-dimensional and more flexible searching port and is of much strong dynamics and extensibility. Users could get related materials from all these databases only by one search at one port and one interface.

The system is running on the Window2000 Server with SQL Server 2000 as its background database environment. ASP is adopted as the main language for programming with the combination of HTML Language and JavaScript as its complement. There are three layers in B/S infrastructure with only one common browser installed on client without any plus software for users. The first layer is the client/browser; the second layer is the Web server and the third is the database server. Direct linkage to Internet through TCP/IP protocol is realized. With a remote web searching interface and a remote data-managing interface established on Web server, searching, display and count are implemented there, thus reducing the cost of maintenance greatly and easing user's operation. Using ASP plus SQL system, the B/S infrastructure is based on TCP/IP standard network protocol and could provide the appropriate foundation and environment, which in turn makes it possible to develop various functions and friendly interface for users.

The database server is the basis for the SAES. Seven database tables are created with three of them for acquiring original data from e-journal, e-book and index and abstract databases, applying the Dublin concept and code in creating the fields of the tables for linking to other databases and extending its functions. 12 elements from the 15 core elements of DC code have been applied as the core elements. The workflow starts from the data collection. Then the cataloguing of e-resources by subject category is followed. The program then automatically performs the matching function of journal citation by 4 sources. The harvesting and marking of DC data are conducted and put into the three database tables. The data processing could be done either in an individual way by logging in or in a batch way using SQL language.

Basically following the Chinese Library Classification (CLC) and other subject-centered practices, a subject category has been built to make it parallel to the practice for printed materials. Some adjustments have been made accordingly.

Z. Chen et al. (Eds.): ICADL 2004, LNCS 3334, pp. 656–657, 2004.
© Springer-Verlag Berlin Heidelberg 2004

Being a one-station mode, the SEAS has the following features:

- Multiple languages and multiple types of resources covered
- A unified port.
- A unified searching interface
- Multiple access points
- Various combined searching modes
- Value-added information
- Abundant display information
- Friendly functions

The SAES is a combination of the various types of resources and multiple access points. Users could access the system via a unified port and conduct searching, browsing and retrieving functions at one searching interface. Users could do a search for specific types of resources in a default state (i.e. the three distinctive categories of databases) and browse the citation information of journals by certain publishers.

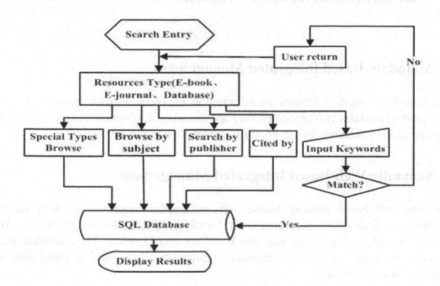

Function flow chart

Statistics shows that in 20 days of running, more than 13348 users accessed the system, a sign indicating the role of the system in providing e-resources information and promoting the use of them, and a sign indicating the importance and necessity of developing such an integration system.

An Essay on the Integrated Management of Digital Resources

Judy L. Cheng and Fred Y. Ye

Dept. of Information Resources Management, Zhejiang University, Hangzhou 310028 China
yye@zju.edu.cn

Abstract. With Comparing metadata-based method, semantic web-based method and ontology-based method for integrated management of digital resources, the authors think that ontology-based method will be the developing direction for integrated management of digital resources.

1 Metadate-Based Integrated Management

Metadata-based method focuses on information organization with artificial system. This method contains two processes, they are metadata description and web resources discovering and running. This method fits information organization.

2 Semantic Web-Based Integrated Management

Semantic web-based method focuses on information organization with natural languages and describes information in forms understandable by machines. The typical examples of semantic web are WordNet and HowNet. They constructed a semantic network for web information organization. It is also a foundation of ontology–based method.

3 Ontology-Based Integrated Management

Ontology–based method comes from formal ontology [1]. The method is composed of three steps and constructed by concept, model and software. Ontology–based method fits knowledge organization.

Reference

[1] Ye, Ying. A study on the formal ontology for information science and technology. *Journal of the China Society for Scientific and Technical Information (Chinese)*, 2003, 22(5): 561-564

Z. Chen et al. (Eds.): ICADL 2004, LNCS 3334, p. 658, 2004.
© Springer-Verlag Berlin Heidelberg 2004

Analysis, Design and Realization of Metadata Managing System for Multimedia Resources*

Xu Wu and Ziwei Ma

Beijing University of Posts and Telecommunications Library, Beijing, 100876
wux@bupt.edu.cn

For the description and management scientifically and in order and for the establishment of digital library information service system with our own features conform to international standards, we design and develop a set of system platform on the basis of multimedia resources. The multimedia resources metadata managing system supports the function of digital collection, processing, bibliography description, storage, organization and publishing of text, pictures or images, audio and video frequency and other multi-media information. The system must first define a set of metadata standard system according to the features of different resources and design metadata model describing these them, order metadata system templates and establish metadata application model through its models. The function of the system templates is to process, describe information resources when bibliographers establish some new multimedia resources on the basis of metadata system defined in advance by the system; secondly, the system describe the metadata of digital resources through metadata description template, identifying subject, classification and related data; thirdly, the system check, and publish data information through data checking and publishing model. During the period of the research of the multimedia metadata model and management system module, we use the domestic and overseas experience for reference. The choice of metadata, description of attributes, validity inspection of DTD and Schema, the standard of description classification, quotation of authority, XML and XSL data format and the upload data through the FTP all conform to the domestic and international standards. The system sets up multimedia resources element attribute descriptive frame on the base of the DC and also provides standard Chinese Library Classification system and authority name control. The bibliography description process can be easily realized with the use of visual operational interface. The pull function should be convenient for bibliographers. The system is highly integrated with other digital library system such as virtual reference service system and MELINETS (Modern Electronic Library Information Net System) of BUPT (Beijing University of Posts and Telecommunications). Mature techniques have been employed during the developing period. Open and standard interface are provided and various data exchanged are supported. The metadata database and object database can be effectively managed with the system management module. The realization of the design and techniques, the standardization and automation of multimedia resources in bibliography description are strengthened and the working efficiency improved.

* This work is supported by Work Committee for Beijing University Libraries.

Z. Chen et al. (Eds.): ICADL 2004, LNCS 3334, p. 659, 2004.
© Springer-Verlag Berlin Heidelberg 2004

Australian Digital Theses Program: Expansion, Partnership and the Future

Andrew Wells and Tony Cargnelutti

The University of New South Wales, Sydney, Australia
{a.wells, t.cargnelutti}@unsw.edu.au

Abstract. The continuing evolution of the Australian Digital Theses (ADT) Program, with the aid of an additional grant from the Australian Federal Government, sees it redeveloping the existing central metadata repository to increase its coverage and utility to the national and international research community. The repository's content will expand to include metadata about all Australian higher degree theses, whether in digital form or not. This goal responds to a clearly stated desire of the Australian research community, and brings together the university, government and corporate sectors, in building an open access service which exposes Australian research.

The ADT[1] began as a research project funded by the Australian Research Council. The project's rationale was to expose this research to wider and global audiences through exploiting the power of the web. Seven Australian university libraries under the leadership of The University of New South Wales Library (UNSW) participated in this project between 1998 and 2001. The project developed and implemented a distributed database model. In 2002, the Council of Australian University Librarians (CAUL) agreed to transform this project into a sustainable program. All Australian university libraries are members of the ADT Program and contribute financially to its ongoing management. In 2004, the Council of New Zealand University Librarians (CONZUL) expressed interest in joining the ADT. The ADT has been active in the international NDLTD (Networked Digital Library of Theses and Dissertations) since 1998. In September 2005, the international ETD (Electronic Theses and Dissertations) Conference[2] will be held at The University of New South Wales in Sydney.

A number of external factors has given the ADT Program an opportunity to increase its coverage and utility to the national and international research communities. These factors were the discovery problem for Australian theses, trend to mandatory digital submission, emerging standards facilitating interoperability and the sharing of metadata, plus the institutional repository movement. Australia's Commonwealth Government funds scientific research and innovation through a program known as Backing Australia's Ability.[3] The current ADT metadata repository expansion has been funded by this program. The expansion project is underway and due for completion in early 2005. The success of the ADT Program can be attributed to the strength of its national and international partnerships. The project has built on a long history of collaboration among Australian university libraries, bringing experience in digital content management to staff and students.

---

[1] http://adt.caul.edu.au/
[2] http://adt.caul.edu.au/etd2005/etd2005.html

Z. Chen et al. (Eds.): ICADL 2004, LNCS 3334, p. 660, 2004.
© Springer-Verlag Berlin Heidelberg 2004

Building Indian Language Digital Library Collections: Some Experiences with Greenstone Software

B.S. Shivaram and T.B. Rajashekar

National Centre for Science Information (NCSI),
Indian Institute of Science,
Bangalore 560 012, India
{shivaram, raja}@ncsi.iisc.ernet.in

With its diverse cultural and linguistic heritage, India today produces significant volume of digital material in Indian languages. This has been facilitated by increasing availability of word processing systems supporting Indian languages and their use in various areas including e-governance; education and research; and mass media. There is need for digital library software for organizing and provision of access to this material. Such software has to meet two prime requirements: Indexing and searching of documents in Indian languages (full text and metadata), and customizing the collection user interface in Indian languages. Further the software should be able to handle Indian language material in different encoding formats and fonts. Majority of Indian language material available online today seem to follow one of the three encoding strategies: ISO 8859-1 and Windows 1252 series character sets, with custom fonts; ad-hoc (font-specific or user defined) encoding schemes; and Unicode character set. Search and retrieval requirements would include features such as word truncation and alphabetical sorting. Cross-language material searching is an advanced search requirement. Greenstone is a very popular open source software used today for creating digital library collections. Main objective of this study was to assess capabilities of this software in creating Indian language digital library collections with above mentioned requirements for indexing, searching and display. We gathered five sample collections in two Indian languages Hindi and Kannada, in different encoding formats, for this study. For each of these collections, we assessed the multilingual support of Greenstone with respect to collection building; search and retrieval; and interface design. We used the 'Collector' approach of Greenstone to build the five collections. We could successfully build the collections. Limitations were found in handling metadata in Indian languages using the 'GLI' approach. We present details of internal mapping of character sets carried out by Greenstone during collection building process. We could successfully carry out simple keyword and Boolean searches on these collections. We discuss details of search features. Viewing results requires installation of suitable fonts at the operating system level and configuration of the browser. We found limitations in sorting. Greenstone does not support cross-language searching. In terms of users interface, Greenstone has in-built support for customizing the interface for well known languages. It also supports designing customized interface for other languages. We could successfully design desired user interface for the test collections in Hindi and Kannada. Overall, Greenstone appears to be a versatile software for building Indian language digital library collections, with some limitations.

Z. Chen et al. (Eds.): ICADL 2004, LNCS 3334, p. 661, 2004.
© Springer-Verlag Berlin Heidelberg 2004

Descriptive Metadata Structure and Extended Rules: A Case Study on Ancient Atlases Metadata Standard

Yunyun Shen[1], Boyue Yao[1], and Xiangyun Feng[2]

[1] Peking University Library, Beijing, 100871, P.R. China
{Shen Yunyun, shenyy}@lib.pku.edu.cn
[2] CALIS Administrative Center, Beijing, 100871, P.R. China

This paper is the summing-up of the study on descriptive metadata for variant resource objects in a national project *Chinese Digital Library Standards (CDLS)*. In this study, the two key issues, metadata structure and extended rules, are focused on while designing the metadata standards aiming at the different objects and their characteristics. They will enhance the interoperability among the metadata standards. This paper takes the metadata standard of ancient atlases as an example to illustrates its structure, elements and extended rules. The main parts of this study include as following:

1) Analysis of ancient atlases: It contains the definition of ancient atlases, the relationship among different atlases, the items of description. This is the basis of designing descriptive elements.
2) Content structure of descriptive metadata: Through the analysis, we find that there are core elements, resource core elements and unique elements in metadata elements. Ancient atlases metadata standard inosculate these three parts. The 13 core elements of ancient atlas descriptive metadata standard are accordant with Dublin Core. According the characteristics of ancient atlases, the other 5 elements are defined. The element set for ancient atlases is tabled.
3) Extended rules: Extended rules include the horizontal and vertical ones. The horizontal rules indicate the extension of element level: using the elements from localized DC in accordance with their semantic definitions; generating the new elements when the core elements cannot meet the special description, and semantic definitions of the new elements cannot overlap that of existing elements; complying with the content structure. The vertical extended rules adopt the mode of qualifiers and "Dumb-Down Principle". This part also illustrates in details how those rules act on the atlases metadata concretely.
4) Open experiment of ancient atlases descriptive metadata standard: The element set needs to be verified through application. A descriptive experimental system for the ancient atlases and other types of resources developed. Meanwhile, the describing rules of ancient atlases are formed and the syntax encoding languages XML, RDF and RDF Schema are applied.

We hope this paper will provide the instruction for designing descriptive metadata standards for different resource objects, and also hope it will become easier for a digital library to keep the integration and standardization of its varying metadata standards.

Z. Chen et al. (Eds.): ICADL 2004, LNCS 3334, p. 662, 2004.
© Springer-Verlag Berlin Heidelberg 2004

Featured Collection Digitization and Cooperation: Case Study of Chinese Mathematics Digital Library

Xiaohui Zheng, Bianai Cheng, Lisheng Feng, and Airong Jiang

Tsinghua University Library, Bejing, 100084, China
{zhengxh, chengba, fenglsh, jiangar}@lib.tsinghua.edu.cn

In more than 90 years history, plenty of featured scientific literature has been accumulated at Tsinghua Univ. Library. From 2001, we participated in the international cooperative initiative EMANI (Electronic Mathematics Archiving Network Initiative) together with SUB Goettingen (Germany), Cornell University Library (USA), MathDoc (France) and the Springer Press. The major idea of this project is the cooperation can promote the digitization of ancient as well as current publications of Mathematics all over the world, to care about the long term preservation of the content in readable form and provide convenient access to distributed digitized materials for users all over the world (See http://www.emani.org).

To coordinate with this international cooperation, we proposed a project aimed at Chinese mathematics digital library (CMDL) with emphasis on ancient works. CMDL grouped members from library, computer science department, electronic engineering department and mathematics department. Members from computer science department developed the management system based on Fedora open source software. Due to the scarcity of web application layer of this software, CS members developed the graphic interface for database configuration and web presentation. Math department and library together acted as the collection provider and evaluation group. Electronic Engineering dept. members provided ancient character OCR technology. Library member designed preservation metadata schema using METS framework. The METS data is essential for a digital repository which is the container for access and preservation of the objects. Also, it's important for interchange of digital objects for viewing and use by other systems. In CMDL project, METS acted as SIP and AIP roles that defined in OAIS. For DIP part, the Open Ebook format was used because the resources mainly are books. The seven parts of the METS package are: header (MetsHdr), descriptive metadata (dmdSec), administrative metadata (amdSec), file section (fileSec), structural map (structMap), structural link (structLink) and behavior section (BehaviorSec). AmdSec is divided into four subsections: techMD (technical metadata), rightsMD (intellectual property rights metadata), sourceMD (analog/digital source metadata), and digiprovMD (digital provenance metadata). TechMD included DC elements except rights, source, date, publisher. In the SourceMD, origital printed info was described in details which contained date, publisher, physical description, holding information, holding history. DigiprovMD clearified digitization time, person, organization, device, and process info. The elements of TechMD were derived from MIX standards including MIMEType, Compression, ColorSpace, CreationMethod, HostComputer, Resolution. In the entire process of our practice on CMDL project we recognize that cooperation has been being more and more substantial importance.

Z. Chen et al. (Eds.): ICADL 2004, LNCS 3334, p. 663, 2004.
© Springer-Verlag Berlin Heidelberg 2004

A Study on Framework and Methods of Online Information Literacy Instruction

Chunhong Zhang[1], Zhenbo Lu[1], and Wu Li[2]

[1] Reference Department, Peking University Library, Beijing, 100871, China
{zhangch, luzb}@lib.pku.edu.cn
[2] Department of Information Management, Peking University, Beijing, 100871, China
liw@calis.edu.cn

Abstract. The paper firstly explains the definition of Online ILI. Then taken Webtraining of PKU library as an example, authors try to put forwards an operable framework and methods of Online ILI considering the conditions in academic libraries in China.

1 Introduction

The online information literacy instruction (ILI) is web-based training or distance education that takes advantage of computer and Internet technology. From instructional contents, online ILI mainly educates patrons how to acquire electronic resources; while from the implementing methods, it emphasizes to fully make use of new media to implement ILI, such as computer and Internet.

2 Framework and Methods of Online ILI

In this part, we will mainly study web training. In our opinion, the content framework of web training prefers to all kinds of contents that web training should offer. And the function framework of web training means all the self-study frameworks such as navigation system, resource linking and user alternation mechanism, etc. There are two ways to implement web training in aboard, one is to build instructional websites, and the other is to implement web training making use of Network Education Platform. Taking the present status in academic libraries in China, it is generally agreed that building instruction websites with Internet technology is a better choice, since this kind of web sites costs less and is easily promoted.

3 Case Study — Webtraining of Peking University Library

The Webtraining System of PKU library was officially released at the end of 2003, which is composed of four parts, which respectively are Retrieval of Electronic Resources, Introduction to Resources and Services in Library, Use of Popular Software and Link to the Other Tutorials. As for implementing method, Webtraining

Z. Chen et al. (Eds.): ICADL 2004, LNCS 3334, pp. 664–665, 2004.

System of PKU Library adopted the model of web files plus PowerPoint presentation based on the successful experience of lots of tutorials, especially TILT.

4 Challenges Facing Before Online ILI

There are also some problems when we implemented our web training such as collaboration, maintenance and evaluation. In order to resolve these problems, we recommend that collaboration mechanism should be set up in a certain scope.

Assessing Users, Uses, and Usage of a Collaborated Digital Library

Natalie Lee-San Pang and Pang-Leang Hiew

School of Information Technology, Monash University Malaysia
{natalie.pang, hiew.pang.leang}@infotech.monash.edu.my

Evaluation for Multiple User Communities, Uses, and Usage

The Tun Hussein Onn Library (thereafter known as THOL), collaborates with the Monash University Library Australia and other education partners of Sunway College in their digital library initiative. THOL, as a collaborated digital library, has several unique characteristics:

☐ Extensive amount of heterogeneous resources, with differentiated access to different users.
☐ Ongoing digitization effort for resources from different libraries
☐ Multifaceted access restrictions
☐ Heavy reliance on online library services and education by remote users

Several Assessment Areas Are Proposed:

☐ Evaluation of usage: Frequency of use, login sessions, articles retrieved, number of remote logins.
☐ Identifying user communities: In our study, frequent users come from institutions which had greater amount of resources and services – implying that user communities were clustered according to their institutional memberships. Education levels, attendance of information skills workshops, user perceptions of information and computer literacy, availability of remote access, reliance on physical library were also significant cluster variables.
☐ Purposes of use: In our study of multiple user communities, there was no one clear purpose of use of the digital library – most users had a diversity of uses such as research, teaching, and leisure needs.
☐ Assessing perceived information skills: Determined in turn by perceived computer literacy, and interaction between computer literacy and attendance of information skills workshops.
☐ Adequacy of digital library resources and services: Users saw the physical library as the gateway to heterogeneous resources. Where online library help is available, there is also lesser reliance on physical library for services.
☐ Knowledge of using the digital library: While this is a significant factor in our study which influences usage frequency, we also found that users who stated a lack of knowledge mostly turned to the Internet to satisfy their information needs.
☐ Problems of using the digital library.

Z. Chen et al. (Eds.): ICADL 2004, LNCS 3334, p. 666, 2004.
© Springer-Verlag Berlin Heidelberg 2004

Deepening and Developing the Conception and Service of the Library

JiaZhen Pan

East China University of Science and Technology, Shanghai, 200237, P. R. China
jzpan@ecust.edu.cn

The famous Indian librarian, Dr. S. R. Ranganathan, proposed a five laws of library during 1931[1], which was taken as classical theory of library ever since. The laws point out the basic principles of library, clarify the object for effort, and obtain widely agreements during the several decades. Based on these laws, American librarian Michael Goman proposed a new five laws of library. Then in 1975 IFLA conference reached same comprehension: The library possesses four social functions: 1) Preserve human cultural heritage; 2) Open social education; 3) Deliver scientific information; and 4) Develop intelligence resources. All this has made huge contributions in promoting the library activities and still serve as basic principals for that. However, in the new situation of knowledge-based economy, the conceptions are subject to further deepening and developing. The computer technology offers good chances and opportunities for libraries to do it while the network technology makes it possible for libraries to be in the front of the information technology. Electronic collections and their searching abilities are good examples. China's policy to develop university and colleague's education also helps the changes. Some new ideas and practices about the library's functions have been formed from the classic and practice laws. They are "service- oriented information provider" comparing the "custodian of books"; "multiple media" comparing the "one medium"; "library without walls" comparing the "own collection"; "the library comes to us" comparing the "we go to the library"; service "just in time" comparing the service "in good time"; "out- sourcing" comparing the "in sourcing" and "global reach" comparing the "local reach",etc. Library is transferring from local library to a global library and must immerge into the global information market. As is put in the UNESCO document No. 105, library is a area should pay special attention. In modern academic organization, the word "Library" is given a new meaning. It will not be a place to collect,... The library will become a dialogue center necessary in modern study, teaching and scientific research between information provider and reader. The library, ... also provide intelligent environment. This has posed challenges for librarians who should be more than traditional ones. Their responsibilities include the traditional techniques of classification, cataloguing, acquisition but also the new ones to train patrons in searching databases and to use the new technology in providing efficient service to patrons, etc. On the other hand the libraries, especially the academic libraries should become center of learning with the assistance by librarians who should therefore involve research work. These new functions and services could be available all around the campuses and beyond with the facilities of network.

Z. Chen et al. (Eds.): ICADL 2004, LNCS 3334, p. 667, 2004.
© Springer-Verlag Berlin Heidelberg 2004

Design an Ideal Digital Reference Service (DRS) Model for Academic Libraries

Jing Guo, Wei Pan, Qiaoying Zheng, Min Huang, Zongying Yang, and Ying Ye

Shanghai Jiao Tong University Libraries,
1954 Hua Shan Road Shanghai, 200030, P.R. China
{jguo, wpan, zheng, mhuang}@lib.sjtu.edu.cn, zyyang@sjtu.edu.cn,
yye@dial.zju.edu.cn

Abstract. An investigation on digital reference service (DRS) has been carried out amongst 30 world top university libraries. This paper summarizes the recommendable elements of DRS in these libraries. Then the basic characteristics are generalized and an ideal DRS model including eight modules for academic libraries will be introduced.

The Recommendable Elements and Basic Characteristics of DRS

In order to find an ideal digital reference service (DRS) model to guide libraries to perfect it, this paper investigate 30 world top university libraries that have advanced DRS. Through the investigation, the authors find out that none of these libraries' DRS is perfect, but each library's DRS has recommendable elements. These elements can be summarized as follows:

(1) Real Time Reference Service: This kind of reference service can adapt for digital libraries and networks. There are about 16 libraries that have such services amongst 30 libraries. Moreover, many libraries are about to develop analogous services.
(2) Cooperative Reference Service: For the sake of limited service resources in single library, cooperative services are tried to adopt by more and more libraries, i.e., Cornell Univ. has a cooperative arrangement with the Washington Univ. reference staff. Shanghai Jiao tong Univ. is taking charge of CVRS (CALIS Virtual Reference Service) project with other four top universities for academic libraries in China.
(3) Subject Reference Service: Users in academic libraries are mostly scholars. So subject services of high quality are indispensable to VRS. Six libraries have set "subject pathfinder" or "subject guide" in their websites to provide subject research assistance. These "path-finders" are designed to bring together some of the most useful sources on a given topic and to help users quickly "find a path" through the almost overwhelming variety of choices. Pathfinders can be useful for class assignments as well as for research. Furthermore, "subject specialist" service is common and welcome.
(4) Special User Reference Service: Service purposes in academic libraries mainly satisfy faculty and students. Different users need particular services. Course collection (or "course reserve") and self-help learning center are set for sharing the opening information resources. For instance, "teacher's lab and classroom" is a kind of DRS

Z. Chen et al. (Eds.): ICADL 2004, LNCS 3334, pp. 668–669, 2004.

for research of faculty and self-study of students in Michigan Univ. Chicago Univ. establishes "the class librarian" to better serve user needs as a student in the College. Reference service for schoolfellows and handicapped should be advocated, too.

(5) Extended Reference Service: Pennsylvania Univ. sets "Ask a college house research consultant program". The program provides services during late night hours and visits residence halls upon request.

(6) Integrated Reference Service: Integrative reference resources and services make users access them via uniform interface, i.e., Hong Kong Univ. has gathered all web forms, such as ILL form, technical help form, into one page for users filling in. Singapore national Univ. has a kind of service called "email alert to latest research", which collects databases, journals and books providing alert services on one page.

Then the authors summarize the basic characteristics of DRS in academic libraries. These characteristics include: ① service means diversification; ② service contents are mostly subject reference guides; ③ service modes comprise information navigation, self-help services, individuation and integrative services, etc; ④ attach importance to information literacy education and user training; ⑤ think much of service management policy including service standards and statistics; ⑥ adjust service elements according to diversifications of user demands in time.

The Ideal Digital Reference Service (DRS) Model

An ideal DRS model (Figure 1) for academic libraries is designed based on research above. This model consists eight modules. The concrete columns and contents of each module include: I self-helpful information center: Such as course collections (reserve), research lab and training resources. II subject research assistance: For example, electronic subject pathfinders or research guides. III resource and service navigation: It means subject resource or categorizing service navigation. IV special librarian service: Special librarians comprise subject specialists, class (grade) librarians and database responsible persons. V individuation service: This kind of service is set for scholars, faculty, students, handicapped and off-campus persons, etc. VI integrated resources and services: For instance, integrated web forms, updated information and email alert services, etc. VII user policy and service statistics. VIII multiform service manners: These kinds of service manners can apply to all service modules, they include: Email, web form, real-chat, phone, knowledgebase or FAQ (frequently-asked questions), in person, schedule an appointment and a collaborative reference, etc.

These eight modules may be divided into three functional parts: service functional part, management and evaluation functional part and perform functional part. Module I to module VI are service modules. Module VII applies to management and evaluation of DRS. Module VIII contains all kinds of manners of DRS. Module VII and Module VIII can apply to all service modules, namely, module I to module VI. The DRS model addresses subject guides and user demands oriented reference service. Nothing but reasonable management strategy and advanced service concept that impenetrate all the modules can ensure the fast development of DRS in practice.

Discussion of Service Innovation Under the Mode of a Digital Library

Xiaoping He[1], Liang Wang[2], and Xi Zhang[2]

[1] Professor, Director, Library of Nanchang University, Jiangxi, China 330029
[2] Division of Information Studies, Library of Nanchang University, Jiangxi, China 330029

Abstract. "service innovation" is the theme that library should study. The library needs kinds of innovation such as mechanism, librarian's quality, reading circumstance and service function innovation.

Under the mode of digital library, "service innovation" is the theme that library should study. Our library makes great efforts to study and practice in order to promote construction with service, to promote development with scientific research. We'll discuss the related ideas, which were built and formed during this course with colleague.

Through the "211" Project for higher education, Nanchang University library's service mode has changed from tradition to modern, and initially set up a modern library. With the development of digital library, the goals that library will carry out are operation automation, information service networklization, information carrier digitalized, data criterion standardization.

Management Needs Mechanism Innovation. In order to break the management mechanism of traditional library thoroughly, fit the development of modern digital library and the change of network environment, some divisions such as reader service division, information service division, information research division, resources construction division are set up.

Improvement of Service Quality Needs Innovation of Librarians' Quality. The goal of digital library is that anyone can acquire the documents he needs anywhere without time limits. Librarians should have ability of reorganizing knowledge so as to be a knowledge navigator. Librarians' quality is improved by training and reeducation. Kinds of lecture activities are hold to stir up the whole librarians' go-aheadism, enthusiasm, and creativity.

Advancement Needs Reading Circumstance Innovation. University library should be a study place that takes reader as center in the process of IT in education. It needs not only the liberal study space with kinds of modern technology equipments but also comfortable convenience reading environment.

We'll endeavor to set up digital library in the guideline of opening, cooperation and sharing.

Z. Chen et al. (Eds.): ICADL 2004, LNCS 3334, p. 670, 2004.
© Springer-Verlag Berlin Heidelberg 2004

Information Services in Digital Library, Fudan's Experience

Yixin Xu, Jun Ying, Xinli Si, Meiqi Mo, and Zhiping Xia

Fudan University Library, Shanghai 200433, China
Yxxu@shmu.edu.cn

In the past 10 years, academic libraries have combined various modern digital technologies with traditional library services to improve their services.

In China, most of the core Chinese journals are included in a few important full-text databases. Core foreign language journals are scatter through different databases or journal platforms. Users need a uniform portal to provide instant access across all databases. Fudan University library periodically engages in survey for collecting users' retrieval behavior and habits for utilizing libraries resources. Based on the survey findings, we built an Internet-based Biomedical Information Resource Assure System (IBIRAS) in year 2000 for which to be updated twice a year. IBIRAS was built under Solaris operation system, JSP and database technologies and served the meta-database for our holdings in all formats. In the situation of Fudan University library, we are investigating the possibility to combine the existing Horizon OPAC system with meta-data searching software to build ultimate portal of the library. It is still rely on professional librarians to continuously invest on evaluation.

Virtual Reference Services (VRS) have become one of the key services and gained considerable attention. VRS usually serves users by E-mail, web form and in real-time system. In April of 2003, an integrated virtual reference service system at Fudan University library was launched. The integrated virtual reference desk system includes E-mail service, Real-time inquiry service, learning center, BBS, Knowledgebase and virtual reference tools. The work flow of the virtual reference desk system includes following steps: Question acquisition →Triage →Answer formulation →Tracking → Resource creation. Library patrons can submit questions at any time through library web site and the questions will be answered online by qualified librarians.

Personalized library platforms emerged on 1998 in America. The generalized name of the system is Mylibrary. However in China, similar researches have just launched among a few large libraries. After detailed investigation for end user needs, Fudan University library decided to build our personalized library from two aspects. One is to build a common portal for all the users and everyone can save his/her personal settings through his account and password. The other aspect is to construct personal library template for particular subject areas that serves particular user group.

Fudan University library has been endeavoring in improving information service for several years. We always remember that the coming generations of users will have their individual needs and preferences, which are awaiting us to discover and meet. We also must better utilize the use of digital library tools to serve the users. And in the end we believe in heart that librarians will always be in the business of removing barriers between users and information.

Z. Chen et al. (Eds.): ICADL 2004, LNCS 3334, p. 671, 2004.
© Springer-Verlag Berlin Heidelberg 2004

Knowledge Management in Library Information Services

Meng Zhan[1], Ying Liu[2], and Gaokang Yao[3]

[1,2] Wuhan University Library, 430072 Luojia Hill, Wuhan, Hubei, China
[3] Department of Information Management, Peking University, 10087, Beijing, China
{mzhan, liuy}@lib.whu.edu.cn, 3yaogaokang@sina.com

1 Introduction

Explicit knowledge is coded knowledge that is saved in various formats, such as books, journals and information in online databases. To incorporate the concept of knowledge management into the management of libraries will change services and management in libraries. In terms of processing, it will increase the division of explicit knowledge and break packets of explicit knowledge into smaller pieces. This will be very beneficial for user retrieval of information as knowledge becomes more complex within branching sub-disciplines, and it will also enhance the effect of the information services in library.

2 Develop a Model of a Resource System Based Knowledge Attributes

Digital resources are stored according to their types in library database. We can see it as a repository that has three layers: the bottom-layer is the layer of object data, there are different kinds of object databases in this layer; the middle-layer is the layer of descriptive metadata, using metadata to describe all kinds of object databases, sub-databases and items; the top-layer is the layer of descriptive knowledge, using the knowledge concept to categorize the attributes of all kind data and mapping them to the addresses of all kinds of data. This three-layered repository is a multi-type repository. There are attribute relationship and address mapping between the three layers. The descriptive knowledge layer will provide information services to the users, and the other two layers will relate with the top-layer in a logical way. After resources are divided by subject, described by metadata and linked to the address, the users can retrieve information from the database using a branching model of knowledge organization. This way of organizing and storing resources can be seen as a method to catalog and recompose the resources. Actually, the key technology is how to divide up the database, catalog and describe the resources, and reorganize link between resources when libraries provide individual services and knowledge services to users.

3 Multi-levels Description and Links Between Explicit Knowledge

The Multi-level description of explicit knowledge includes descriptions of basic information, objects information, general information and unit information. Take a

Z. Chen et al. (Eds.): ICADL 2004, LNCS 3334, pp. 672–674, 2004.
© Springer-Verlag Berlin Heidelberg 2004

book as an example, its basic information is the bibliographic information, and the object information is the digital full text information obtained from scanning. Each type of explicit knowledge, which has been described in multiple levels, can be logically looked as a knowledge unit with certain characteristic attributes. Vertically, these knowledge units have upper and lower linking relationships with the upper-level information that derives from them. This is a kind of one-to-one relationship. Horizontally, those knowledge units with the same characteristic attributes have cross-linking reticular relationships with each other. This is a kind of one-to-many relationship. For instance, if we take The Dream of the Red Chamber published by Yuelu Press, in terms of vertical relationships, the upper level is basic information, i.e. the bibliographic record of this book, and the lower level is object information, i.e. electronic full text. In terms of horizontal relationships, all knowledge units with the same attributive characteristic words "Dream of the Red Chamber" are linked objects of it, such as films, TV programs, graphic novels, songs, research works and book reviews etc. related to The Dream of the Red Chamber. It can be easily seen from the example above about the linking relationship that a kind of cross linkage based on knowledge concepts can be established among all resources through the hierarchical description and linking process. This relationship is independent of the types and carriers of resources. The formation of this relationship can set up a foundation for us to pick up information by following knowledge threads.

4 Researching and Establishing the Knowledge Vocabulary Database

All processes including recognizing, analyzing, storing and abstracting knowledge are based on the knowledge vocabulary database, therefore, the knowledge vocabulary database is very important in the whole process of knowledge management, so the knowledge vocabulary database used in the library information service system should map users' natural language queries to a controlled vocabulary. For instance, in the field of library information services, we can establish the vocabulary by adapting compatible information retrieval languages. We can merge or link the Chinese Library Classification, Law of Scientific Classification, Law of Classified Subject Table and Subject Code List based on knowledge concepts, and establish the knowledge vocabulary database. This knowledge vocabulary can be introduced into retrieval systems to provide the retrieval services based on multi retrieval languages. If the retrieval language used by the user is not the index language, the system can extract results by transferring terms entered by the user to index term with the help of the knowledge-thesaurus full of referring relationships. Users of the intelligent retrieval system can find results in a familiar style without the need to learn a new retrieval language. Furthermore, a retrieval system can build up a dynamic, retractable browser tree with the help of a knowledge-thesaurus and the user can also retrieve documents by browsing. The tree structure of the knowledge thesaurus will be visible to users in a friendly interface.

Reference

1. Hwa-Wei Lee, Reposition Libraries in the Digital and Knowledge Age. Report In Wuhan University 2000

Marketing Academic Digital Library

Jingbo Zhang

Library of East China Normal University,
3663 North Zhongshan Road,
Shanghai, 200062, P.R. China
zhangjb@lib.ecnu.edu.cn

Academic digital library should consider applying modern marketing theory as the significant change in resource form and service means in recent years. Marketing in academic digital library can be regarded as a process of understanding, stimulating and meeting the needs of its users. It must satisfy the selected user market through establishing specific academic resources and services of digital library. The four main principles about assessment of user request, establishing target market, using whole market strategy and emphasizing long-term benefit are very important in marketing academic digital library.

Academic library can use various kinds of marketing strategies to enhance the visibility of digital library and expand its market both in traditional means and network means Traditional promotion strategies such as announcement meeting, flysheet, advertising gift, database guideline, exhibition are still very useful and acceptant in current age. Network technology like email, BBS, website are no doubt the necessary and effective tools to marketing digital library. For expanding market share of digital library, academic library should make efforts in existing market penetration, new market establishment, new product development and other divers management means as described in Ansoff's Market Expansion Matrix. In university, the instruction sessions or training courses of digital resource pertaining to courses, subject or research programs are useful strategies to penetrating the student market or faculty market. Establishing a new kind service or resource may develop a new market or get increase in an existing market. It is also very important to provide multiple accesses to digital resource, integration of digital resource, personalized service, virtual reference, network tutorial or remote training. In addition, academic library can exploit outside opportunities to get extra growth by providing special information services, developing unique digital resource or promoting cooperation with other libraries.

Marketing achievement can be evaluated by various statistics and user feedback from interaction with users. In East China Normal University, there has been some marketing practice in digital library and some evaluation test through usage statistics of certain subject digital resource. It reflects the effectiveness of marketing in academic library.

The problem in marketing academic digital library is the lack of enough competition. Therefore the future development should emphasize to develop evaluation system and promote competition among academic libraries. And academic library should strengthen the cognition of marketing among all library staff and improve their personal skill and cooperation ability in marketing practice.

Z. Chen et al. (Eds.): ICADL 2004, LNCS 3334, p. 675, 2004.
© Springer-Verlag Berlin Heidelberg 2004

Marketing Information Services in the Digital Age: Viewpoints from Academic Libraries in North America and the Asia-Pacific Rim

Michael R. Leach[1] and Chihfeng P. Lin[2]

[1] Physics Research Library & Kummel Library of Geological Sciences, 17 Oxford Street,
Harvard University, Cambridge, MA, USA 02138
mrleach@fas.harvard.edu

[2] Department/Graduate School of Information & Communications, Shih-Hsin University,
Mucha P. O. Box 6-89, Taipei, Taiwan 11603
chihfeng@cc.shu.edu.tw

Abstract. Digital libraries, institutional repositories, electronic journals, aggregator services, and open access publishing are just some of the new digital resources and services that are impacting libraries and information centers around the world. Marketing these new resources and collections is even more important in this new digital age, especially when some are challenging the value and worth of academic libraries. In the past, different audiences and patron groups with different expectations generally required different marketing strategies. But is this true in the digital age? This poster will compare and contrast the marketing strategies of academic libraries in North America and the Asia-Pacific Rim, focusing on shared strategies and new methods of reaching and convincing audiences of the value of academic libraries, which are key players in the new digital age, linking users with an ever more complex array of digital resources and services. The presenters will cover such topics as branding digital resources; imbedding marketing into training and instruction; forms of electronic marketing including newsletters and web logs (blogs); and integrating marketing into user needs surveying.

Z. Chen et al. (Eds.): ICADL 2004, LNCS 3334, p. 676, 2004.
© Springer-Verlag Berlin Heidelberg 2004

Models For Sustainability: Three Case Studies

Naicheng Chang

School of Library, Archive and Information Studies, University College London,
Gower Street, London WC1E 6BT, UK
uczcncc@ucl.ac.uk

Digital library development demonstrates its potential in content creation and collaborative partnership. However, it will take time for digital libraries to achieve critical mass. Therefore sustainability is a crucial element in fulfilling their potential.

The following three initiatives represent distinct characteristics of digital library development and are the basis of this research. **Library of Congress National Digital Library Program (NDLP)** has the mission to sustain and preserve a universal collection of knowledge and creativity for future generations. **University of Michigan Digital Library (UMDL)** is a representative of an academic library with the mission is to support a virtual learning environment and preserve campus-wide materials for long-term access. **Perseus Digital Library (PDL)** based at Tufts University is a representative of a technology-oriented research testbed, the mission of one humanist to use technology to facilitate research and teaching in the humanities.

The conclusion was that building a digital library can be a costly and lengthy process. Funding is an ongoing issue for digital library projects. For most organizations which have digital libraries it is probably the case that they are not capable of setting up and managing sustainable digital collections without assistance outside the department which hosts the library. This issue is particularly obvious when creating collections with large numbers of documents rather than occasional documents. In the higher education sector, the challenges of the digital library do not relate only to the library. They belong to its host institution and need to be resolved at an appropriate institutional level. The three case studies in this research share the core mission of education, which unfortunately does not bring in money; therefore, fundraising is particularly important for them.

Research institutions and government agencies in the US have a long record of cooperation in the digital library arena. Consequently digital library development in the US is more active, devoted and enthusiastic than in the UK in terms of scale and budget, so the results are more encouraging and fruitful. Compared to the US, digital library development in the UK needs more visible commercial and industrial involvement along with government and academic institutions to give it more chance to succeed.

Z. Chen et al. (Eds.): ICADL 2004, LNCS 3334, p. 677, 2004.
© Springer-Verlag Berlin Heidelberg 2004

Research on Academic Personal Portal in Digital Library*

Youhua Chen, Wei Pan, and Peifu Xia

Library of Shanghai Jiaotong Univ.,
1954 Huashan Rd., Shanghai 200030, P.R. China
{yhchen, wpan, pfxia}@lib.sjtu.edu.cn

The requirements of intensive information urge the emergence of portal. Based on the existing research, portal can be described as an integrated system of information, services and applications with the capabilities of single sign-on and seamless link as well as the functions of personalization and customization. Generally speaking, there're three portal modes : (1)Vertical portal, which provides access to a variety of information and services about a particular area of interest; (2)Horizontal portal, often referred to as "mega-portals", which targets the entire Internet community. (3)University or enterprise portals.

At present, many portal projects have been developed in library field, such as ARL scholars portal, SPP(the subject portals project), the AARLIN(Australian Academic Research Libraries Network), MyLibrary@NCState, which will provide effective portal application experiences for the underway academic personal portal projects.

The paper brings forward a single sign-on, module-based and web-based architecture of academic personal portal, which integrates the functions of academic resources personalization and customization, cross-search, personal recommendation, personal database management and personal editing, so that user can access any resource or any application customized in his personal virtual space seamlessly at anytime and anywhere. The system tries to provide a friendly, scalable, secure and intelligentized platform to realize academic personal resources management, discovery, search and usage. Nine functional modules are designed, which include user authentication module, user resources customization module, favorite link module, personalized recommendation module, quick search module, cross-search module, personal database module, personal communication module and system usage statistic module. Among all the modules, the personal database section aims at generating personal database to realize personal resources storing and organizing effectively. Search results from cross-search platform can be stored into personal database automatically with existing metadata formats. For the resources user want to add into database directly, system provide standard metadata formats about multimedia resources of different types(for example, video data, audio data, journal article, movie and so on) for filling in. Thus, users can manage and retrieve all resources of themselves. Article editing tool is embedded into the module so that user can write in the very format of the journal to which he want to submit. During the

---

* The research is supported by Shanghai Jiaotong Univ. social science foundation project: Research on the digital libraries of the world top universities.

Z. Chen et al. (Eds.): ICADL 2004, LNCS 3334, pp. 678–679, 2004.

periods of writing, user can search some articles through a search tool bar and references list can be generated intelligently if the articles have been cited.

Through the detailed explanations on each module, the paper completes the frame of an academic personal portal and presents an outline of personal resources page containing all functional modules. An architecture was designed as following:

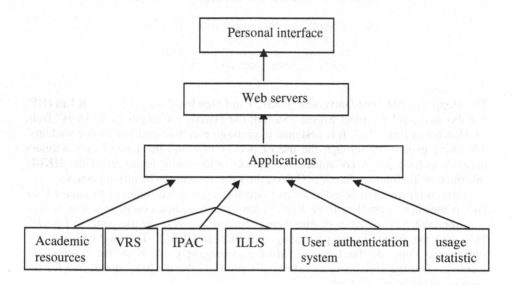

Notes:

- Academic resources includes subscribed databases, e-journals, e-books, organized net resources; resources harvested through protocols, such as OAI; the favorite links or resources user customized;
- VRS, IPAC and ILLS are applications systems seamlessly linking to academic personal portal system;
- Applications process the matching relationships between resources & applications and user profiles; also update user interface based on usage statistics;
- Web servers process the launching at front end;
- Personal interface presents all customized academic resources and applications in suitable display styles.

The system realization needs support so many protocols, standards and apply complicated technologies. About personalization and customization, there have been some mature technologies; While referring to users' behaviors track and analysis as well as personalized knowledge discovery, further research should be developed on agent systems, data mining technology and ontology. If the above problems are settled, the academic personal portal will have a perfect solution.

Surfing the Hong Kong Baptist University e-Campus in 80 Days: A Pilot Pocket PC Project with Hewlett-Packard

Teresa M. L. Kong[1] and Rebekah S. H. Wong[2]

Hong Kong Baptist University Library, Hong Kong,
Special Administrative Region (SAR), China
{teresak, rebekahw}@hkbu.edu.hk
http://www.hkbu.edu.hk/lib

The Hong Kong Baptist University (HKBU) and Hewlett-Packard HK SAR Ltd (HP) collaborated a pilot project named "Surfing the HKBU e-Campus in 80 Days" from 17 March to 4 June 2004. It is designed to promote e-culture and to enhance students' e-learning experience through the use of pocket PCs and the University's wireless network technology. A committee was formed with senior members of the HKBU Information Technology Services Center, the Library, and six faculty members.

Fifty students were selected as participants. They were required to attend User Group meetings; complete three Exploration exercises; and complete a user survey questionnaire. Several types of data were collected to assess the use pattern of pocket PCs, and the feasibility of promoting e-culture at HKBU. The two tables below summarize some of the findings. Most encouragingly, 98% of the respondents recommended the University to extensively promote the usage of the device for the purpose of study and research.

Table 1. How much learned after the Project

RATED SCORES							
10	9	8	7	6	5	4	3 - 0
2 %	2 %	28 %	40 %	14 %	6 %	8 %	0 %

WRITTEN EXPLANATIONS	No. of Respondents
LEARNED	
Different aspects of PPC	24
Library resources and services	4
PARTICULARLY USEFUL LEARNING CHANNELS	
Explorations and their answers	12
Discussions and sharing	3
Additional self-learning efforts	2

Table 2. Time spent on PDA during the Project

Usage	Time spent
Study & academic	30 %
Leisure & recreation	30 %
Web surfing	18 %
PDA Project assignments	9 %
Communication	8 %
Calendar / scheduling	2 %
Miscellaneous	3 %

The findings of the Project help to inform future information technology and service planning efforts in the increasingly important and fast developing area of wireless network technology and handheld devices at HKBU. For further information, please refer the Project website at http://www.hkbu.edu.hk/surfing80.

---

[1] Teresa M.L. Kong is the Assistant Librarian of Multimedia Learning Centre of Hong Kong Baptist University Library.

[2] Rebekah S.H. Wong is the Junior Assistant Librarian of Reference and User Education Section of Hong Kong Baptist University Library.

Z. Chen et al. (Eds.): ICADL 2004, LNCS 3334, p. 680, 2004.
© Springer-Verlag Berlin Heidelberg 2004

The Impact of Copyright Upon Digital Libraries

Min Chou[1] and Oliver G. Zhou[2]

[1] Reference Librarian / Associate Professor, Congressman Frank J. Guarini Library,
New Jersey City University, 2039 Kennedy Boulevard, Jersey City, NJ 07305, U.S.A.
mchou@njcu.edu
[2] Attorney at Law, Law Offices of Oliver Zhou, 350 Broadway, Suite 318,
New York, NY, 10013, U.S.A.
ozhou@verizon.net

1 Introduction

The Internet offers unprecedented opportunities for people to communicate and access to information. Libraries are embracing the new digital medium as it allows massive data storage, faster and more effective data retrieval, and easier content navigation and transfer. This communication revolution helps libraries fulfill their important mission in the society as the information repository and disseminator. The legal landscape of the digital environment, however, is very different from that of the traditional print environment due to the nature of the digital technology. This research explores the shift of legal paradigm and its implications upon the digital library development, and also suggests viable solutions to cope with the trend.

2 Issues and Theories

The recent developments of digital international copyright laws and domestic copyright laws in the United States and other countries have dramatically altered the legal landscape upon which libraries have relied on to operate for centuries, such as fair use and the first sale doctrines. The underlying legal philosophy for this dramatic change is the transformation of contents from sale to lease through licensing mechanism, backed up by the legal enforceability of all shrink-wrap or click-on licensing agreements of American courts and the Digital Millennium Copyright Act (DMCA). Digital content providers have increasingly resorted to the digital fence, digital firewall, and remote disabler to enforce their copyright monopoly under the digital copyright law regime. That affects almost all aspects of library services, including acquisition and collection development, lending, document delivery, electronic reserve, and virtual reference, etc.

This research briefly overviews the current international copyright regime represented by the World Intellectual Property Organization (WIPO). Under the WIPO regime, the United States enacted the DMCA. The DMCA, however, runs afoul to the WIPO treaty's legal principle that each member country can retain the existing exceptions, and create new exceptions. It also deviates from the long held American copyright law tradition by regulating the use of information rather than the devices by which the information is delivered. It legalizes the anti-circumvention measures, eliminates the first sale doctrine, marginalizes the fair use doctrine, and

Z. Chen et al. (Eds.): ICADL 2004, LNCS 3334, pp. 681–682, 2004.
© Springer-Verlag Berlin Heidelberg 2004

makes an automated digital copyright management system become a fortress to block the information access right of the general public. The access controls have enabled copyright owners to charge on a pay-per-view basis, an essential working feature of online business operation models to generate profits to make the e-commerce sustainable. In the last decade, the content industry have first circumvented the first sale doctrine through licensing contracts, and then through the DMCA later, thereby legitimatising the elimination of first sale doctrine and marginalizing the fair use doctrine in cyberspace. All these have definitely a direct impact on digital library development.

3 Methodologies

This research first reviews the historical developments of copyright law from the United States and international perspectives. It then examines the prevailing legal paradigm behind each trend and focuses on the changes made in the digital age. Next, it compares and contrasts the advantages and disadvantages of copyright changes and analyzes their implications to the daily operation of libraries. It concludes with practical strategies for digital libraries to effectively cope with the imposing copyright issues. The underlying methodologies employed in this research are literature review, case studies, comparative studies, statistical data collection and analysis, and qualitative and quantitative analysis.

4 Conclusion

Digital library projects will be incomplete without taking copyright issues into serious consideration. Digital library builders must keep track of current and emerging legal issues of intellectual property rights and how they affect the libraries. Under the DMCA, the first sale doctrine will be no longer applied in the electronic world, and fair use doctrine is at a crossroads. Contractual licensing agreements may replace specific provisions of copyright law as the immediate source of authority to archive, use, and to distribute digital works in a digital library. Facing the ever changing economic and technological settings as well as the uncertain legal precedents in the context of the dynamic American case law system, libraries must carefully review public policies regarding intellectual property, and create policies that respect the copyright law as well as assert legitimate library uses for education and research by relying upon their nonprofit motive. Libraries should take leadership roles in the digital copyright debate and lobby legislators to change the laws for the purposes of creating a more balanced copyright regime between information owners and users. Libraries should work collectively to increase bargaining power to force digital content providers to make concessions to libraries so that libraries can fulfill their mission to promote science and useful arts for the general public.

Online Supervised Learning for Digital Library

Ning Liu[1], Benyu Zhang[2], Jun Yan[3], Wensi Xi[4],
Shuicheng Yan[2], Zheng Chen[2], Fengshan Bai[1], and Wei-Ying Ma[2]

[1] Department of Mathematics, Tsinghua University, Beijing 100084, P.R. China
nliu01@mails.tsinghua.edu.cn
[2] Microsoft Research Asia, 49 Zhichun Road, Beijing, P.R. China
[3] LMAM, School of Mathematical Sciences, Peking University, Beijing, P.R. China
[4] Virginia Polytechnic Institute and State University, Blacksburg, VA 24060, USA

Abstract. We propose an online learning algorithm for digital library. It learns from a data stream and overcomes the inherent problem of other incremental operations. Experiments on RCV1 show the superior performance of it.

1 The Incremental Algorithm and Experimental Results

In the last decade, the dramatic growth of the digital library requires a novel algorithm to overcome the inherent problem of online dimension reduction for document classification tasks. Principal Component Analysis (PCA) and Linear Discriminant Analysis (LDA) are among the most popular linear dimension reduction algorithms. However, PCA is an unsupervised algorithm and is not optimal for classification tasks. LDA is limited by the singularity problem and the number of classes being classified. Moreover, both of them are batch algorithms and can not process continues document streams in the context of digital libraries. On the other hand, feature selection algorithms such as Information Gain (IG) are efficient, greedy and they may not obtain the optimal solution. In this paper, we propose an online supervised learning algorithm that overcomes the shortcomings of the incremental algorithms introduced above. This proposed algorithm aims at adaptively searching for the projection axes on which the data points of different classes are far from each other.

We conducted our experiments on RCV1 collection, which contains over 800,000 samples. The dimension of each sample is about 300,000. We take an online PCA algorithm CCIPCA (Weng J., et al) and IG as baseline. The experimental results were evaluated by F1 measurement, and showed that on 3d subspace, It can outperform CCIPCA by 30% and outperform IG by 20%, while still maintain low complexity.

The full mathematical description and derivation of the proposed algorithm could be found at: http://jyan.nease.net/publications.htm

References

Weng, J., Zhang, Y., & Hwang, W.-S. (2003). Candid Covariance-free Incremental Principal Component Analysis. *IEEE Trans. Pattern Analysis and Machine Intelligence.*

Z. Chen et al. (Eds.): ICADL 2004, LNCS 3334, p. 683, 2004.
© Springer-Verlag Berlin Heidelberg 2004

Implementation of a Personalized Portal for Academic Library

Chenggan Quan, Shuang Wang, and Lin Mai

Xiamen University Library, Xiamen, Fujian, China 361005
ganr1231@sina.com

Abstract. The design and construction of a personalized portal based on Library patrons' requirements and functions of academic libraries with such characters as modularization, personalization and intelligent online help was sketched out in this paper. The framework involves the integration of various information resources and services according to the attributes of subjects. Also, the integration of services and resources based on the way of serving was contained in the system. In addition, this system consists of a trial module that tracks users' behavior and therefore recommends digital collections. The system which provides information seeking, filtering, organizing and delivering is part of a networked digital library project whose principle goal is to present users a convenient way to select, structure and retrieval digital resources from different repositories.

XMUKRP involves the integration of various information resources and services according to the attributes of subjects. Also, the integration of services and resources based on the workflow of serving was contained in the system.

1. Resource discovery. All e-resources were organized by subject area based on the collection's content and recommended to potential users according to their major.

2. Single login. The system remembers all login information for different database provided when the library patrons login in it at the first time. That means most users need remember only one username and password for access to most resources.

3. Single interface. The XMUKRP tried to offer the potential for reducing this to standard interfaces through which most resources could be searched, and in which the results returned were reformed to a standard format.

4. Extendable interface. The page of results provides user a chance to search information in famous search engine such as Google just by right-clicking mice.

5. Personalized interface. Users could not only regroup the resources cataloged by librarian according their favorite or major requirement, whether it is provide by libraries or not, but also organize all resources depend on Dublin Core Metadata in their favorite.

6. Intelligent online help (Figure 2). Nowadays, all resource providers offer online help with the database, however, these helps are seldom or never visited by users because they are too complex and inconvenient. Xiamen University Library reedited the helps and developed an Internet Explorer plug-in which could detect the content users browsing and offer users the relational helps. Also, reference system was involved in this functions that provides users an interface to ask a librarian or exports while they are querying information.

Z. Chen et al. (Eds.): ICADL 2004, LNCS 3334, p. 684, 2004.
© Springer-Verlag Berlin Heidelberg 2004

The System Design of Military Equipment Digital Library

Lu Gao[1], Hongmin Yu[1], Hongfeng Wang[2], and Sumei Zhang[1]

[1] Department of Management Engineering,
[2] Department of Electronic Engineering,
Shijiazhuang Mechanical Engineering College,
Heping West Road 97, Shijiazhuang, Hebei, China 050003
gaosandong@peoplemail.com.cn

Abstract. This paper analyses the characteristics of military equipment information resources and the special demand of military equipment digital library. Based on the general digital library architecture combined the characteristics of military equipment information resource, it builds the architecture of military equipment digital library and the operation mechanism for military equipment digital library is discussed.

The architecture of military equipment digital library as fig. 4 shows. This architecture has following characteristics:

First, reliability improves; Secondly, safety strengthens; Thirdly, flexibility increases.

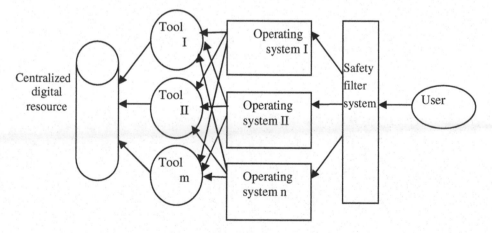

Fig. 1. Digital library general architecture

Because of the particularity of military equipment digital library, its operation mechanism also has own characteristics and demands: operation power mechanism, integration mechanism and safe mechanism.

Z. Chen et al. (Eds.): ICADL 2004, LNCS 3334, p. 685, 2004.

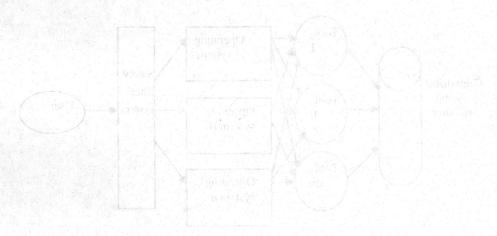

Author Index

Akhter, Ragina   608
Amagasa, Toshiyuki   419

Babu, R. Sathish   290
Bai, Fengshan   683
Bai, Huixian   213
Bai, Yongge   656

Caidi, Nadia   584
Cao, Sanxing   444
Cao, Yukun   641
Cargnelutti Tony   660
Cecelia, Lee Shong Lin   543
Chang, Chew-Hung   553
Chang, Naicheng   677
Chang, Tsui-Yun   574
Chau, Michael   515
Cheang, Chan Wa   355
Chen, Ching-chih   73
Chen, Hsinchun   1, 515
Chen, Lin   643
Chen, Rong-Chang   574
Chen, Su-Shing   61
Chen, Tung-Shou   574
Chen, Youhua   563, 678
Chen, Zheng   683
Cheng, Bianai   663
Cheng, Judy L.   658
Chou, Min   681
Chung, Chin Hyun   646

Dang, Haifeng   213
Deng, Zhihong   255
Deng, ZhiHong   310
Ding, Hao   184
Dong, Li   174
Dong, Mingkai   644

Fan, Jilian   270
Fan, Zhijian   227
Feng, Lisheng   663
Feng, Xiangyun   662
Foo, Schubert Shou-Boon   453, 491
Fox, Edward A.   51, 533
Frommholz, Ingo   133
Fu, Lin   491

Gao, Lu   685
Geng, Yibing   270
Goh, Dion Hoe-Lian   453, 491, 553, 594
Gong, Zhiguo   355
Gu, Lixu   388
Guo, Hui   648
Guo, Jing   668

He, Xiaoping   670
Hedberg, John   553
Hemmje, Matthias   523
Hider, Philip   266
Hiew, Pang-Leang   666
Hiiragi, Wasuke   144
Hu, Xiulin   648
Huang, Chen   220
Huang, Jian   483
Huang, Min   124, 668
Huang, Xiaoqin   643
Huang, Xuanjing   483
Huang, Yun   519
Hubbard, William J.   618
Hughes, Baden   320

Jeong, C.B.   440
Jiang, Airong   155, 174, 663
Jiang, Junjie   429
Jin, Hai   13
Jin, Yi   124

Kageura, Kyo   398
Kang, Bo-Yeong   501
Kang, Dazhou   650
Kang, Yin   642
Keller, Michael A.   84
Kim, Hae-Jung   501
Kim, Jin Ok   646
Kim, Jin Soo   646
Kim, S.H.   440
Kim, Seonho   533
Kiyoki, Yasushi   626
Komlodi, Anita   584
Kong, Teresa M. L.   680
Kumaresan, V.   290

Lam, Wai   280
Leach, Michael R.   676

Lee, Dongwon   408
Lee, Kyung-Soon   398
Lee, Sang-Jo   501
Lee, Shu-Shing   453
Leung, Kevin   236
Li, Feng   255
Li, Jianhua   330
Li, Jianzhong   345
Li, Qiang   330
Li, Wei   510
Li, Wu   664
Li, Xiang   330
Li, Yunfeng   641
Lim, Ee-Peng   553, 594
Lin, Chihfeng P.   676
Lin, Haoming   124, 656
Liu Jian   649
Liu, Gongshen   330
Liu, Jian   649
Liu, Ning   683
Liu, Wei   245
Liu, Ying   672
Liu, Zehua   553
Lu, Jianjiang   650
Lu, Rui   444
Lu, Zhenbo   664
Luo, Chunrong   165

Ma, Wei-Ying   683
Ma, Ziwei   659
Mai, Lin   684
Mehta, Bhaskar   133, 523
Mo, Meiqi   671

Nagarajan, R.   290
Neuhold, Erich   133, 523
Niederée, Claudia   133, 523
Niu, Zhendong   644, 653

On, Byung-Won   408

Pan, JiaZhen   667
Pan, Wei   563, 668, 678
Pan, Xiang   640
Pan, Yunhe   449
Pang, Natalie Lee-San   666
Park, Jong-Seung   458
Park, Seong-Bae   501

Peng, Jia   656
Peng, Jing   651
Poon, Paul W.T.   636
Pu, Hsiao-Tieh   378

Qin, Jian   300
Qiu, Junrui   270
Quan, Chenggan   684

Rahman, Md. Anisur   608
Rajashekar, T.B.   661
Rasmussen, Edie   95
Rauber, Andreas   203
Rauch, Carl   203

Sakaguchi, Tetsuo   144
Sasaki, Hideyasu   626
Shao, Jing   213
Shen, Yunyun   662
Shi, Shengfei   345
Shi, Xuelin   653
Shivaram, B.S.   661
Shreve, Gregory M.   339, 341
Si, Xinli   671
Sølvberg, Ingeborg   184
Song, Hantao   653
Song, Lizhe   653
Stewart, Avaré   133, 523
Storey, Colin   236
Subrahmanyam, Bhagirathi   339
Suen, Eng-Kai   594
Sugimoto, Shigeo   144
Suriya, M.   290
Sun, Aixin   553
Supangat, Yohan   491

Tabata, Koichi   144
Tang, Shiwei   255, 652
Teh, Tiong-Sa   553
Theng, Yin-Leng   453, 553, 594
Tu, Xiangbo   227

U, Leong Hou   355
Uddin, Md. Hanif   608

Wang, Bin   462
Wang, Chaokun   345
Wang, Dake   651

Wang, Fu Lee   368
Wang, Guoren   462
Wang, Hanrong   618
Wang, Hongfeng   685
Wang, Liang   670
Wang, Shuang   684
Wang, Weinong   429
Wang, Yunpeng   648
Wells Andrew   660
Wheeler, Kristin   584
Witten, Ian H.   35
Wong, Rebekah S. H.   680
Wong, Rita   236
Woo, Seon-Mi   473
Wu, Fei   449
Wu, Guomin   449
Wu, Guowen   510, 642
Wu, Jiangqin   649
Wu, Lide   483
Wu, Sai   255
Wu, Xu   659
Wu, Yizi   649
Wuwongse, Vilas   419

Xi, Wensi   683
Xia, Peifu   563, 678
Xia, Zhiping   671
Xiao, Xiaobo   630
Xing, Chunxiao   174, 654
Xu, Baowen   650
Xu, Qiang   25
Xu, Ruxing   563
Xu, Yanfei   510
Xu, Yixin   671

Yan, Jun   683
Yan, Shuicheng   683
Yang, Christopher C.   280, 368
Yang, Dongqing   255, 310, 652
Yang, Xiaochun   462
Yang, Xubo   647
Yang, Yulin   543
Yang, Zongying   195, 568, 668
Yao, Boyue   662
Yao, Gaokang   672
Ye, Fred Y.   658
Ye, Ying   668

Ye, YunMing   519
Ye, Xiuzi   640
Yik, Ernest   236
Yin, Jun   642
Yin, Ming   594
Yin, Ping   310
Ying, Jun   671
Yoo, Chun-Sik   473
Yoshikawa, Masatoshi   419
You, Jinyuan   643
Yu, Ge   462
Yu, Hongmin   685
Yu, Zhengtao   653
Yu, Zhuzheng   641
Yuan, Guojing   568, 656

Zeng, Marcia Lei   339, 341, 574
Zhan, Meng   672
Zhang, Bei   174
Zhang, Benyu   683
Zhang, Chunhong   664
Zhang, Foster   300
Zhang, Huijun   630
Zhang, Jie   644
Zhang, Jingbo   675
Zhang, Jingchang   270
Zhang, Liang   510, 642
Zhang, Ming   255, 310, 652
Zhang, Peiyi   642
Zhang, Sanyuan   640
Zhang, Sumei   685
Zhang, Wenxian   650
Zhang, Xi   670
Zhang, Xiaolin   115
Zhang, Xiaoxing   104
Zhang, Xiya   630
Zhang, Yin   640
Zhang, Ying   165
Zhang, Zhiqiang   654
Zhao, Jihai   220
Zhao, Lin   642
Zhao, Peixiang   652
Zhao, Yang   155
Zheng, Qiaoying   195, 563, 568, 668
Zheng, Qinghua   213
Zheng, Xiaohui   663
Zheng, Zhangfei   227

Zhong, Yang   510
Zhou, Lizhu   174, 654
Zhou, Oliver G.   681
Zhou, Xiangdong   642
Zhou, Zhinong   165

Zhu, Guomin   270
Zhu, Shanfeng   280
Zhu, Wei   195
Zhuang, Yueting   449, 649
Zia, Lee L.   45

Lecture Notes in Computer Science

For information about Vols. 1–3237

please contact your bookseller or Springer

Vol. 3340: C.S. Calude, E. Calude, M.J. Dinneen (Eds.), Developments in Language Theory. XI, 431 pages. 2004.

Vol. 3339: G.I. Webb, X. Yu (Eds.), AI 2004: Advances in Artificial Intelligence. XXII, 1272 pages. 2004. (Subseries LNAI).

Vol. 3338: S.Z. Li, J. Lai, T. Tan, G. Feng, Y. Wang (Eds.), Advances in Biometric Person Authentication. XVI, 707 pages. 2004.

Vol. 3337: J.M. Barreiro, F. Martin-Sanchez, V. Maojo, F. Sanz (Eds.), Biological and Medical Data Analysis. XI, 508 pages. 2004.

Vol. 3336: D. Karagiannis, U. Reimer (Eds.), Practical Aspects of Knowledge Management. X, 523 pages. 2004. (Subseries LNAI).

Vol. 3334: Z. Chen, H. Chen, Q. Miao, Y. Fu, E. Fox, E.-p. Lim (Eds.), Digital Libraries: International Collaboration and Cross-Fertilization. XX, 690 pages. 2004.

Vol. 3333: K. Aizawa, Y. Nakamura, S. Satoh (Eds.), Advances in Multimedia Information Processing - PCM 2004. XXXV, 785 pages. 2004.

Vol. 3332: K. Aizawa, Y. Nakamura, S. Satoh (Eds.), Advances in Multimedia Information Processing - PCM 2004. XXXVI, 1051 pages. 2004.

Vol. 3331: K. Aizawa, Y. Nakamura, S. Satoh (Eds.), Advances in Multimedia Information Processing - PCM 2004. XXXVI, 667 pages. 2004.

Vol. 3329: P.J. Lee (Ed.), Advances in Cryptology - ASIACRYPT 2004. XVI, 546 pages. 2004.

Vol. 3323: G. Antoniou, H. Boley (Eds.), Rules and Rule Markup Languages for the Semantic Web. X, 215 pages. 2004.

Vol. 3322: R. Klette, J. Žunić (Eds.), Combinatorial Image Analysis. XII, 760 pages. 2004.

Vol. 3321: M.J. Maher (Ed.), Advances in Computer Science - ASIAN 2004. XII, 510 pages. 2004.

Vol. 3321: M.J. Maher (Ed.), Advances in Computer Science - ASIAN 2004. XII, 510 pages. 2004.

Vol. 3316: N.R. Pal, N.K. Kasabov, R.K. Mudi, S. Pal, S.K. Parui (Eds.), Neural Information Processing. XXX, 1368 pages. 2004.

Vol. 3315: C. Lemaître, C.A. Reyes, J.A. González (Eds.), Advances in Artificial Intelligence - IBERAMIA 2004. XX, 987 pages. 2004. (Subseries LNAI).

Vol. 3312: A.J. Hu, A.K. Martin (Eds.), Formal Methods in Computer-Aided Design. XI, 445 pages. 2004.

Vol. 3311: V. Roca, F. Rousseau (Eds.), Interactive Multimedia and Next Generation Networks. XIII, 287 pages. 2004.

Vol. 3309: C.-H. Chi, K.-Y. Lam (Eds.), Content Computing. XII, 510 pages. 2004.

Vol. 3308: J. Davies, W. Schulte, M. Barnett (Eds.), Formal Methods and Software Engineering. XIII, 500 pages. 2004.

Vol. 3307: C. Bussler, S.-k. Hong, W. Jun, R. Kaschek, D.. Kinshuk, S. Krishnaswamy, S.W. Loke, D. Oberle, D. Richards, A. Sharma, Y. Sure, B. Thalheim (Eds.), Web Information Systems - WISE 2004 Workshops. XV, 277 pages. 2004.

Vol. 3306: X. Zhou, S. Su, M.P. Papazoglou, M.E. Orlowska, K.G. Jeffery (Eds.), Web Information Systems - WISE 2004. XVII, 745 pages. 2004.

Vol. 3305: P.M.A. Sloot, B. Chopard, A.G. Hoekstra (Eds.), Cellular Automata. XV, 883 pages. 2004.

Vol. 3303: J.A. López, E. Benfenati, W. Dubitzky (Eds.), Knowledge Exploration in Life Science Informatics. X, 249 pages. 2004. (Subseries LNAI).

Vol. 3302: W.-N. Chin (Ed.), Programming Languages and Systems. XIII, 453 pages. 2004.

Vol. 3299: F. Wang (Ed.), Automated Technology for Verification and Analysis. XII, 506 pages. 2004.

Vol. 3298: S.A. McIlraith, D. Plexousakis, F. van Harmelen (Eds.), The Semantic Web - ISWC 2004. XXI, 841 pages. 2004.

Vol. 3295: P. Markopoulos, B. Eggen, E. Aarts, J.L. Crowley (Eds.), Ambient Intelligence. XIII, 388 pages. 2004.

Vol. 3294: C.N. Dean, R.T. Boute (Eds.), Teaching Formal Methods. X, 249 pages. 2004.

Vol. 3293: C.-H. Chi, M. van Steen, C. Wills (Eds.), Web Content Caching and Distribution. IX, 283 pages. 2004.

Vol. 3292: R. Meersman, Z. Tari, A. Corsaro (Eds.), On the Move to Meaningful Internet Systems 2004: OTM 2004 Workshops. XXIII, 885 pages. 2004.

Vol. 3291: R. Meersman, Z. Tari (Eds.), On the Move to Meaningful Internet Systems 2004: CoopIS, DOA, and ODBASE. XXV, 824 pages. 2004.

Vol. 3290: R. Meersman, Z. Tari (Eds.), On the Move to Meaningful Internet Systems 2004: CoopIS, DOA, and ODBASE. XXV, 823 pages. 2004.

Vol. 3289: S. Wang, K. Tanaka, S. Zhou, T.W. Ling, J. Guan, D. Yang, F. Grandi, E. Mangina, I.-Y. Song, H.C. Mayr (Eds.), Conceptual Modeling for Advanced Application Domains. XXII, 692 pages. 2004.

Vol. 3288: P. Atzeni, W. Chu, H. Lu, S. Zhou, T.W. Ling (Eds.), Conceptual Modeling - ER 2004. XXI, 869 pages. 2004.

Vol. 3287: A. Sanfeliu, J.F. Martínez Trinidad, J.A. Carrasco Ochoa (Eds.), Progress in Pattern Recognition, Image Analysis and Applications. XVII, 703 pages. 2004.

Vol. 3286: G. Karsai, E. Visser (Eds.), Generative Programming and Component Engineering. XIII, 491 pages. 2004.

Vol. 3285: S. Manandhar, J. Austin, U.B. Desai, Y. Oyanagi, A. Talukder (Eds.), Applied Computing. XII, 334 pages. 2004.

Vol. 3284: A. Karmouch, L. Korba, E.R.M. Madeira (Eds.), Mobility Aware Technologies and Applications. XII, 382 pages. 2004.

Vol. 3283: F.A. Aagesen, C. Anutariya, V. Wuwongse (Eds.), Intelligence in Communication Systems. XIII, 327 pages. 2004.

Vol. 3282: V. Guruswami, List Decoding of Error-Correcting Codes. XIX, 350 pages. 2004.

Vol. 3281: T. Dingsøyr (Ed.), Software Process Improvement. X, 207 pages. 2004.

Vol. 3280: C. Aykanat, T. Dayar, İ. Körpeoğlu (Eds.), Computer and Information Sciences - ISCIS 2004. XVIII, 1009 pages. 2004.

Vol. 3278: A. Sahai, F. Wu (Eds.), Utility Computing. XI, 272 pages. 2004.

Vol. 3275: P. Perner (Ed.), Advances in Data Mining. VIII, 173 pages. 2004. (Subseries LNAI).

Vol. 3274: R. Guerraoui (Ed.), Distributed Computing. XIII, 465 pages. 2004.

Vol. 3273: T. Baar, A. Strohmeier, A. Moreira, S.J. Mellor (Eds.), <<UML>> 2004 - The Unified Modelling Language. XIII, 454 pages. 2004.

Vol. 3271: J. Vicente, D. Hutchison (Eds.), Management of Multimedia Networks and Services. XIII, 335 pages. 2004.

Vol. 3270: M. Jeckle, R. Kowalczyk, P. Braun (Eds.), Grid Services Engineering and Management. X, 165 pages. 2004.

Vol. 3269: J. Lopez, S. Qing, E. Okamoto (Eds.), Information and Communications Security. XI, 564 pages. 2004.

Vol. 3268: W. Lindner, M. Mesiti, C. Türker, Y. Tzitzikas, A. Vakali (Eds.), Current Trends in Database Technology - EDBT 2004 Workshops. XVIII, 608 pages. 2004.

Vol. 3266: J. Solé-Pareta, M. Smirnov, P.V. Mieghem, J. Domingo-Pascual, E. Monteiro, P. Reichl, B. Stiller, R.J. Gibbens (Eds.), Quality of Service in the Emerging Networking Panorama. XVI, 390 pages. 2004.

Vol. 3265: R.E. Frederking, K.B. Taylor (Eds.), Machine Translation: From Real Users to Research. XI, 392 pages. 2004. (Subseries LNAI).

Vol. 3264: G. Paliouras, Y. Sakakibara (Eds.), Grammatical Inference: Algorithms and Applications. XI, 291 pages. 2004. (Subseries LNAI).

Vol. 3263: M. Weske, P. Liggesmeyer (Eds.), Object-Oriented and Internet-Based Technologies. XII, 239 pages. 2004.

Vol. 3262: M.M. Freire, P. Chemouil, P. Lorenz, A. Gravey (Eds.), Universal Multiservice Networks. XIII, 556 pages. 2004.

Vol. 3261: T. Yakhno (Ed.), Advances in Information Systems. XIV, 617 pages. 2004.

Vol. 3260: I.G.M.M. Niemegeers, S.H. de Groot (Eds.), Personal Wireless Communications. XIV, 478 pages. 2004.

Vol. 3259: J. Dix, J. Leite (Eds.), Computational Logic in Multi-Agent Systems. XII, 251 pages. 2004. (Subseries LNAI).

Vol. 3258: M. Wallace (Ed.), Principles and Practice of Constraint Programming - CP 2004. XVII, 822 pages. 2004.

Vol. 3257: E. Motta, N.R. Shadbolt, A. Stutt, N. Gibbins (Eds.), Engineering Knowledge in the Age of the Semantic Web. XVII, 517 pages. 2004. (Subseries LNAI).

Vol. 3256: H. Ehrig, G. Engels, F. Parisi-Presicce, G. Rozenberg (Eds.), Graph Transformations. XII, 451 pages. 2004.

Vol. 3255: A. Benczúr, J. Demetrovics, G. Gottlob (Eds.), Advances in Databases and Information Systems. XI, 423 pages. 2004.

Vol. 3254: E. Macii, V. Paliouras, O. Koufopavlou (Eds.), Integrated Circuit and System Design. XVI, 910 pages. 2004.

Vol. 3253: Y. Lakhnech, S. Yovine (Eds.), Formal Techniques, Modelling and Analysis of Timed and Fault-Tolerant Systems. X, 397 pages. 2004.

Vol. 3252: H. Jin, Y. Pan, N. Xiao, J. Sun (Eds.), Grid and Cooperative Computing - GCC 2004 Workshops. XVIII, 785 pages. 2004.

Vol. 3251: H. Jin, Y. Pan, N. Xiao, J. Sun (Eds.), Grid and Cooperative Computing - GCC 2004. XXII, 1025 pages. 2004.

Vol. 3250: L.-J. (LJ) Zhang, M. Jeckle (Eds.), Web Services. X, 301 pages. 2004.

Vol. 3249: B. Buchberger, J.A. Campbell (Eds.), Artificial Intelligence and Symbolic Computation. X, 285 pages. 2004. (Subseries LNAI).

Vol. 3246: A. Apostolico, M. Melucci (Eds.), String Processing and Information Retrieval. XIV, 332 pages. 2004.

Vol. 3245: E. Suzuki, S. Arikawa (Eds.), Discovery Science. XIV, 430 pages. 2004. (Subseries LNAI).

Vol. 3244: S. Ben-David, J. Case, A. Maruoka (Eds.), Algorithmic Learning Theory. XIV, 505 pages. 2004. (Subseries LNAI).

Vol. 3243: S. Leonardi (Ed.), Algorithms and Models for the Web-Graph. VIII, 189 pages. 2004.

Vol. 3242: X. Yao, E. Burke, J.A. Lozano, J. Smith, J.J. Merelo-Guervós, J.A. Bullinaria, J. Rowe, P. Tiño, A. Kabán, H.-P. Schwefel (Eds.), Parallel Problem Solving from Nature - PPSN VIII. XX, 1185 pages. 2004.

Vol. 3241: D. Kranzlmüller, P. Kacsuk, J.J. Dongarra (Eds.), Recent Advances in Parallel Virtual Machine and Message Passing Interface. XIII, 452 pages. 2004.

Vol. 3240: I. Jonassen, J. Kim (Eds.), Algorithms in Bioinformatics. IX, 476 pages. 2004. (Subseries LNBI).

Vol. 3239: G. Nicosia, V. Cutello, P.J. Bentley, J. Timmis (Eds.), Artificial Immune Systems. XII, 444 pages. 2004.

Vol. 3238: S. Biundo, T. Frühwirth, G. Palm (Eds.), KI 2004: Advances in Artificial Intelligence. XI, 467 pages. 2004. (Subseries LNAI).